Hannah Arendt in Jerusalem

Hannah Arendt
in Jerusalem

EDITED BY
Steven E. Aschheim

UNIVERSITY OF CALIFORNIA PRESS
Berkeley · *Los Angeles* · *London*

Grateful acknowledgment is made for permission
to reprint previously published material: Albrecht
Wellmer, "Hannah Arendt on Revolution," from
Revue International de Philosophie 2 (1999).
Michael Halberstam, "Hannah Arendt on the To-
talitarian Sublime and Its Promise of Freedom,"
from Michael Halberstam, *Totalitarianism and the
Modern Conception of Politics,* © 1999 Yale Uni-
versity Press. Dana R. Villa, "Totalitarianism, Mo-
dernity, and the Tradition," and "Apologist or Critic?
On Arendt's Relation to Heidegger," revised from
*Politics, Philosophy, Terror: Essays on the Thought
of Hannah Arendt,* © 1999 Princeton University
Press.

University of California Press
Berkeley and Los Angeles, California

University of California Press, Ltd.
London, England

Library of Congress Cataloging-in-Publication Data

Hannah Arendt in Jerusalem / Steven E. Aschheim,
editor.
    p. cm.
  Includes bibliographical references and index.
  ISBN 0-520-22056-0 (cloth : alk. paper)—
  ISBN 0-520-22057-9 (pbk. : alk. paper)
  1. Arendt, Hannah. I. Aschheim, Steven E., 1942–

B945.A694 H36 2001
320.5'092—dc21

                            00-053243

Manufactured in the United States of America
10 09 08 07 06 05 04 03 02 01

10 9 8 7 6 5 4 3 2 1

The paper used in this publication meets the
minimum requirements of ANSI/NISO Z39.48-1992
(R 1997) (*Permanence of Paper*). ♾

Contents

Preface

Steven Aschheim

The contents of this volume represent the fruits of a conference held in Jerusalem between December 9 and December 11, 1997.[1] This was the first international gathering of scholars ever assembled in Israel to consider the life and work of Hannah Arendt. It is not difficult to understand why such an event had not taken place before. In the Introduction that follows, I explain this in greater detail. Here, suffice it to say that Arendt's early critique of Zionism and, even more explosively, her famous (or, better, infamous) 1963 report on the Eichmann trial had essentially rendered her a persona non grata, an object of virtual intellectual taboo in Israel. But many years had since passed, and by 1997, it seemed to me, the time was ripe for initiating a more balanced confrontation.

The gathering, hardly surprisingly, attracted a great deal of international publicity and attention.[2] This was partly because it broached existential issues still precariously close to the national nerve, to cherished collective sensibilities. At stake, among other things, were the contested nature and implications of Zionism, Jewish and German loyalties, and competing narratives of Nazism and the Holocaust. Intellectual combat seemed, therefore, almost inevitable. But beyond these gladiatorial expectations, the enormous interest aroused by the conference—even before it began—pointed more importantly to a felt need for exposure to an unjustifiably neglected thinker whose thought and biography intersect at vital points with the history, self-definition, and predicaments

of Jewish and Israeli society. If in the preceding years there was a resistance, even a refusal, to engage, the urge now seemed almost irresistible
to do so.

A new generation with different needs, perspectives, and problems
had emerged. In a more mature and troubled Israel in search of new directions, and in an intellectual (if not a political) culture increasingly
open to heterodox visions, there was a serious desire to explore and
mine Arendt's oeuvre, its general as well as Jewish components. For
some, this was a receptive interest framed still by a continuing wariness
and opposition. Others were animated by an intimation that precisely in
Arendt's "subversive" insights lay useful keys for comprehending some
of the society's central dilemmas and, perhaps, even for resolving some
of its acute problems. For a few, as some of the papers included here indicate, there was an eagerness not only to grapple with, but to affirm her
critical views on, and alternative approaches to, Zionism and the Palestinian question. At least for some of the Israeli participants, as Amnon
Raz-Krakotzkin put it, the time had come to read Arendt's texts into
present political reality.

At the summing-up session of the conference, a leading Israeli historian, Shulamit Volkov, accounted for Arendt's newly acquired reso-
nance in even more stark and controversial form. While the Holocaust
(and Arendt's reading of it) remain crucial for her overall reception,
Volkov maintained, there is an even more powerful, immediate factor at
work. For Israelis, the most palpable factor is the continuing reality of
the post-1967 military occupation of the West Bank. The key to Arendt's
present relevance and attractiveness consists, above all, in her insight
that under such polarized political conditions, very ordinary people are
capable of thoughtlessly committing quite immoral, even evil, acts.

That summing-up session, held in a packed hall, was, indeed, quite
remarkable. If prior to the conference Arendt's reception in Israel had
been characterized by resistance and refusal, by its celebratory end,
judging by the admittedly selective sample of those in attendance, it had
taken on something of the character of an enthusiastic religious revival.[3]
This was rather disturbing. Stiflingly uncritical embrace is a kind of mirror opposite of, and surely no better than, blind rejection. The conference was intended to begin a process, to facilitate the kind of judicious
examination of Arendt and her world that would go beyond both reflexive negation and cultlike affirmation. It sought to provide as open-ended
a platform as possible for a thoroughgoing and sympathetic, but also al-

ways critical, examination of Arendt's thought and life, especially as it impinged upon her relations with and issues connected to Jerusalem.

This, of course, is the main intention behind our title, *Hannah Arendt in Jerusalem*. The volume seeks—both sympathetically and critically—to reexamine Arendt's project as it relates to this topic. The organization is self-explanatory and needs no further commentary (I have never understood why editors so often take upon themselves the superfluous—and often trivializing—task of summarizing in advance what readers will later encounter in any case). It is structured around and variously highlights Arendt's relevant reworkings of political thought and critical observations on the Western philosophical tradition, her analyses of totalitarianism and Nazism, her complex identity as a German Jew, her early commitment to and later critique of Zionism and the state of Israel, her reading of the Eichmann trial, its repercussions and implications, her relationship to key twentieth-century intellectuals—most notably Gershom Scholem, Karl Jaspers, and Martin Heidegger—and her tensely intimate connections to German culture.

The title, it must be pointed out, is at once literal and figurative. The volume discusses the historical record of Arendt's visits to and observations about the earthly Jerusalem and records the present scholarly reflections upon this thinker that since have taken place within that city. But "Jerusalem" also serves as the metaphor for her reflections upon, and relations to, things Jewish, Judaic, and Zionist. If, in a mildly ironic way, it plays upon the title of her famous work *Eichmann in Jerusalem,* the intention most definitively must not be taken to be, as one irate critic has quite wrongheadedly maintained, somehow also to place *her* on trial in Jerusalem, but rather to allow the possibility of a free, open, and productive encounter with her life, work, and thought.

I hope that this becomes clear as one proceeds through the volume. In her contribution, Agnes Heller insightfully notes that Arendt's works were themselves designed as a kind of political intervention. The conference and the present volume should similarly be regarded as a form of intervention—not in the sense that it seeks to impose any particular agenda, but rather as an attempt to place Arendt within the arena, to expose Arendtian modes and categories to an intellectual and political culture previously (and dogmatically) hostile to the very possibility. Outside of these contours, no single ideological or political line will be found, nor are any of the topics or approaches limited to any geographical or conceptual realm. Fierce criticism and animated approbation—

all informed by a sense of the density and complexity of the issues involved—will be found here. I have left the papers more or less intact, with very little editorial interference, in order to demonstrate the range of thinking and positions on Arendt and to allow them free expression. Her work remains the subject of complex and often deeply disputed evaluations and assessments. Her thought, as this volume also seeks to show, has undergone ever-renewed interpretation and been increasingly appropriated for multiple political and cultural purposes. The papers included here reflect the views of both those who are deeply skeptical of such developments and those who approve.

Would it be too much to hope that through an examination of the whole corpus within this "Jerusalem" context we will not only fill important lacunae in Arendt scholarship, but also help to illuminate, often in surprising and provocative ways, the broader ramifications of her thought and the nature of a highly controversial, stimulating, and provocative life?

The creation and production of a book is always a collective enterprise. This applies especially to the complex dynamics and logistics of conference volumes. I would like to express my gratitude to the many contributors to *Hannah Arendt in Jerusalem,* who have displayed exemplary patience on the sometimes painfully slow road to publication. I hope that the result justifies their powers of endurance. I would also like to thank the various members of the staff of the University of California Press: Bud Bynack, for his excellent copyediting, Stanley Holwitz, Scott Norton, Mary Olivas, and Laura Pasquale. Without their dedication and skill, this volume would never have seen the light of day.

Introduction

Hannah Arendt in Jerusalem

Steven Aschheim

In the intellectual discourse of our day, Hannah Arendt has become something of an icon. The climate of postmodernism and identity politics and the search for a non-ideological, post-totalitarian worldview have endowed her thought with renewed relevance and vitality. In Western Europe and the United States, even in Eastern Europe, her work has become the subject of intense, often celebratory interest and analysis.[1] In Israel, however, this engagement has been conspicuously lacking. This may tell us as much about our own cultural self-understanding and biases as it does about the nature of Arendt's person and thought. In Israel, beginning prior to, but certainly coming to a climax with, the appearance in 1963 of her deeply controversial, explosive book on Eichmann, Arendt has to all intents and purposes been relegated to the status of an adversary, an "enemy" tainted by "self-hating," indeed anti-Semitic, impulses, condemned as a thinker whose tone and work violated some of the society's basic taboos.[2] The experience of reading Arendt, I have been told by a number of sophisticated Israeli intellectuals, still evokes a visceral sense of physical revulsion. This is a distaste that has been marked, moreover, not so much by overt confrontation and refutation as by stark, collective silence and implicit communal excommunication.[3]

It is a quite remarkable but telling fact that none of Hannah Arendt's work was translated into Hebrew until 2000.[4] It will not do to claim, as some have, that other major thinkers of the Cold War period such as Karl Popper and Friedrich Hayek went similarly untranslated. For, quite unlike with these authors, Arendt's life and thought were passionately linked to core predicaments of the modern Jewish experience. Her work analyzed almost all the great issues, often in pioneering and provocative fashion—the complex dynamics of emancipation and assimilation, the tortuous binds of Western Jewish identity and its "psychologized" forms, the phenomenon of nineteenth-century and twentieth-century Jewish intellectual and cultural creativity, the nature of anti-Semitism and totalitarianism, Jewish politics and Zionism, and, above all, the genocidal eruption of Nazism and the Holocaust.[5] It was precisely her *involvement* in these matters, her troubling relevance, that rendered her so threatening. In Israel's still-developing, insecure, and highly ideological culture wary of partial identifications and provisional commitments, critiques, especially in the ironic mode (often made in an offhand, arrogant manner), could not be easily absorbed.

Today, in a later, quite different climate, there are signs of a new generational openness, a willingness to receive and read Arendt somewhat differently, perhaps even to appropriate selected aspects of her thought.[6] But to understand the history and nature of Arendt's reception in Jerusalem to date, we must also examine the closely interrelated ways in which Arendt herself engaged and imagined Jerusalem—actually and metaphorically.[7] In order to do this satisfactorily, it is necessary to place Arendt within the relevant historical context.

Like the figures she vividly brought to life—Rahel Varnhagen, Heinrich Heine, Franz Kafka, Hermann Broch, and many others—Hannah Arendt, her achievements and biases, her creativity and inner conflicts, must be seen as part of the quite extraordinary history of post-emancipation German-Jewish intellectuals and their wider engagement with the imperatives of German culture and its later great breakdown. Arendt not only was a keen analyst of that experience, but was herself a central expression of it.[8] Indeed, much of her acuity derived from the fact that she embodied the tensions and contradictions that fueled so much of its creativity, especially as they manifested themselves in the productive turbulence of the Weimar Republic, in which she spent her formative years. Her Weimar friends, lovers, and adversaries—including Karl Jaspers and Martin Heidegger, Kurt Blumenfeld, Theodor Adorno, Gershom Scholem, and Walter Benjamin—were all incarnations of its manifold, yet related sensibilities.

Arendt was both an explicator and a living example of what Dan Diner, in another context, has termed the "Western" Jewish narrative.[9] Unlike its Eastern European counterpart, which was constructed upon the basis of collective, national experience and a singular self-understanding, this narrative takes as its starting point the individual and the rupture with community and tradition, the engagement with manifold cultural worlds and political affiliations. It highlights ambivalence, multiple loyalties, fissures, breakdowns, and partial reconstitutions. One could argue that perhaps one source of difficulty in absorbing Arendt within Jerusalem was that such a model of fracture and conflict did not sit easily with more organic national narratives cut out of more unified, heroic materials.

But, of course, the situation is more complicated than this. Events around Arendt pushed this classic *Bildungs* intellectual to turn sharply away from that tradition's unworldly, apolitical cultivation of individual interiority.[10] In reaction to the duplicities of Western Jewish social assimilation, which she critiqued as acutely as she diagnosed them, and to the rise of the Nazis and her own experience as a refugee, we should not forget, she advocated what amounted to an activist Zionist solution: a worldly, affirmative politics of collective Jewish existence and national Jewish rights. Witness her militant call for the formation of a Jewish army during World War II.[11] Indeed, throughout the 1930s and 1940s, she entirely devoted herself, not just intellectually, but also practically and professionally, to Jewish and Zionist commitments. It was none other than her later nemesis, Gershom Scholem, who in 1941 described her as "a wonderful woman and an extraordinary Zionist."[12]

If later, controversially, she opposed statehood and wrote highly critical articles about Zionism, she did not question the need for a Jewish homeland, and her historiography of modern Jewish life and anti-Semitism was laden with Zionist assumptions. And even after the great disputes around the Eichmann book—which she described as "the war between me and the Jews"—she wrote to Mary McCarthy concerning the 1967 war: "Any real catastrophe in Israel would affect me more deeply than anything else."[13] Indeed, in the wake of that war, even *her* critical judgment was momentarily suspended, overtaken by the prevalent euphoria of the time. She wrote to Jaspers:

> Israel: In many respects, in most actually, very encouraging. It's really quite wonderful that an entire nation reacts to a victory like that not by bellowing hurrah but with a real orgy of tourism—everybody has to go to have a look at the newly conquered territory. I was in all the formerly Arab territories and never noticed any conqueror behavior in the stream of Israeli

tourists. The Arab population was more hostile than I expected . . . as far as the country itself is concerned, one can clearly see from what great fear it has suddenly been freed. That contributes significantly to improving the national character.[14]

It is precisely because of the complexity of her commitments, her partial "insider" status, and the difficulties of classifying her that Arendt was so unassimilable, baffling to Jewish establishments both within and without Israel.[15] After all, it is far easier to pigeonhole and dismiss classic disaffected intellectuals, or what Isaac Deutscher called universalist non-Jewish Jews. They fit a pattern. Arendt was something else. She is best understood in terms of Michael Walzer's portrait of "connected critics," those figures whose life and thought are characterized not by detachment but rather by passionate, yet essentially ambiguous engagement.[16] It is precisely this relationship that rendered her challenges and the responses to them particularly charged, emotionally overdetermined. Moreover, Arendt's insistence upon what she termed "thinking without banisters," upon critical judgment and non-ideological categories, made her even more difficult to categorize. To make matters worse, she was peppered by what critics both in Israel and elsewhere regarded as an almost perverse desire for originality, a penchant for extreme, nasty, and arrogant, even at times bizarre, declarations.[17] "These Hungarian Jews à la Koestler do not become any more pleasant because one denies Hitler the right to kill them," she proclaimed to Hermann Broch.[18]

On the one hand, the fact of her Jewishness, even her strident affirmation of it, was never in question. "I belong to [the Jews]," she wrote, "beyond dispute or agreement." "One Does Not Escape Jewishness," reads the title of the last chapter of her book on Rahel Varnhagen— her most revealingly personal work, one that, as Arendt herself put it, "was written from the perspective of a Zionist critique of assimilation" and that was well received in Jerusalem.[19] Interestingly, her friend Karl Jaspers objected to the book precisely *because* of this proto-Zionist bias. In working through her own issues of identity, he argued, Arendt had presented Rahel entirely one-dimensionally: "you force everything under the rubric of being a Jew."[20] Arendt, he declared, had ideologically flattened Rahel's "unconditional" humanity and in her antipathy to the Enlightenment had reduced the full force of her own individual personality.

But, of course, Arendt's determined identification was by no means absolute. It was most clear and decisive under conditions of persecution, where, as she put it in her 1959 Lessing Prize address, one had to "resist only in terms of the identity that is under attack." "Politically," she declared in 1946, "I will speak only in the name of the Jews," but she immediately qualified this by adding "whenever circumstances force me to give my nationality." Ultimately, she resisted all totalizing definitions, insisting that no single or homogeneous identities and identifications adequately account for the disclosive complexities of selfhood. When asked by Jaspers whether she was a German or a Jew, she replied: "To be perfectly honest, it doesn't matter to me in the least on the personal and individual level." [21] This problem of group versus individual loyalties, of commitment and criticism, formed an essential part of the tension between Arendt and Jerusalem. It was expressed in Arendt's famous response to Scholem's 1963 admonition that she lacked *ahavat Israel,* love of the Jewish people. "Love," Arendt insisted, is not a collective matter: "I indeed love 'only' my friends and the only kind of love I know of and believe in is the love of persons." [22]

Thus, even her celebrations of aspects of Zionist life contained an unrelenting, insightful edge of critical complexity. The pioneers of the kibbutz, she wrote, "did succeed in creating a new type of Jew, even a kind of aristocracy with their newly established values; their genuine contempt for material wealth, exploitation and bourgeois life; their unique combination of culture and labor; their rigorous realization of social justice within their small circle; and their loving pride in the fertile soil, the work of their hands, together with an utter and surprising lack of any wish for personal possession." Yet, at the same time, she exclaimed, it was as if they had "established themselves on the moon," a laboring community of "innocent obliviousness," one "that did not even stop to think of the very existence of Arabs." [23]

At the same time as she unabashedly confirmed her Jewishness and tried to provide it with political shape and expression, then, Arendt continued to challenge the unreflexive, self-celebratory nature of group affiliations.[24] Indeed, she took great pride in the complex, even subversive nature of her own intertwined commitments. Thus, her second husband, Heinrich Blücher, was not only a non-Jew; he was, to boot, a proletarian and so nonconformist a German Marxist that as an adolescent, he joined the Zionist group the Blau Weiss.[25] As Arendt put it in 1946: "If I had wanted to become respectable I would either have had to give up my interest in Jewish affairs or not marry a non-Jewish man, either option equally inhuman and in a sense crazy." [26] The intimate, sometimes highly erotic, correspondence between Blücher and Arendt documents these unorthodox predilections in critically prejudiced and humorously

self-conscious ways. Writing to him in 1936 about a meeting to found
the World Jewish Congress, Arendt comments that the proceedings were
partly conducted in Hebrew, "which after all my dismal attempts to learn
it, is no language, but a national misfortune! So, my love, don't let
yourself be circumcised." Yet her letters to her friend the great novelist
Hermann Broch and to Blücher were peppered with affectionate Yiddish-
isms. "I am the only German Jewess anywhere that has learned Yiddish," she declared to Blücher—whom she addresses as my "beloved
wonder rabbi."[27]

These multiple loyalties clearly colored Arendt's dialogue with Jerusalem. In 1955, she wrote to Blumenfeld concerning Scholem: "I cannot
tolerate this nationalist chatter that isn't really seriously intended and
that springs from a quite understandable anxiety. And this gossip about
the goyim gets pretty much on my nerves. I should have mentioned that
I actually am married to such a 'Goy' and that one should feel as little
free in my company to talk about this, as one should talk absolutely
'freely' about the Jews in Heinrich's presence."[28]

It is precisely this dual moment, this insider-outsider tension, evident
in the personal and narrative clashes that emerged from deep bonds and
commonalties, that constitutes the complexities of Arendt in Jerusalem.
I would suggest that the source of her achievements, conflicts, and limitations lay in the fact that in her great engagement with the wider world,
especially with German culture, she exemplified the bifurcated Western
Jew that she so acutely diagnosed and critiqued. "The behavior patterns
of assimilated Jews," she wrote in *The Origins of Totalitarianism*, "determined by this continuous concentrated effort to distinguish themselves, created a Jewish type that is recognizable everywhere. Instead of
being defined by nationality or religion, Jews were being transformed
into a social group whose members shared certain psychological attributes and reactions, the sum total of which was to constitute 'Jewishness.' In other words, Judaism became a psychological quality and the
Jewish question became an involved personal problem for every individual Jew."[29]

Arendt's really interesting insights, which both reflected and were
transformed into her larger philosophical vision, concentrated upon
both the "Jewish" and general aspects of Western and Central European
cultural fragmentation, breakdowns, and attempted recoveries. These,
of course, were particularly acutely felt and analyzed during the Weimar
Republic. Little wonder, for instance, that Arendt was so enamored of

Kafka's works.[30] Her insightful analysis of Benjamin and Scholem applies equally to her own thought in matters both Jewish and general:

> Benjamin's choice, baroque in a double sense, has an exact counterpart in Scholem's strange decision to approach Judaism via the Cabala, that is, that part of Hebrew literature which is untransmitted and untransmissible in terms of Jewish tradition, in which it has always had the odor of something downright disreputable. Nothing showed more clearly—so one is inclined to say today—that there was no such thing as a "return" to either the German or the European or the Jewish tradition than the choice of these fields of study. It was an implicit admission that the past spoke directly only through these things that had not been handed down, whose seeming closeness to the present was thus due precisely to their exotic character, which ruled out all claims to a binding authority.[31]

The most clear-sighted of these intellectuals, Arendt added, "were led by their personal [Jewish] conflicts to a much more general and radical problem, namely, to questioning the relevance of the Western tradition as a whole."[32] This, surely, was also meant autobiographically. What ultimately was Arendt's project but the attempt to rethink the Western political and philosophical tradition? (It is worth noting that many establishment Jewish and Israeli intellectuals have remained stuck at the level of problems engendered by Arendt's Jewish narrative. This, at least until now, has constituted a block toward engaging her more general thought.)

Of course, if Arendt's strengths and insights were rooted in this experience, so, too, were many of her weaknesses and limitations. This great critic of assimilationist, bourgeois German Jewry shared many of its basic historical prejudices. She poured all of them into a few pungent sentences in a letter from Jerusalem when she came to report on the Eichmann trial:

> My first impression. On top, the judges, the best of German Jewry. Below them, the persecuting attorneys, Galicians, but still Europeans. Everything is organized by a police force that gives me the creeps, speaks only Hebrew and looks Arabic. Some downright brutal types among them. They would follow any order. And outside the doors, the oriental mob, as if one were in Istanbul or some other half-Asiatic country. In addition, and very visible in Jerusalem, the peies [sidelocked] and caftan Jews, who make life impossible for all the reasonable people here.[33]

But these were, on the whole, private utterances that need not preoccupy us here. What does need attention in the present context is Arendt's willingness, indeed determination, publicly to challenge fundamental precepts of collective narrative and memory. While her defenders argue that she sought to do so as a matter of intellectual principle and honesty, her critics regard this as a kind of tactless perversity, the desire to damage the Jews at their most sensitive and vulnerable points. Throughout this volume, we examine the content, the strengths, and the many weaknesses of Arendt's relevant Jewish writings. Here I do not want to make such an assessment. Rather, I want to try to capture the emotional undergrowth, the atmospheric resonances and subtexts that, I think, provoked such outraged reactions.

It was, of course, over the Eichmann book that the issues were most intensely played out, especially over Arendt's by now very familiar depiction of the behavior of the *Judenräte,* the Jewish councils that cooperated with the Nazis, her allegedly sympathetic portrait of Eichmann, and her book's seeming violation of what Richard Cohen has called "the power of the myth and the sacredness of the memory." [34] The key protagonists themselves were quite aware of the preintellectual, prerational nature of the issues it broached and the extreme emotions it evoked. These ranged from feelings of liberation, of having told the truth in the face of collective pressures, to accusations of self-hatred, of betrayal, of having "crossed over." Mary McCarthy wrote: "To me, *Eichmann in Jerusalem,* despite all the horrors in it, was morally exhilarating. I freely confess that it gave me joy and I too heard a paean in it—not a hate-paean to totalitarianism but a paean of transcendence, heavenly music, like that of the final chorus of *Figaro* or the *Messiah.* . . . The reader 'rose above' the terrible material of the trial or was borne aloft to survey it with his intelligence." And Arendt, though she thought McCarthy's comparisons a little excessive, told her: "You were the only reader to understand what otherwise I have never admitted—namely that I wrote this book in a curious state of euphoria. And that ever since I did it, I feel . . . light-hearted about the whole matter. Don't tell anybody; is it not proof positive that I have no 'soul'?" [35] And, on the other side of the fence, it was not only this apparent lightheartedness, what Scholem called her "heartless, frequently almost sneering and malicious tone . . . touching the very quick of our life" that grated, but the shock that such sentiments could be publicly expressed by someone whom he regarded, as he put it, "wholly as a daughter of our people, and in no other way." [36]

Karl Jaspers (though he thought the book was "magnificent") acutely recognized the relevant gut level of the matter when he curtly dismissed

Arendt's theory that the hostility toward her was motivated by her be-lief that the *Judenrat* members she had criticized occupied positions of power in Israel and by fear of revelations about Zionist-Nazi cooper-ation during the war. "If that were so," Jaspers correctly pointed out, "then people would have some knowledge of these things." Instead, he suggested: "What is revealed here is a deep-seated sense of having been struck a mortal blow. . . . Something in 'Jewry' itself has been struck a blow." [37]

It is worth pointing out that, although it did not evoke anything like the same outcry, the same structural tensions applied to Arendt's Oc-tober 1944 piece "Zionism Reconsidered." [38] Again, what mattered as much as the content of her arguments was the fact that they touched upon the question of solidarity and the limits of loyal, connected criti-cism. Once again, but this time in an unpublished letter, it was Scholem who angrily responded. He fashioned a well-wrought, piercing refu-tation, but what underlies it is the pain and confusion engendered by the fact that this attack was written by a supposed friend. He registered surprise that her arguments were based "not on Zionist but rather ex-treme . . . anti-Zionist grounds." Given Arendt's explicit Zionist com-mitments at the time, Scholem had expected an immanent critique, one that took a position from "within." Instead, as he put it, he found an in-discriminate mix of arguments, stated scornfully and written from the viewpoint of a universalistic morality that existed in practice nowhere but in the heads of disaffected Jewish intellectuals. [39] Years later, in 1968, he wrote an embittered letter to Hans Paeschke in which he made it clear that it was Arendt's fickleness, her disloyalty to her vaunted ideological and group commitments, that above all disturbed him: "I knew Hannah Arendt when she was a socialist or half-communist" (an assertion, by the way, always heatedly denied by Arendt, who consistently claimed that "If I can be said to 'have come from anywhere' it is from the tradi-tion of German philosophy"), "and I knew her when she was a Zionist. I am astounded by her ability to pronounce upon movements in which she was once so deeply engaged, in terms of a distance measured in light years and from such sovereign heights." [40]

Even in his original reply to Arendt's anti-Zionist polemic, Scholem made explicit the fact that this was a confrontation about the nature of ideological commitment: "I confess my guilt with the greatest calm to most of the sins that you have attributed to Zionism. I am a nation-alist and fully unmoved by apparently progressive declarations against a view, that since my earliest youth has been repeatedly declared as super-seded. . . . I am a 'sectarian' and have never been ashamed to present my conviction of sectarianism as decisive and positive."[41]

As the years went by, the rift between the two became even greater. We should not, however, exaggerate this. Viewed in a larger historical perspective, their differences and the intensity with which they expressed them were, I think, linked to a certain kind of kinship and flowed from some profound commonalties. Family quarrels, after all, are often the most strongly felt. Both exemplified the radical revolt against German-Jewish bourgeois modes of assimilation. Both were classical German-Jewish intellectuals, products of the European and Jewish traditions that they subjected to the most withering critiques. (This, I think, in many ways accounts for their current fascination in Western intellectual circles.)[42] Both, as David Suchoff points out, "created new models for the transmission of tradition and the relation between culture and political action. Their writing sought to confront, without repressing, the scandal that Jewish particularity posed to German culture in their period."[43]

Paradoxically, their negative personal evaluations of each other also looked like mirror images. Each regarded the other as megalomaniacally arrogant and self-obsessed. Already in 1957, Arendt wrote that Scholem was "so self-preoccupied that he has no eyes (and not only that: no ears). Basically he believes: The midpoint of the world is Israel; the midpoint of Israel is Jerusalem, the midpoint of Jerusalem is the university and the midpoint of the university is Scholem. And the worst of it is that he really believes that the world has a central point."[44]

Yet, for all that, the differences are not insignificant. Arendt's critical narrative ultimately did depart from a more organic and totalizing national (and Zionist) version. The twentieth-century experience of forced statelessness rendered her suspicious of the logic of all homogenizing politics. Her evolving political thought focused, at least in part, on the dynamic possibilities entailed in multiple new beginnings and on an open, disclosive performativity.[45] In works such as *The Human Condition* and *On Revolution,* she developed an alternative conception designed to enhance the public spaces and dimensions of freedom and the possibilities of action. This was a politics in which plurality was placed at the center. (Whatever else she may have shared with her lover-mentor Martin Heidegger—postmetaphysical thinking, the problematic conservative critique of instrumental modernity and mass society, and so on—Arendt's emphasis on the primacy of the political realm and the intrinsic value of plurality decidedly separated her from him.)[46] As recent readings of her work have emphasized, she held that "a political community that constitutes itself on the basis of a prior, shared, and stable identity threatens to close the spaces of politics, to homogenize or repress the plurality and multiplicity that political action postulates."[47]

It was these emphases, and not meanness or "self-hatred," that lay behind Arendt's repeated (and not unwarranted) warnings about chauvinist Zionist and Israeli attitudes toward the Arabs. She did, one must point out, repeatedly recognize the element of fear that lay behind such egocentric attitudes but held that such fears only increased the dangers. If at times she spoke warmly of certain Israeli achievements, she could also be extremely cutting. Israel, she stated in a 1961 letter, was the "ghetto-mentality with tanks and military parades." For her, clearly, the logic of the nation-state does not solve the problem that totalitarianism raises most acutely. Rather, it both precedes and to some degree reproduces it. "The troublesome majority-minority constellation," she wrote in May 1948, "is insoluble by definition."[48]

We need to examine a still more acute narrative tension between Arendt and Jerusalem, and this in an even more sensitive area. In order to do so, we must make a brief detour. Arendt, we should not forget, became famous, above all, for her work on Nazism and totalitarianism, especially for *The Origins of Totalitarianism,* that extraordinarily idiosyncratic book, so patently wrong-minded in parts, so willfully peculiar in its historical method (or lack of it), yet punctuated by flashes of brilliance and original insight. This work was animated by the conviction that Nazism and Auschwitz—far more than the Soviet experience—were the great transgressive moment in European history. That conviction was certainly evident in many of her essays throughout the 1940s and early 1950s. Upon learning of Auschwitz in 1943, she later reported: "It was really as if an abyss had opened. . . . Something happened there to which we cannot reconcile ourselves. None of us ever can." And as she wrote to Kurt Blumenfeld in 1947, while composing the book: "You see, I cannot get over the extermination factories."[49] Arendt's classical "totalitarian" approach may have employed an essentially comparative method, but unlike that of the later *Historikerstreit* historians, who in the 1980s questioned the radical uniqueness of the Holocaust, it never entailed a hint of relativization—implicitly, the Nazi case was the one really in need of explanation, the ultimate against which other crimes were measured.[50]

Despite all its shortcomings, the appearance in 1951 of *The Origins of Totalitarianism* satisfied an urgent need. Until then, and for at least a decade after that,[51] there were virtually no serious attempts to forge the theoretical, historical, and conceptual tools necessary to illuminate the great cataclysms of the twentieth century. Indeed, to this day, historians find it difficult to integrate these events persuasively and coherently into the flow of this century's history. Arendt was seen to provide an account adequate to the enormity of the materials and problems at hand. To be sure, the term "the Holocaust" had not yet crystallized and does not appear in the book. It may even be that the generalized notion of "totalitarianism" precluded any thoroughgoing, separate analysis of the "Final Solution," with its distinct motivational history. Later critics, such as Saul Friedlander, argued that the "totalitarian framework is the means of destruction, not its basic explanation." Nevertheless, for contemporaries hungry for understanding, the work was regarded as revelatory precisely because, as Alfred Kazin put it, it seemed to address itself "to the gas."[52]

What I want to highlight here, then, is Arendt's crucial role in the formulation and creation of the ubiquitous postwar "discourse on evil," one in which Nazism and Auschwitz have become emblematic of Western culture's conceptions of absolute inhumanity.[53] In 1945, she wrote: "The problem of evil will be the fundamental question of postwar intellectual life in Europe." Indeed, *The Origins of Totalitarianism* can be read as an attempt to try to answer that question, especially through her organizing idea of "radical evil," a notion that gave expression to her conception of the novelty of these events and the impulses that generated them. Here was an unprecedented evil, incomprehensible in terms of traditionally understandable, sinful human motives. She left the definition somewhat vague but concluded that "radical evil has emerged in connection with a system in which all men have become equally superfluous."[54]

Arendt's early awareness of Nazism's radical transgressiveness convinced her that entirely new and often very problematic ways of thinking, new categories of analysis, were required. Her espousal of a dubious model of mass society derived from conservative European social theory,[55] and her total dismissal of German *Sonderweg* explanations based on the notion of German exceptionalism—"Luther or Kant or Hegel or Nietzsche," she wrote, "have not the least responsibility for what is happening in the extermination camps"—may have been extreme and somewhat misguided, but I do not think they were impelled, as has recently been suggested, by her desire to exculpate a guilty culture to which she remained loyal. For her, these conventional explanations were simply inadequate. "Nazism," she insisted, "is actually the break-down of all German and European traditions, the good as well as the bad."[56] Continuity could not thus account for the emergence of an entirely new genocidal mentality. Rather, it was the breakdown of older frameworks, the emergence of new social and political structures and unprecedented expansionary drives, the urge to destroy all previous limits, to render everything possible, that constituted the key.

But how does all this relate to the Arendt-Jerusalem relationship? If, later, there were doubts about placing Nazism and Stalinism under a single rubric, her emphasis on the link between the extermination factories and "radical evil" sat well in Jerusalem. So too, one presumes, did some of her general historiographical impulses. While her depiction of early modern Jewish power and its alliance with the absolutist state and economy raised eyebrows (she dismissed all scapegoat theories as painfully inadequate), her emphasis on situating Jews at the storm center of events, her desire to grasp anti-Semitism at its deadliest level, flowed from her Zionist sensibilities.[57]

But Arendt—to put it mildly—was not Daniel Goldhagen. She was never happy to see these extreme events portrayed in terms of a simple dichotomy between wildly anti-Semitic German killers and Jewish victims. From the beginning, she was impelled by the conviction that the method and the nature of the killings went beyond essentialized anthropological distinctions and raised explanatory and moral issues of urgent universal concern.[58] She insisted that Jew hatred was a necessary but not sufficient condition for genocide. "Neither the fate of European Jewry nor the establishment of death factories," she wrote, "can be fully explained and grasped in terms of anti-Semitism."[59] This jelled less easily with Zionist sensibilities, as did her repeated assertion that anti-Semitism is not an eternal, ahistorical given. Moreover, her contempt for explanations that resorted to German national character or history did not sit comfortably with popular and even some scholarly Israeli and Jewish archetypal images, and perhaps it still does not.[60]

In its stead, she insisted from the beginning upon general rather than national categories of historical and psychological analysis, viewing events in terms of universal processes and "human" capacities. In 1945, she stated: "The reality is that 'the Nazis are men like ourselves'; the nightmare is that they have . . . proven beyond doubt what man is capable of."[61] Whatever the validity of this position, her later, much contested rendering of Eichmann in "ordinary" terms as a dull, essentially "thoughtless" bureaucrat flowed from these assumptions and deeply threatened the older, perhaps more demonizing view that constituted the prevailing model and that perhaps still does. There are scholarly disputes as to whether or not there is continuity in Arendt's various imaginings of evil,[62] but, clearly, the apparent shift from its "radical" to "banal" expression was not well received, even as it was not always well understood. In the eyes of many, Arendt was seen, quite mistakenly, I believe, to slight the enormity of the event, to domesticate its monstrous unspeakability.

This was a real source of narrative tension. At the same time as she formulated this discourse of evil, Arendt also presciently problematized and sought to demystify it. Indeed, in her treatment of the *Judenräte,* her apparent blurring of the almost sacrosanct distinction between perpetrators and victims seemed to violate fundamental sensibilities, even though she contextualized this blurring as part of a general moral collapse under the extreme conditions of totalitarian society. Moreover, very early on, Arendt warned that the uniqueness of the atrocities could create a self-righteous cult of victimization, one that indeed has occurred. (Witness the absurd current competition in comparative victimization as a tool of identity politics.) She wrote the following extremely harsh words in August 1946:

> Human beings simply can't be as innocent as they all were in the face of the gas chambers (the most repulsive usurer was as innocent as the newborn child because no crime deserves such a punishment). We are simply not equipped to deal, on a human, political level, with a guilt that is beyond crime and an innocence that is beyond goodness or virtue . . . we Jews are burdened by millions of innocents, by reasons of which every Jew alive today can see himself as innocence personified.[63]

Arendt, then, was not prepared to insulate or grant absolute privilege to Jewish history and suffering, despite her emphasis on the radical novelty of the exterminations. Even in the context of analyzing the murders, she insisted on locating Zionism within a wider victimizing context. While she maintained that "the State of Israel . . . in no way arose exclusively from . . . necessity,"[64] she kept very much in mind the tragic price of that necessity. As she put it in *The Origins of Totalitarianism:* "After the war it turned out that the Jewish question, which was considered the only insoluble one, was indeed solved—namely, by means of a colonized and then conquered territory—but this solved neither the problem of the minorities nor the stateless. On the contrary, like virtually all other events of our century, the solution of the Jewish question merely produced a new category of refugees, the Arabs, thereby increasing the number of the stateless and rightless by another 700,000 to 800,000 people."[65]

Viewed historically, it seems that Arendt was indeed unassimilable in Jerusalem, at least during the earlier years, when the state and Israeli society were coming into being. Nation building encourages organic, heroic, homogeneous narratives. It could not, I suggest, easily absorb her iconoclasms or afford her ambiguities, her blurring of boundaries. It may be, however, that now, in a more secure, mature, increasingly self-critical and self-ironizing intellectual culture—especially as it cohabits with an ever more intolerant and dogmatic polity—there can be greater receptivity not only to Arendt's insights into the modern Jewish experience and the Nazi genocide, but also to her general observations concerning the dangers of homogeneity and the importance of a free, plural political space.[66]

At any rate, we in Jerusalem need no longer demonize Arendt. Nor, on the other hand, must we canonize her. I am not suggesting that we name an express train in her honor or place her face on a postage stamp, as was done in Germany.[67] And Karl Jaspers's 1963 prediction is certainly still premature. He wrote then to Arendt: "A time will come that you will not live to see, when the Jews will erect a monument to you in Israel . . . and they will proudly claim you as their own."[68] As far as I know, there is not yet even a sculpture. But, surely, the time for greater critical and sympathetic engagement is upon us.

HANNAH ARENDT

Politics and Philosophy

Hannah Arendt on Tradition and New Beginnings

Agnes Heller

Wer auf die Welt kommt, baut ein neues Haus,
Er geht und lasst es einem zweiten.
Der wird sich's anders zubereiten
Und niemand baut es aus.

Goethe

I begin with a quotation from Goethe, for I think that this poetic aphorism illuminates Arendt's vision of history, of politics, and of the world. To fence off criticism right at the beginning, I know that the metaphor "building a house" is associated in Arendt's philosophy with work or creation, and not with action. In Goethe's poem, however, it stands for both, yet in a paradoxical form, as an aporia. Goethe says that everyone who is born will build a *new* house—will build their own world—and that it is this new house that another will inherit, and this other will change the house, yet no one will finish it, accomplish it.

What is paradoxical in the aphorism? Surely, it sounds impossible that everyone who comes into the world will build a new house, whereas the same everyone will inherit the house from the previous generation, only to refurbish and to rebuild it. If everyone did build a new house, there would be as many worlds as people on earth, but how can the other then rebuild the house he or she has inherited—in other words, share a world with others? And if everyone did in fact rebuild the house that is inherited, and there would be just one world, although a world of difference, how could everyone who comes into the world still build an entirely new house?

As we shall see, this is the paradox Arendt constantly faces. She suggests in the preface of her first collection of philosophical essays, *Be-*

tween Past and Future,[1] that we are squeezed between the old and the new. Humans have been thrown into a world of pull and push, but they can disrupt the continuity. Beginning anew as the interruption of continuity is the essence of human action. But only continuity can be interrupted, for interruption cannot be interrupted. Political action cuts the thread that binds actors to tradition. Yet it is also true that a loss of tradition means a loss of what Arendt called "treasure,"[2] or rather of *the* treasure, the past: If there is no treasure to inherit, there is no continuity at all, no past, no future, just the eternal recurrence of the same. How can this be? How can one begin something absolutely new at any time and also preserve and cherish the treasures of the past?

There is no Hegelian dialectic between continuity and discontinuity in Arendt's work because the contradiction is not sublated. And Arendt tells us why she rejects philosophical sublation. She says that one could sublate this contradiction between continuity and discontinuity only if one told a single story about history. But those who tell one single story about history, the master thinkers of the grand narrative, cannot assume the political perspective. They must switch to the historical perspective, instead. Political perspective enhances the comprehension of action, action in its own right, whereas the historical perspective is the attitude of mere contemplation. To switch from the political to the historical was —before Hegel—already Kant's way to avoid the paradox, Arendt assures us. She prefers switching back to the political position, a position of comprehension and reflection: comprehending political action and reflecting on tradition.[3]

But one can assume the position of comprehension and reflection only if one does not undertake the grand project to tell one single story about history and instead decides to tell many different stories of new beginnings and of traditions. These stories should not be merely different in topic, but also different in kind. Stories that are both different in topic and different in kind are stories of traditions and new beginnings that can never be completely fitted together, because if taken together and told in one breath, they would still not yield one comprehensive story or theory about the "category" of new beginnings and tradition and their relation as such. The content of the "category" will constantly change. Arendt tells her stories without pretending that her stories are the only true ones to be told about this or that event. Yet she is passionately involved in her stories, and, of course, she believes in their verisimilitude, in the sense of the German *fürwahrhalten,* the expression so much

liked by Kant, and also in their political significance and effect. For stories thus told are also acts of political intervention.

Almost all Arendt's books are also acts of political intervention. Stories also can be acts of a new beginning in political thinking. But as it is
the case in every new beginning in the world of politics, intervention
through story telling is also a shot in the dark, a gesture of courage and
daring, a provocation. Arendt was aware of the fallibility and the
fragility of her stories. But stories that are not fallible and fragile, stories
that are not also shots in the dark, stories that merely contemplate action, rather than comprehending it, cannot give actions their due, nor
can they invite others to act—not even to tell alternative stories. In a
story of progressive development or regressive self-destruction, that is,
in a narrative with a tendency toward the consummation that is its end,
liberty plays only the role of the midwife or the gravedigger. Freedom
can fare even worse, as in the ancient Stoic or Gnostic vision of *heimarmene,* the uncontrollable fate, the eternal recurrence of the same, where
there remains only a pathetic place for the vestiges of a negative and
merely subjective freedom. Augustine pitted *pronoia* (divine providence)
against *heimarmene,* whereas Arendt pits natality—birth, a new beginning—as freedom against it.

It is not inconsistency, but the essence of Arendt's way of seeing things
that the relation between new beginnings and tradition is not depicted
in the same fashion in her different narratives, that both new beginnings
and tradition appear in different lights, and that their contrasts and /
or their connections are always presented in different forms. Arendt is
comprehending, thinking; she is thinking in stories. She chooses certain
stories not for their own sake, but in the spirit of political intervention.
She normally knows ahead of time what she is seeking in them, even if—
sometimes—she also finds or discovers something unexpected. The best
and deepest of Arendt's stories are those in which she does not violate
her texts by a certain preconception but rather allows the story to tell
itself, or, at least, to speak its own lines.

In what follows, I will discuss briefly three different Arendtian stories, the first from *The Origins of Totalitarianism,* the second from *The
Human Condition,* and the third from *On Revolution.* One of Arendt's
greatest achievements is the way in which, in stories like these, the meanings of the concept of new beginnings and the concept of tradition shift
and do not let themselves be fitted together in a unified and comprehensive theory. In a world that is brittle, the stories better remain brittle,

too. Arendt's stories are always about here and now, because they are also stories of the just here and the just now, of the *nunc stans* of discontinuity, where they are situated. If abstracted from their situation, they lose much of their theoretical and rhetorical power. It is *as stories* that they are a treasure to preserve, a living tradition of contemporary thinking.

I start with a quotation from *The Origins of Totalitarianism.*

> It is almost impossible even now to describe what actually happened in Europe on August 14, 1914. The days before and the days after the first World War are separated not like the end of an old, and the beginning of a new period, but like the day before and the day after an explosion. . . . The first explosion seems to have touched off a chain reaction in which we have been caught ever since and which nobody seems to be able to stop. . . . The first World War exploded the European comity of nations beyond repair. Nothing which was being done . . . no matter how many people foretold the consequences could be undone or prevented. Every event had the finality of a last judgment, a judgment that was passed neither by God nor by the devil, but looked rather like the expression of some unredeemably stupid phantasy.[4]

August 14, 1914, is described here by Arendt as a crack, or rather an abyss, as the *nunc stans* squeezed between past and future. Europeans began something entirely new then, the fateful twentieth century, and they abandoned their treasure, the tradition of the European comity of the nineteenth century. There is no question that World War I is also a case of natality. In politics, explosions are not natural phenomena. They are initiated by action, more precisely, by political action. For Arendt, everything that takes place between two or more persons without employing a material as mediation except the human voice, speech acts included, is an action. All actions bring uncertainties into the world. Their results are unpredictable. The actor takes a chance, embarks on a deed in broad daylight. In the general sense of action, it was political action that caused August 14, 1914, an explosion the results of which no one could foresee. Something new had been initiated, and the actors, squeezed between an already accomplished past and a present not yet present, had acted freely.

But for Arendt, liberation, freedom, the constitution of freedoms are very distinct actions or events. Free acts initiated World War I, but those acts resulted in a chain of fateful and irreversible events. This is why Arendt's well-known enthusiasm for all kinds of new beginnings and free action can hardly be detected in this text: not just because something happened that the actors did not foresee, since this eventuality inheres in the essence of political action, but because the chain reaction simply had run its course. There was no space for political action.

Thus, in Arendt's mind—and this we need to take for granted—World War I had absolutely nothing to do with politics. Arendt tells here a story in which the possibility of new beginning is absent. But how far did the consequences of this period extend? How long did it last? In fact, Arendt hints at two different chains of consequences for the period. The first is the development of the war itself, which resulted in the phenomenon of statelessness and in the decline of the nation-state. These events became unstoppable, ran their course, and in this sense left no territory for political action as a new beginning.

The second chain of consequences is the twentieth century in its entirety, with all its vicissitudes, horrors, and also eventual triumphs. Still, although the twentieth century in its entirety was triggered by World War I, there have been several new beginnings during the twentieth century, all the same. But if there were new beginnings, why was the event of August 14 beyond repair? Because it changed the world. And every new beginning in Europe took place in this world, in a world that resulted from World War I, even if political action itself is not "worlding" and always initiates something entirely new. Arendt tells no unilinear story here, for totalitarianism has a multiple parentage, not one single fateful "cause." Arendt could have titled her book—in Nietzsche's spirit—*On the Genealogy of Totalitarianism.* Although one could not speak of a "necessary development" leading from World War I to the emergence of totalitarianism, the world in which fateful new initiatives had been taken that finally empowered European totalitarian regimes was the offspring of the explosion of 1914.

In the quotation above, Arendt speaks of the last judgment of some unredeemably stupid fatality. She is not the last to describe World War I in such terms. François Furet, in his last book, *The Passing of an Illusion,* writes that World War I was and remains for our understanding entirely irrational, that it just happened, had no meaning, and it served no purpose.[5] What is most important in Arendt's description, however, is the word "stupid." An action is normally not entirely understandable, does not necessarily serve any purpose, yet, in Arendt's mind, a political action should not be and cannot be stupid. Why not?

If I wanted to forge a consistent political theory of action for Arendt—as some scholars have done—I would stop here for a while and try to fit her various texts together. For example, I could say that Arendt associates action with thinking, that a proper actor thinks about what she is doing. In this sense, an Arendtian actor proper cannot be stupid. And if the actor cannot be stupid, neither can be an action, and so on. This could be said, but I do not think that it would hit the mark. In the attempt to make Arendt consistent, I would translate her political concept of action into a metaphysical concept. I would then speak about the "idea" of an authentic, real action, and whether I used the term "idea" or not, I would differentiate between the appearance of an action and real action. Although no one escapes metaphysics entirely, Arendt's constant shifts in her understanding of action and tradition are not due to an inconsistency that can be straightened out. She comprehends the situation and comprehends it politically. In the above-cited text, Arendt speaks about the beginning of the twentieth century in Europe. In this story, there is a new beginning that does not deserve enthusiasm because of its stupidity and because it was calling for disaster. This is all. And this is well said.

In the final section of the book, Arendt discusses—in 1973, long after the publication of *The Human Condition*—the longevity of Soviet totalitarianism. She says:

> there remains the fact that the crisis of our time and its central experience have brought forth an *entirely new form of government* which as a potentiality and as an ever present danger is only too likely to stay with us from now on. . . . But there remains also the truth that every end in history necessarily contains a new beginning; the beginning is the promise, the only "message" which the end can ever produce. Beginning, before it becomes a historical event, is the supreme capacity of man; politically, it is identical with man's freedom. . . . The beginning is guaranteed by each new birth; it is indeed every man.[6]

Let me briefly analyze this passage, where historical realism and the rhetorics of freedom so beautifully blend.

Just as in the first quotation, Arendt here, too, comprehends the incomprehensible, the beginning of the twentieth century. Yet she also foretells something that (so she says) cannot be foretold—the end of the twentieth century. There is a discrepancy between the first and the second half of her chain of thought, but this theoretical discrepancy is, again, no inconsistency. In the first, she speaks of the past in the present, and in the second, she speaks about the future in the present.

Totalitarian states introduced something into the modern world that can be described as radically new. Arendt situates this nasty novel development in the "crisis of our time" in general. Totalitarianism was not initiated by action, in a strictly Arendtian understanding. In contrast to

World War I, it emerged from some ideologically motivated and strictly goal-oriented series of activities, which, in Arendt's terms, could be associated with work, rather than with action. I think that Arendt is absolutely right in her insistence on describing the well-established totalitarian regimes as antipolitical. I am, however, not entirely convinced that the preparation for those regimes, their initiation at least, could be entirely excluded from the cluster of political action. Even resistance against totalitarian party formations at a very early stage of their development belongs to this development and can be described in terms of action. Arendt in fact conceded that much in her beautiful essay on Rosa Luxemburg.

In Arendt's philosophical conception, action is, in the main, identical with freedom. But what is freedom? There is no political action without political affiliation, without a cause to support, without decisions, without an idea, in the everyday sense of the word. The Arendtian *pure* action (a very Kantian expression) is entirely free, free from everything, not just from constraints, but also from the situation in which it occurs. But actions, political actions included, are never "pure." Arendt knows this very well. She does not put the emphasis on pure action, on action as pure initiation and pure freedom, just to make a pleasing typology or to exclude from action everything that is impure—including the mixture of action and the modern or totalitarian frenzy to mold the whole world into a preset shape. Arendt speaks of pure action for the sake of the future. Nothing but the concept of pure action can offer hope for the almost impossible, for the omnipresence of the eruption of freedom everywhere, in every situation and at any time.

We need to think in context. Arendt speaks to those who look at the Soviet Union and say "a new beginning is impossible, the conditions are absent, one should consider the overwhelming power of the party, of the secret police and the army; whoever speaks of the possibility of freedom is just daydreaming." And Arendt answers: "pure action does not depend on the conditions, it is possible also in a world of secret police, of the rule of the party; for it is possible everywhere and in all times, with the birth of every man." The sentence that it is a historical necessity, that every end contains a new beginning, although written by Arendt, is not written in her deepest spirit. Here she only overdetermines her point that the concept of pure action stands, in this context, for hope. And, indeed, less than fifteen years later the (Berlin) wall came tumbling down.

Yet once upon a time, not very long ago, the totalitarian regimes did in fact begin something new, and this new kind of political domina-

tion, which is by now already old, remains with us. Totalitarianism remains with us, even if all totalitarian regimes vanish. Totalitarianism is
written in our memory. It is preserved in the psychological archive, and
its reemergence is from now on a constant possibility. Totalitarianism is
a tradition as a warning. This is by no means a tradition to cherish. And
still, those events and horrors should not be forgotten, if for no other
but the momentous reason that their victims should be mourned and
remembered.

Let me now turn to a second Arendtian story, the story that she
tells in *The Human Condition.* This is the only book of Arendt's that can
also be read as a truncated grand narrative told about the decline of the
West. After all, among the three manifestations of *vita activa,* action
(primarily as political action) occupied a pride of place in the world of
ancient Greece and Rome, while work, that is, creativity, became the
guiding star of early moderns. It is only in contemporary society, the
"jobholding society," that labor, the sheer reproduction of life, becomes
man's main concern. This reading is, in my mind, not entirely wrong,
but one-sided.

In this book, which is frequently quoted as Arendt's chief work, the
story turns around a project of fundamental ontology (since "the human
condition" is another term for Dasein) yet is combined with Heidegger's later insights. This is Arendt's most Heideggerian book. The Kantian allusion in her description of pure action is overdetermined by the
allusion to Heidegger's concept of the "originary" (*ursprünglich*). Heidegger employs the fiction of originary thinking (*Ursprüngliches Denken*). "Originary thinking" is a complex, basic term. On the one hand,
the philosophical poetry of three pre-Socratic philosophers shows traces
of originary thinking, thinking before metaphysics, a kind of unconcealment (truth) entirely different from the concept of truth that is at least
partially responsible for *Gestell,* the enframed mind and world of modernity. Still, originary thinking is not a fact of past history. One can
engage oneself in originary thinking at any time, also here and now.
One can always originate. This is what hope means for Heidegger. In
Arendt—since she is writing about active life here—originary thinking
is replaced by originary action. Politically, this makes all the difference.
Originary action is identified by Arendt as a concept of the political
where being free and being originary / originating coalesce. In the philosophy of political liberty, Arendt puts the emphasis on appearances.
Action appears as interaction. It appears in the public space, in the light
of the day, as Hegel put it, in high visibility.

The structure of the book, not its content, shows Heidegger's strong presence. If one translates the structural and narrative position of the Heideggerian originary thinking into Arendt's thought of originary action, one gets the following results. I will simplify at the beginning and will complicate matters only later. Thus runs the story: Pure action, pure political action, was originally present at the birth of Europe among the Greeks and the Romans. It later became marginalized because work, and later labor, occupied the pride of place in the *vita activa* of the Europeans. But it is always possible to act, and it remains possible here and now, in the midst of the jobholding society, since it is possible anytime. One can always engage in action, and something absolutely new can always appear.

If this simplified summary is in the main true to Arendt's intentions, it means that in *The Human Condition,* new beginnings and tradition roughly coalesce. I say "roughly," for in Arendt's work there are always shifts and reversals; there is never a complete fit. But, after all, what is the tradition one should cherish and preserve or eventually revitalize? It is action, originary action. One can clearly see from this perspective how the narrative of the book becomes a vehicle of political intervention. Arendt's intervention does not merely tell readers something philosophical about political action in the ancient world but also instructs them that there is always the possibility to act.

In order to make a strong case, Arendt had to expand the concept of action from the field of political philosophy to the field of fundamental ontology. Action is not just political action, which can disappear altogether in dark times. All kinds of interactions between human actors are actions in the fundamental-ontological sense of the word. After all, in chapter 33, while ruminating on the irreversibility of action and the power to forgive, Arendt discusses Jesus of Nazareth and love as examples of an absolute new beginning, yet she immediately adds that love is one of the most unpolitical powers. It looks as if beginning anew itself, whether directly political or not, would be the tradition to cherish. The most significant tradition is then the tradition of interruptions.

The difference between political action proper and action in general is, however, important. Action as such has an ontological status, whereas political action is tied to the condition of freedom. It is in the fact of natality, says Arendt, that "the faculty of action is ontologically rooted." It seems, however, as if the full essence of this ontological foundation came to light only at the times when originary political action was no more the order of the day. "Only the full experience of this capacity [Arendt means the capacity for new beginnings, the ability to interrupt and to begin something new] can bestow upon human affairs faith and hope, those two essential characteristics of human existence which Greek antiquity ignored altogether." Thus, the Greek polis, where the public realm for political action was widely open, where political actors put everything at risk in the sphere of appearances, knew far *less* about the ontological essence of natality than we now know.

In scrutinizing the character of *vita activa* in the modern age (chapter 6 of the book), Arendt strongly insists that we have *not* lost our capacities—neither the capacity to create nor the capacity to act. This sounds odd at first glance. For if the faculties of *vita activa* are fundamental-ontological existentials, insisting on their omnipresence is redundant. This must be taken for granted. But omnipresent faculties can also change their appearances. In insisting that they still exist, Arendt needs to speak first of all about the forms in which they now appear. She writes: "Similarly, the capacity for action, at least in the sense of releasing processes, is still with us, although it has become the exclusive prerogative of the scientists . . . it seems only proper that their deeds should eventually have turned out to have greater news value, to be of greater political significance, than the administrative and the diplomatic doings of most so-called statesmen."[7] Beginning anew, natality, the ontological constant, appears now as initiation in scientific inquiry. It seems, then, that beginning anew in political action would be just a historically variable kind of the *genus proximum* of natality. But if this is so, what is the tradition to cherish? Can an ontological capacity be called a tradition? Hardly. Only a particular kind of understanding, the interpretation of an ontological capacity, can be called tradition.

Tradition lives in recollection. It lives in stories. It seems to me as if beginning anew itself would have been identified by Arendt with the very tradition we should cherish, at least in this book. Moreover, I have also expressed my doubt whether an ontological constant per se could qualify for the position of tradition. Now I modify, or rather expand, my earlier conclusion. The tradition to cherish is not beginning anew as such, but the stories told about beginning anew. Here, political action again occupies the pride of place. We know about work (creation) directly because creative activity is objectivized as a thing (e.g. a temple), but we know about political actions and their grandeur exclusively from the stories that immortalize them. Political stories are stories of freedom, yet—Arendt would now add—they are also the stories of faith and

hope. The new scientific discoveries initiated in laboratories are not political in character but, *per analogiam,* can be perceived as if they were
because they have great "news value," because one can tell stories about
them, more and better stories than about the so-called statesmen, who
initiate nothing, whose acts are not deeds and therefore not worthy to
be narrated.

The hand is Esau's hand, but the voice is Jacob's voice. Hannah
Arendt's visible enthusiasm is so much vested in the public political action of the Greeks and Romans that one would hardly accept a conclusion that suggests looking for scientific inventions in their place. Political action, public action, the act of freedom that cannot be detected by
fundamental ontology, only in the stories of people's political histories,
is the tradition of beginning anew that Arendt enlivens here in the story
she is telling about the human condition. Let me return to the parallel
nature of Heidegger's originary thinking and Arendt's originary action.
The capacity to initiate can always appear as political action proper.
One can never say that it is impossible. And Arendt's books themselves
provide such testimony.

The Human Condition is no less an act of political intervention than
The Origins of Totalitarianism. It is an intervention through telling the
story of the glory of political action—the action Arendt places highest
among all the human capacities to act. It is a story told to the contemporary actor who may think its grandeur and may also begin. For thinking in the originary way—so we learn from the last sentences of the
book—is also the return to origins. Whatever she says about love or scientific discovery, Arendt has faith in the new beginning of political action proper, above all. She vests her hope in originary action as the tradition of *vita activa,* which, although not ontologically rooted, is not
entirely lost.

This is the topic of *On Revolution.* No wonder that while tradition
and new beginnings do not manifest their paradoxical character in *The
Human Condition,* they do so in *On Revolution.*

In the story of the American Revolution, the concepts of interruption,
of new beginning, of natality become strictly political. They all stand for
revolution. Politically, beginning anew *is* revolution. But revolution contains as its necessary aspect the constitution of liberties. Beginning anew
as political revolution is also the act of foundation. This is why liberation is not yet liberty. Liberation is an act of breaking chains, of crushing tyrants, of leaving behind the past in one stroke. It offers the possibil-

ity of the constitution of liberties, yet not all acts of liberation are followed by the foundation of liberties. Arendt's juxtaposition of the French Revolution and the American Revolution rests—among others—on this in many contexts equally important distinction.

Freedom is interruption and also beginning anew. It is a new beginning that must endure. It is the absolutely new, the beginning that, so Arendt says, "would justify starting to count time in the year of the revolution." [8] But this sentence implies a paradox. One starts to count time in the year of the revolution. But this time goes on and on, as long as the institutions of liberty endure. How can the spirit of taking initiatives, the permanency of revolutionary action, prevail after liberties have already been constituted? To put it bluntly: Can freedom be a tradition to which one constantly returns, instead of becoming a tradition that simply endures?

Arendt tells us the story of the greatest—in her mind—revolution mankind ever initiated, a revolution that, however, in the long run, has not lived up to the task: "the second task of the revolution, to assure the survival of the spirit out of which the act of foundation sprang, to realize the principle which inspired it . . . was frustrated from the beginning." [9] Arendt employs again the word we know so well from *Between Past and Future*: she speaks of the "lost treasure," the lost tradition. But what is the tradition here, the treasure? The public spirit, the enthusiasm in the pursuit of public happiness, the spirit of freedom, the permanency of action. Without making references to him, Arendt here echoes Hegel—institutions become positive, and thus dead, if their spirit leaves them.

Arendt does not accept the paradox of freedom in matters of political liberty. She insists that every time the spirit of beginning anew thins out, some mistake has been made in the act of foundation (e.g. the American Founding Fathers did not recognize the importance of townships while forging the constitution). She clings to models of direct democracy, such as the revolutionary councils in Hungary in 1956. She in fact neglects the circumstance that this revolution lasted for only ten days. I would add that after the system changed in 1989, all actions taken for the sake of a new beginning, for the revitalization of the council system, were catastrophically defeated, although the memory of revolutionary councils was kept alive, and thus the treasure was not entirely lost.

I said that Arendt was not ready to accept the paradox of freedom if it came to political action, although otherwise she did accept it. She says: "The perplexity was very simple, and stated in logical terms, it seemed unsolvable: if the foundation was the aim and the end of the revolution, then the revolutionary spirit was not only the spirit of beginning something new but of starting something permanent and enduring." [10] But things can be logically paradoxical, yet political actors can still brush aside the paradox.

Was Arendt right? Can one brush aside one of the manifestations of the modern paradox of freedom politically?

If one takes the position of observation, the paradox cannot be brushed aside, but in action, it can be. And telling stories about action is, as we have seen, already an act of practical intervention.

I think that Arendt was in fact wrong when she believed and made us believe that one can invent institutions (e.g. revolutionary councils) that keep the spirit of revolution alive. These—alternative—institutions are only short-lived, precisely because the spirit of revolution cannot be kept alive on the same level of enthusiasm for a long time, or, alternatively, and this is worse, they can become terroristic, in cases when the spirit of revolution is translated into the language of fundamentalism, as in the totalitarian movements. Direct democracy and constant activism are by no means guarantees of freedom. There are, of course, no guarantees of freedom whatsoever; neither are there guarantees for the preservation of political liberties. Arendt knew all this, but sometimes she forgot what she knew.

Yet Arendt was right when she brushed aside the paradox of freedom in the case of political liberties. For even if the constitution of liberties is the foundation of a city so that it should endure, not all institutions of this city need to endure. One can constantly return to the beginning and start many things anew and from scratch without destroying the foundations of the city's freedom. To talk about the paradox of freedom politically is problematic. A paradox cannot be resolved. Yet the treasure (the tradition) on the one hand, and the gestures of interruption, of beginning anew, on the other, can still be held, at least approximately, in proper balance. If the tradition gets the upper hand, the spirit of freedom withers. If taking the initiative gets the upper hand, one enters the state of crisis or chaos, and one takes an enormous risk. Arendt knew only too well how to perform the balancing act. She practiced it in her book *Crises of the Republic* and in her other writings of the 1970s. She became involved in the acts of beginning anew as also in the acts of conservation and preservation.

This is why she could never be pigeonholed. Was she a revolutionary?

Was she conservative? She was both: in one situation, rather a revolutionary, in another, rather a conservative. In one question, a revolutionary, in another question, a conservative. Her deep understanding of the paradox of freedom and of the commitment to something that Goethe called "*die Forderung des Tages,*" the obligation of the day, made her the libertarian, both revolutionary and conservative. This is—in my mind—her most enduring legacy.

Hannah Arendt
on Revolution

Albrecht Wellmer

In her essay *On Revolution*,[1] Hannah Arendt has tried to settle accounts with both the liberal-democratic and the Marxist traditions, that is, with the two dominant traditions of modern political thought that, in one way or the other, can be traced back to the European Enlightenment. Arendt's basic thesis is that both liberal democrats and Marxists have misunderstood the drama of modern revolutions because they have not understood that what was actually revolutionary in modern revolutions was the repeatedly failed attempt of a *"constitutio libertatis"*—the attempt to establish a political space of public freedom in which people as free and equal citizens would take their common concerns into their own hands. Both the liberals and the Marxists equally harbored a conception of the political according to which the final goal of politics would be something *beyond* politics—the unencumbered pursuit of private happiness, the realization of social justice, or the free association of the producers in a classless society. Arendt's critique of Marxist politics has already become a locus classicus and requires no further justification. Her critique of liberal and social democracy in modern industrial societies seems more provocative from a present point of view. I want to raise the question of whether the provocation is still a genuine one.

Arendt develops her basic categories, in terms of which she will renarrate the history of modern revolutions, by using the paradigm of the American Revolution, which in her view was the only halfway successful revolution in modernity. Only in the American Revolution did the ultimate goal of the revolutionary people in all modern revolutions—the constitution of a space of public freedom—actually become a reality in a large modern state, thanks to fortunate circumstances, a long tradition of self-government, and the political ingenuity of the Founding Fathers. Moreover, and this is the issue for Arendt, in the American Revolution, a space of freedom was established not only in the "negative" sense of a constitutional guarantee of equal basic rights for all citizens, but also in the "positive," strictly political sense of a federal system of institutions in which the self-government of citizens from the local level to the level of national polity became a reality that was anchored in the experiences and habits of citizens and that, at the same time, could be experienced *as* a reality ever anew in everyday praxis. Based on the American model, Arendt develops the idea of a system of councils as the alternative to the traditional liberal-democratic and Marxist conceptions of the state.

In the great revolutions following the American Revolution, in particular the French and Russian Revolutions, Arendt claims that the idea of a council system was spontaneously rediscovered by the revolutionary people in order then to be repressed according to an always identical brutal logic, either by a revolutionary elite that had come to power or by a conservative establishment that regained power. Only the American Revolution led to the establishment of a federal system of self-government in which, until today, elements were retained of the tradition of local self-government. That tradition had once constituted the terminus a quo of the American Revolution, and in it memories survived of the "public happiness" of free and equal persons acting in concert, a "public happiness" that had been experienced in the townships and wards of the prerevolutionary epoch, as well as on the national level in the period when the American republic was being founded.

Of course, as Arendt observes, in America too, shortly after the Revolution, tendencies grew ever stronger in the direction of establishing a state based on partisan political parties and thus ultimately of developing a modern mass democracy. What is characteristic of modern mass democracy for Arendt, however, is the fact that its citizens are free only in a "negative" sense because they have lost their political freedom—the freedom of self-government based on common action and shared deliberation—to their delegates, to large political parties, to representative bodies, to a powerful bureaucracy, and to organized interest groups. The Marxist dictatorship, according to Arendt, to a certain extent merely drew out the consequences of a development within the liberal-

democratic party system. In a way, it merely completed the political in-
fantilization (*Entmündigung*) of the citizens and the depoliticization of
the political that Arendt perceived as an inherent tendency of modern
mass democracy—a tendency in which she saw a mortal danger for
freedom in the modern world.

What is interesting in Arendt's theory is not this diagnosis—which
is not particularly original—but the way she tries to underpin it by
means of a conceptual strategy intended to question fundamentally the
political self-articulation of modern societies, to question, as it were, the
deep grammar of modern political discourse. Political freedom, she argues, was the center of gravity in all modern revolutions, but it was a
secret center of gravity, since the idea itself was hardly ever adequately
articulated in the established political discourse of modernity, so that the
most important revolutionary events of modernity were usually perceived, remembered, and thought about only in a distorted way by theorists, by political common sense, and even by the participants themselves. Arendt's critique of liberal democracy therefore is radical in a
philosophical sense of the word: What she demands of her contemporaries is a radical break with the central categories by which modern
democratic societies have articulated themselves politically. By setting
these categories in motion and locating them in a new structural context, Arendt first of all tries to articulate an idea of political freedom
that, in her view, was more or less latently at work in the revolutions of
modernity, but that was always at odds with the mainstream of modern
political thought. Arendt's basic objection against this mainstream of
modern political thought is that it was forgetful of politics itself and
therefore could not possibly articulate an idea of *political* freedom.

Arendt has often been described as a neo-Aristotelian philosopher
of praxis. This description, however, although not completely false, is
deeply misleading. To be sure, the traces of Aristotle's practical philosophy in Arendt's concept of the political are so evident and unmistakable
that they hardly need mentioning. Think of Arendt's oppositions[2] between the sphere of action and of "acting in concert," on the one hand,
and the sphere of "work" (*poiesis*) and "labour," on the other; between
the rationality of practical deliberation and the rationality of scientific
discourse, technical production, economic planning, or bureaucratic administration; between the public sphere of the "*isonomia*"—of free and
equal citizens—and the social sphere of labor or the private sphere of an
individual pursuit of happiness. All these oppositions echo Aristotelian

distinctions, and seen this way, Arendt might be justly perceived as a philosopher who tried to resurrect and reinvigorate an ancient tradition of political thought that had largely been lost in modernity.

But she certainly is not simply a neo-Aristotelian. Her political thought would be better described as the site of a dramatic encounter between Aristotle, Kant, and Heidegger, all of whom she brings face to face with the catastrophes of civilization in our time. Arendt's recourse to Aristotle, for instance, amounts to a radical critique of Heidegger's politics or antipolitics, while it also rests on a deeply Heideggerian rethinking of Aristotelian categories. In a way, she writes the political philosophy that, in her view, Heidegger, as a post-Kantian thinker, *should* have written instead of flirting with the Nazis. The profound originality of Arendt's political thought can be grasped only if it is seen how she uses Aristotelian, Kantian, and Heideggerian categories to bring them into a new constellation, thereby revealing herself as a deeply modern thinker.

1

Traces of a Heideggerian rethinking of Aristotelian categories become obvious when Arendt describes the *constitutio libertatis* as the opening up of a common world, as a break with the continuum of history, a radically new beginning. Her critique of the "philosophy of history"— by which she means the Hegelian heritage in Marxism—and of the belief in historical "progress" are elements of a philosophy of finitude in whose light the constitution of a space of public freedom appears as a contingent performative act by those who decide to act together as free and equal citizens. In that light, this space of political freedom necessarily appears limited and local, "fenced in," as Arendt says. The space of public freedom is in essence finite, the shining forth of a light in which, for historic moments, the creaturely life of human beings "gleams." That life then opens itself onto a public world in which the actors can appear in their irreducible individuality and, in acting together, can begin something new, and in which the common world that is the habitat of our ordinary private and social life is endowed with a meaning and significance it otherwise lacks. At the end of *On Revolution,* Arendt recalls Sophocles' Theseus, through whose mouth Sophocles tells us "what it was that enabled ordinary men, young and old, to bear life's burden: it was the polis, the space of men's free deeds and living words, which could endow life with splendor—*tòn bion lampròn poieisthai.*" [3]

2

Arendt's thesis that political freedom can exist only in a limited space[4] seems to mark a radical break with the liberal-democratic tradition and its universalism of human and citizens' rights. And so it does. What has to be understood, however, is what this break really means. Arendt does not dispute the universalism of human rights in a moral—that is, prepolitical—sense, and she even acknowledges the internal link, characteristic of Kant and the liberal tradition, between the universalism of human rights and a modern conception of citizens' rights, for she takes it to be a human (i.e. moral) right to have citizens' rights.[5] However, in contrast with the liberal tradition, Arendt considers citizens' rights not as the substance, but only as a necessary precondition of political freedom. According to her, it is a fateful disaster to confuse a constitutionally based guarantee of citizens' rights with the constitution of political freedom. Again this thesis must be understood in the right way. Although at first sight it may appear to anticipate later communitarian theories, its point, as we shall see, is quite different from that of standard communitarian or "republican" arguments.

An indication of this difference might already be seen in another "universalist" presupposition that can also be found in Arendt's conception of politics: Her conception of political freedom is "universalist" in that she takes it to signify a universal human possibility. According to Arendt, the idea of and the desire for political freedom are rooted in the "elementary conditions of action."[6] This might be called the "anthropological universalism" inherent in her conception of political freedom. This latent universalism comes out clearly in the following passage: "What has been concealed by the terrible catastrophes of the revolutions of the twentieth century is nothing more or less than the first, truly revolutionary hope of the European and ultimately perhaps of all peoples of the earth for a new form of state, which would allow each person in the midst of mass societies to participate in the public issues of the day."[7] What this passage shows is that the "particularistic" aspects of Arendt's idea of political freedom must be seen against the background of a moral, as well as an anthropological, universalism.

3

At this point, it is important to be fully aware of the radically modern aspects of Arendt's opposition between "negative" and "positive" freedom. Arendt is no more a communitarian than she is a liberal. Communitarians wish to preserve or restore particular—national, cultural, or religious—traditions and value systems as the only possible ground of social solidarity and of collective identity, while the liberal *dispositif* rests on the awareness of an irrevocable break regarding the power of tradition in the transition to modernity. As far as this opposition between liberals and communitarians is concerned, Arendt would side with the liberals, in spite of the fact that her critique of liberalism has been repeatedly claimed for the communitarian project. According to Arendt, since the time of the Romans, the space of the political actually had been safeguarded in the course of Western civilization by the "trinity of authority, religion and tradition." [8] Modernity, however, came into being as a break with this "founding" trinity, so that for us, no return to the premodern conditions of politics, and in particular no restoration of the binding power of tradition, is possible.

Perhaps one might say that the awareness of this falling apart of the "Roman trinity" of authority, religion, and tradition has led to the second-order political tradition of liberal democracy. Consequently, in her critique of liberalism, Arendt could be said to share a common ground with the liberal "tradition." Accordingly, her critique of liberalism does not rest simply on an appeal to the Greek polis or the virtues of civic republicanism. Arendt's critique of liberalism instead rests on a deconstruction of the whole "metaphysical" tradition of political thought up to Aristotle and Plato. Arendt's deconstruction of Western political thought since the time of the Greek polis has an undeniable affinity with Heidegger's deconstruction of Western metaphysics since its Greek inception, as Dana Villa has shown convincingly. [9] This means, however, that Arendt traces the shortcomings of liberal thought and its forgetfulness of the political in favor of the "social," the "private," and the sphere of instrumental action, to a tendency of Western political thought, emerging already with Plato and Aristotle, to distort the essential character of praxis and of the political. As I said before, however, this critique of liberalism can be understood only if it is seen as sharing a common ground with the liberal tradition, an antitraditional conception of human and citizens' rights. Sharing this common ground with liberalism, Arendt was immune to all regressive dreams of community and community-engendering values—whether they be national, religious, or even ethnic in nature. It was the potential of the new, of what still was to come into existence in the modern world, that she tried to think with her idea of republican freedom. In this sense, she was truly a revolutionary thinker.

4

What, then, does Arendt's break with the liberal-democratic *dispositif* really mean? She herself often articulates it in terms of an opposition between "direct" and "representative" democracy, between a system of councils and a parliamentary party system. This opposition is as illuminating as it is misleading. Misleading it is, because if it were taken literally, it would be naive (it is the naiveté of political anarchism). The political institutions of complex modern societies can no longer be construed along the simple model of a system of councils. I therefore take the idea of a council system to be a metaphor for a network of autonomous or partially autonomous institutions, organizations, and associations in each of which something takes place like the self-government of free and equal participants—free and equal in various dimensions, with various tasks and with various forms for recruiting members, a network whose units might be both horizontally and vertically connected, related to or dependent upon one another. Complex structural bodies of this kind can represent both the institutions of a federal political system (from the local to the national level) and the associations, organizations, and institutions of a democratic "civil society," in contrast to "formal" political institutions. I thus think that with her concept of a council system, Arendt must have meant both: the political institutions of a federal political system *and* a network of autonomous or partially autonomous associations and organizations along the lines of civil society.

Arendt's basic point, then, is that the taste for freedom and the experience of freedom can derive only from the diverse forms of active participation in common concerns. The idea of political freedom therefore has to be spelled out in terms of a network of institutions and associations in such a way that freedom must begin in and become a lived experience in which the "common issues" are still tangible to those involved and, as their own immediate concerns, can be negotiated in an autonomous manner. It seems obvious that political freedom, seen this way, means something other and something more than a constitutionally based guarantee of basic citizens' rights. These are, as Arendt observes, a precondition of freedom, but not (political) freedom itself.

5

If Arendt's idea of a council system is interpreted along the lines I have suggested, it becomes obvious that her opposition between "direct" and "representative" democracy cannot really be understood as signifying an alternative of two entirely different political systems, but that it must be spelled out as signifying a set of alternatives within liberal democracy itself, a merely "formal" versus a "substantive" or "participatory" version of democracy. Arendt herself, as has often been pointed out, was occasionally tempted to interpret important conceptual distinctions in a "concretistic" way: direct versus representative democracy, the "political" versus the "social," and so on. This has made it difficult to see what her real objections against liberal democracy were—and has made it relatively easy to claim her critique of a "rights-based" liberal democracy for communitarian or republican theories.

What I have suggested so far instead points to the possibility of integrating her idea of political freedom into a rights-based theory of democracy, in the sense in which both John Rawls and Jürgen Habermas have recently emphasized the interdependence of "private" and "public" autonomy for any viable modern conception of democracy.[10] So one might wonder whether Arendt's idea of political freedom still poses any substantial challenge to the more advanced forms of democratic theory today. I think one should be aware that my previous suggestions do not really answer this question, since they hardly have touched the conceptual issues involved in Arendt's critique of the liberal-democratic *dispositif*. I have only tried to prepare a way for answering the question I raised by ruling out a naive-anarchistic reading of Arendt. The question itself—Does Arendt's conception of political freedom still pose a challenge to contemporary democratic theory?—has still to be answered. I shall try to answer this question by relating Arendt's idea of public freedom to the debate, which I have already alluded to, between John Rawls and Jürgen Habermas about the interdependence between "private" and "public" autonomy.

6

Both Rawls and Habermas have claimed that the very conception of citizens' rights, adequately understood, first of all must comprise democratic rights of participation together with those of "negative" liberty, and that secondly, "liberal" and "democratic" rights must be conceived as being internally related in such a way that private ("negative") and public ("positive") freedom mutually imply each other, so that, strictly speaking, the one is unthinkable without the other. It seems obvious that at least Rawls does not mean by "public autonomy" what Arendt means by "public freedom," since for Rawls, "public autonomy" would have to be spelled out in terms of passive and active voting rights, of representative bodies, democratic procedures, and so on—that is, in terms that are certainly insufficient for reformulating Arendt's ideas of "direct" democracy, of the "acting in concert" of free and equal citizens, of a *communicative* public freedom, as I would like to call it, following Habermas. The latter, in contrast to Rawls, has explicitly tried to integrate an Arendtian conception of public freedom and of "communicative power" into a rights-based theory of deliberative democracy. Therefore it is Habermas's theory that I would like to take as a test case for approaching the question I have set out to answer.

Habermas has tried to overcome the shortcomings of traditional liberal theories of democracy by combining a principle of equal liberal and democratic rights with a principle of rational discourse. It is this basic idea that implies an interdependence between private and public autonomy in Habermas's theory. As I have tried to show elsewhere,[11] it suggests a kind of "circular" relationship between the two ideas of autonomy: the one meaning "negative liberty" in the traditional liberal sense, the other meaning a democratically constituted sovereignty of the people. The "circle" is this: There can be no democratic self-government of the people without an institutionalization of individual rights, and there can be no genuine institutionalization of individual rights if it is not always newly worked out, revised, and reinterpreted in the medium of democratic discourse, that is, democratically decided upon by the people themselves. Consequently, what *precedes* democratic discourse is only the *principle* of equal basic rights, but not—as in traditional liberal theory—a specific interpretation and institutionalization of these rights. In Habermas's theory of liberal democracy, the emphasis shifts from the word "liberal" to the word "democracy." His thesis is that the very principle of equal basic rights demands a deliberative democracy, a process of democratic will formation as the condition of its adequate realization. And in this context, a democratic public sphere—a sphere of uninhibited public discourse, as distinct from the sphere of formal political institutions—indeed signifies for Habermas an essential precondition of an adequate functioning of democratic institutions.

Arendt, of course, would not disagree with this. In contrast to Habermas, however, she argues that although public freedom presupposes a guarantee of individual rights, the reverse is not true. What could she mean by that? Obviously, Arendt believes that a "state of law" (*Rechts-staat*), even with democratic representation and equal democratic rights of participation, is possible—and actually is realized in many societies of our time—without public freedom having any sort of substantial reality. But now one might argue that Habermas probably would not totally disagree with this as an empirical diagnosis. His conception of democracy is a normative one, and he certainly would not deny that rational discourse is blocked in many ways in existing democracies. So the difference cannot just be a difference concerning the evaluation of existing democracies according to a normative conception of democracy. The difference must be a conceptual one after all. Arendt's thesis, indeed, is that a theory focusing on "rights" and "justice"—as Habermas's theory still does—cannot arrive at an adequate conception of political freedom. In this respect—but I think *only* in this respect—her theory is close to communitarian or republican theories. What Arendt would say is that an adequate conception of political freedom cannot be arrived at even by combining a principle of rights with a principle of rational discourse. To show why she would say that, I want to come back to her "revolutionary particularism."

To start with, I would argue that Arendt's conception of revolution must be understood in terms of its internal relationship to the concept of "institution"—in the double sense of institution as a (collective) act and as the result of this act (i.e. a system of institutions). Not only is the institution (the institutionalization) of public freedom (the *constitutio libertatis*) the terminus ad quem of revolutions in Arendt's sense, but at the same time, for Arendt, the institutions of freedom are inherently related to revolution as their terminus a quo. This means that, on the one hand, the inherent goal of what Arendt calls revolution is an institution—an institutionalization—of freedom, which can emerge only from the common willing of people who begin to act in concert and thereby transform their common world and create a space of public freedom. On the other hand, the internal correlation of "revolution" and "institution" also means that a performative and inventive element belongs to the preservation of republican institutions, so that the spirit of revolution becomes something like a condition of the permanence of republican institutions. Arendt, consequently, insists on elements of contingency and performativity in the founding and preservation of political freedom.

What is at stake here is not merely that democratic constitutions do not have any metaphysical or transcendental foundations, but rather what Arendt has in mind when she speaks about the "opening up" of a public world, about a "new beginning," a break with the continuum of history. Institutions of freedom must be *invented*—and their preservation in some sense amounts to their continuous reinvention. The establishment of such institutions can more or less succeed or fail, and their invention, where successful, will bring about a new grammar of political discourse, new experiences and attitudes, while, conversely, they remain dependent on such experiences and attitudes, on judgment and political virtue.

The extent to which and the forms in which public freedom can become a reality in the modern world depend on historical contingencies as well as on cultural traditions, on experiences as well as on the commitment, imagination, and courage of the individuals involved. And what should be added is that the institutions of public freedom have to maintain themselves against the requirements of the material reproduction of society, against the pressures caused by contingent historical circumstances and vis-à-vis the desiderata of social justice. In any case, the constitution of political freedom does not mean (only) an institutionalization of basic rights but demands an understanding and a use of such rights according to a "standard" that cannot be read off these rights themselves, even if we think their scope to be determined in the medium of rational (democratic) discourse. Rational discourse regarding rights—at least in its Habermasian sense—can have only justice as its standard. Arendt's idea of public freedom, in contrast, aims at an optimum concerning the self-organization of the people, which is not the same as a maximum of justice but in a way redefines the parameters of justice itself.

Inasmuch as the institutions of public freedom become a common project, their preservation and reinvention become ends in themselves, through which the problems of "rights" and of "justice" will be seen in a new light or, as one might say, will be "focused" in a new way. Arendt emphasizes the "agonistic" and—with Aristotle—the "doxastic" features of such a space of public freedom, and although the agon here takes place in the medium of speech, that is, nonviolently, it seems to be something different from "rational discourse" in Habermas's sense. This is so not only because in this agon, doxa and persuasion reign—and this means that there are specific virtues that count and are persuasive in this public domain: courage, imagination, experience, and judgment—but, above all, because action and deliberation are intertwined with each other. Deliberation is the deliberation of those who will decide and act, and whose action will always be a new beginning, the consequences of which the actors will not be able to control fully. Elements of contingency and performativity thus belong to the deliberative agon in a space of public freedom. So although the space of public freedom may be characterized as a space of "rational" deliberation, an understanding of what "rational" means here presupposes an explication of what is the point and what are the essential features of such a space. To put it differently: As long as the rationality of democratic discourse is basically understood only in terms of equal-participation rights and of its internal reference to the problems of "rights" and of "justice," the idea of public freedom can signify only a sphere of public *discourse* in which matters of common interest are debated, for instance in the media. For Arendt, in contrast, the sphere of public freedom also signifies a sphere of *action,* of self-organization, of direct democracy. In such a sphere, deliberation and action are intertwined with each other, and an essential theme of deliberation will be the constitution and preservation of public freedom itself.

7

I have pointed out before that Arendt's opposition between liberal democracy and republican freedom, between representative and direct democracy, does not make sense if it is understood in a "concretistic" way, as an opposition between two mutually exclusive types of political system. And I have also pointed out that Arendt herself was not quite immune to the temptation to interpret the opposition in this way. The opposition, however, does make sense if it is relocated into the interior of modern mass democracies. In this case, the opposition indicates a spectrum of possibilities within liberal and social democracy itself. At one end of this spectrum would be a centralistic state with formally democratic institutions such as a representative body and general active and passive voting rights—and perhaps a manipulation of public opinion by the mass media. At the other end of this spectrum would be a democratic culture of self-determination that could be experienced and would be alive on the level of everyday life, together with a corresponding culture of public debate. What Arendt, I think, shows is that such a democratic culture of public debate can exist only inasmuch as it is anchored in a political praxis of self-determination that reaches down to the level of everyday life. For only such a praxis of "direct" democracy can generate the attitudes, the experiences, the virtues, and the faculty of judgment on which a viable democratic culture of public debate depends.

I think it can now be seen in which sense Arendt's idea of political freedom transcends the parameters of the liberal-democratic *dispositif,* even in its Habermasian version. Arendt's claim is that a deliberative democracy, to deserve its name, presupposes strong elements of "direct" democracy, and what this means cannot be sufficiently spelled out in terms of equal *rights* of participation, but only in terms of a specific *mode* of participation. This, however, affects the concept of democratic legitimacy itself. It becomes obvious now that the idea of a rational consensus based on an equal right of democratic participation is not sufficient to establish a standard of democratic legitimacy. For what "we"—the people, the democratic sovereign—can rationally agree upon depends not least upon how this "we" has organized itself in the institutions of a political system. If Arendt, however, is right in claiming that the idea of public freedom was the hidden agenda in all modern revolutions, then a standard of democratic legitimacy is thereby established that eludes any attempt to reconstruct it solely in terms of "rights" and of "rational discourse." It demands a *constitutio libertatis* as the "construction," realization, and preservation of a system of institutions in which and through which public freedom would become a reality and a matter of experience and, at the same time, a common value that would affect the parameters of public debate as well as democratic decision processes at any level of the political system. This value, Arendt would contend, is not just one value among all those values that may compete with one another in the will formation of democratic societies. It is instead that value on the realization of which it depends whether and to what extent democracy is a form of government in which the power really rests with the people, or whether, in the words of Benjamin Rush quoted by Arendt, although "all power is derived from the people, they possess it only on the days of their elections. After this it is the property of their rulers." [12]

In the chapters of *On Revolution* in which Arendt deals with the American Revolution, she has made it clear that a *constitutio libertatis* on the large scale of a modern nation-state is not least a highly intricate problem of inventing and "constructing" a system of institutions that would balance elements of direct democracy with the necessities of central government, of efficient administration, and of a unitary legal system. I have not said anything about this problem of construction, which, as Arendt well saw, remains a permanent one *within* democratic societies, today even more so as it reemerges on the level of supranational associations. I do not want to deny that Arendt's way of dealing with this problem of construction is rather questionable in several respects. But my goal here was not to point to undeniable weaknesses of Arendt's political theory. My goal was rather to point to Arendt's conceptual contributions to a postmetaphysical understanding of democracy. If we call the realization of that value I spoke about a moment ago—I mean "public freedom" in Arendt's sense—"participatory democracy," it becomes clear that Arendt's idea of public freedom has indeed been around for quite a while in the political imagination of modern societies. What is original in Arendt's work is not the idea itself, but the way she has re-articulated it against the dominant traditions of modern political—and antipolitical—thought. If I am not mistaken in my reading of Arendt, her ideas still pose a challenge to contemporary political thought.

The Arendt Cult

Hannah Arendt as
Political Commentator

Walter Laqueur

Hannah Arendt (1906–1975) was a woman of many parts. She was a philosopher, historian, sociologist, and journalist; she wrote poetry but also wrote on technology; she had an interest in theology but also reviewed Kafka, Benjamin, and Brecht. The following reflections do not refer to her life's work, but merely one, albeit central, aspect, that of a political analyst and commentator.

No other twentieth-century philosopher and political thinker has at the present time as wide an echo. The Library of Congress Catalogue shows more than fifty books written about her and also comparing her with fellow thinkers such as Margaret Duras, Camus, Jürgen Habermas, Leo Strauss, and others. There are books with titles such as *Hannah Arendt and the Philosophy of Natality* and *Hannah Arendt, Hegel, and Marx*. Northern Light, an Internet search engine, registers 15,065 hits concerning Hannah Arendt, another search engine only 2965, but the numbers grow with every passing week. The number of articles about her in scholarly journals is probably in excess of one thousand. In 1998, a long study of her political views by Martine Leibowici was published in Paris. Dr. Caroline Kealey has written a basic paper on Hannah Arendt dealing with topics such as cyberspace and the Arendtian model of the Internet. On another Internet site we find "Hannah in 3D." The German railway runs a Hannah Arendt Express from Karlsruhe to Hannover, the German postal services have a Hannah Arendt stamp (DM 1.70), and there are streets named for Hannah Arendt, for instance in Hannover and Marburg, even though the connection between her and Marburg was tenuous—she studied there for less than a year. There are Hannah Arendt *Vereine,* and the University of Bremen bestows an annual Hannah Arendt Award. Not to be outdone, neighboring Hamburg has another Hannah Arendt Prize for DM 300,000, one of the highest in Europe. The Leo Baeck Award, in comparison, is for a mere DM 25,000, but then, it is donated by the Jewish communities, in contrast to the Hamburg award. There is an Arendt institute in Saxony. In the Great Synagogue in Essen, there is a semipermanent exhibition devoted to Hannah Arendt. German and French television collaborated in 1997 on a long program on Arendt based mainly on her correspondence with Heidegger and her husband. There were several more discussions on Arendt on German television in 1998.

All of this tends to show that Hannah Arendt has been more successful than any other German philosopher, living or dead. There is, to the best of my knowledge, no Max Weber Express on the German railways, nor is one of the Lufthansa planes named after Schopenhauer, Nietzsche, or Hegel. (There are many *Kantstrassen,* though.)

In brief, it has become the fashion, particularly in Germany, to invoke her authority on every conceivable topic, and the attitude toward her writings is quite uncritical, even when she was quite manifestly wrong. Virtually all contemporary German authors seem to believe that her writings on the Eichmann trial expressed deep insights and were profoundly honest and courageous, and that as a result she was persecuted by the Jewish establishment, if not the Elders of Zion.[1]

On the Internet, there are various Arendt lists, including an elaborate Japanese site by a Mr. Nakayama. Those who write in to them report that they have "passionate" feelings about Hannah Arendt and that reading her works has "changed their life." This kind of feeling and language one used to find more often in connection with novelists such as Hermann Hesse, rather than philosophers and political thinkers.

But it is also true that the cult (for which Hannah Arendt, needless to say, cannot be made responsible) has attracted a fair amount of contradiction and even ridicule. Professional philosophers such as, for instance, Isaiah Berlin and Stuart Hampshire have expressed the view that seldom in our time has so much been made of so little, not because they violently disagreed with Hannah Arendt's ideas, but because they found them devoid of originality, depth, and a systematic character.

As for Hannah Arendt's political writings, beginning with *The Origins of Totalitarianism,* they were more warmly welcomed by literary figures such as Dwight McDonald and Mary McCarthy than by the professionals in this field.[2]

The Arendt cult is a riddle, and while one can point to certain trends accounting for it, I doubt whether a full explanation is possible at the present time. Above all, there is the attraction she has exuded for women writers, for whom she has become a heroine, the greatest female philosopher of our time, perhaps of all times, which she might well be. The bibliographies show that many, if not most, of the studies dealing with Arendt were written by women.

But she was not a feminist, and the radical feminists of today sharply reject her for having written "crippled books," for having been "nourished on male ideology," for "accepting male supremacy," for "machismo in her vision," for "embracing the exclusively male Athenian polis" as an ideal society, and, generally speaking, for not having paid enough attention to the "body," to women's interests, and to their oppression.[3] But the opposition of these radical critics notwithstanding, there is much sympathy and support for her, especially in academe.

Even Israelis seem to have forgiven *Eichmann in Jerusalem,* and there have been academic conferences on this subject in Jerusalem and Potsdam, with adulatory papers abounding. Arab postmodernists praise her for her anti-Zionism. Rainer Wimmer has written a book entitled *Four Jewish Philosophers: Rosa Luxemburg, Simone Weil, Edith Stein, and Hannah Arendt.* "*Jüdische Philosophinnen*": it is doubtful whether any of these four would have wanted to be classified this way.

Only a few years ago, Hannah Arendt was derided by some politically correct thinkers as a sexist, a racist, and, of course, an early Cold Warrior. But now she has many admirers among the Left, despite her distinctly unfashionable views about the Third World and its inhabitants, her lack of interest in Marxism, her emphasis on the need for maintaining standards in university education (she wanted jeans banned in the classroom), and her critical views on the early civil rights movement. She was deeply conservative in most respects, but this did not prevent her from writing Danny Cohn Bendit in 1968, when he was leading the Paris students on the barricades, that his father would have been proud of him.

But she also has admirers among conservatives, despite her sympathies for revolution and revolutionaries. These sympathies were always emotional and romantic, rather than rational and philosophical. The best example was perhaps her love affair with Rosa Luxemburg, who is remembered today mainly for what she wrote about the swallows outside her prison windows, her dissociation from her Jewish origins ("do not come to me with your specific Jewish worries"), and her prophetic words about the future of the Russian Revolution. After her assassination, Lenin wrote about her that she was an "eagle of the revolution." She was certainly a radical, devoted fighter for her cause, and in view of the tragic circumstances of her death, she became a romantic heroine. But as a theorist (and it was precisely this aspect which, Arendt claimed, attracted her—she wrote about her "brilliant insights into the political structures of imperialism"), Luxemburg was not an eagle. Her *Accumulation of Capital* (on the automatic breakdown of capitalism) was second-rate and disproved by subsequent developments. What she wrote about nationalism, the most important political issue of the time, was wholly insensitive and politically suicidal. As a Marxist theorist, a contemporary of Luxemburg such as the Austrian Rudolf Hilferding was head and shoulders above her. But Hilferding, later for a while the German minister of finance, was not, alas, a romantic figure, and Arendt had no interest in him. And so in the final analysis, the conservatives are probably correct in taking Arendt's revolutionary enthusiasm not too seriously. She was not really impressed by Luxemburg's theories, but by her courage and style.

There is a fascinating discrepancy between Arendt the political philosopher and the poverty of her judgment concerning current politics. She was not alone in this respect, and some did worse than her—Sartre, for instance, who became after the war a great philosopher on the basis of a book that hardly anyone had ever read, a hero of the Resistance, to which he had not really belonged, the leading intellectual in France and by far the most influential. It is difficult even in retrospect to explain the intensity and spread of the Sartre cult during almost two decades.[4] But Sartre was a literary figure, and his fame was not rooted in the field of political philosophy. What of Marcuse, another vanished cult figure of yesteryear, who had predicted that after the Second World War the world would be divided into two camps—the soviet-communist one, and the neofascist camp, including America and Western Europe?[5]

It is also true that Arendt's two great teachers, Heidegger and Jaspers, were not among the most astute political thinkers of their time. Heideggerian politics have been discussed ad nauseam. Jaspers's record was better. He was among the very few Germans after the war who publicly insisted on Germany's guilt. But the same Jaspers wrote a sensationalist pamphlet in 1966 in which he predicted imminent disaster for Germany, Europe, and the world because Germany was drifting back to something akin to Nazism. He compared the present period in the history of Bonn to the last phase of the Weimar Republic. Within a couple of years, the Social Democrats were in power, though, and Nazism has not returned to Germany yet. These pearls of political wisdom were published in the United States with a foreword by Hannah Arendt in which she claimed that this was the politically most important book to have appeared in Germany since the war. (She may have had misgivings, because only part of the Jaspers book appeared in English, but if so, she kept these doubts to herself.) Extenuating circumstances could be adduced for Jaspers. He led a retired life, almost that of a hermit, his contact with the outside world was very restricted, and he derived his information from two or three newspapers he read. Nor, like Heidegger, did he ever regard himself as a political philosopher. Arendt, on the other hand, belonged to another generation, one for which politics was absolutely central.

The book that made her famous was, of course, *The Origins of Totalitarianism*. It is a big work, based on wide reading, and it was the first in the field. It made the essential argument that totalitarianism is in crucial respects different from earlier forms of dictatorship. It made useful points with regard to propaganda, terror, and the differences between Nazism and Italian fascism. It was not a pathbreaking book, because during the previous decade others had pointed to the specific character of totalitarianism—Ernst Fraenkel and Franz Neumann, Waldemar Gurian and Franz Borkenau, Boris Souvarine, Rudolf Hilferding, and others, including Russian writers such as Georgi Fyodotov. What was new and ingenious in Arendt's book was not relevant to her topic—the long and far-fetched discourses on the Dreyfus trial and French anti-Semitism, on D'Israeli, Cecil Rhodes, Lawrence of Arabia, and British imperialism—for it was not in these countries that totalitarianism came to power. On the other hand, there was virtually nothing on the Soviet Union and the Soviet empire, and the few asides were misleading, such as the equation between fascism and communism.

More than forty years later, this idea was taken up by the late François Furet, and it was perhaps no accident that he became the second Arendt Award winner. Having exaggerated the affinities between Nazism and Stalinism in the first edition of her book, she retreated from it posthaste following the events in Hungary in 1956. This had shown her the time limits of Stalinism, and she saw freedom just around the corner. But there was still a long way to go. Several decades were to pass before the empire broke down, and its consequences have not been fully overcome to this day. If in 1949 she could not even imagine how totalitarianism could ever be overthrown, except perhaps by military defeat, and if she feared that it would succeed in creating a new breed of totalitarian man not dissimilar to what is found in Orwell's *1984*, she switched within a few years from excessive pessimism to exaggerated optimism.

In a similar way, she retreated from the "radical evil" she had detected in totalitarianism to the "banality of evil" as revealed in the Eichmann trial fifteen years later. Arendt was aware of the fact that a book on totalitarianism that did not discuss Marxism-Leninism and the Soviet Union was, to say the least, incomplete. She wanted to write a companion volume but never found the time or the inspiration to do it. She exaggerated the atomization of society under totalitarianism, a fact noted even at the time by critics such as Daniel Bell, Raymond Aron, and others. Seen in retrospect, her book is still of historical interest, inasmuch as the development of our thinking on totalitarianism is concerned. But the reputation of *Origins* as a pathbreaking, let alone definitive, work seems unwarranted.

One of Arendt's first ventures into politics was the idea to establish a Jewish army, or at the very least Jewish armed units. This idea first appeared at the time of the Spanish Civil War. It reemerged in November 1941, when Arendt was in New York and propagated this project in a series of open letters and articles. The Jews needed an army to establish their antifascist credentials, but also for their own self-esteem and as the starting point for Jewish politics. She wanted the Jews to fight as a European people but did not make it clear how this could be achieved as long as the Jews of Europe were under Nazi rule and British Jews were serving in the British Army. The Jews of Palestine were trying to have their army, but it took them three years to get a mere brigade.

Five years earlier, Heinrich Blücher, Arendt's future husband, had written her a long letter in which he had stressed how important it was that the Jews should be in the forefront of the armed struggle for the world revolution. This could well have been the origin of the idea of a Jewish army. In a letter dated August 1936, he had said that if the day ever came when the world media would announce that Mordehai Veiteles, a commander in the Jewish volunteer battalion, had been killed fighting in Spain, on that day, the dirty grin on the face of world reaction would disappear and give way to apprehension and fear.

The story of Hannah Arendt's Jewish army campaign has been told by her biographer Elisabeth Young-Bruehl. The only major support she received was from the emissaries of Irgun in America, and this was not the help she wanted. Palestine was at the time the only place where a reservoir of people existed willing and able to join a Jewish army, but at the same time, such an army was bound to provoke Arab opposition. Since Arendt was also preaching that the future of the Jews in Palestine depended on Arab good will, and since the Arabs would undoubtedly oppose it, the idea of a Jewish army was inconsistent with the general policy she advocated.

Arendt despised Ben-Gurion, who had not studied political philosophy but instinctively understood that the beginning of "Jewish politics" was not an army, but a state. In any case, how could an army exist, free-floating in midair, without the support of a state? Such lack of a sense of reality was not a sudden aberration. It was typical of her political judgment.

Hannah Arendt had been attracted during the war, if not earlier, by the ideas of "Brit Shalom," the group of Zionist intellectuals who advocated close collaboration between Jews and Arabs in Palestine and, if a state was needed, a binational state. Among the members of this group were some of the finest minds of their generation, people with the highest moral authority, and their idealism was unquestioned by friends and foes alike. The best-known and unofficial leader of the group was Dr. Judah Leib Magnes, the president of the Hebrew University.[6]

However, "Brit Shalom," or as it was later called, the League for Jewish-Arab Rapprochement, remained a tiny group because its ideas had no mass appeal. And this lack of appeal was based not least on the fact that there was literally no one on the Arab side willing even to consider a binational state. (The few willing even to talk about it, like Fakhri Nashashibi, were killed as traitors.) The Arab leadership had no wish to consider further Jewish immigration into Palestine—it wanted the Jews to leave. Arendt was wholly unfamiliar with the political realities in Palestine. She did not know the language, which on more than one occasion she pronounced unlearnable. But this did not prevent her from holding firm opinions about the subject and writing position papers for Magnes, some of which were subsequently published. The best known of these essays was "Zionism Reconsidered," which appeared in *Menorah* in 1945.[7]

The article was a powerful statement of the dangers that would threaten the Jewish state if it came into being without the good will of the Arabs. Arendt predicted a bloody conflict that would go on for a long time. As she saw it, the concept of a nation-state was out of date. She suggested an alternative: the Zionists should "organize the Jewish people in order to negotiate on the basis of a great revolutionary move-

ment," an alliance "with all progressive forces in Europe." What revolutionary movement, what progressive forces? She never bothered to
make it clear. Arendt had one more piece of advice: one should give
one's "utmost attention" to the Soviet experience. She referred to the
"entirely new and successful approach to nationality conflicts," organizing people on the basis of national equality, that the Bolsheviks had
practiced. The Caucasus, the Crimea, Moldova, Central Asia as models
of national conflict resolution—the idea seems admittedly more breath-
taking now than at the time. But how could the author of *The Origins
of Totalitarianism* have failed to understand even in 1945 that such conflict resolution by brute force was impossible in a democratic society?

A binational state might have appeared an excellent solution on the
level of abstract argument, but how could a serious student of history
have failed to understand even in 1945 that the long-term chances of
success for such a scheme were slim, even if there had been a partner
among the Palestinian Arabs? In what country other than Switzerland
had such a concept been workable?

Her reflections about Jews, Zionism, and the solution of the "Arab
questions" were not just farfetched or utopian. Much of the time she did
not know what she was writing about. Thus, "among all the misconceptions harbored by the Zionist movement . . . this false notion of the
non-European character of the Jews has had most probably the most far
reaching and worst consequences. Not only did the Zionists break the
necessary solidarity of European peoples—necessary not only for the
weak but for the strong as well; incredibly they would deprive the Jews
of the only historical and cultural homeland they positively can have; for
Palestine with the whole Mediterranean basin has always belonged to
the European continent." In these few lines, about everything is wrong.
The Zionists, a few Romantic eccentrics apart, had never stressed the
"non-European character of the Jews." On the contrary, they had always envisaged Palestine as a haven for European Jewry. But by 1945,
it should have been clear that the great majority of the European Jewish
communities had perished and that the character of Jewish Palestine
would be largely Oriental in character. As for Palestine belonging to Europe, this concept was of course anathema to the Arabs, and it could not
possibly have become the basis of Jewish-Arab understanding and collaboration, which, Arendt stressed, was absolutely essential.

Hannah Arendt could have conceded that there was no solution to
the Palestinian confrontation, that there was an insoluble conflict between two peoples, that it was all going to end in a horrible tragedy. In

the circumstances, she could have decided that from now on, she would devote her time to philosophical and historical study. Instead, she went on carping and fault finding, querulous and almost always negative. She had no constructive advice to offer as to how to prevent a conflict, but neither was she willing to be silent. As she wrote in an article in May 1948: "What is the point of the establishment of sovereignty whose only sovereign right would be to commit collective suicide?"

Hannah Arendt's political horizon, like that of her husband, was limited to Europe, or, to be precise, to Western Europe, and thus she had reached the conclusion early on that the age of nationalism and the nation-state was over. It was not quite correct even with regard to Western Europe. As for the rest of the world, it could not have been more mistaken.

Hannah Arendt's comments on current affairs appear most frequently in her correspondence with Jaspers, and above all in her letters to her husband, Heinrich Blücher. Blücher was, in some respects, her mentor in contemporary politics, and she could let herself go more in letters to him than in the correspondence with other friends. These letters, which have been available since 1995, seem not to have been consulted by most authors writing about Arendt in recent years.[8]

Striking, above all, is her panicky fear of a new world war. When her husband wrote her in May 1952 that she should not proceed to Berlin because she might be caught in a trap, she immediately accepted his advice and canceled an appearance that had already been made. In October 1955, she wrote Blücher that she felt infinitely relieved having escaped (*entkommen*) from Israel to Turkey because of the general war hysteria she had encountered.

In October 1956, at the time of the Hungarian and Suez crises, she thought a world war imminent and was prepared to fly back from Europe, even though she believed that "we Americans will always get out in the very last moment" ("But one can never know"). On one occasion, she sadly wrote Jaspers that the situation was such that she was not sure that she would ever see him again. On the Cuba crisis, Jaspers took a steadfast position—Kennedy was right; one could not afford to let the Russians get away with it. Arendt, too, claimed (after the event) that this time she did not have the slightest worry that it would come to a war. In her enthusiasm, she continued giving advice on how the Berlin wall could have been prevented: "if the Berliners had just called in the fire department when the wall was built they could have washed away the whole thing" (letter to Jaspers, October 29, 1963). At the same time, she was advocating neutrality for Germany. Arendt wrote on more than one occasion that she assumed that Europe would drift toward a new Rapallo, that is to say, toward neutralism and perhaps even an agreement with Russia. Again, on a number of occasions, she wrote her husband that everything was finished—NATO, the United Nations. Berlin, too, was lost (July 1959); France was corrupt beyond redemption, but she still very much enjoyed Paris. How wonderful and prosperous and vital and joyous was Paris (letter to Blücher, May 1958). How well she felt; the newspapers were so intelligent and unprovincial. One felt the "smell of American stupidity doubly and threefold coming here." West Germany was a failure, the Bonn republic was not better than Weimar, "decline is written all over its face" (June 1965). But despite her dark prognostications, she felt exceedingly well in Germany. She knew the people and they trusted her, and she spoke the same language. Despite her advanced years, male Germans, especially the blond ones among them, found her most attractive (letter to Blücher, March 2, 1950).

But she was not more optimistic about the United States. She firmly believed that Senator McCarthy had a good chance to be elected president in 1956. The presidents were all fools or knaves, and she also distrusted Kennedy. The domestic situation was horrible; the educational system, the social services, everything had broken down. She reported to Jaspers in July 1963: "Most people of good will are all very pessimistic. A Jewish friend who is very active on behalf of the Negroes said yesterday: We are all lost." She added that she was not quite that pessimistic— the police were still functioning. But in 1968, she finally thought that the end had come ("the flood" as she said in a letter to Mary McCarthy in December 1968), and she and her husband were actively considering emigrating to Switzerland.

Such misjudgments about America were quite common among refugees from Europe in the 1950s and 1960s, and it is not difficult to see why. Most of them were basically unpolitical people. They were newcomers to America and did not feel certain things in their bones that were altogether obvious to native Americans of far lesser intellectual sophistication. Their European experiences in the 1930s had traumatized them. Most of their social intercourse was with fellow émigrés, their panic moods feeding and reinforcing each other. Few had an opportunity to come to know the real America. To mention just a minor, but significant, fact, few could drive a car (including Hannah Arendt, Marcuse, Leo Strauss, and most of the Frankfurt School), which by necessity limited their radius of movement. And thus imagination had to compensate for lack of knowledge of reality. Hannah Arendt, one of the younger among them, was still a prime example.

How to explain Hannah Arendt's frequent, almost consistent misjudgments? She detested ex-Communists, even though her own husband had been one, but in retrospect, it could well be that the fact that she never passed through a Marxist phase was one of the reasons for this weakness. Marxism was certainly not the only way to gain a more realistic understanding concerning world affairs, and in its extreme forms, it led those attached to it horribly astray. But it also helped to provide a political education concerning such things as power and reality, which Hannah Arendt, a highly emotional person with a strong inclination toward impressionistic, Romantic, and even metaphysical influences, sadly lacked. In all her writings, one will look in vain for one politician of whom she approved, except, of course, those in opposition, like Rosa Luxemburg and Bernard Lazare. In the world of politics as she saw it, everything was always possible.

In one of the first letters to Heinrich Blücher, she had written "*quant à moi, je n'en comprends rien du tout de la politique actuelle*" (September 11, 1937). Which did not prevent her from commenting on current affairs passionately for the rest of her life. Joseph Meier, one of her close associates during the early years in New York, said in an interview many years later: "We thought philosophy and politics were identical. We thought that if we had the right idea and the will to realize it, our victory was certain. But we were overtaken by the historical facts." Hannah Arendt was not given to such introspection and self-criticism.

Much, perhaps too much, has been written about Hannah Arendt's attitude toward things Jewish. In the famous exchange of letters with Scholem, he wrote that "I regard you wholly as a daughter of our people," and she replied, "the truth is that I never pretended to be anything else." She was not really interested in Jewish history, and her doctorate was on Saint Augustine, not on Jewish medieval thinkers. She did write about Rahel Varnhagen, but this study had mainly to do with the difficulties facing someone trying to get away from Jewish traditions and surroundings. Hannah Arendt became a Zionist, but she never intended to go to Palestine, and her loyalty was really to the man who had converted her, Kurt Blumenfeld, rather than to the cause. From the German literature about Hannah Arendt, it would appear as if she served her people faithfully, almost sacrificing herself, working for Jewish and Zionist organizations for twenty years after her emigration. But the truth was more prosaic. It was very difficult for emigrants to get any work, and these were the only jobs Hannah Arendt could get.

It appears from her letters that while many of her friends were Jews, she did not like Jews as a group, and there were always generalizations such as "the Jews are against me" or "the Jews behave badly." Even some of those closest to her occasionally upbraided her for her anti-Semitism. Thus, she reports to her husband a serious confrontation with her child-hood friend Aennchen (Anne Weil) about Hannah's anti-Semitism (letter to Blücher, Paris, May 22, 1952), and Jaspers in a long and very thoughtful letter told her that her book about Rahel Varnhagen was not only wrong in parts, but was a "bonanza for anti-Semites" (Jaspers to Arendt, August 23, 1952).

This animosity toward Jews as a group was of long standing, and it was by no means restricted to Israel and the Israelis. Thus, on the occasion of her very first visit to Germany after the war, she wrote about the horrible so-called Jewish communities. But about the French Jews, she wrote her husband in the same vein as for the American Jewish establishment: they were corrupt and really out of their minds. According to a "reliable source," she claimed, Judge Michael Musmanno, who had published a (negative) review of her Eichmann book in the *New York Times,* had received extra payment for his hatchet job from the United Jewish Appeal. In other words, the judge (who had officiated at the Nuremberg trial) had been bribed by the Elders of Zion (letter to Jaspers, February 19, 1966). There was a streak of paranoia in Arendt on such occasions. Perhaps she had read too much anti-Semitic literature for her own good.[9]

Much of the outrage she felt was directed against the Israelis. In autumn of 1955, Arendt participated in a conference in Milan arranged by the Congress of Cultural Freedom. In a letter to Blücher (September 17, 1955) she writes that she had noted a "typically Israeli attitude" among members of the Israeli delegation: "They walk around with pinched lips, jealous because of the great (past) achievements of the Italians." This is a curious observation, simply because there was no Israeli delegation at the conference, only one individual from Israel, Yakov Talmon, the distinguished historian of modern Europe. I happened to be there as an observer, and I knew Talmon well. He was an admirer of European culture second to none. He may have suffered from toothache those days, but the idea that he went around flaunting his disdain for Italian architecture and painting is simply hilarious. I have no explanation for Hannah

Arendt's remarks. But it could be not untypical for her powers of observation. She had a powerful imagination and saw what she wanted to see.

Her yardsticks for Jewish behavior in history and politics were very high indeed. She expected from them heroism, yet she counseled pacifism, as in Palestine. In November 1955, Arendt went to Israel for the first time. She had been in Palestine once before, twenty years earlier. Everyone she met (with only a handful of exceptions) was utterly stupid, the climate was horrible, the pressure under which people were living was tremendous. Politically, it was hopeless. The decline in the kibbutzim, the general decrepitude, could be observed as much in the dirt of the dining rooms as in the depravity in human relations.

There is a revealing passage in a letter to Jaspers dated April 13, 1961, describing the scene at the Eichmann trial: "On top, the judges, the best of German Jewry. Below them, the prosecution, Galicians, but still Europeans. Everything is organized by a police force that gives me the creeps, speaks only Hebrew, but looks Arabic. Some downright brutal types among them. They would obey any order. And outside the doors the oriental mob as if one were in Istanbul, or some other half-Asiatic country."

It was a tactless description, politically incorrect and factually only half-true. But it was not entirely wrong, and it brings up the old issue of *ahavat Israel,* the love of her people, or, rather, the absence of such love, for which Scholem had upbraided Arendt in a famous, often-quoted letter. Arendt replied rightly and honestly that she never loved any collective. If there was any feeling of solidarity and sometimes even pride, it was for "our crowd," and how could it have been different? How could Hannah Arendt (or Scholem, at that) see kindred spirits in a group of new immigrants from, say, Morocco or Kurdistan, fine people, no doubt, but with whom she had no common traditions, ties, cultural interests, or even language? True, Scholem's criticism of Arendt's lack of a feeling of Jewish solidarity had been made in a different context, namely that of Eastern European Jewry, but it raised a more general issue for which there is no easy answer.

The contrast between the dirt and the hopelessness of Israel and civilized Europe was so stark that Hannah Arendt "almost shouted with happiness" when she arrived in Zurich, a city alive, humane, pleasant. Here one could live comfortably. But, if possible, she liked Germany even better. Germany was prosperous, sparkling clean, a brand-new country. Every chair in every restaurant looked as if it had come from the factory the previous day. Everything looked modern and solid. Everyone was living well.

Hannah Arendt felt infinitely better in Germany than in Israel, and her stay six years later during the Eichmann trial only confirmed her earlier impressions. Jerusalem was a loud and horrible place, full of an Oriental mob such as can be seen everywhere in the Middle East, with the European element very much on the decline. In front of the courthouse, a mob of young Oriental and *Peiesjuden,* young orthodox Jews with sidelocks, such as can be found whenever there is some sensation. The general Balkanization was very much in evidence in Israel, with honest and clean people at a premium. The country—not very interesting, artificially blown up (letter to Heinrich Blücher, April 15, 1961). In contrast, almost everything in Germany was *wunderschön und reizend,* the forests, the Rhine River, the cities, the nice young people bringing her roses and violets. She was a star, being feted everywhere . . . invited to give well-paid lectures, made a member of various academies.

There is no denying that Zurich is a more civilized city than Tel Aviv is or was, the Rhine is a more impressive river than the Yarmuk, and the Black Forest compares favorably with most hills in Israel. Jerusalem was not a wonderful place in those pre–Teddy Kollek days. Few ministers of the Israeli government had their homes there. Germany was not only a cleaner country; it had more theaters, universities, orchestras, and libraries than Israel, and the standard of living was (and is) definitely higher. Many Israelis felt relieved when they arrived in Europe on a holiday, away from the Israeli pressure cooker. And the fact that so many of them went to Europe each year shows the depth of the attraction. But in the case of Hannah Arendt, it was not just a case of aesthetic pleasure; it was a question of belonging, and in her case, there could be no doubt.

Hannah Arendt went to Israel once again, shortly after the Six Days' War of 1967, and at that time there were fewer complaints. In some respects, she found the military victory quite wonderful, and the way a whole nation reacted to the victory not by bellowing hurrah, but with an orgy of mass tourism. She still had family ties in Israel, but there was no intellectual interest and few emotional ties. And yet, when the Yom Kippur War came and the existence of Israel seemed to be at stake for a little while, she was genuinely worried, could not work for a while, and offered money to Jewish organizations and to her family in Tel Aviv. The heart has its reasons that reason does not know (Pascal, *Pensées* 4).

Despite all the bitter attacks, it was not as if she did not care about Israel. In a letter to Scholem in 1946 (April 21, 1946, Scholem archives), she had mentioned her panic fear for the Jewish community in Palestine, a panic fear of many years. Whence this misjudgment? Because she did not know the situation on the ground. When she went to Israel, she made German-speaking relations and friends, but it is doubtful whether she ever talked to anyone belonging to the "generation of 1948," and it is intriguing to think what she would have made of the Sabra, the native-born Israeli, and the Palmach, the paramilitary force of the era prior to the founding of the state of Israel. Both might be weak on philosophy, but in many ways they correspond to Arendt's ideal of freedom-loving, courageous, fighting citizens who are, furthermore, Jews.

She had read Herzl and Pinsker and Bernard Lazare, just as she had read Jefferson and Madison and *The Federalist Papers*. But she was not familiar with the real America and the real Israel, and hence her mis-judgments and her panic.[10]

What can be said in defense of Hannah Arendt as a political oracle? And does she need a defense in the first place? It can be argued that her present fame rests on her philosophical writings, and that her political comments in her letters and even in her books are irrelevant. Why take seriously what was written perhaps on the spur of a momentary mood, without much reflection? But this explanation is not quite satisfactory, for the letters provide the subtext of her published articles and books, and while Hannah Arendt was indeed a woman of strong emotions, they also help to understand the origins of her reasoning and views. The Arendt cult certainly does not rest in the main on her philosophical writ-ings. What bothers one are not her philosophical views, but the phenom-enon that could be found most clearly in *Eichmann in Jerusalem*, less the essence of what she said than the undue generalizations, the exaggera-tions, the violence and aggression in her attacks, the one-sidedness of her judgment. This tendency was noted even by sympathetic observers early on. In a long review of the French edition of *Origins* published in *Critique* in 1954, Raymond Aron wrote that "without being aware of it, Mrs. Arendt affects a tone of haughty superiority regarding things and men." In later years and books, this tone became even more pro-nounced, and at times insufferable.

One would certainly judge her less harshly were it not for the conceit and the contempt, which appear all along. Outside her own circle of friends, there were, as she saw it, few people who were not stupid or who did not suffer from some major character deficiencies, and this not just with regard to her enemies, but to people who had done her favors and helped her in her career. The following report, dated 1955, is not untypical: "The Europeans, the greatest riffraff which God created in his wrath. Yesterday I also met Raymond Aron and Manes Sperber and so on. All of them [treated me] with great respect and a little fear. I am very nice because I fear that my contempt appears all too visibly" (letter to Blücher, September 13, 1955).

"The Europeans"—surely she did not include Heidegger and Jaspers. And why the contempt for Raymond Aron, whose basic philosophical views were not remote from hers (he had been instrumental in publishing *Origins* in France)? As a political thinker, he was at least her equal, and his political judgment was infinitely better than hers. He was usually right, and she was often wrong. The list of alleged fools in Hannah Arendt's letters is truly enormous. One sometimes tends to think that she had no judgment at all, but then, from time to time, there would be a brilliant observation or a clever judgment. In her friends, she was willing to forgive almost everything. Those outside her circle were judged by a wholly different standard.

The best she could say about people outside her circle was that someone was decent, but not too bright, or if he was bright, she usually added "but I cannot trust him," assuming apparently that intelligence and untrustworthiness went hand in hand.

She expressed contempt for the conceit of German professors, but in this respect, as in others, she was very like these professors, as far as the need for praise was concerned. Her letters to her husband are one long chain of reports about academic successes, and Heinrich Blücher regularly reported back that someone or other in her circle or from outside had said that she was the greatest.

But what if she was not a saint—are these not venial sins? Raymond Aron also liked eulogies, and who is wholly indifferent to praise? The problem is not sanctity, even though a moral philosopher, like a man of the cloth, might be measured by somewhat more exacting standards than other mortals. An art historian can be mistaken from time to time in judging the origins of a picture. But we shall not think highly of an expert who is very often mistaken, and the same seems to me true with regard to a political philosopher unable to judge political realities. Should Hannah Arendt have stuck to the realm of the abstract? This takes one back to the question originally asked: Is political philosophy a discipline wholly separate from the real world?

It is easier in many ways to explain Hannah Arendt's Jewish problems. She was anything but religious, and her Zionism was not very deep. If she was disappointed by the way things turned out in Israel, the same was true for most German Zionists of her generation. She was deeply immersed in German culture, Bialik, the great Hebrew writer, meant nothing to her, and what was there of Jewish philosophy to pre-occupy her? The same dilemma faced most twentieth-century Jewish intellectuals. With his much deeper roots in Jewish tradition, Isaiah Berlin admitted his lack of interest in Jewish religious teachings and philosophy, and Raymond Aron did not get involved in Jewish or Israeli affairs before de Gaulle made his famous derogatory speech in 1967.

At one time, Hannah Arendt admired kibbutz life but knew instinctively that this was not for her; nor is it certain whether she would have been accepted as senior lecturer at the Hebrew University. Scholem might appeal to her Jewish heart, and, of course, she was a daughter of the Jewish people. She also knew that it would have been unseemly to escape from a beleaguered fortress, as the Jewish community was during the Hitler era. Nor would it have been a practical possibility.

But what was the meaning of this kind of belonging? It was not a specific problem pertaining to Hannah Arendt, or one facing German Jewry. Western and Central European Jewry had lost most of its establishment and most of the intellectual elite for the preceding one hundred and fifty years. They were assimilated, intermarried, and gradually disappeared. The Scholems, who found their way back from a secular and non-Zionist background, were a tiny minority. If Hannah Arendt had no particular interest in Israel, the same was true for the overwhelming majority of Jewish intellectuals.

What will remain of the Arendt legacy? Of the cult, probably very little—in America, not much more than of Marcuse, Sartre, and Simone de Beauvoir, cult figures of an earlier age. In Germany, it will probably persist longer, for there seems to be an objective need for a progressive German Jewish cult figure, and Hannah Arendt seems to fit this role ideally—she was deeply attached to German culture, her name is closely connected with two of the greatest German philosophers of the twentieth century, and she was Jewish by origin, but critical of Zionism and of many Jews. She was vaguely in sympathy with the Left and with revolution, whatever that meant. She liked "radicals" but was not a Marxist and thus is ideally placed in an age in which Marxism has lost its appeal for German intellectuals. She was *persona gratissima* with the German "functionalists" because of her concept of the "banality of evil," which made it possible to put the blame for the mass murder at the door of all kind of middle-level bureaucrats. The evildoer disappears, or becomes so banal as to be hardly worthy of our attention, and is replaced by all kind of underlings with a bookkeeper mentality. Hitler turns into a boring *Spiessbürger*.[11]

In a letter to Jaspers, she had once written that the margins of society were the only possible place at the present time for a decent human being. But the margins of society were exactly the place where the potential cult figures of the intellectual establishment had to be positioned. In the two hundred years that have passed since Rahel Varnhagen's suffering from the double misfortune of being both a woman and of Jewish origin, those erstwhile handicaps have become something like a prerequisite for success. Hannah Arendt would not have become the cult figure she is in Germany but for being a woman and of Jewish origin. If poor Rahel Varnhagen could only choose between being a pariah or a parvenu, her biographer, largely by force of changed historical circumstances, was bound to acquire in her country of origin the status of a saint or a genius, but in any case that a cult figure. Hannah Arendt never realized what destiny had in store for her.

But the cult, needless to say, is not all there is to her legacy. She had a powerful intellect and considerable literary gifts. What she wrote must have appealed to numerous people. A comparison with the leading philosophical figures of the 1980s and 1990s such as the leading lights of the postmodern age makes her appear a thinker of almost giant stature, a true argonaut of the spirit. She was among the last of a highly educated generation, and it is not difficult to imagine what she would have made of the quasi-philosophical fads and fashions that became fashionable in the past twenty years.

Nor was she always wrong in her political judgments. Even though the world has not gone under, even if America and Europe have not collapsed yet, and a third world war has failed to break out, and Nazism has not taken over in Germany, political problems abound, will persist, and may become aggravated. What she wrote about Israel was untrue when she wrote it, but she discerned certain negative trends that became more blatant in the two decades after her death, and with some justification she could now say, "I told you so." That these trends were not preordained belongs to another discussion.

The cult will go the way of all cults, but her legacy will not be forgotten soon. She will be remembered not as a political commentator, or even as a political philosopher, but as an outstanding critic of her age, sometimes profound, sometimes wholly misdirected, frequently annoying, but almost always stimulating.

Theodicy in Jerusalem

Susan Neiman

I must admit that I shall be in fullest sympathy with a
Zeitgeist that would bring the intellectuals to the point of no
longer considering the tremendous body of past philosophy
as the "errors of the past."
                        —*Arendt, "Religion and the Intellectuals"*

Whose trial was it?

The question haunts the pages of *Eichmann in Jerusalem* and much of
the controversy surrounding it. Arendt charged that in soliciting victims'
testimony, the state of Israel was trying the history of anti-Semitism,
rather than the particular deeds of a particular criminal, as simple justice demands. Arendt's critics found her discussion of the role of the *Judenräte* even more gratuitous. Her insistence on confronting the question of Jewish complicity in this context suggested that not Eichmann,
but the *Judenräte* were on trial and led many to conclude that Arendt
had taken it on herself to indict the victims. That *Eichmann in Jerusalem* provoked enormous controversy at its publication when the issues
it broached had been little discussed in the Jewish or German communities is no surprise. More puzzling is the violent passion the book continues to inspire some thirty-five years later, when we can hardly be said
to suffer from a dearth of discussion of the Holocaust. The ferocity of
discussion cannot be explained by the book's apparent content. Thus, it
remains unstilled by further examination of historical data or by the
suggestion that Arendt was simply careless in her choice of expression.[1]

In what follows, I shall offer a reading of the book in terms that are
unavailable on its surface. Discussion of her notion of the banality of evil
has emphasized her attempt to capture the specifically modern character of evil. I do not intend to evaluate her view, shared by many, that the

Holocaust involves a radically unique form of evil, or the success of her attempts to characterize its nature. Without deciding the question of whether the twentieth century presents something fundamentally new in the quality of evil, I wish to situate the question in an older one. Much about the book and the debate it engenders becomes clearer when we cease to view it as a faulty piece of historical writing, or even an incomplete sketch in moral theory. What was on trial was not (only) German war crimes, or Jewish complicity in them, but Creation itself. Among other things, this explains why Arendt's critics were right to sense she was engaged in more than the simple reporting she claimed. There is no doubt that Arendt undertook to defend something whose justification should make us more than a little uneasy. It was not, however, Adolf Eichmann, but a world that contained him.

My argument proceeds as follows. I begin with a summary of the modern problem of evil in order to place the issues raised by Arendt in traditional context. I then discuss Arendt's use of theological discourse and her remarks about philosophy in order to outline the constraints her project must face: If Arendt's work provides a (substitute for) theodicy, it does so in radically modern form. Her decided antipathy to Hegelian attempts to justify Creation through history is as much rooted in Kantian metaphysics as in the experience of the Shoah and must entail rejecting any hint of suggestion that this world is the best of all possible ones. I proceed to examine her discussion of evil as a piece of moral psychology and philosophy whose goal is to preserve individual moral responsibility without relying on a notion of intention. Finally, I discuss the ways in which that discussion serves practical and theoretical ends. It responds to concrete political dangers Arendt correctly anticipated while providing a metaphysical framework that allows us to preserve the stance she ascribed to Lessing: not entirely at home in the world, but committed to it (*MDT*, 5).

The problem of evil can be divided into three separate questions:

(1) Defining the nature of evil.

(2) Explaining how people (knowingly) commit evil actions.

(3) Understanding how (a benevolent and powerful) God could create a world containing innocent suffering.

For most modern readers, these are thoroughly different projects, so that the eighteenth-century designation of all of them as somehow belonging together can seem simply confused. That human cruelty and natural disaster were both called evils may appear but a historical mistake—perhaps a natural mistake in a group of theists, for whom everything is ultimately in God's hands, but one we've been forced to correct. Even optimists among us no longer expect benevolence and intelligibility from the natural world but confine our hopes to encountering them occasionally among human beings. Thus, the case of Eichmann may seem to have nothing in common with the traditional problem of evil but an accident of name. So Arendt, it could be urged, never deeply addresses any of the three questions listed above. "Banal" is not a definition of evil, but at best a description of it. More than one reader has found it not merely offensive, but lacking in the rigor or structure that a well-developed account should provide. It is arguable that no one has succeeded in giving an interesting definition of evil. Augustine's appeal to privation is more a piece of theodicy than of explication. To say that evil is not-Being is to say something formal about its Creator. It hardly counts as having said something about the subject itself. But whether or not other definitions of evil were more illuminating, Arendt's own cannot be adequate.[2]

Her contribution to the second project can seem equally unsatisfactory. We may be willing to forego a definition of evil in exchange for an explanation of the actions that are unquestionably so. But her answer to the question of what allows people to engage in evil actions is thoroughly schematic. Historically, she adds little to the accounts that were available in 1963 of the process by which the Nazis created a system of compliant extermination. Philosophically, she sketches an idea about judgment and thoughtlessness that says next to nothing about why some of us turn out to be Eichmann and others Anton Schmidt—particularly unsettling in view of the fact that some of us turn out to be Heidegger. I will argue that Arendt's discussion of moral judgment is less sketchy than has been thought. Nevertheless, as attempts to give detailed analyses of the two modern questions concerning the problem of evil, Arendt's account is hard to view as successful.[3] Yet the work continues to evoke levels of response that find in it depth and significance, touching nerves that show that it is surely addressing something.

How could it be the third question? The suggestion that Arendt's project might have its roots in the eighteenth century can seem to result not merely from conceptual confusion, but from morally revolting conceptual confusion. Discussing in similar terms what we now radically separate as moral evil and natural suffering would leave God's responsibility for both a matter for speculation. Perhaps atheists, more than others, recoil from a line of thinking that could make God, at best, a *Mitläufer*.

But if contemplating God's culpability for Auschwitz seems too noxious to consider, we must recall that the problems facing Leibniz were hardly easier. In focusing on the freedom of Judas as the act most in need of explanation, the Christian philosopher forces himself to contemplate God's complicity in the murder of the Christ. And though he himself rejected the doctrine, Leibniz felt bound to defend even a God who condemns unbaptized babies to eternal damnation, as Calvinists believed. Arendt's deep and repeated conviction that totalitarian governments succeed in creating Hell on earth can also be read backward: if unspeakable torture is inflicted without ground in one realm, the sense of Creation is precarious in all of them.

The term "theodicy"—from *theos,* as in "God," and *dike,* as in "justice"—was introduced by Leibniz in 1710 in the book of the same name. His justification of God was undertaken against the charge of gross negligence so persuasively stated by Pierre Bayle: A God whose Creation includes the set of crimes and misfortunes of which human history is constructed can be worshipped only in an act of blind faith. Leibniz's attempt to answer him by insisting evils are just and intelligible was seen as flawed in inception. After the Lisbon earthquake, at the very latest, it was merely the object of sport.

Contemporary readers no longer demand an account of natural evils and have no wish to give God the responsibility for moral ones. Indeed, insofar as God is admitted at all, He is not admitted into explanation. It is worth remembering that the very development that split the two questions decisively began by connecting them. Rousseau's second *Discourse* is the first great attempt to examine evil as a political and psychological phenomenon. Rousseau replaced theological with historical discourse, yet he did so in answer to a cosmological problem. He thereby initiated a discussion of the social bases of evil in which we can recognize our own problems, but he was driven by concerns that strike us as remote.

They are not. As Arendt wrote: "behind the theodicies of the modern age, that is, in the justifications of God, there lurks of course the suspicion that life as we know it stands in great need of being justified" *(Lectures,* 24). She was lecturing on Kant, for whom the connection between the various aspects of the problem of evil is not only historical, but conceptual. His essay "On the Failure of All Future Attempts at Theodicy" comments extensively on the Book of Job and decisively disallows, on moral and political grounds, just the sort of rejuvenation of Leibnizian solutions Hegel would attempt a generation later. But if Kant removed the problem from the realm of the (decently) answerable, and surely from one in which theological categories can be used to discuss it, he left it all the more firmly anchored in the structure of reality. The problem of evil is, for Kant, a necessary one. It cannot be resolved by theology (for which suffering could be understood as punishment and hence justified) or by a messianic vision of history (for which suffering could be understood as necessary and hence redeemed). A past in which Adam ate no apples, or a future in which a classless society is realized, are big contingencies, but contingencies for all that. Kant, by contrast, defines the problem of evil in metaphysical terms. A world in which reason and nature have equally pressing claims is one that is *systematically* out of joint. The absence of all but accidental connection between virtue and happiness cannot be resolved by reducing one to the other; but this is the source of permanent tension both in theory and in practice.

Whether or not we follow Kant in thinking that a disjunction between happiness and virtue structures the human condition, it is clear that the structure changes. The way in which all the assumptions on which civilized understanding is founded were threatened by Auschwitz is not the way in which they were threatened by the Lisbon earthquake, and it is hardly my purpose to deny a difference between them. I do insist that we understand that development against a background of commonality. To trace what has changed in our understanding of ourselves and our place in the world, we must keep in focus something permanent.[4]

It starts as a matter of tone: of everything that happens before and after argument begins. Arendt's writings are charged with theological language. It is hard to think of a twentieth-century philosopher whose work as often uses concepts like "soul" and "hell" and "redemption" and "blasphemy," or a nonobservant Jew who more naturally refers to the *Avinu Malkenu* or Yom Kippur prayers on the Talmudic legend of the thirty-six righteous souls. Arendt never hesitates to take up Eichmann's New Testament allusion and subtitle her chapter on the Wannsee Conference "Pontius Pilate" or to return Scholem's charge that she is short on *ahavat Israel* with the observation that the people of Israel have replaced that love of God in which their greatness once consisted with simple narcissism. Lest one take her use of sacred language as metaphorical, Arendt is explicit:

> When I used the image of Hell, I did not mean this allegorically but literally: it seems rather obvious that men who have lost their faith in Paradise will not be able to establish it on earth; but it is not so certain that those who have lost their belief in Hell as a place of the hereafter may not be willing and able to establish on earth exact imitations of what people used to believe about

Hell. In this sense I think that a description of the camps as Hell on earth is more "objective," that is, more adequate to their essence than statements of a purely sociological or psychological nature. ("Reply to Eric Voegelin," in *EU*, 404)[5]

One suspects that Arendt would have been just as happy to defend a literal analysis of the word "soul." Indeed, the features Arendt holds to be most definitive of the human, natality and plurality, are just those that distinguish us from the God of Abraham: He is eternal, and He is one. The warning against the tendency to overstep human limits in the wrong sort of attempt to imitate God is an old one. In any case, there is even more direct testimony of an attitude toward religion that, like so much in Arendt's work, is deeply and persuasively Kantian. She dismisses atheists as "fools who pretend to know what no man can know" (*MDT*, 67) and writes more explicitly to Jaspers: "Personally, I make my way through the world (and indeed rather better than worse) with a kind of (childish? because unquestioned?) trust in God (as distinguished from faith, which always believes to know and thus lands in doubts and paradoxes). Of course, one can't do anything with this but be happy about it" (March 4, 1951). Much like Kant himself, Arendt disallows any role for private faith in the public realm. Throughout his final years, Kant was clearly longing to assert the same argument from design he had conclusively undermined. His self-restraint on this score, like Arendt's, was based not primarily in epistemological concerns: Any claims about God and his workings must exceed the limits of human reason. Far more important are political ones: Asserting the goodness of Creation would both validate the existing order and undermine human freedom to change it.[6]

The tension between a clear, but nearly private inclination to think in sacred categories and a healthy suspicion of the transcendent, which leads to a resolute insistence on secular ones, can seem to result from bad faith. I believe it does not. Kant may have closed the eighteenth century by insisting on the separation of philosophical and theological discourse, but Nietzsche closed the nineteenth by insisting on their inextricability. Little could be further from a denial of God's presence than the claim that He is dead. Some readings of Nietzsche, or positivism, explain the tension by insisting we have not yet heard the news: grammatical errors, or the shadows of the dead God, still cloud our ability to think clearly. But the persistence of the sacred in the most serious of secular discourse suggests the entanglement to be more than a mere mistake. It is common enough to say that Hegel replaces the theological no-

tion of providence with the secular notion of history.[7] The trouble with
statements like these is their assumption of a linear notion of the history
of ideas, implying that having once made this turn, we could be done
with God—at least intellectually—once and for all. Hegel asserts just
the opposite when asserting that philosophy should *become* theodicy
and acknowledging his roots in Leibniz. Rousseau wasn't done with cosmology when he invented psychology in order to cope with it; nor was
his ongoing preoccupation simply an oversight, that is, itself a psychological matter. It is, of course, too soon to reflect on what closed the
twentieth century, but Arendt's work is a better place than most to begin. Much of its power derives from its refusal to respect traditional dis-
ciplinary boundaries and her consequent ability to live with creative
confusion. Her use of philosophical theology is an unexplored instance
of these capacities.

But before arguing that *Eichmann in Jerusalem* can be read as theodicy, we may require an argument that it can be read as philosophy at all.
Here one might ask: How can a book about the nature of evil, the conditions of freedom, and the relations between thought and action *not*
be read as philosophy? The fact that it wasn't published by a university
press is unimportant when we recall how many enduring philosophical
essays were first published in the *Berlinische Monatsschrift,* the eighteenth century's version of the *New Yorker.* But *Eichmann in Jerusalem*
presents graver problems. The first is Arendt's own word that it is not
philosophy and she is not a philosopher. The second is its relentless particularity—relentless not only because it tries to confine itself to descriptions of particular deeds committed by particular agents, but because
it time and again criticizes the prosecution for failing to do so. Writing
to Mary McCarthy, Arendt claims there are no ideas, but only facts, in
what she disingenuously continues to call a report (*BF,* September 20,
1963).[8] She is merciless in attacking Ben-Gurion and prosecutor Hausner for concentrating on "general issues of greater import" rather than
on the question of the individual guilt of the accused (*EiJ,* 5, 18). Lest
there remain ambiguity about her intentions, Arendt adds in the "Post-
script": "This book is [not] . . . finally and least of all, a theoretical trea-
tise on the nature of evil. The focus of every trial is upon the person of
the defendant, a man of flesh and blood with an individual history, with
an always unique set of qualities, peculiarities, behavior patterns and
circumstances" (*EiJ,* 285).

It is possible to dismiss such remarks by denying that authors' wishes
about their texts have greater claims to fulfillment than any others, but

there is a good deal more to be said. Concerning the question of particularity: *Eichmann in Jerusalem* is a work about judgment, the capacity to relate the universal to the particular.[9] Arendt's final book was to have been devoted to the question, but one wonders how much further she would have come on the subject than Kant himself. While his *Critique of Judgment* devotes four hundred pages to central and interesting features of judgment, he comes no closer to a theoretical account of it than he did when first mentioning the faculty in the *Critique of Pure Reason.* There, in a statement Arendt was fond of quoting, he tells us that judgment is a peculiar talent that cannot be taught, but only practiced, and that those who are deficient in it are ordinarily called stupid—a failure for which there is no remedy.[10] This suggests, as we will see, that a general account of how judgment works will be impossible, for one cannot give general rules for applying the universal to the particular. One can, as Kant does, give a set of maxims that specify the general exhortation to think for oneself,[11] or one can work with exemplars.

The latter course is the one taken by *Eichmann in Jerusalem.* Precisely because it focuses on "a man of flesh and blood with an individual history," it can serve as a case from which we might learn. We understand judgment through examining particular and individual instances of it, in all their specificity. Here, bad judgment can be just as instructive as its opposite. In this sense, Eichmann provides "a lesson, neither an explanation nor a theory" (*EiJ*, 288). Just because it is a lesson that confines itself to the particular, it may succeed in conveying Arendt's central moral message, namely, that it is only individuals who act. The connection between the general capacity to apply the universal to the particular and the judicial act of deciding which actions are instances of what law is more than an etymological one, and it is no accident that the history of philosophy is full of legal metaphors. Except for the *Apology,* however, it stops short of considering a real trial. Perhaps because it seems increasingly clear that the hard question is not whether we can find shared general principles, but whether we can learn to apply them, philosophy must turn to the particular. (Nothing displays this more chillingly than Eichmann's own ability to cite Kant with a certain amount of accuracy.) In short, this book can be read as a work of philosophy not only because it is a philosopher's discussion of general philosophical questions as reflected in one particular case, but because just this particularity is the route philosophy must take if it is to understand the nature of judgment.

Writing to Jaspers, Arendt describes her concern to free the Western tradition from the suspicion of having contributed to totalitarianism (March 4, 1951). That she can only do so as a philosopher seems clear. It's no accident that she refers to Kant's claim that "we can therefore be sure that however cold or contemptuously critical may be the attitude of those who judge a science not by its nature but by its accidental effects, we shall always return to metaphysics as to a beloved with whom we have had a quarrel" *(Critique of Pure Reason,* A850/B878, quoted in *Thinking,* 9). In other words, you don't have to be a student of Heidegger to be ambivalent about philosophy. Arendt's strongest expression of revulsion toward the subject occurs in discussing the intellectual embrace of Nazism: Precisely the capacity to use well-trained wit to provide interesting rationalizations of Nazism made philosophy permanently suspect.[12] But in just the discussion in which, for these reasons, she most vehemently rejects her interviewer's inclination to call her a philosopher, Arendt undercuts her own position. Defending her claim to have bid farewell to philosophy, she appeals to what she calls philosophy's essential hostility to the political—from which she immediately excepts Kant (Gaus, V, 45). Later she would generalize to describe Kant as "so singularly free of all the specifically philosophical vices" (T, 83). Be that as it may, this is fairly respectable company to keep for one who insists she has said farewell to philosophy.

Arendt's criticisms of philosophy cannot be examined here in detail.[13] I wish only to note that for every statement expressing her aversion to philosophy there is another recording her devotion to it; and that though she had excellent historical grounds for wanting to distance herself from the subject, she is hardly the first philosopher to have quite general ones for doing so. There are even those who view ambivalence toward philosophy as a criterion of seriousness, and certainly of good taste in it. Nor is this only a modern phenomenon, but one that can be seen in Socrates' false, ironic, pathological, and nonetheless serious humility. To say that true love of wisdom requires acknowledgment that the object of desire is unattainable is to say that philosophy can never be done without pain or paradox.

I have claimed that Arendt's theological language is neither allegorical nor atavistic, that her protestations against being called a philosopher must be read with their negations. This puts us in position to consider the work as theodicy, but only with the severest of constraints. Arendt herself defines theodicies as "those strange justifications of God or Being which, ever since the seventeenth century, philosophers felt were needed to reconcile man's mind to the world in which he was to spend his life" (*W*, 21). Arendt's distanced description requires discussion, as does her use of the word "reconcile."

Recall that traditional theodicy undertakes to defend God from the charges of negligence or cruelty evoked by the presence of innocent suffering in the Creation for which He is responsible. The defense can take two strategies. It can argue that the crime itself is not as grave as charged, or it can argue that the accused could not have acted otherwise. The first is the route taken by those who claim that apparent evils are only apparent. The second is the attempt to prove the Creator free of blame. Traditional methods of absolution will be hard to apply. The claim that an agent wasn't knowledgeable enough to anticipate the consequences of his actions, or powerful enough to prevent them, can sound feeble enough in ordinary courtrooms but will be intolerable when applied to the Creator Himself. The assertion that evils are not truly real can express the urge to escape reality that, Arendt tells us, has infected philosophy since Plato. If one doesn't take this route, one is left with the attempt to absolve the Creator by arguing that the evils we experience are necessary in service of the greater good of the whole—in short, that ends justify means. Few claims were attacked by Arendt as often and consistently as this one. This is clearly one source of her deep rejection of every form of Hegelianism, which she read not only as entailing justification of any evil that can be said to be necessary in the order of the world as a whole, but consequently as denying contingency itself.[14] For Hegel, evils are necessary, thus justified.

Combating such claims was an ongoing and diverse task. Arendt opened a 1942 meeting attacking Revisionist Zionism by charging: "They have all made a secret pact with the *Weltgeist*."[15] Historiography itself, she wrote, is necessarily salvation and frequently justification. In making history his central metaphysical concept, Hegel offered redemption from the melancholy haphazardness human affairs seems to present (*EU*, 402; *BPF*, 85). Hegel's claim to give us a more determinate version of Leibniz's theodicy is the claim that only time is missing to show the world order to be necessary: While it may not yet be the best possible creation, it surely will become so. Arendt's earliest philosophical commitments might have been enough to preserve her from any of this, for nothing is more repugnant to a Kantian than a philosophy that offers the "insight" that the real world is as it ought to be (Hegel, quoted in *W*, 47). But all such views become intolerable, at the latest, through the Shoah. Indeed, one question at issue in the question of the uniqueness of

Auschwitz is the refutation of whatever remains of Hegelianism. Were we presented with a relapse to barbarism, we might yet maintain something close to Lessing's position: The ways of Providence are peculiarly crooked, but it may be possible to trace within them a forward path. If civilization itself presents thoroughly new forms of evil, seeking meaning in history seems merely madness.[16]

If the attempt to find determinate meaning within the historical process has become unacceptable since Auschwitz, Arendt attributes all assignment of such meaning to the "superstitious belief in necessity, be this a necessity of doom or salvation" ("Understanding and Politics," in *EU*, 326). Narratives of history as inevitable decline are to be just as surely rejected as narratives of inevitable progress. Neither leaves room for the forces of fortune, contingency, and accident on which Arendt insists. On these depend freedom, the capacity for beginning both represented and realized every time a human being is born into the world. One cannot have it both ways. "Finally we shall be left with the only alternative there is in these matters—we can either say with Hegel: *Die Weltgeschichte ist das Weltgericht,* leaving the ultimate judgment to success, or we can maintain with Kant the autonomy of the minds of men and their possible independence of things as they are or have come into being" (*T*, 216).

Just the possibility to be independent of things as they are is at issue in *Eichmann in Jerusalem*. This is why Arendt opens the book by accusing *both* prosecutor Hausner and defense attorney Servatius of Hegelianism and bad history, "clearly at cross-purposes with putting Eichmann on trial" (*EiJ*, 19–20). To suggest that the cunning of history might use the Holocaust to create the state of Israel is not only to suggest that there are ends through which any means could be justified, but to veer toward the worst resources of anti-Semitism. And if anything about this history was necessary, then Eichmann, or any other individual actor in it, must be just the helpless vehicle of larger forces that his counsel had claimed.

Every form of Hegelian theodicy must therefore be rejected: Arendt cannot accept a response to evil that would excuse or redeem it. Yet she writes, more autobiographically than prophetically, that "the problem of evil will be the fundamental question of postwar intellectual life in Europe—as death became the fundamental problem after the last war" ("Nightmare and Flight," *EU*, 134). A grant application in 1969 says that "behind all these seemingly academic problems looms the ques-

tion: how can we approach the problem of evil in an entirely secular setting?" [17] The problem is not secularity, but contingency, for Hegel provides quite enough of the former. What alternatives remain?

Arendt does not correctly describe Kant's view about the impossibility of theodicy in equating it with "Job's position: God's ways are inscrutable" (*Lectures,* 30).[18] She is, however, quite right in identifying the
question that would have been at issue had Kant written a theodicy as
the question of whether human beings fit into the world.[19] Arendt herself tried a number of formulations of the relation for which she needs
to make room. Love of the world, rightly seen by Young-Bruehl as central, is necessary, but not quite sufficient, just because she knows love
can be less than open-eyed. To show that we are at home in the world
would make us too comfortable for anyone so profoundly cosmopolitan,
as she recognizes when refraining from attributing such a standpoint to
Lessing. To provide a framework that would reconcile us to reality could
support a passive stance which threatens to acquiesce in it (*BPF,* 86).
Perhaps her most successful formulation of the goal to which our efforts
should be directed occurs in a dedication to Jaspers: "to find my way
around in reality without selling my soul to it the way people in earlier
times sold their souls to the devil" ("Dedication to Jaspers," *EU,* 2183).

The goal of her investigation, then, is a framework that helps us find
our way about in the world without making us too comfortable within
it. To seek a framework in which to set evil is to seek something less than
a full theoretical explanation of it. Several readers have argued that such
an explanation is missing not only in *Eichmann in Jerusalem,* but in the
later *Thinking,* which was meant to provide the former volume's theoretical underpinnings.[20] These criticisms do not vitiate Arendt's goal.
Quite the contrary. Too exhaustive a theoretical explanation would re-
strict the room of the inexplicable that accompanies any act that takes
place in the realm of freedom. To claim that evil is comprehensible in
principle is not to claim that any instance of it is transparent. It is rather
to deny that supernatural forces, divine or demonic, are required to account for it. It is also to say that while natural processes are responsible
for it, natural processes can be just as easily used to avoid it. The faculty
of judgment we were given to relate our ideas about the world to the
particulars that compose it is fundamentally sound.[21]

Part of the significance of the fungus metaphor she uses in her letter
to Scholem is its place in the realm of natural science: "Evil possesses
neither depth nor any demonic dimension. It can overgrow and lay
waste the whole world precisely because it spreads like a fungus on the

surface" (*V,* 36).[22] Arendt, of course, is far too sophisticated and too determined to avoid causal explanations in the moral realm to suggest
that, like bacteria, evil could be given a genuinely scientific explanation.
But the metaphor expresses the ways in which Arendt attempts to defuse
the *conceptually* threatening element in the novelty of modern evil. Biological warfare could destroy humankind, but it is not the bacteria that
thereby call the value of life into question. That something so paltry
could cause such devastation may be the source of a certain kind of horror, but it is a horror that is close to disgust.

The fungus metaphor thus signals evil that can be comprehended. It
also indicates an object in which intention plays no role. Here Arendt's
discussion most radically diverges from philosophical tradition. Intention, or motive, has been viewed as the heart and soul of action, the
thing that determines its very meaning. Kant's greengrocer example ex-
hibits this well: a shopkeeper facing competition may decide to increase
his clientele by acquiring a reputation for honesty so that even children
can buy from him. Here "the people are served honestly," but we are
loathe to call this a moral action (*Groundwork of the Metaphysics of
Morals,* 397). The persistent possibility of self-deception, rather than
any commitment to two-world metaphysics, fuels Kant's emphasis on
our capacity to do the right thing for the wrong reasons. Thus he concludes that the only unconditioned good is the good will. Even should
misfortune prevent it from ever accomplishing anything, the good will
"would still shine like a jewel for its own sake as something which has
its full value in itself" (*Groundwork,* 394).

What's wrong with good intentions? For a start, they pave the road
to hell.[23] It's significant that Arendt alludes to the English aphorism,
rather than the more elegant but less stark German one: the opposite of
"good" is "good intention." Here, Arendt's claim to be engaged in simple observation seems quite justified. Not only were Eichmann's intentions not wicked, in the sense of stemming from hatred or other base or
abhorrent motives; they were thoroughly disconnected from the consequences of his actions. To shut one's eyes to Nazism, and even to profit
from it, was *not* to intend the chain of events that ended at Auschwitz.
The Holocaust was nevertheless the consequence of a series of discrete
actions whose agents could have done otherwise. "We didn't mean it
that way" (*So haben wir es nicht gemeint*) is just as true, and just as unacceptable, as "We didn't know at all" (*Das haben wir alles nicht ge-
wusst*). So much the worse for intention.

That is to say: Arendt is hardly attempting to mitigate the guilt of

Eichmann or of anyone like him. On the contrary: she is insisting on the
need for a moral theory that locates guilt and responsibility in something other than intention. It is the observation of what she termed the
total moral collapse of European society that makes that need acute. If
a good will were unconditionally valuable, there would be nothing
wrong with "inner emigration." Kant does, of course, distinguish good
will from merely wishing, but his critique of consequentialism emphasizes the degree to which the consequences of actions may be out of our
hands. The potential for the abuse of such claims in the land often
charged with confining freedom, and hence responsibility, to the realm
of the spirit is all too clear. Kant's claim that good will may be rendered
useless by "some special disfavor of destiny" comes perilously close to
Eichmann's tale of bad luck. As in her discussion of the claims of the inner emigrants, Arendt insists on the insignificance of sincerity. What is
important is not whether one's claims to have been inwardly opposed to
the Final Solution are genuine, but the complete irrelevance of one's inner state. If your good will can shine like a jewel while your neighbor is
being deported, it cannot be the thing that matters.

I believe that it is concern to show the irrelevance of intention that
leads Arendt to the very controversial introduction of the *Judenräte,*
whose role in the context of discussion has not been satisfactorily explained.[24] Nor is it accidental that she discusses the behavior of the *Judenräte* and that of the "inner emigrants" in one breath (*EiJ,* 121–28).
The point is not to equate their intentions, but to show the equal irrelevance of intention. Eichmann's motive may have been nothing but extraordinary diligence in looking out for his personal advancement. The
inner emigrants may have been less diligent, hence less energetic, hence
less culpable. The members of the *Judenräte* were acting not only from
motives that are not, in themselves, particularly reprehensible, but from
those that are positively admirable. Arendt never seriously questions the
claim that the members of the *Judenräte* acted in what they believed to
be the best interests of the Jewish people, intending to save lives and prevent pain by any means in their control. Yet their very well intended actions had the result of enabling the murder of the Jews to occur with a
thoroughness and efficiency it would otherwise have lacked.

It is this sort of data—combined with the fact that the core of Eichmann's defense was the absence of bad intentions, allowing him to plead
"not guilty in the sense of the indictment"—that lead Arendt to conclude that intention is not the issue. In questioning Eichmann's sincerity,
Arendt maintained that the judges missed the greatest moral and even

legal challenge of the case. Their judgment rested on the moral assumption that intention is the locus of praise and blame. The difference between murder and manslaughter rests on the defendant's ability to convince a court that he didn't really mean it, where "meaning it" signifies that he neither acted out of base motives nor desired the consequences of his action. "On nothing, perhaps, has civilized jurisprudence prided itself more than this taking into account of the subjective factor" (*EiJ*, 277). Trials like Eichmann's force us to conclude that the lack of bad intentions does not even mitigate—it plays exactly no role. So it led her to ask: "Is evil doing (the sins of omission, as well as commission) possible in default of not just 'base motives' (as the law calls them) but of any motives whatever, of any particular prompting of interest or volition? Is wickedness, however we may define it, this being 'determined to prove a villain,' *not* a necessary condition for evil doing?" (*T*, 4). Arendt might have put the issue in stronger terms. It is not only the motive for an action that is irrelevant to its being a good or an evil one, but every other feature of the agent's intended aim. That one could have done nothing other than sign a paper, without experiencing vile emotions, without willing—or even being comfortable contemplating—the consequences to which it led, and nevertheless be guilty of murder is a fact that shows the limits of traditional categories. In the Third Reich, the *meaning* of action was not determined by intentionality.

It may be unsurprising that much twentieth-century moral and legal philosophy has been devoted to understanding the notion of intention—with uncertain results. The opacity of much discussion of the question signals equivocation in the concept itself. Here, ordinary intuitions and philosophical reflection can be equally murky. Even should we return, *per impossibile,* to a Cartesian understanding of intention as private mental state, which mental state would it be? The attitude with which one undertakes an action? The state of affairs one hopes to achieve by it? Is intention fundamentally cognitive, my ability to understand the consequences of my action? Or is it primarily volitional, my desire that those consequences should come about? Both features are contained in the ordinary use of the concept and often sidestepped in philosophical analysis of it. Classical discussion relies less on the metaphysics of inner states than on the assumption of a stable distinction between *what* you did and *why* you did it. Just this distinction is thrown into question both by contemporary thought on the subject and by contemporary practice. It cannot be my purpose to begin to survey or clarify this discussion, nor to argue that Arendt's conception of intention is itself clear. The incompleteness of her account of judgment has been well argued by others.[25] I wish here only to argue that it will seem more substantial when understood in conjunction with an (equally incomplete) account of intention. In each of its features, judgment is to be contrasted with intention. While neither her notion of judgment nor her notion of intention is ever adequately elaborated, the contrast between the two forms a rich and suggestive signpost for further thought.

Are there cases where classical notions of intention still have force? Arendt writes of the judgment demanded in situations that are radically new. The uniqueness of the Shoah is not, again, a question that will be treated in this essay, though I suspect that the breakdown of the notion of intention is connected with the general breakdown of moral categories that event engendered. Moral categories, like others, presuppose a framework that gives them reference and function. Where the framework is broken, categories within it lose meaning and weight. If the concept of intention is pointless for understanding and judging crimes like Eichmann's, it may be because the Shoah threatens all ordinary projects of making sense.[26]

It clearly threatens our notions of the person, in more ways than one. As the subject was destroyed by the murderers, so notions of subjectivity themselves become void. Arendt's readers will understand the following in frightening form: "Why do I want to tell him about an intention too, as well as telling him what I did?—Not because the intention was also something which was going on at that time. But because I want to tell him something about *myself,* which goes beyond what happened at that time" (Wittgenstein, *Philosophical Investigations,* # 659). Wittgenstein's response to the hopelessness of specifying an adequate account of intention is to call on intention itself: what I want when appealing to intentions is to tell you something crucial of myself. It is easy enough to think of hosts of ordinary cases this captures. Eichmann's nearly alarming willingness to cooperate with the prosecution was also a desire for just that. And Arendt's claim that evil can be banal is the claim not just that the self that undertakes it may be thoroughly undemonic, but that it can be literally insignificant: it simply drops out. Eichmann's eerie complaints to an Israeli examiner about the failures in his SS career— which Arendt uses as evidence for his utter thoughtlessness—are just as uninteresting as the prosecution's tale of fanatical hatred. For moral purposes, it matters little whether the correct version of events is the sort offered by writers like Daniel Goldhagen or the sort provided by Eichmann himself. Intentionality takes place in the world of the subjective, while for Arendt, guilt and innocence are objective matters—radically objective. If mass murderers' intentions can be unexceptionable, we are not to conclude that nobody is responsible for anything, but to locate responsibility elsewhere.

If the focus on intention often results from observation of those who do the right thing for the wrong reasons, Arendt is concerned with those who do the wrong thing for the right reasons—or, at least, not the wrong ones. This is the modern question, against which questions of bad faith simply pale.[27] It is precisely the question of judgment. For Arendt, a Kantian account of moral worth requires both too little and too much. It requires too little because it can too easily allow us to have no other attitude toward the worst consequences of our actions but the feckless one of not intending them. It requires too much because it devalues those actions undertaken for motives that are less than pure. In Kant's example, "the people are served honestly" by the calculating green-grocer. How much better European history would have been if the people had been served honestly by agents less concerned with purity of intention! All the more so since intentions are ultimately unknowable—as Kant quite rightly insists, and as the phenomena of self-deception underscore, we can never be sure of our own good intentions, much less those of others.

By contrast, judgment takes place in the world we share with others.[28] There is no room behind a judgment that needs to be evaluated or explored—a judgment is constituted by the act of judging itself. The centrality of the category of action and the privileging of the political are of a piece with Arendt's shift to the question of judgment. The inaccessibility of judgment is part of its unreliability. In general, Arendt distrusts moral emotions as not merely private, but passive, and hence manipulable.[29] The *feeling* of guilt, so easily manipulable for so many purposes, is such an unreliable index of the agent's real guilt that it may indicate the opposite: As the case of Eichmann showed, it may often be criminals who enjoy the sense of clear conscience, while it is the best people who are capable of self-reproach (*T*, 5). Compassion and pity are suspect as bases for political action because, as Lessing noted, "we feel something akin to compassion for the evildoer also" (*MDT*, 12). Just this feeling could be successfully exploited by Himmler, whom Arendt described as the member of the Nazi hierarchy most gifted at solving problems of conscience. Since an effort was made to remove simple sadists from the troops expected to murder, "the problem was how to overcome not so much their conscience as the animal pity by which all normal men are affected in the presence of physical suffering." Himmler overcame this, she writes, "by turning those instincts around, as it were, in directing them toward the self. So that instead of saying: what horrible things I did to people! the murderers would be able to say: what horrible things I had to watch in the pursuance of my duties, how heavily the task weighed upon my shoulders!" (*EiJ*, 106).

Himmler's reversal plays on the ways in which guilt is and is not taken to be an inner state. On the one hand, if conscience is a matter of feeling, the presence of feelings that are grand or sublime—that may even run counter to the natural pity that Rousseau insists we share with mere animals—are enough to attest to the murderers' conscience. The "terrifyingly normal" SS officer didn't know or feel that he did wrong because he relied on intentional criteria. Introspection into his soul reveals nothing he can regard as base or wicked motives. So Arendt writes that evil lost the quality by which one recognizes it, the quality of temptation—indeed, the temptation was to do just the opposite (*EiJ*, 150). Arendt is determined to take at face value Eichmann's description of the revulsion he felt when watching an instance of mass murder. It probably caused him pain. Rightly manipulated, the very pain it caused could be used to support the Nazis' resolve in carrying through murder, for it clearly did nothing to stop them.

In her 1948 essay "The Concentration Camps," Arendt argues against "the attempt to understand the behavior of concentration camp inmates and SS men psychologically, when the very thing that must be realized is that the psyche (or character) can be destroyed." Arendt's strong distinction between public and private must incline her to disregard the psychological as a morally relevant focus of action in any case: Your intention is, at most, your business. It may also be the case that intention is fundamentally backward-looking or timeless. Focusing on an action's intention means focusing on its origin, instead of its end. Judgment is a series of concrete and particular actions that take place in time and is hence opposed to the essentialist thrust of the intentional. If guilt and responsibility are located in intention, it makes sense to ask if one is, fundamentally, good or evil. If they are instead located in judgment, the question can never be answered once and for all.

This leads, I think, to Arendt's strongest reason to move from intention to judgment. One solution to the problems involved in analyzing intention as an inner state has been an attempt to analyze it as disposition or potential. Whether or not this analysis is successful, the focus on intention obscures just the "*abyss*" between potential and actual evil that

Arendt was determined to preserve (*EiJ*, 278). Suppose intention cannot be discovered by introspection. The only test of your intention to commit a crime is your potential, under appropriate circumstances, to commit that crime. Arendt is well aware that, under circumstances like Eichmann's, many around him would have acted as he did—and this is not a fact about Germans. Her awareness of that potential led to the charge that she posits an "Eichmann in all of us." Her vehement rejection of it depends on her insistence that guilt and innocence are "objective matters," as she states in her imagined address to Eichmann: "We are concerned only with what you did, and not with the possible noncriminal nature of your inner life and of your motives or with the criminal potentialities of those around you" (*EiJ*, 278). Time and again, she rejected the notion of collective guilt as based on sentiment, which substitutes an attempt at sincerity for a search for truth. Where all are guilty, no one really is. It is worse than ironic that her denial of the moral relevance of intention should have been taken as an attempt to erase responsibility or to show that evil is "merely structural." Replacing intention with judgment is precisely the attempt to delimit the gap between the actual crimes of Eichmann and the potential crimes of others, the gap that make guilt and innocence matters not of feeling, but of fact.

Cosmological fact, no less. In accepting as sincere Eichmann's claim to have acted without evil intention, Arendt is so very far from exonerating him that she takes his guilt to be a matter not of the death of millions of people, but of a violation of the order of mankind (*EiJ*, 272). Her insistence on the radical objectivity of guilt and innocence leads to a (once again Kantian) position few modern thinkers would express:

> We refuse, and consider as barbaric, the propositions "that a great crime offends nature, so that the very earth cries out for vengeance; that evil violates a natural harmony which only retribution can restore; that a wronged collectivity owes a duty to the moral order to punish the criminal" (Yosal Rogat). And yet I think it is undeniable that it was precisely on the ground of these long-forgotten propositions that Eichmann was brought to justice to begin with, and that they were, in fact, the supreme justification for the death penalty. (*EiJ*, 277)

To say that guilt and innocence are objective is not to say they are easy to determine. Nothing in Arendt's discussion makes sympathetic readers so uneasy as the indeterminacy of the faculty of judgment. Arendt offers no criterion for telling good judgments from bad ones, no guidelines for making good judgments except Kant's extraordinarily general ones, and no advice about teaching judgment except Kant's remark that one cannot. The appeal to another authority from Königsberg cannot be enough to allay our uneasiness with Arendt's account, even when accompanied by the quite accurate reflection that, in principle, one cannot give a rule for applying rules (*T,* 69). Three factors may, however, make the absence of a recipe for good judgment seem less disturbing.

First is the fact that its source is not, or not only, the general helplessness of a philosopher, but the astuteness of a careful observer.[30] Arendt's awareness of the difficulties of moral judgment rests on keen attention to the ways in which the Third Reich destroyed it. So she recorded the shock that lay in the recognition "not of what our enemies did, but of what our friends did," and wrote, in a 1945 essay originally titled "German Guilt":

> Whether any person in Germany is a Nazi or an anti-Nazi can be determined only by the One who knows the secrets of the human heart, which no human eye can penetrate. . . . The most extreme slogan which this war has evoked, among the Allies, that the only "good German" is a "dead German," has this much basis in fact: the only way in which we can identify an anti-Nazi is when the Nazis have hanged him. There is no other reliable token. (*EU,* 124)

Arendt is not the first to point out the fact that Nazism was devoted to blurring moral distinctions, implicating those who would elsewhere have remained merely victims or bystanders, absolving those one would elsewhere clearly condemn. Nazism thrived by effacing distinctions between guilt and innocence, indeed, by trying to create conditions in which the very concepts lose their sense.[31] She may be the first to insist that we need a new moral theory to cope with it. The solution cannot be to acquiesce in obfuscation—either by erasing all distinctions and concluding that everyone, or everyone of a certain group, is guilty, or by attempting to determine guilt by seeking formulas.

Nothing provides a better lesson in the vanity of the attempt to derive moral judgment by formal rules than the procedures of denazification the Allies introduced in postwar Germany. Arendt takes those procedures to have been (more or less) well-intentioned attempts to introduce moral judgment into a society desperately in need of it. The problem was not that these procedures were too crude, refinable by doing more of the same thing more carefully. Their crudity was irreparable, vitiating the entire process, because "they helped to conceal and thus to perpetuate moral confusion." Arendt continues:

> The injustices of the denazification system were simple and monotonous: the city-employed garbage collector, who under Hitler had to become a party member or look for another job, was caught in the denazification net, while

his superiors either went scot-free because they knew how to manage these matters, or else suffered the same penalty as he—to them, of course, a much less serious matter. Worse than these daily injustices was the fact that the system, devised to draw clear moral and political distinctions in the chaos of a completely disorganized people, actually tended to blur even the few genuine distinctions that had survived the Nazi regime. Active opponents of the regime naturally had to enter a Nazi organization in order to camouflage their illegal activities, and those members of any such resistance movement as had existed in Germany were caught in the same net as their enemies, to the great pleasure of the latter. ("The Aftermath of Nazi Rule," *EU,* 257)

The utter failure of denazification would be well worth further study by those impatient with trying to make moral distinctions through a "net" of fixed rules. The solution cannot of course be to abandon efforts at moral judgment, but to answer the fascist attempt to abolish moral distinctions by making more of them.

Arendt's insistence on the indeterminacy of moral judgment is thus based on the hardest of observation. If it doesn't give us formulas, it's because formulas do not work. Moreover, the contrast between judgment and intention shows that we are, at least, better off when locating guilt in judgment than when locating it in intention. If judgment cannot be taught, it can at least be shown—unlike intention, which is in principle inaccessible. Moreover, judgment can be practiced, which means that we can do more toward being good than merely wanting to become so. Where intention is the locus of goodness, we can answer the question of how one becomes good only with a mystery: by willing it. Not surprisingly, theology has had more to say about this mystery than philosophy, though the answer seems to be that one waits for grace. Locating goodness in judgment, however, gives one something to do.

One can study exemplars. One studies exemplars not only because one cannot obtain general formulas, but because judgment concerns that very particular individual that totalitarianism is concerned to destroy. It is one of history's happier ironies that this attempt to destroy human freedom was belied by just the unpredictability of response to totalitarianism itself. Here Arendt, like others, was struck by utter contingency: Who sold their soul and who did not, at what price and in what manner, stood completely undetermined by prior experience or education or origin, or anything else that seems amenable to causal explanation.[32] If the goal of totalitarianism is to make human individuality superfluous, it is focus on the individual case that will constitute a response.[33] Exemplars like Eichmann show us *what it means* to make wrong moral judgment. Exemplars like Anton Schmidt show us the opposite. We can do *more* than Arendt does on this score, but we cannot do something fundamentally different. At issue is not something that lies behind the set of judgments that make up character, but all the sorts of detail history and literature can present to fill out a life. These are not primarily inner qualities, which is as it should be, for what is at stake is something in which the inner and the outer are so thoroughly suffused that one cannot imagine the one without the other.

Arendt called it "dignity." Writing of the Nazis' success in implicating German Jews by persuading them to accept categories that privileged them, Arendt writes of a modern tendency to suppose "that there existed a law of human nature compelling everybody to lose his dignity in the face of disaster" (*EiJ*, 131). To disprove such a law, one need but show the variety of all the actions that might be thought to fall under it, but don't. Both dignity and judgment resist attempts at placement. Neither can be traced to a singular feeling. They are instead constituted by discrete, often ordinary actions, without being reducible to any of them. Like dignity, however, good judgment must be manifest: You do not have it if you fail to show it.

If the argument I have outlined is correct, Arendt's account of judgment, while embryonic, is much richer than often supposed. It is based on three considerations. The first is empirical observation of both the breakdown of moral judgment and the utter inadequacy of general rules for restoring it that occurred in Nazi and postwar Germany. The second is the contrast with intention, that complex of private and passive phenomena that proved useless in either preventing guilt or determining it. The third is reflection on the totalitarian destruction of the unrepeatably particular in every human individual that moral judgment must strain to preserve. All these considerations could be taken to explicate and extend Arendt's notion of judgment so that the notion could become a fullfledged account. (The difficulties of elucidating the concept of intention have, after all, prevented neither moral philosophy nor legal practice from relying on it to locate guilt and innocence.) Still, one may ask: What does any of this have to do with theodicy?

The possibility of an account of evil is the possibility of intelligibility. I have examined Arendt's discussion in some detail because the account has to work, that is, to provide a better understanding of the facts—in this case, the way in which the greatest crimes can be carried out by men who have none of the marks of the criminal. If the account is successful, it will serve two functions. The first is political: An account of evil allows us to act. Where sin is neither original nor inevitable, it may be avoided.

If we understand the causes of evil and the forces that conceal it, we have some chance of recognizing it in the future. The chance may not be great, but it is the only one we have: To insist that evil is demonic is not only to insist that it is fundamentally mysterious, but thereby to relegate it to religion, rather than to politics. Arendt's discussion has been said to focus on the criminal, rather than on the victim. Insofar as this is the case, it is not because her sympathies lie more with the one than with the other, but because her concern is more with the future than with the past. In this, as elsewhere, she remains resolutely anti-Hegelian. Her concern is not to vindicate reality, but to make room for resisting it, room provided by the very un-Hegelian insistence on the role of fortune in the past and contingency in the future.

Understanding and justification are nevertheless related.[34] For Arendt, thinking and being alive are reciprocal metaphors. Each is absolutely noninstrumental, and each is a good in itself.[35] If they are to be justified, it will therefore be together. This does not mean that one could be justified through the other—as if thinking were justified because it helps us to live better, or, even more absurdly, life were acceptable as long as it enables us to think. The meaning of each must be sought, and found, in the activity itself. Yet Arendt compares the feeling of understanding to the feeling of being at home (Gaus, V, 47). Like the experience of natural beauty, our capacity to comprehend what seemed incomprehensible is evidence for the idea that we and the world were made for each other. And this, as the *Critique of Judgment* showed us, is as close to the argument from design as we should ever come.

Even this is far too close for the view of Jean Améry, who worked to show the complete paralysis of human reason in the face of evil by showing that the intellectual was less equipped to cope with Auschwitz than those whose moral and instrumental reasoning were less developed.[36] Améry thus offers what I take to be the only genuine alternative to Arendt's position. This is the claim that the refusal to comprehend Auschwitz is the only moral response to it, for successful comprehension would be evidence of an intelligible world. Any proof that reason can understand evil is thus a hint of a proof of the argument from design, and such hints are indecent. My purpose here is not to evaluate these positions, but to state what is at stake in them: Both Arendt's insistence on the comprehensibility of radical evil and much of the attack on it rest not on epistemological but on moral demands.

Arendt's attempt to deny that reason leaves us helpless when confronted with horror is, then, a validation: Our natural faculties are corruptible, but not inherently corrupt. Nor are they, as Hume so well argued, principally impotent. We have means both to understand the world and to act in it. Substituting judgment for intention provides no guarantee for the results of moral reasoning, but it does save the prospect of it. And this is to save a great deal. It is sometimes claimed that the Holocaust threatens our very notion of rationality in at least two ways: The extermination of the Jews proceeded to the detriment of the German war effort and hence was counter to instrumentally rational interests of the Nazis themselves, and Jewish survival in the Third Reich was so utterly fortuitous as to make all attempts at calculation meaningless.[37] To use Rawls's distinction: Arendt is less concerned with the rational than with the reasonable—more precisely, with its possible destruction.[38] Her own description of Eichmann as "not stupid but thoughtless" is less helpful in marking the difference we draw between the choices involved in instrumental reasoning and those involved in that determination of ends, a difference that is basic to moral reasoning, but the latter choices are her primary concern. Conscience broke down under Nazism. It proved to be a fully inadequate instrument in helping agents negotiate decent behavior. Not only could it easily remain private and passive; it simply provided no touchstone for anything at all. Collective guilt, *qua* feeling, was worth nothing to the victims, nor was its absence a clue to the absence of real guilt. Most murderers could, like Eichmann, introspect all motives and find their consciences perfectly clear. We could thus conclude that conscience, or moral reasoning, is perfectly useless for guiding us in navigating the world, or that, in considering it as inward phenomenon, we have misdescribed its structure and form. Arendt's discussion of judgment is an argument for the latter alternative.

Evil is not demonic if we can give a naturalistic account of both its development and the forces that allow us to resist it. Arendt's contrast between the banal and the demonic is her most important. Writing about the problem of evil in 1946, she described gnosticism as the most dangerous, attractive, and widespread heresy of tomorrow ("Nightmare and Flight," *EU*, 135). Here, Arendt was brilliant, prescient, and very nearly literal. Denying that evil is demonic means, first, attacking the tendency of totalitarianism to make everything possible. The search for omnipotence that enabled the Nazis to create facts that continue to elude our imagination is what must be undermined. And here, citing Brecht, she maintains that comedy is more effective than tragedy, for the latter reinforces the apocalyptic quality that lends evil the sense of sublime.

Arendt sought a formulation of the nature of evil that resists all images of "Satanic greatness," combats "all impulses to mythologize the horrible." [39] Let's be more explicit: Mythology involves a mixture of the sacred and the erotic that infects too many discussions of the Third Reich. Like Hell itself, the demonic can be given a literal interpretation: gnosticism today involves what Susan Sontag identified as fascination with fascism. To call evil banal is to call it boring. And if nothing about it is interesting, it can become no object of temptation. A fungus, after all, is anything but erotic.

The other side of fascination with fascism is the sacralization of the Holocaust, which serves as the historical event whose foundational status threatens to replace the revelation at Sinai. It thus stands at risk of becoming both the event most constitutive of Jewish identity and the telos toward which Jewish history was directed. The urge to leave the Holocaust untouched by explanation can appear as the urge to leave the mystery intact, sometimes frankly described as a need to avoid desacralizing the Holocaust. Arendt must find such urges loathsome. She is far too decided a monotheist to grant supernatural powers to sin or suffering, far too good an observer of history to permit the desire for transcendence political space. To deny that the forces of evil have depth or dimension is to say that gnosticism is false. But then, as she wrote to Kurt Blumenfeld: "The world as God created it seems to me a good one."

That this is the question at issue is clear from her discussion of Anton Schmidt. Arendt maintains that only good, not evil, is the bearer of depth. Thus, it is entirely fitting that the tone she takes in discussing Eichmann is the ironic distance that enraged many readers. Moral passion emerges only when she discusses the man who was Eichmann's counterpart. Here, her uses of rhetoric approach the sublime. Arendt describes the hush that fell over the crowded courtroom at the story of the German sergeant who sacrificed his life to help Jewish partisans—a hush "like a sudden burst of light in the midst of impenetrable, unfathomable darkness." She concludes her discussion thus:

> The lesson of such stories is simple and within everybody's grasp. Politically speaking, it is that under conditions of terror most people will comply but *some people will not*, just as the lesson of the countries in which the Final Solution was proposed is that "it could happen" in most places but *it did not happen everywhere*. Humanly speaking, no more is required, and no more can reasonably be asked, for this planet to remain a place fit for human habitation. (*EiJ*, 233)

The passage cannot but recall the righteous thirty-six whose presence in the world, according to Jewish legend, is enough to guarantee our continued existence.[40] Those who think the Anton Schmidts are too few in number to redeem the world should recall that God would have spared Sodom and Gomorrah for the sake of a mere ten—in the story that Arendt recommends to Eichmann's attention in her final chapter. If it is the righteous among us who make the earth habitable, someone like Eichmann threatens its moral balance. And so she concludes the address she would have made him:

> Just as you supported and carried out a policy of not wanting to share the earth with the Jewish people and the people of a number of other nations—as though you and your superiors had any right to determine who should and who should not inhabit the world—we find that no one, that is, no member of the human race, can be expected to want to share the earth with you. This is the reason, and the only reason, you must hang. (EiJ, 279)

In a passage replete with allusion to one of Kant's best essays, Arendt describes understanding the world as providing orientation in it. Understanding results in meaning, "which we originate in the very process of living insofar as we try to reconcile ourselves to what we do and what we suffer" ("Understanding and Politics," EU, 325). This is something less than justification and something more than hope. Améry called it trust in the world, and he could not regain it. To show the unimaginable to be comprehensible is a feat that ransoms both Creation and our own capacities, and it does indeed suggest they were made for each other. No wonder that Eichmann in Jerusalem produced in Mary McCarthy an exhilaration akin to hearing Figaro or The Messiah, "both of which are concerned with redemption" (BF, 166). Arendt's reply deserves closest attention: "you were the only reader to understand what otherwise I have never admitted—namely that I wrote this book in a curious state of euphoria. And that ever since I did it, I feel—after 20 years—light-hearted about the whole matter. Don't tell anybody; is it not proof positive that I have no 'soul'?" (BF, 168).

One wishes tones of voice could be heard in a letter, for the passage is open to several: irony, defiance, and even fear. How could it be otherwise? One concerned with redemption will feel the risk of perdition. One capable of awe will know the threat of sacrilege. Distinguishing between respect and false piety will be, like most matters of consequence, a question of judgment, and here Arendt herself could err.[41] Yet euphoria can be explained only by the sense of wonder and gratitude for all that is that Arendt saw as the beginning of thought itself. We may find ourselves at home, after all.

THE ORIGINS OF

TOTALITARIANISM

RECONSIDERED

Arendt and *The Origins of Totalitarianism*

An Anglocentric View

Bernard Crick

Many have written more clearly about the dynamics of modern despotisms, about the causes and nature of both the Nazi and the Communist concentration camps, and about the fundamental conditions of European civic republicanism and its seeming decay into individualistic consumerism. But no one other than Arendt has tried so hard to see the links between these different phenomena and to set up a mirror by which European civilization can recognize its faults and perhaps seize a last chance to set its house in order before some other great disaster, or at best a gradual decay of civic spirit and public values, a privatization of all concern, befalls us.

However, until at least a decade after her death in 1975, Hannah Arendt's reputation stood far higher in the United States than in Great Britain. Perhaps this is due to the greater openness of American higher education to thinkers who do not fit easily in the Procrustean beds of the conventional academic disciplines. Thus the greater interchange there between academia and quality or intellectual journalism, and also the greater openness of New York than the Oxbridge-London triangle to the ideas of the refugee generation from Germany. So in the United States there have for a long time been more people willing and able to cross what in the United Kingdom is still the great editorial divide (despite Orwell) between politics and literature, not to mention a certain lingering intellectual parochialism.

The first British edition of her famous *The Origins of Totalitarianism*

(New York, 1951) was titled *The Burden of Our Times*. That title could hardly have seized the attention of historians and political scientists, nor was the publisher, Fred Warburg, knowing or known in academic pastures. Secker & Warburg had sprung to prominence and prosperity as Orwell's last publisher and as having the English rights to Thomas Mann and Kafka. Warburg was surely at least half right to see Arendt in such company, that of deep-thinking intellectual writers who are probably more influential in shaping the concepts by which we perceive the world than are social scientists and professional historians.

So the book, as well as being long and difficult and by an unknown author, appeared in Britain with a title of ambiguous connotation, even if in some ways "burden of our times" made better sense than "origins of totalitarianism"—but only when one had got into the book. Only a literary reviewer, Al Alvarez, was fully perceptive as well as unreservedly enthusiastic about what she was trying to say. She was writing, indeed, about the dreadful burden of guilt and horrified astonishment of our times. *How* could such things be done at all that were done so deliberately and in such cold blood in the camps? After all, most people in the wartime United States and United Kingdom, hearing rumors or reading dramatic underground reports of what was happening, simply did not believe them, and it is facile to attribute most of this unbelief simply to anti-Semitism or prudent skepticism about Zionist propaganda. Few people believed that human beings could do such things to other human beings, deliberately, cold-bloodedly, en masse, even as the atomic bomb was being produced, even as mass obliteration bombing was pounding German cities, regardless of precise military targets.

Arendt was not writing primarily, as historians and some sociologists mistakenly thought (and then faulted her because of this thought), about *why* this happened, thus to be read as an empirical, historical account of the causes of totalitarianism, rather than a detailed speculation about how it could have happened at all. Many were, indeed (and still are), skeptical about the very concept of totalitarianism that then appeared to be, following the American title, the subject matter in all subsequent editions and revisions. The historians have told us that the more one knows about Stalinism and particularly Hitlerism, the more exceptions one finds to the idea of total control, remnants of the past continuing, or powerful entrenched rivalries within the state. Elsewhere I have argued that while the concept does not work descriptively, and no "totalitarian" system has ever exercised total control over society, yet the ideological attempt to do so was real and accounts for most of the ruthlessness, the lack of normal political and human restraints, of Nazism and Bolshevism, not to mention Maoism and Pol Pot's Khmer Rouge.[1]

I know of no British political thinker who reviewed the original *Burden of Our Times*. When political theorists did come to look at it, the then-prevailing tone of logical positivism or linguistic analysis would have shared Isaiah Berlin's ex cathedra judgment. He once said to me, apropos kind words about my *In Defense of Politics* (the second edition of which carried an explicit acknowledgment or dawning recognition of Arendt's influence): "We seem to agree on most things except your admiration for De Jouvenel and Miss Arendt. Could you summarize either of their arguments for me in brief propositions?" "That's a tall order." "Indeed, can't be done. Sheer metaphysical free-association. Fairy gold, Bernard, fairy gold, I beg you to notice." But I still beg to differ. She irritated him mightily, for when the *Observer* sometime back then in the early 1960s had a silly one-off feature, "Most Over-Rated Authors of the Year," Berlin contributed not with a paragraph of more or less reasoned denunciation, but with two words: "Hannah Arendt." Ipse dixit.

There are things to irritate. She could be verbose, repetitive, and eager to say everything at once, and every time, but this may have arisen quite simply because when she started writing and was writing in different journals, she was aware that she did not have a continuing readership. So major premises had to repeated, but often in different words to avoid the appearance of repetition—a literary practice that subsequently exposed her, in the days of her fame, either to charges of inconsistency or to readings far too precise by seminar philosophers. The essay is a different genre than the monograph. Modern philosophers, keen on precision and mainly writing for each other, usually avoid it. But she was a contemplative thinker who most often chose the essay as a form because she was also a speculative thinker: To her, the very process of thinking was philosophy. I think she was at her best as a contemplative, speculative essayist. *Between Past and Future* (1968), *Men in Dark Times* (1970), and *Crises of the Republic* (1972) were, indeed, all collections of essays. I think her least successful books were when she tried to be a fully systematic thinker, as in her final and unfinished purely philosophical volumes, *The Life of the Mind* (1978).

Even her most elaborate book, perhaps even her most important book, *The Human Condition,* while it looks systematic, is more like a set of variations on two great themes, some harmonizing well, others discordant and thus "unsuccessful," but all provoking what she valued and gave us above all, active thought. Even her two most contentious books, *Eichmann in Jerusalem: A Report on the Banality of Evil* and *On Revolution* are only essays, far from monographic and comprehensive treatments. Only her short book *On Violence* achieves the symmetry of form and content of great political writing. Isaiah Berlin, who wrote as well as Joseph Conrad, might have made some allowance for the difficulties of writing philosophical English as a second language in maturity. So in the image that he popularized, she is a supreme example of a fox appearing to be a hedgehog. With Berlin, I think that the story of human freedom is one of many foxes, the plurality of thoughts and thinking in a civilized, civic context, rather than invocation of one or other of those hedgehogging, all-consuming big thoughts, but I would have liked to persuade him that she was a great fox for freedom, if her more than occasional vices of exposition can be forgiven and the reasons for her inconsistencies understood. Her pretensions can at times irritate: a bad old Germanic vice of appearing to think that through philology, the original meanings of concepts should be returned to, for example. In fact she knew better but liked to parade her erudition, pretending to be a hedgehog. And it took a long time before those in the British empiricist tradition could see that her existentialism, taken pure from Jaspers and tainted for a while by Heidegger, was more than the card castle of neologisms that passed for philosophy in Sartre, was closer to the humanism of Kant, forever moving between Newton and Rousseau ("the wonder at the starry heavens above *and* the moral law within").

One step forward, two steps back. *The Origins of Totalitarianism,* her first published book, looks the most systematic, but it is not. Part 1, "Antisemitism," and Part 2, "Imperialism," are somewhat loosely connected to Part 3, "Totalitarianism," which contained her basic concern, our common burden of failure and guilt: how the Holocaust could ever have happened. She saw this as not necessarily a unique event over the whole sweep of human history in terms of numbers (she was irritated at arguments that treated it "as a Jewish possession"), but as unique horror and shame for our times in that it negated, came near to destroying, the liberal hopes of progress ascendant in Europe and America before the First World War. Not that she thought these liberal ideas unflawed, as we will see, even if they could not be held responsible for what happened in the camps simply because of their alleged philosophical "emptiness" or by their deification of the self-contained individual (in some strained sense "lonely" or "anomic")—as some conservative and even a few socialist theorists maintained. Her explanation begins with the historical breakdown of liberal expectations of progress and of a rational and peaceful international order.

The First World War, she argued, smashed the old system—whatever its causes, profound or contingent. The idea of total war could become applied to social change. And the Great War released two irrational, demonlike forces destroying civic structures and rational expectations, especially in Germany: mass unemployment and hyperinflation. The peace settlement was based on nationalism, rather than constitutionalism, and in turbulent conditions, nationalism could easily turn to racialism as scapegoats were sought for economic and political failure. Racialism and anti-Semitism explained much (not all) of what then happened, why the drive to exterminate a hated and scapegoat minority, and one particularly large minority, not just in Germany.

Part of her bold explanation has led to misunderstanding. She was not saying that English, French, Belgian, or even German imperialism was a direct cause of Nazism, but that, first, the dream of an imposed universality created a new type and scale of thinking (she quoted Cecil Rhodes saying he "dreamed in centuries and thought in continents"), and, second, such incidents as the Congo massacres and exploitation to death showed that a contempt for human life could coexist with modernity or, more subtly and terribly, that such lives were thought not to be human. It then became "proved" to the Nazi racialists in the extermination camps (no longer mere concentration camps) that Jews were not human, for they did not revolt, they dug their own graves, and individuals when degraded and rendered utterly desperate lost all mutual care and sociability, which, to Arendt, is the very mark of humanity. Humanity is not a biological given; it is a cultural achievement that can become lost if we cease to reenact it daily.

Part of the "totalitarian thesis" was, of course, simply the perception that there was something grimly in common between Hitlerism and Stalinism. She was not the first to have this insight and was more than a little cavalier not to have noted (could she really have not noticed?) that certain intellectuals and political writers, all outside the academy, had had this dark thought even in the 1930s—notably Franz Borkenau, André Gide, Arthur Koestler, André Malraux, George Orwell, and Ignazio Silone. Certainly, as so many have said, the book is gravely unbalanced between a detailed treatment of Germany and the generalized and sketchy treatment of Russia. But the thesis was sound in one vital respect. She could deal with the seeming rationality of the irrational by invoking, in a special sense, the concept of *ideology:* how crazy ideas of the gutter or the library desk top could become state policy in both regimes and could animate mass movements. Never before had two sets of ideas that claimed to be comprehensive and predictive explanations of all human conduct become state policy. And there were only the two ideologies, both modern: the ideology of racial determinism and the ideology of economic determinism. All other purported ideologies—better to use another word, say, "doctrines"—were in fact (thank god, or common sense), however good or bad, partial. Some reject this "partiality," others accept it as part of the good plurality of existence. As she wrote in the first edition:

> While the totalitarian regimes are thus resolutely and cynically emptying the world of the only thing that makes sense to the utilitarian expectations of common sense, they impose upon it at the same time a kind of supersense which the ideologies always meant when they claimed to have found the key to history or the answer to the riddles of the universe. Over and above the senselessness of totalitarian society is enthroned the ridiculous supersense of its ideological superstition. Ideologies are harmless, uncritical and arbitrary opinions only as long as they are not believed in seriously. Once their claim to total validity is taken literally they become the nuclei of logical systems in which, as in the systems of paranoiacs, everything follows comprehensibly and even compulsorily once the first premise is accepted. The insanity of such systems lies not only in their first premise but in the very logicality with which they are constructed. The curious logicality of all isms, their simple-minded trust in the survival value of stubborn devotion without regard for specific, varying factors, already harbors the first germs of the totalitarian contempt for reality and factuality.[2]

Let a historian prefer Karl Bracher's, Alan Bullock's, or even A. J. P. Taylor's account of *how* Hitler came to power to Arendt's. But this does not meet her main point. What did Hitler do *when* he came to power? Hitler was (in part) a clever nationalist politician (vide Taylor), and he was also (in part) a cunning demagogue who pursued a "tactic of legality," saying one thing to the party and another to the public (vide Bullock), but neither explanation seems to give an adequate account either of what happened when Hitler came to power or of his motives.

The historian is on firmer ground to claim that Arendt gives no clear explanation of how the Nazis came to power. She virtually says so herself. "There is an abyss between men of brilliant and facile conceptions and men of brutal deeds and active bestiality which no intellectual explanation is able to bridge." Nazism and Marxism might have been as futile as Freemasonry and Single Tax, had conditions not proved ripe.

There is an element of terrible accident about—not "it all," for some terrible something would have happened amid such breakdown. But what actually happened? The formation of ideologies can be described. The breakdown of old systems can be described. And what then happens can be described. But there are no inevitable connections between them. Arendt never implies that there are. Her critics either have not read her closely or else are just using other formulations of the origins and conditions of totalitarianism, often crude, rigid, and deterministic, as sticks to beat both her and the concept. Or often they are angered, even if not Marxist, by the key comparison: of course Marxism is nothing at all like Nazism, they argue, has no totalitarian qualities, and is, of course, a much more comprehensive and total view of human history than was ever Nazism, and it happens either to be true or to be the only ideology scientific enough for liberal tolerance or respect.

An appearance of determinism could be given to Arendt's argument because, quite naturally, she concentrates on an account of the growth in the nineteenth century of those elements of thought that became important in Nazism in the twentieth century, and she gives all too few glimpses of the nonstarters and the ideologies of the salon and of the gutter that got nowhere. Think of all the horses with money on them that lose. She is, quite properly, writing history backward: she selects what is relevant to understanding the mentality of the Nazis and of the Communists under Stalin, and she is not writing a general account of nineteenth-century extreme political sects. She would have been both wise and prudent to have said this more explicitly, or to have given a few examples of the "also rans." That would have shown the historian that she was not arguing a direct causal connection between the thought of Gobineau and the deeds of Hitler, or between the thought of Marx and the deeds of Stalin, but only showing how it was, having come to power for whatever reasons (profound and contingent), that they were able and eager to think not in power-preserving and power-enjoying terms, like traditional autocrats, but in world-transforming terms.

Both Margaret Canovan and I have argued that *The Origins of Totalitarianism*, for all its faults and its bold, but discomforting and alarming—not only to the empiricist—leaps from history to sociology to philosophy, and its mixture of factuality and speculation, is still her key work, possibly her master work. It is a magisterial, if untidy mixture of deep passion and cool analysis, so that many or most of her other works are like huge footnotes to resolve difficulties left behind in the postwar urgency and immediacy of its exposition.[3]

The Human Condition can then be seen as the clearest account of her political philosophy, only implicit or presumed in *The Origins:* how political action is the absolute antithesis of totalitarian systems. But it is also an account of the decay of that tradition. Once there was the Greco-Roman idea of citizenship as the highest attribute of human excellence, free men acting together in agreed, concerted action determined by public debate. (And in our times women too, of course, but she did not labor the point nor see the source as tainted by the age-old gender ostracism.) To her, the essence of the human condition is the *vita activa,* where citizens interact, not the *vita contemplative* of the philosophers or the religious, still less the view of man as *animal laborans,* the *mere* creature of necessity. We must *labor* to stay alive, but there is *work,* too, which she defined, leaning too much on a special definition that, if it works at all, only appears to work in English and German, as things that we make with our hands to last as if for their own sake, not simply to consume out of biological necessity. This distinction is far from clear. Works of art can obviously be both made and certainly traded as consumer goods and can go out of fashion very quickly. Think of what Thorstein Veblen once had to say about "conspicuous consumption" and class differentiation. But the important thing is that she saw political action as part of the *vita activa,* not of the necessity of labor. Political acts are free acts; they are spontaneous interactions. Their value lies in themselves. To act freely is good in itself, keeping in mind that political action is always action in concert with others. And her sharp distinction between labor and work enables her to see (whatever words are used) that *both* Marxism and laissez-faire economics are variant restless and illimitable forms of worship or sanctification of labor for its own sake, rather than limiting its space to what is necessary for a fully human life of action in the public realm, creative work, friendships, and contemplation—all higher values than mere labor.

She attacks modern liberalism for overvaluing the realm of privacy as against the public realm, just as she spoke carefully of civil rights rather than individual rights. To be protected by law from state intervention never lasts unless individuals are willing and able to busy themselves in the making of those laws. Her *Eichmann in Jerusalem: A Report on the Banality of Evil* of 1961 angered many or most fellow Jews, quite apart from the misunderstanding that she meant that evil is banal, rather than that evil men acted as if it were and organized mass killing bureaucratically not flamboyantly. She further provoked anger by her sad historical point that there was virtually no tradition of political action in the stateless people that might have led to resistance to the rounding up. Certainly more and more accounts of brave resistance have been uncovered by Israeli historians determined to disprove her and to read the citizen ethos of modern Israel back into the ghettos of central Europe, but such acts remain exceptional, and if they show what could have been done, they make her sad point—after all the double point—that mass resistance did not take place even when it was suspected what was happening, and that most of those rounded up believed that concentration camps were concentration, not extermination, camps.

Also, in the *Eichmann* book, she provoked anger by her seemingly heartless view that even when effective resistance was impossible, it should have been attempted precisely to demonstrate human freedom and dignity in defiance even of necessity, somewhat as the Stoic faces death. She recalled that Cicero held that a free man, if captured and enslaved with no possibility of escape whatever, then *should* commit suicide—the last free action possible, when possible—rather than see his humanity inevitably debased. The religious may say that there is always a soul that should not take its own life, though a rationally calculated sacrifice likely to save another is always permissible, indeed often commendable. But Arendt's free-thinking or even pagan existentialism saw our very sense of unique and individual human existence as being in social relationships, how we interact with others, others with each of us. If these conditions of sociability are removed, we cease to be human. So we should at least assert our freedom while we can, even hopelessly, perhaps to set an example, but we cannot even ask to be sure that the brave example will be remembered, therefore honored, or possibly even effective in the future. She was not a utilitarian. It is a hard doctrine to swallow, or for many to understand. But to try to make an ethic out of the contrary is even harder. Any duty of action or resistance that depends on guarantees of probable success is a poor defense in desperate times.

Thus, though she is often thought of as a modern Aristotelian, she rejects his teleology—even a polis with well-ordered institutions will not necessarily increase in betterment, so much depends on free human action (and sometimes accident, Machiavelli would add—say, Caesare Borgia's sudden death, John F. Kennedy's, or, for example, John Smith's when a traditional leader of my old Labour Party). Also, she rejects what is perhaps his instrumentalism: that free political action in the long run ordinarily succeeds. (He might have noticed, living under the pikes of Macedonia, that it didn't.) She astonishingly sees political action as

valuable in itself. Quite simply, I think we should live with that astonishment of delight in premeditated free actions, as when we are moved
by an unexpected work of art. We do not always say, "What for?" or
"How much is it?"[4]

So she stands in a tradition of classical republicanism but has deep
worries that this is being eaten away by consumerism, and even representative government can be an invitation to leave politics to others, or
to see politics as simply a matter of voting in elections. Like Jefferson,
she worried that the formal constitution even of the United States left
too little space for political participation. She viewed referenda, for instance, as inherently manipulative, not especially democratic ways of
containing, managing, and narrowing debate rather than encouraging
and broadening it. Ernest Gellner once expressed this more simply and
scathingly as "the binary view of politics." He proclaimed himself "at
least a trinitarian, or else there is always some excluded middle." Well,
say "other," not necessarily "middle." Therefore a rash appendix was
added to an edition of *The Origins* just after the Hungarian Revolution
that saw hope in what was the old utopia of Proudhon socialism, workers' councils, rather than representative democracy. And some topical
essays showed interest and some sympathy with the student radicalism
of the 1960s, but only because it was challenging "thoughtless" institutions, that is, institutions simply carrying on without thought as to
what was their real purpose or what they could do better. She quickly
saw that most of the students knew no better.

So the Left could not claim her. But conservatives could not either. If
she showed a deep understanding of the strength of tradition, it was often in a pessimistic mode—how difficult it is by thought and reason to
invent new institutions. And to her, the American Revolution was a revolution, not just a rhetorical term for a war of colonial independence: It
had been the "world's best hope," indeed, for civic republicanism, perhaps the "last hope." If she could sound like Michael Oakeshott for a
moment when she argues that the idea of starting with a blueprint and
putting it into practice is preposterous, it was not because tradition
determines or is always the major conditioning factor, and therefore
political invention, let alone revolution, is impossible, but precisely because the invention of new political institutions is needed, and for them
to last, they must arise from a plurality of political actors with different
experiences debating among themselves publicly until they can reach a
consensus to act together.

She can give some comfort to contemporary communitarians or radical pluralists, as long as the community works with a political tradition, both internally and externally, and as long as the individual has the conscious courage to act alone should the community seek, except in times of direst and immediate emergency, to stifle public debate. In *The Human Condition,* she remarks that nothing in nature is more dissimilar and unique than one man from another, but that nothing is more alike. But what most generally can resolve this metaphysical paradox is not, say, a belief that we are all children of one father, but that we can all act like, indeed be, citizens.

Always the life of the citizen and the life of the mind: the greatest fault is quite simply not to think what we are doing and to think that we cannot think otherwise and then act otherwise. Her own position is never quite clear. Certainly it is anti-Platonist: There are no final solutions or single rational imperatives of any kind. But there are some moral limits and imperatives on *how* we should act in politics, as well as acting politically—these she seems to draw from Kant and Jaspers, a refined modern humanism. Canovan well says that "it is not so much a position as an internal dialogue, continually going back and forth between alternative standpoints." In a literal sense, this is free thinking. Perhaps this makes her rather careless of her philosophic presuppositions in essays on current problems, although in other essays, she can parade them somewhat pretentiously. In more than one place, however, she expresses her preference for the "political writer," who has had some experience of the political world, rather than the "political philosopher." She herself took on the role of a "public intellectual" that got her into many scrapes when activists, unfamiliar with her writings, could not understand her special use of terms. (She was not careful to start each time again as if from the beginning.) But what was always important to her is the thinking mind offering reasoned justifications for actions based on reflection. And "justifications" could never be (to get close to the present) mere sound bites or appeals to self-interest or a politics dominated by unwillingness to pay for any public improvements. Thinking, to her, is quite simply the antithesis of thoughtlessness, accepting things as they are, speaking, acting or voting as we are expected to, by order, by custom, or by appeals to personal loyalty.

Yet freedom is not breaking from tradition, whether in a society or a party, but is understanding the tradition one is in as a preliminary to action. If radical breaks are needed, they are then more likely to be successful. We do not reach final conclusions, but by public debate, citizen activity, and the dispersal of power (she sees the very concept of "sovereignty" as inimical to freedom), a plurality of voices can achieve not The Good, but always some betterment—not necessarily continual betterment, mind you. Our "dark times" have seen quite as many downs as ups. Colonial liberation, indeed, but then new tyrannies. Mass enfranchisement and much economic progress, but still dehumanizing poverty and dehumanizing indifference to it, growing consumerism, and neglect of the opportunities of citizenship.

Is it her possibly too idealistic and demanding concept of citizenship and human nature that makes me stress her pessimism? I think not. There are many reasons for pessimism if we think what is happening to trivialize the tradition and to corrupt the institutions of free politics. It is clear how worried she would be when, as I write, the leaders of both main parties in two great countries have been bending much of their energies in election campaigns into persuading their colleagues not to debate matters of public interest except by rote. Political parties and pressure groups have now too often developed as devices for limiting debate, rather than for encouraging it. Arendt might see great dangers in this. But she certainly can help us to put contingent events (not to use words like "trivial" or "thoughtless" again) in the broader context of the nature of our civilization—to see, in William Morris's homely words, "what it is around us." At least she helps us to struggle when we sometimes wonder what good it does to look the facts squarely in the face. We should read or reread her, both for memory of what is lost and for some hope of what still could be in the new century.

Hannah Arendt on the Totalitarian Sublime and Its Promise of Freedom

Michael Halberstam

Hannah Arendt's critics have frequently seen a political aestheticism at work in her writings that fails to take account of historical fact and political reality. "Arendt is an aesthete," one such critic suggested, "*elle n'aime que les trains qui partent*." This charge, intended to be substantive, consigns Arendt's political philosophy to the tradition of Romantic German thought that has been variously understood as a politics of cultural despair (Fritz Stern), as the aesthetic ideology (Terry Eagleton), as the quest for the aesthetic state (Josef Chytry), or as a metaphysical, irrationalist approach to politics that proceeds from ideas to social and political reality, rather than the other way around (Isaiah Berlin). Isaiah Berlin once remarked rather scathingly that Arendt "produces no arguments, no evidence of serious philosophical or historical thought. It is all a stream of metaphysical associations."[1] The charge that Arendt's work reflects the peculiarly antipolitical substitution of nonpolitical concerns for political ones characteristic of the German tradition from Schiller to Heidegger and beyond squarely calls into question Arendt's central claim of contributing to the rediscovery and rehabilitation of politics.

In reading Arendt's *The Origins of Totalitarianism,* and especially her final chapter, "Ideology and Terror," it seems hard to disagree with Berlin's remark that her work is excessively speculative or even mystical. Arendt writes metaphorically that under totalitarian rule, "the essence of government itself has become motion."[2] Totalitarianism destroys "the space between men . . . pressing men against each other. In totalitarianism a "radical evil" surfaces that is inherent in modern politics. "Something seems to be involved in modern politics that actually should never be involved in politics as we used to understand it, namely all or nothing." The totalitarian subject is one who has lost "the very capacity for experience." "Total terror, the essence of totalitarian government, exists neither for nor against men. It is supposed to provide the forces of nature or history with an incomparable instrument to accelerate their movement."[3]

Placed at the end of *The Origins of Totalitarianism,* the essay "Ideology and Terror" presents what appears to be a confusing theory of ideology.[4] Moreover, it makes terror the essence of totalitarian rule in what is now frequently regarded as an empirically unfounded comparison between the everyday life of the ethnic German under the National Socialist regime and the experience of the Soviet citizen under the Stalinist terror. Historians agree that the average ethnic German was not terrorized by the constant threat of deportation and death, as was even the most powerful Russian party member during Stalin's rule in the mid-1930s.[5] Such doubts about the actual levels of threat experienced by the ethnic German population under National Socialism raise suspicions that the terror thesis—and with it, the comparative concept of totalitarianism—constitutes an apologetic for crimes committed under the Nazi regime. The terror thesis, it is argued, falsely presents the German population as passive sufferers, rather than willing participants in the murderous political cult of German nationalist supremacy. George Mosse, for example, argues that the terror thesis is "a new version of the older occupation theory," suggesting "a confrontation of leader and people" that did not, in fact, take place—at least not in the comprehensive way suggested.[6] Is Arendt's theory of totalitarianism then also "altogether worthless," as the headline to a recent article in *Die Zeit* suggested regarding her Eichmann book?

Arendt's model of totalitarianism, to be sure, must be reexamined in light of recent historical scholarship.[7] This may well raise problems with her basic conclusions.[8] At the same time, the terror thesis cannot, in my view, be so unequivocally rejected as some of the arguments suggest.[9] Moreover, as Friedrich Pohlman argues, Arendt's account of totalitarianism should be understood as a model or an ideal type, "as a theoretical construct that attempts to highlight tendencies inherent in these systems so that the real dictatorships represent only an approximation of the model."[10] Arendt's theory "ultimately aims at a *philosophical and anthropological attempt to define totalitarianism.*"[11] While there was no rule of "total terror" permeating all levels and groups of German society throughout Hitler's reign, conceiving National Socialism as a regime of "total terror" is intended to mark a basic tendency of the system and to characterize the experience of living within it. Such an account may still be rejected as fundamentally misleading. However, some philosophical and historical reflection on the idea of terror can give us greater appreciation for Arendt's insights and render her thesis richer than expected.

When Arendt speaks of terror as the ruling principle of totalitarianism, she does not merely refer to levels of actual threat experienced by the population or to the actions of a secret police. Arendt's phenomenological thesis is that the experience of terror describes the *mood* of totalitarianism. In other words, terror accounts for the way in which the totalitarian subject stands in the world. Her description sheds light on the flight from reality on the part of totalitarian movements, their displacement of ordinary judgment and common sense, their self-destructiveness, their strange appeal, and their connection with modern emancipatory social movements.

Whether Arendt's model can stand up to criticism or be helpful to contemporary historical understanding is a question we must finally leave for historians to judge. In order to understand it, however, I suggest we do need to turn to aesthetic categories—categories that prominently figure in the German tradition of political and cultural criticism. Karl Marx once remarked that the essence of Hegel's philosophy was to be found in Hegel's aesthetics, and that he, Marx, sought to wrest these insights from the still waters of aesthetic theory and introduce their explosive potential into politics.[12] Arendt appreciated the political relevance of the aesthetic in her analysis of totalitarianism.

First, some general hermeneutical remarks about Arendt's approach are in order. Despite Arendt's continuous insistence that she was no philosopher and did not wish to build a system of political philosophy,[13] we understand her poorly if we take her unwillingness to systematize as a nontheoretical stance. It is instead the result of a highly theoretical position and stems from her profound philosophical appreciation of the problematic relation between theory and practice and of the relation between conceptual representation and sensible apprehension—an approach that emerged out of her studies with Karl Jaspers and Martin Heidegger.[14] In defending Arendt against her critics, some have tried to defuse the complexities and the theory-laden quality of Arendt's approach in an attempt to bring her into the Anglo-American mainstream. "As far as explicit commitments go," writes Margaret Canovan, "[Arendt's] . . . intention was often the phenomenological one of trying to be true to experience."[15] Canovan's remark can be misleading, if we take "experience" to mean what a narrowly positivist empirical social science takes it to be. The attempt to minimize Arendt's departure from a straightforward descriptive empiricism misses the specific character of what I take to be Arendt's aesthetic approach to politics. Being true to experience, for Arendt, means articulating a self-world relationship, a certain way of standing in the world, that appears against a historical background and includes an attention to spiritual self-understandings. When reading Arendt, we have to recognize that her statements about her own work have to be reviewed cautiously. Arendt persistently positions herself within the particular political and historical context of European intellectual politics that is suffused with the rhetoric of German Idealism—as is, of course, Marxist theory. She frequently draws on sources she does not explicitly adduce and gives readings that draw from a particular tradition while cutting against or inflecting it at the same time. Dana Villa's analysis of Arendt's complicated and often less than explicit relationship to Heidegger's philosophy well exemplifies this feature of her work.[16] With the dedication to Heidegger left off of *The Human Condition,* for example, we have little indication that the philosophical impetus for this work dates back to Heidegger's lectures on Aristotle that Arendt attended during the summer of 1924.

Arendt's "Ideology and Terror" and its thesis about the essence of totalitarianism have to be understood in light of these interpretive caveats. The essay speaks quite philosophically to the conditions for the possibility of experience in general. The capacity of totalitarian regimes to construct a fictitious world through ideology and terror raises the problem of the nature of reality and our proper access to it. Arendt's thesis, which I will try to reconstruct here, is that the experience of terror is descriptive of the mood of totalitarianism—in other words, that terror shapes the extreme self-world relationship of the subject under totalitarianism. In "Ideology and Terror," Arendt advances a thesis that draws on a variety of influential sources of political and cultural criticism in the German tradition that also frame her analysis of totalitarian movements and regimes. Her refusal to highlight these sources while simultaneously drawing on them in her analysis of ideology might be seen as an expression of her unwillingness to buy into the Idealist claims of a tradition that posits history as something taking place in the realm of ideas alone, even though she recognized the significance of these sources for understanding the *cultural* phenomenon that totalitarianism represents.

HEGEL'S CRITIQUE OF THE WILL

Arendt's account of totalitarianism recalls Hegel's famous section "Terror and Absolute Freedom" in *The Phenomenology of Spirit,* where Hegel provides an analysis of the terror unleashed by the Jacobins during the French Revolution. Others have noted the significance of Hegel's analysis for understanding the political terror of the twentieth century. "Hegel's study of Terror," writes Charles Taylor, "touches a question that has a relevance beyond his time. The Stalinist terror had some of the same properties as those which Hegel singled out in the Jacobin one: liquidation become banal, the fastening on intentions and other subjective deviations, the self-feeding destructiveness." [17] According to Hegel, the destructive fury of the revolutionary terror has a logic. The terror is an unintended consequence of the attempt to base the state on an altogether unprecedented foundation: on absolute freedom. "The modern aspiration to remake the world entirely according to the prescriptions of rational will is [what Hegel calls] the aspiration to 'absolute freedom,'" writes Taylor. [18] Hegel views the French Revolution as the first attempt at establishing human (social) existence on a nonarbitrary foundation, on the foundation of Spirit (*Geist*). This vision of society as a human construct turns man into "a creative god who resides completely in his works; these works are the terrestrial city." [19] The manifestation of absolute freedom as terror, however, shows the indispensability of traditional institutions and norms as the setting within which reason does its work. [20]

The dynamic of absolute freedom reflects Rousseau's idea of the general will. According to Rousseau, the social contract that constitutes a general will gives expression to the sovereignty of the people. It realizes the demand for an absolute self-determination, for an absolute freedom from all other-determination, whether it be natural, cultural, historical, or religious. [21] In Rousseau's own famous justification, "in giving himself to all, each person gives himself to no one. And since there is no associate over whom he does not acquire the same right that he would grant others over himself, he gains that equivalent of everything he loses, along with a greater amount of force to preserve what he has." [22]

We might equally recall Immanuel Kant's later rendering of this same

Enlightenment project of constructing civil society on the basis of reason alone in his "Idea for a Universal History." [23] There, Kant expresses
the demand for absolute freedom to the same effect, only in a slightly
different language: Nature, according to Kant, has willed that man fully
develop out of himself through his own reason whatever exceeds the
purely material aspect of his life, that he live, in other words, "entirely
in his own work." For Kant, as for Rousseau, "human nature" proceeds
to the development of a "second nature" (Kant) that "produces a moral
and collective body" (Rousseau) that arises when a person, through a
voluntary act, takes up a common standpoint, the standpoint of all, and
contracts with others to place himself or herself under the laws of a common association that accords an equal voice to every person. [24] When in
society, we henceforth act *as if* we were all united in an all-encompassing
collective project.

According to Hegel, the ideal of absolute freedom as expressed by the
social contract is a genuine achievement of historical self-consciousness.
In understanding themselves in such terms, individuals raise themselves
in their existence to the level of the universal, to the level of thought. But
this ideal fails in that it is too abstract. [25] The general will does not provide positive content to collective projects or specify concrete purposes.
The social contract as such does not motivate any particular course of
action. Moreover, where the social world is understood as "the work
of men"(Vico) and taken in every aspect as a creation of each and every
one of its individual members—for only in this way can each person be
bound voluntarily to this new order of freedom—all that genuinely dif-
ferentiates society into separate parts with separate wills, such as, for example, different classes or groups with different purposes, has to be seen
as a challenge to the new order. The ideal of absolute freedom militates
against the differentiation of society and the plurality of human exis-
tences or wills, and so, ultimately, against individual separateness that
might find expression in civil liberties, or against preexisting differences
that might have been protected by established group privileges.

Although the state is identified with the general will—the absolute
freedom of the will of the people—this nevertheless does not suffice for it
to act, for as we have said, the general will takes up within itself only the
negative freedom from all determination that is not self-imposed. The
ideal of freedom as the self-assertion of an unconstrained will can issue
forth in concrete state action where the state in fact has a concrete will,
a concrete personality endowed with the capacity for action. "Just as the

individual self-consciousness does not find itself in this *universal work* of absolute freedom *qua* existent Substance," writes Hegel in *The Phenomenology of Spirit*,

> so little does it find itself in the *deeds* proper and *individual* actions of the will of this freedom. Before the universal can perform a deed it must concentrate itself into the One of individuality and put at the head an individual self-consciousness; for the universal will is only an *actual* will in a self, which is a One. But thereby all other individuals are excluded from the entirety of this deed and have only a limited share in it, so that the deed would not be a deed of the *actual universal* self-consciousness. Universal freedom, therefore, can produce neither a positive work nor a deed; there is left for it only *negative* action; it is merely the *fury* of destruction.[26]

Where the general will is applied directly and without mediation to the actions of a state, a single individual becomes its stand-in. The free will of the leader becomes the concrete representative of the will to absolute freedom. As the incarnation of the general will, the leader can be limited neither by existing conditions nor by other subordinate wills.

Arendt describes the logic of totalitarian state action in terms very similar to Hegel's. Totalitarian terror is connected to the exhilarating belief that everything is possible. This fantasy of transcending the limits of the possible is at least partially realized in a monstrous, twisted manner by totalitarian movements. Radical change, even the complete transformation of society, is indeed possible where consequences don't matter, where vast resources are indiscriminately applied in order to make propaganda predictions come out right, and where predictions can always be realized by a mad and perverse willingness to take "the destructive way out of all impasses."[27] "It is one of Hannah Arendt's fundamental insights," writes Pohlmann, "that totalitarian societies are by no means to be understood as systems of authority that are totally subject to consistent norms. They are rather *contrivances for destroying normative order*, which means that they disable the *basic conditions for human socialization processes*."[28]

Like Hegel, Arendt connects the modern aspiration toward progress and human emancipation to the state terror. In the preface to the first edition of *The Origins of Totalitarianism*, she writes that "Progress and Doom are two sides of the same medal." What gets indicted here is not political freedom, but the demand that a notion of freedom conceived metaphysically in terms of the unboundedness of human will can serve as the basis for a conception of political freedom. Arendt's development of her critique of this conception of freedom in the essay "What Is Freedom?" is profoundly related to her analysis of totalitarianism. "That the faculty of will and will-power in and by itself," she writes in that essay, "unconnected with any other faculties, is an essentially nonpolitical and even anti-political capacity is perhaps nowhere else so manifest as in the absurdities to which Rousseau was driven and in the curious cheerfulness with which he accepted them. Politically, this identification of freedom with sovereignty is perhaps the most pernicious and dangerous consequence of the philosophical equation of freedom and free will." [29]

The irony of history—and this potentially offensive thesis of Arendt's must be faced up to on pain of dismissal—is that totalitarianism springs from the same soil as the modern conception of freedom. Totalitarian movements participate in a dynamic of modernization the flip side of which constitutes a disintegration of traditional social structures and institutions. The process of structural disintegration subjects individuals to homogenizing pressures that both "press individuals together" and at the same time "isolate." That is, they "massify" and "atomize" the population, setting the stage for the rise of totalitarian movements. Totalitarian movements perpetuate and exacerbate the lawlessness of revolutionary social transformation. Totalitarian regimes "retain terror as a power functioning outside of the law." [30] Laws stabilize society and fix social relations within certain institutional and normative parameters. By contrast, totalitarianism thrives on keeping the movement of disintegration going.

Arendt's indebtedness to Hegel's account of the French revolutionary terror is not surprising. [31] The highly abstract and speculative story Hegel tells has its roots in the culturally conservative German critique of the French Enlightenment. But it also incorporates elements of a religion-based critique of the modern philosophy of man. In a 1951 letter to Jaspers, Arendt speaks of "the radical evil of totalitarianism." "What radical evil really is I don't know," she writes to Jaspers,

> but it seems to me it somehow has to do with the following phenomenon: making human beings as human beings superfluous. This happens as soon as all unpredictability—which, in human beings, is the equivalent of spontaneity—is eliminated. And all this in turn arises from—or, better, goes along with—the delusion of the omnipotence (not simply with the lust for power) of an individual man. If an individual man *qua* man were omnipotent, then there is in fact no reason why men in the plural should exist at all—just as in monotheism it is only God's impotence that makes him ONE. So, in this same way, the omnipotence of an individual man would make men superfluous. [32]

Although Arendt is not advancing a theological position, she, like Hegel, nevertheless draws on the perspective afforded by a theologically rooted critique of modernity. Her exchange with the philosopher Eric Voegelin is illuminating in this regard. In his review of *The Origins of Totalitarianism*, Voegelin had expressed his sympathy with aspects of Arendt's analysis: "The spiritual disease of agnosticism is the peculiar problem of the modern masses," he wrote, "and man-made paradises and man-made hells are its symptoms and the masses have the disease whether they are in their paradise or in their hell." [33] Voegelin, however, also had criticized Arendt for failing to follow through on these insights.

> The author, thus, is aware of the problem; but, oddly enough, the knowledge does not affect her treatment of the materials. If the spiritual disease is the decisive feature that distinguishes modern masses from those of earlier centuries, then one would expect the study of totalitarianism not to be delimited by the institutional breakdown of national societies and the growth of socially superfluous masses, but rather by the genesis of the spiritual disease, especially since the response to the institutional breakdown clearly bears the marks of the disease. Then the origins of totalitarianism would not have to be sought primarily in the fate of the national state and attendant social and economic changes since the eighteenth century, but rather in the rise of immanentist sectarianism since the high Middle Ages; and the totalitarian movements would not be simply revolutionary movements of functionally dislocated people, but immanentist creed movements in which mediaeval heresies have come to their fruition. [34]

While Arendt insists on the phenomenological and sociological strand in her historical analysis, Voegelin is right in seeing in her account of the logic of totalitarianism certain elements of the Catholic critique of modernity and of a Romantic secularization of properly religious experiences. In her exchange with Voegelin, Arendt explicitly disavowed a secularization thesis, a historical account of totalitarianism that fails to perceive what is new about this form of government and understands it in essentialist terms. [35] Totalitarianism, Arendt seems to be persistently inveighing, has little to do with the "religious feeling without a religion," that Freud is so deeply suspicious of in his most political essay *Civilization and Its Discontents* (1929). Upon closer examination, however, we find that Arendt's reflections on totalitarian terror and ideology are deeply concerned with the question of spiritual feeling, or *Geistesgefühl*, which Immanuel Kant already had set out to critique in his treatment of the sublime in *Observations on the Feeling of the Beautiful and the Sublime* and in the *Critique of Aesthetic Judgment*. [36]

THE EXPERIENCE OF THE SUBLIME,
ITS HISTORY AND SIGNIFICANCE

"The entirely new and unprecedented forms of totalitarian organization and course of action," writes Arendt in a crucial passage of "Ideology and Terror,"

> must rest on one of the few basic experiences which men can have whenever they live together, and are concerned with public affairs. If there is a basic experience which finds its political expression in totalitarian domination, then, in view of the novelty of the totalitarian form of government, this must be an experience which, for whatever reason, has never before served as the foundation of a body politic and whose general mood—although it may be familiar in every other respect—never before has pervaded, and directed the handling of, public affairs.[37]

According to Arendt, the paradoxical nature of totalitarianism and the "basic experience" it rests upon is the experience of a "loss of the very capacity for experience."[38] It is the experience of an utter loss of world. The spontaneity of the human being is destroyed. The person is reduced to a bundle of reactions and is radically divested of its capacity for action. Arendt describes the loss of all intersubjectivity and capacity to communicate, the radical isolation and loneliness of the totalitarian subject, but also the way in which the pain of the "ice-cold reasoning" and the "mighty tentacle of dialectics" that "seizes you as in a vice grip" give rise to a peculiar elation of transcending the chaotic situation wrought by the regime of terror in its dislocation and destruction of all social stability.

When Arendt speaks of terror as the essence of totalitarianism and connects the terror of totalitarian rule to the worldlessness of the totalitarian subject, she is drawing upon a type of experience that is well articulated in the realm of aesthetics. Her account suggests that what enters the theater of politics is an experience that has its proper origins in a different sphere. The political relevance of this experience, the experience of the sublime, was already recognized by Edmund Burke in his *Reflections on the Origin of Our Ideas of the Sublime and the Beautiful*. Burke introduces the sublime in its familiar relationship with terror and gives it a place in aesthetics alongside that of the beautiful as a "positive pain" that gives enjoyment.

> No passion so effectually robs the mind of all its powers of acting and reasoning as fear. For fear being an apprehension of pain or death, it operates in a manner that resembles actual pain. Whatever therefore is terrible, with re-

gard to sight, is sublime too, whether this cause of terror, be endued with greatness of dimensions or not; for it is impossible to look on any thing as trifling, or contemptible, that may be dangerous. There are many animals, who though far from being large, are yet capable of raising ideas of the sublime, because they are considered as objects of terror. As serpents and poisonous animals of almost all kinds. And to things of great dimensions, if we annex an adventitious idea of terror, they become without comparison greater. A level plain of a vast extent on land, is certainly no mean idea; the prospect of such a plain may be as extensive as a prospect of the ocean; but can it ever fill the mind with any thing so great as the ocean itself? This is owing to several causes, but it is owing to none more than this, that the ocean is an object of no small terror. Indeed terror is in all cases whatsoever, either more openly or latently the ruling principle of the sublime.[39]

Burke's complete description of the sublime goes on to delineate most of the elements familiar to us. The sublime is a passion that has us experience a "positive pain." Solitude encourages this passion, whereas beauty is the "passion which belongs to society." A certain aesthetic distance from the danger encountered makes possible the enjoyment of the terrible. And yet, the specter of death itself gives rise to the passion of the sublime. "Vast power" is sublime. Shapelessness and obscurity contribute to the sublime. While the experience of beauty is of a "sensible perfection," and of "clear" but "confused" sensible ideas (according to Alexander Baumgarten), the sublime is taken to be heightened by "dark, uncertain, confused," and "obscure" representations. Burke explains the sublime in naturalistic terms, as "an unnatural tension of the nerves."[40]

The sublime designates a certain mood or sensibility that first got named in the early seventeenth century in connection with the awe and terror inspired by nature. Henry More voices the rapture that the conception of infinite space elicited in the seventeenth century:

Wherefore with leave th' infinite I'll sing
Of Time, of Space: or without leave; I'm brent
And all my spirits move with pleasant trembeling.
With eagre rage, my heart for joy doth spring.[41]

Encouraged by the new cosmology's transition from the closed world to the infinite universe, the experience of nature's immensity became increasingly invested in the popular imagination with attributes reserved for God. Shaftesbury draws directly on Nicholas of Cusa's idea of the finite world as an "*explicatio* or unfolding of the divine essence" in his view of the natural world as an unfolding of divine mind itself. "The 'Abyss of SPACE,' experienced ecstatically, becomes 'the Seat of thy extensive being.'" In the sublime experience of the immensity of space, divine infinity itself was thought to have become visible in the natural world. One Elizabeth Carter, for example, in a letter of 1762, remarks: "I am afraid I shall miss my church tomorrow, but the sea is to me a sermon and prayers, and at once doctrine and devotion." [42]

By the time Burke was writing in the eighteenth century, the sublime had firmly established itself as an aesthetic category in Britain and Germany and became one of the central experiences claimed by every side in the contest for a new philosophy of man. Not just nature, but raw and unschooled human genius, insofar as it cannot be rationally comprehended in its infinite power to create, was said to inspire the passion of the sublime. The human creative genius became the exemplar of the new man. In this way, the sublime came to serve as a foundational experience, not just for the Romantic vision, but also in a somewhat tempered manner in Kant's critical philosophy.

Unlike Burke, Kant does not understand the sublime merely as a subjective feeling that is to be explained psychologically. [43] The sublime has a transcendental significance, for it recommends to the subject an overall relationship to sensibility on the level of sensibility itself. Kant's account of the movement of the sublime feeling is as rich as any Romantic's. [44] While the experience of beauty is an experience in which the subject feels a harmony within itself and with the object of experience, the sublime is the experience of a dislocation with regard to what presents itself to the senses. Kant emphasizes the peculiar freedom that the sublime experience gives rise to, despite the violence it does to our lower faculties of sensibility and imagination. It is the experience of an unburdening of the self from the cares and concerns of the everyday. "Nature," he writes, "is not judged to be sublime in our aesthetical judgments in so far as it excites fear, but because it calls up that power in us (which is not nature) of regarding as small the things we *care about* (goods, health, and life)." In the movement of the sublime, the subject undergoes a humiliation of the imagination and the faculties of sense, is cast back upon the self and referred to its own rational capacity to grasp the infinite, supersensible purposiveness that gives meaning to the unity of nature and of self and world. It is a movement of sensibility that does violence to the very capacity for grasping the world on the level of sensibility.

The object that occasions the movement of the sublime is monstrous, colossal, shapeless, formless, overflows the bounds of the imagination, and fails to be grasped in sensible intuition because it resists an empirical synthesis. The experience is merely occasioned by the object. It is not really an experience of an object at all, as Burke would have it. [45] Kant construes it as a reflective experience in which the inability of sense and imagination to grasp what presents itself gives a peculiar pleasure, for it makes the subject aware of its existence, even as it stands apart from the world of the senses. The subject is both repelled and attracted by the experience. The inadequacy of sensibility to grasp the object gives way to a movement of transcendence wherein the subject identifies itself with the infinite.

Arendt's characterization of the peculiar disinterestedness of the totalitarian subject, even in its own life, and of the paradoxical "experience of loss of the capacity for experience" takes up the moments of this complex reflective experience in which Kant and much of the German tradition after him attempt to locate the transcendence of the subject toward its own capacity for experiencing the infinite, the absolute, the idea, an experience or capacity associated with the freedom of the will.

For Kant, as for the German tradition, the experience of the sublime is the locus of the self in which the self experiences its own transcendence over the everyday. Kant is well aware of the danger of this moment. That is precisely why he engages in a critique of taste that deploys this spiritual feeling in an uncritical manner. Already in his early essay on the beautiful and the sublime, he had transformed the notion of the sublime and grounded it in the feeling of human moral worth. And in the *Critique of Judgment,* this concern is at issue, as well. "This pure, elevating, merely negative presentation of morality," he writes against Hamman and Herder in the *Critique of Judgment,* "brings with it, on the other hand, no danger of *fanaticism, which is a belief in our capacity of seeing something beyond all bounds of sensibility,* i.e. of dreaming in accordance with fundamental propositions (or of going mad with reason); and this is so just because this presentation is merely negative. For the *inscrutableness of the idea of freedom* quite cuts it off from any positive presentation." [46] In other words, Kant's claim is that the experience of the sublime, when understood as a reflective experience, reveals our capacity for transcendence, but not any incarnation of spirit here on earth. "That was not a line pursued by the British aestheticians, or a tack taken by the Germans of the *Sturm und Drang.* While they stressed wonder and awe, and even developed complex psychological accounts of the experience, they first of all found the ground for such an experience in the objects of nature, and second, if they related it to subjectivity, found the relation not in human moral grandeur, but rather in human genius and creativity." [47]

Arendt's critique of the modern conception of freedom is directed at precisely this identification of freedom with the experience of sublime transcendence, with an otherworldly freedom that cannot be the basis for political action, an experience that instead unhinges judgment and the modalities of an "enlarged capacity" of thought that arise when projecting oneself toward others in the realm of concrete human affairs. "Inwardness as a place of absolute freedom within one's own self," she writes in "What Is Freedom?" was discovered "in late antiquity by those who had no place of their own in the world and hence lacked a worldly condition which, from early antiquity to almost the middle of the nineteenth century, was unanimously held to be a prerequisite for freedom." [48] Modernity, according to Arendt, falsely identifies political freedom with the (inward) freedom of the will. While Arendt agrees with Kant's great "insight that freedom is no more ascertainable to the inner sense and within the field of inner experience than it is to the senses with which we know and understand the world," she rejects his solution to the problem of freedom, since it takes the subject of freedom out of the world altogether. Consistent with the philosophical tradition's articulation of the experience of the sublime, Arendt suggests that this existential stance—fostered under totalitarianism by a comprehensive upending of social structures and norms backed by the threat of police terror—destroys the subject's capacity for distinguishing between fiction and reality. [49]

THE STATE AS THE SUBLIME OBJECT

Our master narrative, which traces the migration of divine attributes to nature, to the sovereign individual, and finally to an association with the expectations and attitudes toward the sovereignty of the modern state— a secularization of sorts carried forward by the spiritual and cultural role accorded to the experience of the sublime—might sound far too abstract to serve as a frame for what Arendt calls her phenomenal approach, which, as she is fond of repeating, starts from facts and events, instead of historical essences. As we have seen, Arendt vehemently rejected a straightforward secularization thesis. Nevertheless, her analysis of totalitarianism undoubtedly seizes upon the career of the *Geistesgefühl* of the sublime within the modern tradition, implicates the disclosive power accorded to this mood, and explores its significance for the intrinsic relationship between totalitarian ideology and totalitarian terror.

In her criticism of the existential tradition, Arendt persistently challenges its privileging of this standpoint as a vantage from which the identity of the self or of the community should be constructed. Not just Kant, but Kierkegaard, Nietzsche, Dostoyevsky, Heidegger, and Sartre[50] all relate the most profound self-experience to the sublime movement of feeling, which encourages a radical leave-taking from the cares and concerns of the everyday—a leave-taking from "the burden of our time"— and a desperate projection toward some as yet still merely imagined extraordinary existence, which for lack of a controlling power can momentarily find its concrete expression only in the comprehensive destruction of its own prevailing situation.[51] Such identities display a "peculiar cheerfulness" that makes them suspect and renders them beyond the reach of conventional ethics—ethics that, although oppressive, nevertheless may at times provide limits of last resort when basic social arrangements and institutions have broken down. We should note, of course, that each of these thinkers was also characteristically self-conscious and critical of identities authorized by this type of comprehensive dislocation alone.[52]

In her strongest passage against Heidegger's philosophy, in the essay "What Is Existential Philosophy?" that was published in 1947 at the same time that she was writing *The Origins of Totalitarianism,* Arendt rehearses precisely the kind of criticism she applies to the "radical evil" of totalitarianism in the letter to Jaspers: "Heidegger's conception of Dasein," Arendt argues, "puts man in the place of God."[53] In a footnote to her discussion of Heidegger, Arendt explains Heidegger's foray into National Socialism by pointing to his affinity with the Romantics: "[Heidegger's] entire mode of behavior [during the Third Reich]," she writes,

> has such exact parallels in German Romanticism that one can hardly believe them to result from the sheer coincidence of a purely personal failure of character. Heidegger is really (let us hope) the last Romantic—an immensely talented Friedrich Schlegel or Adam Müller, as it were, whose complete lack of responsibility is attributable to a spiritual playfulness that stems in part from delusions of genius and in part from despair.[54]

To be sure, Arendt distances Heidegger from totalitarianism by this remark, because she insists on a distinction between early nineteenth-century ideologies and the character and significance of totalitarian ideology. At the same time, this move reiterates the connection between the wholesale privileging of a certain existential stance or self-world relationship and the disastrous course of twentieth-century politics.

Adam Müller's nationalist political tract *The Idea of the State* (1809), in which he developed the representative Romantic theory of politics,[55] displays striking similarities with Arendt's characterization of totalitarian ideology. Müller's first political work, composed, like Nietzsche's *Birth of Tragedy*, during a Franco-Prussian war, figures the state as a sublime object and puts forth many of the elements of totalitarian ideology. The National Socialists explicitly claimed Müller's political tract as their heritage. In a review essay published in two parts in the *Kölner Zeitung* in 1932, Hannah Arendt addresses the "Adam Müller Renaissance" spurred by the German nationalist revival. "When National Socialism relates itself to Adam Müller," writes Arendt, "it intends more specifically his theory of man in the 'community' [*Gemeinschaft*]. Müller's concept of the community is indeed irridescent [*schillernd*], part biological, part historical, part religious." [56]

Müller demands that we reject the dead, abstract, and legalistic concepts of the French Enlightenment's theory of the individual and its relationship to the state. He seeks to return "movement" and "life" to the state. The state is to be understood naturally and organically and, most importantly, as idea. [57] Müller urges a holy marriage of the individual with the state in which all opposition is dissolved into a higher unity. Though he pays homage to the citizen's individuality or authenticity (*Eigenheit*; Heidegger uses *eigen, eigentlich* for "authentic"), this authenticity expresses itself in the subordination / coordination of the individual into the organism of the whole (*Einordnung in den Organismus des Ganzen*), "which brings the citizen into more universal relations and thereby places his own individuality on firmer, securer, freer ground." [58]

The state gets invested with all the attributes of the sublime experience. It is originary. There is nothing outside the state, and it is boundless and comprehends all changes in forms of government. Müller explicitly acknowledges the religious origins of the experiences he invokes: "The state rests entirely within itself. It originates independently of human arbitrariness and invention, immediately and contemporaneously with man, where man originates, namely from nature, or, as the ancients said, from God." [59]

Müller's state is in perpetual motion, fusing individuals into an organic whole that is itself the unmediated life of the idea. It is in war that the bourgeois differentiation of society into different spheres reveals itself as bankrupt. How can such a state act? How can it "stand for a single Man" when its existence is at stake? [60] "The state," he writes, "is the totality of all human affairs and their synthesis into an organic whole. If we cut even the most insignificant part of the human nature off from this connection forever, if we separate the human character in any aspect from that of the citizen (*vom bürgerlichen*), we can no longer experience / feel [*empfinden*] the state as a form of life or as idea." [61] This idea is nothing but the natural development of the state in its organic form. The state is not a contract made by men but is a force of nature itself.

The elements of Müller's theory of the state enter into Arendt's account of ideology: totalitarian ideology, which elides the efficacy of human judgment and describes history, including totalitarianism's own accession to power, as an inexorable logic inherent in history or nature itself, represents a heightening of these moments. "An ideology," writes Arendt in "Ideology and Terror,"

> is quite literally what its name indicates: it is the logic of an idea. Its subject matter is history, to which the idea is applied; the result of this application is not a body of statements about something that *is,* but the unfolding of a process which is in constant change. The ideology treats the course of events as though it followed the same "law" as the logical exposition of its "idea." [62]

The "idea" of an ideology is not Platonic in the sense that it provides a sort of regulative ideal. Totalitarian ideology treats history as the unfolding of "a movement which is the consequence of the idea itself and needs no outside factor to set it into motion." [63] The fanaticism Kant fears, namely, of an identification of the (symbolic) object occasioning the sublime movement of reflection with the absolute itself, is exactly what Müller proposes and what Arendt portrays as occurring under totalitarian rule. Every action of the totalitarian state becomes not just a reference toward a higher law, but the embodiment of the absolute law of nature / history, of movement / life itself.[64]

The National Socialists clearly saw their own sensibilities reflected in Adam Müller's theory of the state. Arendt, however, questions such an unambiguous relegation of Müller to the canon of National Socialist thinkers. Her reasons are illuminating, since they display the already familiar concern with the concretization of the absolute characteristic of a politics of the sublime. Müller was finally a Catholic, and as such he still held to the ultimately transcendent nature and authority of religious practice and prescription. "What Müller intends as a Catholic," Arendt explains, "is intended nonreligiously, naturalistically by National Socialism." He did not entirely divorce his quasi-religious veneration of the state from religious traditions and institutions, as the National Socialists did. As a result, Müller's state could still be fallible. It had to live up to an ideal that it did not automatically embody.[65] Moreover, Müller's positions, as Arendt argues, have to be understood within their historical context. They were first of all strategic. Müller sought first of all to sanctify the existing order—the waning aristocratic class to which he so desperately sought to be admitted—a project entirely at odds with the totalitarian evacuation of tradition. These distinguishing features of Müller's political engagement invited the Nazi "constitutional lawyer" Carl Schmitt's most virulent scorn.

CONCLUSION

I have argued that Arendt's account of totalitarianism subtly (or surreptitiously, if one prefers) draws on an aesthetic category that has helped define the German tradition of thought, its philosophical anthropology, and its aesthetic approach to politics. Arendt figures the totalitarian sensibility as a species of the sublime. The notion of "terror" is therefore used ambiguously in Arendt's theory. It designates the literal terrorization of society by the totalitarian machinery for making war on its own population by the secret police, the system of special tribunals, political prisons, concentration camps, and so forth. At the same time "terror" designates synechdochically a complex sensibility of existential dislocation that, according to Arendt, affects the population broadly under totalitarian rule.[66] "Terror, in the sense we were speaking of it," she writes in one of her unpublished essays, "is not so much something which people may fear, but a way of life." [67] Arendt's suggestion, which illuminates the peculiar mixture of terrible coercion and enthusiastic cooperation that characterizes the popular response to totalitarian rule, is that these two senses and experiences of terror conspire. This aspect of Arendt's account of totalitarianism is offered from within the tradition of German philosophical anthropology and also from within the tradition of nationalist feeling.[68]

The connections argued for here are frequently only implicit in Arendt's work. She does not use the word "sublime" in her theory of totalitarian terror. The intuitive cogency of Arendt's account, however, significantly depends upon the rich connections she makes, at a sophisticated philosophical level, with an intellectual history that has profoundly shaped European politics during the nineteenth and twentieth centuries. The question we may raise is whether entering into the debate about totalitarianism on the grounds of this intellectual tradition, which, it seems to me, Arendt does, is itself corrupting, as Isaiah Berlin suggests. We might recall the debate between the Jesuit and revolutionary Marxist Naphta and the humanist Settembrini in Thomas Mann's *Magic*

Mountain, which Arendt read together with Heidegger in 1924.[69] Something peculiar happens as soon as a protagonist enters the infectious atmosphere of the magic mountaintop at Davos. The air itself is infectious, and once engaged in the cure, all participants become sick. Even the down-to-earth engineer Castorp begins to be seduced by the magnetic rhetoric of the radical revolutionary Naphta, and the humanist Settembrini has few resources to stay the ship.

Totalitarianism, Modernity, and the Tradition

Dana R. Villa

To what extent does Hannah Arendt view totalitarianism as a distinctively modern phenomenon, one that reveals essential aspects of our time? What is the connection between her conception of totalitarianism and the phenomenology of human activities laid out in *The Human Condition*? Finally, what is the link between the critique of the Western tradition of political philosophy she mounts in that book and her view of the "essence" of totalitarianism? Does Arendt believe that totalitarianism, most often regarded as the nihilistic negation of our tradition, is, in fact, a partial product of that tradition?[1] If so, what possible (and plausible) connection can there be between Plato and Aristotle and Hitler and Stalin?

These are, obviously, large, complex, and controversial questions. I can't pretend to offer adequate answers to them in the compass of a single essay. Instead, what I propose to do is sketch brief responses to the first two, so that I might devote the bulk of what follows to the third—the question of a possible link between the "great tradition" of Western political thought and totalitarianism. I choose to focus on this question out of a desire to clarify some suggestions I made in my book *Arendt and Heidegger: The Fate of the Political*.

My focus is, admittedly, the result of an anxiety. I fear that readers of my interpretation of Arendt's thought might come away with the impression that she saw some mysterious inner logic working itself out in the course of the sequence from Plato to Marx, a nihilistic logic that led to the "devaluation of the highest values" and hence to the horrors of the twentieth century. So viewed, Arendt could be clumped in with Nietzsche, Heidegger, and other inverters of the Hegelian metanarrative of historical progress, for example, Max Horkheimer and Theodor Adorno, Leo Strauss, and Eric Voegelin.[2]

To see Arendt's views on totalitarianism, modernity, and the tradition as fitting snugly within the confines of this genre of *Geistesgeschichte* is to do her a great disservice. Throughout her work, from *The Origins of Totalitarianism* to *The Life of the Mind,* she was at war with all Hegelian-type teleologies, whether of progress or of doom. Moreover, she was extremely skeptical of all causal explanations of totalitarianism, explanations that isolated one or several determining factors that allegedly "produced" totalitarianism.[3] Thus, she hardly thought that totalitarianism was, in any significant sense, the "result" of what Plato or Aristotle, Machiavelli or Hobbes, Nietzsche or Heidegger wrote, or of the "dialectic of enlightenment" (her distance from Strauss and the Frankfurt School on this issue is vast).[4] She frequently expressed more than mild contempt for the methodological idealism and historicist determinism underlying such approaches.[5]

But neither did she think that elements that truly were crucial "conditions of possibility" for the advent of totalitarianism—racism, imperialism, the decline of the nation-state, anti-Semitism—caused it to occur as a kind of logical consequence. Totalitarianism remained for her a monstrous, unprecedented event, one that "exploded our traditional categories of political thought (totalitarian domination is unlike all forms of tyranny and despotism we know of) and the standards of our moral judgment (totalitarian crimes are very inadequately described as 'murder' and totalitarian criminals can hardly be punished as 'murderers')."[6] Its chief characteristic was "a horrible originality which no far-fetched historical parallels can alleviate."[7] To view totalitarianism as the predictable outcome of any configuration of causal forces perpetuates the denial of human freedom that Arendt identifies as the sine qua non of totalitarian ideology and action.[8]

However, these caveats notwithstanding, Arendt *did* see a connection (albeit not a causal one) between totalitarianism and the tradition, just as she saw a connection between totalitarianism and the spirit of the modern age. We must try to make sense of these connections while avoiding turning Arendt into something she was not, namely, a philosophical idealist à la Heidegger.

TOTALITARIANISM AND MODERNITY

What, then, made totalitarianism an essentially *modern* phenomenon, in Arendt's view? First and foremost, one cannot exaggerate the strength of her conviction that totalitarianism was something radically novel, a new form of political regime that could not be grasped by the traditional categories of tyranny, dictatorship, or authoritarianism.[9] Hence her quest to understand the "essence" or nature of totalitarianism as a form of government, rather than as an updated (peculiarly German or Russian) version of despotism. As she insists in *The Origins of Totalitarianism* and the essays "On the Nature of Totalitarianism" and "Ideology and Terror," total domination is qualitatively different from tyrannical domination. Rule by terror is different in nature from rule based on fear.[10]

Fear serves the tyrant's interest by radically isolating his subjects, exposing them to an overwhelming anxiety born of loneliness. Rule by fear makes a "desert" of the public realm, a desert in which isolated individuals despair of concerted action and resistance, experiencing daily their impotence and helplessness.[11] Yet action is still possible here as strategic reaction: Complete obedience and the avoidance of all "questionable" activities provides the principle of survival. Thus, in tyrannies, fear is a "principle of action" in Montesquieu's sense of an "animating principle," just as virtue is the principle animating republics and honor that of monarchies.[12]

Rule by terror, however, goes much further. It is not satisfied with exploiting the human experience of radical loneliness and the impotence it creates. Nor is it satisfied with banishing plural individuals from the public sphere. Rather, rule by terror aims at eliminating the incalculable from human existence: It seeks to expunge not merely *public* freedom, but freedom as such.[13] It does this by systematically destroying the legal boundaries that separate public from private, thereby destroying the space required for individuality, as well as for action. Rule by terror reveals not merely the *impotence* of the ruled, but their sheer *superfluousness*.[14] This is the *differentia specifica* of totalitarian power.

Arendt believed that in totalitarianism, she had discovered a regime whose principle, in Montesquieu's sense, was terror. She did not deny that other regime forms have used terror in the past. None, however, made it their organizing principle, their raison d'être.[15] Totalitarianism is radically novel because terror "is the very essence of such a government." It is a form of regime that aims at eliminating the incalculable by remarking reality in accordance with the logic of its ruling ideology.[16]

Totalitarian regimes use terror to execute what their ideologies assume are the judgments of Nature or History. They do this, however, only *after* they have eliminated all genuine or potential political opposition. Terror is "deployed as an incomparable instrument of acceleration," as a way of speeding up the allegedly unquestionable "laws of motion" of Nature or History. "Decadent and dying classes," "inferior races," individuals who are "unfit to live": from the totalitarian point of view, all are destined for the ash heap of history. The purpose of terror is to carry out the death sentence of Nature or History with greater dispatch, to facilitate the removal of obstacles to this destiny and thus make mankind a "walking embodiment" of the laws of motion of Nature or History.[17]

Yet even this formulation is misleading, because it leads us to think of terror in traditional terms, as merely a (deplorable) *means* of political power. According to Arendt, we will be incapable of understanding totalitarianism as a political phenomenon as long as we attempt to fit it within such a utilitarian framework. For terror to be a means, an instrument, it must serve the perpetrator's interest. Yet what interest is there in maintaining an elaborate and costly apparatus of terror such as the Nazi concentration camp system when the regime's very survival depends upon getting the most out of its dwindling resources?[18]

In this and other respects, it is not really the case that "the means has become the end." In Arendt's view, this formulation is "only a confession, disguised as a paradox, that the category of means and ends no longer work; that terror is apparently without an end."[19] Terror is the essence of the totalitarian form of government because it stands as a kind of end in itself. Its meaning cannot be grasped in strategic or utilitarian terms, in terms of *raison d'état* or the maintenance of power.[20] To say, as Arendt does, that terror is an "incomparable instrument" is to say that millions were sacrificed—and even the regime, the party, and, ultimately, the nation itself—for the sake of an *idea* of reality as an endlessly destructive process. Terror not only accelerates the "laws of motion" of History or Nature; it expresses their innermost murderous essence. It is the "means" by which a recalcitrant reality is made to conform to the axiomatic logic of a single *idea* (human history as the history of class struggle, the natural process as the evolution and perfection of the species).[21]

Arendt is adamant that totalitarian terror explodes "the very alternative upon which all definitions of the essence of governments have been based in political philosophy, that is the alternative between lawful and lawless government, between arbitrary and legitimate power."[22] If, as Arendt writes, "lawfulness is the essence of non-tyrannical government and lawlessness is the essence of tyranny," then totalitarianism confronts political theory with the conundrum of a regime whose essence is terror guided by "law."[23]

What needs to be stressed here is how, in Arendt's view, totalitarian terror is neither arbitrary nor self-serving. It is *not* tyrannical illegitimacy blown up to gigantic proportions.[24] On the contrary, she insists that totalitarian regimes are characterized by a strict and unvarying adherence to the "laws" of Nature or History that allegedly stand above positive laws. Indeed,

> it is the monstrous, yet seemingly unanswerable claim of totalitarian rule that, far from being "lawless," it goes to the sources of authority from which positive laws received their ultimate legitimation, that far from being arbitrary, it is more obedient to these superhuman forces than any government ever was before, and that far from wielding its power in the interest of one man, it is quite prepared to sacrifice everybody's vital, immediate interests to the execution of what it assumes to be the law of History or the law of Nature.[25]

The surface impression of tyrannical lawlessness given by these regimes' contempt for positive law (including their own constitutions) is belied by a restless activism that has only one purpose: accelerating "the laws of motion" that will ultimately produce a new and beautified species, a world without class divisions or inferior races.[26] Far from being lawless, totalitarianism is distinguished by a peculiar and intense *lawfulness*. This lawfulness "pretends to have found a way to establish the rule of justice on earth—something which the legality of positive law could never attain."[27]

As a regime whose goal is the fabrication of a "perfected" mankind through the terroristic execution of such "laws," totalitarianism is unprecedented and unquestionably modern. But it is modern in a deeper sense, in that it gives exaggerated expression to what Arendt considers to be the defining spirit of the age, namely, a hubristic belief in the limitless nature of human power. For Arendt, the modern age is one of boundless self-assertion growing out of a resentment of the human condition, a resentment of all the limits that define human existence (mortality, labor, and natural necessity, earth-boundedness, etc.). Unwilling to accept what he hasn't made himself, modern man transforms reality by means of modern science and technology, making it over in the hope of creating a totally humanized world in which he can (finally) be at home.

What Arendt calls "the modern triumph of *homo faber*" in *The Human Condition* thus gives birth to the modernist credo that "everything is possible"—that there are no limits to humanity's capacity to mimic and exploit natural processes, and thus no limits to the reshaping of reality that we might accomplish. This hubris finds expression in the totalitarian project of "fabricating mankind," the violent reshaping of available human material so that, in the end, classes, races, and individuals no longer exist, but only specimens of the (perfected) species.[28] In such a world, the incalculable truly has been eliminated.

One of the oddities of totalitarianism is that it couples this distinctively modern hubris with an equally modern determinism. As Margaret Canovan points out, Arendt thought that modern man was tempted to "purchase unlimited power at the cost of siding with inhuman forces and giving necessity a helping hand."[29] Totalitarian regimes demonstrate what happens when human beings surrender, without reservation, to this temptation. Submission to a racist "law of nature" (with its imperative of genocide) or historical "laws of motion" (which predict the extinction not only of capitalism but also of all class enemies of the proletariat) creates a feeling of power in the totalitarian leader and follower. Both feel themselves to be instruments of a suprahuman necessity, a necessity manifest in the historical laws of motion and the destruction they wreak.[30]

Arendt, then, sees totalitarian regimes as animated by a ruthless desire to remove all the obstacles that the "human artifice"—the civilized world of relatively permanent political and social structures—puts in the way of the forces of Nature or History. Hence the defining role of terror in totalitarian regimes. Terror "razes the boundaries of man-made law" and makes it possible for "the force of nature or of history to race freely through mankind, unhindered by any spontaneous human action."[31] Only through the systematic elimination of legally and institutionally articulated spaces of freedom can a totalitarian regime destroy the capacity for action implicit in the simple fact of human plurality. Indeed, in Arendt's analysis, human plurality and freedom are the primary phenomena that must be overcome if "mankind" (understood as "One Man of gigantic dimensions") is to be created.[32] Only then can reality be brought into line with the logic of a single idea.[33]

This is the goal of total domination, the complete organization of the "infinite plurality and differentiation of human beings as if all of humanity were just one individual." [34] As such, total domination was achieved only in the concentration and extermination camps, for it was there, under "scientifically controlled conditions," that experiments aimed at the utter elimination of spontaneity and freedom from human existence were able to take place.[35]

In the camps, human beings were reduced by terror into mere specimens of the human animal. Human personality was transformed into a "mere thing," into something *less* than animal, "an always constant collection of reactions and reflexes." [36] Totally conditioned by terror, shorn of their uniqueness and spontaneity, the inmates were the barely living proof that *human nature can be transformed through the application of human power.*[37] It is for this reason that Arendt refers to the camps as "the true central institution of totalitarian organizational power" and as "laboratories in which the fundamental belief of totalitarianism that everything is possible is being verified." [38]

Arendt's analysis of the three-step process necessary for making total domination a reality is well known, but little appreciated.[39] Suffice it to note here that this process—the destruction of the juridical person through the deprivation of rights and citizenship, followed by the destruction of the moral person through the creation of conditions in which conscience can no longer function, culminating in the destruction of individuality performed by the camps themselves—is eminently repeatable and limited to no particular group (ethnic, religious, or political). It constitutes instead a moving and expansive apparatus that aims not at "despotic rule over men," but at their replacement by as many bundles of conditioned reflexes as necessary.[40]

Thus, in the perfect totalitarian society, for which the camps provide the paradigm, terror binds individuals so tightly together that "all channels of communication" disappear, and neither spontaneity nor individuality has space for expression. Frozen by terror, human beings are pliable raw material, incapable of offering resistance to the laws of motion of Nature or History as these "rage through mankind," performing their never-ending task of violently shaping human beings into their final, radically deindividualized form. As Arendt writes in "Mankind and Terror," the ultimate political goal of totalitarianism was "to form and maintain a society, whether dominated by a particular race or one in which classes and nations no longer exist, in which every individual would be nothing other than a specimen of the species." [41] In other words, the "perfection" of the human species entails the destruction of humanity, both as a concept and as the phenomenological reality of unique individuals.

TOTALITARIANISM AND *THE HUMAN CONDITION*

In Arendt's reflections on the "perfected" totalitarian regime—on the regime in which totalitarian logic is carried through to the end, and the goal of total domination achieved—we see the clearest links to the phenomenology of human activities presented in *The Human Condition*. If totalitarianism displayed in exaggerated form how the modern extremist aspiration ("everything is possible") could lead to a radical destruction of freedom, then one central purpose of *The Human Condition* is to remind us that freedom's preservation demands relatively permanent laws and institutions, the sort of stable human artifices that totalitarianism makes impossible. Totalitarianism taught Arendt how absolutely indispensable such a realm of stability was and how destructive the principle of unlimited dynamism instantiated in the restless activism of the totalitarian movements themselves could be.

The Human Condition turns from the danger of totalitarian dynamism to consider other "world destroying" forces that the modern age has unleashed. Among these are the tremendous growth in the forces of production and consumption brought about by the rise of capitalism. This growth, together with the hegemony of the economic that it creates, threatens to swallow up all other relatively autonomous spheres of human activity. Thus, it, too, fosters the eradication of human plurality, freedom, and uniqueness. Arendt is deeply convinced that it is only within the protective confines of the framework of artificial laws and institutions that human plurality can be preserved from the automatism that characterizes the life of subsistence, biological reproduction, and the endless cycle of production and consumption. Only within the framework of artificial laws and institutions is the automatism of nature kept at bay and the realms of freedom and necessity kept distinct.

The image of fragile "islands of freedom" surrounded by a sea of automatic, natural processes is a recurrent one in Arendt's work.[42] Both totalitarianism and modern technological capitalism, with its transformation of man into the *animal laborans,* do their utmost to swamp this artifice in processes of destruction or reproduction. Arendt reminds us of the differences between action, work, and labor in order to underline just how dangerous it is to forget that an individual's life is human to the extent that it has the possibility of a limited transcendence of natural or pseudonatural processes. In Arendt's view, action—speech and deeds in the public realm—is the vehicle by which we achieve this limited transcendence and thereby a unique identity. To be deprived of this opportunity—an opportunity provided by an intact public realm—is to be deprived of the chance of living a fully human life.[43] If the goal of totalitarianism is to reduce human beings to mere examples of the species, technological capitalism has a parallel, if immeasurably less horrible, logic. Both are insults to the human status in that they strive to replace human plurality and spontaneity with a kind of oneness (whether of the species or of the "household" blown up to national proportions)[44] while moving us ever closer to rhythms of nature and necessity.

Arendt's indictment of the "laboring society" in *The Human Condition* seems to place her in the company of such totalizing critics of capitalist modernity as Herbert Marcuse. Consider, for example, the following passage from the last part of *The Human Condition:*

> even now, laboring is too lofty, too ambitious a word for what we are doing, or think we are doing, in the world we have come to live in. The last stage of the laboring society, the society of jobholders, demands of its members a sheer automatic functioning, as though individual life had actually been submerged in the over-all life process of the species and the only active decision still required of the individual were to let go, so to speak, to abandon his individuality, the still individually sensed pain and trouble of living, and acquiesce in a dazed, "tranquilized," functional type of behavior. . . . It is quite conceivable that the modern age—which began with such an unprecedented and promising outburst of human activity—may end in the deadliest, most sterile passivity history has ever known.[45]

The echoes of Nietzsche, Weber, and Heidegger here are almost overwhelming, as is the temptation to describe what Arendt is talking about as a kind of "soft" totalitarianism. For what, finally, is the difference between the real thing and its capitalist, technological shadow if the end result is the same: the "destruction of the common world," the eradication of freedom understood as speech and deeds in the public realm, and the ultimate assimilation of human beings to nature and necessity? Add to this the aforementioned emphasis on "resentment of the human condition" common to both the modern and totalitarian projects, and it is easy to accuse Arendt of diminishing, rather than enhancing, our understanding of modernity and totalitarianism's place within it.

Of course, Arendt herself would have repudiated any such conflation. She was far too aware of the "horrible originality" of totalitarianism to read it back into some broader, world-historical movement. Here we confront the irreducible difference between her approach and that of her teacher, Heidegger, whose own brand of *Seinsgeschichte* encouraged such conflation in pupils such as Marcuse. Nothing links totalitarianism and capitalist, technological modernity on the morphological level, in Arendt's view. If totalitarian domination is to be radically distinguished from tyranny and authoritarianism, it is, needless to say, altogether different in structure and movement from society as a "national household." The sole link between them (aside from the hubris that drives both)[46] is that each represents a threat to the continuing reality the human artifice and, thus, to freedom.

As we've seen, the totalitarian project is nothing less than the radical denaturing and deindividualization of human beings in order to produce a new and supremely pliable animal species, mankind.[47] Compared with this denaturing, even the most economically integrated, politically docile "national household" represents an extremely limited loss: the diminishment of public spirit and the capacity for political action. From the perspective of Arendt's quasi-Aristotelian ranking of the *bioi*, or ways of life, such a loss is still great, since it undermines the very thing that, in her view, makes life worth living.[48] It does not, however, come close to approximating the "hell on earth" established by totalitarian regimes and their never-ending reign of terror. It is one thing to be rendered relatively "worldless" by political or economic forces, quite another to be subject to the "law of killing" that Arendt saw as the core of totalitarianism.[49]

Contra Marcuse, Horkheimer and Adorno, and some postmodernists, then, totalitarianism is not a trope for the modern age, or the culmination of an epoch that was always already nihilistic. Totalitarianism is, in Arendt's view, a distinctly pathological form of modern politics, a pathology of modernity that illuminates modernity, but that cannot, in the end, be identified with it (even if, as George Kateb notes, Arendt sees the story of modern Europe as a story of pathologies, with Nazi and Stalinist totalitarianism as "the climactic pathology").[50] Despite the harshness of her critique of the modern age in *The Human Condition*, and despite her conviction that the rootlessness of the modern masses provided the soil for totalitarianism to take root, there is no inner link between the "worldlessness" of the modern age and the "essence" of totalitarianism, namely, terror.

The most we can say is that, for Arendt, the modern age creates unprecedented alienation and loneliness; that the experience of radical loneliness or uprootedness deprives people not only of a "place in the world," but their sense of identity and their feeling for the world (their "common sense"); that, bereft of the sense that relates him to the world and to others, the modern individual is all too likely to turn to an ideology that, with impeccable logic, explains the past, present, and future by deductions from a single premise (for example, the history of the world is the history of class struggle).[51] Having lost contact with fellow humans and with the surrounding reality (a contact underwritten by a stable and vibrant public realm), the modern individual loses the capacity for both thought and experience. Hence the susceptibility to totalitarian fictions. It is in this sense that totalitarianism can be said to base itself on the worldlessness inherent in loneliness, on "the experience of not belonging to the world at all, which is among the most radical and desperate experiences of man."[52]

The reflections on the "worldlessness" of the modern masses in *The Origins of Totalitarianism* obviously prepare the way for the phenomenology of action and the public realm in *The Human Condition*. Arendt moves from the most pathological expression of worldlessness—intense loneliness and the embrace of totalitarian fiction—to a description of how political action on the public stage endows the world with meaning *and* offers the individual the chance to achieve both recognition and identity through the creation of a public self.[53] What matter most to her in *The Origins of Totalitarianism* are the pathological political possibilities opened up by the loss of a tangible, worldly reality. What drives her phenomenological descriptions in *The Human Condition* is the desire to show how a strong sense of the public world manifests itself in political action and the stories, judgments, and understanding such action inspires.[54]

A common fear, then, links *The Origins of Totalitarianism* to *The Human Condition*. Both texts locate the basic threat to our political health in the loss of a sense of the public world, a public reality, among vast numbers of people. As long as we fail to confront the implications of this loss of a "common sense," we will fail to understand why racism, imperialism, anti-Semitism, and totalitarianism had such enormous appeal in the late modern age and why they encountered such minimal resistance. We will be unable to understand the peculiar mix of gullibility and cynicism that characterized European society between the wars and that characterizes our own contemporary political culture.[55] Finally, we will be unable to "think what we are doing" as we make politics, the public sphere, and the claims of justice ever more subservient to the demands of the market, technology, and the "national" (now international) household.

TOTALITARIANISM AND THE TRADITION

The Origins of Totalitarianism is notable for its lack of attention to affiliation between totalitarian ideologies and canonical sources. In part, this had to do with Arendt's contempt for the "gutter-born ideology" that was National Socialism, with its "crack-pot" ideas cobbled together from the most dubious of sources. Thus, in the preface to the first edition of *The Origins of Totalitarianism*, Arendt writes that a "subterranean stream of Western history has finally come to the surface and usurped the dignity of our tradition." [56] If an intellectual of the first rank (for instance, Heidegger) supported the Nazis, it was only his fantasy of what the movement represented, and not any intrinsic depth of the ideology, that accounted for the attraction.[57] Yet when she contemplates the case of Stalinism, things are not so easy.

Here, totalitarianism could claim a distinguished intellectual pedigree, one grounded in the towering work of Karl Marx and embodying some of the most cherished moral aspirations of European modernity. Moreover, although intellectually revolutionary, Marxism "was unquestionably a product of the mainstream Western tradition of political thought." [58] Contemplating the implications of this fact in the 1950s led Arendt to the conclusion that "to accuse Marx of totalitarianism amounts to accusing the Western tradition itself of necessarily [!] ending in the monstrosity of this novel form of government." [59] Thoughts along these lines led her to dwell increasingly upon the problem of "the missing link between the unprecedentedness of our present situation and certain commonly accepted traditional categories of political thought." [60]

Arendt never wrote the book "Totalitarian Elements in Marxism" she suggested to the Guggenheim Foundation in 1952, in the proposal for which the last quote is to be found. Yet her detective work expanded, leading her to a rereading of the canon from Plato to Marx. The results of this rereading can be found in the essays that make up *Between Past and Future* and, of course, in *The Human Condition* itself. In turning to these texts, I want to restate Arendt's question: What are the links between "certain commonly accepted traditional categories of political thought" and totalitarianism?

Answering this question is easier if we, like Arendt, begin with Marx.

At the center of Marx's thought, from the "Economic and Philosophical Manuscripts" of 1844 through the *Grundrisse* and *Capital,* is the notion that man creates himself through labor. As Arendt emphasizes in *The Human Condition,* Marx utterly conflates labor (the endless cycle of production and consumption required for the maintenance of human life) with work (the creation of lasting artifacts that add to the "thing-world" that stands between man and nature).[61] In viewing labor as the vehicle for the historical self-creation of mankind (the means by which we realize our "species essence"—*Gattungswesen*), Marx makes human emancipation dependent upon the evolution of man's "metabolism with nature," blurring the all-important line between the man-made realm of freedom (the political realm) and the nature-determined realm of necessity (the "household" or economic sphere).

Even more telling for Arendt is the way Marx frames action—praxis—as a form of work or fabrication. While for the greater part of the life of the species history has been something that happens to man, the advent of capitalism (with its tremendous increase in social forces of production and the means to dominate nature) allegedly makes possible political action that will hasten the next phase in social evolution (as predicted by the Marxian science of political economy). As a *political* movement, then, communism is presented by Marx as realizing the possibility of *making* history with will and intention. Arendt saw this identification of action with work and the making of history as the crucial link between Marx's theory and totalitarian practice: "Marxism could be developed into a totalitarian ideology because of its perversion, or misunderstanding, of political action as the making of history."[62]

As Arendt notes in a number of places, all processes of making or fabrication are inherently violent, the creation of the envisaged end product demanding the violent working over of raw materials by the producer.[63] In her view, it is a relatively short conceptual step from Marx's notion of revolutionary praxis as the making of history to the totalitarian project of fabricating mankind. Not only are both processes necessarily violent—"you can't make an omelet without breaking eggs"—they both aim at the eradication of the basic human condition of plurality, which, for Arendt, is the ground of all genuine political action.[64] Whether in the seemingly benign formula of Marx (the overcoming of class division leading to the withering away of the state and the flowering of a truly general will) or that of totalitarianism, the fabrication of the "end" of history demands the "violent molding of plural men to a single purpose."[65] Both Marx and totalitarianism view human plurality (and the myriad purposes, interests, and perspectives that derive from it) as the chief obstacle to the eventual realization of the (predetermined) telos of history. Hence their shared misunderstanding of action as work, a misunderstanding that facilitates acceptance of the idea that individuals, classes, and other groups must be sacrificed for the good of the species.[66]

The "work model of action" is often viewed as an isolated conceptualization peculiar to Marx and Marxist thought.[67] Arendt doesn't see it this way. In her view, Marx's "mistake" has a long and impressive history in Western thought, one that reaches back to the political theories of Plato and Aristotle. It is in Plato and Aristotle that we find the first, founding examples of what Arendt calls the "traditional substitution of making for acting."[68] This transposition has the greatest effect on the concepts of action, freedom, and judgment within the Western tradition of political philosophy.

In the chapter devoted to action in *The Human Condition,* Arendt stresses that action performed in the public sphere, in the context of human plurality, is never sovereign, never in control of its range of effects or its ultimate meaning. Unlike fabrication, action does not shape material in order to bring about a preconceived end. Rather, action is a kind of insertion into the human world, an insertion that is immediately caught up in what Arendt calls "the web of human affairs."[69] This web, born of plurality, renders the effects of action boundless and creates the impression of futility when we judge action simply in terms of its success or failure. The truth of the matter is that political action rarely, if ever, achieves its goal. Moreover, "because the actor always moves among and in relation to other acting beings, he is never merely a 'doer' but always and at the same time a sufferer. To do and to suffer are like opposite sides of the same coin, and the story that an act starts is composed of its consequent deeds and sufferings."[70]

Action's futility and boundlessness, and the uncertainty of its outcome account for what Arendt calls "the frailty of human affairs." This frailty can be offset somewhat by the creation of relatively permanent laws and institutions that provide boundaries and shape for the public sphere, the arena of action.[71] Yet as long as human plurality is respected through the political form of equal citizenship characteristic of democracies or free republics, this frailty and its frustrations cannot be eliminated. It is for this reason that "Plato thought that human affairs (*ta ton anthropon pragmata*), the outcome of action (praxis), should not be treated with great seriousness."[72] Insofar as he and Aristotle *do* take politics seriously, they focus on lawmaking and city building in their political philosophies, promoting these activities to the highest rank of political life, since here men "act like craftsmen: the result of their action is a tangible product, and its process has a clearly recognizable end."[73] As Arendt observes, "It is as though [Plato and Aristotle] had said that if men only renounce their capacity for action, with its futility, boundlessness, and uncertainty of outcome, there could be a remedy for the frailty of human affairs."[74]

Plato and Aristotle's desire to think action as a kind of making—to "rephrase" political action as an activity as little dependent upon or affected by human plurality as fabrication—does not exhaust itself in their choice of political phenomena worthy of study. On the contrary, it leads them to create an optic on political life in which the freedom, meaning, and goal of action are reinterpreted so that the "unsettling" effects of human plurality (and democratic or republican citizenship) can be contained, if not outright eliminated. Both Plato and Aristotle make the concept of rule central to their political philosophies, both attempt to introduce something akin to the concept of authority into Greek thinking about politics, and both try to "naturalize" these innovations (which were less than palatable, from an Athenian democratic perspective) by relying heavily upon the supposed analogy between just political action and expert craftsmanship.[75]

In Plato's political dialogues (the *Republic,* the *Statesman,* and the *Laws*), this analogy receives its most systematic and authoritative articulation. Plato justifies the separation of knowing from doing and the identification of knowledge with command and of action with obedience by appealing to the expert knowledge of the physician or carpenter (or, in the *Statesman,* the expert "weaver"). If political judgment is acknowledged to be a kind of expert knowledge or *techne,* rather than a generalizable capacity of deliberating citizens, then the argument against the debilitating effects of plurality is all but won.[76] Just rulers would be a knowledge elite, unified not merely by prudence or statesmanship, but by their acquaintance with moral truth, the natural order culminating in the vision of the Good.[77] Their subjects would be similarly unified in their obedient execution of the commands issued by what Arendt calls Plato's "tyranny of reason."[78]

The "expert knowledge" argument is made more persuasive by Plato's use of an analogy drawn from the productive arts. Just as the craftsman envisages his end product as an ideal before the actual process of fabrication, so the Platonic political actor orients his action in light of the ideal standards provided by the forms of justice, the Good, and so on. The Platonic ruler is a "political artist of character," sculpting the plastic material of his subjects into an ordered and unified whole, all in accordance with the original, ideal model.[79]

Plato's interpretation of his doctrine of ideas to provide a set of "unwavering, 'absolute' standards for political and moral behavior and judgment in the same sense that the 'idea' of a bed in general is the standard for the making and judging the fitness of all particular beds" not only imports the metaphorics of making into the realm of action (the plural, political realm), it also sets the pattern for the Western idea of authority and legitimacy.[80] According to Arendt, the distinguishing characteristic of all genuinely authoritarian government (as opposed to tyranny) is that its source of authority is always "a force external and superior to its own power; it is always this source, this external source which transcends the political realm, from which the authorities derive their 'authority,' that is, their legitimacy, and against which their power can be checked." This appeal to transcendent standards repudiates any charge of arbitrariness on the part of the sovereign political actor. The latter's actions do not embody the human capacity to initiate a radically new beginning. Instead, they manifest the human capacity to *correspond* to a larger necessity or order of being.[81]

Plato's interpretation of action as making and his authoritarian appeal to transcendent standards thus crucially depend on one another. Together, they provide a way out of the "frailty of human affairs" and the "futility, boundlessness, and uncertainty of outcome" that characterize political action. With the substitution of making for acting, politics is "degraded" into a "means to obtain an allegedly 'higher' end."[82] This instrumentalization of action is the inevitable outcome of its assimilation to making, since "the process of making is itself entirely determined by the categories of means and end."[83] A "technical" relation is thereby set up between theory and practice, first principles and action.[84] With this configuration (and its implied overcoming of the fact of human plurality), it becomes possible to escape the philosopher's sense that the freedom manifest in initiatory action is, in fact, a kind of bondage, dragging the agent down into a web of unintended consequences from which no actor cannot escape.

The genius of Plato—and the reason why his interpretation of action along "productionist" lines could become authoritative for an entire tradition—is that his "substitution of making for acting" made it possible to see the political actor not only as relatively sovereign, but as limited only by the availability of adequate means to realize preconceived ends. From Plato and Aristotle to Machiavelli and Hobbes, and thence to Marx and Weber, the means / end category reigns supreme in Western political thought. Indeed, as Arendt notes, the persistence and success of the transformation of action into a mode of making is "easily attested by the whole terminology of political theory and political thought, which indeed makes it almost impossible to discuss these matters without using the category of means and ends and thinking in terms of instrumentality." [85] From our perspective, the problem of political action simply *is* the problem of means and ends, the nature of freedom is indissolubly associated with notions of mastery and control, and political judgment is viewed as the privileged possession of experts, moral or otherwise. The reality of human plurality—the very ground of political freedom, action, and the public realm, in Arendt's view—has been eviscerated.

What does all this have to do with totalitarianism? It is certainly not the case that Arendt wants to accuse Plato of being a totalitarian *avant la lettre,* in the manner of Karl Popper or Andre Glucksmann.[86] While her essay "What Is Authority?" makes a strong case for viewing Plato as the originator of a particular tradition of authoritarianism, tyranny, and totalitarianism, her entire analysis is framed by a set of strict distinctions between authoritarianism, tyranny, and totalitarianism.[87] Rather, the paradigmatic importance of Plato resides in his influence upon a tradition of political thought that is deeply suspicious of the idea that human freedom manifests itself in spontaneous, unruly action in the public realm. From the standpoint of the tradition, the freedom of political action (the human ability to *begin*—but not control—radically new sequences of events) is merely a phantom, the possibility that freedom and nonsovereignty coincide a patent absurdity.

When we note how, after Plato, "the concept of action was interpreted in terms of making and fabrication," how the political realm came to be seen as means to "obtain an allegedly higher end," and how the phenomenon of human plurality is consistently effaced by the appeal to the metaphorics of making and the fiction of some sovereign agent who embodies the general interest (the philosopher-kings, Hobbes's sovereign representative, Rousseau's general will, Hegel's rational state, Marx's proletariat, etc.), we are forced to conclude that totalitarianism represents not the negation of the tradition, but a radicalization of some of its most cherished and foundational tropes.

The will to efface plurality, to overcome the "haphazardness" of spontaneity, to identify freedom with control, judgment with *episteme,* and legitimacy with obedience to a "higher law" are all distinguishing characteristics of the Western tradition of political thought (as Arendt understands it) and of totalitarianism.[88] The totalitarian project of fabricating mankind, of "producing" the species through the execution of the law of Nature or the law of History, is unthinkable outside the metaphorics Plato installed at the root of our tradition. The antipolitics of the "state as artwork" find their most radical formulation in the totalitarian project of a violent, endless working over of the "plastic material" of humanity itself.[89]

It is, of course, a long way from a regime based on correspondence with a metaphysical Truth to a regime that views Truth, like reality itself, as something to be fabricated, and from a regime that bases itself on reason to a regime that appeals to the logic of an ideology or myth.[90] Similarly, it is a long way from Platonic restraint (manifest in the conclusion to book 9 of the *Republic* [592c], where the goal of actualizing the ideally just polity in this world is explicitly dismissed as a political project) to the modernist / totalitarian credo that "everything is possible."[91] Yet Arendt's ruminations on totalitarianism's effacement of human plurality, spontaneity, and freedom in the name of a kitsch aestheticism ("beautifying" the species by getting rid of the ugly, inferior, or historically anachronistic) and a "higher" law led her inexorably to the reexamination of the fundamental categories of Western political thought. In the course of this reexamination, she discovered what Philippe Lacoue-Labarthe has called the "nonpolitical essence of the political" in the West, namely, an interpretation of acting as making, guided by an ideal of political community that is at war with the human condition of plurality.[92]

BETWEEN FEAR AND TERROR

None of the reflections I have described above undermined Arendt's basic conviction (expressed most vividly in her essay "Ideology and Terror") that totalitarianism is a radically novel form of government. Unlike authoritarian, tyrannical, or despotic regimes, totalitarianism relies fundamentally on terror—not only as a means, but as a kind of end in itself.[93] But despite this irreducible gap between the tradition (and the authoritarian and quasi-authoritarian forms of government it tends to endorse), on the one hand, and totalitarian regimes, on the other, the fact remains that Arendt devoted great theoretical energy and ingenuity to the task of tracing totalitarian impulses back to the spirit of modernity and the core of the tradition. We should view this theoretical labor, enormous in its ambition, if finally one-sided in its insight, as part of the salutary project of reminding us that (in Arendt's words) the "crisis of our century" was, in fact, "no mere threat from the outside." [94]

But why is this insight one-sided? First because Arendt's engagement with the tradition is highly selective. Intent on drawing out the way the Platonic metaphorics of making echo and reecho in our tradition of political thought, she devotes little attention to the liberal tradition and the theory of rights that animates it. The rights-based individualism of *that* tradition (the Levelers, Locke, Kant, Thoreau, Emerson, and Mill) is, of course, the greatest bar to the limitless instrumentalization of politics and the tendency to treat human beings as material in need of publicly imposed form. It matters not whether the formative project is Platonic soulcraft, Aristotelian habituation to virtue, the inculcation of civic virtue, or the totalitarian sculpting of a "perfected" body politic. Rights-based individualism stands as the obvious and most successful response to any politics, theoretical or practical, that desires to overcome plurality and the "frailty of human affairs."

Why didn't Arendt recognize the obvious? In part out of ignorance (she is at her weakest and most spare in her readings of liberal theorists), in part out of prejudice (she tended to conflate liberalism with "the bourgeoisie" and bourgeois hypocrisy, as did many a Weimar intellectual). Her blindness, however, is mainly a function of a persistent theme of her political thought, one that is first articulated in *The Origins of Totalitarianism*. This is her emphasis on the pervasive experience of loneliness (or worldlessness) encountered by "superfluous masses" created by the modern age.

Convinced that capitalist expropriation, the dissolution of a stable class structure, and the decline of the nation-state (to say nothing of modern science's release of pseudonatural forces to human artifice) all fostered the experience of worldlessness and a corresponding sense of meaninglessness, Arendt focused on the one activity she thought could make us worldly once again. That activity is, of course, political action, by which Arendt meant the sharing of words and deeds on a public stage, the experience of acting together with peers in the founding and preservation of a space for politics.

For Arendt, political action is not simply a sad necessity forced upon responsible individuals if they want to avoid disasters such as totalitarianism. It is, rather, the thing that makes life worth living, the thing that bestows meaning, identity, and coherence on an individual's life.[95] In political action—the worldly activity par excellence—we realize our humanity. No other activity has the same capacity to create meaning—to endow the human artifice with meaning—and no other activity can provide the kind of happiness found in the "joy in action."[96]

The "politics of meaning" sketched out negatively in Arendt's analysis of the preconditions of totalitarianism and positively in her mature theory of political action is what has made her such an attractive theorist to so many different contemporary political sensibilities. The disenchantment of communitarians, feminists, "deliberative democrats," and postmodernists, not only with liberal politics, but with liberal theory attests to a shared desire for a vision of politics that, while not perfectionist, does far more than merely "avoid the worst" (to use Judith Shklar's phrase).[97] While these groups hardly share Arendt's relative unconcern with the topic of justice, they do share her sense that the reality of the public realm has been seriously, if not fatally, undermined.

It is tempting to dismiss as hopelessly romantic both Arendt's focus on the public realm as a space where meaning is created and her critique of the modern age as responsible for the "loss" or "destruction" of this space. But before we do so, we should remember the original experience upon which Hannah Arendt built her political thought. This experience is not that of peers "acting together, acting in concert," as in the Greek polis. It is, instead, the experience of terror under totalitarianism. Arendt's virtually lifelong focus on the public sphere and the life of action grew out of her encounter with this radical negation of public reality and human freedom. Her interest in the "positive" freedom of political action as opposed to the "negative" freedom of civil rights arose from a context in which totalitarian political forces had little trouble overwhelming the protective boundaries of positive law and enlisting "rootless" and "homeless" masses in their cause.[98]

I want to suggest that it makes a difference—perhaps all the difference—if one builds one's political theory on the experience of terror and loneliness or the experience of fear and cruelty. The enormous gap between Arendt's political theory and Judith Shklar's influential "liberalism of fear" can be explained in a number of ways, but in the final analysis it is the difference between totalitarian terror and the fear characteristic of tyrannical government that tells the tale.

What is this difference? What does it signify? In answering these questions, it is helpful to turn to a passage in Arendt's essay "On the Nature of Totalitarianism." She writes:

> As long as totalitarian rule has not conquered the whole earth and, with the iron band of terror, melded all individual men into one mankind, terror in its double function as the essence of the government and the principle—not of action, but of motion—cannot be fully realized. To add to this a principle of action, such as fear, would be contradictory. For even fear is still (according to Montesquieu) a principle of action and as such unpredictable in its consequences. Fear is always connected with isolation—which can be either its result or its origin—and the concomitant experiences of impotence and helplessness. The space freedom needs for its realization is transformed into a desert when the arbitrariness of tyrants destroys the boundaries of laws that hedge in and guarantee to each the realm of freedom. Fear is the principle of human movements in this desert of neighborlessness and loneliness; as such, however, it is still a principle which guides the actions of individual men, who therefore retain a minimal, fearful contact with other men. The desert in which these individual, fearfully atomized men move retains an image, though a distorted one, of that space which human freedom needs.[99]

This remarkable passage concludes a lengthy analysis of Montesquieu's discussion in *The Spirit of the Laws,* book 2 of the principles of action animating different forms of government. Her point vis-à-vis Montesquieu—and also vis-à-vis his disciple, Shklar—is that there is something worse than fear, and something worse than cruelty.

However dehumanizing cruelty and the fear it inspires are, they are not, finally, the "worst thing we do to each other."[100] The worst thing, the true *summum malum,* according to Arendt, is the totalitarian attempt to deprive human beings not only of their freedom and dignity, but of their *world.* In the passage above, Arendt is saying that even the subjects of a tyrannical regime still have a world, a simulacrum of the space for freedom. Insofar as they have a world—insofar as something stands between them and natural or pseudonatural forces—they retain something of their humanity.

Because totalitarian terror effectively levels the protective walls of the human artifice, exposing human beings to the violence of nature-like forces, it can be said to qualitatively exceed the kinds of degradations Shklar discusses. To lose the world is to become a member of an animal species, whereas to live in fear is to be consigned to a degraded humanity. If cruelty is, as Shklar maintains, the center of a secular notion of evil, totalitarian terror is, in fact, a form of *radical* evil.

From Arendt's perspective, Shklar's insistence that we "put cruelty first" on the list of vices we, as good liberals, must combat remains at the level of "ordinary vices" (such as betrayal, hypocrisy, and misanthropy). Shklar's liberalism of fear begins, in other words, within a recognizable, if deeply flawed and often revolting moral world. It hopes to lessen the amount of cruelty and fear human beings must face. In contrast, to begin, as Arendt did, with the experience of totalitarian terror is to enter a world in which "all our categories of thought and standards for judgment seem to explode in our hands the instant we try to apply them."[101] The ordinary vices and the abuses they prompt are not at the heart of totalitarianism: They do not even begin to make sense of the radical evil committed by such regimes.

This Arendtian point is confirmed, to a degree, by the pathetic inadequacy of viewing the totalitarian attempt to "fabricate mankind" as merely an "abuse of public power" or as Machiavellian *raison d'état* run amok. This qualitative gap between totalitarian evil and "ordinary" cruelty is why Arendt turned toward action in the public world, rather than toward a consideration of liberal constitutionalism and civil rights, after *The Origins of Totalitarianism*.[102] The specter of radical worldlessness and the negation of spontaneity—of a literal dehumanization—moved her attention away from legal structures and procedural mechanisms to the activity that, in her eyes, embodied and preserved our humanity. She moved, in short, from a phenomenology of terror and worldlessness to a phenomenology of worldly freedom, from negation to affirmation. No doubt this accounts for the "inspirational" character of her political thought. Yet, as I've tried to suggest, this inspiration comes at a heavy price.

If Arendt's attempts to link totalitarianism to the spirit of the modern age and the roots of the tradition sometimes strain credulity, we must remember her original goal of converting trauma into understanding in *The Origins of Totalitarianism*. That aim remained unfulfilled, in her view, as long as political theorists failed to confront the massive potential for evil lurking in the various formative projects of the tradition and the modern assimilation of human beings to natural and pseudonatural processes. Rights, positive law, constitutional frameworks—all contribute mightily to containing the tendency to treat human beings as raw material. Yet, from Arendt's perspective, liberalism fails to imagine or comprehend the worst and therefore fails to see that the preservation of rights and procedural safeguards ultimately depends on worldliness.[103] This, at any rate, is the fundamental and shaping conviction behind her political thought, and the reason why it will always remain, for better or worse, beyond the pale of a more sober liberalism.

HANNAH ARENDT AND JEWISHNESS:

IDENTITY, HISTORY, AND ZIONISM

In Search of the Mother Tongue

Hannah Arendt's
German-Jewish Literature

Liliane Weissberg

Over the past few years, Hannah Arendt's work has received renewed attention, and publications and conferences that focus on her life and work continue to multiply. The decline of communism and the search for female role models have perhaps contributed to the increased interest in a critic who thought and wrote about the nature of totalitarian regimes and who could serve as a focus for feminist scholarship, even if her interest in the women's movement was virtually nonexistent.[1]

There are still areas, however, where Arendt's work remains peculiarly unexplored. Little attention has been paid to Arendt as a literary critic, for example, despite the fact that her work abounds with references to literature in the traditional sense. Political theorists such as Peter Fuss, Lisa Disch, and Seyla Benhabib have mentioned Arendt's frequent citations of literary figures—for instance, Herman Melville's Billy Budd—and point to her discussions of authors like Isak Dinesen and Hermann Broch.[2] Arendt's oeuvre seems to focus on the act of storytelling, moreover, both in its practical and theoretical dimensions. In her well-known *Origins of Totalitarianism* and in many of her other books, Arendt offers life stories to elucidate her argument, and she defines her political theory as supported by such "examples."[3]

In the present paper, however, I would like to explore a different question. I am interested in Arendt's concept of a particular tradition, that of a "German-Jewish literature." Arendt had a firm understanding of German-Jewish identity, and she conceived of a specific literature that would be able to reflect it. What is the context for this "representation," however, and what is its nature? What are its consequences for her political theory or her—and our—understanding of literature?

I would like to explore these questions by concentrating on Arendt's discussion of three authors, Rahel Varnhagen, Franz Kafka, and Walter Benjamin; however, I will not begin with a reading of Arendt's books or essays on these writers, but with a reference to a public interview.

1

In 1963, Arendt published a series of articles about the trial of Adolf Eichmann, "Eichmann in Jerusalem," in the *New Yorker*. In the following year, a revised version of this text appeared in book form in the United States and in Germany.[4] In both countries, Arendt's report received much publicity, and shortly after these publications, the journalist Günter Gaus took the opportunity to invite Arendt for a television interview.[5]

Gaus begins this conversation with an apparently innocent question, asking Arendt whether she understood her position as a female philosopher as an unusual "role" (9). Much to Gaus's surprise, and despite his protesting intervention—"I regard you as a philosopher" (9)—Arendt rejects this definition. While there may be a place for a female philosopher in the future—"It does not have to remain a masculine occupation! It may happen, indeed, that a woman will become a philosopher someday"—Arendt does not claim this place or role for herself (9). This has little to do with the "female qualities" that Arendt demands for women and that would exclude them from certain professions. A philosopher, in search of knowledge, does not issue orders, which is, according to Arendt, an entirely manly occupation (10). Arendt does not explore the relationship between philosophy and the authoritative voice further here, and the implicit allusion to the military seems oddly placed in a conversation that takes its instigation from the publication of her book on Eichmann.

Arendt's rejection of the position of the philosopher for herself does not center on the issue of the feminine, but on the definition of philosophy. She refers to Plato and Kant to draw a distinction between philosophy and political theory, and it is the latter field that she stakes out for herself. Philosophy, she explains, can claim political neutrality, and the philosopher can endeavor to speak in the name of humanity itself. Political science calls upon a person to take a position. Arendt, who treats philosophy as an occupation of her past, chose to become an acting and active person, but also realizes that she has fallen from a state of innocence. In regard to Arendt's personal life, this fall from innocence has led to her emigration; for Arendt the political theorist, the search for knowledge leads to a satisfaction like that of feeling at home, a *Heimatgefühl* (11).

But it would be too easy to view political science simply as a striving for a home and assign to it the full force of reconciliation. The separation between the public and the private sphere exists from the very beginning. Arendt's relatives were actively engaged in Jewish community issues, yet at home her mother was not religious and never told Arendt that she was a Jew. Arendt refers to this silence as a linguistic issue. The word *Jude* was never mentioned in her home, Arendt explains. It was not part of her mother's tongue or of the German language from which she would later derive not only the comfort of home, but also the ability to think and write without clichés (22–23). Indeed, Arendt encountered the word *Jude* first in the context of anti-Semitic remarks—not in her home, but in the street, and not from her parent, but from other children. The phrase that Arendt uses to refer to this encounter—"Following this event, I was, so to say, 'enlightened' [*aufgeklärt*]"—speaks of enlightenment in quotation marks (23). The children's anti-Semitic remarks result in a parental explanation that is likened to instruction about the facts of life. For Arendt, learning to know that she is Jewish is related to learning to know that she is a sexual being.

If political science appears to be philosophy after the Fall, Judaism itself is gendered. It is linked here to womanhood in a constellation that is far from new. Since the Middle Ages, Jews and women were often compared in regard to their legal status, their social standing, and even the biological constitution of their bodies.[6] But Arendt responds to the discovery of being a woman *and* a Jew once again, and perhaps surprisingly now, with the study of philosophy. And while she acknowledges these studies in the interview with Gaus, she puts them aside with a gesture that mirrors her earlier response in regard to womanhood and her own "enlightenment": "At that time, I was only concerned with how to do it, if one is a Jewish woman? And how it is in general done. You have to realize that I had no idea. I had great problems because of this, which could not be solved easily. Greek is another matter altogether. I have always loved Greek poetry" (18). The seemingly neutral, innocent philosophy is always already the bearer of conflict. Arendt may be eager to participate in a paradisiacal discourse of philosophical abstraction, but in her longing for enlightenment, the Fall is already inscribed.

Arendt's early encounter with anti-Semitic remarks is not the only reference to the street in her conversation with Gaus. The street reappears in the interview in recollections of 1933 as the place where Arendt encountered Nazi activities. She responded to this encounter by studying the language of anti-Semitism at the instigation of Kurt Blumenfeld and other members of the German Zionist organization. She searched in newspapers and other records for a vocabulary that was not her own, but one that confirmed her in what she was, even retrospectively. Her rejoinder to Gaus echoes one of her letters to Gershom Scholem, written in response to his reading of the Eichmann book: "To be Jewish belongs to the irrefutable conditions of my life, and I had never tried to change any such fact, not even in my childhood." [7] And the street appears again in her response to Gaus's questions within the context of a more positive experience. Returning to Germany shortly after the war, Arendt is happy to hear German spoken in the street—it is a happiness beyond words, quite "indescribable" (25). Indeed, this statement echoes an earlier letter written to her husband, Heinrich Blücher, in which Arendt relates her first postwar visit to Berlin, her bus ride through various sections of the city, while recording the sights of ruins as well as her delight in the surviving and resistant Berlin dialect: "But: what still remains are the inhabitants of Berlin. Unchanged, wonderful, humane, full of humor, clever, very clever even. This was for the first time like coming home." [8]

In a city of ruins, the peculiar Berlin slang of the street acquires a recuperative, healing function. But these same streets and this same language can offer disappointments as well, and at the same time. In describing for Gaus the political events after 1949, Arendt stresses the difference between her own German language and that of others. The contemporary language of German streets may be devoid of anti-Semitic remarks, but it is poorer than expected. The word *Jude* was earlier meant to expose. Silence now is meant to cover the deeds of the true perpetrators, precisely in and as a general admission of German guilt. Arendt confronts this silence, not with Greek, but with German poetry. Poetry gives Arendt the language of reflection to respond to, discuss, and analyze this eloquent silence for what it is: a declaration of guilt in a posture of innocence.

Theodor Adorno once declared that after Auschwitz, the writing of poetry has become barbaric.[9] Arendt saves the poetry of her mother tongue precisely to come to terms with Auschwitz, the terrible consequence of anti-Semitism, the fact that exceeded and still exceeds her imagination, the "abyss" confirming and transgressing her own personal experience.[10] No other fact can show the transition from word to action in a more blatant way; no other fact can prove the difference between some intellectual's ideas and human deeds, the separation between philosophy and political theory marked by *Einfall* ("idea," "breaking," "falling into") and *Abgrund* ("abyss") and the horrible fact of dangerous *Einfälle,* "breaking the ground." Rephrasing Karl Kraus, who had once claimed that in regard to Hitler, nothing came to his mind,[11] Arendt describes her disappointment in those intellectuals who pursued their *Einfälle* even in regard to him (21). Philosophy is not only political science in its state of innocence; the safety of its home ground is a treacherous one and in constant danger of the contamination of the street.

Thus, Arendt does not call for a silence to end all poetry after the Holocaust, but for a language to investigate silence and question a tradition that may have begun with nothing else but a child's uttered word. Memory, the *An-denken* of German poetry and language, coincides with the individual's wish to act. Not philosophy, but human action can finally provide the answer for an anti-Semitism, which appears here, first of all, as a matter of language itself. Arendt describes such an action by referring again to her own childhood memories:

> You see, all Jewish children encountered anti-Semitism. And it had poisoned the souls of many children. The difference with us was that my mother always insisted that we never humble ourselves. That one must defend oneself! When my teachers made anti-Semitic remarks—usually they were not directed at me, but at my classmates, particularly at the Eastern Jewesses—I was instructed to stand up immediately, to leave the class and to go home, and report everything [*zu Protokoll . . . geben*]. Then, my mother would write one of her many certified letters, and, with that, my involvement in the affair ended completely. I had a day off from school, and that was quite nice for me. But if such remarks were made by children, I was not allowed to report on it at home. This did not count. Whatever is said by children, one can respond to this [*wehren*] oneself. In this way, these things have never become a problem for me. There existed rules of behavior by which my dignity was, so to speak, protected, absolutely protected, at home. (17)

Despite the fact that Arendt encounters anti-Semitic remarks from children first, she is not allowed to recount them at home, but has to respond to them herself. Her mother's letters are directed toward the adult teachers, for whom innocence can no longer be claimed as it can for children. Arendt herself is in the position of a witness, her mother assumes that of a judge. A word, put in writing, reverts to its speaker and becomes a means of accusation and defense. Turning words into writing signifies action, and while Arendt denies her mother a philosophical

mind ("My mother had no talent for abstract thoughts"), she cannot deny her a political position. Oddly enough, this childhood scene of
legal action prefigures Arendt's own involvement in the Eichmann trial.
Eichmann in Jerusalem was criticized by many Jewish organizations
as an indictment of Jews because Arendt did not understand them as
innocent victims only. Some Jews seemed to cooperate with the National Socialist institutions, and Arendt's discussion of the *Judenräte*
was hotly debated in the reviews to her book.[12] Many Jews, however,
did not act at all, and simply accepted passively what they would view
as their "fate." For Arendt, however, even resistance would have been a
form of action, one that could not only alter the position of a victim, but
also counter the model of a "banal" behavior, such as that of Eichmann
himself.[13]

Arendt's own earlier trial provides an example for such an action. It
takes place among women. Her father had died when she was still quite
young, and the position of authority and legal action was assigned to her
mother. Writing letters is a woman's affair. The mother protects her
daughter with her letter and acts on her behalf, as well as on behalf of
those other "Eastern" girls. The birth of the letter becomes a public scene
of self-definition. But Arendt's mother does not act by accepting Judaism
in a positive way. She proceeds with an aggressive defense, a *sich wehren,*
and refutes anti-Semitic claims to protect the honor [*Würde*] of the individual. Being respected as a Jew is equated to being respected as a human being.

2

Listening to Arendt's memories, Günter Gaus finally poses a more general question: How would Arendt describe her relationship to Germany?
What remains, Arendt answers, is the mother tongue. Arendt gave this
answer once before, in almost the same words, to her former teacher, the
philosopher Karl Jaspers. Jaspers wanted to know whether she would
view herself as of "German essence," and Arendt responded by shifting
the argument to a linguistic concern: "what remains is the language."[14]

In Arendt's childhood narrative, language, indeed, is the ultimate
force. The language of the mother becomes a written word that responds
to the spoken one and turns into a weapon in and as a letter. This letter
is literature and political action in one, and it defines a person's identity.
The motherly act of writing, reconstructed in memory, assumes, moreover, the status of an original scene that imagines a nonpassive feminin-

ity and an actively defensive Judaism while transcending both in the name of a general human right.

And the mother's act of writing becomes a lesson for the daughter. After these early encounters with letters, Arendt's interest in the epistolary genre continued to remain strong. Around 1929, even before the completion of her dissertation, Arendt began her work on the biography of Rahel Varnhagen, a Jewish woman and the author of thousands of letters, who lived in Berlin in the early nineteenth century. Soon, she would describe Rahel as her "closest friend" [15] and explore her published collections—above all, the *Buch des Andenkens* (Rahel: A book of memories for her friends)—as well as much of her unpublished work in the Berlin Staatsbibliothek. Arendt worked on Rahel's biography until 1933 in Berlin, took the project to Paris when she emigrated, and completed it there before her move to New York. It was published first in English translation in 1958, as *Rahel Varnhagen: The Life of a Jewess,* and finally in German in the following year. [16] With this book, Arendt undertook a curious experiment. She wanted to write a life story "from the inside." [17] Far from attempting a psychological analysis, she envisioned a text that would be constructed from excerpts of Rahel's many letters, a montage of quotations that would attempt to capture Rahel's voice. Thus, Rahel would become the author of her own biography, by providing the raw material of it in her letters.

But Arendt's book becomes also an exploration in social theory. Arendt had first encountered the term "conscious pariah" in a book on anti-Semitism by Bernard Lazare, [18] but it is in *Rahel Varnhagen* that she develops her own concept of the pariah as a social outsider. For Arendt, Rahel was a pariah with the choice of only two options. She could either accept her status and live a life in a limited and limiting Jewish world or choose assimilation to German society. At first, Rahel chose assimilation, and her letters document her efforts to gain education and *Bildung,* to marry outside the narrow Jewish circle, to leave Judaism behind, to become not only a German citizen (*Bürgerin*) or a bourgeois (also *Bürgerin*), but even an aristocrat. Arendt recounts here briefly Rahel's attempts to assimilate:

> It was essential to try each successive step. The change of name was of crucial importance; it made her, she thought, "outwardly another person." After that came baptism, since the change of name had proved insufficient and "no reason exists to want to remain in the semblance of the religion of [her] birth." What counted was to "adhere in external matters as well to the class" whose customs, opinions, culture and convictions she wished to identity with.

The most important thing, she believed, was "to baptize the children as well. They . . . must learn to think of that crazy episode of history as no different from other aspects of history in general." [19]

"But was Rahel really prepared to take all the consequences and radically extirpate her own identity?" (255), Arendt asks at the end. For Arendt, the answer is clearly negative, and she calls the last chapter of her book "One Does Not Escape Jewishness." At first, Rahel's letters document the failure of her undertaking, the fact that she could not achieve much more than the status of a parvenu. Ultimately, however, Rahel rejected this parvenu position to return to a consciously chosen pariah existence. "Rahel had remained a Jew and a pariah," Arendt writes, and she adds, echoing her interpretation of her mother's insistence on general human rights: "Only because she clung to both conditions did she find a place in the history of European humanity" (258). Despite all the historic limitations that have doomed Rahel to failure, her attempts to escape the restrictions imposed on her life are exemplary, as is her final embrace of her Jewish fate. There is a legacy of social analysis and protest that is Rahel's to bestow, and Arendt sees it most poignantly realized in one of Rahel's younger friends, the poet Heinrich Heine.[20]

A century later, German Jews would articulate different options. Arendt's privileged author of the twentieth century is not a woman, but a writer who was, like her former classmates (at least geographically), an "Eastern Jew"—Franz Kafka. In her essay "The Jew as Pariah: The Hidden Tradition," published first in 1944, Arendt describes Kafka as an author who attempted an "immense revolution" or turn of the thought that still marked Rahel's letters. Rahel viewed herself as an outsider, and Kafka's fictional characters are seemingly outsiders as well.[21] Like Rahel, they are unwilling to accept their social position. But while Rahel acknowledges her pariah existence to be able to escape it, Kafka's heroes question it. They do not doubt themselves; they do not ask themselves whether they would fit into their social surroundings. Instead, they question the reality of this social sphere. It is their social environment that seems strange and at times outlandish. "Kafka turns everything on its head, right at the very beginning of his literary production," [22] Arendt writes, "yet of all who have dealt with this age-long conflict Kafka is the first to have started from the basic truth that 'society is a nobody in a dress-suit.'" (82 n.). Thus, Kafka may not really be concerned whether the social exclusion of one of his characters was just or justified. Instead, his characters question the authority implicit in each act of exclusion.

Why does society or any of its representatives exclude people, treat them differently, issue orders for them?

Within the context of Arendt's argument, it may not be accidental that Kafka himself was intimately acquainted with legal procedures in his professional work for an insurance company. Indeed, much of his fiction centers upon the law, as well. But in her discussion of Kafka's novels in her essay "The Jew as Pariah: The Hidden Tradition," Arendt touches only briefly on *The Trial*. Instead, she focuses on Kafka's other major novel, *The Castle,* but she returns to this book in a second, later essay on the author, entitled "Franz Kafka," that covers more of his literary oeuvre. According to Arendt, Kafka's heroes are endowed with a "contemplative faculty as an instrument of self-preservation" and "face society with an attitude of outspoken aggression." [23]

Arendt's reading of Kafka's novel seems rather peculiar. The book's hero, the land surveyor K., arrives in a village that seems located in a foreign land. He fails to measure and establish borders but is intrigued by the mysterious castle and the villagers' peculiarities. He wants to go about his business, but he is detained. He lingers on and waits for instructions from the nearby castle on how to proceed. K. does not emerge as an acting person; quite the contrary. He is hindered from acting. But do his very thoughts give evidence of aggression? Is thought here already a form of action, a kind of protest, and a *Wehren* of sorts?

For Arendt, K. becomes a Jew who lacks the pariah's awkwardness, his or her vain hopes for recognition. K.'s protest in *The Castle* appears in the course of the novel as a rejection and a refusal to obey. Rahel authored thousands of letters in the hope of assimilating to German society and literature, but Kafka's hero is not interested in writing any letters at all. Instead, he expects a letter to be issued by an unknown authority. It is this letter that will define his tasks. But more than a simple letter of employment, it will also elucidate K.'s own position in the village and his relationship to the castle and its unknown, but ruling inhabitant. But K.'s waiting seems to be in vain. For a long time, the letter does not arrive, though a telephone transmits messages that are both inaudible and fleeting, nothing more than a temporary hum.

Just as K. seems to be doomed to remain in a passive position, he is offered his awaited epistolary sentence. The unknown authority grants him a choice. The decision is his. He can either become a villager or continue to insist on his—however tenuous—relationship to the castle. For Arendt, K.'s alternative signifies the predicament of the situation of Ger-

man Judaism per se: "No better analogy could have been found to illus-
trate the entire dilemma of the modern would-be assimilationist Jew. He,
too, is faced with the same alternative, whether to belong ostensibly to
the people, but really to the rulers—as their creature and tool—or
utterly and forever to renounce their protection and seek his fortune
with the masses." [24] Thus, the lines between Rahel and Kafka's hero are
clearly drawn. Whereas Rahel relates her efforts to assimilate in her letters, Kafka's novel submits a letter that represents "the true drama of assimilation" (84–85). K. makes his decision, not as a writer, but as a
reader, and reading itself, as Arendt persists to show, is no passive activity. By reading and by reflecting about the consequences of the text,
K. intervenes in an aggressively reflecting way and enters the political
arena. He chooses to resist. Objecting to both alternatives, K. submits
to neither. He follows, in the end, the example set by Arendt's mother
and rejects any decision that would mark him as an Other, as different
still, for the sake of general human rights. Arendt concludes: "[Kafka]
speaks for the average small-time Jew who really wants no more than his
rights as a human being: home, work, family and citizenship" (85).

But this Jew's word is not conveyed without abstraction. K. speaks a
language in which any ethnic coloring is absent. In Rahel's letters, the
reader is still able to find a Yiddish word, an odd grammatical construction, and an orthography unusual even for her time. For Arendt,
Kafka acquires importance, not just because of his claim for general human rights, but also because of his rejection of any Jewish slang or *Jargon*. In that, as well, Kafka becomes a descendent and heir of the Enlightenment.[25] He writes without repetitions or elaborate constructions.
His language is simple and clear. He does not want language to draw attention to itself, but to offer Truth instead. The "real drama of [Jewish]
assimilation," Arendt seems to suggest, can be rendered only in this pure
and simple German language, and perhaps the opposite holds as well.
Language this pure and simple may be able to emerge only as the result
of attempted assimilation. Thus, as Kafka articulates the German-Jewish
predicament, he sets new standards for the discussion of German-Jewish
identity, and for that of German literature, as well. In regard to German
literature, however, Kafka may have founded a school, but it includes
few masters. Arendt insists that Kafka's language has tempted others to
try their voice in imitation. None of his successors, however, have succeeded in matching or even rivaling him. In Kafka, therefore, assimilation seems to fail itself. He is, as Arendt writes, an incomparable author.

For Arendt, Kafka is not only a storyteller par excellence who represents his time. He assumes an almost clairvoyant position: he is ahead of
(his) time, or perhaps even beyond any chronological considerations.
While his language conveys Truth, his literature is "true," as well. This
is not a literature that could reconcile its readers with Auschwitz, but
it could offer its readers the language needed to talk about the Holocaust. Moreover, Kafka's literature does not lose in meaning, despite the
recent German past. "Kafka's world is doubtlessly a frightening world,"
Arendt writes.

> But that it is more than a nightmare, that it is, in a structural sense, rather
> uncannily adequate to the reality in which we are forced to live today, this
> we know better now, I assume, than twenty years ago. The magnificence of
> his art is that it can be as moving and unsettling now as it was then, that the
> horror of the "Penal Colony" has lost nothing of its immediacy because of
> the reality of the gas chambers.[26]

3

With Kafka, one may thus assume, German-Jewish literature has found
both its proper contemporary representative and its last word. Despite
K.'s doubts, Arendt cites a reality—that of the gas chambers—in which
even the possibility of doubt would find its end. But despite Arendt's
own description of Kafka's work as "incomparable," it lives on in constant comparison to the work of other authors in Arendt's texts. Nowhere is Arendt's urge to compare Kafka with another author more obvious than in her essay on Walter Benjamin, which was published in the
New Yorker in 1968, five years after her report on the Eichmann trial.[27]

For Arendt, Kafka is an author who could represent his and our time
equally well. His work is both timeless and written for the future. Although ten years younger than Kafka, Benjamin seems to belong to another time, the nineteenth century, and to have entered the twentieth century more or less by accident. Living in the past, Benjamin is, nonetheless,
able to develop a concept of modernity and sketch a philosophy of history that would capture the problems outlined in Kafka's work.

As in her book on Rahel Varnhagen, Arendt concentrates in her essay
on Benjamin's biography and tries to explain his work by relating it to his
life. She describes his vain attempts to make a living as a writer and refers to his interest in book collecting, which outpaced his declining fortune and left him without funds more often than not. These anecdotes

not only are remarks about an individual but cast a nostalgic glance at a bygone era of potentially successful gentleman scholars. For Arendt, Benjamin's lifestyle and demeanor poignantly represent the German-Jewish bourgeois upper middle class at the point of its disappearance.

His story is one not only of economic miscalculations, but, more important, of political ones. In his essay on the storyteller, Benjamin predicts the end of narrative due to the absence of experience, and, more specifically, the experience of death. In Arendt's essay, Benjamin's death not only takes a central position, but is integrated in a general narrative of lucky coincidences and mishaps. Benjamin's life becomes a tale about the good and bad turns of fate, of decisions made much too late or neglected entirely. But while Benjamin may seem to be the "type" of a bourgeois Jewish scholar, his work is "absolutely incomparable," and Arendt borrows here a phrase from Hugo von Hofmannsthal's evaluation of Benjamin's essays (155).

Benjamin wrote an essayist literature both fragmentary and allegorical, and he brought together passages from other texts in a process of montage. Arendt reads Benjamin's constellations of quotations as an extension of his collection of books. But when Benjamin replaced material goods with literature, his collection achieved a new abstractness and adjusted to new modes of exchange. For Arendt, this procedure is still reminiscent of the nineteenth century, and Benjamin emerges in her essay as a flaneur of words. At the same time, his project of montage gives evidence of his early interest in surrealism and contemporary aesthetics of the collage, the ready-made, the photographic image. Such a project not only questions tradition, but tries to review history from the present. It constructs an image whose historical significance would lie within the new. Arendt quotes Benjamin here to illuminate this process: "The genuine picture may be old, but the genuine thought is new. It is of the present. This present may be meager, granted. But no matter what it is like, one must firmly take it by the horns to be able to consult the past. It is the bull whose blood must fill the pit if the shades of the departed are to appear at its edge" (199).

This is the process that Arendt defines as unique. But it also bears a certain resemblance to one of Arendt's own projects, her biography of Rahel Varnhagen, which she intended to construct from quotations as well. In Paris in the 1930s, Benjamin had a chance to read Arendt's manuscript in progress and urge her to complete it.[28] But while Arendt was eager to design an interior monologue of sons and insisted on the integrity of her subject both as person and as author, Benjamin had no individual biography in mind. He wanted to construct "dialectical images,"[29] to reflect on the world of objects and their circulation. Thus, Arendt did not view him as a critic, but as a diver who would rescue words the way that she would try to rescue biographical tales. But herein, too, the incomparable Benjamin could, indeed, be compared, and he appears in unlikely company: "Without realizing it, Benjamin actually had more in common with Heidegger's remarkable sense for living eyes and living bone that had sea-changed into pearls and coral, and as such could be saved and lifted into the present only by doing violence to their context in interpreting them with 'the deadly impact' of new thoughts, than he did with the dialectical subtleties of his Marxist friends" (201). For the political theorist Arendt, Martin Heidegger's and Benjamin's searches for Truth seem to unite both beyond the question of political orientation. And it is precisely Benjamin's position as a pearl diver—one that he seems to share with Heidegger—that provides him with his own form of resistance. In a gesture that may well be implicitly intended to save Heidegger from his National Socialist past, Arendt thus points at a mode of reflection and writing that would, under Benjamin's pen, serve the cause of exploring German-Jewish identity. Benjamin, too, seems to have been offered two alternatives, those of Jewish religion and orthodox Marxism, and he was willing to reject both. Thus, he defined his own choice between the castle and the village.

Benjamin enters the twentieth century in the same way that Kafka's hero encounters an alien village. The new time and the new geographical space seem to deny assimilation to both, albeit on different terms. But while Rahel seems never quite able to achieve assimilation, K. and Benjamin indicate its possibility in a time past and a place lost. And in his own search for Truth, Benjamin's language, too, remains simple and pure as it proceeds to link and build upon quotations. In its purity, it resembles Kafka's style, and those of the many children's books that Benjamin collected, as well.

Arendt points again and again at the affinities between Benjamin and Kafka, and her wish to draw the two close to each other becomes strikingly evident in the mode of her own research. Her files on Walter Benjamin, which are deposited at the Library of Congress in Washington, contain sketches and notes by Benjamin, as well as his and Arendt's notes on Kafka's work.[30] Thus united under the same cover, it is difficult to separate Arendt's comments on Kafka's fictional heroes from her remarks on

Benjamin's work. Arendt structured her essay on Benjamin, moreover, to parallel Benjamin's own essay on the Prague author. The poem about the little hunchback, for example, which first appeared in Benjamin's memoirs *Berliner Kindheit um Neunzehnhundert* (Berlin childhood around 1900) first, receives a central location in his essay on Franz Kafka.[31] Arendt directs it back to Benjamin's life, where it becomes the epigraph of her own work:

> When I go down to the cellar
> There to draw some wine
> A little hunchback who's in there
> Grabs that jug of mine.
>
> When I go into my kitchen
> There my soup to make
> A little hunchback who's in there
> My little pot did break.
>
> . . . .
>
> O dear child, I beg of you
> Pray for the little hunchback too. (158–59)

The little hunchback trips the child in the role of an adult, thus drawing wine and making soup. His signature is one of mischief. He may cause damage inadvertently and is a sorry figure, one that should be included in a prayer for protection.

In *Berliner Kindheit,* Benjamin recalls his mother's references to a "little hunchback" who would play tricks on persons and objects in the house, and the memories of the tales about the little hunchback indeed conclude the memoirs of his youth. In his essay on Franz Kafka, Benjamin calls these verses a "folk song." [32] In her essay on Benjamin, Arendt returns this poem to the realm of childhood, and it becomes Benjamin's own letter, sent to him by his mother. This letter is no longer written in response to his teacher's actions but comments on his own fateful clumsiness. The letter, sent by the mother and transmitted via Kafka, is finally addressed to a person whose "aggressive thought" would have to remain in the realm of childlike innocence.

Thus, Arendt sees it as her task to protect Benjamin's person as well as his philosophy. The philosopher and the acting political theorist are made to meet. Arendt not only sponsored the postwar English publication of Kafka's work; she championed the publication of Benjamin's essays, as well, and did so despite the resistance of Theodor W. Adorno, whose exiled Institute for Social Research had sponsored much of Benjamin's later work, but who was not eager to sponsor its early publication.[33] If death has been inscribed in Arendt's account of Benjamin's life and work, this work becomes, indeed, the inheritance of German Jewry itself. Arendt describes Benjamin's work as a space in which a hidden tradition could reveal itself, in which Benjamin, an incomparable writer and an awkward child at once, could find refuge, and to whom she has offered shelter in her own text.

Arendt prepared this and other essays for a collection *Men in Dark Times* in 1968, and she sent a draft of the manuscript to her friend, the writer Mary McCarthy. In her comments, McCarthy concentrates on the figure of the little hunchback. She turns this hunchback into a figure of a German fairy tale and gives it a name: Rumpelstiltzchen.[34] This figure merges with Benjamin in her remarks about Arendt's text:

> Of course you are coaxing them to tell you (and us) their secret name. This book is very maternal, Hannah—*mütterlich,* if that is a word. You've made me think a lot about the Germans and how you / they are different from us. It's the only work of yours I would call "German," and this may have something to do with the role friendship plays in it, workmanly friendship, of apprentices starting out with their bundle on a pole and doing a piece of the road together.[35]

According to McCarthy, Arendt's essay provides a curatorial space that turns Benjamin into a figure ready for apprenticeship, as well as motherly protection. But she seems to turn Benjamin into a figure of a German fairy tale, as well. In describing Arendt's own text within a definite "German" tradition, McCarthy completes, perhaps, a striving for assimilation that Arendt had resisted finding in Benjamin's own work.

In his essay on Kafka, Benjamin had quoted the little hunchback to insist on a common German and Jewish inheritance. "In his depth," he writes, "Kafka touches the ground which neither 'mythical divination' nor 'existential theology' supplied him with. It is the core of folk tradition, the German as well as the Jewish" (134). Arendt, however, designs a German-Jewish tradition that is much different from a description of a common ground. Rahel, the author of letters, Kafka, the novelist of Truth, Benjamin, the childlike, but Truth-seeking philosopher—become examples of a German-Jewish identity for which resistance—*Wehren*—provides its signature. This German Jew, imagined after the Holocaust and in response to the experience of a failed assimilation, emerges, perhaps, as the political scientist par excellence. But Rahel, Kafka, and Benjamin mark Arendt's position as well, both as a thinker and within an imaginary family constellation. Within this constellation, little space is offered to any fatherhood. If Judaism is transmitted through the mother,

German-Jewish identity here is transmitted through the mother's hand. In her childhood anecdote, Arendt relates the mother's act of letter writing. In her essay on Benjamin, she finally moves into the mother's position herself, protecting the child by a letter that finally reaches us as the claim of German-Jewish literature. It is the mother who becomes the first author of a German-Jewish literature and who has the last word. What remains is, indeed, the mother's tongue.

Binationalism and Jewish Identity

Hannah Arendt and the Question of Palestine

Amnon Raz-Krakotzkin

In a series of essays published in the 1940s, Hannah Arendt came out against the political position adopted at the time by the Zionist movement, a policy that demonstrated the demand to establish an independent Jewish state in Palestine as the main and ultimate goal of Zionism. Previously, this demand was made only by right-wing "Revisionist" representatives and was rejected by the leaders of the majority Labor movement and of the Jewish Agency as being wrong and dangerous. Arendt condemned the new political line for ignoring the rights and will of the Palestinians and viewed it as a shift toward a right-wing nationalistic attitude. She sharply rejected the idea of a Jewish state and warned that it would lead to dispossession of the Palestinians and would consequently also risk the very existence of the Jewish community.[1]

Instead, Arendt supported a binational solution and tried to advance an agreement that would ensure a Jewish homeland within the framework of a binational state.[2] She followed a line that was first forged in the 1920s by a small group of intellectuals who founded the association of "Brit Shalom" in order to advance an agreement with Arab leaders on Jewish settlement and on a binational solution. The dispersal of that organization in the early 1930s was followed by other initiatives in the same direction. In that period, the late 1930s, and during the 1940s, the adherents of the idea were gathered in an organization called "Ichud" ("Union") that tried to advance a solution based on the rights of the Palestinians.[3] It was a small group whose political impact was very limited, although among its members were some of the most outstanding intellectuals, including Hugo Bergmann, Gershom Scholem (until the early 1930s), Judah Leib Magnes, Ernst Simon, Hans Kohn, Arthur Ruppin, and Martin Buber. Like many of them, Arendt came from a German-Jewish milieu, but, unlike them, she did not settle in Palestine. Observing the political situation from a distance, she supplied a comprehensive analysis of Zionist political discourse absent from the writings of other representatives of the idea.

In the first paragraph of her famous essay "Zionism Reconsidered," Arendt described the implications of two current Zionist resolutions that expressed the new political approach adopted by Zionist leadership during the Second World War. One was the Biltmore Program (1942), which demanded the establishment of "a free Jewish commonwealth in Palestine" after the war. That attitude was further sharpened and given an extreme formulation in the Atlantic City resolution by the American Jewish Conference (later confirmed by the World Zionist Organization) in 1944, which raised the demand for a "free and democratic Jewish commonwealth ... which shall embrace the whole of Palestine, undivided and undiminished." Analyzing these declarations, Arendt claimed:

> The Atlantic City resolution goes even a step further than the Biltmore Program in which the Jewish minority had granted minority rights to the Arab majority. This time the Arabs were simply not mentioned in the resolution, which obviously leaves them the choice between voluntary emigration or second-class citizenship ... it seems to admit that only opportunist reasons had previously prevented the Zionist movement from stating its final aims. These aims now appear to be completely identical with those of the extremists as far as the future political constitution of Palestine is concerned. It is a deadly blow to those Jewish parties in Palestine itself that have tirelessly preached the necessity of an understanding between the Arab and the Jewish peoples. On the other hand it will considerably strengthen the majority under the leadership of Ben-Gurion, which, through the pressure of many injustices in Palestine and the terrible catastrophes in Europe, have turned more than ever nationalistic.[4]

On the same grounds, Arendt also objected to the 1947 UN partition resolution and voiced a warning against its consequences.[5] She predicted that it would inevitably lead to the expulsion of the Palestinians and to violation of their rights, and consequently to a war that would also threaten the very existence of the Jewish community. She collaborated with Judah Leib Magnes, the first chancellor of the Hebrew University and the most enthusiastic adherent of binationalism, in order to prevent the acceptance of the partition plan, and she assisted his ineffective efforts to suggest and advance alternative proposals based on agreement with Arab representatives. In March 1948, when the war was evident, they both supported the short-lived American initiative to nominate an international trusteeship that would rule until an agreement was achieved and ensure the rights of the population.[6]

This position led to a wide-ranging and penetrating analysis in which Arendt identified, revealed, and examined different aspects of the dominant Zionist ideology and praxis. But it should be emphasized that the critical, binational position was an integral part of Arendt's commitment to Zionism and her involvement in Zionist efforts to save Jewish youth from Germany. Arendt, who was not interested in "Jewish affairs" until the 1930s, began Zionist activity after the rise of the Nazis to power in Germany and regarded Zionism as the only effective and authentic way to struggle against anti-Semitism. She considered it as the approach demanded by the critique of modern political discourse, an opportunity to define "Jewish politics," and a means for the Jews to take responsibility and also to develop political values. She developed her binational views as she thought about and wrote *The Origins of Totalitarianism,* and her political activity should thus be considered as part of the same project, an attempt to implement the conclusions of her historical analysis in a concrete realm. According to that, Zionism was the only relevant and respected activity, but on the condition that it would provide a different political attitude, one that would challenge European colonial discourse and regard reality from the standpoint of the victim. Zionism should manifest the responsibility of the victim to the conditions that enabled their exclusion and extermination. As will be discussed later, she did not accept Zionism as a political-theological myth, but as a political option. On these grounds, she criticized "the conversion of the Jews to a nation" as the assimilation of the same values that enabled their exclusion.

Binationalism was therefore the necessary conclusion of the analysis of anti-Semitism, the nation-state, and colonialism, the issues discussed in *The Origins of Totalitarianism.* Seen thus, the rights and perspective of the Palestinians were an integral part of the discussion of Jewish rights and self-definition and of the vision of Jewish political emancipation. At the same time, it was an approach that challenged dominant modern political concepts in which both anti-Semitism and imperialism were acceptable. In her writings against the partition plan, Arendt warned against the blindness of the Jewish leadership, who had surrendered to colonial interests, including those of the Soviets (who were the most enthusiastic supporters of the partition solution and later supplied military aid to the Jewish forces). She condemned Zionist reliance on imperialist power as an adoption of the same principles that enabled the political influence and victory of anti-Semitism. She claimed that the actual policy of the Zionist movement demonstrated the failure of its leadership to understand anti-Semitism as a historical—and not natural—phenomenon, and to perceive that its origins were grounded in the foundations of modern reality and modern consciousness.

These writings have sometimes received the attention of experts on Hannah Arendt, but they have had hardly any effect on the political discourse in Israel. This is usually the case with the political writings of the "Brit Shalom" circle. The concept of binationalism was presented as unrealistic, and its adherents—although outstanding and distinguished intellectuals—were described as naive dreamers who ignored political reality. Later republication of Martin Buber's writings on the issue (by Paul Mendes Flohr) and those of Gershom Scholem (by Avraham Shapira) were received as a cultural contribution, reflecting the morality of Zionism, but as politically irrelevant.[7] Arendt's writings, in particular, were hardly discussed and were not even translated, although her exclusion from the Zionist discourse was on different grounds and was related to the "Eichmann in Jerusalem" affair.

Undoubtedly, many of the insights and critical observations contained in these essays should be regarded as obsolete. They were introduced in a concrete political context that has changed drastically. They were written when the Jews were a minority, less than a third of the population in Palestine, and when a sort of binational state did exist: the British colonial administration still ruled. The establishment of the state of Israel and the temporary "partition" of Palestine that followed the 1948 war (though not according to the UN resolution) seemed to bring the idea of binationalism to an end.

Arendt certainly did not suggest a coherent political attitude or a satisfactory alternative. She herself, like most of the other advocates of the idea, did not return to this option later and even changed her mind. It may be suggested that because, at least for the time being, her pessimistic predictions on the chance of the Jewish homeland to survive have been proved wrong, the motivation for the political activity has disappeared. Like other advocates of binationalism, Arendt saw the idea more as a matter of Jewish identity than as a commitment to or solidarity with Arab victims. Later, according to similar presuppositions, Arendt supported the Jewish Defense League of Meir Kahane. Even though at that time he was not yet famous as being an extreme anti-Arab racist, it indicates that her main motivation remained Jewish interests.[8]

Yet, even if we accept her limitations, the principles Arendt laid down, as well as many of her brilliant observations, are still relevant. Reading Arendt's writings into the present context illuminates different aspects of the discussion of Zionism and the question of Palestine and enables us to redefine political values and political goals. In this context, the concept of binationalism and the sense of responsibility on which Arendt insisted are even more relevant and important from the perspective of the present, when the Jewish state dominates the entire land, operating various systems of exclusion and dispossession with regard to the Arab inhabitants. It can thus direct us toward a different definition of Jewish collectivity, one that is based on the fulfillment of Palestinian rights. Arendt regarded herself as a political thinker, and following her therefore demands thinking politically, namely, reading her texts into the present reality.

First of all, we must realize that these ideas became "unrealistic" when "reality" proved Arendt's observations and predictions to be correct and precise. In other words, Arendt became irrelevant when what she foresaw came to be real. The establishment of the state of Israel as a Jewish state caused the destruction of the Arab entity and the expulsion and escape of hundreds of thousands of Palestinians. It then led to the confiscation of most Arab land, which was henceforth declared to be Jewish national property. The definition of Israel as a Jewish state turned its Arab citizens, those who were not expelled from its territory in 1948, into second-class citizens. To say that the binationalist arrangement was not realistic means therefore that in order to establish a Jewish state and to ensure Jewish hegemony and Jewish majority, expulsion and exclusion were inevitable.

This perspective sheds a different light on the commonly accepted Zionist version of events, according to which the Palestinians are to be blamed for their tragedy because of their refusal to accept the partition plan.[9] Arendt predicted the evacuation as the result of the UN resolution, not its rejection. In other words, from her perspective, it was not the refusal of the Palestinians, but the forced implementation of partition against the agreement of the inhabitants, that caused the tragedy. Arendt considered the Palestinian position to be reasonable, even though she did not accept it as it was. The fact that the Palestinians refused the resolution does not mean that they did not suggest other alternatives that preserved the minority rights of the Jews and enabled a limited immigration.

Arendt's prediction preceded the conclusions of later historians and the so-called Israeli New Historians who challenged the dominant perception that denied any responsibility from the Jewish side.[10] Arendt's perspective also shifts the focus from the question whether the expulsion was planned in advance by the Zionist institutions or was caused by a spontaneous development of the war. Arendt's perspective clarifies that it was embodied within the partition plan. In other words, the establishment of a Jewish state and its dramatic growth made the dispossession of the Palestinians inevitable. For the present discussion, this clarification is of greater importance than the concrete questions that still define the historiographic discourse. We have to remember that according to the resolution, even within the borders of the Jewish state, the Arabs were to be almost equal in number to the Jews, whereas Israel continually rejected the refugees' right of return, according to resolutions of the same institution, the United Nations assembly. There were no measures taken or even any previous discussions on the status of Palestinian residents of the Jewish state, and the minority that was not expelled was for many years subject to military government and multiple restrictions. It is impossible to imagine the ensuing Jewish mass immigration to Israel without expulsion and dispossession. Moreover, from the beginning, Israel related to the UN resolution exclusively as though it referred to the founding of a Jewish state and ignored the other state implied by the partition plan. The principle of partition was removed from the Israeli Declaration of Independence, where the UN resolution is described as the international recognition of the Jewish state. The Palestinian state was forgotten and denied.

"Blaming the victims" was a charge directed against Arendt herself on a different occasion, when she claimed that Jews as pariahs should feel responsible for what society had done to them.[11] Her analysis of the Eichmann trial was misinterpreted as an accusation of the Jews. But in that case, Arendt demanded that the Jews should take responsibility for their own deeds and develop a political approach stemming from the experience of the victims and the analysis of their victimization. But blaming the victims continued to be the foundation of Zionist historical perception.

Arendt preceded critical discussions of Zionism on other levels, as well. She criticized the attitude of the socialist pioneer settlers who followed similar values and excluded the Palestinians from their social vision. Although on several occasions she praised the kibbutz movement and the different social experiments initiated by Zionist settlers, at the same time, she criticized them for their total political indifference, namely, their lack of responsibility toward the implications of the project for the economic reality of the Palestinians. She condemned the concept of "Hebrew labor"(*avodah ivrit*) for excluding the Arab workers and blamed the leftist movements for their lack of solidarity with the Palestinians.[12] She concluded by claiming that "Jewish class struggle in Palestine was for the most part a fight against Arab workers. To be anti-capitalist in Palestine almost always meant to be practically anti-Arab." She described the isolated world that these "radicals" were trying to create for themselves as an island that ignored the rest of humanity. "Palestine functioned as an ideal place, out of the bleak world, where one might realize one's ideals and find a personal solution for political and social conflicts." [13]

This does not mean that a binational state was a realistic option in 1947. It was not. In any case, this is not the issue. It seems to me meaningless to discuss now historical options that are no longer relevant. The purpose is not simplistically to "condemn" Zionism, and we certainly cannot ignore the context of the events. But the historical evaluation of the birth of Israel and the Palestinian tragedy are crucial, since the historical perception continues to direct political discourse and to determine its boundaries. The political concepts that were criticized by Arendt continue to be implemented today, and the historical clarification can thus clarify their continuing effect.

On the same lines, the critical stance should thus be updated and take into consideration contemporary reality. In that context, binationalism does not refer necessarily to a binational state but is the framework of principles that should direct the process of reconciliation. From the Jewish point of view, the present use of Arendt's analysis determines the context of responsibility to include the Palestinians and the refugee question. It is not a question of guilt, but a question of awareness and responsibility that should direct us toward the future. It is a critical stand based on a different vision.

We are reading Arendt in Jerusalem, a city that for many years has been under closure, preventing the reentry of Palestinians. In the name of a peace process, a reality of oppression and apartheid is established, at least for the time being. Following Arendt, we have to observe that in the Israeli public debate, the term "peace" still does not mean primarily the fulfillment of Palestinian rights, including the rights of the refugees, but rather the principle of separation, the same principle she opposed in the 1940s. This is one of the obvious characteristics of Israel even today, within what is considered as a peace process. This concept preserves the exclusion of the Palestinian perspective from the discussion of Jewish identity, enables one to ignore their political rights, and obviates the need to challenge the dominant historical narrative. This prevents confronting Palestinian history and the Palestinian tragedy as part of Zionist history and the immediate context of responsibility and solidarity.[14]

Paradoxically, from our perspective, the two options that were submitted by the UN delegation to the General Assembly in 1947—the plan to establish Palestine as a federation (the plan of the minority delegates that was favored by Magnes and Arendt but was immediately opposed) and the plan of partition—can both be considered as binational. From our perspective, both considered equal rights for both peoples and ensured procedures of partnership between them, seen as crucial for its success. Under the present circumstances, these values are the foundation of any solution of the conflict. The question now is not only how to prevent expulsion, but how to ensure Palestinian national and civil rights.

This can be achieved in various ways, in the framework of a two-states solution or in one state. But in any case, the concept of binationalism is essential for the process of reconciliation. In both solutions, national definition would depend on the recognition of the other, including the rights of the Palestinian refugees and awareness of the Jewish question. In both cases, it is necessary to establish procedures that will ensure equal distribution of goods such as land and water. Any other solution preserves the present status of the Palestinians as an inferior group, as well as the process of apartheid. The principle of binationalism is therefore the starting point for imagining and developing different political alternatives. It is not necessarily a fixed solution, but at least a direction that fosters resistance to the present situation.

The problem embodied in the concept of a Jewish state remains as it was, even within the framework of a solution that will ensure a Palestinian state in the occupied territories (the compromise that is favored by the Palestinians and some Israelis, but that for the moment seems to be an illusion). That is because it determines the exclusion of the Palestinian citizens of Israel and demonstrates the dual system of the Israeli regime, a regime that grants legal authority to the Jewish Agency and thus guarantees the inferiority and marginalization of the Arab citizens. In her objection to the concept, Arendt pointed out that the main issue is not the separation of religion from the state, but rather the distinction between national identity and the state. Even if we do not reject the concept of a Jewish state itself (in a two-state arrangement), her observations beg one to consider its implications. Israel is not the only state in which minorities are excluded, but the unique nature and history of the national conflict throws light on the general question of the nation-state. In this sense, the concept of binationalism is a critical tool that can be relevant for the discussion of other contexts, as well.

Binationalism is therefore a set of values, not necessarily a concrete political arrangement. But it demands the separation of national identity from the state and the regard of the other as an integral part of self-definition. The Jewish experience that led Arendt to Zionism and to binationalism, the persecution of the Jews in Europe, is crucial for the redefinition of Jewish identity. It reminds us that the emancipation of the Jews necessarily includes the emancipation of the Palestinians and the inclusion of their memories and aspirations in the history and future plans for the region.

In this context, the question that should be raised is how to define a Jewish collectivity in Palestine that will be based on the recognition of the rights of the Palestinians, including the rights of the refugees. Arendt's insights direct us to the awareness that it is impossible to distinguish the discussion of Jewish identity from discussion of the continuous national conflict and from responsibility for the Palestinian tragedy. Binationalism therefore is the evident context for any political and cultural discussion.

Arendt's writing on Zionism and the Palestinian question in the 1940s can receive another dimension through a comparison with Gershom Scholem's attitudes concerning the Jewish question and binationalism, attitudes that they both shared, though not simultaneously. Their different attitudes toward their common friend, Walter Benjamin, open further perspectives for political and cultural discussion.

Arendt in her critical writings took a stance similar to that expressed by Scholem in the 1920s, while he was a member of "Brit Shalom." This was not the only resemblance between their attitudes concerning the Jewish question. Yet from a similar analysis and similar assumptions, they took very different directions. It is not my intention here to summarize their complicated relationship, but to use the comparison for the clarification of several aspects of Zionist consciousness with respect to the issue at stake here.

In his early writings, Scholem opposed the reliance of Zionism on the Balfour declaration and on colonial power. For Scholem, a follower of Ahad Ha'am's "cultural Zionism," the main purpose of the Zionist movement as he viewed it in those years was to establish a spiritual center, not an independent state. In order to fulfill this goal, he called for an agreement with the Arabs. This for him was a precondition for the authentic revival of Judaism. From this point of view he regarded a binational arrangement as the ideal solution. It was the only alternative to the chauvinism (which he sometimes presented as "messianism" or "Sabbatianism") that he attributed mainly to right-wing movements, as well as to some declarations of Labor leaders. Like his partners in "Brit Shalom," many of them of German origin, he regarded binationalism as a conclusion of his Zionist vision. For him, as for Arendt (who was not familiar with the reality in Palestine), binationalism was first of all part of the Jewish identity. In 1931, after the Arab riots of 1929, he blamed Zionism for the national tension and linked it to the alliance of Zionism with colonial powers.[15] Instead, Zionism should join the "awakening East," he claimed.

Scholem's binationalistic approach preserved an obvious notion of a forthcoming catastrophe, a notion that directed his anticolonial stand at that time. He expected an apocalyptic war between the awakening East and the declining West. He was aware of the dangers and was not sure that Zionism would be able to survive. But he definitely demonstrated that the precondition for Zionism was its stand "on the right side of the barricades,"[16] that is, against the colonial powers.

Yet the catastrophe occurred elsewhere, and Scholem changed his interests and redefined his Zionist attitude. Unlike many of the other adherents of binationalism, Scholem withdrew from all political involvement and did not participate in later initiatives such as the "Ichud." The cause for this shift was probably the rise of the Nazis to power. The question of Palestine did not interest him anymore, and he adopted the dominant Zionist attitude he had previously rejected and condemned. He could no longer ignore the question of rescue, but this led him to neglect the perspective of the Palestinians. Scholem no longer rejected the principles of statehood and shelter.

It was not only that he abandoned his political activity. At the same time, he turned his academic focus of research from early and medieval Jewish mysticism, to which he had previously dedicated his attention, to questions of messianism, especially to Sabbatianism. In the following decades, he enriched us with enlightening research and stimulating insights on several aspects of these phenomena and their implications. But the scholarly project was at the same time a discussion of the essence of Zionism and its relation to the traditional messianic notion. Within his research and in individual essays, Scholem also formulated his vision of

Zionism as national-theological redemption. He located Zionism within the myth of redemption, defined as political and national.[17] Nationalism here was not distinguished from religion, but modernized interpretation of the theological realm.[18]

Scholem's attitude toward messianism was ambivalent. On the one hand, he regarded Zionism as the dialectic fulfillment of a redemptive process and of the national attributes of messianism. Yet he also regarded Zionism as the overcoming of apocalyptic tendencies. Therefore, even though he often warned against the dangers and "the price" of messianism, he had a constitutive role in the shaping of the perception of messianic imagination in Jewish tradition as "national," and consequently the view of Zionism as the fulfillment of Jewish expectations throughout the ages.

This redemptive dimension left no room for the people already on the land itself and enabled the exclusion of its population in the way described so brilliantly by Arendt. Scholem did indeed warn against messianism, but at the same time, he designed the conception that regarded the present as the final stage of national redemption. He opposed radical national-religious movements, but in his description of Jewish history, the land preserved its mythical connotation. His intentions were certainly different, but his assumptions did not offer a different approach, and they even motivated right-wing national-religious tendencies. The Arabs had no place, certainly no value, in his national imagination.

The same circumstances that mark the shift in Scholem's political sensitivity, the victory of the Nazis, led Hannah Arendt to dedicate her intellectual and political commitment to Zionism and thus to support the binational option. It was based on values similar to those that Scholem had expressed two decades earlier. Her reconsideration of Zionism in the 1940s advanced the same values and was grounded in the same intellectual context. But it was directed against the political-historical construction that was shaped and designed in those years by Scholem himself.[19]

As Richard Bernstein has correctly emphasized, Arendt hardly considered the theological dimensions of Zionism and ignored the religious components of Jewish identity.[20] In this, she differed from the other supporters of the binational option, many of whom were preoccupied with theological issues and considered Zionism as the precondition for a spiritual revival of the Jews. Arendt perceived Zionism as the authentic Jewish reaction to anti-Semitism and subordinated her reconsideration of Zionism to that principle. She rejected the national interpretation of the

concept of messianism and attempted to distinguish national activity
from theological discourse.[21] She did not pay attention to and was not
aware of the theological implications of Jewish settlement in the Holy
Land. She regarded the Jewish state as the realization of what Theodor
Herzl had called for in his book with that same title, and Herzl had tried
to overcome this theological aspect, as well. For her, as for Herzl, Zionism was not a "return," but a movement for shelter and dignity. But Zionist ideology and self-image was in practice extremely different, and
much of Zionist national identity was based upon the perception that
Jewish existence in Palestine was the return of the Jews to their homeland, conceived as the restoration of ancient sovereignty. This is the essence of the Zionist metanarrative, which continues to define the boundaries of Israeli-Jewish culture.

   This is not to say that Arendt's vocabulary was purely "political."
Her own political analysis, and especially her image of the Jew as pariah,
contains obviously theological concepts. Moreover, it rests on a framework and concepts similar to those developed by Scholem himself.[22]
Scholem and Arendt were very close in their views concerning Jewish
history and Jewish existence, yet they reached different conclusions.
They both criticized what they considered to be an "assimilationist" approach (the "parvenu," in Arendt's terms) and shared the belief that the
emancipation of the Jews entailed accepting responsibility and commitment to political activity within the framework of "peoplehood." They
both tried to define a "nonassimilationist" Jewish way of action and
looked for a "hidden" Jewish tradition, one that would direct a "popular revival" of the Jew toward modern reality. Zionism was regarded by
both Scholem and Arendt (by her, only temporarily) as the only authentic Jewish way.

   For both Scholem and Arendt, the Jewish heretic—the subversive figure who challenges tradition and authority—had a constitutive role in
the definition of what they regarded as "Jewish politics." The heretical
Jew was portrayed by both as the authentic nonreligious Jew and as the
one who conducts the historical process and conserves the genuine hidden tradition. According to Scholem's description, the Marranos, and
later the Sabbatian heretics, were those who carried on the dialectical
process of secularization and defined a "third road" between assimilation and orthodoxy.[23] The "heretics" kept the vital authentic element of
Judaism, the one that was also the origin of Cabalah, and transferred it
into an active political myth, which led first to the Enlightenment and

then to its dialectical fulfillment in Zionism. The *heretikon* had become the carrier of tradition, as well as the one who subverts it.

Arendt's pariah functioned in the same way that Marranos and messianic figures had done in Scholem's description of Jewish history. Arendt regarded the pariah as the only authentic representative of Jewish action in the modern world.[24] The pariah's struggle rests on Jewish experience, but she considered its implications to be global, since it challenges the whole system of imperialism and discrimination. Arendt accepted Zionism as a redemptive act and regarded it as the most significant pariah attitude in modern Jewish history.

The historical perception of Jewish history according to which Arendt defined this kind of action relied on Scholem's work. Arendt praised Scholem's *Major Trends in Jewish Mysticism* and especially emphasized the "Mystic's justification of action" against the passivity ascribed to the Jews. It was not Cabalah itself, but the idea of Cabalah that fascinated her, an idea she interpreted as a critique of dominant modern consciousness. Following Scholem, she considered Cabalah (Scholem's *Major Trends in Jewish Mysticism*) as a guide to the definition of the Jew in the modern world,[25] though the components of this Jew always remained very vague.

Arendt also accepted Scholem's description of Sabbatianism as a political movement and, following him, regarded Sabbatianism and Zionism as the only Jewish political movements in the whole period of exile.[26] In this way, she created a link between Zionism and Sabbatianism, even though she did not accept the attitude that considered Zionism as the dialectical fulfillment of Jewish history. Like Scholem, Arendt described Sabbatianism and Zionism as two stages of the secularization of Judaism: the first as a rupture that enabled secularization, a catastrophe that broke the authority of religion as a complete cultural system and the past / future organization of time. This was a precondition for the redefinition of Jewish identity, one that replaced what she considered to be "Jewish passivity."[27]

Yet the context in which these Jewish subversive figures functioned was different: for Scholem, they were the mediators in the dialectical evolution of Jewish history and led to its fulfillment in the Zionist context. The Jewish "return to history" did not involve taking a stance toward non-Jewish history. Arendt evaluated the position of pariahs as Jews, but as such, they were those who subverted European hegemonic values. She tried to define Jewish identity and what she called "Jewish politics" in secularized terms, based on the struggle against anti-Semitism. This was her criterion of political judgment.

Arendt's later criticism of Zionism was based on this framework. She attacked the Zionist Palestinian policy for being assimilationist instead of revolting against the values of dominant European culture. Zionism had become, in her words, "a movement of escape" and had adopted the same values that led to the centrality of anti-Semitism. She therefore emphasized the binational perspective and regarded—at least temporarily—equality between Jews and Arabs as one of the major values that Zionism should adopt.

The different paths of Arendt and Scholem concerning these issues can be illuminated by their attitudes toward Walter Benjamin and especially by their different interpretations of his *Theses on the Philosophy of History,* a text that he entrusted to Arendt and her husband. Their different uses of Benjamin's concept of history in relation to the question of Zionism can advance the discussion on binationalism further.

Scholem described Benjamin as a modern version of the former Jewish Sabbatians, a rebellious Marrano. His book dedicated to their friendship is similar in form and content to several monographs he dedicated to earlier Jewish heretics.[28] He therefore claimed that Benjamin's Marxism was only a superficial mask, and he tried to isolate what he described as his genuine Jewish-mystical thought in the same way he distinguished between the authentic Jewish and what he regarded as the external, Christian part of the Marranos and heretic Sabbatians. He interpreted it as relating exclusively to those lost to Jewish history. The practice of "remembrance," as developed by Benjamin, was directed by Scholem exclusively toward Jewish phenomena, or to what he considered to be so. By so doing, he actually denied the implications of Benjamin's concept of history, the perspective of the victims. He elaborated on several aspects of the sources of Benjamin's writings and illuminated some of his observations but at the same time coopted him into the national myth.

In a paragraph considering Nathan of Gaza's perception of Christ as a hidden messiah, he commented: "There is something impressive about the messianic élan of Nathan's refusal to acknowledge that the 'lost souls' of Jewish history were irrevocably lost. This idea of Nathan's was—actually or implicitly—only part of an even more radical conception: nothing and nobody is irrevocably lost, and everything will ultimately be saved and reinstated in holiness."[29]

The resemblance between this paragraph and Benjamin's position is obvious. Yet while in his writings from the 1920s Scholem used a similar approach in order to emphasize Palestinian rights, in his later phase, it was associated only with Jewish history. In many places in his writings, Scholem insisted on the superiority of the national vision over the universalist one and criticized Hermann Cohen for his interpretation of messianism as a universal vision.

Arendt, on the other hand, ignored Benjamin's theological perception and his notion of redemption. Instead, she tried to give him a political interpretation. She described Benjamin as neither a Zionist nor a Marxist and at the same time both,[30] a description that fitted her own position. In her critique of Zionism and her sensitivity to the Palestinian cause, she relied obviously and heavily on Benjamin's concept of history. She used Benjamin in order to criticize the Zionist context, which was based on an opposite (or at least different) interpretation of the same theological terms he used. She criticized Zionism for adopting the historical image of the victors and demanded that we "brush history against the grain" in the name of "the tradition of the oppressed."

Arendt therefore points to the relevance of Benjamin's concept of history as a critical tool of Zionist historical consciousness as designed and represented by, among others, Scholem himself.[31] She paved the way for using this critical attitude for the reexamination of Zionism as constituted in the same terminology and according to the same concepts. This complex directs us toward the application of Benjamin's sensitivity in the concrete realm, as a perspective that does not deny the notion of redemption but attempts to enlarge its boundaries.

The experience of the "peace process" according to the 1993 Oslo Accord between Israel and the Palestinians led many observers, the most prominent among them being Edward Said, to the conclusion that a binational state is the only option for a compromise based on the fulfillment of Palestinian rights. That is because the process led to a limited Palestinian autonomy in part of the occupied territories and left the various restrictions on the Palestinian population. As I already claimed, it seems that in the present context, even the two-state solution demands a binational position.

In order to give this process meaning, it is necessary to examine the structure of the cultural discourse and the implications of the position designed by Scholem. To do this, we cannot ignore the theological aspects that define the limits of the discourse and the historical perception. Rather, we should give them a different meaning. By accepting Scholem's concepts uncritically, Arendt could not consider these theological aspects. Yet they are crucial for a different definition of Jewish existence in a way that enables us to evaluate the Palestinian right of self-determination and of coexistence based on equality. It is a precondition for the normalization of Jewish existence in the Middle East. Therefore, the concept of binationalism, as was formulated by Arendt through her critical observations, is a precondition to secularization of the state and for a different definition of the Jewish existence in Palestine.

Arendt's distinction between "state" and "nationhood" is of great importance in this case. It reminds us that the definition of Israel as the state of the Jewish people excludes the Palestinian minority and maintains their inferior status. It shows that the terms of the debate in Israel must be over the separation of national identity from the image of the state in order to establish it as the state of all its citizens.[32] The definition of the state as a Jewish state and its acceptance as the triumphal conclusion of Jewish history prevent any solution based on the principles of equality and partnership. In order to promote such an attitude, despite its many difficulties, it is necessary to define Jewish collective identity in Palestine apart from the theological-messianic myth.

We still do not have satisfactory answers concerning the political issues, and the questions generated by the concept of binationalism are indeed multileveled and complicated. But the concept of binationalism creates a new discursive framework. To keep our critical thinking and to define the context of responsibility are not satisfactory political actions, only a point of departure. We must develop a different concept of history in which the Palestinian right of self-determination will be part of Jewish consciousness, a concept of history that could be recognized and accepted by Palestinians.

Hannah Arendt, the Early "Post-Zionist"

Moshe Zimmermann

Hannah Arendt did not belong to the establishment of prominent Zionist thinkers, nor did she belong to the very exclusive group of leading Zionist politicians. She also claimed that she became a Zionist "only because of Hitler, of course" (which is incorrect).[1] In the biographies of Hannah Arendt, the Zionist chapter is therefore generally rather marginal, though her reflections on the Jewish question, including Zionism, "preceded her entry into world politics" and should thus be considered as a key to the understanding of her work in general.[2] Moreover, she deserves attention on the part of historians of Zionism on two grounds: (1) Hannah Arendt had excellent insights concerning Zionism, insights that provide us with a good answer as to the origins of some of the misconceptions or aberrations of Zionism. (2) Israel is a society skeptical about "new" trends in historical interpretation. Hannah Arendt's writings about Zionism provide so-called post-Zionists with good arguments, or at least with a wonderful alibi. Quoting Hannah Arendt on Zionism can provide a historian with the needed safe haven, because beyond her sharp, radical criticism there was deep conviction, expressed in 1963, that "I am not against Israel on principle," that a catastrophe for Israel "would be perhaps the final catastrophe for the whole Jewish people," and, as late as October 1967, that "any real catastrophe in Israel would affect me more deeply than almost anything else."[3] And yet, no Israeli pupil's syllabus mentions Hannah Arendt. She is far from belonging to the Zionist "Hall of Fame," and despite her open embrace of

Zionism in principle, her critical attitude goes far beyond what is tolerated by Israeli educators.

THE DEATH OF ZIONISM

An excellent example of a quasi-post-Zionist statement made by Hannah Arendt is provided in a letter (dated January 9, 1957) to Kurt Blumenfeld, the well-known leader of German Zionism until Hitler's rise to power in 1933 and her master in matters of Zionism, who practically recruited her to the movement in the late 1920s:[4] "at the present moment the Zionist movement is dead. It decayed partly because of victory (creation of the state, which was the goal) and partly because of the fundamental change in the nature of the Jewish question after Hitler. There is no European Jewry any more, maybe forever. . . . It seems to me that at the present moment there is no chance for a renaissance of Zionism."

This was a clear verdict, passed some forty years ago. Interestingly enough, what seemed to be clear to Hannah Arendt in 1957 is still unacceptable to many adherents of Zionism: Zionism, as originally and traditionally perceived by the European Zionists, could not survive the crises it underwent in the 1940s and 1950s.

Of the two alternative explanations for the decay of Zionism provided by Hannah Arendt in her letter to Blumenfeld—the fact that the goal was achieved (i.e. the creation of the Zionist state) and the fundamental change in the nature of "the Jewish question" confronting Zionism—the latter undoubtedly carries more weight. The Jewish question, the *Judenfrage,* at the root of Zionism underwent such a radical metamorphosis that the proposed Zionist solution to the old problem lost much of its relevance, even before 1948.

The combination of Jewish preference for the United States, where most Jewish emigrants from Europe had already settled since 1881, the Holocaust, which eliminated the main reservoir of Zionist immigration, and the existence of an "iron curtain" changed the nature of the *Judenfrage* so radically that after 1946 the Zionist movement was no longer a relevant answer—if it ever was one. Hannah Arendt was indeed a strong believer in a Eurocentric Zionism. If one adds yet another, later element to the three already mentioned, the influx of non-European Jews into Israel since 1948, one can understand why the whole enterprise seemed doomed to her by 1957.

In her article "Krise des Zionismus," written in 1942—a short time after the Biltmore conference that defined the creation of a Jewish state

(commonwealth) as the aim of Zionism and after she came to the conclusion that "a third of [the Jewish people] is very near its total extermination"—Arendt was clear that "The crisis of Zionism revolves around
the fact that Herzl's concept needs an immediate revision." [5] Yet she
needed about fifteen years more in order to find out that the crisis was
so severe that it could not be overcome: Not only were approximately
six million European Jews lost, but half of Israeli society was of non-
European, "Oriental" origin. Zionism, already destined for failure in
1942, had little chance after 1948. This does not necessarily mean a retrospective value judgment concerning the quality of European versus
Oriental Jewry. It should be considered a factual statement only, to be
evaluated—for better or for worse—by the reader of these quotations
years after they were written.

ANTI-SEMITISM AND ZIONISM

According to Arendt, the basic problem of Zionism is not its deviation
from the Herzlian vision, but Herzlian Zionism itself. Herzl "did not realize that the country he dreamt of [inspired by German sources] did not
exist . . . even if there had been a country without a people." [6] From the
start, therefore, she believed in and fought for an alternative Zionism in
the spirit of Bernard Lazare. In principle, she agreed with Herzl that
Zionism was the only attempt to encounter anti-Semitism politically, yet
she not only snubbed Herzl's Zionism, calling it a "transportation enterprise," [7] she also did not accept his basic assumptions concerning the nature of anti-Semitism or the way to dispose of it through emigration. For
her, "anti-Semitism was discredited thanks to Hitler," not because of Zionism's success,[8] and it was not to be fought by joining hands with anti-
Semites in Europe in order to implement the Zionist solution. Nor did
she accept Herzl's conception of the Jewish state as *the* answer per se to
anti-Semitism, which is why she also criticized Weizmann for his remark
about Israel being the answer to anti-Semitism.[9] As early as 1942, it was
clear to Hannah Arendt that every Jew must know "he is not safe from
anti-Semites even in Palestine." [10] Of course, in 1942, this referred to the
lucky victory of Montgomery over Rommel—but later this sentence became relevant within a new context.

We know that Zionism in Palestine / Israel could not and *did not* solve
the problem of anti-Semitism, and indeed we can see today that Zionism only helped the center of anti-Semitism to shift from Europe to the
Middle East. Before World War II, Europe was the stronghold of anti-

Semitism. Today, it is the Arab world surrounding Israel. Zionism thus became a "transportation enterprise" for anti-Semitism as well, and not only because the Europeans learned a lesson from history and tried to eliminate this dubious merchandise. Arab anti-Semitism, nearly nonexistent before Zionist migration to Palestine, is today—thanks to the Zionist challenge—the most dangerous brand of anti-Semitism, joining forces, of course, with anti-Semitism in other countries, thus turning Diaspora Jews into hostages of the Arab-Israeli conflict, and not necessarily the victims of local animosity.

As Zionism demonstrated its inability actually to eliminate anti-Semitism, it was cynical enough to turn this failure into an instrument of stabilizing the Zionist belief in "the eternal and ubiquitous enemy" and in its claim as the only solution of the "Jewish question." This again called for Arendt's criticism. As early as 1941, she warned against those "in our own camp" who believe "that we were always only the victims" because it is "untrue that we were always and everywhere only the innocent persecuted ones." [11] The belief in eternal and ubiquitous anti-Semitism, in the "basic mistrust of all other nations," which she defined as a potential danger in 1946–47 ("if the whole world is ultimately against us," she argued, "then we are lost"), indeed became the safe excuse for so many Zionists in confronting the problems they themselves had helped to create.[12] The belief that "the whole world is against oneself and this is the proof of the dumbness of the world"[13] is, of course, very tempting for a system that ignores any criticism against it in principle. Moreover, it seems to be a crushing argument in favor of Jewish existence in an Israel allegedly able to defend itself as the alternative to "defenseless" Diaspora vulnerability. This was also the idea behind the Eichmann trial—as Hannah Arendt told Jaspers before the trial started: "there'll be an effort to show Israeli youth . . . that Jews who aren't Israelis will wind up in situations where they'll let themselves be slaughtered like sheep." [14] When the trial started, she told her husband of her conviction that Gideon Hausner and David Ben-Gurion wanted the Israelis to believe "that the murder of Jews is just the normal occupation of non-Jews." [15] Her public declaration was slightly more moderate: They (Ben-Gurion and company) wanted to "convince them that only in Israel could a Jew be safe and live an honorable life." [16] As she wrote to her husband while on a visit to Israel, she tried to refrain from "burning her mouth" with public utterances.

Against this background, Hannah Arendt's observation in 1945 seems accurate and prophetic: "Zionists fled into a doctrine of eternal anti-Semitism," according to which every Gentile living with Jews must become "a conscious or subconscious Jew-hater," thus denying "the Jewish part of responsibility for existing conditions" (especially in Palestine), evading a thorough examination of Zionism's theory of anti-Semitism, and entering a phase of "racist chauvinism" that does not differ "from other master race theories," or so she says in her 1948 article "Save the Jewish Homeland." [17] The paradox is that anti-Semitism was so dear to Zionist philosophy that it used it even in a way that undermined Herzl's basic belief that the problem of anti-Semitism could be solved by the creation of the Jewish homeland / state: "general Gentile hostility, a phenomenon that Herzl thought was directed only at Galut [Diaspora] Jewry . . . is now assumed by Zionists to be an unalterable, eternal fact of Jewish history that repeats itself . . . even in Palestine." [18]

IMPERIALISM AND ZIONISM

The Herzlian fixation on an alliance with imperialism instead of with oppressed and discriminated groups and peoples was Zionism's "original sin." This is at least one reason why Arendt preferred Bernard Lazare to Theodor Herzl. This unholy alliance went on long after Herzl: the unfounded Zionist boasting about *Komemiut* (independence and self-reliance) revealed itself only as a facade for Zionism's growing dependence on imperial powers between World War I and 1947 or 1956, and perhaps until 1989, the end of the Cold War. Arendt's dissatisfaction with the "juristic fiction" of the Balfour Declaration and the mandate system [19] was consistent and remained relevant in principle after May 14, 1948, as well.

There were further fatal aberrations. Very early, Hannah Arendt was aware that Zionism, eager for or at least oriented toward confrontation with the Arabs, was going to *create* the conflict, a conflict that would undermine Zionism itself. In "Zionism Reconsidered," submitted to *Commentary* in 1944 and subsequently rejected, Hannah Arendt blamed the Zionists in a manner hinting at an early "post-Zionism" for doing their best to create that insoluble "tragic conflict." [20] Beginning in 1936, the Zionists in Palestine had started an opportunistic policy in which "the smaller injustice (against Palestinian Arabs) should be accepted in favor of a 'higher Justice' towards the Jews," she wrote in August 1944. [21] Even the best Zionists (i.e. the socialists) "established themselves on the moon" instead of in the Near East, [22] thus allowing the inevitable catastrophe to occur. In so doing, they became coresponsible for those terrorist measures taken by the radical right (the slaughter of approximately one hundred and fifty civilians in the Arab village of Deir Jassin in April 1948, or the attack on Arab workers in the Haifa refineries) that served to deepen the gap between Jews and Arabs, making reconciliation impossible. "The present [leftist] executive of the Jewish Agency . . . have by now amply demonstrated that they are either unwilling or incapable of preventing the terrorists from making political decisions for the whole Yishuv," she said in 1948 in a sentence that may sum up the history of Zionism since 1967, no less than the history of the Yishuv, the Jewish settlement in Palestine, up to 1948.[23]

After 1948, this criticism remained true not only with regard to "the Arab enemy" outside Israel, but also concerning the Arab citizens of the state of Israel, those who did not flee during the war. "They handle the Arabs who did not leave the country in such a manner, that this alone suffices to mobilize the whole world against [Israel]."[24] This is an important observation: Zionism first needed an enemy in order to justify its existence and policies. Constructing the outside enemy (the Arab world) then led to the next construct, that of "the enemy from within," the alleged "fifth column." The negative repercussions worldwide to Israel's discriminatory policy toward its Arabs were perceived in Israel as a confirmation of the Goyim's intrinsic, everlasting hatred of the Jews / Israel so essential to Zionism. In its own way, the Eichmann trial, according to Arendt, later served Israel in combining this "eternal anti-Semitism" with the "insoluble conflict" with the Arabs. Hannah Arendt rightly suspected the organizers of the "Show-trial" of making an effort to show "that the Arabs were hand in glove with the Nazis,"[25] which put infinite blame on the Arabs.

CHAUVINISM AND ZIONISM

The European experience taught Hannah Arendt to doubt minority agreements of any kind in the search for a solution to the Middle East problem and, above all, to doubt the national state, with its basis in Romantic nationalism of central European origin.[26] Zionism, Hannah Arendt realized, had developed exactly along these frightening lines. As early as 1945, she had reached the conclusion that Zionism, with its beginnings as a social-revolutionary movement, "a serious attempt at a new social order," the one element of Zionism which she wholeheartedly supported, had turned into a nationalistic, chauvinistic movement instead, a repetition of the negative experience of European nations, an experience that should have taught the Jewish nation a better lesson.[27] Arendt believed in an alternative solution without relinquishing the idea of a national home. She looked for "a political form for a Jewish home-land that would transcend the European conflict between the 'nation' and the 'modern state.'"[28] This was a logical conclusion reached by an expert on the history of ideologies and nationalism, a conclusion that came too early for postwar Zionists and that is still unacceptable to many Israelis at the beginning of the twenty-first century.

An observation on the basic beliefs of Zionism as they developed to-ward 1948 reveals the potential dead ends toward which Zionist policy was heading. The Biltmore conference in 1942 not only paved the way for the creation of a state, Arendt claimed. Zionism was also headed to a decadent warriors' state,[29] not unprecedented in European history: "And even if the Jews were to win the war" of independence, the "growth of a Jewish culture would cease to be the concern of the whole people; social experiments would have to be discarded as impractical luxuries; political thought would center around military strategy . . . the Palestin-ian Jews would degenerate into one of those small warrior tribes about whose possibilities and importance history has amply informed us since the days of Sparta."

This warning expressed in 1948 was far from being an overstatement, and not just from the point of view of so-called post-Zionists of the 1990s. The psychological outcome was indeed, by necessity, the para-dox so characteristic of Jewish-Israeli society after 1948: "Everyone is afraid of the war *and* is a warmonger."[30]

Hannah Arendt's criticism of the Israeli approach to the Arab world sought to remain constructive, not defeatist. "Can the Jewish-Arab question be solved?" she asked in December 1943.[31] Her affirmative an-swer was to be found in the creation of a federation in the Near East or around the Mediterranean (or a British commonwealth), starting with a federal structure for Palestine itself.[32] This was not only criticism of Zi-onist prospects in 1943, of the national state and minority rights, or, later, of the deliberations leading to the creation of the state of Israel, which she considered a "pseudo sovereignty,"[33] but also is the most plausible proposal to be implemented, even today, as the myth of the sovereign state loses its hold. Arendt was already cognizant of the dan-ger of Balkanization in 1950, as the title of her essay "Federation or Bal-kanization?" shows, having the pre–World War I or post–World War II situation in mind, not knowing of course how relevant this term would become again toward the end of the twentieth century.[34]

Taking into account Hannah Arendt's dislike of aggressive, anti-Arab Zionism, one may be bewildered by the enthusiasm she expressed during World War II for the creation of a "Jewish army."[35] But the contradiction is not a real one: She pleaded for a Jewish army fighting in the war side-by-side with other armies against the Nazi army in order, first, to "substitute the law of extermination . . . with the law of fighting" for a people "a third of which is very near its total extermination,"[36] and, second, to secure the Jews, or Zionism, a place at the conference table after the war, the status of a nation with equal rights. It was a short-range, emergency policy, no more. What she never had in mind was a Jewish army prepared to fight against the Arabs. In her eyes, the lack of an army in 1942 in the face of the Germans was suicide, not the lack of an army to face the Arabs.

RIGHT-WING RADICALISM AND ZIONISM

Arendt's opposition to Jewish suicide is also reflected in her outright opposition to the militant ideas of the "Bergson group"—the American-Jewish supporters of the Yishuv dissidents ("Faschisten eines unterdrückten Volkes") that long before the Hamas cherished the idea of creating suicide squads—Jewish suicide squads.[37] Arendt's attitude toward the Bergson group and its heirs does not leave much room for doubt: She was suspicious of the extreme Zionist right early enough and emphatically cautioned against it: "The general mood of the country . . . has been such, that terrorism and the growth of totalitarian methods are . . . secretly applauded."[38] When writing this in 1948, Arendt had in mind a very clear picture of the term "totalitarianism."

Arendt's criticism of the extreme right was directed not only against the Peter Bergson–Hillel Kook group, but also against Menachem Begin, the political leader of Israel's right-wing revisionist party Herut. The open letter in the New York Times of December 4, 1948, that she helped formulate expresses her fear explicitly: This letter, signed among others by Albert Einstein, a potential candidate for presidency of the state of Israel, says clearly: The Herut party is "closely akin in its organization, methods, political philosophy and social appeal, to the Nazi and Fascist parties."[39]

But the similarities between the worst enemies of the Jews and Zionism do not—according to Arendt—concern the extreme Zionist right alone. In Eichmann in Jerusalem she referred to the irony of the prose-

cution—Gideon Hausner, Ben-Gurion's "errand boy," denouncing "the
infamous Nuremberg laws" that forbade German-Jewish intermarriage
in Nazi Germany in 1935, while at the same time the state of Israel and
its population "seemed agreed upon the desirability of having a law
which prohibits intermarriage."[40] Even if she exaggerated in 1963, she
was certainly anticipating the incredible call in Israeli papers in 1981 of
Rabbi Kahane to impose a Jewish version of the Nuremberg laws. Incidentally, Hannah Arendt's remark that Eichmann's notion of Judaism
was based on his reading of Jewish-Zionist authors is also far from flat-
tering to Zionism.[41]

Hannah Arendt did not have to wait until 1963 or 1977 to repeatedly
stress the fact that the foundations of Zionism were prone from the start
to a development in the direction of revisionism.[42] Her warnings go
back to the 1940s, when she wrote that the ideological roots of nationalistic revisionism were to be found at the heart of classical Zionism,
starting with Herzl and his contemporaries. She wouldn't have been surprised by the 1977 *Mahapach* (landslide), which occurred two years after she died, or by Benjamin Netanyahu's brand of Zionism.

THE HOLOCAUST *(SHOAH)* AND ZIONISM

A special topic, at the heart of Zionism since the end of World War II,
is the Shoah. Its place in collective Israeli memory became more and
more important as time passed and the catastrophic events became
history. Here again, Hannah Arendt had already criticized the relationship between the Shoah and Zionism while this relationship was only *in
nascendi*.

Perhaps the most pertinent observation about this connection concerns Zionism's retrospective claim of farsightedness, as if Zionists
were the only group within Judaism to predict the coming of the Holocaust. Arendt's assessment of this presumptuous claim is just as valid today as it was more than fifty years ago and points to the logical flaw of
Zionism's argument:

> Zionists occasionally boast of their foresight. Compared with the earthquake
> that has shaken the world in our time, those predictions read like prophecies
> of a storm in a teacup. The fierce outburst of popular hatred which Zionism
> predicted, and which fitted well with its general distrust of the peoples and
> over-confidence in Governments, did not take place. Rather . . . it was re-
> placed by concerted government action, which proved infinitely more detri-
> mental than any popular outburst of Jew-hatred had ever been.[43]

What follows from this assessment was articulated by Hannah Arendt only indirectly. This retrospective boast of foresight camouflaged the real miscalculation of Zionism: The Shoah eliminated the population that was the raison d'être of Zionism, thus forcing the Zionist movement either to give up or to invent new goals without admitting it. That "the European element was considerably pushed back"[44] was clear in the early 1960s, and not only to Arendt. Its profound influence on the nature of Zionism, however, became apparent only after 1977.

There are two further aspects of the Shoah-Israel connection that attracted Arendt's criticism. The first was the identification of heroism (*Gevura*) and resistance to Nazism during the Holocaust with Zionism—a central pillar of Israeli identity.[45] Yad Vashem, the Holocaust memorial and the central institution assigned by law to commemorate the Holocaust, distinguished between *Shoa* and *Gevura,* thus associating Diaspora tradition and slaughter on the one hand and *Gevura* and Zionism on the other. Before and after the Eichmann trial, the role of non-Zionist participation in the arena of *Gevura* was suppressed in public discourse in order to promote the heroic self-image of Zionism. The second aspect of criticism was the attempt to hold both ends of the rope: inconsistently looking at the whole of Jewish history as a series of catastrophes (including the Holocaust), but at the same time adhering to the slogan of the uniqueness of the Shoah.[46] Arendt, as we know, never accepted the Zionist interpretation of Jewish history as an endless *Leidensgeschichte,* a history of suffering, with the Holocaust as yet another, albeit extreme, event within it.

DIASPORA AND ISRAEL

For Zionism, the Shoah only accentuated a problem it attempted to solve in its own monopolistic way—the problem of the Jewish Diaspora, the *Galut.* Zionism as interpreted by Ben-Gurion and even more by Begin was reduced to the total repatriation of Jews into Israel, the eventual disappearance of the Jewish Diaspora. The *modus vivendi* between Israel and the Diaspora was thus to be only a temporary, utilitarian one. Arendt argued differently. As long as there was a European Jewry, she believed, a "Palestinian policy must be derived from a general policy of European Jewry, and not the other way around, that Palestinian policy must decide general Jewish policy."[47] With the destruction of European Jewry, the question of primacy, of European versus Palestinian Jewry, was replaced by the question of cooperation with other diasporas versus isolation.[48] For Hannah Arendt, it became clear as early as 1944: "Zionists shut themselves off from the destiny of the Jews all over the world." Palestinocentric Zionism meant friction, isolation ("crazy isolationism") of the "Israeli diaspora [sic]," not the unity of the Jewish people.[49] This observation was to remain valid for the following years, and its dramatic confirmation was in evidence more than fifty years later, when the adherents of what is today called Zionism, the majority of the Israeli Jews and their parliamentary representatives, risked a schism between Israeli and Diaspora Jewry by introducing a "conversion law," a law based on religious orthodoxy that will decide who is not a Jew in Israel, a step certain to alienate liberal Judaism in the Diaspora.

ASSIMILATION AND ZIONISM

An additional Zionist myth questioned by Hannah Arendt concerned the heart of Jewish history—the myth of Zionism as an alternative, the only alternative, to assimilation. That she was critical of the German-Jewish politics of assimilation was already evident before 1933, when she wrote the Rahel Varnhagen biography.[50] But there is an interesting twist in her argument. She considered Zionism to be the real but legitimate assimilation: "The hollow word-struggles between Zionism and assimilationism have completely distorted the simple fact that the Zionists, in a sense, were the only ones who sincerely wanted assimilation, namely 'normalization' of the people ('to be a people like all other peoples') whereas the assimilationists wanted the Jewish people to retain their unique position."[51] She turned this myth on its head: Zionism is the real assimilation, whereas Diaspora is anti-assimilation, or dissimilation, a term she did not use. She explained this change of heart in favor of Jewish assimilation when practiced by Zionism in a private letter to her friend Karl Jaspers: "Palestine . . . represents the only logically consistent effort at assimilation." What is so attractive and consistent in this effort is not that it is an attempt at a collective, rather than individual, assimilation while retaining a collective Jewish identity, or the admitted departure from her own "critique [that] was politically naive as to what it was criticizing,"[52] but the key concept "normality." "The Zionists are the only people," she told Jaspers two years following the publication of "Zionism Reconsidered," "who no longer believe in the idea of the chosen people."[53] The assimilation of the European or German Jews was not a genuine one because they did not relinquish the idea of their being the chosen people, "the salt of the earth."[54] This may also explain her consequent critique of Israeli Zionism (after 1967), which positioned the ideology of "the chosen people" at the forefront.

ISRAEL AS THE "NEW GHETTO"

Moreover, not only was the Diaspora less assimilationist than Zionism, but the real ghetto, the "new Ghetto"—entirely different from the one described by Herzl—had moved from Europe to Israel.

Judging from the hindsight of 1998, any observer of the history of Zionism must refer to the origins and position of religious Zionism. After all, Zionism was a movement alienating itself from traditional Jewish religiosity, "a negation of Galut," in its own words. What, then, brought about the shift in the Zionist approach to religion, and when did this shift occur? Was it in 1977, when Begin formed his government, together with all the religious Jewish parties? Was it following the "liberation" of the West Bank in 1967, or was it even earlier? Hannah Arendt warned against the fatal combination of "ultra-nationalism, religious mysticism and a propaganda of racial superiority" as early as 1948.[55] She never underestimated the power of religion or orthodoxy in Israel, even when secularization seemed to be triumphant. An observation she made in 1955 concerns the "internal terror of orthodoxy": To her mind, the surprising and crucial fact was then, as it is today, "that nobody really is against it, so that the black gang with lust for power becomes ever more impertinent."[56] She did not wait until after 1977 to pass this judgment. Twenty years before Rabbi Kahane proposed his law against "mixed" marriages, Arendt defined the nature of the discussion on this very topic as revolving solely around the "racial question."[57] The strengthening of orthodoxy and the combination of religion and nationalism from 1967 or 1977 on only confirmed Arendt's earlier fears.

The failure to practice "normal" assimilation in Israel paradoxically led to the creation of a Diaspora-like Jewish existence: a new Jewish ghetto in the national homeland itself. In reply to a question by Hannah Arendt, Kurt Blumenfeld said: "How does the tendency toward ghettoization stand? . . . [It is] a question I asked as an early Zionist."[58] Hannah Arendt wholeheartedly agreed: "Politically it is even more hopeless than I thought," she wrote to Blücher, her husband, in 1955, "the *Galut und* ghetto mentality in full bloom."[59] This impression was even stronger when she covered Eichmann's trial less than a decade later: "the ghetto mentality with tanks and military parades."[60]

Arendt was accused of anti-Zionism.[61] This accusation depends, however, on the definition of Zionism. As early as 1946, she explained, "I really am afraid for Palestine" and expressed her fear of the "suicidal attitudes" there.[62] The relevant historical parallel was indeed frightening. As she wrote in 1946, "the parallels [of Herzlian Zionism] with the Sabbatai Zevi episode," the seventeenth-century Jewish messianic movement, "have become terribly close."[63]

She was very much against a belligerent Zionism, which she considered suicidal, but in the face of the reigning myth of heroism, this attitude held by her, as well as by others, meant defeatism, betrayal, anti-Zionism. The fact that she was also critical of the Arab stand and attitude in the conflict and that she was an admirer of a movement she considered "not merely colonization but a serious attempt at a new social order" was often ignored.[64] For her, the outstanding achievements of Zionism were the kibbutz and the Hebrew University. "These two institutions . . . inspired the non-nationalist, anti-chauvinist trend and opposition in [sic!] Zionism. The University was supposed to represent the universalism of Judaism . . . [and the kibbutzim] to build a new type of society . . . within the highest tradition of Judaism."[65] But this very admiration of facets of Zionism that proved to be either marginal or waning led her to even greater frustration. Many admirers of Israel, even after the rise of the Likud party to power in 1977, did not see that the kibbutz and its myth were totally destroyed. Arendt did see it coming more than twenty years earlier when she asserted: "the *kibbutzim* play no role whatsoever anymore"[66] and even thirty years earlier when she remarked that "the *kibbutzim* have offered no serious obstacle to terrorism [meaning Irgun, etc.]."[67] Neither did the Hebrew University offer an obstacle to Zionist aberrations.

There still is no room for "post-Zionists" like Hannah Arendt in a pupils' syllabus in Israel. On the evidence, it's clear why—and also why there should be.

Hannah Arendt's Zionism?

Richard J. Bernstein

Hannah Arendt never seriously considered *Aliyah,* "going up," the term used for emigration to Palestine / Israel, not before she fled Germany in 1933, not during her years in Paris when she worked for Youth Aliyah, and not when she finally escaped from Europe in 1941. In the early 1940s, she called for the formation of a Jewish army to fight the Nazis. She wrote passionately about her vision of a Jewish homeland in Palestine. But along with Judah Magnes, she actively opposed the founding of a Jewish nation-state. Indeed, if Hannah Arendt's political recommendations had been followed, the state of Israel might never have been founded. For many persons, these facts about Hannah Arendt—that she never considered *Aliyah* and that she actively opposed the founding of the state of Israel—are all that need to be said about Arendt's alleged Zionism. I believe that this would be a serious mistake, and I hope to show why in this paper.

There are a variety of ways of approaching the question of Arendt and Zionism. It is important to get the historical record straight: to examine carefully what she did (and did not do) and what she said (and did not say), and to follow carefully the events to which she was responding. To ask, in an unqualified manner, "Was Hannah Arendt ever a Zionist and when?" obscures basic issues. We need to make more discriminating judgments. We need to clarify what precisely attracted her to Zionism (especially which version of Zionism, and when this occurred), as well as what repelled her about Zionist ideology and became the target of her stinging critique.[1] In this paper, however, I want to frame my discussion by asking what, if anything, we might still learn from Arendt. What is there that might still be relevant to our contemporary situation and assessment of Zionism? When I speak of "our" in this context, I mean those who are presently citizens of Israel (Jews and non-Jews) and those living outside of the state of Israel—especially those who still identify themselves with the Jewish people. If I had to pick an epigraph for my presentation, it would be taken from Arendt herself. In 1948, responding to a harsh attack by Ben Halpern, who accused her of being a "collaborationist," she declared that "we deal in politics only with warnings and not with prophecies" (*JP*, 238). It is her warnings that most concern me, although, unfortunately, she was all too prophetic about some of the dangers that have plagued—and continue to plague—the state of Israel.

In order to set the context for my exploration, I do, however, want to remind you of some of the essential facts of her life. By her own admission, Arendt grew up in a German home where the word "Jew" was scarcely mentioned. As a precocious, talented German secular Jewess, her intellectual passion was for German poetry, language, and philosophy, as well as for Christian thinkers such as Kierkegaard and St. Augustine. She tells us that as a young girl she found the Jewish question "boring." As a university student, she had no real interest in Zionism. She was, however, extremely impressed when she first met Kurt Blumenfeld in the 1920s. They became lifelong friends, although this friendship became strained, especially after the Eichmann trial. During the late 1920s, when the Nazis were rapidly gaining power—a time when Arendt started working on her biography of Rahel Varnhagen—her interest in Jewish issues began to develop. She was especially interested in studying the ominous forms of European *political* ideological anti-Semitism that originated during the last decades of the nineteenth century—anti-Semitic political movements that influenced the character of twentieth-century anti-Semitism and Nazi ideology. She never joined the German Zionist movement. Arendt never really was a "joiner." She was always fiercely independent. But she had many close friends who were Zionists. Consequently, in 1933, when she was asked to do some illegal work by the German Zionists—to collect and copy anti-Semitic propaganda from the Prussian State Library, she readily agreed. She was, however, apprehended, arrested, interrogated, and finally released after eight days without ever divulging what she had been doing. Arendt tells the story of her interrogation and release with humor. But if she had not been so lucky, if she had encountered a less sympathetic interrogating officer, the consequences might have been disastrous. Shortly after her release, she quickly fled from Germany illegally with her mother. At the time, Arendt was twenty-seven. From 1933 until she became a naturalized U.S. citizen in 1951, she was officially a "stateless person." Years later, looking back to the events of 1933, she said:

> I realized what I then expressed time and again in the sentence: If one is attacked as a Jew, one must defend oneself as a Jew. Not as a German, not as a world-citizen, not as an upholder of the Rights of Man, or whatever. But: What can I specifically do as a Jew? Second, it was now my clear intention to work with an organization. For the first time. To work with the Zionists. They were the only ones who were ready. . . . Belonging to Judaism had become my own problem, and my problem was political. Purely political! I wanted to go into practical work, exclusively and only Jewish work. With this in mind I then looked for work in France. (*EU*, 11–12)

For the twenty-year period after she left Germany, Arendt worked almost exclusively for Jewish and Zionist organizations. Her first visit to Palestine took place in 1935, when she escorted a group of Youth Aliyah trainees. And in the first decade of her life in New York, she wrote primarily about Jewish and Zionist questions. She felt that Kurt Blumenfeld and Heinrich Blücher, her second husband, were her mentors in learning about politics and history. In a letter to another mentor, Karl Jaspers, dated January 29, 1946, she wrote: "My literary existence . . . has two major roots: First, thanks to my husband, I have learned to think politically and see historically; and, second, I have refused to abandon the Jewish question as the focal point of my historical and political thinking" (*HAKJ*, 31).

But when she was a philosophy student at Marburg and Heidelberg in the 1920s, she had virtually no interest in politics and history. This interest developed only when—as she put it—she was hit over the head by History. We can begin to understand the context for Arendt's original attraction to Zionism. In her own intellectual and personal journey, she came to the conclusion that the great failure of the Jewish people in the modern age was a political one. She argued that the Jewish people lacked political experience and failed to understand the political transformations that were taking place throughout Europe that were drawing them into the very storm center of events. Consequently, Jews were completely unprepared to respond to the extraordinary political events.

It was politics, and politics alone, that provided any real hope for a solution to the Jewish question. For Arendt, this meant fighting for the

rights of Jews to live as Jews and opposing political anti-Semitism wherever it existed. She sharply criticized the tendencies of Jewish parvenus
who sought to avoid politics and tried to win social privileges for themselves. Although thoroughly secular in her outlook, Arendt was scorn-
ful and contemptuous of those "exceptional Jews" who thought that Jewish emancipation meant assimilation. The "logic" of active assimilation
meant appropriating and internalizing the very anti-Semitism directed
against Jews. Arendt argued that this confusion of emancipation with assimilation was self-deceitful, hypocritical, and ultimately self-defeating.

In these respects—in her critique of Jewish assimilation and her insistence on a political solution to the Jewish question—Arendt shared a
common platform with the Zionists. Her great hero, however, was not
Theodor Herzl, but a French Jew, Bernard Lazare. It was her allegiance
to Lazare (and to Blumenfeld) that shaped her orientation toward Zionism. For Arendt, Lazare was an exemplar of what he characterized as
"the conscious pariah." The conscious pariah is the independent outsider who takes responsibility for the pariah status thrust upon him,
who becomes a rebel and a "champion of an oppressed people. His fight
for freedom is part and parcel of that which all the down-trodden of Europe must needs wage to achieve national and social liberation" (*JP,* 76).
Like Lazare, Arendt was deeply skeptical of the role that European Jewish leaders were playing in their communities. In order to protect their
uneasy and unstable social status, to secure the privileges that they had
been granted, they discouraged grassroots political activity. Lazare's
experience of French politics—especially during the Dreyfus Affair—
had taught him that "whenever the enemy seeks control, he makes a
point of using some oppressed element of the population as his lackeys
and henchmen, rewarding them with special privileges, as a kind of sop"
(*JP,* 77).

This is a lesson that Arendt never forgot. For Lazare, unlike for Herzl,
"the territorial question was secondary—a mere outcome of the primary demand that 'the Jews should be emancipated as a people and in
the form of a nation'" (*JP,* 128). Like Lazare, Arendt emphasized the
need for Jews to join in coalition with the downtrodden people in order
to fight for their political freedom. And like Lazare, Arendt never conceived of a Jewish homeland as an exclusive alternative to Jews gaining their rights as Jews in their own European communities. Although
Arendt expressed her admiration for Herzl's dedication to the Zionist
movement, she was extremely critical of his "top-down" idea of political
alliances, his mistrust of the Jewish populace, and his belief that "it is

the anti-Semites who will be our staunchest friends, and the anti-Semitic countries which will be our allies" (*JP,* 128 n. 10).

During the time when Arendt most identified with the Zionists, then, it was not because of any deep spiritual or emotional attachment to Zionism. She never was part of a Zionist youth movement, and she was always critical of all ideologies. She allied herself with the Zionists primarily because of her conviction that the Jews must fight for their political rights as Jews.

There is a subtle dialectical relation between Arendt's hopes for a Jewish politics and her more general understanding of those islands of political freedom that arise in the rare and fragile moments when the "lost treasure" of the revolutionary spirit bursts forth. Politics, as Arendt came to understand it, arises spontaneously when a people create their own public spaces. Politics requires equality—what the Greeks called "isonomy"—among those who form a political community where individuals debate, deliberate, argue, and act collectively. This is the sort of political action based on the condition of plurality that Arendt hoped might be achieved by the Jewish people. And she was bitterly disappointed when she witnessed what she considered the betrayal of such a politics by the Zionists. In short, it was politics that initially was the basis of her sympathy and her identification with Zionism, and it was politics that was the basis for her sharp—and increasingly bitter—critique of the direction that the Zionist movement was taking during the 1940s.

The occasion that provoked her bitter attack on Zionism was the resolution adopted unanimously at the October 1944 meeting of the American Zionists (and later affirmed by the World Zionist Organization). In "Zionism Reconsidered," she outlined her version of the development, decline, and betrayal of the revolutionary potential of the Zionist movement by the Zionists themselves. The biting rhetoric of "Zionism Reconsidered" was so vehement that *Commentary* refused to publish the article because one of the editors claimed that it "contained too many anti-Semitic implications." What was it that so provoked Arendt's ire? She strongly objected to the resolution that demanded a "free and democratic Jewish commonwealth . . . [that] shall embrace the whole of Palestine, undivided and undiminished" (*JP,* 131). This resolution marked a turning point in Zionist history. It went further than the Biltmore Program of 1942 in which—as she sarcastically phrases it—"the Jewish minority had granted minority rights to the Arab majority. This time the Arabs were simply not mentioned in the resolution, which obviously leaves them the choice between voluntary emigration or second-class citizenship"(*JP,* 131). The 1944 resolution represented the victory of the Revisionist program—despite its alleged repudiation by the General Zionists. More generally, Arendt felt that Zionists were failing to confront honestly what was becoming the most intractable problem in the Middle East—Arab-Jewish relations. But even in her damning critique of what she took to be the triumph of Revisionism, she reminded her readers of the origins of Zionism as "the genuine national revolutionary movement which sprang from the Jewish masses" (*JP,* 142). It was this revolutionary movement that she felt was now being betrayed.

What Arendt asserted so firmly in 1950 is as true (perhaps even more so) today: "Peace in the Near East is essential to the State of Israel, to the Arab people and to the Western World. Peace, as distinguished from an armistice, cannot be imposed from the outside, it can only be the result of negotiations, of mutual compromise and eventual agreement between Jews and Arabs" (*JP,* 193). Arendt was extremely sardonic, even brutal, in her critical analyses. For example, in her discussion of refugee populations and stateless people in the twentieth century in *The Origins of Totalitarianism,* she remarked:

> After the [Second World] war it turned out that the Jewish question, which was considered the only insoluble one, was indeed solved—namely by means of a colonialized and then conquered territory—but this solved neither the problems of the minorities nor the stateless. On the contrary, like virtually all other events of our century, the solution of the Jewish question merely produced a new category of refugees, the Arabs, thereby increasing the number of stateless and rightless by another 700,000 to 800,000 people. (*OT,* 290)

But it was not just the failure of Jewish-Arab relations that concerned her. It was the growth of a chauvinistic nationalism that she feared. She supported the political platform of the Judah Magnes's Ihud group when they called for a Jewish homeland and opposed an independent sovereign state of Israel. Arendt had a visceral reaction against all ideologies, including Zionist ideology. She felt that the European experience since the Versailles treaties demonstrated that nation-states—especially those artificially created—become increasingly intolerant to minority populations within their territorial borders. She declared that "nationalism is bad enough when it trusts in nothing but the rude force of the nation. A nationalism that necessarily and admittedly depends upon the force of a foreign nation is certainly worse" (*JP,* 132–33).

In May 1948, Arendt was still speaking out for the possibility of a

Jewish homeland, rather than a Jewish state. Not as a prophecy, but as a warning, she said:

> And even if the Jews were to win the war, its end would find the unique pos-
> sibilities and the unique achievements of Zionism in Palestine destroyed. The
> land to come into being would be something quite other than the dream of
> world Jewry, Zionist and non-Zionist. The "victorious" Jews would live
> surrounded by an entirely hostile Arab population, secluded inside ever-
> threatened borders, absorbed with physical self-defense to a degree that
> would submerge all other interests and activities. The growth of a Jewish cul-
> ture would cease to be the concern of the whole people; social experiments
> would have to be discarded as impractical luxuries; political thought would
> center around military strategy; economic development would be determined
> exclusively by the needs of war. And all this would be the fate of a nation
> that—no matter how many immigrants it could still absorb and how far it
> extended its boundaries (the whole of Palestine and Transjordan is the insane
> Revisionist demand)—would still remain a very small people greatly out-
> numbered by hostile neighbors. (*JP,* 187)

If Arendt so staunchly opposed the founding of a sovereign state of Israel, what was the alternative that she advocated? As I have already in- dicated, she strongly identified herself with the Ihud movement. This was the one brief period in her life when Arendt herself was actively engaged in politics. Judah Magnes even wanted Arendt to become the spokesperson for Ihud in the United States. But Arendt refused a role of leadership. Despite her insights into action and politics, Arendt her- self—as she acknowledged—was not a "political actor." Her intellec- tual strength was as a critic—a judging spectator. Arendt, like Magnes, favored the creation of a federated state that would be based upon local Jewish-Arab councils. She even argued that such a federated state was "much more realistic" than an independent sovereign nation-state. In 1948 she wrote:

> The alternative proposition of a federated state, also recently endorsed by
> Dr. Magnes, is much more realistic; despite the fact that it establishes a
> common government for two different peoples, it avoids the troublesome
> majority-minority constellation, which is insoluble by definition. A federated
> structure, moreover, would have to rest on Jewish-Arab community councils,
> which would mean that Jewish-Arab conflict would be resolved on the low-
> est and most promising level of proximity and neighborliness. A federated
> state, finally, could be the natural stepping-stone for any later, federated struc-
> ture in the Near East and the Mediterranean area. (*JP,* 191)

Shortly before Magnes's death on October 27, 1948, she wrote to him: "Will you permit me to tell you how grateful I am that the past year has brought me the privilege of knowing you. . . . Politics in our century is almost a business of despair and I have always been tempted to run away from it. I wanted you to know that your example prevented me from despairing and will prevent me for many years to come." And in the last major article that Arendt ever wrote dealing explicitly with Zionism—an article that she had written at the suggestion of Magnes and that she dedicated to him after his death—she once again warned about the dangers of chauvinistic nationalism for both Jews and Arabs. She referred to the vision of Ahad Ha'am, who "saw in Palestine the Jewish cultural center which would inspire the spiritual development of all Jews in other countries, but would not need ethnic homogeneity and national sovereignty" (*JP*, 213). She noted that "as far back as the nineties of the last century, Ahad Ha' Am' insisted on the presence in Palestine of an Arab native population and the necessity for peace" (*JP*, 213).

Even at this time, when Arendt was most active and vociferous in advocating a federated alternative to the founding of an independent sovereign nation-state of Israel, Arendt did not think of herself as an "anti-Zionist," but rather as a member of the loyal opposition. In a letter to Magnes (September 17, 1948) she urged that "the most urgent task of *Ihud* in Palestine now is not to support Ben-Gurion as a kind of lesser evil, but rather to form and insist on a consistent opposition within the limits of a loyal opposition." "Every believer in a democratic government knows the importance of a loyal opposition" (*JP*, 184).

This last point is crucial, not only for understanding Arendt's complex attitude toward Zionism, but especially for understanding her thinking about action and politics. Politics in the normative sense, that is, politics as it ought to be practiced and, according to Arendt, as it has been practiced at those rare moments when the revolutionary spirit has burst forth, presupposes genuine plurality. Politics involves active agonistic debate, discussion, and deliberation. Politics involves a contest of a plurality of perspectives that are publicly displayed and tested in public spaces. These are the public spaces in which freedom becomes a tangible reality. Politics dies when unanimity takes over—a unanimity that is intolerant toward dissent. The great danger to politics is a homogenization, a leveling out in which differences are not tolerated—where "loyal opposition" is marginalized, suppressed, or violently repressed.

The words that Hannah Arendt wrote fifty years ago are as striking and relevant today as they were in 1948. Let me conclude by quoting them:

> Unanimity of opinion is a very ominous phenomenon, and one characteristic of our modern mass age. It destroys social and personal life, which is based

on the fact that we are different by nature and conviction. To hold different opinions and to be aware that other people think differently on the same issue shields us from god-like certainty which stops all discussion and reduces social relationships to those of an ant heap. A unanimous public opinion tends to eliminate bodily those who differ, for mass unanimity is not the result of agreement, but an expression of fanaticism and hysteria. In contrast to agreement, unanimity does not stop at certain well-defined objects, but spreads like an infection into every related issue. (*JP*, 182)

EICHMANN IN JERUSALEM

Eichmann in Jerusalem

Justice and History

Michael R. Marrus

Seeking to understand the sometimes reckless argumentation of *Eichmann in Jerusalem,* Jewish scholars have regularly peered into the deep pool of German-Jewish identity, one of the most overused sources, in my view, to explain Jewish responses to their victimization during the Second World War. The key to understanding her distortions, Gershom Scholem contended in his famous letter to Arendt in 1963, was the absence of *ahavat Israel,* love of the Jewish people. "In you, dear Hannah, as in so many intellectuals who came here from the German Left, I find little trace of this," Scholem wrote. In a similar vein, "Hannah Arendt's Self-Hatred" was the title of Holocaust survivor Yisrael Gutman's learned critique of 1966, which denounced her "prejudiced" evaluation of the trial. Arendt "chose a narrative framework for the Holocaust that was consistent with her own profound cultural-biographical ambivalences as an assimilated German Jew," writes historian Richard Wolin, in a recent assessment.[1]

Debate over this point is unlikely ever to be settled, for evidence can easily be mustered to demonstrate the opposite contention—namely, Arendt's unequivocal Jewish identification, however different her notion of Jewishness may have been from that of her critics on this score. She was, after all, the intellectual who opened her first lecture in Germany after the war, as Alfred Kazin remembers, with the words: "I am a German Jew driven from my homeland by the Nazis."[2] Author of a sophisticated study of the nineteenth-century Jewish *salonnarde* Rahel Varnhagen,

Arendt considered herself a fierce critic of assimilation; one of the chapters carried the pointedly communicative title "One Does Not Escape Jewishness." [3]

.   Avoiding this well-traveled ground, I would like to approach her view of the Eichmann trial from one vantage point that I think is sometimes overlooked—legal argumentation, which in fact preoccupied Arendt from the very moment she heard of Eichmann's capture and considered covering the trial for the *New Yorker*. This is not to ignore some obvious instances of personal antipathies, blinkered views, and simple prejudices in her narrative—which was intended, one must recall, as a journalistic account, and not a learned evaluation. It is rather to suggest that Arendt's "agenda," as we say, was quite different from our own, in which identity politics comes so quickly to the fore. In thinking of the Eichmann trial, I suggest, Arendt operated very much in the shadow of the Nuremberg tribunal and therefore had a point of reference quite different from that of many of her critics. She was primarily concerned with how legal systems, both at Nuremberg and in Jerusalem, could "deal with the facts of administrative massacres organized by the state apparatus"—what she understood as a radically new order of criminality, one of the outstanding characteristics of modern times.[4]

Months before she went to Jerusalem, Arendt ruminated on the trial that the Israelis were busy preparing. It was her *Doktorvater*, Karl Jaspers, not Arendt, who worried about the legal basis for the proceeding and who hoped the Israelis would seek some sort of international process. Nahum Goldmann took the same view, as did a number of prominent Diaspora Jews. Unhesitatingly, Arendt took up the case for Israeli jurisdiction. Using the first-person plural, she proposed a response on behalf of the Jewish state in three points, each of which looked back to Nuremberg:

1. We kidnapped a man who was indicted in the first trial in Nuremberg. [She was, of course, quite wrong on this score.] He escaped arrest then. The Nuremberg court dealt with cases of crimes against humanity. Eichmann was an outlaw—a *hostis humani generis*, the way pirates used to be. 2. We abducted him from Argentina because Argentina has the worst possible record for the extradition of war criminals, even when extradition has been requested. And that in the face of repeated insistence not only of the victorious powers but also of the United Nations that anyone accused in Nuremberg be arrested and extradited. 3. We did not take the man to Germany, but to our own country. Germany could have demanded his extradition. What we would have done in that case is uncertain. The man should have appeared before the

Nuremberg court, a special court. There is no successor court to carry on the special court's mission. If the Germans were of the opinion that their regular courts were such successors, then they should have demanded Eichmann's extradition. As things stand, there doesn't seem to be anyone but us eager to bring a wanted criminal to trial. So we'll go ahead and do it.[5]

Well known as an opponent of Israeli policies, Arendt nevertheless insisted that the Jewish state had special standing in the case. "Israel has the right to speak for the victims, because the large majority of them (300,000) are living in Israel as citizens. The trial will take place in the country in which the injured parties and those who happened to survive are."[6]

Assuming, as is entirely likely, that Arendt had read David Ben-Gurion's article in *The New York Times Magazine* that appeared less than a week before writing those lines, she did not rise to the bait set by the Israeli prime minister, who proclaimed that "only a Jew with an inferiority complex" would doubt, as Jaspers, among many others, had doubted, that Israel should undertake the trial herself.[7] International courts "had always failed," Arendt observed just after the appearance of Ben-Gurion's article. "As long as such a court does not exist, international law holds that any court in the world is competent—so why not Israel?" Long before the trial had begun, Arendt argued that the real issue was not the Israelis' jurisdiction, but rather the nature of the crimes with which Eichmann would be charged—what she would refer to as "the new crime of administrative massacre," identified for the first time, she claimed, at Nuremberg.[8] From the very beginning, she insisted that the assault on European Jewry had universal implications. That was why she kept returning to the concept of *hostis humani generis* ("enemy of humanity," as she wanted it translated). "The crucial point is that although the crime at issue was committed primarily against the Jews, it is in no way limited to the Jews or the Jewish question"—a notion to which few, I think, would object today.[9] How would the balance be struck between the two elements of Eichmann's criminality? How would the Israelis balance the particular and the universal? The task would not be easy, she seemed to imply in a letter to Jaspers in December 1960. "We have no tools to hand except legal ones with which we have to judge and pass sentence on something that cannot even be adequately represented either in legal terms or in political terms."[10]

Three months later, installed in the Moriyah Hotel on King George Street in Jerusalem, Arendt found herself steeped in the atmosphere of the historic trial. Notwithstanding her disdain for its showlike aspects, her overall impression of the court was positive: Arendt commented on "the scrupulous fairness of all technical arrangements for the trial," and this despite what she felt had been the prime minister's publicly expressed contempt for "legal niceties." [11] Among her strongest impressions was the dignity and fair-mindedness of the judges, especially Moshe Landau, who presided over the proceedings—"superb," she wrote to Jaspers. "Marvelous man! Modest, intelligent, very open, knows America well; you'd like him a lot." [12] To be sure, it helped that the judges were German Jews, indeed "the best of German Jewry"—"sober and intense," no-nonsense in their style, and impatient with the prosecution's "attempt to drag out these hearings forever." "They are so obviously three good and honest men that one is not surprised that none of them yields to the greatest temptation to playact in this setting—that of pretending that they, all three born and educated in Germany, must wait for the Hebrew translation." As was notorious with German Jews, Arendt refused to defer to the official language of the state and hence of the trial. She was struck by "the comedy of speaking Hebrew when everyone involved knows German and thinks in German." The German translation was execrable—"sheer comedy, frequently incomprehensible," she observed. [13]

Arendt's real animus was reserved for the prosecution, and therein lies her principal critique of the trial as a whole. At issue was not only Gideon Hausner's showmanship, what Arendt deemed his crudity of speech—"a typical Galician Jew," she wrote to Jaspers. "Probably one of those people who don't know any language." [14] Her essential criticism of the prosecution's case, and hence of the trial as a whole, was that it refused to identify Eichmann's crime as a "crime against humanity"— or more specifically as it related to Eichmann, "crimes against mankind committed on the body of the Jewish people." [15] Gideon Hausner, Arendt felt, set his course in a very different direction from the outset of the trial.

For Hausner, drawing on what Arendt felt was Ben-Gurion's behind-the-scenes directives and guided by a Zionist view of history, anti-Semitism was the focus of the proceedings against Eichmann. "It is not an individual that is in the dock at this historic trial, and not the Nazi regime alone," she quoted the chief prosecutor as saying, "but anti-Semitism throughout history." Having embarked on this path, and committed to Ben-Gurion's stated goal of instructing, indeed shaming, the world, and educating Israeli youth on the catastrophe that had befallen the Jewish people during the Second World War, the prosecution orchestrated the trial as a history lesson on the grandest possible scale. And the lesson was not what Arendt wanted to see taught, the story of political modernity, but rather the travails of the Jewish people, beginning with Pharaoh in Egypt. "It was bad history and cheap rhetoric," she wrote. "Worse, it was clearly at cross-purposes with putting Eichmann on trial." [16] Later, she sat through more pertinent evidence, terrible accounts by survivors of what they had endured at the hands of the Nazis. But here, too, she questioned the relevance of their testimony to the specific case of Adolf Eichmann. Like many in attendance, and like the judges themselves, Arendt smoldered—even though the stories were horrifying, even though the pain of the witnesses was sometimes palpable, and even though Arendt herself was stunned by some of what she heard. "Everyone, everyone should have his day in court," she wrote as her impatience mounted. [17]

Left out of the proceedings, Arendt felt, was an identification of the singularity of the events that were recounted, and hence the uncommon character of Eichmann's deeds. His "was no ordinary crime," she insisted. Eichmann was no "common criminal," as she felt the prosecution had portrayed him, a garden-variety anti-Semite, driven by fanaticism and covering his path with lies and deceit. Rather, Eichmann was the quintessential example of the totalitarian bureaucrat—unable to speak except in officialese [Amtssprache], unable to think outside the framework of his bureaucratic function, unable to contemplate wider issues of right and wrong or a transcendent morality, ignorant "of everything that was not directly, technically and bureaucratically, connected with his job." In a word: banal. [18]

What was extraordinary, as Arendt understood it, was not Eichmann, but the vast criminal enterprise of which he was a part. As evidence first presented at Nuremberg showed, this criminality involved "unheard-of atrocities, the blotting out of whole peoples, the 'clearance' of whole regions of their native population, that is, not only crimes that 'no conception of military necessity could sustain' but crimes that were in fact independent of the war and that announced a policy of systematic murder to be continued in time of peace." [19] Beginning with Nuremberg, the great challenge to the international community had been to come to terms with this new order of criminality, of a scale and of a significance that the world had not seen or understood before. Such crimes were "against the human status," "an attack on human diversity as such." [20]

"The purpose of a trial is to render justice, and nothing else," Arendt wrote in her final reflections on the proceedings in Jerusalem.[21] But justice required a clear-minded identification of the crime and a specific determination of the responsibility of the accused. *Eichmann in Jerusalem* is an extended essay on these very questions.

The problem posed by this new order of criminality was the difficulty of bringing to justice vast armies of criminals and those who were complicit in great crimes, particularly given that they had no consciousness of guilt. Having pondered the totalitarian phenomenon for several decades, Arendt had long contended that criminal responsibility was widely diffused throughout the Third Reich. "The totalitarian policy," she had written in 1945, "has achieved the result of making the existence of each individual in Germany depend either upon committing crimes or upon complicity in crimes."[22] The crimes of Nazism posed such a great challenge to the judicial process because the perpetrators were legion, embracing practically "the whole of respectable society [that] had in one way or another succumbed to Hitler."[23] Nuremberg had gone wrong, she believed, because while it had groped toward the identification of a new order of criminality, it had failed to specify the ubiquitous character of Nazi criminality and the unprecedented ways in which "crimes against humanity" had been carried out. Notably, it had failed to assess the degree to which all of German society had been fashioned into a criminal enterprise. At Nuremberg, for example, there was a great effort to establish a handful of organizations as being the agents of a criminal conspiracy. But "the truth of the matter," said Arendt, in her characteristically declamatory mode, "is that there existed not a single organization or public institution in Germany, at least during the war years, that did *not* become involved in criminal actions and transactions."[24]

Arendt had no doubt that the Nazis' assault on European Jewry was a "supreme crime" with which the regime crossed the threshold into "crimes against humanity." "It was when the Nazi regime declared that the German people not only were unwilling to have any Jews in Germany but wished to make the entire Jewish people disappear from the face of the earth that the new crime, the crime against humanity . . . appeared."[25] In 1961, fresh from a reading of Raul Hilberg's *Destruction of the European Jews*—a book that she had read as background for her reportage and that she acknowledged, but with insufficient generosity—Arendt understood Eichmann's involvement in the assault on European

Jewry as one part of a vast, bureaucratic anti-Jewish effort, orchestrated on a continental scale, involving front-line perpetrators, but also armies of officials behind the scenes, passive collaborators and zealous Quislings—and even, in some cases, organizations of the victims themselves.

How to deal with what had happened to the Jews was the great challenge posed both at Nuremberg and in Jerusalem. While "fumbling" in its definitions of the new order of criminality, Nuremberg attempted an understanding of the new reality. The "crimes against humanity" with which many had been accused there had not been covered by international or municipal law, she felt, or, perhaps more accurately, had not been fully understood by contemporaries. Nuremberg had failed fully to identify such crimes not because it had ignored the Jews—it had certainly not done that—but because the American trial plan, enshrined in the Nuremberg Charter, had focused on aggression as "the supreme international crime"—"differing only from other war crimes in that it contains within itself the accumulated evil of the whole," as the judges of the International Military Tribunal put it.[26]

The Eichmann trial was an improvement on the proceedings at Nuremberg because it put the new order of criminality "at the center of the . . . proceedings," and hence prominently before the world. Arendt's main criticism of the Eichmann trial was that it did not go far enough in this direction. The trial ought to have pronounced Eichmann an enemy of humanity, and not just of the Jewish people. It ought to have understood his acts as part of a new order of criminality, explicable, Arendt felt, in terms of a new kind of totalitarian criminal purpose—"to determine who should and who should not inhabit the world." It ought to have placed his criminality in the context of "the almost ubiquitous complicity" of German society.[27]

Arendt's quarrel with the prosecution of Adolf Eichmann was thus that it had failed to point out the universal and historical significance of what had occurred. By limiting its understanding of what had happened to one event (admittedly an important one) in the long history of attacks on the Jewish people, the prosecution had narrowed the vision of the court. The court ought to have understood Eichmann as she herself understood him, as a representative of the totalitarian society that modernity could produce. It ought to have seen him in all his thoughtlessness, lack of imagination, and bureaucratic ambition, rather than as a particularly fanatic champion of anti-Semitism. The Israelis ought to have spoken for all of humanity, whose present and future were menaced by

Auschwitz as surely as were those of the Jews. As she insisted, "these modern, state-employed mass murderers must be prosecuted because they violated the order of mankind, and not because they killed millions of people." [28]

Finally, Arendt argued that the Eichmann trial ought to have alerted humanity to the universal threat represented in Nazism. Indeed, there was some urgency in getting it right with Eichmann and the kinds of crime he had committed. While the Nazis had launched such an attack primarily against the Jews, they had set a precedent that others might well follow in the future. Modern society, Arendt felt, retains a capacity for genocide that was hardly eliminated with the destruction of Nazism. "The frightening coincidence of the modern population explosion with the discovery of technical devices that, through automation, will make large sections of the population 'superfluous' even in terms of labor, and that, through nuclear energy, make it possible to deal with this twofold threat by the use of instruments beside which Hitler's gassing installations look like an evil child's fumbling toys, should be enough to make us tremble." [29] This vision may perhaps be implausible today. As I recall, it was not uncommon in 1961.

Arendt touched many exposed nerves, of course, and to some degree invited the intense polemic that appeared in response to her book. She wanted to distance herself from the Jewish vantage point and self-consciously embraced the posture of the Jewish nonconformist, a Jewish rebel who told "the truth in a hostile environment." [30] And she could be very irritating. Having worked things out to her satisfaction, she had a tendency to pontificate, rather than to argue, and certainly rather than to muster evidence. As Walter Laqueur once observed, she had "a somewhat cavalier attitude toward facts." [31] Her account of the Eichmann trial took her down paths with which she was unfamiliar and involved her in serious inaccuracies in depicting both the Nazis and their victims.

I do not believe that Arendt's claims about the universal significance of the Holocaust should be dismissed as the product of a self-hating German Jew, however. The implication of her work has a warning to her own people and to others. "If evil is banal," writes her biographer, "no faulty nature or original sinfulness is required to become enmeshed in it; indeed the best, not knowing what they do, are likely to become enmeshed for the sake of a future good." [32] Consider the remarkable admonition she offered in 1945: "In political terms, the idea of humanity, excluding no people and assigning a monopoly of guilt to no one, is the only guarantee that one 'superior race' after another may not feel obligated to follow the 'natural law' of the right of the powerful, and exterminate 'inferior races unworthy of survival'; so that at the end of an 'imperialistic age' we should find ourselves in a stage which would make the Nazis look like crude precursors of future political methods."[33] This was a dark vision, but one that made some sense in the wake of what had happened to the Jewish people at the hands of the Nazis.

Malicious Clerks

*The Nazi Security Police
and the Banality of Evil*

Yaacov Lozowick

For many, the name Adolf Eichmann is synonymous with the Nazi murder of six million Jews. Alongside Adolf Hitler and Heinrich Himmler, he is probably the most infamous of the Nazi murderers. Unlike with them, the aura linked to his name is that of the ultimate evil that may lurk in each and every one of us. Hitler is somehow inexplicable—Joachim Fest called him a nonperson—and Himmler was the all-powerful chief of the SS. Eichmann was a mere flesh and blood lieutenant colonel: It is he we seek under our bed, not they.

There are historical reasons for this. Nazi defendants at the International Military Tribunal at Nuremberg and at subsequent trials have customarily deposited their dirt at the doorsteps of whoever was absent. Eichmann disappeared after the war and there were documents to prove that he *had* been at the center of the policy of murder, and so he was the convenient scapegoat for any number of unpleasant deeds. The tendency to inflate Eichmann's responsibility was enhanced by the Israeli prosecutors at his trial in Jerusalem in 1961: They were convinced he had been the moving force behind the "Final Solution" and set out to prove so.[1] The fact that they overestimated his importance needs to be seen within its historical context, for at the time even the historians were just beginning to sort out the chronology of the Holocaust, which was not yet known by that name.[2]

At least as significant for the enduring infamy of the man, however, was the presence of one of the spectators at his trial. Professor Hannah

Arendt, brilliant, Jewish, born in Germany, refugee of the Nazis, was sent by the *New Yorker* to report on the trial. Her studies, including the seminal *Origins of Totalitarianism*,[3] uniquely equipped her. It is not an everyday event when a scholar of her stature serves as a reporter.

Arendt did not let down her editors. The reports, collected in the small book *Eichmann in Jerusalem*, have been published at least twelve times since 1963. The words of the subtitle have become a catch phrase: *A Report on the Banality of Evil*.[4] The essence of her thesis is chillingly simple. There was nothing unusually bestial about Eichmann, who was basically a rather mediocre person. He was merely symptomatic of a new type of reality, one where banal characters can be swept up in the enthusiasm of large historical movements to such an extent that they lose the ability to distinguish between right and wrong. In her own words:

> Behind the comedy of the soul experts lay the hard fact that this was obviously no case of moral let alone legal insanity. . . . Worse, his was also no case of insane hatred of Jews, of fanatical anti-Semitism or indoctrination of any kind. He "personally" had extraordinary diligence in looking out for his personal advancement, he had no motives at all. And this diligence in itself was in no way criminal; he certainly would never have murdered his superior in order to inherit his post. He *merely,* to put the matter colloquially, *never realized what he was doing.* . . . That such remoteness from reality and such thoughtlessness can wreak more havoc than all the evil instincts taken together which, perhaps, are inherent in man—that was, in fact, the lesson one could learn in Jerusalem.[5]

In other words, Arendt rejected the biblical story of Genesis that attributes the ability to distinguish between right and wrong to the very core of being human. Instead, she implied that Eichmann represented a potential face of the future. Her basic tenet, that Eichmann and his ilk were somehow sincerely unaware of the criminality of their actions, needs to be read in the context of her interpretation of totalitarianism, particularly the eleventh chapter of *Origins*, "The Totalitarian Movement," where she discusses the role of propaganda and interpretation of reality, and the second subchapter there, where she postulates a pyramid of ever higher circles of members. The higher one climbs and the closer to power, the further one is from reality and from contact with the nontotalitarian society and world. The chill of her thesis lies in the frightening ordinariness and banality of his horrific evil.

This powerful warning was only too eagerly adopted by what the Germans call *Multiplikatoren:* journalists, academics, clergy, and educators,[6] many of whose intellectual stature was below that of Arendt. At times, their interpretation of her position far exceeded what she was willing to accept. She had never meant to say, for example, that every one of us could potentially descend to mass murder, rather that every group includes individuals, possibly even many of them, who are capable of such a regression. When she expressed such reservations about her own thesis, she was not always heeded.

When I embarked upon my own research of Eichmann and his colleagues, I had no doubts about the validity of Arendt's position. True, it was clear that some of the historical descriptions in her book were not accurate. Primarily, however, it was my wish to deal with an oft-stated Nazi excuse for their activities: that they had merely followed orders and hence should be regarded as good citizens. That this statement was patently untrue seemed to me self-evident. Whatever he *did* say, Hitler certainly never told his underlings *how* to kill the Jews, nor, by the same token, could Himmler or Heydrich have had the technical knowledge required to instruct their men how to run gas chambers. The crucial additions of their underlings to the decision-making process and the actual formation of policy were what I wished to delineate. I was casting about for a group of bureaucrats to study in order to learn about the strata of policy formulators who must be found between the ultimate decision makers and the implementers of policy in the field, and Eichmann and his staff seemed an obvious choice.

As I delved ever deeper into the documents, however, my unease grew, until at last I reluctantly had no choice but to admit that Hannah Arendt was wrong. There was very little that was banal about Eichmann or any of his accomplices, and the little that could be found was not relevant to what they had done. Arendt's point of departure was wrong. Although she was primarily a philosopher, she had written a historical analysis—and without checking her facts. Moreover, she had refrained from taking into account much potentially relevant information. Above all, her position was the result of ideological considerations, not careful scholarship. This was even more true in the case of most of her followers.

The organization that the men chose to join—and it was their choice—was an unusual one, even in the 1930s. The Nazi Security Police was the first unified police force in German history. Its leaders consciously and openly abandoned the role of protecting society from elements that had shown themselves to be criminal, preferring the aggressive pursuit of groups who—according to the ideology of the pursuers—might potentially become disruptive.[7] It was a police force that made use of tools far more potent than those available to most police organizations. The two most significant of these were protective custody, which meant the authority to arrest anyone for unlimited duration, irrespective of evidence or lack thereof, and the concentration camps, where terror reigned beyond the protection of the law. These tools were eagerly wielded by police officers who cared more about social goals than about the rights of the individual. These officers intermingled with and were influenced by an ever growing number of SS officers whose ideological affinity was central in forming their actions.[8]

A central tenet in the thinking of Arendt and her followers has always been that ideology was at most of secondary importance for the murderers, its significance being greatly exceeded by universal characteristics such as camaraderie, ambition, and opportunism. Yet Eichmann and many of his closest colleagues were affiliated with nationalistic, anti-Semitic organizations before they joined the party or the SS, and earlier than 1932, so that opportunism was not their main motive. Perhaps the best illustration of Arendt's carelessness on this point is that of the Schlaraffia club in Linz: Arendt would have us believe that this was a harmless *bürgerlich* club, committed to having fun, and that Eichmann was about to join when Kaltenbrunner carried him off to join the SS. Eichmann himself, *after the war,* told a different tale: What had impressed him about the Schlaraffia members was that they accepted no Jews. "*Ich war imponiert,*" he said: "I was immensely impressed."[9]

From about 1936 on, Eichmann and his colleagues in the SD wrote a long series of reports about the Jews of the Third Reich and international Judaism. In more than one case, Eichmann dealt at length with the Hagana, the paramilitary organization of the Jews in Palestine. If one were to believe him, the word *Hagana* means "secret" (it actually means "defense"), and the organization secretly controlled both the British and the French intelligence services. Reading these reports, one finds many of the standard canards of Nazi anti-Semitism, except that the formulations are more sophisticated than usual.[10] If he and his colleagues were earnestly writing and talking this way at the time merely out of opportunism, they certainly managed to hide the fact well: These were the very indoctrinators themselves.

By 1938, many of these men were impatiently casting about for a mode to carry out the ideas they had been developing. The *Anschluß* in Austria offered Eichmann a way out of his frustration. He—and the staff he collected around him—far exceeded both the instructions he had received when he was sent to Vienna in March 1938 and their expected results. Given the chance to abuse the almost unlimited power at their disposal, Eichmann and his staff were arrogant, brutally violent, malicious—and innovative. Their brutality is vividly described in the first chapter of Hans Safrian's book *Die Eichmann Männer*.[11] More significant, however, is the fact that they understood how to utilize the terror of the Jews of Vienna in order to stampede them out of the country and leave much of their possessions behind. These junior SS men were no mere cogs in a machine.

A second significant development in 1938 was that the growing involvement in real action left less and less time for ideological training and reflection. This was perceived and rued at the time by the men of the SD.[12] Postwar scholars ought to have taken note of this before proclaiming that the relative lack of ideological discourse in the bureaucratic correspondence of busy officials was proof of their indifference. Thus we can see that a year before the outbreak of the war, an organization was in position which was fully poised to inflict great damage on the Jews of Europe, should the opportunity arrive. If there were any mindless bureaucrats in its ranks, they left no mark.

Decisions of policy are made at the top of bureaucracies, but the ongoing management is the task of the middle echelons. This is also true regarding the policy of murdering the Jews. As of early 1942, the staff of Department IV B 4 managed the "Final Solution" in the *Reich*. The officers of the department ensured the uninterrupted supply of trains and coordinated the arrest of Jews in communities according to the schedule of these trains. They prepared detailed ordinances for the local police forces so that the execution of policy would be as smooth as possible. When they encountered complications, they supplied solutions.[13] They informed the local authorities who was to be deported and which categories of people were as yet not to be deported. While doing so, they also served as the conduit for pressure from the implementers of policy in the field to the upper echelons to expand these categories, lest the pace of the deportations decrease.[14] They stood between the death camps and prying eyes of foreigners by supplying their colleagues in the Foreign Ministry with convenient excuses and fairy tales with which to respond to foreign queries.[15] They authorized executions, selected Jewish community workers in Berlin to be sent to their deaths, and supplied logistic support to Sonderkommando 1005, the ghoulish units whose task was to destroy the evidence of murder by exhuming mass graves and burning the corpses.[16] They also helped to prepare the ground for the deportations of the Jews from countries where the "Final Solution" had not yet been applied, whether by aiding and abetting the Foreign Ministry or by directing the local representatives of the Nazi regime.[17]

They were aware of what they were doing at all stages. This is clear from a reading of the many letters they wrote, in which they disseminated lies to the outside world while simultaneously being crystal clear to insiders. This documentation was there to be read by Hannah Arendt, had she so wished. However, one of the more interesting bodies of evidence was indeed created only a few years after she had invented the banality of evil. These were the interrogations carried out by the prosecution in West Berlin, beginning in the mid-1960s, as they prepared to bring some of Eichmann's subordinate officers to trial.[18] The prosecutors repeatedly interrogated as many surviving members of Eichmann's staff as they could find, cross-referenced the evidence, and came back with further questions. Among their findings: Everyone had known precisely what was going on, and the fate of the Jews had even been the source of various gruesome in-house jokes. Clearly articulated hatred of the Jews was a motivating force. When called upon to face the remaining Jews of Berlin, they did so with contempt and brutality. The inculcation of young secretaries was perhaps the most significant of all: These were young women straight out of school. We would assume that they, of all people, having graduated from the Nazi school system, should have been the most willing to participate in the killing of the Jews—and yet, it was not so. These young women needed a period of adjustment before they were able to overcome the residues of their natural abhorrence of murder. Meanwhile, some of the officers stated clearly their understanding that should Germany ever lose the war, no one would ever forgive them their crimes.[19]

Having described these clerks of malice as they operated at the center, in Berlin, we then turn to the outposts of the empire. The German forces of occupation in the Netherlands set up a system whereby the government was not Dutch, but rather German. The SS was one of the German agencies that participated in the ruling of the land, but it was not the only one.[20]

The relationship between the SS in the Netherlands and their purported superiors in Berlin was not always hierarchical. The SS in the Netherlands, while undoubtedly acting under directives coming from Berlin, needs to be seen as one of the local German agencies, fully functioning within the framework of the local German government. This is particularly clear with regard to the deportation of the Jews. At times, the SS in The Hague and Amsterdam were as fully aware of the policy as their counterparts in Berlin. Throughout the period, Eichmann and his staff were reduced to the marginal positions of suppliers of trains or technical advisors. Only at rare instances was there any need for Eichmann's staff to goad the SS men on the scene in the Netherlands to make greater efforts to carry out deportations.

Policy making was not the only sphere in which the influence from Berlin was limited. It is clear that various SS officers in the Netherlands needed no directives from Germany to engage in the torture of Jews who stood before them. The independence of SS clerks in the Netherlands is also evident in the way they routinely interpreted directives from Berlin as strictly as possible, especially regarding the deportation of Jews. Like their peers in Berlin, they, too, could appreciate what they considered to be a good joke at the expense of their terrorized victims.[21] Like their peers in Berlin, there was nothing banal about them: They had hated Jews for years and were only too glad to contribute toward solving this most vexing of problems.

Turning to France, we are removed one step further from the center. For political reasons of their own, the Nazis had allowed the French to maintain a partial sovereignty. Having done so, they were committed to abiding by their own ground rules.

From very early on, the SS in France were aware of a crucial aspect of the situation there: For Nazi Germany, the French were an untrustworthy ally.[22] This may come as a faint surprise to some students of the period. Early postwar French portrayals of themselves were of the great resisters to the Nazis. Since the mid-1970s, this myth has been repeatedly attacked and for all practical purposes destroyed, so that the Vichy government—and, to some extent, French society—are now seen as having collaborated in the Nazi persecution of the Jews, and at times even having outpaced it.[23] My present research has no quarrel with the broad outlines of this historical portrayal, yet it also highlights a significant point: The partnership between Vichy and Third Reich was not an equal one.

Regarding the policy of deporting the Jews to their deaths, the partnership was not only unequal; it was deeply and essentially flawed. The French authorities were openly anti-Semitic, and at times they eagerly encouraged and assisted in the deportations. Yet even at the height of the cooperation, both sides were aware of their differences. The French authorities never intended the deportations to include Jews of French citizenship. Their resolve to deport non-French Jews was the result of political considerations, not deep-seated ideological ones. A careful reading of the documentation shows that the SS officers were aware of these differences at all times and felt compelled to act appropriately.[24] As time went on and there were fewer and fewer non-French Jews to deport, the friction grew. The central significance for a discussion of Arendt's thesis is that there can be no doubt that by 1943, at the latest, top French functionaries known to be anti-Semites were nonetheless disagreeing with the SS officers. The SS could not have been under the illusion that their own interpretation of their actions was the only one possible—nor, to hark back to Arendt's formulation, is it plausible that they didn't realize what they were doing.

This distinction between the French and Germans is even more obvious in light of internal developments within the ranks of the Paris SS during the summer of 1942. At the very peak of anti-Jewish activities, Theodore Dannecker, Eichmann's associate since 1937, was ousted, and an anonymous younger officer, Heinz Roethke, was brought in to take his place.[25] The pace of the operation was not affected in the slightest. While the SS cast about—unsuccessfully—for fully reliable French associates, they had no problem finding German ones when the need arose.

Mindless bureaucracies, it would seem, are a figment of the imagination, to be found in learned books, but not in reality. A further proof for this can be found in the story of the Italian intervention in southern France after the autumn of 1942. For various reasons, one of them being abhorrence of the Nazi policy of murder, the Italian authorities in southern France took upon themselves to interfere with and impede the deportations. The central figure in this story was a high Italian police officer by the name of Guido Lospinoso. Using the same tools as the SS—bureaucratic procedures—Lospinoso and his colleagues succeeded in staving off the Nazis for many months. They were so successful that months passed before the SS even became aware that Lospinoso was pulling their legs.[26]

The story in France, therefore, was the following: German, French, and Italian bureaucrats were all aware of what was happening to the Jews. Each group related to this according to its own criteria and agenda. Everyone brought to their tasks dedication and conscious decision making. There were no mindless bureaucrats.

One could continue this historical survey and look at the activities of Eichmann and his men in Greece, in Hungary, in Bulgaria, and elsewhere,[27] but this would merely be an enumeration of additional facts of the same kind.

The historical data collected for this research seems to cut the ground from beneath Hannah Arendt's thesis. Eichmann and his cohorts knew very well what they were doing and were quite aware that their activity would be considered criminal in any but their own political context. The reasons they chose for participating in murder must have been varied, but there is much evidence that ideology played a central role. They wished to create a new world order, and they wished to have no Jews in it. One can, obviously, explain this in terms of "structures" and other academic terms culled from the social sciences and thereby defuse the issue from particularistic shadows touching, for example, upon Germans or Jews. Yet by doing so, one may reveal more about the describer than about the described.

Essentially, we are dealing with an aspect of the nature of evil. To me, it is obvious that there is nothing banal about it. Wherein, therefore, lies the great power of Arendt's thesis? Why are so many people attracted to an explanation of evil that makes of it something familiar and commonplace? Is there something comforting in accepting commonalties with the murderers of the SS?

One explanation is that accepting Eichmann into the club is a way to keep his ideology out. The Nazis divided humanity into groups, rated them, and persecuted them accordingly. According to this point of view, we must refrain forever from any such gradations, even if by doing so we must blur distinctions that really exist. Our propensity is to talk not about Germans and Jews, but rather about perpetrators and victims who happened to be members of the above groups, but who could just as easily have come from other groups. Supposedly the part of Eichmann's personality that enabled him to do what he did was the part of him that is universally human. This thesis suggests that any person given the proper conditions could become a murderer in the Nazi cast, irrespective of his or her national, social, or cultural identity. As I have tried to show, this line of explanation seems to overlook too many of the facts.

A second explanation is that we need to understand Eichmann in rational terms such as ambition, obedience, peer pressure, and ignorance so that we will not have to face the irrational, such as pure malice and naked evil. Being rational-minded and academic, we are at a loss to deal with religious and moral terms, which rightly do not belong in the history books unless as phenomena to be described and analyzed—never as explanations themselves.

The findings of this research have underlined the singularity of the Nazi behavior and seem to call for a new metaphor: that of the alpinists. It is a banal commonplace that human beings can be nasty to one another, and varying degrees of cruelty are unfortunately widespread. The ability to be nasty, however, does not tell us much about the ability to commit bureaucratic murder. To focus the point more clearly, this research has demonstrated that even the ability of a person to become a high-ranking fascist police officer does not mean that he also has the innate ability to become a participant in systematic mass murder. Just as most of us can easily climb a hill, but scaling the Alps is forever beyond our abilities, so also one must be cautious in drawing conclusions from Eichmann and his actions about our potential for evil. His evil, and that of his peers, is far less common than some would have us believe.

And if this is the case, it is the task of those who would understand to continue the search for the explanations, elusive as they may be.

Hannah Arendt's Interpretation of the Holocaust as a Challenge to Human Existence

The Intellectual Background

Hans Mommsen

Hannah Arendt's *Eichmann in Jerusalem* was widely reviewed, and the controversy it initiated among the West German public has itself become an object of historical investigation. The book and the articles that preceded it instigated an extremely polemical debate, including the endeavor to prevent publications favorable to her views. The extreme position presented by Hannah Arendt no longer seems exceptional, however, although intensified international Holocaust research has since then extended the factual foundations for the arguments of both Arendt and her opponents. Thus, it is appropriate to present a new evaluation of what was in 1963 regarded as an unjustified and almost incomprehensible offense against the Holocaust victims.[1]

It was not so much the details of Arendt's book that caused the furor—although they are debatable, nonetheless, because she frequently relied on insufficient study of the available primary sources to support the far-reaching conclusions she drew and because she tended to overdraw her arguments in a polemical fashion. The controversy erupted, first, because Hannah Arendt challenged the predominant interpretation of the origins and the implementation of the genocide and in doing so broke long-cherished political taboos. The Zionist interpretation that perceived the Holocaust as the culmination of the anti-Semitic indoctrination of the Western world was put into doubt by Arendt's attempt to view the genocide mainly as the outcome of bureaucratic and technical mechanisms and to a lesser degree a result of racial fanaticism and long-term political planning on the part of the German dictator. Although Arendt was not aware that her frontal attack against the then-prevailing interpretation of the origins of the Holocaust would be inevitably regarded as deliberately disparaging the Jewish community, both the private dimension of the conflict, which led to a break with almost all former Jewish friends, including Gershom Scholem,[2] and its public repercussions were immense.

Recent Holocaust research points to a high degree of interaction between bureaucratic and ideological factors, as well as between the central agencies of the regime and local and regional perpetrators. Thus, the picture painted by Hannah Arendt of the role of Adolf Eichmann found the support of many historians, although her conclusion that he was characterized by an almost amoral mentality appears to be still controversial.[3]

The second source of controversy revolved (and still revolves) around the notion of the "banality of evil." This notion emerged in discourse with Heinrich Blücher and Karl Jaspers.[4] Arendt did not deny the inhuman character of the Holocaust, but argued that its evil was not the outcome of a superior will to power or demonism but originated under rather trivial conditions, in some respect in a sphere of action that lay below moral considerations. It is fully comprehensible that the victims had immense difficulties accepting an interpretation of the Holocaust in which mass annihilation appeared not as a long-planned result of a devilish plan to kill European Jewry, but rather as a complex process comprising not only leading agencies in Berlin, especially the Reich Main Security Office, but also local SS units and the concentration camp guards.[5]

Arendt, who was not a trained historian and was far from employing a genetic methodological approach, presented an innovative interpretation that in some respects anticipated the arguments of the functionalist school that developed in the later 1960s. She arrived at her conclusions on the basis of a critical evaluation of the trial documents, in the process modifying her position as laid down in *The Origins of Totalitarianism.*[6] The fact that her arguments were not always logically consistent added to the many misunderstandings of her true intentions. Although Hannah Arendt wielded an impressive array of documentary evidence—she was very influenced by Raul Hilberg's pioneering 1961 book, without mentioning the extent of her dependence upon it—in essence she used the historical material to sustain her arguments.[7] For Arendt *The Origins of Totalitarianism* and the Eichmann book were exceptional excursions into the field of historical research. Nevertheless, her rather impressionistic approach to the history of the Holocaust enabled her to arrive at a series of principal conclusions that anticipated the results of subsequent historical scholarship.

Eichmann's original report, which had been written when he was still in Argentina, already supported Arendt's presumption that the defendant lacked any of the demonic qualities attributed to him by the prosecution.[8] Arriving in Jerusalem, Arendt became deeply convinced of the personal and moral mediocrity of the defendant during the trial. This stood in almost unbridgeable contrast to the guilt attributed to him as the alleged main perpetrator.

In December 1960, Arendt wrote to Jaspers that Eichmann could have undermined the strategy of the court by pointing at the lack of resistance against the destruction of European Jews, either by the Western powers, which did not support the emigration schemes of the Rublee committee that had been formed at the Evian conference, or by the Jewish notables, who, as she reproachfully remarked to Karl Jaspers, had participated "in organizing their own destruction."[9] Conversely, she regarded Eichmann's subaltern mentality and bureaucratic mediocrity as proof of what she called the "banality of evil," a variation on the term "absolute evil" employed in *The Origins of Totalitarianism*.[10]

The controversy over the role of the Jewish councils and the leaders of the Jewish organizations in Central and Western Europe touched a major issue and violated a taboo of which Arendt had been aware for a long time.[11] The critical analysis presented by Raul Hilberg of the reactions of the Jewish councils to the German persecutors may have underpinned her critical judgment on the role the Jewish leadership had played in the destruction process. It is, however, important to be aware of the fact that Arendt raised this issue not so much because of her repeated disputes with representatives of the Zionist camp, but because of her earlier observation, that under totalitarian conditions, the victims were deprived of their capability to resist or to flee from the terror and were turned into immobilized and apathetic human beings.[12]

The dehumanization not only of the perpetrators, but of the victims, too, appeared to Arendt one of the most terrifying experiences of totalitarian rule. This, and not so much the intention to raise moral objections against the victims and survivors alike, induced her to focus on the controversial reaction of the Jewish communities against the Nazi onslaught and their attempts to achieve some arrangements with the persecutors.

Also, the leitmotiv of the Eichmann report, the "banality of evil," was already in her mind before she decided to go to Jerusalem. In a letter to

Karl Jaspers on December 2, 1960, in which she informed him that she intended to observe the proceedings of the court and write for the *New Yorker,* she wrote that she did not want to miss the chance to study "this walking disaster face to face in all his bizarre vacuousness." [13]

What did she have in mind, when she coined the term "nothingness" in order to circumscribe the events of the Holocaust? Certainly, it was not her intention to downgrade the annihilation of Jews as an unsurpassed atrocity and crime. Conversely, she was convinced of the uniqueness of the anti-Jewish genocide, and she rejected any attempt to put it into a continuous line of anti-Jewish assaults and anti-Semitic movements in world history, as was done by the prosecution. [14]

Already in *The Origins of Totalitarianism* she had located the Holocaust as a crucial element of totalitarian dictatorship because it represented the climax of what she called "the anti-political principle." [15] The term itself had been coined by Heinrich Blücher and then strongly endorsed by Jaspers, who thought it emphasized that the genocide policy was not the outcome of a diabolic and demonic force. [16] The implied concept, which Blücher later regretted having introduced into the debate, can be correctly interpreted only against the background of German Idealist philosophy. It implied a departure from the notion of history as the embodiment of ethical values.

As the worst culmination of terror and devastation, the Holocaust revealed that the nature of totalitarian rule consisted in the destruction of politics as such because it destroyed in the long run any possibility of political communication and of meaningful political action. Consequently, Hannah Arendt stressed the point that the implementation of the Holocaust was far from being the outcome of any specific political or economic interests. The fact that the annihilation ran counter to any given interest, be it the war economy or the scarcity of manpower, made it obvious that the Holocaust, as well as similar annihilation processes in Stalinist Russia and the Third Reich, were destroying the moral foundations of the human community and were principally of an ahistorical and amoral nature. [17]

The meaning of all this is clear. On the basis of her Idealist definition of politics—here Arendt remained within the German philosophical tradition and was certainly influenced by the antihistoricist mentality of most of the Weimar intellectuals—she was convinced that the essential nature of totalitarian regimes consisted in the unlimited devastation of the *conditio humana* and the replacement of politics by terror, intimidation, and propaganda. [18] Undoubtedly, she added a crucial new aspect to our understanding of the specific elements of the political process ultimately leading to self-destruction.

Hannah Arendt would argue that totalitarian rule would not only destroy the very conditions for peaceful and rational communication among people, but also uproot any confidence in the body politic as such. With arguments like this, Hannah Arendt came near to those of Helmuth James von Moltke, who was convinced that the resisters, after having overthrown the dictatorship, as such had to devote all their energies to restoring "the image of man in the hearts of our fellow citizens."[19] This demand sprang from the experience of the cynical use of power in the Nazi system, which destroyed the confidence of the people in the function of politics as such and foreclosed any readiness to take over public responsibility.[20]

The dehumanizing effect of totalitarian rule culminated in the Holocaust, which deprived the victims of their humanity and transformed them into the "outlawed," with the status of "*Vogelfreiheit.*"[21] By using this term, Arendt wanted to underline the fact that the implementation of the Holocaust occurred within a quasi-amoral sphere, as far as the perspective and mentality of the perpetrators were concerned. Thus, the Holocaust involved a new dimension of human action that consisted in annihilation without any discernible motivation and that at the same time tended to place victims and persecutors on the same existential level.

Hannah Arendt discussed this issue in connection with the question of whether an international court would have been more adequate than the Israel trial and whether Eichmann should not have been treated as *hostis humani generis* because his deeds lay outside any ordinary criminality.[22] By formulating an alternative motivation for the death sentence against Eichmann, she returned to this argument.[23] Her alternative proposal looks somewhat artificial but must be perceived within the context of her intention to stress the universalistic character of the Holocaust, which, as she wrote to Jaspers in February 1961, although it had been a crime essentially committed against Jews, was not restricted to "the Jews or the Jewish question."[24] This was, however, not an attempt to put the genocide into a comparative perspective and to diminish its uniqueness, but to stipulate its principally ahistorical and amoral nature.

Arguments like this reflected Arendt's peculiar interpretation of the character of totalitarian systems, which she believed tend toward the dissolution of the body politic and lead in the long run into dissolution and destabilization of their own rule because their basically arbitrary character aims at creating a new fictitious world and at the destruction of any given historical inheritance. The Nazi dictatorship was especially characterized in her eyes by the unremitting endeavor "to create a merely fictitious new world."[25]

She perceived totalitarian dictatorship not primarily as a consistent hierarchy of subordinated functionaries, as others had tended to see it, but as drawing much of its remarkable outward efficiency from the ability to bypass existing bureaucratic structures. Therein lay the mechanism that prevented totalitarian "self-moving movement"[26] and its political and social energies from being reintegrated into the framework of the normative state. Simultaneously, totalitarianism's competing bureaucratic apparatus would act on its own and add to the destructive energies of the system.

The Jerusalem trial seemed to justify all these assumptions and to prove that the process of anti-Jewish destruction was in many respects self-propelling after having been set in motion. Actually, Eichmann presented himself exactly as the subaltern agent who controlled the destruction machinery without any feeling of remorse, equipped by bureaucratic cold-bloodedness and having no moral self-reflexivity whatsoever. In conjunction with this, Hannah Arendt arrived at the conclusion that the role of anti-Semitic ideology was less important than she previously had thought. In a letter to Mary McCarthy on September 20, 1963, she pointed out that she had exaggerated the impact of ideology in *The Origins of Totalitarianism*. When the extermination made headway, she argued, the impact of anti-Semitism was of decreasing importance and the annihilation became a more or less self-sustaining process.[27]

For the same reason, she could argue that the Nazi regime, after having achieved the slaughter of the Jews, would turn against other groups of victims, as well.[28] This observation appears to be correct. The use of euthanasia provides a striking example. This was eventually extended to include elderly people in Germany. What better illustrates the insatiable nature of the liquidation machinery?[29] The fact that Eichmann did not show any remorse for his deeds and regarded them as the fulfillment of an ordinary job without regard for its ethical dimensions endorsed Arendt's argument for the "unprecedentedness" of this human tragedy.[30] The mainly anonymous process resulting in the murder of almost six million Jews emerged from the self-moving dynamic of totalitarian rule and was primarily the consequence neither of racial fanaticism nor of long-term planning processes. From this vantage point, Arendt maintained that the Holocaust was to be perceived as an aberration from the fundamentals of human civilization and not just a previously unheard-of accumulation of ordinary crimes.

Simultaneously, she stressed that the transpersonal element of the Holocaust, which she interpreted as the self-destruction of humanity, never would have come to its end with the liquidation of the Jews, but would have involved other groups, as well, as the targeting of the Sinti and Roma peoples commonly known as Gypsies and of members of the Slavic peoples already indicated. In conjunction with this, she put the main weight on the functional, and not the ideological, causes of the Holocaust, although ideological causes had predominated in the explanations advanced in *The Origins of Totalitarianism,* although she distinguished sharply between nineteenth-century anti-Semitism and the Nazi racist ideology, which needed to present an enemy as a corollary of totalitarian terror.[31]

Arendt, however, overlooked the fact that her criticism of the trial in *Eichmann in Jerusalem,* that the indictment should have involved crimes against humanity and not against the Jewish people alone, inevitably created the erroneous impression that she intended to express contempt for the court itself. Actually, she argued in this way because she was deliberately accentuating the paradigmatic importance of the Holocaust and its universalist nature. Hence, she rejected sharply any attempt to integrate the Nazi genocide into the continuity of the Jewish history. Conversely, she perceived the abominable fate of the Jewish victims and those of other suppressed groups in the totalitarian states within the broader context of the general destruction of human values as she saw it reflected in the fate of millions of refugees and displaced persons, who stood as a symbol for a fundamental threat to mankind.

The existential category of the *Verlassenheit,* the loss of one's homeland, family, and social ties, as well as of the material conditions for survival,[32] was taken from the existential philosophy with which she was so familiar since her Heidelberg days. In some respects, she sided with the myth of the 1920s that, out of the decay of the bourgeois world, new social and political structures, something like a new beginning, might arise.[33] For her, one precondition for this new beginning consisted in a readiness to accept shared general responsibility for the catastrophe of the Jewish people, even by the victims, and particularly by the leaders of the Jewish community in Israel as well as in the Diaspora.

Ideas like these may explain why Hannah Arendt put so much weight on the controversial issue of the cooperation of the Jewish councils and other Jewish organizations with the Nazi persecutors. Before she had studied the available documents in connection with the projected report on the Eichmann trial, she already had in this respect made up her mind.[34] Obviously, she did not sufficiently comprehend the actual conditions under which the persecuted Jewish communities tried to survive, especially in Eastern Europe. But her crucial argument was not so much directed against the Jewish functionaries, but referred instead to the way that, as she had already written in *The Origins of Totalitarianism,* the Nazi machinery of destruction successfully turned the criminal activities involved into routine procedures that suffocated any moral protest, either from bystanders or from those who were induced to become perpetrators, as the recent discussion over the role of the police battalions is revealing again.[35]

While Hannah Arendt's specific understanding of the Holocaust enabled her to reach some remarkable critical observations, it also led her to a great number of overstatements that partly derived from her polemical temper but also were the result of her method of deductive thinking. Trained in dialectic thought and starting from ontological categories, she fell in some respects victim to what she called "the self-coercion of deductive thought" (*den Selbstzwang des deduzierenden Denkens*).[36] Yet her critical commentaries—particularly concerning the Jewish reaction to the Nazi onslaught—had all the time contained a hidden self-criticism, and this should be taken into account if she is erroneously attacked as a defector from the Jewish camp.

Between Justice and Politics

*The Competition of Storytellers
in the Eichmann Trial*

Leora Bilsky

"History" contains the word "story," and every historian is also a story-teller. When history is put on trial, who is the storyteller then?

The case of the state of Israel against Adolf Eichmann was brought nto trial in Jerusalem in 1961 and was concluded with the judgment of the court.[1] The judgment was pronounced unanimously—the court spoke with one voice, providing the official (hi)story. Judges, however, are not the only storytellers in trials. Lawyers have their own share of storytelling. Their stories are built mainly upon choosing the framework of the trial's narrative and upon deciding who will tell it.[2]

Gideon Hausner, the attorney general in Eichmann's trial, took it upon himself to be the master storyteller. He claimed to speak with the voice of six million victims, six million accusers.[3] Hannah Arendt, who came as a reporter for the *New Yorker,* was also a storyteller of the Eichmann trial. However, Arendt was not an official actor in the legal drama, and she deliberately took it upon herself to provide a counternarrative, the story that was not told but should have been told in the courtroom.

If ever there was a "competition of storytellers," it was strongly evident here. Arendt rewrote the attorney general's accusations, challenged his choice of witnesses, objected to the direction in which he led the trial, reinterpreted the crime, and, finally, could not resist the temptation to produce her own judgment.[4]

In *Eichmann in Jerusalem,* Arendt criticizes Hausner's decisions time and again. Hausner, for his part, mentions Arendt only once in *Justice in Jerusalem*. He cites an article that criticizes "Miss Arendt" and adds in a footnote that her book was refuted by many reviewers; hence it does not deserve a further discussion in his book.[5] In their zeal to produce the "correct"[6] story, both, at times, forgot the limits of storytelling and sought to occupy the position of the sole author.[7] It is for this reason that I conduct an imagined dialogue between Arendt and Hausner that will explore their views about the relation between story, history, and judgment as exemplified in the Eichmann trial.

I will focus on two aspects of their respective stories. One might be called the "framework" of the narrative, its temporal and spatial boundaries. With respect to temporal boundaries, Hausner's story stretches to include the whole of Jewish history, while Arendt begins her story in the nineteenth century. With respect to spatial boundaries, Hausner's story focuses on the Jewish people, while Arendt's concern is humanity.[8] The second way in which I will compare their narratives concerns the question of who is to tell the story—that is, whether the story will be told through written documents or through the oral testimonies of survivors.

THE MISSING CHAPTER

The two storytellers, Hausner and Arendt, came into direct confrontation over the exclusion of one particular chapter from the Eichmann trial.

"After fifty sessions, we reached the chapter on Hungarian Jewry," Hausner writes in his book. "The shadow of another [earlier] trial now fell over our courtroom."

Hausner is referring to the Kastner affair, which was brought to court in 1952 as a libel trial against Malchiel Gruenvald, a Hungarian Jew who imputed collaboration and treason to Dr. Rudolf (Rezso) Kastner.[9] During 1943–44, while Kastner negotiated with Eichmann over his proposal to exchange "trucks for lives," approximately four hundred thousand Hungarian Jews were led in trains to Auschwitz. At the same time, Kastner managed to rescue a train with 1685 Jews, including many of his friends and relatives. The defense attorney, Samuel Tamir, managed to turn the libel trial against his client Gruenvald into a political trial of the behavior of the Labour Party (MAPAI) during the war. In his verdict, Judge Halevi of the trial court condemned Kastner's collaboration with the Nazis, using the infamous phrase "Kastner sold his soul to the devil."

Subsequently, the appellate court cleared Kastner's name, but it was too late for Kastner, who was assassinated while the appeal was proceeding.[10]

Thus, the first time an Israeli court had to confront the Holocaust, it was a Jewish leader who was put on trial, not the Nazi perpetrators.[11] The later trial of Adolf Eichmann was carefully separated from the previous trial of Kastner. The prosecution tried to create an acoustic separation between the trials. This, however, could not conceal the fact that many of the main actors in the trials (judges, attorneys, and witnesses) were repeat players.[12] In fact, so clearly interwoven were the trials that the attorney general had to approach his witnesses in advance and ask them, for the sake of national unity, not to drag the bitter controversy over the Kastner affair into the trial of Eichmann. As Hausner recalls: "I had appealed to everyone to abstain from internal reckoning, since this was the trial of the exterminator and not of his victims."[13]

Traces of the Kastner affair still infiltrated into the Eichmann trial. Hansi Brand, who was Kastner's partner in the rescue committee in Budapest and in the negotiations with Eichmann, testified at Eichmann's trial. Judge Halevi, who sat in judgment in both trials, questioned her whether the Aid and Rescue Committee considered the possibility of assassinating Eichmann. Brand rejected the implicit accusation in the judge's question (Why didn't you rebel?), answering him: "We were a rescue committee and none of us was a hero. Our goal was to try and save these people. We did not know if killing Eichmann would bring relief . . . we were sure . . . that someone else would replace him and the system will keep on moving, maybe even faster."[14]

This answer brought back the public controversy that erupted around Kastner's trial about the legitimacy of negotiating with the Nazis. Likewise, during the testimony of Pinchas Freudiger, one of the leaders of the Orthodox community in Budapest and a member of the *Judenrat* (Jewish council), a spectator from the audience stood up and shouted at the witness in Hungarian: "You soothed us so that we should not run away while you were saving your families." Traces of this incident did not find their way into the official transcript of the testimonies in the trial.[15]

Hannah Arendt was quick to notice this staged silence. What was erased from the official transcript quickly found its way into her report.[16] Indeed, she devoted twenty-two pages of her book, its most controversial pages, to discussing the cooperation of the Jewish leadership in general and the cooperation of Kastner in particular with the Nazis, even though the issue was never raised during the trial.[17]

Arendt was right on target, as can be gleaned from Hausner's report of a conversation that he had prior to the trial with the leaders of the Jewish resistance of the Warsaw ghetto, Yitzhak Zuckerman and Zvia Luvetkin Zuckerman: "'What will you say about the Jewish Councils?' Yitzhak asked me. . . . 'This is going to be the trial of the murderer, not of his victims,' I replied. 'But you will not be able to avoid the issue,' Zvia said. . . . 'No,' I replied, 'and what we shall bring forth will be the truth. No embellishments.' 'That is good,' said Yitzhak. 'The whole truth must be told.'" [18]

Hausner did not keep his promise. This may well be because in the early 1960s, Israeli society was just recovering from the painful stage of accusing the victims for their own disaster and moving on to blame the victimizers. The 1950s atmosphere of pointing a blaming finger at the survivors, culminating in the Kastner trial, contributed to their effective silencing.[19] The Eichmann trial can be understood as an organized attempt to use the legal system to facilitate this move.[20]

Why was Arendt so strongly opposed to this attempt? Why was it so important to her to include the Kastner affair and the behavior of the Jewish leadership in the trial of the "exterminator," as Hausner called him? Arendt provides an explanation for including this chapter in the report in a private letter to Karl Jaspers: "I'm afraid that Eichmann will be able to prove . . . to what a huge degree the Jews helped organize their own destruction. That is, of course, the naked truth, but this truth, if it is not really explained, could stir up more anti-Semitism than ten kidnappings." [21] However, this explanation cannot stand closer scrutiny because when Eichmann's attorney decided *not* to raise the issue in the trial, Arendt went on and raised it on her own initiative.

At the time of the publication of her report, Arendt was harshly criticized for including this chapter.[22] She chose not to answer her critics. Yet Arendt does have an answer to which she refers in a letter to Mary McCarthy dated October 1963.[23] She tells McCarthy that she intends to write an essay about "truth and politics" as an implicit answer to her critics. Indeed, she published this essay in the *New Yorker* in February 1967. The essay will serve as a basis for my discussion of Arendt's position on the role of the trial and of her reasons for including this chapter in her report.

JUSTICE VERSUS POLITICS

The essay's title, "Truth and Politics," points to its topic, a study of their ancient conflict. In her earlier report, Arendt presented the Eichmann trial as a dramatic struggle between the two age-old antagonists, politics and justice, personified in the characters of Gideon Hausner and Justice Moshe Landau. She accused Hausner of serving the dictates of politics instead of searching for truth and justice. Arendt argued that justice demanded that the trial concentrate on the acts of Adolf Eichmann the accused, while politics called for opening the stage to the testimonies of survivors about the "suffering of the Jewish people." Arendt herself did not remain an impartial spectator. Instead, she claimed to take the side of justice. Hausner's divergences from the narrow framework of a criminal trial in his constant attempts to "draw the big picture" of the Jewish tragedy were, therefore, criticized by Arendt as signs of his political agenda.[24] In her criticism of Hausner we witness an inversion of roles: Arendt, the historian, took the side of justice and accused Hausner, the prosecutor, for adopting the role of the historian.

A closer reading of *Eichmann in Jerusalem* reveals that the opposition between justice and politics might be a misleading clue to understanding the controversy between Arendt and Hausner. It is apparent that Arendt herself did not obey the "dictates of justice" when she decided to "enlarge the picture" of the trial and discuss the Jewish cooperation with the Nazis. Indeed, Arendt offers an entirely different explanation for bringing up this issue in the Eichmann book. She writes: "I have dwelt on this chapter of the story, which the Jerusalem trial failed to put before the eyes of the world in its true dimensions, because it offers the most striking insight into the totality of the moral collapse the Nazis caused in respectable European society—not only in Germany but in almost all countries, not only among the persecutors but also among the victims." [25]

This is a very different explanation from the one she initially gave to Jaspers for including this chapter. What is conspicuously missing from Arendt's explanation is the simple "demand of justice" to concentrate on the acts of Eichmann. It indicates that the real controversy between Arendt and Hausner was about which "big picture" to draw, about the proper historical framework of the trial's story. Both Arendt and Hausner understood that Eichmann's trial could not be contained within the scope of narrow legalistic considerations. They tried to supply the historical narrative as the basis for judging Eichmann's acts. The trial was important for both of them because they understood that it occupied the no-man's land between past and future, a place where human beings are called to reflect back upon their common past and try to comprehend it.[26] Their historical narratives, however, differed in substantial ways. Before

I proceed to examine the two contrasting narratives, I would like to turn first to theory about the relation between story, history, and judgment.

THEORY: STORY, HISTORY, JUDGMENT

Since the beginning of the 1980s, we have witnessed the growth of a new movement in legal scholarship known as the law and literature movement.[27] The topics that the proponents of the movement study range from the art of storytelling in the courtroom, to structuralist analysis of courtroom decisions, to the production of "counterstories" that unmask the racial and gendered faces of legal discourse. A similar development can be traced in historiography.[28]

Not withstanding the interesting parallels that can be drawn between these legal and historiographical movements, I will not pursue this line of inquiry here. I would like to explore, instead, the juncture between the two disciplines as it occurred in the trial of Adolf Eichmann. Historic trials, which are also trials of history, stand at the crossroads where law and history meet. Indeed, this was the perception of the Eichmann trial from its beginning.[29] The judges, who were aware of public expectations that their judgment would provide the "official history" of the Holocaust, warned against this tendency and carefully delimited their jurisdiction.[30] However, no one, not the judges, the lawyers, or the public at large, could divorce history from the courtroom altogether. The crucial questions turned out to be "What kind of history?" and "Who will tell this (hi)story?"

In order to understand the relations between law, history, and narrative, let us divide the issue into three smaller questions. What is the relation between story and judgment? What is the relation between historical narratives and judgment? And finally, what is the relation between law and narrative? I turn to three writers from the three disciplines involved (literary criticism, historiography, and legal scholarship) who attempted to answer these questions. Surprisingly, a common theme emerges from their writings.

Walter Benjamin offers his reflections on the connection between story and judgment in *The Storyteller,* an essay about the disappearing art of storytelling: "All this points to the nature of every real story. It contains, openly or covertly, something useful. The usefulness may, in one case, consist in a moral; in another, in some practical advice; in a third, in a proverb or maxim. In every case the storyteller is a man who has counsel for his readers." [31]

Stories, for Benjamin, far from being merely a pleasurable pastime, are practical devices that provide their listeners with orientation and direction in the world. This is so because each story contains a moment of judgment that is shared by the storyteller and her listeners. The advice, the proverb, or the maxims that can be discerned in the story are all instances of judgment. Benjamin chose to use the term "advice" to stress the practical aspects of such judgments. According to Benjamin, the counsel that the story provides "is less an answer to a question than a proposal concerning the continuation of a story, which is just unfolding." As human beings, our judgments are not mere reflections on things past; they are important precisely because they can also guide us into the future.[32] The disappearing art of storytelling in our modern age is taken by Benjamin, therefore, to be a sign of a loss of way and direction for humanity.

Hayden White examines a special kind of story, the kind that offers a historical account of past events. White explains that today, for a historical account to acquire the highest status of history telling, it has to be formulated as a narrative, rather than, say, as a collection of annals or a chronicle. White asks, therefore, what additional value a narrative form gives to a historical account in comparison with these other forms. He suggests that it is the value of moral judgment. "The demand for closure in the historical story is a demand . . . for moral meaning, a demand that sequences of real events be assessed as to their significance as elements of a moral drama."[33]

Although the narrative form offers closure, White argues that reality itself does not display the formal coherence of a narrative with well-defined beginning, middle, and end. For this reason, to represent reality in the form of a narrative requires the introduction of another order of things—a normative order implicit in every historical narrative. In other words, it is the presence of judgment implicit in the form of the historical narrative that provides it with closure.

The narrative form offers normative closure to a historical account but also introduces the problem of authority because "Insofar as historical stories can be completed, can be given a narrative closure . . . they give to reality the odor of the *ideal*. This is why the plot of a historical narrative is always an embarrassment and has to be 'found' in the events rather than put there by narrative techniques." Thus, narrative is shown by White to be both a solution to a problem (the desire for closure) and a source of a new problem (undermining the authority of the historian). We will return to this subject later, when we examine how the narrative form was both a solution and an embarrassment for Hausner and Arendt.

Robert Cover's description of the relation of a legal system to the social narratives surrounding it is the mirror image of White's formulation: "In this normative world, law and narrative are inseparably related. Every prescription is insistent in its demand to be located in discourse— to be supplied with history and destiny, beginning and end, explanation and purpose. And every narrative is insistent in its demand for its prescriptive point." [34]

Cover argues that as a body of prescriptions, law is made meaningful only with the help of stories in which it is embedded and in light of the human experiences from which it springs. Recognizing the thick embeddedness of the normative world of law in a web of communal narratives points to the central problem that occupies Cover. He studies the contest of narratives among different social groups for recognition by the state's law and the contest of different groups over the meaning of that law. This understanding of the presence of the social group in the production of law's stories has important ramifications for understanding the contest between Hausner and Arendt. Their contest might reflect the fact that Hausner and Arendt imagined different social groups when they told their narratives about Eichmann's crimes. [35]

We can now try to bring together the three perspectives: the need for a form (literature), the search for meaning (history), and the duty to judge (law). White explains the relations among them in the following way: "we cannot but be struck by the frequency with which narrativity . . . presupposes the existence of a legal system against which the typical agents of a narrative account militate. . . . The more historically self-conscious the writer of any form of historiography, the more the question of the social system and the law which sustains it, the authority of this law and its justification, and threats to the law occupy his attention." [36]

The Nazi regime turned this formulation into the hardest problem confronting the storyteller, the historian, and the judge. They all had to grapple with a reality of discontinuity—a sense of a growing abyss separating the past from the present. Judging the unprecedented could not be left to the tools of traditional criminal law, which presupposes human experiences radically different from the ones under consideration. In order to construct new laws adequate to the new social reality under Nazi totalitarianism, one had to formulate a historical narrative of the period. In order to formulate such a narrative, however, one had to presuppose a common normative world that could provide the tools for judgment. But this normative world collapsed under the Nazi regime. Thus, we are caught in what seems to be a vicious circle. This circle, however, is not the result of a logical paradox. It instead stems from the reality of a "limit experience." It was indeed the experience of the limit produced by the Holocaust that challenged novelists, historians, and judges alike.[37]

This problem made the courtroom a great challenge but also a possible solution. A trial forces us to judge a past event, to formulate the historical narrative on which to base our judgment, and to reflect on the precedent to take with us into the future. Arendt, who was preoccupied with these questions, wrote in a letter to Jaspers: "It seems to me to be in the nature of this case that we have no tools except the legal ones with which we have to judge and pass sentence on something that cannot even be adequately represented within legal terms or in political terms. That is precisely what makes the process itself, namely the trial, so exciting." [38]

Arendt realized that traditional frameworks of judgment, social narratives, and historical accounts were missing when we tried to judge the Holocaust. Eichmann's trial confronted us with the problem of judging "without banisters," as Arendt's vivid phrase would have it. The need to judge past events by putting their disorder under the well-ordered categories of law was strongly felt in this trial, as it is in all trials. Only in this trial, the legal categories were deficient and the historical narratives that locate them were not yet formulated. The Eichmann trial, however, offered a great opportunity for the lawyer and the historian precisely because it functioned as a meeting place where the need to tell the story, to judge the criminal, and to offer the history all coincided. It forced the participants, as well as the audience, to begin the painful process of articulating the story and judging the past in order to continue into the future. Let us turn now to examine how Arendt and Hausner confronted this challenge.

TWO CONTRASTING HISTORICAL FRAMEWORKS

Hausner advocated bridging the abyss between past and future with the tools of traditional Jewish historiography. His narrative was based on a structure of a repetition: Jews have always been persecuted for anti-Semitic reasons; every generation has its own Pharaoh.[39] Hausner sought to connect the latest catastrophe to anti-Semitic persecutions of Diaspora Jews over the ages. He also linked the Holocaust to the enemies of today, namely, to the Palestinian leader Haj Amin Husseini.[40] For this purpose, Hausner had to demarcate clearly the line between victims and perpetrators. Adolf Eichmann was depicted as the incarnation of the persecutors of old, Pharaoh and Haman. The frame of the story was the long history of victimization and persecution of the Jews, and it was meant to illuminate the Jewish story that was largely missing from the Nuremberg trials.[41] Accordingly, the prosecution chose to focus its case on the legal category of "crimes against the Jewish people."[42] In Hausner's clear-cut division of victims and victimizers there was no place for dwelling on the murky category of Jewish cooperation with the Nazis, the phenomenon of the *Judenräte*. Arendt criticized this historical narrative: "It was bad history and cheap rhetoric; worse, it was clearly at cross purposes with putting Eichmann on trial, suggesting that perhaps he was only an innocent executor of some mysteriously foreordained destiny, or, for that matter, even of anti-Semitism, which perhaps was necessary to blaze the trail of 'the bloodstained road traveled by this people' to fulfill its destiny."[43]

For Arendt, traditional Jewish frames of meaning could not supply the needed explanation for the new phenomena because they sought to highlight present-day analogies to the old story of anti-Semitism. Instead, she wanted to understand Eichmann's actions with the tools of modern historiography, in terms of the immediate historical circumstances, and not in terms of the relation between God and a chosen people. She suggested locating the modern catastrophe within the European context of the rise of the totalitarian state. Her tools were not analogies, but distinctions. Indeed, she was careful to distinguish Eichmann the man from the mythical figures of Pharaoh and Haman. Eichmann was depicted in her book as the product of his own age—the age of bureaucracy, science, and ideology.

AUTHOR AND AUTHORITY

Contrasting the historical frameworks of Hausner and Arendt helps expose their narrative element. Both accounts offer coherence and structure to the "facts" by supplying them with narrative closure. However, the narration of the facts also introduces the problem of authority that I mentioned before.[44] If Arendt and Hausner are storytellers of sorts, whose story is to be preferred as the "true" story? Both shy away from confronting this problem. Hausner relies on the legal tools for endowing his account with "objectivity."[45] Arendt, being an outsider to the legal drama, relies on her position as a reporter of facts to minimize her presence as the narrator of facts. Indeed, this stance can explain her choice to subtitle the book a "report" on the banality of evil. The same attitude is also manifested in a letter to McCarthy in which Arendt writes: "As I see it, there are no 'ideas' in this Report, there are only facts with a few conclusions, and these conclusions usually appear at the end of each chapter." [46]

This circumvention of the problem later proved to be unsatisfying to Arendt, who returned to the problem of narrative authority in "Truth and Politics." This time, she elaborated her views on historiography as narration. Arendt argues that there is no necessary conflict between "factual truth" and "narrative" as long as the historian respects the facts while acknowledging the importance of ordering them into a narrative form. Arendt thinks that there are "facts" independent of opinions and interpretations, though she also thinks that facts in themselves do not determine the historical narrative. Her solution to the problem is that "facts" function as limits on our historical narration. They are the "ground on which we stand" and the "sky that stretches above us." Arendt explains that "even if we admit that every generation has the right to write its own history, we admit no more than that it has the right to rearrange the facts in accordance with its own perspective; we don't admit the right to touch the factual matter itself." [47] This subtler formulation, however, is not of much help for our purposes, because the controversy was precisely on how to rearrange the facts, under which framework, and from what perspective. Arendt and Hausner did not offer the reasons for preferring one narrative framework to the other. They chose to circumvent the problem by stressing their position as fact finders and minimizing their role as narrators. In order to evaluate their choices as storytellers, we need to reconstruct their reasons for choosing their respective historical frameworks. To this end, I suggest we examine Arendt and Hausner's views about the role of the trial in relating the past to the future.

WAYS OF RECONCILIATION IN THE COURTROOM

With very different stories, both Arendt and Hausner hoped that the trial would bring about reconciliation. Hausner writes, "only through knowledge could understanding and reconciliation with the past be achieved." [48] And Arendt explains that "to the extent that the teller

of factual truth is also a storyteller, he brings about that 'reconciliation with reality.' "[49] In other words, reconciliation can be achieved only
when the facts are placed into a humanly comprehensible narrative.[50]
In Arendt's view reconciliation with the past through storytelling also
provides a solid basis for judgment.[51] Arendt and Hausner strongly
disagree, however, about the way in which this reconciliation should
take place.

Hausner's choice of frame can be understood in light of what happened in the trial of Kastner.[52] The district court's infamous phrase, that
"Kastner sold his soul to the devil," did not bring about closure or
catharsis.[53] The Kastner trial was like a traumatic repetition of the past,
a reopening of the wound that could not bring about reconciliation. One
of the purposes of Eichmann's trial was to use the structure of the trial
in order to invert the past symbolically, turning the persecuted victims
into the prosecutors, and by this to offer a resolution to that painful
past.[54] For this purpose, the line between victims and perpetrators had
to be clearly demarcated.[55] And for this reason, the attorney general appealed to the witnesses to "abstain from internal reckoning."

Arendt sought to bring about reconciliation with the past in a very
different way. She worried about the omission of the story of the *Judenräte* in Eichmann's trial. In her report, she admits that these were not
simple lies, since she did not expose any new facts that were previously
unknown to Israeli society: "these issues . . . are discussed quite openly
and with astonishing frankness in Israeli schoolbooks."[56] But this was
precisely the reason why the omissions in the trial seemed all the more
dangerous to Arendt. As she explained in "Truth and Politics," even
though the facts she insisted on discussing were "publicly known . . . yet
the same public that knows them can successfully, and often spontaneously, taboo their public discussion and treat them as though they were
what they are not—namely, secrets."[57] In other words, Arendt's understanding of the collective aspects of memory made her fear that the
omissions in Eichmann's trial will produce in the Israeli collective memory what she had called "holes of oblivion" in *The Origins of Totalitarianism.* She traces this danger back to the fragility of factual truth that
we encounter in trials: "it is established by witnesses and depends upon
testimony; it exists only to the extent that it is spoken about."[58]

Arendt's concern with collective self-deception can be linked to her
political philosophy. Arendt is a philosopher of action—she opposes all
determinist schools of history because she believes in human natality, in

the possibility to begin anew. In "Truth and Politics," Arendt writes that
the fact of human natality, the immanent "it might have been otherwise"
that is inherent in any factual event, is what frustrates historians who try
to master the story once and for all. But it is precisely this understanding of human natality that convinces her to include what she calls the
"darkest chapter of the story," the chapter on the Jewish *Judenräte*.
Arendt writes: "Not the past—and all factual truth, of course, concerns
the past—or the present, insofar as it is the outcome of the past, but the
future is open for action." [59] By this she means that our only hope for
learning and changing (and here she is also thinking as a daughter of the
Jewish people) is to confront the past as it was, without defense mechanisms, but with an understanding that the future is still open for change:
"If the past and present are treated as parts of the future—that is,
changed back into their former state of potentiality—the political realm
is deprived not only of its main stabilizing force, but of the starting point
from which to change, to begin something new." [60]

We are thus offered two different forms of reconciliation with the
past. Hausner advocates splitting the story in two and focusing on the
story of the victims in judging Eichmann. He adopts this approach because of what happened in Kastner's trial, where the blaming of the victim ended in a political assassination with no sense of resolution. Arendt
does not believe in this solution of "collective forgetfulness" of the
"darkest chapter." She argues that it is precisely such an attitude that
condemns us to reiterations. [61] Instead, she advocates communication
and storytelling of the ways in which Jews (and others) were led to cooperate with the Nazi system, so that this painful experience will acquire
a permanent place and hence become part of the nation's history.

These differences in approach are connected to a larger view of history. For Hausner, the persecution of Jews throughout the ages is a historical constant, the product of historical determinism, that can be
changed only with the establishment of a Jewish state. The lesson that
he draws from the Holocaust is, therefore, the particularistic lesson of
empowering the Jews by protecting their state. Indeed, the trial of Eichmann by the sovereign state of Israel serves as the embodiment of this
lesson. For Arendt, on the other hand, the persecution of the Jews is
taken as a warning sign to humanity at large of the dangers of the totalitarian state. In her story, there are no nations that are protected from
these dangers a priori. The horror of the totalitarian system is precisely
its ability to implicate perpetrators, bystanders, and victims. Because she
believes that these experiences might be repeated in the future, she draws

the lesson of the need to strengthen the international community by developing a new legal category of "crimes against humanity."

LAW FRAMES HISTORY

The opposition between the narratives of Arendt and Hausner is also shaped by their choice of legal categories. Hausner's narrative stresses continuity and repetitions by pointing out historical precedents to Nazi crimes against the Jews. The legal framework of "crimes against the Jewish people" that he advocates emphasizes the unique victimhood of the Jewish people. His story also suggests a direction for the future—the way to overcome the Jewish fate—is to establish a lasting Jewish state that will have the jurisdiction to prosecute these crimes. Arendt, on the other hand, offers a historical narrative that highlights the lack of historical precedents. Instead of focusing on the victims, she directs our attention to the crime, thus decentering the issue of anti-Semitism in the trial. She replaces the thesis of Jewish uniqueness with the proposition that "the physical extermination of the Jewish people, was a crime against humanity, perpetrated upon the body of the Jewish people." She adds a rebuttal to Hausner's narrative, saying, "only the choice of victims, not the nature of the crime, could be derived from the long history of Jew-hatred and anti-Semitism." [62] In confronting the future, Arendt seeks to construct a *legal* precedent that will withstand the very real possibility that such crimes will be repeated in the future on other people and in other places.[63] Her preferred legal category is therefore "crimes against humanity."

The question of frame turns out to be a question of center and periphery. The frame that Hausner advocated puts anti-Semitism and the Jewish victims at the center, while Arendt's frame puts totalitarianism, and Eichmann as its typical actor, at the center.[64] This difference is often understood as stemming from the opposition between particularism on Hausner's side and universalism on Arendt's side. However, if we read Arendt's historical narrative in conjunction with her choice of legal category, this explanation will prove to be insufficient. In my view, Arendt sought to integrate the two perspectives of universalism and particularism. She espoused bridging the two by offering a universalistic approach while speaking within the particularity of the Jewish experience. The dichotomy between universalism and particularism dissolves once we examine the choice of legal category against the choice of a narrative framework.

The mistake lies in the attempt to evaluate Arendt's historical narrative under the framework of the legal category of "crimes against the Jewish people" that she has rejected. Only under Hausner's legal framework, which highlights the uniqueness of Jewish victimhood, could the introduction of a chapter on the behavior of the Jewish leadership, as suggested by Arendt, have carried anti-Semitic implications. Under this legal framework, a chapter discussing the cooperation of Jewish leaders with the Nazis would tend to reflect on the nature of the Jewish people, instead of on the general circumstances under Nazi regime. This is so because the legal framework of "crimes against the Jewish people" does not call for comparisons with the behavior of other people under the Nazi rule. In contrast, Arendt's choice of the legal category of "crimes against humanity" shaped her historical narrative. It allowed her to introduce the chapter on the Jewish councils into her narrative in a way that encourages comparisons with the behavior of different nations and groups under Nazi totalitarianism. We can see that the choice of "crimes against humanity" does not, necessarily, call for abstracting away the particularities of the Jewish story. On the contrary, it could help put the behavior of Jewish leaders in context by showing the totality of the moral collapse all over Europe in all occupied nations. Accordingly, Arendt writes that "the deliberate attempt at the trial to tell only the Jewish side of the story distorted the truth, even the Jewish truth." [65] On the universalist side, Arendt's legal framework allowed her to tell the story of the Jewish people in order to draw from it implications for international law. In particular, her story exposed the weakness of an international system established on the protection of individuals' rights without providing real protections to groups.

VICTIMS AS STORYTELLERS: VOICES VERSUS DOCUMENTS

The discussion of the legal and historical framework of the Eichmann trial has led us back to an earlier trial. We saw how the shadow of the Kastner trial shaped, to a large degree, the positions taken by Arendt and Hausner about the proper framework, legal and historical, for Eichmann's trial. A crucial question remains to be decided—Who should tell the story? In answering this question, we confront the shadow of another legal precedent—that of the Nuremberg trials.

Nuremberg set a precedent of letting the documents tell the story. Arendt strongly recommends this way for the Eichmann trial, as well. For the purposes of a trial, documents seem to provide a more reliable source. There is no need to depend on the memory of witnesses many years after the event. A document cannot be broken down in cross-examination. It speaks in a steady voice that cannot be silenced or interrupted. Moreover, Arendt fears that oral testimonies by survivors will open the door to the suffering of the victims—a suffering that has no measure and cannot be comprehended. She came to Eichmann's trial with the hope that the legal categories would provide some measure of understanding.[66] The only hope of achieving such understanding, Arendt wrote, is by concentrating on the acts of the accused, not on the immeasurable suffering of the victims.[67]

Hausner was well aware of these difficulties. He wrote in his book that by choosing to build the case of the prosecution on the oral testimony of survivors, he risked weakening its position.[68] Moreover, in preparing the witnesses to give testimony in trial, he confronted their difficulties of telling a story with a beginning, middle, and ending. In particular, the witnesses found it difficult to impose on their past experiences a temporal frame of continuity between past and present. He faced the phenomenon that Lawrence Langer calls "deep memory."[69] Hausner wrote: "At a pretrial conference they would sometimes stop conveying facts in an intelligible manner and begin speaking as if through a fog. The narrative, which had been precise and lucid up to this point, became detached and obscured. They found it difficult to describe in concrete terms phenomena from a different world."[70]

Indeed, one of the most famous testimonies in the trial, that of Yehiel Dinur, who used the pen name K-Zetnik, which means "camp inmate" in German, had this character about it, just before the witness collapsed on the witness stand.[71] Notwithstanding these difficulties, Hausner decided to tell the story of the Jewish Holocaust through the testimonies of survivors.[72]

How are we to understand this disagreement? We can take our cue from the metaphors of "hearing" and "seeing" as signaling two ways to get to the truth. What could bring law closer to justice—an auditory or a visual approach? In arguing their different views Hausner and Arendt were reenacting the old conflict between Jewish and Greek traditions.[73] Hausner's decision to prefer the human voice is compatible with the Jewish tradition that gives priority to voice and hearing over sight. Arendt's preference for sight, for written documents, is in accord with the Greek tradition that privileges seeing. In *The Life of the Mind,* Arendt articulates the difference between the two traditions: "The Hebrew God can be heard but not seen, and truth therefore becomes invisible: 'Thou shalt not make unto thee my graven image or any likeness of any thing that is in heaven above or that is on earth beneath.' The *invisibility* of truth in the Hebrew religion is as axiomatic as its ineffability in Greek philosophy from which all other later philosophy derived its axiomatic assumptions."

In her philosophical writings, Arendt advocated the sight metaphor as the safer road to truth and objectivity. This is because "seeing" inscribes a distance between subject and object, thus ensuring the "independence" of judgment. In contrast, she thought that "in hearing, the percipient is at the mercy of something or somebody else." [74] If we try to translate this insight to the context of the Eichmann trial, we can say that Arendt feared that the oral testimonies of human suffering will destroy the crucial distance between speaker and listener. This distance is needed for objective judgment, and without it the audience is overwhelmed with emotions.

When Arendt turned to examine more closely the human faculty of judgment under the influence of the Eichmann trial, she came to reject the metaphor of seeing as insufficient to explain its operation. [75] However, in her Eichmann report, Arendt still upheld the epistemic paradigm for judgment and equated justice with the search for the objective truth. No wonder that she opposed so strongly the use of the oral testimony of victims and preferred the objectivity of documents. Indeed, looking at the matter within an epistemic framework, Hausner's decision seems questionable. However, I suggest that the epistemic framework was not the only one that guided Hausner.

As an experienced legal practitioner, Hausner brought to the courtroom an understanding of the performative aspects of a trial. Every lawyer knows that trials are rarely an accurate representation of the past. More often, they provide a reenactment of events of the past in a concentrated and dramatized form. [76] The performative aspects of a trial can help reveal a truth about the past that might otherwise remain detached and obscured. But they also can contribute to the symbolic reenactment of the original crime within the courtroom. [77]

Hausner understood that the role of Eichmann's trial was not exhausted by the need to tell the truth about an untold story. He sought to create legal procedures that would reveal the nature of the new crimes. The novelty of the Nazis' crimes was not only in their plan to eliminate a nation, an entire human group, from the face of the earth in their crimes against the human status of diversity, as Arendt called it, but

also in their efforts to produce a crime without a witness. For this purpose, a whole system of distancing and concealment was erected, from
walls and fences to language rules.[78] This is what she had called "the
holes of oblivion." Paradoxically, however, her insistence that the court
establish the truth through the more objective tools of documents could
have served to repeat the silencing that was intended by the Nazis, the
erasure of the human voice as a reliable witness.[79]

In Nuremberg, the court allowed the testimony of the camera, showing a film about the liberation of the concentration camps.[80] But the
camera depicted the victims as voiceless *Figuren*—as horrific figures
that do not speak.[81] Arendt was one of the first to expose this aspect
of concentration camps. The camps, she wrote, were not just factories
of death, but were also meant to supply living "proofs" of Nazi ideology, proofs that some people are subhuman. This was accomplished by
starving and torturing the prisoners until they lost their capacity for action. Disconnecting the bond between action and speech produced an
essential part of this dehumanization process.[82] If Hausner had chosen
to rely solely on documents and pictures, he would have denied the voice
of the victims once again. In this sense, giving the stage to the testimonies of victims carried an ethical message of "giving voice." Hausner
was willing to take the legal risks and open the stage to the victims in
order to transform them from statistical figures into human beings with
a voice and a story. It was largely as a result of this procedural decision
that the Eichmann trial "created" the Holocaust in the consciousness of
the world.

VICTIMS AS STORYTELLERS: STORYTELLING IN A LEGAL SETTING

The moral obligation to bear witness was strongly felt by the survivors
themselves, and the need to give their testimonies a public stage is beyond dispute. The difficult question is whether the courtroom is the
proper forum for such an endeavor. What is the added value of a courtroom to the testimony of survivors? Is this value worth the risks of turning the trial into a political trial, risks that Arendt was so careful to expose? I do not think that we can offer a general answer to this question
that is derived from the nature of trials as such. In my view, the answer
has to be a combination of an understanding of the structural characteristics of a trial together with an understanding of the specific historical and social context in which it unfolds.[83] I would, therefore, limit my

reflections about the value of courtroom testimonies of Holocaust survivors to the historical and social circumstances surrounding the Eichmann trial.

Eichmann's trial provided a public stage for testimonies of survivors
that was qualitatively different from films and books. A trial has the
function of authorizing the movement from private to public by weav-
ing the private story into the web of communal stories that are then authorized by the judgment of the court. This aspect of a trial was especially important in the Eichmann trial, given the nature of the reception
of Holocaust survivors in Israel during the 1950s. Israeli society during
that time perceived the survivors who did not belong to the Jewish underground resistance as suspect ("What did you do in order to survive?
Judenrat? Kapo?"). Survivors had the negative images of people who
were morally corrupted under the Nazi regime or people who were
psychologically disturbed. This mode of pointing a blaming finger at the
victims can be gleaned from the debate in the Israeli parliament about
the enactment of the Law of Punishment of Nazis and their collaborators and from the various criminal trials that were held against survivors
under this law.[84] The Kastner trial was a culmination of these attitudes.
As a result of this public atmosphere, the survivors chose not to tell their
stories in public. To change such negative public images and to break the
silence that followed, it was not enough to provide a public stage for survivors' testimonies in the media or in political forums. The whole conceptual framework under which survivors were seen as suspects had to
be changed in order to begin to listen to what they had to tell.[85] The
Eichmann trial, with its well-defined roles of accuser and accused, could
facilitate this change because for the first time, the survivors were linked
with the accusing party and not with the accused. Moreover, for the first
time, the survivors were standing side by side with Israelis against a common enemy—Adolf Eichmann. Hausner's opening statement exemplified this change. This structural change could help survivors develop a
positive self-image that was needed in order to overcome the shame and
begin to talk in public. Moreover, by offering a metanarrative in terms
of chronology and geography, the victims could better understand the
meaning of their own experiences. By basing the case of the prosecution
on the testimonies of survivors, the trial presented the victims as reliable
witnesses and conferred authority on their words.[86] Finally, because each
trial is also a communal endeavor of taking responsibility in the literal
sense, of responding to testimonies with a legal judgment, the Eichmann

trial offered a double gesture of imputing responsibility to the perpetrator by responding to the words of the victims.

By deciding to prove Eichmann's guilt through the testimonies of Holocaust survivors, Hausner offered a unique interpretation of the meaning of justice, an interpretation that insists not only on telling the untold
story, but also on the importance of who will tell the story. This procedural decision is perhaps the lasting contribution of Eichmann's trial to
the development of international law, which today tries to make more
room to hear the stories of individual victims within legal proceedings.
The theoretical questions that the issue of giving voice to victims in trials raise are only now beginning to be addressed. One of the most important questions, I believe, is how to rethink the role of a courtroom in
enhancing the recognition of silenced groups such as victims of atrocities as part of the process of "doing justice." [87]

Arendt eventually began to change her mind in respect to the role of
victims' testimonies,[88] and it might well be that this change was induced
by Hausner's procedural decision. We witness this change in her report
when she exclaims after the testimony of Zindel Grynszpan, contrary
to all her previous warnings, that "everybody should have his day in
court," [89] meaning—every victim! I believe that at this point, Arendt
suddenly realizes the significance of a trial as a public forum where human action receives its name and story. It is at this point that she aban-
dons the epistemic framework into which she tried to fit the trial and is
reminded of her own ethics of storytelling.

CONCLUSION

Aware of the dangers to the collective memory of a society presented
by "holes of oblivion," Arendt opposed the legal framework that was
provided by Hausner because it excluded the chapter on the *Judenräte*.
However, in relation to the question of who should tell the story, it was
Hausner who insisted on giving voice to the victims, precisely because
of his awareness of an existing hole of oblivion in Israeli collective memory. Arendt's conclusion of the chapter called "Evidence and Witnesses"
seems to acknowledge the importance of this move: "The holes of oblivion do not exist. Nothing human is that perfect, and there are simply too
many people in the world to make oblivion possible. One man will always be left alive to tell the story." [90]

I would add that it is more likely that we need at least two people to

tell *this* story, with different frames and distinct voices. The two frameworks employed by Arendt and Hausner are incompatible, and therefore they allow us to see (and hear) different things. We should not look
for the meaning of this period and for the definitive judgment of Eichmann in either Hausner's narrative or Arendt's. Instead of choosing between them, we should learn to recognize the importance of the contest
of narratives as such to the possibility of judgment in the wake of the
Holocaust.

A Generation's Response to *Eichmann in Jerusalem*

Richard I. Cohen

No single study of the Holocaust has come close to attracting the kind of public attention *Eichmann in Jerusalem* received, although the sales of Daniel Goldhagen's *Hitler's Willing Executioners* have far exceeded those of Hannah Arendt's provocative work.[1] From its original publication in the *New Yorker* magazine in 1963 until today, *Eichmann in Jerusalem* continues to arouse interest, disagreement, and controversy. Though its historical value as a study of the events of the Holocaust is seriously questioned today by historians and totally dismissed by some, most prominently by Raul Hilberg,[2] it continues to be regarded as a landmark in the writing on the period. A generation and more have passed since its original publication. That generation witnessed the penetration of the Holocaust into academic and public discourse and the emergence of schools of interpretation that emphasized, on the one hand, the high degree of consistency in Nazi anti-Semitic policies driven by Hitler's "blueprint" (the "intentionalist" view), and, on the other, a "functionalist" view that stressed the lack of a master anti-Semitic plan and a far more "twisted" route to the Final Solution. That generation also faced the historical debates that have become known as the *Historikerstreit,* disagreements over whether and how to compare ("relativize," some claimed) Auschwitz and Nazism with other phenomena in history and whether there was a particular German historical road to such phenomena. Notwithstanding, *Eichmann in Jerusalem* has reappeared in English and German editions, has been the subject of special issues of academic journals, and continues to be highlighted in discussions on Holocaust historiography, as in the recent controversy over *Hitler's Willing Executioners*.[3] I am concerned here with the staying power of the book, the elements that originally provoked the enormous controversy, and its ability to sustain interest, although professional historians deride its factual value.

The still-explosive controversy surrounding *Hitler's Willing Executioners*, though seldom framed in this manner, can be seen as an expression of the age-old philosophical and historiosophical question about the nature of individual actions and whether they can be interpreted as a result of a particular national ethic, environment, or structure, in the sense that Herbert Spencer used these terms, or warrant a more nuanced analysis. Goldhagen not only reawakened the functionalist and intentionalist debate relating to the understanding of the Final Solution, but also brought us back to the heart of the Arendt polemic of the 1960s, which revolved around a seminal issue of modern times: the question of human freedom in historical action.

But the initial response to *Eichmann in Jerusalem* did not focus solely on Arendt's concept of the "banality of evil"[4]—the notion that a rather simple individual within a terrorized political situation could become engaged in acts of great evil without really construing the meaning of those actions—but also revolved around her assessment of Jewish complicity in the Final Solution.[5] Though this argument had already been presented in Raul Hilberg's *The Destruction of the European Jews*, published in 1961, it was Arendt's formulation that sparked the tremendous uproar. Sensitivity to her argument has remained rather constant throughout this last generation, especially to a certain historiosophical aspect of it: Arendt's assertion that Jewish leadership was partially responsible for the demise of the Jews assumed that they were not merely victims of the historical process. Apparently accepting Salo Baron's critique of the "lachrymose notion" of Jewish history, Arendt challenged the historical "image" of the Jew as a passive victim, even with respect to a period that would have appeared to have been the ultimate moment of the victimized Jew. In raising this claim, Arendt remained true to the interpretation of anti-Semitism she presented in *The Origins of Totalitarianism*. There, she argued that events relating to Jews, including those in which they were the victims, cannot be comprehended without considering the ways in which Jews themselves contributed to that outcome. This thesis did become the object of—sometimes heated—criticism.[6] *Eichmann in Jerusalem* most certainly did, precisely because of its direct association with the events of the Holocaust.

Placing the Jew within the context of an anti-Semitic development in a role other than that of a purely innocent victim has run the danger of stirring up Jewish and non-Jewish sensitivities—as if to challenge "sacred truths." Mutatis mutandis, and, on a much smaller scale, Israel Yuval, an Israeli scholar, aroused a storm when he argued recently that the acts of Jewish sanctification of the Name (suicides committed by Jewish families during the period of the Crusades) triggered in some way Christian beliefs that Jews used Christian blood for the making of their unleavened bread for the Passover holiday.[7] Or, in a different direction, consider the response of elements of the Israeli academy and society to various arguments presented by those designated as post-Zionist historians, wherein the "image" of a David fighting a Goliath is turned around, and Israel's policy toward the Arab population is seen in a diametrically opposite manner. What these responses have in common with the Arendt controversy is the rejection of a sacrosanct model that intuitively viewed "the Jews" as victims of the behavior of others and its replacement by a model that sees Jews acting in history and affecting their own fate, similar to the behavior of other ethnic, national, or religious groups—even in the face of genocide.[8] Placing the response to *Eichmann in Jerusalem* within the perspective of other historical controversies surrounding Jewish behavior should not blur the fact that other parallels to these volatile responses can be found in the ways in which national entities respond to criticism of their past, as can be seen in the case of French society's response to the claims made with regard to the collaboration of French officials and society during the Vichy period. Thus, by challenging or even condemning an important aspect of Jewish collective memory, raised at times to an almost theological premise—Jews as victims of history—an interpretation mutually held by non-Jews, and by focusing on individual freedom, *Eichmann in Jerusalem* presented an alternative reading to the history of the twentieth century that was bound to sustain controversy.

In sharpening a theoretical construction based on Hilberg's massive documentation of the bureaucratic process, by showing Eichmann to be a man without personal drive or motivation—a truly "ordinary man" (to use Christopher Browning's term,[9] which followed Arendt's "banality")—and by turning Hilberg's account of the Jewish leadership's alleged collaboration into "the darkest chapter of the whole dark story," Arendt radically reversed what had become the accepted truths on the Holocaust and transformed basic notions of man's individual culpability and of the Jew's place in history. Shot through with innuendoes that bridged the gap between perpetrator and victim, Arendt's account

pitted the Jewish community structure against the individual, the former
bearing unique responsibility for the destruction process. The collective
abandonment of the individual constituted for her a continuation of the
path taken by the German-Jewish leadership in their negotiations with
the Nazis—and a continuation of the paradigm of Jewish self-denial that
there were always other Jews to be found who fully fulfilled the "image"
of the Jew, while they did not. This, in a similar vein, was the way she
wrote of Berlin Jews in the early nineteenth century: "And just as every
anti-Semite knew his personal exceptional Jews in Berlin, so every Berlin
Jew knew at least two eastern Jews in comparison with whom he felt
himself to be an exception." [10] Moreover, by believing in "eternal anti-
Semitism"—what we have termed the collective memory of the Jew as
victim—and lacking political clairvoyance, "the Jewish leadership," according to Arendt, became predisposed to aid the Nazis in their efforts.

Arendt's formulations that so scintillated in the 1960s became clar-
ion calls for a whole generation, reappearing in new contexts and debates, even when her evidence was found wanting. Christopher Browning rejected her example of Eichmann as a "banal bureaucrat" but
found the concept "valid for understanding many Holocaust perpetrators." Writing in a period engaged with debates about postmodernism,
Gertrude Himmelfarb alluded to the same issue: "To 'structuralize' Nazism is to trivialize and 'de-moralize' it, to make evil banal. It is also to
'de-historicize' it, to belie the facts of history." [11] Two years later, Daniel
Goldhagen would add to this, maintaining, while pointing in the direction of *Eichmann in Jerusalem*, "Even though the full character of the
perpetrators' social and cultural existence is hard to recover, the unreal
images of them as isolated, frightened, thoughtless beings performing
their tasks reluctantly are erroneous." [12] But these formulations, and
many others that can be gleaned from the recent writing on Arendt,
were clearly of a different order, less charged and more sympathetic,
than those that characterized the controversy in the 1960s.

Let us recall that the appearance of Arendt's *Eichmann in Jerusalem*
in 1963 sparked an unparalleled public airing of historical issues relating to the Holocaust. For the first time since the war, laymen, journalists, intellectuals, jurists, social scientists, and historians—of both Jewish and non-Jewish extraction—placed the events of the Holocaust in
central focus. In several books and well over two hundred articles and
essays, they analyzed and challenged Arendt's unique portrayal of Eichmann, her understanding of evil in a totalitarian society, and her moral
condemnation of Jewish leadership in war-stricken Europe. Not all of

Arendt's critics were negatively inclined, and some praised her essay as a brilliant exposition of humanity's predicament in the face of totalitarianism, but their opinion was muted by those who condemned the work for its disrespectful treatment of the Jewish victims. While Arendt's favorable critics tended to accept her universalistic yardstick for measuring the moral culpability of Germans and Jews, her deriders rejected it as an affront to the memory of the murdered. In so doing, Arendt's critics presented their own image of the Holocaust, anchored in personal experience and background, philosophy, or ideological orientation, and often constructed an almost mythical approach to the war years.

JEWISH RESPONSES TO *EICHMANN IN JERUSALEM*

Prior to the Eichmann trial, public discussions of the Holocaust had been sparse, though Jewish journals aired many of the more sensitive themes that appeared in Arendt's book, including those that were to prove so explosive in her formulation. But the Holocaust had not penetrated into Jewish public consciousness and remained the purview of those immediately affected. Various authors bewailed that fact in anguished tones, while others claimed that the wide support for the state of Israel transferred the focus and postponed the encounter with those trying years. Arendt's strong reservations about the behavior of Jewish leaders during the Holocaust and her critique of Israel's rationale for holding the trial united both phenomena in a single framework, engendering a unique outpouring of emotion and dissatisfaction. On one level, her work jolted individuals out of a certain complacency toward their immediate past, but, on a deeper level, it undermined received myths and memories of the past, shaking the foundations of a postwar Weltanschauung that had begun to integrate the Holocaust and the creation of the state of Israel as seminal moments in the history of the Jewish people.

The "archetypal terms," to follow Steven Aschheim's appellation,[13] for scores of individuals who confronted Arendt in the 1960s were built upon clear differentiations between good and evil, horror and banality, Nazism and humanity, perpetrators and victims, the powerful and the powerless. Nazis were sworn anti-Semites of the worst kind who performed unbearable and unforgivable cruelties. The Jews were a powerless people who faced an unbending enemy driven to fulfill the worst crime in the history of humanity. Two years after *Eichmann in Jerusalem* appeared, the Yiddish writer Aron Zeitlin argued that there was no point in debating Arendt's thesis, but rather one must simply show that she is the devil's representative, striving endlessly to reverse the order of the world by revealing that the devil is a mask for the good and just one, while goodness and justice are guises of the devil. Zeitlin's strategy for placing Arendt beyond the pale was to uphold a total dichotomy between the enemy and the victim. Zeitlin echoed the feelings of many others. To sharpen his argument and redirect the world to its previous order, he advocated the use of extreme language: Language reveals meaning. Thus, Nazis were to be described in terminology derived from the world of animals and monsters. By using primitive language, he was able to recast the archetype in its most pristine form—Nazis were monsters, and their victims *Zadikkim* (saints) whose sacredness had to be preserved. This differentiation had to be maintained for the postwar generation, and anyone who dared upset it deserved to be damned. In rejecting totally Arendt's theses, Zeitlin never once mentioned her by name, excommunicating her in a traditional way by removing her, so to speak, from the book of life.[14]

It was not only the archetypes of good and evil that Arendt's detractors assumed were being trampled upon, but also the memory of the past. *Eichmann in Jerusalem* was a troubling book not simply because of its historical description, but because it allowed "scientific objectivity" and conceptualization to stand on a higher rung than the honor or memory of the victims. For some, memory was inevitably intertwined with personal associations that had been ruptured by the events, while for others, it entailed a link to a past that connected their present world to that of their ancestors. Herein lies the difference between responses to Arendt's claims in the 1960s and in the following decades. What respondents in the 1960s rejected outright as disrespect to the dead, later writers would find acceptable and meaningful in trying to place the Holocaust within a comparative context. But in the initial response, the private and public need to allow the past to remain untampered with was common. Friedrich Brodnitz, the son of Julius, a central figure in the German-Jewish Central-Verein (the Central Union of German Citizens of Jewish Faith), put it in the following manner: "We must leave the victims of Hitler, leaders and led, the honor of martyrdom, which by their death was taken from them." [15] Thus, faced with a provocative attempt to dismantle the memory of the past and taint the dead, readers of *Eichmann in Jerusalem* looked for ways to discredit Arendt, ways that turned her formulations into expressions of a misguided individual who lacked a "soul" and *ahavat Israel,* "the love of Israel" (Gershom Scholem), and was motivated by a "neurotic consistency for its own sake" (Ernst Simon) and Jewish self-hatred (Marie Syrkin). Indeed, for some, criticism of the dead was tantamount to serving the goals of anti-Semites, for, as one Jewish journalist crassly put it, "In fact, like those she so viciously condemns for contributing to their own doom, Miss Arendt now does yeoman's service in digging future Jewish graves to the applause of the world's unconverted anti-Semites." [16] Representing Arendt in these terms was an effort to preserve the "archetypal images" and memory of the Holocaust from criticism and to muzzle all efforts to convert the Holocaust into merely the object of another discipline, analyzed along the common lines of study. Moreover, it attempted to turn Arendt against Arendt—to reinvoke her interpretation of totalitarianism in the *Origins,* in which all forms of opposition were understood to be well-nigh impossible. Thus, already in this controversy, the issues to be reverberated in the *Historikerstreit* appeared in a less nuanced and filtered form.

The torrent of public outrage and condemnation aroused the suspicion that an organized campaign against Arendt was being conducted, a claim made by the author on several occasions. Arendt found it hard to believe that the simultaneous outburst against her work was authentic. She pointed an accusing finger at three individuals, leveling at each of them a particular accusation. Siegfried Moses (former state comptroller of Israel and the head of the Council of Jews from Germany) was considered responsible for coordinating the attacks of former leaders of German Jewry "now dispersed all over the world." [17] David Ben-Gurion, the prime minister of Israel during the Eichmann trial, was considered responsible for reversing the favorable attitude toward the book and preventing its Hebrew translation.[18] And Arnold Forster, a leading figure in B'nai B'rith's Anti-Defamation League (ADL), was considered responsible for crafting patterns of hostile response to her book. Their combined success, she argued, stemmed from a traditional Jewish response to criticism of their leaders or of the Jewish people: In such circumstances, Jews must, out of fear, stand together. Arendt further argued that these leading Jewish figures presented an image of a book that she had not written.

Arendt's contention of a concerted campaign, though somewhat exaggerated, was not unfounded. The Jewish "establishment" that she so derided actually undertook organizational efforts to uphold received myths and accepted truths, but even an organized campaign is insufficient to explain the scope of the response. Looking at the "organization" from another vantage point, one is often struck by the unified nature of the responses. Indeed, Siegfried Moses tried to prevent her from publishing the series of articles as a book,[19] yet, independent of his efforts, the criticism leveled at *Eichmann in Jerusalem* by Jews from Germany could have easily created the impression that it was part of a planned scheme to dismiss the book's veracity. Jews from Germany were among the first to respond to the work. They included individuals who had been active in Germany during the 1930s, as well as others who emigrated before or after the rise of Nazism.

German Jewry was severely criticized by Arendt, in particular for conducting negotiations with the National Socialists on the *Haavara* agreement, whereby Jews in Germany transferred money into a special German account that was used to purchase German export goods that the *Haavara* later sold in Palestine, providing money to buy "capitalist" emigration certificates for German Jews so they could depart for Palestine. She also viewed negatively its fantasylike image of the regime and its maintaining illusions as to a future existence in Germany. Their spiritual leader, Rabbi Leo Baeck, was depicted in the *New Yorker* series as the "Führer" of the Jews in the eyes of Germans and Jews. In responding to her book, Jews from Germany placed these issues at the center of their attention, revealing no visible differences, be they from the United States, England, Israel, or Germany. Their past experience as Jews of German extraction was the formative factor in their almost uniform response. This lent their critiques an image of an organized response, but, in effect, it was their individual appropriation of and profound attachment to a collective past memory that provoked the similarity. Their perception was anchored in their German-Jewish past, and few turned to issues outside of this purview.

Pitting Arendt's understanding of humanity's dilemma under totalitarianism, as she explored it in *The Origins,* against her contentions vis-à-vis the Jews in *Eichmann in Jerusalem,* Jews from Germany wished to emphasize the lack of compassion in the latter work. They wondered how a scholar who knew full well the ways in which totalitarian society has the power and means to crush the individual's freedom could nevertheless view the Jewish leadership as a critical organ in the overall destruction process. Jews from Germany were aware of Arendt's international reputation and tried to emphasize the discrepancy in her presentations. Not all of them responded in the same spirit, yet all felt that Arendt's misrepresentation of German Jewry, in particular its leaders, needed rectification. Arendt's personal biography was not insignificant in this encounter. Being a Jew from Germany who was fortunate enough to have been able to view the historical developments from a secure distance added insult to injury. Thus, for German Jews, Zionists or non-Zionists, Arendt's underlying motives were regarded as suspect.

Yet underneath these sensitivities lay a deeper one. The response of Jews from Germany sheds light on a characteristic attitude of individuals who have undergone a major trauma and whose identity has become deeply intertwined with that experience. They deny the outsider's ability to penetrate authentically into their experience, perceiving that only someone who has experienced a similar event can reach the depths of true understanding. Writing almost twenty-five years later, Walter Laqueur remarked: "Arendt loved to judge. . . . And thus she rushed in where wiser men and women feared to tread, writing about extreme situations in which she in her life had never experienced, a writer by temperament always inclined to overstatement . . . at her weakest when analyzing concrete situations and real people." [20]

Despite the occasional favorable response, *Eichmann in Jerusalem* touched a very sensitive nerve among German Jews. Jews who had deep pride in their German-Jewish heritage and profoundly bemoaned the extinction of the German-Jewish experience focused on those aspects of their past that were seemingly tainted by Arendt's treatment. Responding as Jews of German extraction, they dealt almost singularly with issues of a German-Jewish nature. They thus found themselves grappling not only with historical interpretation and factual accuracy, but with the motivations that occasioned a fellow German Jew to write as she did. Few were attracted to her conceptual framework, with regard to either Eichmann or the Jewish community, and they placed clear boundaries on the nature of historical analysis of the Holocaust. Moral judgment was deemed an affront to their past. History was seen as a deterministic process—Jews responded in the only way possible. Robert Weltsch, the editor of the *Leo Baeck Year Book,* the flagship of the Leo Baeck Institute "for the study of the history and culture of German-speaking Central European Jewry," put it this way: "The only thing German Jews could do—and did—was to try to protect their own interests as well as they could, to negotiate about the possibility of maintaining a livelihood." [21]

This line of argument was upheld by many in the controversy, and most passionately by a group of well-known Yiddish journalists in America and Israel. None were survivors, but they all drank from the fountain of Yiddish culture in Eastern Europe and served a community of readers who related to that world with deep emotion and nostalgia.

Consequently, the Holocaust entailed for them both the demise of their culture and elimination of many family connections. The "Yiddishists" were thus emotionally attached to the survivors and manifested similar responses to the more vociferous element of that group. In their shrill call to researchers of the period to show greater empathy when dealing with the *hurban* (the destruction) and the *kedoshim* (martyrs), they employed uncontrolled anger, bitter sarcasm, and outright hatred toward Hannah Arendt. Virulent personal attacks, second to none in the entire polemic, left little room for reasoned argument.

In trying to comprehend how one could create such a naive image of Eichmann and an equally monstrous one of the Jewish leaders, the Yiddishists were compelled to enter into the psyche and "soul" (*neshome*) of Hannah Arendt. Pained that a Jew who had escaped the trauma could write as she did, all agreed that her "soul" lacked a drop of Jewish feeling. As B. Z. Goldberg put it with the sharpest of metaphors: "How can she with her manicured nails scrape into the very fine souls (*neshomes*) of the victims of the camps?"[22] Shlomo Bickel compared her to the "intelligent wise-men" (Bruno Bettelheim and Raul Hilberg), who preceded her in defaming the victims while specializing in understanding the German, and not the Jewish, soul. The "banality of evil" was thus merely paradoxical sophistry at the expense of the victims. Goldberg also maintained that Arendt made shameful use of Hilberg's facts in order to justify her masochistic desire to stain the Jewish people. Her twisting of accurate facts was said to be an outcome of Arendt's self-hate and the Prussian spirit that hangs over her, integral elements of her subconscious, the self-hatred being a common trait of German Jews that in her case bordered on the pathological. These pseudopsychological inquiries were accompanied by such antagonism that one assessment associated her with Nazi-like thinking capable of claiming that the Jews were to blame for the killing of Nazis. This uncontrolled dismissal of Arendt was reawakened after the publication in 1965 of Jacob Robinson's *And the Crooked Shall Be Made Straight*, upon which occasion Zeitlin poured out his wrath and compared her to the devil.

Adopting the most extreme expressions to manifest their contempt for a critical judgment of the victims, this small circle of Yiddish authors constantly reverted to unbarred denunciations of Hannah Arendt. Here was a voice that came from profound anguish unconnected whatsoever with an organized campaign. It was the encounter with a challenge to the historical self-identification with the Jew as victim. Writing for an audience for whom the victims were regarded as *kedoshim,* they allowed themselves to unleash a raw, primitive, and unsophisticated view of the Holocaust, leaving no ambiguities open. Their view of the past was un- adulterated: Eichmann and the Nazis were monsters of history who committed a heinous crime against a powerless foe, who succumbed gal- lantly. In her quest to understand Eichmann's rationale, Hannah Arendt broke an internal code of communication, evoking the passions of those who steadfastly held to it. To guarantee the preservation of their view of the past and reimplant its image, the Yiddishists called for further schol- arship. In the meantime, they could only hope that their total negation of *Eichmann in Jerusalem* would assuage those offended by it.

In looking at the response of Jews in Western countries, Jews who generally lacked an acute degree of personal attachment and identifi- cation with the events of the Holocaust, one enters into an arena of the polemic that has received the most attention and was called years later by Irving Howe "a civil war." [23] Here was a more amorphous group whose respondents came from many walks of life and were often the product of an Anglo-Saxon tradition. Some had reached a certain prominence in various literary and academic circles, while others, often overlooked in the controversy, were contributors to various general and Jewish magazines and journals. Of liberal, and at times Marxist, back- grounds, these figures had rarely before related publicly to the Holo- caust yet had pursued a consistent interest in social-political themes intrinsically connected with the consequences and ramifications of to- talitarian society. Arendt's work on totalitarianism had served as the primer for many of the intellectuals in their understanding of those de- velopments. As Alfred Kazin put it: "*The Origins* . . . left its haunting and influential vibration on literary intellectuals with an overdeveloped sense of the past as *the great* tradition." [24] The appearance of *Eichmann in Jerusalem* was a disturbing and jolting book for this individualistic group. Arendt pushed the questions of the Holocaust to the forefront of public attention, forcing many to take a stand on issues that had lain dormant. The exposure demanded a confrontation with one's Judaism and Jewishness, what was for some of these circles an "estranged" exis- tence. Irving Howe well expressed this interrelationship in his autobi- ography two decades later: "Efforts to grapple with the Holocaust, all doomed to one or another degree of failure, soon led to timid reconsid- erations of what it meant to be Jewish." [25]

In this most amorphous group, several views stand out, reflecting a much larger constituency of opinions. Though respondents aired issues relating to the right of Israel to try Eichmann in the name of the Jewish people, these and corollary issues remained extraneous to the controversy. Hypotheses relating to the Holocaust stirred excitement and interest, generating a confrontation with the past. Daniel Bell, the noted sociologist, in an article supportive of Arendt's theses, pointed to two hurdles in discussing the Holocaust: Placing the phenomenon in universalistic categories seldom occurs, and a person's Jewishness is of utmost importance in evaluating the past. Bell pinpointed the differences between Arendt and her critics, even among the American intellectuals. The question of "Jewish collaboration" is an exemplary problem.

Lionel Abel, the literary critic, emerged as a vigorous dissident. Abel claimed that the Jewish leadership's failure to save the community lay at the root of Arendt's moral condemnation, for had it succeeded, its acts would have appeared morally upright.[26] Abel went on to question the possibilities of resistance in a totalitarian society, wondering whether there existed a "correct" Jewish response. Pursuing further Arendt's example of a Greek woman whom the Nazis ordered to decide which of her three children should be killed (*Origins,* p. 452), Abel regarded this as the paradigm of the Jewish leadership's predicament. Abel claimed that Arendt failed in *Eichmann in Jerusalem* to take into consideration the case of the Greek woman and offered no political or moral alternative in her "aesthetic" judgment of the leaders when condemning them for not warning their communities and affording them an opportunity to escape. For Abel, faced with the dilemma of choosing between murder and murder, any act of "collaboration" that promised a possibility of survival, even the strategy chosen by Chaim Rumkowsky in Lodz, turning the ghetto into a productive labor space in possible exchange for human lives, was morally legitimate.[27]

Arendt's critics refused to accept the moral yardstick she employed in judging the leadership. They regarded her expectations as unfounded and beyond human capability, while often conceding to her the factual basis of her arguments. They, too, were perplexed by a seeming contradiction in her work. Why would Arendt, who so successfully explicated the insurmountable difficulties of fighting totalitarianism, not view in kind the response of the Jewish leadership? In facing this contradiction, individuals again resorted to a personal argument, seeing her position as an outgrowth of a vendetta against the Jewish people—"Is the answer Jewish self-hatred or possibly the assimilated Jew's aversion to all manifestations of organized Jewish life?"[28] Marie Syrkin, a leading American Zionist, asked rhetorically.

By turning to this form of discourse, the apparent discrepancy in her presentations was dissolved and one could dispense with *Eichmann in Jerusalem* and allow the original interpretation of the past to remain as the received tradition—a totalitarian society cripples all opposition and forces total obedience. In contrast, the critics claimed, Arendt placed inhuman demands on the Jews, implying, as Norman Podhoretz, the editor of *Commentary* put it, that

> Jews be better than other people . . . braver, wiser, nobler, more dignified. . . . But the truth is—*must* be—that the Jews under Hitler acted as men will act when they are set upon by murderers, no better and no worse; the Final Solution reveals nothing about the victims except that they were mortal beings and helplessly vulnerable in their weakness. . . . The Nazis destroyed a third of the Jewish people. In the name of all that is humane, will the remnant never let up on itself?[29]

A small group of authors, often on the periphery of the Jewish community, showed staunch support of Arendt's critique of the Jewish leadership, utilizing her arguments to repudiate the Jewish establishment in general. Elements as diverse as the anti-Zionist American Council for Judaism (ACJ) and the New Left found in her report grist for their mill, as her antagonists had promised. The ACJ, which had offered Arendt their auspices to respond to her critics, published an article, "Deals between Nazis and Zionists," based on descriptions in *Eichmann in Jerusalem*. Relishing her details on the *Haavarah* agreement, the article reiterated the organization's classic position on Zionism, seeing it as an egoistic movement that placed its own interests above those of the Jewish people.

Another author chastised Arendt's critics for hurrying to condemn her, regardless of the historical evidence, which tilted clearly against the Jewish police and its councils. Commenting sarcastically on Jewish fabrication of history for ulterior motives, he wrote: "And since there are some six million dead, there are enough legends to go round to assure official fund-raising activities for decades to come."[30] However, the political potential in this critique was fully enunciated by Norman Fruchter, who adopted the thesis that Jewish leadership was responsible for facilitating the destruction process in the spirit of Jewish passivity and conservatism, symptomatic of Jewish history. But he was especially concerned with and critical of the contemporary Jewish leadership, which he claimed had attacked Arendt without sufficient evidence to remove responsibility from the Jewish leadership and protect the historical image of the Jew as victim. In so doing, he believed, the Jewish community failed to learn the necessary moral lessons of the period that would assist modern mankind in the struggle against the return of totalitarianism.[31]

Could Eichmann be both a Nazi and a simple bureaucrat? Arendt's staunchest critics found this impossible, citing as evidence Eichmann's activity in Hungary in 1944 and Hilberg's documentation that Eichmann would not rest until he fulfilled his mission with regard to the Jews. In trying to unravel the interrelationship between an individual's ideology and his actions, disagreement reigned, with Norman Podhoretz asserting that anti-Semitism was a sine qua non of every inductee to the party. Others took a less definitive position, stating that Arendt's description of totalitarianism lacked a certain dynamism, nullifying the possibility that through years of involvement in the Nazi bureaucracy, an individual like Eichmann could have become an ardent anti-Semite. His personality must have certainly fitted him for the Nazi bureaucracy, but the latter cannot be seen as the sole factor in his development. Without personalities of his kind, the bureaucracy would not have functioned, and individuals must be judged for their actions. Thus, Lionel Abel's depiction of Eichmann as a "morally monstrous" person appealed to many because it fitted well with the public image of the demonic nature of the Nazis.

However, throughout the controversy, sensing their inability to mount a factual refutation of Arendt's work, participants from every corner voiced the need for comprehensive scholarship on the Holocaust. Jacob Robinson, an international legal expert who was actively involved in the prosecution of Eichmann, supplied fuel for respondents by publishing at the outset of the polemics a short essay under the auspices of the ADL intended to contradict the essence of *Eichmann in Jerusalem*. Its purpose was clearly stated: "ADL believes that it would be tragic and a disservice to Jewish—and world—history if this work would go unchallenged, to be accepted as gospel." But this was merely a stop-gap measure. The problem went much deeper and required more serious attention. This same reasoning encouraged Robinson to compose the full-length response to Arendt he published in 1965. *And the Crooked Shall Be Made Straight* reversed the polemic.[32] It concentrated on a *factual* rebuttal of the main components of the controversy—the nature of Eichmann and his activity, Jewish behavior during the war, and the legality of the trial—and it contained a country-by-country description of the destruction process with special reference to Eichmann's role. Quarrying evidence from myriad sources, Robinson took issue with every implied and outright criticism of Jewish life and each implication of Eichmann's insignificance in the destruction process. Upholding the judges' decision on every account, Robinson determined that Eichmann was driven by an "implacable lust for annihilation," while the "overriding purpose of Jewish activity everywhere in Nazi Europe was survival with dignity." In attempting to make the crooked straight, Robinson did not put forward his own conception of the Holocaust but sought to rebuild the classic, sacred image of the period in which "murderers with the power to murder descended upon a defenseless people and murdered a large part of it." [33]

Did Robinson succeed? Judging from the twenty-odd reviews of his book, it would appear not. Certainly, some avid advocates (Moses Decter, Marie Syrkin, Gertrud Ezorsky, etc.) acclaimed his work as the telling confirmation of Arendt's insensitivity and inability to treat the period historically. Yet even they were aware of its problematic public image. Robinson's work so discredited a distinguished scholar that it became suspect in itself. As Decter put it: "one can only hope that *its* reputation, as a quiet, unpretentious and non-polemical devastation of Arendt, will gradually spread and undercut her influence." [34] But other Arendt antagonists recognized Robinson's failure to treat Arendt's philosophical theories adequately, wondering whether a jurist was the appropriate person to provide *the* definitive response. Respondents knowing full well the complicated nature of the historical events questioned whether Robinson's mythic, Manichean presentation would appear any more authentic than Arendt's critique. Howard Morley Sachar noted accurately the pitfalls inherent in Robinson's perspective, particularly "when an historian is animated primarily by a desire to present evidence which will document conclusions he has already drawn, to salvage the 'honor' of a people who do not in fact need exoneration." [35]

Robinson could not clear the air completely, and in response to his book, the recurrent call for historical research continued to assert itself. [36] Memories of the dead and of the myths of the past, invoked to curtail Arendt's immediate influence, were being called into question by the same people who enlisted them. Seeing their own image in Robinson's mirror, they retracted. The period seemed to be ripe for a more critical attitude toward the past.

NON-JEWISH RESPONSES TO
EICHMANN IN JERUSALEM

Two of Arendt's principal supporters, Mary McCarthy and Dwight Mac-donald, remarked sarcastically that non-Jewish and Jewish perspectives permeated the controversy, while several of her antagonists (e.g. Syrkin and Abel) contended that command of the historical events, or the lack of it, was the sole dividing factor. Indeed, the controversy was not limited to the Jewish community, and wherever the book was discussed, non-Jewish writers entered the fray. In isolating non-Jewish from Jewish responses and apparently following the former view, we are interested in seeing whether a different perspective on the Holocaust was inculcated among non-Jews and Jews, to what extent a unique Jewish response emerged from the controversy, what parallels existed with the non-Jewish response, and whether different perspectives prevailed on how the victims were to be judged morally and on the lessons to be learned from the past.

Most non-Jewish observers were troubled by the moral and social implications of Arendt's study, with the cardinal issue being "the banality of evil." For many, the reasoning seemed to follow a similar pattern. Man's inhumanity to man was not a twentieth-century creation; however, modern technology has enabled man to develop methods of mass murder unique in the history of mankind. Murder committed in this new framework is thus characterized by a growing gap between its planning and execution, raising the question of the responsibility of the planner and the executioner and the meaning of evil in such a society. Ruminations on these themes led to considerations of the way one can derive lessons from such situations and inevitably to discussions on the nature of man. In this vein, Arendt's presentation of Eichmann's banality appeared more frightful than the prosecutor's demonic depiction and challenged classical thought that established a direct relation between the murderer and his action. *Eichmann in Jerusalem* unveiled an individual who symbolized the Nazi bureaucracy, revealing no signs of sadistic behavior, hatred of the Jews, or any other fanaticism. Modern technology allowed the bureaucracy to function in such a way that individuals were oblivious to the meaning of their actions of utter evil, performed without sensing the least remorse, feeling, or political inclination. These facts appeared to Robert Lowell "all the more appalling. . . . His life is as close to living in hell as I can imagine, and I'm able to see it as such because Arendt has not dabbled in melodrama."[37] Eichmann was simply

expected to fulfill his orders and was in turn rewarded for his profi-
ciency—murder was no different from any other occupation. Thus,
Arendt's Eichmann loomed for these critics more evil than Hausner's.
Dwight Macdonald, who years earlier had taken issue with the concept
of collective guilt and had warned against the modern state's power over
the individual's actions, found Arendt's portrayal akin to his way of
thinking: "That five million Jews could have been slaughtered by contemptible mediocrities like Eichmann must be hard to accept; it trivial-
izes the horror, robs it of meaning. It must be especially hard to take the
fact that Eichmann wasn't even a serious anti-Semite—in fact, wasn't
serious anything." [38]

As a paradigm of the danger latent in modern man, Arendt's portrait
of Eichmann was seen as a warning to mankind of how political passivity could engender such foul phenomena. Possibly the fear of McCarthy-
ism was still very much in their minds. Mary McCarthy, among others,
read the book in this way. She, too, removed it from its particular context
and turned it into a parable for modern man. As such, it represented for
her a brave political analysis that should awaken in individuals a concern
for freedom of thought at all costs as a precondition for a just society.
Mary McCarthy believed Arendt was completely vindicated, and highly
commended her for her unswerving quest for truth, bringing her to assert that possibly only Christians, educated on principles of compassion,
could adequately recognize Arendt's compassionate writing. Clearly,
McCarthy's deep friendship with Arendt figured prominently in her decision to enter the controversy and to combat the arguments presented
by Lionel Abel. [39]

Eichmann and the problem he raised did not completely overshadow
the discussion of Jewish behavior during the Holocaust but played a
prominent part in its understanding, as well. Relying heavily on Bettelheim and Hilberg, various authors agreed that the depersonalization ef-
fected by the totalitarian regime weakened even the ability of the victims
to act differently, adding to the cruelty of the Nazi deeds. Almost fore-
casting the source of contention during the *Historikerstreit,* commentators wove together the theses of Bettelheim, Hilberg, and Arendt and
emphasized how Jewish goals came awfully close to those of the Nazis:
Resistance was well-nigh impossible, collaboration was rampant, and
moral decadence had set in among the leadership. Thus, Arendt's discussion was viewed less as a critique of the Jewish community than as further indication of the terror embedded in the system: "a more plausible
theory would attribute their actions to a mean—but human—desire to

buy immunity for themselves." In other words, Arendt's arguments seemed to them "perfectly plausible," "self-evidently true," and undeserving of the Jewish community's demagogic criticism, intended to block a historical discussion on these themes.[40]

Specifically, these writers cringed at the parochial nature of the ad hominem attacks against Arendt, and Dwight Macdonald singled out Scholem's remark as a symptom of Jewish inability to place the Holocaust in a universal perspective. Macdonald's assessment of Jewish sensitivity to Arendt's analysis records a significant difference between non-Jewish and Jewish responses to *Eichmann in Jerusalem:* "[They] reproach her because she lacks a special feeling in favor of her fellow Jews. But such a prejudice would have made it impossible for her to speculate on how the catastrophe might have been less complete, had the Jewish leadership followed different policies, or to attempt a realistic interpretation of the Nazi horror as the work of men (who can be understood) and not 'monsters' and demons (who cannot)."[41]

Such remarks indicate that as the Jewish polemicists assumed and feared, Arendt's theoretical prowess was accepted at face value, and she was accorded blanket trust for her historical narrative. These journalists and intellectuals, distant from the experiential aspect of the Holocaust, were attracted to the same elements in *Eichmann in Jerusalem*—witty language, daring conceptualizations, and original conclusions—that aroused distrust among their Jewish counterparts. Because Arendt's conceptual arguments appealed to them, they dwelt with concern on their significance for modern times in a universalistic mode while laconically summarizing the historical description of the destruction. The tragedy of European Jewry aroused little emotional involvement and fueled few expressions of remorse over the silence of the Church or the ineffectiveness of the Allies in saving Jews from destruction. As one non-Jewish writer questioned: "And what about the part the Jews played in their own destruction through the willing help they offered the Nazis? If Eichmann was guilty of aiding in mass murder, are not those Jews also guilty who supplied listing of the members of countless Jewish communities, in the order in which they were to be deported?"[42]

Non-Jewish response was not uniform, however. Judge Michael Musmanno, the former American prosecutor at the Nuremberg trials, published a scathing review in the *New York Times Book Review* two weeks after *Eichmann in Jerusalem* was published. A review of such vitriolic nature appearing in the leading American newspaper contributed a definite dimension to the controversy.[43] Musmanno presented a mythic approach to the tragedy of European Jewry in which the Nazis loom as the demonic force in the history of mankind and the six million Jews appear as defenseless, innocent individuals who valiantly faced the powerful Nazi machine. Musmanno minced no words in his description: "and if Eichmann's acts did not prove him to be one of the most malignant and multifarious murderers of all time, then facts have no meaning, records have no bearing, documents are useless."[44] The American prosecutor placed before the American public the archetypal image of the Nazis and dismissed Arendt's conceptualizations as an aberration. Musmanno's rejection of Eichmann's (and the Nazis') "normality" was supported by two distinguished Englishmen, Hugh Trevor-Roper and Richard Crossman. A noted historian who made several seminal contributions to the history of the Third Reich, Trevor-Roper established a clear link between Eichmann's activity and the role of the Jewish leadership, arguing that Arendt minimized the responsibility of the Germans at the expense of the Jewish leaders. Trevor-Roper, who fully accepted Hilberg's assessment of the Nazi bureaucracy, reasoned that the typical bureaucratic figure was the mainspring of the "Final Solution." Eichmann may have begun as a "banal" personality but over the years became converted into an ardent Nazi who pursued the Jews relentlessly.[45] Thus, any attempt to change the order of responsibility appeared to Trevor-Roper a travesty of the historical event: "If the Jewish leaders were so compliant, that, to her, partially excuses Eichmann who, being a 'banal' man, receiving only orders from above and compliance from beneath, could hardly be expected to doubt the rightness of what he did."[46] Trevor-Roper went on to emphasize the obstacles inherent in the system to effective resistance and implied that Arendt's ambivalent and critical attitude toward the Jews directed her writing on these themes. Richard Crossman, an M.P., went further. Seeing Eichmann's banality as a strategy for blaming the Jews, Crossman found only one explanation for Arendt's way of writing—self-hatred. He queried: "Does the fact that she has done so suggest that anti-Semitism is endemic in the Jew as well as in the Gentile unconscious?"[47]

This small group of authors differed from other non-Jewish writers both in their basic disagreement with the thrust of the book and in the specific way they understood their points of dispute. Generally accepting the terrorizing nature of totalitarianism, they used it as a starting point to disagree with Arendt on its implications for the behavior of the victims. In so doing, they were prone to question the purity of Arendt's argument.

Eichmann in Jerusalem was first published in Germany in 1964, after the controversy had already simmered in the United States. Because arguments for and against the book were already known, and a large number of the negative articles had been written by Jews, the publication came on the wave of deep emotion. In Germany, however, the book failed initially to arouse much of a stir, and only a dozen or so articles appeared, illuminating a somewhat different angle than that adopted by other non-Jewish writers. Uniquely German issues arose. Regardless of their view of the book, German authors seemed to be bound by what was "permissible" and "forbidden" to them, as Germans, to write. Unlike all other commentators, they sensed a barrier that could not be overstepped, especially when it came to the internal Jewish issues in the book. This was also evident in Friedrich Arnold Krummacher's collection of essays published in 1964, which failed to include a cross section of opinion, overlooking articles clearly supportive of Arendt's theses (e.g. those by Macdonald, McCarthy, Bell, etc.).[48] Furthermore, most of the German respondents showed particular interest in Arendt's moral criticism of the attempted coup of July 20, 1944, an event of minor importance for other respondents in the controversy. They chastised Arendt for failing to comprehend the feelings of the rebelling officers, stressing only their egoism and self-serving motivations. Instead, German authors described the rebels' deep revulsion of the atrocities in the East and their view of Hitler as a criminal murderer.

Prior to the German publication of the book, various individuals in the American and German press, including the distinguished German historian Golo Mann, tried to convince Arendt to defer its publication, at least until such time as offensive mistakes were corrected. Mention of these efforts appeared widely in German discussions of the book as part of an internal dialogue on the spiritual preparedness of the German public to confront a work that trespassed several taboos. Arendt's depiction of Eichmann was for the German readers the most troubling. Though offended by the book's anti-German animus, German commentators considered Arendt's portrayal of Eichmann as authentic and a close replica of their image of him and other SS personalities. Moreover, Eichmann seemed to be a model for contemporary successors. Some, like Rolf Schroers, saw Eichmann's personality type persisting in modern German society, his characteristics apparent to every German reader. Schroers cautioned his fellow Germans against letting up their quest for penitence, encouraging them to continue the battle against the characteristics of Eichmann's personality.[49] Though Golo Mann found Arendt's description of Eichmann more plausible than the one offered by the prosecutor Gideon Hausner, he attributed to Eichmann more offensiveness and intelligence than Arendt did.[50] Similarly, the Holocaust historian Wolfgang Scheffler was not at odds with Arendt's theoretical presentation of Eichmann yet reached the conclusion that Eichmann was not as "normal" as portrayed.[51] For these German writers, acceptance of "the banality of evil" was fraught with internal havoc. It allowed one to turn the Nazi period into a normal possibility, and not an aberration in which anti-Semitism ruled mercilessly. Eichmann's "normality" constituted a threat to the self-understanding of those in postwar Germany who based its rehabilitation on a total rupture with the world of National Socialism.

Jewish behavior in respect to issues of both collaboration and resistance was perceived within the overall perspective of totalitarianism and the resistance of other peoples. But on another level, Germans touched these problems with particular care. They appreciated the sensitivity of Jewish respondents to Arendt in their refusal to regard Eichmann's behavior as "normal," while proposing a moratorium on such discussions for the Germans themselves, As H. Köpke put it: "We Germans have every reason to show discretion in this aspect of the discussion."[52] Gingerly treading on these themes, German authors found fault with Arendt's personal bias. H. E. Holthusen accused her of consciously overlooking evidence contradictory to her thesis with regard to Jewish resistance activity, justifiably arousing strong criticism from Jewish circles.[53] Rolf Schroers emphasized the importance of seeing Jewish developments in a comparative perspective. The unique position Jews were thrust into during the Nazi period made their battle against anti-Semitism all the more difficult and precarious, he argued. Against the background of German society's behavior, Jewish passivity took on a different meaning, a dimension that completely escaped Arendt. This theme was reiterated by Golo Mann. He, too, insisted on placing Jewish response in a comparative perspective. He claimed that Jewish assessment of Nazi intentions appeared no different from that of the French or English. They were neither more nor less politically savvy. Mann further criticized Arendt's placing more onus on the Jews than on the Germans, pursuing what he thought to be a growing and disturbing trend to reduce German responsibility, but he believed she surpassed all. Almost echoing the caustic comments of certain Jewish respondents to her book, Mann concluded: "One step forward and the Jews will have persecuted and exterminated themselves, and by chance only a few Nazis also took part in it."[54]

Wolfgang Scheffler dealt specifically with Arendt's claims about collaboration and the relation between the Nazi authorities and German Jews. Scheffler emphasized the efforts made by the Nazis to take over the Jewish organizations in Germany while praising the tremendous efforts of the community to aid the needy. He, too, could not understand Arendt's willingness to judge the victims of Nazism. Scheffler also rejected the encompassing dismissal of Jewish leadership across Europe, taking issue with Hilberg's evidence and Arendt's willingness to create a sweeping generalization that failed to take into consideration the variables of different countries. Ghettos in Poland shared very little with Nazi Germany, he pointed out. All in all, no German writer utilized Arendt's Jewishness to grant them legitimacy to criticize Jewish behavior during the Third Reich, and none even intimated a moral collapse of the Jewish leadership. Totalitarianism and Nazism were solely to blame, he argued.

The early German critique of *Eichmann in Jerusalem* provides an interesting perspective on the controversy in general and is exceptionally illuminating in light of the changing perspectives on the book within the dynamic historiographical debates in the 1980s and 1990s in Germany and elsewhere. Completely in contradiction to what Jewish writers had anticipated the German response to be, it showed utmost compassion with the Jewish fate and blamed Arendt for a lack of sensitivity in the way many Jewish writers had previously done.

Interestingly enough, *Eichmann in Jerusalem* was republished in 1986, at the height of the *Historikerstreit,* with a new introduction by Hans Mommsen.[55] In a totally different atmosphere from that of the 1960s, the republication heralded new currents in thinking and historical interpretation of the Holocaust. Mommsen, who had by then become a leading representative of the functionalist approach to the evolution of National Socialism, now saw Arendt's interpretation of Jewish behavior as astute and insightful. While pointing out some of Arendt's "many statements which are obviously not sufficiently thought through," Mommsen retraced his earlier positions on Hitler's role in the "Jewish question" and in his introduction to the new German edition seems to have accepted some of the conclusions elaborated on in *Eichmann in Jerusalem,* especially with regard to the nature of the Jewish victims: The character of totalitarian society and terror, he argued, was such that it "virtually conditions all the groups of the population so that they are equally fit for the role of the perpetrators as well as for the role of the victims," concurring that "the mentality of perpetrators and victims" was "assimilated." This change of orientation in the appraisal of Arendt's book emanated from the reassessment of attitudes toward the study of totalitarianism and the Holocaust in Germany and elsewhere. Clearly, what German writers regarded as taboo in the 1960s had become legitimate in the 1980s.

Elements of Arendt's formulations now seemed to political theorists, historians of ideas, and specialists in the study of the Holocaust much more appealing, and they were discussed without the burden of the original controversy and the sense of delicacy toward the sensibilities of the survivors. Arendt passed away in 1975, and several years later, her first biography appeared by Elisabeth Young-Bruehl. Written with deep empathy for Arendt's life and life's work, the biography devoted a long and informative chapter to the controversy on *Eichmann in Jerusalem,* clearly intimating that the entire storm was trumped up, while glossing over the intricacies of some of Arendt's arguments for her contemporaries. But the reception of *Eichmann in Jerusalem* had already taken a turn in a more positive direction with the publication of Ron Feldman's collection of Arendt's essays in 1978, which was only partially devoted to the Eichmann book, but which was structured in such a way that all of Arendt's earlier writings on Jewish themes led to it. Feldman argued that "the controversy . . . obscured for too long the real depth of her contribution to understanding the Jewish experience in the modern age." [56] This direction was pursued more extensively almost two decades later by Richard Bernstein, who also attempted to explain the growing engagement with Arendt's thought and life since her death.[57]

In these works, as in many others, *Eichmann in Jerusalem* is given pride of place, in particular Arendt's notions of the "banality of evil" and her understanding of Jewish leadership during the Holocaust.[58] New interpretations were offered for her theses, stressing their universalistic implications without a specific link to the historical context of World War II. As Dana Villa remarked: "What Arendt fears is not the 'Eichmann in us all' nor even a 'loss of values,' but the increasingly automatic quality of our judgments." [59] In a similar vein, Alan Milchman and Alan Rosenberg found the notion of "thoughtlessness" associated with the banality of evil "one of the central features of the desk killer," a feature that "remains a hallmark of modernity." [60] In this reassessment, historians of the Holocaust have generally refrained from referring to Arendt's historical descriptions because of their factual inaccuracy, though they would at times find value (as did Mommsen and Browning) in her theoretical approach. These conflicting and contrasting assessments, a few among many in the recent literature, highlight the remarkable staying power of Arendt's report.

CONCLUSION

Postwar preoccupation with the conflicting models of historical explanation concerning the role of individuals and ideas within social processes and structures remains at the heart of our historical and philosophical tradition. These concerns were also central to Arendt's treatment of Eichmann and human freedom and enabled her work to survive controversies and historical duels based on new research and archival studies. The sharpness of her images and pronouncements presented in a theoretical framework that challenges, jars, and overturns received discourse enabled her work to rise above many others, however "historically" problematic it may have been. So, too, with regard to her claims vis-à-vis the Jewish victims.

Arendt seemingly wrote in the name of pure history, *sine ira et studio*, placing no barriers on the quest to penetrate the inner motivations of a Nazi bureaucrat and avoiding lingering on the traumatic emphases of the Jewish tragedy. Eichmann and the Nazis were studied as human beings who performed mass murder. Their Jewish victims were also presented as human beings, not saints, and they figured in history not simply as passive entities, but as significant characters who affected their own fate. Even in the Holocaust, their actions, or lack of them, played a role in their ultimate demise. Consequently, the past was for Arendt an open road that offered different routes for the traveler. She rejected a deterministic outlook on the decisions made by Eichmann and the Jews. For Eichmann, the road was clear and unsophisticated. Surrendering his moral decisions to the bureaucracy, he simply performed his duties. He and the Jews, especially their leaders, could have chosen differently, and they, like all actors in history, she believed, must face moral judgment.

To others, this represented an oversophisticated understanding of the past, one that apparently normalized mass murder and glossed over the inner Jewish tragedies. Fearing a minimization of German responsibility, as we have seen, critics presented the Holocaust in archetypal terms: the Nazis were monsters, the Jews powerless martyrs. Because Jewish actions were predetermined by the Nazi onslaught, Jewish behavior was often deemed beyond reproach, and judgment of such victims seemed morally reprehensible. Yet, in contrast, moral judgment of the Nazis was said to constitute a moral responsibility for all mankind, especially

Jews. To "understand" the Holocaust in this way meant to recognize that Eichmann possessed an alternative that his victims lacked.

Responses to Arendt thus centered on issues of the Holocaust, and not on issues raised by the trial. The history of the reception of *Eichmann in Jerusalem* shows how different groups focused on issues that touched their particular experiences. Memory and respect for the past and for their forefathers' traditions and culture were strong motivating factors. Many a Jewish intellectual who previously refrained from dealing publicly with such issues joined the fray with a special intensity, revealing intertwining feelings of guilt and nostalgia. Many, educated in universal principles of scholarship, could not employ those principles in response to the book, warned against them, and often joined a common refrain of personal invective against the author. In refuting her, they and others reveled in a language of discreditation that fed the desired myths. Few in the controversy brought new evidence to bear in refuting Arendt, and most relied on the power of the myth and the sacredness of the memory to delegitimize the author and her work and bring the broken vessels back to their former state.

Yet, a generation later, the controversy over *Eichmann in Jerusalem* has given way to a greater appreciation of the author and to her theoretical contribution to understanding the nature of evil in modern society and the problem of individual choice and freedom of action. A generation of interest in her work has shown that the memory of the dead and the stereotypical archetypes of Jews and Germans in the Third Reich could not overcome the fascination with a theoretical presentation that attempted to answer the salient questions of our time.

ARENDT AND GERMAN CULTURE

Love and *Bildung*
for Hannah Arendt

Gabriel Motzkin

There is a story that has been told about German-Jewish culture, which is that German Jews were uniquely interested in *Bildung*. They adopted the ideal of self-cultivation, of being educated people, as a symbol of the status which they had achieved.[1] According to this story, they used *Bildung* to compensate for the lack of social definition, for their being what Hannah Arendt so trenchantly called pariahs.[2] *Bildung* gave them an entrée into a universal social class, one not defined by birth. Yet this universal class was not defined by achievement, for the way *Bildung* was to be acquired is qualitative, and not quantitative. *Bildung* was supposed to reflect one's inner worth.

This story became popular in post–World War II German-Jewish historiography. Its narrative was perhaps inevitably tinged with an ambivalent nostalgia, a retrospective yearning for a finer past that was constrained by an awareness of that past's tragic culmination. Not all German-Jewish intellectuals of the postwar era shared this nostalgia. Many postwar intellectual trajectories can be evaluated in terms of a deep skepticism toward the ideal of *Bildung,* a skepticism that also permeated Hannah Arendt's prewar portrayal of Rahel Varnhagen's emotional biography.

Why were many twentieth-century intellectuals skeptical about *Bildung*? *Bildung* assumed that intellectual worth is reflected in emotional experience, that the purpose of acquiring culture is to become a better person, and that there then must be something inherent in culture that

improves people. Very few people are left who believe that. One aspect
of the ideology of *Bildung*, however, has survived its demise as an ideal
for the acquisition of culture: *Bildung* has been transformed into what
our forebears would have called a sentimental ideal. The ideal of *Bildung* continues to affect the conception of the emotional life. The idea
that life is a process of emotional learning—that there is a process
of emotional cultivation, that people can work on themselves by learning from their experiences—continues to be popular. Love has been de-
coupled from intellectual cultivation and cultural self-improvement.
While one cannot acquire cultivation, one can learn how to love.

Clearly, this ideal of the emotional life, especially in its democratic
form, according to which the option of emotional self-cultivation is
available to everyone, is not universal. It is an emancipatory ideal, for in
its modern form, it provides access to society, as mediated through relationships, for anyone who can love sincerely or learn from love. The social cement is construed to be made up of emotional relationships.

This ideal of emotional *Bildung* was grafted onto an older and quite
different tradition of love, one that distinguished quite sharply between
sacred and profane love, between the love of another and the love of
God. In the Christian tradition, profane love was usually viewed quite
negatively, excepting the middle form of love of the community. There
are many theories about when and why this changed, when profane love
began to be viewed as a positive phenomenon. There is a predominantly
French theory according to which this occurred in the Middle Ages and
signified the love outside of marriage, adulterous love, which was viewed
as the love that provides freedom.[3] If Christian love, in its Augustinian
variant, signified the possibility of freedom from the world, profane love
signified the possibility of freedom from society. Thus, the Christian contempt of the secular world led to the coupling in our Western culture of
the ideals of love and freedom. Women, especially, could be free only if
they could be free to love. Here freedom meant the denial of social roles.
There is a lot of literature about whether this conception ever characterized a real society, or even whether this conception characterized the
lords and ladies of medieval courts.[4] What is certainly true is that many
people in our time have chosen to tell this particular story about the
past, a story in which the origin of both romantic love and women's
emancipation lies in the positive evaluation of adultery.

There is another story that can be told about love. In this story, the
real issue is the question of identity and difference, Jacob wrestling with
the angel, a dialectical story of two people as being both identical and

opposite, of the way in which two people are supposed to yearn for union and sometimes are able to find it. If the first story is about adultery, the second story is about the search for self-affirmation, about finding out whether the other is like oneself or different from oneself, about a kind of incest. It is a story about self-discovery, about the conditions of identity. Rather than being a story about love and freedom, it is a story about love and identity, and it is a story that, according to Hannah Arendt, was fatal for Rahel Levin's chances for happiness, because, since it is a story about identity, it got mixed up with the stories about German and Jew, or, in this case, about German and Jewess. Since this story is a story about self-discovery, it raises questions such as the lover's link to reality and whether one can find oneself through relationships. In this story, emotional *Bildung* is grafted onto the tradition of identity and difference, onto the question of incest. Indeed, one can say that Rahel's love affairs were doomed because they did not contain enough incest, because German and Jewess were so ineluctably separated that the fulfillment of incest could only be sensed at a spiritual level, what we call the communion of minds and souls. In this story, the question of adultery is quite simply irrelevant. Social convention does obtrude in this story as it does in the adulterous one, not because of adultery, but rather because of difference.

1

In her protracted youth, Hannah Arendt wrote two books about love, one about sacred love, *Der Liebesbegriff bei St. Augustin,* and the other about profane love, *Rahel Varnhagen.*[5] In the first book, she began with love as desire and creation and wound up with the question of love and the social life. In the second book, she began with love as emancipation and wound up with the issue of social life and the failure of love.

There are two cardinal differences between these books. The doctoral thesis on Augustine is a book about loving. It investigates the structural change in loving caused by changing the object that one loves. *Rahel Varnhagen* is a book about wanting to be loved and therefore looks at love from the point of view, not of a subject, but rather of a subject who is trying to be a love object. We have very few books about what God feels when he is loved that begin "For God so wanted to be loved by the world that he gave his only begotten son." That sacrifice, that wanting to be loved, is one link in Arendt's view between being a woman and being an assimilating Jew.

The second difference between these two books follows from the first: While they both consider what would become a constant strain in Arendt's work, the question of the relations between universal and particular, the first book is really about the way in which the emotion of loving can be universalized, how loving the Divine can become loving one's neighbor, loving the community, or even loving humanity. The second book raises the question of whether one can become a full individual, a free individual, through the emotion of being loved, whether there is a path that can lead from the universal to the particular, from the community to the individual. Arendt's conclusion in this book is not optimistic.

In both books, the world is ultimately the cause of loss of oneself. In both books, one believes that one has found oneself, but one has really forgotten oneself (*Serm.* 142, 3).[6] The dialectics of love is not a dialectics of memory, but rather one of forgetting. For the creation of authentic love, what is it that must be forgotten? Augustine is quite clear: the world. There is a forgetting into the world and a forgetting that is directed out of the world.

In the direction out of the world, "finding oneself is the same as finding God," but that can be done only through "a self-denying love," the kind of love that can never succeed when it is profane love.[7] In the world, we also deny ourselves, also forget ourselves, and therein there is no difference when we turn to God, but in the world, this emotion, as Rahel found, can have no possible success, for it is predicated on the desire to be loved, or what, from the point of view of the love object, appears as the unworthiness of the love subject. We, as the subjects of Divine love, already know our unworthiness, from which, however, the Christian communion has liberated us.

There is a self-denial that takes place in the time of this world and a self-denial that takes place in eternity. The lover lives only in future eternity. In forgetting the world, he ceases to be an individual, ceases to be himself. He despises his past, forgets it, forgets his origin. This self-forgetting is identical with transcendence: The lover transcends the present into the absolute future. The transcended person can view his own being only privatively, as having been diminished, devoured by time (*devoratus temporibus,* Conf., 10). Transcendence means transcending time, forgetting time. By transcending through love, I do not lose myself, as I imagine I can lose myself in time. I have instead transcended the human as such. Love of self has been transformed through denial of self into inherence in God. Man is fundamentally not in possession of himself and is constantly exposed to the danger of losing himself.[8] The aim of loving God is security through independence from the world.

Arendt's linkage of love to future eternity, desire to future being, makes memory the opposite of desire.[9] Augustine conceived of the Platonic memory of past eternity as the origin of generativeness. This memory is the memory of a possibility that can be realized now and so links up with the psychology of desire. It makes what has been in the past into a future possibility. So far, Arendt's Augustine sounds like Heidegger. However, for Arendt's Augustine, past memory also contradicts the present and thus buttresses a rejection of the present world, hardly a Heideggerian position. For me, the idea that we can reexperience the past through memory is a fiction of memory, but this possibility of reexperience is fundamental for Augustine, Rahel Levin, Heidegger, and Arendt. Reexperience, however, makes memory depend on the prior possibility of forgetting that something has been forgotten, the possibility that remembering who one is depends on having forgotten who one is. Heidegger retains the notion that forgetting is more fundamental than remembering for life in this world. For Heidegger, forgetting means forgetting death, and not God. Heidegger replaces God by death, deriving time from death, and not from life.

Heidegger's duality between death and things is quite different from Augustine's duality of two worlds, one of eternity and one of history, and two origins, one in eternity and the other the origin in this world. History is the consciousness of a common human origin and makes possible the extension of self-denying love to all humans. Self-denying love does not distinguish between humans: "it loves all humans with an absolute lack of distinction."[10] This lack of differentiation between others first makes possible a relation to the world of "we were," that is, a history. However, this universalization of the love of the neighbor has been made possible on the basis of the complete isolation of the self. The origin in God, which can be realized only in isolation, makes possible the love of others. Thus, a relation has been established between an absolute individual, a lover, and a beloved that has no particularity: all other humans. Indeed, "I love in the other precisely what he is not from himself."[11]

Self-denying love destroys Rahel because she has no genuine faith that can transvalue self-destruction into a positive act. What for Augustine is the highest reality, that in us which we are not, is ultimately for Rahel, as depicted by Arendt, an illusion. Rahel can either love sexually a visible person or idealize an invisible person whom she can help make.

However, the invisible person is ultimately an illusion: The ultimately real dialogue is a dialogue with her historical particularity, a dialogue that for her is present only as an internal dialogue.

Arendt concludes her first work with the idea that "only the past can make the pure selfhood of belief into a community of faith." [12] History is necessary as the link between the individual and society, and the lack of a past would make such a link impossible. In contrast, the future is individual. Therefore, her theory of memory was designed to show how memory is made possible by the future. For this way of thinking, a great distance exists between memory and history: memory means the memory of eternity, deriving its origin from a transcendent sphere, whereas history means the history of the human community as having a common origin in this world. Forgetting makes memory possible by creating a hiatus between the past and the present, whereas history incarnates a principle of continuity. Hence, history's principle of emancipation is different from memory's: "Reciprocal love dissolves mutual dependence." [13] In contrast to the freedom from the world, Arendt discerns in Augustine another ideal, one of freedom *in* the world as the opposite of dependence. It is because people are no longer dependent on each other in the community of believers that they can love each other.

Uncomfortable with Heidegger's solipsism, Arendt sought to turn Augustine's concept of love in a social direction. This social ideal of love is quite different from the personal ideal of love in that it characterizes love as self-affirmation, in contrast to the ideal of love as dissolving the self. It should be noted that self-affirmation is not a personal ideal, but rather a prerequisite for a just society. Thus, Arendt has already transformed the ideal of love as *Bildung*, as self-formation, from a personally oriented ideal into a socially oriented ideal, but at a price, namely, a bifurcation between the metaphysical and the social conceptions of love, between the care of the self and the love for others. Thus, we are left with a tension between these two ideals, for the personal ideal of love as isolation, which for Augustine is Christianity's specific contribution, first becomes a historical possibility through Christianity. By entering history, it makes it possible for man to escape the history of the *genus humanum*. [14]

2

Arendt's biography of Rahel Varnhagen could be read as a polemic against the idea of love as *Bildung*, which it certainly is, but it is also an admission that *both* the types of love that she had sketched in her dissertation could not succeed. For Rahel, there is no possibility of escape from the world, but there is also no real possibility of joining it. The pariah is the reciprocal of the ideal of escape from the world, and the parvenu is the reciprocal of the ideal of joining it. The transformation from pariah to parvenu takes place in a virtual world, since the pariah is not of the world and never becomes part of it. Instead of the ideal of loving in the other what the other is not, Rahel's ideal is to be loved for that which she is not, that is, to be loved as if her particular situation did not exist. Her lover must ignore her Jewishness, but she will occasionally assert it, if only negatively, as something from which she is distancing herself.

One could argue a love that works for the lover and a love that works for the beloved are quite different, and that there is no reason why the failure of being the loved one should entail the failure of being the lover. However, that was not Arendt's view. Clearly, the love of humanity in the book on Saint Augustine required reciprocity—its fatal ambiguity— for one is commanded to love all human beings, but this kind of reciprocity can exist only in the community of believers. Clearly, also, the love of God required reciprocity. The basis for self-denial, ultimately for self-sacrifice, is God's sacrifice of his only begotten Son. The relation with God is unique in that no passivity exists in it. Both participants are lovers. Even in the relation with humanity, the point is to love the other for what he is not so as to seduce the other, to turn him into a believer, into a lover, into the one that is proximate, that is closest.

However, the question in Rahel is more a question of being loved, of love becoming marriage, a question of identity, and it is no coincidence that Rahel wound up with Varnhagen. It is a question whether such an exchange of reciprocal egotisms can succeed, that is, whether one can agree mutually on reciprocally being loved, whether a perfectly receptive communion of souls can exist, rather than a perfectly active one. Arendt's answer is negative. It is the passivity of the ideal of being loved that paralyzes Rahel, that makes her turn to marriage as a rest home for the emotionally impaired.

But why does she need the rest home? Or why does she need to be loved? Arendt's answer is not nature, but history. "If we do not understand it, our history will become our personal destiny." In other words, Rahel, by seeking to escape her Jewishness, has made it impossible to do so, for she has sought transcendence in history. She has sought to deny her past in her historical experience, and by doing so has made her mis-

take. Her only escape from history would be by seeking an identity outside of it. But Arendt is iffy, if not ironic about this possibility: History
bashes "the product of nature on the head." [15] History is far stronger
than nature, and the social is far stronger than the eternal. Rahel could
maintain her freedom only by asserting some dual identity, between nature and society, between being Jewish and being German, and the problem of her history was that her society systematically eviscerated the
possibility of keeping a position between two identities. Yet is not that
possibility what the book on Augustine envisioned as the essence of being human, what would surface in Arendt's later work as the tension
of universal and particular, or as the internal dialogue? In certain social and historical conditions, the possibility of being human is denied
to some people, because the possibility of duality is denied. Hannah
Arendt's ideal of authenticity was quite different from Heidegger's: Hers
depends on a consciousness of duality. Against Romanticism, alienation
is not overcoming an internal duality, but rather the suppression of one
of the alternatives.

This suppression, however, creates a situation of imbalance, of the
loss of reality, a loss that appears as a gain, a hyperreality. Because the
Romantics could not really love the object, unlike Augustine, they created a pure ideal of loving, one for which the love object does not matter. "Romantic love liberates the lover from the reality of his beloved." [16]
By removing specificity from the world, this kind of love liberates the
lover from her own specificity and thus turns her into a universal lover.
But this secularization of the ideal of detachment from the world through
love makes it impossible to be loved. It is fatal that world detachment
and being loved, Romantic love and the yearning for acceptance, cannot
be reconciled. Because Romantic love treats being loved as unimportant,
it is worked out in individual biographies in such a way that being loved
becomes all-important, for it is ultimately the only validation of having
loved in the past. Instead of the mutual loving between God and the
soul, the relation here is one of mutual deficiency, of loving no one, and
therefore seeking to be loved by everyone. Not only is there here a betrayal of the loved one; there is also a self-betrayal, and this self-betrayal
engaged Arendt's full attention.

Detachment from reality creates a type of memory, just as approaching reality creates a different type of memory. That memory is a contradiction for the soul, disturbing the soul with reality as a counterinstance,
recalling the soul to the present. That memory draws the soul out of its
reverie. It destroys Romantic love. Rousseau introduced another, senti-

mental, concept of memory, memory not as the memory of outer reality, but as the memory of inner states of the soul. This kind of memory "obliterates the contours of the remembered event." By destroying the possibility of connection to reality, "sentimental remembering is the best method for completely forgetting one's own destiny. It presupposes that the present itself is instantly converted into a 'sentimental' past." [17] In other words, this kind of memory makes history impossible. By preferring states of mind to objects and outer events, it seeks to eroticize the self, rather than the object, and transposes the condition of being loved as an object into loving as a subject, as if loving and being loved were the same thing. "For Rousseau the present always first rises up out of memory, and it is immediately drawn into the inner self, where everything is eternally present and converted back into potentiality." [18] This kind of memory seeks to construe the soul's love of God as the basic form of love for the world, for it removes the notion of a common history. It suggests that the relation to the absolute that is achieved through self-isolation can be taken as a basis for love in this world, the reason being that the point of love of others is not the love of others, but rather the self-love of the sentimental self. Augustine also believed that self-love is the origin of love, but his notion of love was that love should progress by getting rid of the notion of the self.

In contrast to Romanticism, Arendt dissolves the connection between love and memory. She is rather seeking the connection between love and what she terms history, that is, the external human world: "thus the power and autonomy of the soul are secured." "Secured at the price of truth." "Introspection engenders mendacity." Here autonomy is contrasted with authenticity. It is the quest for autonomy from the world that leads to mendacity, to lying—in *Eichmann in Jerusalem*, she writes: "it is sometimes difficult not to believe that mendacity has become an integral part of the German national character." [19] There, mendacity destroys memory, while for Rahel, "lying takes up the heritage of introspection." [20] Mendacity thus begins with forgetting what memory really is. It involves detachment from reality for the purpose of the construction of an inner self that turns out, however, to be a fictional and empty self.

The desire to lie, which Arendt views as the desire to separate from the world, involves seeking to be different from what one is. "For the possibilities of being different from what one is are infinite. Once one has negated oneself, however, there are no longer any particular choices. There is only one aim: always, at any given moment, to be different from what one is; never to assert oneself, but with infinite pliancy to become anything else, so long as it is not oneself." [21] Once again, this is the same mechanism as in the Augustinian model, but stated in such a way that one is unsure whether this passage should be read as a negation of the Augustinian model or simply as an elucidation of the consequences when love is not directed toward a transcendent object such as God or humanity, but rather toward self-creation. The quest for individual difference blanches the self's particularity, its individuality. The self seeks to be different and ceases to be itself. It adopts a universal stance that is characterized by a sort of passivity with respect to the many indifferent choices that it now faces. This attitude is characterized by longing, but its longing is for a subjective condition of happiness, not for an objective state of grace. This longing leads to Rahel's "inclination to generalize" — Arendt here is quoting Rahel about herself. Rahel's condition is one of deficiency, of "hoping for happiness," "hunger for people," the kind of thing that we know as the desire to be in love without there being anyone to be in love with. [22]

This leads Rahel to displace her interest from the reality of her life to her "narrated emotions." In the narrated world, the passive lover recaptures the sense of action: The confession replaces the erotic act, and by doing so it destroys the gap between private and public that Arendt thought was requisite for a robust conception of love. The distinction between the soul's love for God and man's love of the world can be transposed into a salutary distinction between the private and the public. The confessional, narrative mode overcomes this distinction. Detachment from one's own reality now returns as the attempt "to lend everything subjective an aura of objectivity, publicity, extreme interest." Arendt castigates Schlegel as shameless because he misuses the revelation of the "ultimate intimacy" to denote the "breakthrough of the infinite." "This generation now insisted that it betray its secrets privately." [23] The worst erotic sin is telling the story of one's lives and loves to somebody else, even to another lover. For Arendt, confession is not an affirmation of love. Confession is instead a betrayal of love.

The fundamental question about this detachment from reality is whether love can constitute the self. Rahel uses love for self-definition, and Arendt is claiming that human relations cannot be used in this way. While love can individualize, Arendt claims that this kind of individualization outside of any social framework is not authentic. "She could not do anything specifically individual, but since Finckenstein's love had made her a specific person without a specific world and without specific patterns, outlined only by love; since she had entered upon the adven-

ture of particularity without having been taken in by any particular society, the sole stake she could offer for any action was her own self." [24]
Augustine had argued that the loving human being is between two
worlds. He is on the threshold of eternity, a place with its own temporality and particular passion. Rahel is also between two worlds, one that
she is fleeing and one to which she wishes to belong, but the order is reversed because both worlds are in history.

Augustine's second kind of love, loving the next, the neighbor, was a
historical commandment: One cannot deny the neighbor. The world of
history cannot be shaken off, unlike desire, which can be transformed
into the love of God. Rahel rejected her historical, Jewish world and in
turn was rejected by the Gentile world to which she wished to belong.
What if one had left this world, filled with self-denying love, only to be
rejected by God, because God does not love you back? You would then
be a parvenu in heaven. No more pariahlike situation can be imagined.
Well, the Gentiles did not love Rahel back, and that is understandable
from a Christian point of view, for it is loving that requires sacrifice, not
loving back. God has always already sacrificed himself and has always
already loved mankind, forcing himself into history because of his love.
Mankind is called to love back in the assurance that it is loved. But Rahel loved *because* she wanted to be loved back. She sacrificed herself to
a false god, the society god in place of the social God, because she thought
that her god might love her back. Alas, society could not love her back
because her society was not founded on love. The parvenu turned her
eros to the desire for acceptance, and maybe society can accept only
those people who are not erotically involved with it. Maybe. A philo-
Semitic society can desire Jews or be repelled by them, but it cannot accept them, because it always has the possibility of being anti-Semitic.
This was Rahel's and Arendt's bitter lesson: that a provisional acceptance is no acceptance at all.

German as Pariah, Jew as Pariah

Hannah Arendt and Karl Jaspers

Anson Rabinbach

On several occasions, Hannah Arendt expressed her reverence for her teacher and friend Karl Jaspers, most notably in her 1958 *laudatio* delivered when Jaspers was awarded the German Book Trade's Peace Prize.[1] In that speech, she identified the quality that she so clearly admired in Jaspers and that sustained her loyalty over so many decades as his "*humanitas,*" which she defined as "the valid personality which, once acquired, never leaves a man, even though all other gifts of body and mind may succumb to the destructiveness of time." Characteristically, Arendt emphasized Jaspers's quality in both individual and public terms as a "living act and voice" that accompanies the work of the philosopher. According to Arendt, "*humanitas* is never acquired in solitude and never by giving one's work to the public. It can be achieved only by one who has thrown his life and his person into the 'venture into the public realm.'"[2] It is hardly surprising that Arendt's praise for Jaspers primarily concerns his affirmation of the pubic realm and underscores her conviction that there is no great difference between the substance of Jaspers's philosophy and his "activity as a philosopher." Nothing of the sort could of course be said about her other famous philosophical mentor, Martin Heidegger, who unmistakably comes to mind when Arendt remarks that for Jaspers, "responsibility is not a burden and has nothing whatsoever to do with moral imperatives."[3] Even from this brief encomium, it is clear that Arendt considered Jaspers to be "at home" in what she called "this space forever illuminated anew by a speaking and listening thoughtfulness," rather than by thinking in the more rigorous philosophical sense that she always accorded to Heidegger, despite his descent into political madness. On numerous occasions, Arendt contrasted Jaspers's Socratic ideal of the communicative philosopher with the dangerous, but more authentically philosophical, solitude of thinkers like Plato and Heidegger. As Margaret Canovan aptly summarizes, "When Arendt is focusing on Plato or Heidegger she is inclined to fear that philosophy is intrinsically solitary, antipolitical, and sympathetic to coercion, whereas when she concentrates on Socrates or Jaspers she is tempted to believe that true philosophy may be communicative and in harmony with free politics."[4]

The correspondence between Hannah Arendt and Karl Jaspers that began in 1926 and ended only with Jaspers's death in 1969 attests to a friendship that underwent periods of greater and lesser intensity, that often reached heights of intellectual brilliance, but that also descended to trivia and gossip, not to mention an inexhaustible variety of physical ailments. This long friendship between such temperamentally opposite individuals, the passionately engaged and identified Jewess and the Protestant German patriot who once called himself a "*norddeutsche Eisklotz*," a North German ice block, had many facets: mentor and student, older man and younger woman, Heidelberg professor and American public intellectual, each of which would alone merit discussion. Here, I choose to concentrate on one perhaps understated yet striking theme in their letters and in Jaspers's writings of the mid-1940s, the juxtaposition—at times explicit, at times implicit—of the status of Jews and Germans as pariahs. What I propose is that Arendt's interpretation of the Jews as a pariah people, which appears at the very outset of their correspondence and is in her (and Jaspers's) judgment a "negative" concept, became, after the war, the source of Jaspers's hope for a new, post-Hitlerian German identity. This transposition is, I believe, most clearly expressed in Jaspers's *Die Schuldfrage* (1946), which appeared in English as *The Question of German Guilt*, where, in an astonishing reversal, the Germans are described as a people deprived of their statehood and excluded from the community of nations because of the enormous suffering they had inflicted on others, above all, the Jews.[5]

In one of their first exchanges in the spring of 1930, Arendt had sent Jaspers a copy of a lecture based on her still-uncompleted book on Rahel Varnhagen. Though the lecture is not preserved, Jaspers's reaction is recorded: "You objectify 'Jewish existence' existentially—and in so doing, so perhaps cut existential thinking off at the roots. The concept of being-thrown-back-on-oneself can no longer be taken altogether seriously if it is *grounded* in terms of the fate of the Jews instead of being rooted in itself. Philosophically, the contrast between floating free and being rooted strikes me as very shaky indeed." [6]

Jaspers's comment obviously reflects his skepticism at Arendt's application of Heideggerian concepts to the Jewish condition of "rootlessness," a strategy that turns anti-Semitism's first article of defamation into the authentic Jewish condition of being and into the possibility of freedom. The Jewish pariah appears here in the language of Heidelberg existentialism, and we can perhaps understand why her teacher questioned her use of the phrase "Jewish existence" as a particular destiny, since he believed, as did most German mandarins of his day, that such "'Jewishness' is a *façon de parler* or a manifestation of selfhood originally negative in its outlook and not comprehensible from the historical situation." [7] To Jaspers's criticisms, Arendt replied that her "lecture is only a *preliminary* work meant to show that on the foundation of being Jewish a certain possibility of existence *can* arise that I have tentatively and for the time being called fatefulness. This fatefulness arises from the very fact of 'foundationlessness' and can occur *only* in a separation from Judaism." [8] Arendt's response clearly presupposed her famous distinction between the "Parvenu" and the "Pariah," which regards the former as the "negative" basis of the latter. In contrast to the self-deception of the parvenu, who aspires to commerce and culture, the self-conscious pariah lives in the authentic awareness that only an outsider embodies the humanity that society otherwise denies. [9] It should also be noted that the prideful self-consciousness attributed to the pariah in this exchange contrasts with her more pessimistic assessment in "The Jew as Pariah" (1944), where the high price of the pariah's social exclusion and "reckless magnanimity" is "political vulnerability" and "senseless suffering." [10]

On New Year's Day 1933, Arendt responded to Jaspers's most political book, *Max Weber,* an encomium to his teacher and an appeal to the more noble traditions of his tragic German patriotism. Jaspers's Weber is the liberal nationalist avatar of charismatic "leadership," which underscored the fact that Weber's paradigm of power required that room be made for the "authentic leader" who has an inner capacity for truth, lacks illusions, and holds an "authentic belief in one's own people." Although Jaspers warned against "false messiahs," he approvingly quoted Weber's famous remark of 1918: "to restore Germany to its old preeminence I would certainly align myself with any power on earth, even with

the devil himself, but not with the power of stupidity." [11] Arendt's dis-
comfort with Jaspers's nationalist rhetoric is palpable as she writes of
her difficulty in commenting on his characterization of Weber as the embodiment of the "German essence" or his glorification of Weber's "imposing Patriotism." With a hitherto unexpressed frankness, she wrote:

> You will understand that as a Jew I can say neither yes nor no, and that my
> assent would be as inappropriate as an argument against it. I do not have to
> keep my distance as long as you are talking about the "meaning of the Ger-
> man world power" and its mission for the "culture of the future." I can iden-
> tify with this German mission, though I do not feel myself unquestioningly
> identical with it. For me, Germany means my mother tongue, philosophy and
> literature. I can and must stand by all that. But I am obliged to keep my dis-
> tance, I can neither be for nor against when I read Max Weber's wonderful
> sentence where he says that to put Germany back on her feet he would form
> an alliance with the devil himself. And it is this sentence which seems to me
> to reveal the critical point here. [12]

Jaspers's reply, sent just four weeks before the alliance between German
nationalists and the devil was sealed by the handshake between Hinden-
burg and Hitler, was astonishment: "How tricky (*Fatale Sache*) this
business with the German character is. I find it odd that you as a Jew
want to set yourself apart from what is German." [13]

On the eve of Hitler's assumption of power, before the Nazi dictatorship, the war, and the Holocaust, neither Jaspers nor Arendt was willing to forego their conventional and, in retrospect, still fundamentally
intact ego ideals, Max Weber, the German liberal nationalist scholar,
and Rahel, the German-Jewish *salonnarde* of the Napoleonic era. After
1945, however, these respective postures became for both philosophers
untenable.

I have already alluded to Arendt's more pessimistic view of the pariah
in 1944, and her public battles during and after the war with leading
Zionists over her antipathy to a Jewish state are well known. [14] But Jaspers's own transformation remains largely obscure, and very little is
known about his activities in Heidelberg during the war, especially after
he was banned from teaching in 1938. Nonetheless, it seems certain that
Weber's ghost continued to haunt him, as is evident from a comment that
may be taken as a succinct statement of Jaspers's own thoughts, especially after 1935. In 1962, Jaspers speculated that had Max Weber lived
to experience National Socialism, and particularly the Saar plebiscite, he
would have then seen that "a state, that can contribute nothing more of
dignity to the nation, does not deserve his recognition as a German." [15]

Dolf Sternberger, Jaspers's former student and the cofounder (along with the literary critic Werner Krauss and Alfred Weber) of one of the first intellectual journals in postwar Germany, *Die Wandlung,* recalled that "only the experience of Hitler's dictatorship made Karl Jaspers into a political philosopher." Indeed, "a different Jaspers emerged out of the obscurity of oppression."[16] The title of Jaspers's first postwar lecture, "Von der geistigen Situation in Deutschland" (On the spiritual situation in Germany) self-consciously commented on Jaspers's 1931 *Von der geistigen Situation der Zeit,* a book that exemplified the melancholic pathos and nostalgia for "substance" and "authority" typical of the conservative revolution of the 1930s.[17]

The pronouncement that the Germans are a "pariah people" is perhaps the most important, yet overlooked theme in Jaspers's post-Hitler thought. In his opening remarks to the 1945–46 lectures, Jaspers emphasized his purpose to provide moral guidelines for German reconstruction "through the drafting of an *ethos,* that remains for us—even if this is the Ethos of a people regarded by the world as a pariah people."[18] As it did for Arendt just three years earlier, the concept of the pariah was inspired by Weber's admiration for the "tarrying endurance of the Jews." In his *Ancient Judaism,* Weber portrayed the ethos of the pariah people as one of social exclusion and worldliness. The suffering of the Jews in exile was the path to inner purity and collective redemption. In her 1944 essay, Arendt modified that judgment by pointing out that exclusion from power was a powerful impulse to private humanity, but all the more dangerous for the vulnerability that the Jews had to endure. For Jaspers in 1946, the Germans, their state destroyed, their country under foreign rule, their leaders in flight or in custody, now occupied a position not unlike the one occupied by the Jews—they, too, were at risk, and they had begun their own political diaspora.

Jaspers's *Die Schuldfrage* was an attempt to provide a guide to the wanderings of the German spirit in its new incarnation as a stateless specter.[19] As Arendt recognized, the new global human solidarity envisioned by Jaspers was a restatement of Kant's ideal of "perpetual peace" and a rethinking of his conjectural history in "Weltbürgerlicher Absicht" (Cosmopolitan standpoint). "Jaspers is as far as I know," Arendt wrote, "the first and the only philosopher who ever protested against solitude, to whom solitude appeared 'pernicious.'"[20] Thinking is a practice that occurs *between* individuals, and communication is not secondary to truth, not mere representation or dialogue, but the essential mode of philosophizing itself.

In 1945, Jaspers called Germans to a new "order of responsibility" that was possible only by cooperating with the occupying power. In the 1950s and mid-1960s, he stood at the center of controversies over reparations, rearmament, and the statute of limitations on Nazi crimes. For some conservatives, for example Carl Schmitt, Jaspers was a traitor to the nation and responsible for initiating the "guilt culture" of West Germany.[21] Conversely, for Theodor Adorno, Jaspers was responsible for the nebulous rhetoric of postwar existentialism and its apologetic "jargon of authenticity." In retrospect, he was neither. *Die Schuldfrage* established the new narrative of a "European German," and Karl Jaspers was the one philosopher of repute who had remained in Germany throughout the entire National Socialist era who never had collaborated with the regime and who was, I should add, married to a Jewish woman.

Still, Jaspers never abandoned his prewar Weberian nationalism. In an autobiographical sketch written in 1957, Jaspers recalled that he was one of the few who believed "since 1933 it was probable, and since 1939 certain, that the events in Germany meant the end of Germany. *Finis Germaniae.*" What would such a complete breakdown of the German polity represent? First, the end of Germany as a political entity. Neither the German empire nor the Third Reich was more than a "short-time political episode." Second, what is still German "lives in the great spiritual realm."[22] The defeat of Hitler and the end of German political existence, Jaspers believed, could now bring into existence the true German—the universal citizen.

Jaspers was well aware of the obvious paradox that German guilt was imposed by force of arms and that Germans were dependent on the will of the occupying powers, "which liberated us from the National Socialist yoke."[23] But he also recognized that the victors were peoples who recognized "human rights." The obstacle to their acceptance was the defeated condition of Germany itself. Political responsibility, he maintained, emerges only in authentic communication among autonomous individuals, a possibility that was by Jaspers's own admission practically nonexistent in the atmosphere of ruin, hunger, grief, dissolution, hypocrisy, and four-power occupation that existed at that time. "We have lost almost everything," he wrote, "state, economy, the secure basis of our physical existence, and even worse than that: the valid norms that bind us all together, moral dignity, the unifying self-consciousness of a people."[24]

Publicly, Jaspers took it upon himself to advocate a moral reversal (*Umkehr*) and repudiation (*Abkehr*) of the nation-state thinking that characterized previous generations of German academic philosophers.[25] However, if in his public statements Jaspers affirmed the legitimacy of Germany's defeat and spoke of its liberation, in his day-to-day activities he was actively opposed to the American occupation of the University of Heidelberg. Though he kept these details from Arendt, his primary allegiance was to the rector, Karl Heinz Bauer, whom the Americans suspected because he had written a textbook entitled *Rassenhygiene* (Racial hygiene).[26] Jaspers strongly supported and took credit for drafting the university senate's declaration against the efforts to purge the university of Nazi sympathizers by the American denazification officer, a Frankfurt-born German Jew, Daniel Penham.[27] This is not necessarily contradictory, since Jaspers fiercely defended the university's independence from all political interference, but it does point to an often overlooked dimension of *Die Schuldfrage,* its attempt to distinguish public from private domains of German guilt.

Jaspers's agenda in *Die Schuldfrage* was first and foremost to separate political responsibility from the four famous and distinct concepts of guilt that the book addresses: criminal guilt, political guilt, moral guilt, and metaphysical guilt. Each of these is weighted differently, and it becomes clear almost from the outset that he is far less concerned with the first than with the last three. Moreover, it is really with the third and fourth categories, moral and metaphysical guilt, that Jaspers is most seriously preoccupied.

Given the widespread German resistance to the legal and moral basis of the Nuremberg trials, Jaspers's few sentences devoted to criminal guilt, defined as "objectively demonstrable actions that transgressed against clearly defined laws," are barely adequate. Nonetheless, Jaspers strongly affirmed the legitimacy of the trials, which, in his view, revealed the "monstrous" consequence of the crimes committed by the Nazis. Political guilt refers to those whose political office implies responsibility for the acts of state taken by a particular regime. But, it also includes every citizen of that state, since "each human being is responsible for how he is ruled" (17).[28]

In contrast to political responsibility, which affects all decisions undertaken in the name of the members of a polity whether or not they tacitly consent, moral guilt is borne only by individual conscience and requires "penance and renewal" (*Buße und Erneuerung*). Finally, metaphysical guilt is by far the most ambiguous, referring to a basic solidarity between human beings that makes each responsible for all the justice and injustice in the world and, "in particular, for the crimes that are committed in their presence and with their knowledge." This guilt, however, is borne by neither states nor individuals, but "by God alone" (18).

Law might affect criminal and political guilt, but not moral or metaphysical guilt. The former are determined "externally," by the victors (as punishment, as juridical restrictions on Nazi officeholders, as general proscription on political organization). The latter are matters of individual conscience, since "no one can morally judge another" (23). Moral and metaphysical guilt remain outside the sphere of legal action. Collective guilt is thus a contradiction in terms: "*It is against all sense to make a whole people responsible for a crime,*" and "*it is against all sense to indict an entire people morally*" (24). Since only political responsibility is in any sense collective, collective guilt has meaning only as political responsibility, never as moral or criminal guilt. Although Germans are responsible for the political acts of the Nazi regime, they are not criminally liable for them, nor can they be made to bear the full weight of their moral or "metaphysical" responsibility by others. "Only in the consciousness of guilt," Jaspers concludes, can damaged "consciousness of solidarity and responsibility emerge, without which freedom is impossible" (82).

But Jaspers also warns that to declare Germany a "pariah nation," to punish its people, as "inferior, without worth, and criminal, an ejection of humanity," as was suggested by the circle around Treasury Secretary Henry Morgenthau, is unjust and inhuman (31). Did Jaspers believe that the Germans were being unjustly placed by the occupiers in the position of the Jews? Or did he welcome the new pariah status of the Germans as an opportunity? The two readings are not, of course, entirely incompatible. Guilt had to be assumed in order for it not to be imposed. Germans had to assume the burdens of pariahdom in order to achieve the moral and metaphysical reckoning that *Die Schuldfrage* demands. The question of German guilt is conceived as a "wager," but not one without risk. If the wager failed, the exclusion of Germany from the world community was certain. Germany would suffer a permanent loss of sovereignty. Germany would then be delivered up to the political whim of the victors and relegated to the permanent status of a pariah nation. Jaspers warned of the consequence of not accomplishing this task: "This path is the only one that might protect our soul from a pariah existence" (10).

Jaspers complained to Arendt that in Germany, the reaction to *Die Schuldfrage* was almost nonexistent, and he often spoke of the bitterness and isolation he had to endure because of it: "Publicly I'm left in peace. But behind my back people slander me: the Communists call me a forward guard of National Socialism; the sullen losers, a traitor to my country."[29] Penham reported that "in the course of a lecture delivered by Professor Jaspers ["On the Spiritual Situation of Germany"], the students started laughing and scraping their feet on the floor at the mention of democracy in connection [with] the spiritual situation in Germany." Jaspers interrupted the lecture, declaring that he would not tolerate such a demonstration.[30]

Arendt was alert to the chief weaknesses of Jaspers's *Die Schuldfrage,* though she muted her criticisms, perhaps because, as she later admitted, Jaspers was always "better" than what he wrote.[31] According to her biographer, Elisabeth Young-Bruehl, Arendt was put off by what she perceived as strong residues of Jaspers's prewar Weberian nationalism, as well as by his Protestant emphasis on the atonement of the German people through acknowledgment of guilt.[32] Its very sobriety, as Arendt recognized, was in no small part exculpation by understatement. In August 1946, she wrote him of her reactions to *Die Schuldfrage,* in the course of which she also promised to help find a publisher for the book in the United States.[33] She questioned whether moral or metaphysical guilt could ever be sufficient for any political community that is not restricted to one group or class and that would act against threats to the heterogeneity of the social fabric, and for pluralism and tolerance.[34] In fact there is good reason to doubt whether Jaspers himself actually believed that Germans were capable of the moral solidarity that would qualify them to become "citizens" in the cosmopolitan sense that Arendt imagined. Her husband, Heinrich Blücher, was even more impatient with the book, confessing to Arendt that "despite all beauty and nobility, the guilt brochure of Jaspers is a damned and Hegelized, Christian-pietist-sanctimonious nationalizing bilge."[35] She also reported that Blücher was even more insistent than she that "assuming responsibility has to consist of more than an acceptance of defeat and of the consequences following on that."[36] Specifically, Arendt believed that such an assumption of responsibility, which was a precondition for the continuing existence of the German people (not the nation), had to be "accompanied by a positive political statement of intentions addressed to the victims."[37] Arendt also proposed that it include a constitutional guarantee that any Jew, regardless of birth or residence, could become an equal citizen of any future German republic.

Most important, Arendt rejected Jaspers's definition of criminal guilt as inappropriate to encompass the kind of murder committed by the regime. For Arendt, the very inclusion of mass extermination as a crime was "questionable." "The Nazi crimes, it seems to me," she wrote, "explode the limits of the law; and that is precisely what constitutes their monstrousness. For these crimes, no punishment is severe enough. It may well be essential to hang Göring, but it is totally inadequate. That is, this guilt, in contrast to all criminal guilt, oversteps and shatters any and all legal systems. That is the reason why the Nazis in Nuremberg are so smug." [38] In response, Jaspers pointed out the dangers of dismissing the guilt of the Nazis as so monstrous as to take on the dimension of the "demonic." "You say that what the Nazis did cannot be comprehended as 'crime'—I'm not altogether comfortable with your view, because a guilt that goes beyond all criminal guilt inevitably takes on a streak of 'greatness'—of satanic greatness. . . . It seems to me that we have to see these things in their total banality." [39] Ironically, Arendt may have forgotten the source of that phrase fifteen years later, when, in a striking turnabout, she made use of that term to describe Eichmann and provoked the famous intellectual controversy over her *Report on the Banality of Evil.*

Jaspers's reliance on the concept of the pariah in *Die Schuldfrage* was, in no small way, an attempt to bridge what he called the "difference" between them that had caused such tension more than fifteen years earlier, and the incident of 1930 was still much on his mind, as a letter of May 1947 that refers to how he had "become aware of a difference between us" reveals.[40] As we've seen, in a striking transposition of Arendt's image of the Jewish pariah coming to self-consciousness through social exclusion and alienation, the status of pariahdom had became Jaspers's recipe for the Germans. As Weber and Arendt had demonstrated, social isolation was not without its benefits. Exclusion from power was a powerful impulse to private humanity. Jaspers was aware that to locate German redemption in the figure of the pariah was to identify with the historical image of the Jews in much the same terms (destiny as chance) that Arendt had spoken of in her 1930 lecture. Jaspers then had protested against her conviction that a people's negative historical destiny could be the source of collective identity: Existential concepts were not, he emphasized, determined by historical events. In *Die Schuldfrage,* it is precisely collective responsibility for crimes that binds Germans together. It is hardly incidental, then, that in 1947, Jaspers returned to their earlier

controversy with the rather surprising admission that he had not yet entirely divested himself of the thought that Germans and German Jews
might still share the same identity:

> It may be that for me the consciousness of being a German and the fact that
> from childhood on I have taken for granted that German Jews are Ger-
> mans—both these things together have become a question to which I have a
> final answer on an emotional level but it is not one I can formulate in words.
> About 1932 [sic] (I'm not sure of the year anymore) you and I became aware
> of a difference between us that I did not perceive as a personal one even then,
> a difference that is not absolute in itself but is by no means trivial either. That
> it exists at all (it's the same between my wife and me, and we discuss it again
> every so often) is only a sign that we are working toward a state of the world
> in which such problems will cease to matter.[41]

At this crucial point Jaspers invokes the traditional ideal of the *Kul-
turnation* as Jacob Burckhardt might have framed it. As we have already
seen, his concept of "Germanness" retains its cultural, not its political
or territorial, definition. If he now conceded, as he did not in 1930, that
Jews and Germans did not share the same fate or belong to the same
community in 1945, perhaps with the emergence of the German pariah
and the simultaneous disappearance of both the German power state and
the Jewish parvenu and pariah (Rahel Varnhagen), a chance for Jewish-
German symbiosis actually existed, perhaps for the first time. The negative "existence" that Jaspers had denied was the "foundationless" core
of the Jewish destiny was now—he insisted—Germany's fate. Arendt
especially found "devastating" his sentence "Now that Germany is destroyed I feel at ease as a German for the first time" because, she recalled,
Blücher had said exactly the same thing a year earlier.[42] But she again
rejected Jaspers's suggestion that either then or now, Jews and Germans
were somehow in the same situation: "I recall our disagreement very
well. In the course of it, you once said (or wrote) to me that we were all
in the same boat. I can't remember now whether I answered you or only
thought to myself that with Hitler as captain (this was before '33) we
Jews would not be in the same boat. That was wrong, too, because under the circumstances you weren't in the boat much longer either or, if
you were, then only as a prisoner."[43]

As Jaspers embraced the ideal of the German pariah, Arendt seemed,
if not to abandon the Jewish pariah, at least to recognize some of the difficulties with its normative significance. Just as Jaspers's concept of the
pariah was linked to the fate of Germany as a "cultural" nation, Arendt's
Jewish pariah was bound up with her own version of Zionism. And she

began to realize that her vision of Zionism was no longer as defensible as it had once been. In her essay "The Moral of History," published in January 1946, she wrote: "The events of recent years have proved that the 'excepted Jew' is more the Jew than the exception; no Jew feels quite happy anymore about being assured that he is an exception. The extraordinary catastrophe has converged once again all those who fancied themselves extraordinarily favored beings into quite ordinary mortals." [44] More emphatically, she defended her view that German Jews no longer wanted to be considered German: "If the German Jews don't want to be Germans anymore, that certainly can't be held against us, but it does of course look a little funny. What they really want to say by that gesture is that they have no intention of assuming any share of political responsibility for Germany; and in that they are right again. And that alone is the key point." [45]

In the early 1950s, when Arendt once again contemplated publishing the book on Rahel, she admitted to Jaspers that it was "particularly alien to me now." [46] To Jaspers she acknowledged that the concepts of pariah and parvenu could only peripherally account for anti-Semitism, and she feared that if she now belatedly published the book on Rahel, "people of good will will see a connection, which does not in fact exist, between these things and the eradication of the Jews. All this was capable of fostering social hatred of the Jews and did foster it, just as it fostered on the other side a specifically German breed of Zionism." Even more important, Arendt admitted that it had been "written from the perspective of a Zionist critique of assimilation, which I had adopted as my own and which I still consider basically justified today. But that critique was as politically naive as what it was criticizing." [47]

How that naiveté expressed itself, Arendt did not say, but it is clear that after the Biltmore conference of 1942, Arendt was convinced that the future of Zionism rested, as Richard Bernstein has argued, "on the outdated nineteenth-century concept of a nation-state as a model for the Jewish state that was potentially dangerous." [48] In essence, Arendt abandoned Zionism at precisely the same moment that she recognized that the categories of the pariah and the parvenu had in fact contributed to the making of a particularly German-Jewish dilemma, the dilemma of creating an "identity" out of a "negative existence." Ironically, Jaspers saw in the collapse of the German nation-state the hope for a stateless existence that, like the stateless existence of the ancient Jews, could bring about a humanization from the negative experience of the collapse. At the same moment, Arendt recognized that the statelessness of the Jews was too high a price and had made it impossible for them to think of an alternative to its recreation in Palestine.

Die Schuldfrage had other weaknesses, as well. In 1950, Jaspers sent a copy to his old friend Heidegger with the recommendation that it might be useful for him to read it in connection "with your word about the 'shame,'" a reference to a letter that Heidegger sent in March 1950 confessing to being "ashamed" at not visiting Jaspers again.[49] But Jaspers did not publicly confront Heidegger, despite his own conviction in an unsent letter that "what occurred between us is something public through your National Socialist actions; only publicly, it appears to me, can the conditions be restored."[50] Despite two occasions on which he was publicly challenged to do so, Jaspers never criticized Heidegger's stance in any public forum, and he made sure his autobiographical chapter on Heidegger was withheld until both men were dead. In part, the reasons for his reticence can be found in *Die Schuldfrage* itself, where Jaspers demands "collective responsibility" but consigns the "moral and metaphysical" notions of guilt to the private sphere, while criminal and political guilt alone remain public matters. The separation of German guilt into two distinct spheres, moral / metaphysical and criminal / political, gave tacit support to the so-called silent *Vergangenheitsbewältigung,* coming to terms with the past, of the immediate postwar years.

What were the consequences of the reversal that occurred for the first time in Jaspers's text, and subsequently in popular attitudes, between Arendt's vision of the Jews as coming into their own in the psychological consciousness of being a pariah people and Jaspers's recipe for the Germans? Was Jaspers's ambivalence about the German pariah an attempt to assimilate his Weberian nationalism to Arendt's original formulation of Jewish existence as a "negative" and "foundationless" fate? Could the Germans, having cast off the nation-state that inflicted such suffering on humanity, now become, like the Jews, a stateless people with a cosmopolitan humanity?

After German unification, an event Jaspers still considered unthinkable in his *Freiheit und Wiedervereinigung* (Freedom and reunification, 1960), we can ask whether the language of *Die Schuldfrage* contributed to the lingering disquiet over Germany's apparently permanent status as a "pariah nation." Jaspers's contention that Germans were now placed in a historical role analogous to that of the Jews seemed to underscore the widespread resentment of many Germans who attributed Germany's postwar division and "dismemberment" to retroactive punishment for its historical crimes. Did the perhaps unconscious shifting of the pariah mantel from Jews to Germans reinforce German feelings of victimhood vis à vis other nations? Did it not also open the way for some Germans to consider their state a hostage to Jewish memory, as both the anti-Zionism of the German student Left and the *Historikerstreit* of 1986 revealed? Did Jaspers's concept of "metaphysical guilt" contribute to the permanent "oversensitivity" of many German liberals and Left intellectuals to all forms of oppression, leading to a compulsive projection of the "fascist imaginary" on contemporary events?

Finally, did Jaspers's emphasis on Germany's overcoming the pariah status and on reentering the community of nations, coupled with his expectation that this condition was ultimately transitory, serve those who argued that German unification was the inescapable conclusion of his argument? As former chancellor Willy Brandt remarked in his perceptive forward to a new edition of Jaspers's *Freiheit und Wiedervereinigung,* the claim that "knowledge of Auschwitz forbids German unity" (a claim made by Günter Grass, among others) contained a serious misjudgment, ignoring the expressly "antinational" character of National Socialism, which sacrificed Germans and Germany to its racial imperium.[51] The unification of Germany demonstrated that Jaspers's framing of the problem of German guilt in the context of Germany's having become a political pariah nation ultimately reasserted the importance of a return to the nation-state and national identity, however unintentionally. In the end, Jaspers remained more the student of Max Weber than the teacher of Hannah Arendt. All of these questions point toward what Dan Diner has called the "negative symbiosis" of post-Holocaust Germans and Jews, a negative symbiosis that, despite all good will, could never fully be overcome, either in politics or in this remarkable German-Jewish friendship.[52]

The Grammar of Prudence

Arendt, Jaspers, and the
Appraisal of Max Weber

Peter Baehr

On April 20, 1950, Karl Jaspers wrote to Hannah Arendt, "I had a remarkable dream last night. We were together at Max Weber's. You, Hannah, arrived late, were warmly welcomed. The stairway led through a ravine. The apartment was Weber's old one. He had just returned from a world trip, had brought back political documents and artworks, particularly from the Far East. He gave us some of them, you the best ones because you understood more of politics than I" (no. 100, 148; April 20, 1950).[1] Just over two months later, Arendt replied. "Prompted by your dream," she wrote, "I've read a lot of Max Weber. I felt so idiotically flattered by it that I was ashamed of myself. Weber's intellectual sobriety is impossible to match, at least for me. With me there's always something dogmatic left hanging around somewhere. (That's what you get when Jews start writing history)" (no. 101, 150; June 25, 1950).

So continued the exchange between Jaspers and Arendt over a problem—condensed in the name of Max Weber—that had first emerged specifically in their correspondence as early as January 1933 and that retained its salience until roughly three years before Jaspers's death in 1969. The chief characteristics of this exchange are nicely epitomized in the remarks that I have quoted. On the one hand, Jaspers hoped that Arendt would draw near to Weber, crossing the "ravine" that divided her from him, that she would, in other words, recognize and learn from Weber's example as both a particular kind of German and a particular kind of theorist. On the other hand, Arendt deflected these hopes by means of a certain self-deprecation. What I want to show, however, is that Arendt never did take that "stairway" evoked in Jaspers's dream and that "intellectual sobriety" was among the least of the quarrels she had with his Heidelberg mentor. To put it more pointedly, I will argue that, some similarities notwithstanding, few authors of the twentieth century offered a more comprehensive alternative to Weber's political and sociological thought than Arendt did.

I shall begin by examining how Jaspers summoned Weber's name to delineate a certain idea of Germanness and how Arendt responded to Jaspers's attempts to encompass her within this idea. We will see that she was much more forthright in rejecting Jaspers's interpretation of Germany than she was in confronting his view of Max Weber, and this also has to be explained. Then, I answer a couple of related hermeneutical questions. If, as I claim, Arendt and Weber were so markedly at variance as theorists, why did this not emerge in the Arendt-Jaspers correspondence, where Weber's name is so often invoked? And how did Hannah Arendt respond to Jaspers on the Weber question in a way that minimized conflict between her and her erstwhile supervisor? In answering this latter question, we will see some of the major axes of difference that typify Arendt's and Weber's approaches to political and sociological questions.

"GENEALOGICAL INVESTIGATIONS": WEBER AND GERMANY IN THE ARENDT-JASPERS CORRESPONDENCE

An appreciation of the complexity of the Arendt-Jaspers relationship is impeded by a widely held view of it as vigorously candid and open, entirely unconstrained by fear of censure, almost the very model of the Habermasian ideal speech situation or of Jaspers's own ideal of "*grenzenlose Kommunikation,*" limitless communication. And such a simplification, common as it is,[2] has an authoritative source: Hannah Arendt herself. Speaking in a Toronto seminar convened just over three years before her death, she remarked that intellectual exchange with Jaspers was completely unreserved: "you don't keep anything back. You don't think, 'Oh, I shouldn't say that, it will hurt him.' The confidence in the friendship is so great that you know nothing can hurt."[3] Moreover, with this affirmation of friendship, Arendt was only admitting in public what she had already told Karl Jaspers himself when she remarked on that "always fresh joy of being able to speak without reservation, a happi-

ness that I otherwise know only at home" (no. 99, 147; April 10, 1950).
Jaspers reciprocated. In his "Philosophical Autobiography," composed
in 1953 but only published in 1957, he observed that "with her I was
able to discuss once again in a fashion which I had desired all my life,
namely in a spirit of 'complete unreservedness' and 'abandon' and
'trust.' " [4]

But is this fully credible? For Jaspers, at least, there *were* matters that
hurt, and Arendt was scrupulous as a correspondent not to pursue them
in any extensive way. Her relationship with Heidegger, for example, had
to be handled with caution for fear of offending Jaspers.[5] A more important area of reserve, however, concerned Max Weber (1864–1920), the
great polymath of Wilhelmine Germany, for whom Jaspers felt the kind
of personal, filial reverence that Arendt felt for Jaspers. More significant, Weber symbolized for Jaspers a cluster of deeply cherished commitments to putative "German" qualities of "rationality and humanity
originating in passion" residing in "the secret soul of the German people," [6] to a European, rather than an autarkic, racist destiny for the German nation, and to a "spiritual and moral existence which holds its
ground by power but also places this power under its own conditions." [7]

Jaspers was concerned both to invoke Weber as a particular kind of
European German and to reassure Arendt that a Germany modeled on
Weber's moral-political vision would have been welcoming for Jews and
Gentiles alike. From the beginning, Arendt was blunt, rejecting not Max
Weber himself, but the allegorical use to which he was put by Jaspers.
"It does not bother me," she writes on January 1, 1933,

> that you portray Max Weber as the great German but, rather, that you find
> the "German essence" [*das "deutsche Wesen"*][8] in him and identify that es-
> sence with "rationality and humanity originating in passion." I have the same
> difficulty with that as I do with Max Weber's imposing patriotism itself. You
> will understand that I as a Jew can say neither yes nor no and that my agree-
> ment on this would be as inappropriate as an argument against it. . . . For
> me, Germany means my mother tongue, philosophy, and literature. I can and
> must stand by all that. But I am obliged to keep my distance, I can neither be
> for nor against when I read Max Weber's wonderful sentence where he says
> that to put Germany back on her feet he would form an alliance with the
> devil himself. (no. 22, 16)

Two days later, Jaspers penned a reply admitting to being puzzled
"that you as a Jew want to set yourself apart from what is German" and
seeking to clarify his earlier statements. By saying that the "German
character [*Wesen*] is rationality, etc., I am not saying that rationality is

exclusively German." What Jaspers had meant to do through the example of Weber was to give the word "German" an "ethical content"
(no. 23; 17–18; January 3, 1933). If only Arendt would add to her sense
of Germany a "historical-political destiny" in a unified Europe, then
there would be no difference between them.[9] But Arendt was neither
persuaded nor mollified. Continuing her correspondence in this most
fateful month—Adolf Hitler became chancellor of Germany on January 30—she reaffirmed her unease and dissatisfaction with the expression "German essence," a concept that is not simply open to misuse, but
"almost identical" with it. "I am of course a German in the sense that
I wrote of before," she continues. "But I can't simply add a German historical and political destiny to that. I know only too well how late and
how fragmentary the Jews' participation in that destiny has been, how
much by chance they entered into what was then a foreign history"
(no. 24, 18–19; January 6, 1933). Five letters—short notes, really, dealing with miscellaneous matters—then followed over just as many years,
ending with a letter from Jaspers in September 1938. The Weber and
German questions are not dealt with, and the correspondence shows
every sign of trailing off into oblivion.

When it resumed again in October 1945, with Germany now in ruins, it was not long before Jaspers returned to the theme he had rehearsed twelve years earlier. During the Nazi interregnum, he had told
his Jewish wife "I am Germany" in an effort to reaffirm the "common
ground" on which both a German Gentile and a German Jew stood
(no. 41, 46; June 27, 1946) and to contest the Nazi appropriation of
their country's traditions. After the war, Gertrud Jaspers had reported
this "glib" assertion (Gertrud Jaspers's term) to Arendt, who added her
own observation about Jaspers's self-assessment. Though it was tempting, given the recent history of National Socialism, Arendt wrote to
Gertrud Jaspers, to see her husband as the real and alternative Germany,
it was an impulse that common sense must resist. After all, "Germany is
no single person. It is either the German people, whatever their qualities
may be, or it is a geographical-historical concept" (no. 39, 41; May 30,
1946). Jaspers was something more significant than a quintessential German, whatever that might be. He was an extraordinary "human being,"
a comment to which she would return in the 1958 *laudatio* address that
accompanied Jaspers's award of the German Peace Prize, where she celebrated a man who remained "firm in the midst of the catastrophe."[10] Karl
Jaspers, clearly privy to the letter sent to his wife, conceded to Arendt
that, yes, in hindsight, the expression "I am Germany" was politically

meaningless. When he had first uttered this formulation, he had done so
not out of a grandiloquent sense of his own importance, but rather to reaffirm his solidarity with Gertrud Jaspers. When his wife had welcomed
the solidarity but rejected the phrase, he had immediately concurred
that she was right to do so. "I am not German in any crucially different
way from the way she is German. . . . Now that Germany is destroyed—
in a sense and to a degree and in a finality that hardly anyone here has
really grasped—I feel at ease as a German for the first time (when I gave
my Max Weber book the subtitle 'The German essence . . .' I had to
overcome inner resistance, and did it in the situation of that time). In
what sense we are Germans—and it is in no absolute sense—I would
like to be able to articulate" (no. 41, 46; June 27, 1946).[11] And Jaspers
persisted in his attempts at articulation, though with little evidence that
he was now at last "at ease."

There is no need to trace the various, enduring manifestations of Jaspers's attempts to persuade Arendt that she was "both a Jew and a German" of a particular type,[12] but one more example is illuminating. The
context is a letter from Arendt of May 3, 1947, that discusses the extent
of German complicity in the killing of the Jews, a complicity that cannot, she avers, be limited to the hard-core Nazi and SS elite. It also en-
compassed units of "regular troops" that "represented a cross-section of
the people" (no. 57, 84). Arendt's letter also contains a revised version
of the dedicatory essay to him that was to accompany the publication of
Sechs Essays (1948).[13] In the course of his remarks on the dedication,
Jaspers returns to his "consciousness of being a German" and his inclu-
sive conception of Germanness itself. Since his childhood, he says, he
has taken it for granted that "German Jews are Germans—both these
things together have become a question to which I have a final answer
on an emotional level, but it is not one I can formulate in words." He
goes on:

> About 1932 (I'm not sure of the year anymore) you and I became aware of a
> difference between us that I did not perceive as a personal one even then, a
> difference that is not absolute in itself but is by no means trivial either. That
> it exists at all (it's the same between my wife and me, and we discuss it again
> every so often) is only a sign that we are working toward a state of the world
> in which such problems will cease to matter. I will never subscribe to a concept
> of Germanness by which my Jewish friends cannot be German or by which
> the Swiss and the Dutch, Erasmus and Spinoza and Rembrandt and Burck-
> hardt are not Germans.[14] I affirmed with Max Weber the idea of a German
> political greatness, and at the same time regarded Switzerland and Holland

as German entities that fortunately lay beyond political risk and kept German qualities viable that were threatened in the German Reich (as in 1914). That this German Reich has not only failed but has also by its criminal action brought about the demise of what is best in Germany does not destroy that other possibility, which retains its place among our noble memories (from Freiherr vom Stein to Max Weber). Our only failing has been to grossly overestimate that possibility. . . . I don't know what "the Germans" really are today. (no. 58, 87–88; May 16, 1947).

Judiciously sidestepping the references to Weber, Arendt answered by saying that she recalled their "disagreement very well," and then went on to add, citing the United States as her model:

In conditions of freedom every individual should be able to decide what he would like to be, German or Jew or whatever. . . . If the German Jews don't want to be Germans anymore, that certainly can't be held against us, but it does of course look a little funny. What they really want to say by that gesture is that they have no intention of assuming any share of political responsibility for Germany; and in that they are right again.

In the immediate postwar situation, she found it was understandable that Jews looked to Palestine, not Germany, for their sense of political identity, "even though I don't intend ever to go there and am almost totally convinced that things will not work out there." What Arendt would have liked to see was an "end to genealogical investigations," for it would be much better if "everyone could freely choose where he would like to exercise his political rights and responsibilities and in which cultural tradition he feels most comfortable" (no. 59, 90–91; June 30, 1947).

"MY SECRET GERMAN FRIEND
FROM THE EIGHTEENTH CENTURY"

But it is precisely this impulse toward "genealogical investigation" that Jaspers found so difficult to renounce, even as his own discomfiture with the Federal Republic increased and as he finally decided to leave Heidelberg to assume a chair in philosophy at the University of Basel in March 1948.[15] Moreover, in December 1949, Jaspers actually widened the compass of his genealogical search by contacting Arendt's husband, Heinrich Blücher, and seeking to enlist him too in the cause of "Germany." In his first letter to the man whom he would come to call his "secret German friend from the eighteenth century" (no. 100, 149; April 20, 1950), Jaspers writes enigmatically: "I know you now only as a German, too. Germans are rare" (no. 95, 143; December 28, 1949). More robustly antinationalist than even his wife, if such a thing were possible, Blücher waited over two and a half years to reply substantively and in person to Jaspers's communication.[16] When he did respond, his own reservations were voiced respectfully, but frankly: "What has always separated me from the Germans is that none of them, with a few major exceptions, has ever been seriously concerned about freedom; and, if you'll excuse me for saying so, that is what separates you from the Germans, too" (no. 132, 190; August 5, 1952). Refusing to take no for an answer, Jaspers reaffirmed his sense that he and Blücher "are German, which is our heritage and to which we somehow ultimately belong" (no. 178, 271; November 13, 1955), a sentiment he repeated to Hannah Arendt in a subsequent letter.[17] Blücher, however, remained firm: "How do I perceive myself as a German in these times? My answer has to be: not at all. As Hölderlin once said, the time of kings is past; and now the time of nations is past" (no. 181, 278; February 14, 1956).

However, what must surely be the apotheosis of Jaspers's attempts to pressure both Arendt and Blücher into accepting his version of Germany came when Hannah Arendt was on a visit to Basel. During her stay, Jaspers wrote a letter to Blücher discussing some topics on which the two men had corresponded but then concluded with the following lament: "From Germany—which in [Hannah's] conversation she likes to confuse with the people visible in the Federal Republic today—she has pulled away even more, is more indifferent toward it. That pains me somewhat. I feel she is mistaken about herself, even though she truly has, together with you, achieved a state in which she exists with her feet on the ground, even though deprived of the ground of her origins" (no. 253, 383–84; October 28, 1959). What is unusual about this particular communication is the hand in which it is written: "Hannah has copied this letter because my handwriting would be so difficult for you to read." There could be no clearer way of making Arendt feel the full weight of Jaspers's pained feelings than getting her to write them down verbatim.[18]

OF DEVOTION AND LOYALTY

Up to this point, I have sought to trace the perplexity that the idea of Germany occasioned in Jaspers's work. I have noted, too, the linkage of that idea to Max Weber, summoned by Jaspers as the exemplar of qualities diametrically opposed to those that had so disastrously overtaken

Germany since the foundation of the *Kaiserreich* in 1871. But if one examines the correspondence closely, one finds that while Arendt was willing to confront Jaspers very directly on the German question, she was very reluctant indeed to do the same with Max Weber, particularly in the postwar exchanges. Whereas Jaspers's letters on Germany often invoke Weber's name, Arendt's responses hardly ever do. Presently, I will examine the various kinds of evasion that characterize Arendt's treatment of Weber, both in the correspondence and in her work intended for a public audience. Before I proceed toward this investigation, however, it is necessary to explain *why* Arendt proceeded with the caution and discretion that she did.

Arendt's candor with Jaspers met its limits, it can be conjectured, in the reverence and loyalty she felt for him. Such esteem manifested itself in a number of ways, from the material help in the form of the regular food packages she sent him and his wife in the immediate postwar period of Germany scarcity, to the onerous tasks of overseeing, until her own death in 1975, the English-language translation, publication, editing, and financial management of Jaspers's writings, to the handsome encomia she offered him in three dedicatory essays, in public lectures, interviews, symposia, and books,[19] and in the salutation that begins all of her letters from July 9, 1946, onward: "*Lieber Verehrtester*" (Dear esteemed one). In the 1958 *laudatio* address, her former *Doktorvater* (doctoral thesis advisor) is described as "inviolable, untemptable, unswayable," and one who offered "an affirmation of the public realm," unique to a philosopher.[20] To this kind of homage, Arendt added the immense loyalty that she reserved for all her friends, including Heidegger, Benjamin, and Broch, and that prompted her to adopt one of Jaspers's own favorite motifs in a celebration of his eighty-fifth birthday: Loyalty is the sign of truth.[21]

It is important to add that such devotion and loyalty could lead Arendt to immense efforts to reassure Jaspers of how deep her commitment was to him, so deep, in fact, that it could bridge the perennial question that seemed to divide them. When Jaspers confesses that "I will never cease claiming you as a 'German,'" Arendt responds in a spirit of magnanimity, seeking to comfort her disconsolate friend. The occasion is Jaspers's seventieth birthday: "I want to thank you for seventy years of your life, for your existence, which would be cause enough for gratitude. I want to thank you for the early years in Heidelberg when you were my teacher. . . . I have never forgotten since then that the world and Germany, whatever else they may be, are the world in which you live and the country that produced you." She adds:

> I think I can promise you that I will never cease to be a German in your sense of the word; that is, that I will not deny anything, not your Germany and Heinrich's, not the tradition I grew up in or the language in which I think and in which the poems I love best were written. I won't lay false claims to either a Jewish or an American past. (no. 140, 206–7; February 19, 1953)[22]

The significance of these sentiments of devotion and loyalty for the Weber question is that Weber was Germany for Jaspers, just as Jaspers was to tell Marianne Weber that "Max Weber was truth itself."[23] Or, to express the matter in a different idiom, Weber was an overdetermined symbol for Jaspers, not only of the latent Germany that actual events seemed continually to confound, but of a man who incarnated attributes that were central to Jaspers's *Existenz* philosophy.[24] More specifically, Weber was adduced in the correspondence with Arendt as a kind of moral touchstone of four qualities that Jaspers prized above all others.

The first quality Jaspers emphasizes is Weber's celebratory and unflagging commitment to personal freedom, a liberty that can be shown—in the case of suicide—to encompass even the rejection of life itself.[25] Second, Jaspers describes Weber as a man of "unlimited honesty" that surpassed that of his nearest rivals, Nietzsche and Kierkegaard. Weber was "the archetypical modern man who opens himself completely to absolute inner chaos, to the battle between warring powers, and who doesn't allow himself any secret cheating but lives passionately, struggles with himself, and has no goal. He felt that all of science and learning taken together was totally incapable of providing fulfillment in life" (no. 396, 636; April 29, 1966). Third, Weber is portrayed as the embodiment of "'independent thinking,' the meaning of which I would like to illuminate by discussing your work" (no. 396, 637; April 29, 1966). And fourth, Jaspers dilates on Weber's scrupulous standards in his dealings with other people. Jaspers put the matter in a characteristically personal way: "In the last year of his life—we saw him during a last visit in Heidelberg, two months before his death—he was in a 'manic' but completely disciplined state. . . . When he left after dark he spoke his last words to me, ones that have always been an encouragement to me, apropos of my *Psychologie der Weltanschauungen*, which had just been published. I told you about that before. It was as if he forgot nothing, not even the smallest human courtesies, in those last months when his life exceeded all bounds" (no. 396, 637; April 29, 1966).[26]

Because all these outstanding qualities were distilled in Jaspers's admiring image of Max Weber, Arendt was loathe to tackle explicitly the man who embodied them. Taking the offensive against Weber would have been tantamount to an assault on Jaspers. More than this, it would have been to attack devotion and loyalty themselves, sentiments whose value and importance she valued as much as he did. In any case, Arendt felt no compulsive need to be proved "right," particularly where the issue of friendship was at stake.[27] Equally, the more Jaspers linked Arendt to Weber, as he did in the projected book on independent thinking, the more difficult it was for her personally to extricate herself from that association. This was because Arendt knew Jaspers was paying her the supreme compliment, which it would have been churlish and hurtful to rebut, even if to have done so would, ironically, have proved Jaspers's point about independent thinking.[28]

Such a reconstruction of Arendt's attitudes and action raises a very obvious question. Were there demonstrable grounds for Arendt to believe that her friendship with Jaspers *could* have been endangered, or at least harmed and damaged, over the question of Max Weber? In the first place, Jaspers himself once openly rehearsed his fear of a break with Arendt and, significantly, invoked Weber precisely in that context. The context was Golo Mann's twin attack on *Eichmann in Jerusalem* and, in very personal terms, on its author. Jaspers was appalled by Mann's conduct and reflected on the need for solidarity, even where disagreements are profound and pronounced.

> I'm reminded of Max Weber; our relationship was never put to the ultimate test. I have my doubts sometimes, but then recall his extraordinary willingness to listen, and I cease to doubt, but I really don't know. Something remained hidden with him. And looking back into the past, I thought about still other people. I thought: Could Hannah ever destroy the bond between us? We have disagreed so often and on crucial matters, or at least so it seemed. No, I said to myself, that is impossible. Even to voice that doubt is inadmissible. For it leads to the point where *everything* crumbles. (no. 345, 541; December 13, 1963)[29]

Second, Hannah Arendt knew full well what to expect when Jaspers felt strongly about a writer. His vitriolic condemnation of Marx ("an 'evil' person" whose "dictatorial character" was "filled with hate"),[30] whom she had partially defended, sunk to depths of loathing matched only by his hagiographic celebration of Spinoza ("this pure soul, this great realist, the first human being to attempt to become a citizen of the world . . . this down-to-earth passion"),[31] whom she had mildly slighted.

Judgments of such apodictic ferocity suggested that some subjects—the Weber question chiefly among them—were best left alone or handled in a conciliatory manner. It is also notable that in the case of Marx, Arendt *did* retreat from her original position when faced with Jaspers's rhetorical fusillade.

Though many of Arendt's statements in her published works reveal a high regard for Marx,[32] and though she flatly rejected Jaspers's contention that Marx was "the intellectually responsible originator of what prepared the way for totalitarianism" (no. 138, 205; December 29, 1952), in the correspondence, she did eventually back down from an earlier, qualified defense of him. What prompted Jaspers's denunciation was Arendt's view of Marx as intellectually misguided, but honorable in his "passion for justice," which had a "powerful" affinity with Kant's (no. 106, 160; December 25, 1950). Incredulous that Marx could be associated with his beloved Kant, Jaspers insisted on a different comparison: Ezekiel (no. 107, 163; January 7, 1951). Arendt's response was to give some ground ("I've thought the whole thing over again"), saying that Heinrich Blücher agreed fully with Jaspers's estimation, but adding for good measure that she meant to defend Marx not as "a philosopher, but as a rebel and a revolutionary" (no. 109, 167; March 4, 1951). Such a concession failed, however, to appease Jaspers. On the contrary, he kept up the attack in letters to both Blücher and Arendt. Finally, Arendt capitulated, limply acknowledging: "The more I read Marx, the more I see that you were right. He's not interested either in freedom or in justice. (And he's a terrible pain in the neck in addition.) In spite of that, a good springboard for talking about certain general problems" (no. 142, 216; May 13, 1953).

If Jaspers could entertain such powerful passions for men he had never known personally, what might his response have been to a critique of Max Weber? Particularly when, and this is my third observation, even the mildest of comments about Weber could trigger an indignant rebuke. A case in point concerns the passing remark that Arendt made in a footnote to chapter 6 of *The Human Condition*. Her theme is the loss of certitude that accompanied the rise of both Cartesian doubt and the Calvinistic conviction that one's irrevocable fate—salvation or damnation—could be known only by God, and never by man. To which Arendt appends the observation:

> Max Weber, who, despite some errors in detail which by now have been corrected, is still the only historian who raised the question of the modern age with the depth and relevance corresponding to its importance, was also

aware that it was not a simple loss of faith that caused the reversal in the estimate of work and labor, but the loss of the *certitudo salutis,* of the certainty
of salvation. In our context, it would appear that this certainty was only one
among the many certainties lost with the arrival of the modern age.[33]

A fairly innocuous and restrained judgment, one might think,[34] but not
to Jaspers. In a letter to Arendt of December 1, 1960, congratulating her
on the German publication of the *Vita Activa,* Jaspers devoted half of his
comments to this footnote. Homing in on the statement about Weber's
errors that have since been corrected, Jaspers demands evidence for this
assertion, insists that the "Protestant Ethic" essay is one that is almost
universally misunderstood, and then declares:

> The point is not unimportant to me, because what is involved here is the es-
> sence of Max Weber's scholarly achievement. Max Weber may be subject to
> correction in many other works, if one cares to express it that way, and I have
> my objections to raise with him, too, as I did during his lifetime. But in this
> one work (and this is not the case with his other volumes on the sociology of
> religion) one has to point up the error after total immersion and after follow-
> ing Max Weber step by step in his cognitive process. (no. 270, 407–8)

Arendt's response to the insinuation that she was incompetent to judge
Weber was to write about more pressing issues, the Eichmann trial foremost among them.

THE GRAMMAR OF PRUDENCE

I have been trying to explain why Arendt, her disagreements with Weber notwithstanding, desisted from tackling him head-on in the correspondence that passed between her and Jaspers. With one exception,
Arendt never offered a direct critique of Weber in writings aimed at a
public audience, either. As we will see presently, seeking to refute Weber
was neither her concern nor her strategy. At the same time, Arendt's relationship with Jaspers had to cope with the awkward fact that her own
work comprised a far-reaching alternative to his mentor's. So let us now
turn to examine how Arendt avoided such a critique, in both the correspondence and her books and essays.

To begin with, Arendt responded to Jaspers's comments by simply ignoring them. For instance, in a letter critically analyzing the German
version of "Ideology and Terror," Jaspers suggests that an ideal-type approach to totalitarian government might shed new light on it. He asks:
"What would you think if I adapted your insight in the following way?"
and then proceeds to do just that, drawing on a brief methodological

discussion in the *Protestant Ethic and the Spirit of Capitalism* on the ideal type (no. 141, 208–9; April 3, 1953).[35] Arendt let the question and the suggestion pass. Yet in the *Philosophical Autobiography*, composed in the same year this letter to Arendt was written,[36] Jaspers makes a remark that suggests that Arendt had acted on at least some of his methodological concerns. Writing of Arendt, he notes: "Better than I had ever been able before, I learned from her to see . . . the structures of totalitarianism: now and then slightly hesitating, but only because she had not yet familiarized herself with the categories, methods of research, and insights of Max Weber."[37] The curious implication is, then, that Arendt had by this time familiarized herself with Weberian categories and methods of research. But not only does this contradict the letter on "Ideology and Terror" I previously quoted; there is also nothing in the correspondence or in the rest of her work aside from some references to the *Protestant Ethic* to show that Arendt took the slightest interest in Weber's method, let alone sought to emulate it.[38] "Methodological quarreling," as Arendt once remarked to Heinrich Blücher, was something to which she had the strongest aversion, and Weber's methodology in particular appears to have been for her the least arresting aspect of his work.[39]

Second, Arendt criticized what others had done to Weber's concepts, thus seeming to exculpate Weber himself. To see such exoneration in play, consider Arendt's remarks in an article entitled "Religion and Politics" published in 1953, the year of Jaspers's letter to Arendt on the "ideal type" already quoted. One of Arendt's prime polemical targets in this essay is the positivism of the social sciences and, relatedly, the use of the ideal-type method.

> To take a convenient example, Max Weber coined his ideal type of the "charismatic leader" after the model of Jesus of Nazareth; pupils of Karl Mannheim [she is referring to Hans Gerth] found no difficulty in applying the same category to Hitler. From the viewpoint of the social scientist, Hitler and Jesus were identical because they fulfilled the same social function. It is obvious that such a conclusion is possible only for people who refuse to listen to what either Jesus or Hitler said.

And in a footnote she adds: "By taking this example, I do not mean to imply that Max Weber himself could ever have been guilty of such monstrous identifications."[40] Probably not, but the obvious retort to Arendt is, first, that such identifications are exactly what the ideal type, as a value-neutral concept, invites. (Weber specifically employed the term "charisma" to include maniacs and swindlers, as well as people whom conventional morality deems righteous.) Second, fundamental to charisma is that its bearer is viewed as extraordinary by his adherents (which Hitler indubitably was). Finally, Weber is explicit that though charismatic phenomena are "often most evident in the religious realm" they are "in principle . . . universal."[41]

Moreover, 1953 is the same year that Arendt distanced herself from another basic Weberian stipulation, though without mentioning Weber by name. In her reply to Eric Voegelin's critical remarks on *The Origins of Totalitarianism,* Arendt clarifies her difference from the social scientific "tradition of *sine ira et studio* [without indignation or partisanship] of whose greatness I was fully aware." The death camps, she contends, cannot be described clinically. Some moral evaluation is absolutely necessary, not out of the desire to moralize, but simply to be true to the phenomenon:

> When I used the image of Hell, I did not mean this allegorically but literally: it seems rather obvious that men who have lost their faith in Paradise will not be able to establish it on earth; but it is not so certain that those who have lost their belief in Hell as a place of the hereafter may not be willing to be able to establish on earth exact imitations of what people used to believe about Hell. In this sense I think that a description of the camps as Hell on earth is more "objective," that is, more adequate to their essence than statements of a purely sociological or psychological nature.[42]

Next, Arendt's praise for Weber's scholarship was always for the historical works, never for his sociological writings or his political opinions, areas in which her disagreements must have been most acute.[43] Hence, on February 17, 1956, as she was working on the *Vita Activa,* she wrote: "I've read a great deal of Max Weber in recent weeks. And with great pleasure I wanted you to know that! 'Agrarian relations in antiquity'[44] is a wonderful piece of work, and 'The Protestant Ethic and the Spirit of Capitalism' is one of incredible genius. I knew it already, but only now am I able to grasp everything he perceived. There's nothing in the literature after it that begins to approach it" (no. 182, 282).[45] It might be objected that *The Protestant Ethic* is indeed a sociological work, but Arendt herself appears not to have shared such a view. Weber accepted "sociology" as a designation of his own work only in 1909,[46] some four years after *The Protestant Ethic* was first published.[47] Finally, Arendt did not criticize Weber's political opinions or theories even when she had the evident opportunity to do so. Since Arendt was above all a political theorist, and one whose views were markedly at variance with Weber's, this anomaly is worth considering in greater detail.

Of all the differences between Arendt and Weber, none is more salient and profound than their contrasting views of politics. Weber defined politics primarily as an activity of leadership—particularly the leadership of the state—and insisted that its "decisive means . . . is violence." [48] Like all political institutions, the state as "a relation of men dominating men" requires justifications of various kinds. Whether these are traditional, charismatic, or rational-legal, they are always an exercise of "domination," a mode of power with which a following willingly and voluntarily complies. In modern democracies, politics consists of the relationship between leaders, whose authority rests on a plebiscitary foundation, and the "masses," that largely amorphous and emotional body of men and women whose only real purpose is to endorse the election of the party demagogue or, should he fail, to ensure his expulsion from office. With that limited involvement and imprimatur, the masses' role is exhausted. [49]

It is true that Arendt accepted much of Weber's description of the realities of modern political life, including its plebiscitary component. But where Weber recommended Caesarist governance and the party machine as a formation that offered the opportunity for talented leaders to impose their values on an otherwise shapeless mass, Arendt sharply opposed this mode of rule. Her stance on politics differed fundamentally from Weber's by offering alternative views of "power" (considered by Weber as a type of compulsion, by Arendt as a matter of collective agency) [50] of "the masses" (whose equation with "the people" Arendt describes as "pernicious") [51] and of "domination" or "rulership" (*Herrschaft*, to Weber, the heart of politics, to Arendt, a substitute for it based on a model of "fabrication"). [52] Similarly, Arendt countered Weber's description of the relationship between politics and ethics. Weber's emphasis was on the "numerous instances [that] the attainment of 'good' ends is bound to the fact that one must be willing to pay the price of using morally dubious means or at least dangerous ones." [53] For Arendt, to the contrary, "Every good action for the sake of a bad end actually adds to the world a portion of goodness; every bad action for the sake of a good end actually adds to the world a portion of badness. In other words, whereas for doing and producing ends are totally dominant over means, just the opposite is true for acting: the means are always the decisive factor." [54]

But what, then, is "action," which, together with the related concepts of "freedom" and "plurality" and "power," is an elemental characteristic of politics as Arendt understood it? Once more, Arendt distinguished her position from Weber and, incidentally, from the sociological tradition he influenced. Thus, in contrast with theories that posit action tele-ologically as a means-end relationship or as a "system," Arendt under-stood it as the ability to initiate a new course of events. Action realizes the human potential for freedom, albeit under conditions of "plurality," that is, the diverse human agents in front of whom the action takes place and whose presence confers on it some meaning.

On Arendt's account, furthermore, action is a category of politics, not of sociology. It is inherently interpersonal and public, so that the dis-tinction between private "action" and "social action"[55] is stipulatively irrelevant. It is closely related to, though not synonymous with, the fac-ulty of speech, because it is through speech that the actor reveals his or her unique identity, a faculty irreducible to the "function" a person per-forms. Far from action being subject to a stabilizing "normative orienta-tion" (Talcott Parsons), or being the result of a "motive" or "orientation" (Max Weber) or of a "project" (Alfred Schutz), it is a corollary of "na-tality": the fact that we are born as members of a species whose charac-ter is to make beginnings.

Moreover, a categorical feature of action is its indeterminacy and ir-reversibility. No person ever knows exactly what he or she has initiated, and the "meaning" of that action is not a force that impels them on, but a retrospective judgment by the spectator (this can include the actor, as well), who weaves the strands of many actions into a story that, as "his-tory" or remembrance, preserves the actor's words and deeds.[56] What social scientists were typically writing about when they employed the concept of action, Arendt thought, was actually the largely instrumental practice of "doing-as-making" which *is*, of course, project-dependent, guided by rules, and pursued for a definite end. But this confusion be-tween "acting" (*praxis*) and "making" (*poiēsis*)[57] was precisely one Arendt was keen to avoid. Failure to do so would only deepen the ten-dency, already strongly rooted in philosophy and the human sciences, to taint politics with the imagery of fabrication, to see it as merely a tool, rather than as an activity in its own right, thus collapsing "action" into "work."[58]

Let us now return to the Arendt-Jaspers correspondence and two oc-casions on which Arendt evaded confronting directly Weber's political views. The first emerges from a letter from Jaspers concerning Arendt's article on the Hungarian uprising of 1956:

> Of the many observations in your essay, one in particular has preoccupied me: What you say about the emergence of 'councils' in all the revolutions of the last hundred years and what you view as very positive.[59] I can recall the pe-

riod of the workers and soldiers' councils in Germany. What was astounding was that for that short period absolute order prevailed, as if by itself. Max Weber was a member of the Heidelberg Workers and Soldiers' Council, and he asked one day: Who, I'd like to know, is actually governing here? . . . What exactly did you have in mind in valuing the councils so highly? (no. 219, 338; December 19, 1957)

Arendt did not respond, even though Weber's incredulity, when faced with an organization functioning at variance with his model of plebiscitary-leader democracy, must have spoken volumes to her about the limitations of his political imagination.

The second opportunity for Arendt to have openly challenged Weber's ideas—this time over his nationalism—came in 1964. Like her husband, Heinrich Blücher, Arendt was virulently opposed to nationalism. As she once put it, "What, after all, has contributed more to the catastrophic decline of Europe than the insane nationalism which accompanied the decline of the nation state in the era of imperialism?"[60] Weber's yearning for a powerful Germany was surely, from Arendt's point of view, in part symptomatic of this highly repellent tendency. Had he not, in the famous May 1895 Freiburg inaugural lecture, asserted that "the economic policy of a German state, and the standard of value adopted by a German economic theorist, can . . . be nothing other than a German policy and a German standard"?[61] Had he not also remarked in August 1914, this determined critic of the *Gesinnungsethiker* (the follower of the ethic of conviction), "For *no matter* what the outcome—*this war is great and wonderful*"?[62] Yet Weber's nationalism became a real issue for Arendt in the postwar correspondence only when it threatened to taint Jaspers's—not Weber's—credibility. The context of Arendt's anxiety was the "very nationalist-sounding passages" to be found in Jaspers's 1932 study on Max Weber, then in the process of being translated by Ralph Manheim.[63] Far from taking Weber to task, Arendt confined herself to expunging some passages that might have damaged Jaspers's reputation and to encouraging him to offer a context for other passages that were to remain. And even here, especially here, Arendt proceeded with the greatest tact and caution by making it appear that the instigators of concern were Helen Wolff and Manheim, rather than her (no. 348, 546; February 19, 1964; no. 351, 550–51; April 20, 1964). Moreover, in response to some of Jaspers's comments on Weber's nationalism, Arendt replied obliquely, "I wish we could talk about Max Weber" (no. 351, 551)—a remark that conveniently allowed her, by

means of indefinite postponement, to escape the onerous task of deliv-
ering a written judgment there and then.

Finally, when Arendt did, for the one and only time, criticize Weber's
own handling of a concept—that of power—her strategy was to subsume
it under a list of similar misapprehensions by Voltaire, Clausewitz, Robert Strausz-Hupé, C. Wright Mills, and Bertrand de Jouvenel. Whether
intentional or not, the effect of this approach was to produce a critique
of Weber that is highly muted. Weber appears not in his own right, worthy of detailed rebuttal, but as part of a broader tradition, and it is this
that constitutes the target of Arendt's strictures.[64]

CONCLUSIONS

Arendt and Jaspers conversed in their letters about many important figures. Yet although Max Weber appears more often in the Arendt-Jaspers
correspondence than any other great scholar, with the exception of Kant
and Heidegger, the dialogue about him was highly unusual and asymmet-
rical. How, then, are we to characterize it? We might initially be tempted
to say that Jaspers "spoke" about Weber and Arendt "listened," but this
fails to do justice to the subtlety of what was happening between them,
to the way that ideas are actually lived, to the web of loyalties, fears, and
passions that pervade the exchanges of highly creative and complex individuals. After all, Jaspers also "listened," seeking minutely to discern
the nuances of Arendt's feelings about Germany and Weber. Equally,
Arendt "spoke," trying to find the words to reconcile her moral and political convictions with her devotion to an old friend and mentor. Even
to engage in such a struggle reveals a tact and delicacy, a commitment
to friendship, that is deeply touching. It is also worth reinforcing the
point that Arendt's evasiveness on the Weber question was no intellectual capitulation. As we have seen, while she gave ground or remained
silent in the correspondence, her writings intended for a public audience
revealed a very different stance, comprising a far-reaching alternative to
Weber's theories and emphases.[65]

To this interpretation, however, a number of caveats must be entered.
First, it is no part of my argument that Arendt deliberately sought to
provide an alternative to Weber's ideas, for that would suggest that Weber influenced her thinking, albeit negatively, in a profound way. There
is no evidence whatsoever for such a contention. The point is not that
Weber affected Arendt in any important sense, or that she concertedly

set out to refute him, but rather that she had to reconcile her strongly contrastive approach with an awkward reality: devotion to Karl Jaspers, to whom criticism of Weber by others was anathema. Nor is my argument inconsistent with the obvious truth that, in some respects, and to some degree, Weber and Arendt shared similar attitudes. Both insisted on treating politics as a sphere sui generis. Both found employment for the concept of the "pariah." Both attacked emanationist philosophies, or what Arendt referred to as "two-world" theories, and excoriated doctrines of "progress." Both warned about the dangers of bureaucracy, particularly its tendency to colonize and depoliticize the public realm. Both defended the importance of intellectual integrity and the imperative of "saying what is."

The main inadequacy of such a catalogue, however, is that its plausibility resides not in any congruence of substantive arguments or propositions, but only in the very formal and general level at which the comparisons are pitched. As such, it hides more than it reveals. Carl Schmitt, too, insisted on the independence of the political, but no observer is going to claim credibly that Arendt was a Schmittian. Arendt may have feared the spread of bureaucracy, but in this she was hardly alone, and her source was quite evidently Kafka, not Weber. Intellectual and political integrity were vitally important for Arendt, but while she saw Rosa Luxemburg as an exemplar of these virtues, Weber maintained that the Spartacists were benighted fanatics.

Finally, to examine Arendt's evasions over the Weber question is not to deny that she was fully capable of being combative and robust with Jaspers on many issues, especially where her own authority to make judgments was not in question, as it was not, for instance, on the United States of America and on the Jewish question, or where her passion for Heidegger clashed with her friendship for Jaspers. Least of all do I wish to overemphasize the Weber question in the totality of their intellectual exchange. I have been focusing simply on one aspect of it that has been neglected in Arendt scholarship. My central points are only that the Jaspersian ideal of "limitless communication"[66] reached very tangible impediments in the case of Max Weber and that love and loyalty affect communication in complex ways. That some of the most profound forms of expression and dialogue do not conform to norms of transparency, "sincerity," and consistency may offend some philosophers. But it may also add weight to Arendt's suspicion that philosophy and human experience are constantly at war.

Apologist or Critic?

On Arendt's Relation to Heidegger

Dana R. Villa

The fact that Hannah Arendt was Martin Heidegger's student was never a secret. Nor was his philosophy's influence upon her analysis of totalitarianism and her thinking about politics. What *was* a secret, at least until the publication of Elisabeth Young-Bruehl's biography in 1984, was that she and Heidegger were lovers while Arendt was his student in Marburg during the period from 1924 to 1929. She moved to Heidelberg to work with Jaspers in 1926.[1]

Young-Bruehl's revelations raised some eyebrows, but they were set in the context of a remarkable life story, together with an account of Arendt's intellectual development and her primary contributions to political thought in the twentieth century. As a result, no controversy was engendered. Indeed, the overall effect of the revelation about the relationship with Heidegger was simply to make an already colorful life appear that much more dramatic.

Things took quite a different turn in 1995, when Elzbieta Ettinger published her brief account of their relationship.[2] Because Ettinger had been able to peruse the Arendt-Heidegger correspondence, she could claim that something new was being revealed: the "fact" of Arendt's life-long, self-effacing devotion to Heidegger. According to Ettinger, this devotion led Arendt to become Heidegger's "agent" in the United States after the war, generating translations of his work and "whitewashing" the nature and extent of his complicity with the Nazis. Such, at least, were the conclusions Ettinger had drawn from materials that have only recently become available to the public in a volume edited by Ursula Ludz.[3]

Reviewers hostile to Arendt seized upon the slim reed of Ettinger's psychologizing restatement of Young-Bruehl's basic facts, charging that Arendt was a German-Jewish intellectual snob, more in love with German *Geist* and its representative (Heidegger) than with her own people. Richard Wolin, writing in the *New Republic,* drew a dark parallel between Arendt's alleged exculpatory treatment of the "banal" Adolf Eichmann and her supposed "exoneration" of Heidegger in her 1969 birthday tribute, "Martin Heidegger at Eighty." A debate about the damage to Arendt's moral and intellectual reputation spilled over into the popular press, with articles in the *New York Times,* the *Nation,* and the *Chronicle of Higher Education,* to name only the most prominent.

I will refrain from rehashing the details of the so-called Hannah Arendt scandal. I do, however, want to challenge the primary idea that the controversy put in wide circulation, namely, that Arendt was a "disciple" of Heidegger's, a thinker without any critical distance on the thought of the master. This idea, which undergirds Ettinger's account, helped give new life to the charge that Arendt was, in Wolin's phrase, a "left Heideggerian," a thinker as hostile to democracy and constitutional government as was her teacher. It also made plausible Ettinger's contention, repeated by Wolin, that a good deal of Arendt's energies in the 1950s and 1960s were devoted to restoring Heidegger's damaged reputation.

Due to space limitations, I cannot give anything like an adequate biographical account of Arendt's distanced and often skeptical view of Heidegger the man. (Readers anxious for such an account will find Young-Bruehl a far more reliable guide to the ups and downs of their personal and intellectual relationship than Ettinger.)[4] What I propose to do, instead, is to focus on the two moments in Arendt's work when Heidegger's philosophical legacy is most strongly and most controversially felt. The first is *The Human Condition* (1958), generally described as her "most Heideggerian book." The second is the essay "Martin Heidegger at Eighty," in which Arendt allegedly exonerates Heidegger of his Nazi involvement.

Both texts reveal a far more complicated and critical attitude toward Heidegger than is usually allowed. *The Human Condition* is, in its own way, just as critical of Heidegger as it is of Plato and Marx. Similarly, "Martin Heidegger at Eighty," while containing an unfortunate and ill-informed sentence (in a footnote), turns out to be less an exercise in apologetics than a rumination on the dangers of "extraordinary think-ing." Both texts show that while Arendt took Heidegger seriously as a thinker (perhaps too seriously), she never approached him uncritically— even when she was paying tribute to him.

THE APPROPRIATION OF HEIDEGGER'S
THOUGHT IN *THE HUMAN CONDITION*

Thanks to Ettinger, we know that Arendt intended to dedicate *The Human Condition* to Heidegger. Indeed, she wrote Heidegger a letter to this effect, noting that "the book evolved directly from the first Marburg days, and it owes you just about everything in every regard."[5] This cer-tainly sounds like the kind of statement a disciple would make, and taken at face value, it seems to support Wolin's contention that Arendt was nothing more than a "left Heideggerian."

There is little doubt that *The Human Condition* is a work deeply in-fluenced by Heidegger. The real question is: What is the nature of this influence? Does Arendt slavishly follow in the master's footsteps, jetti-soning only his reactionary politics and cultural sensibility? Or does she use Heidegger violently, twisting his thought in directions he would not have recognized, overcoming her teacher in a manner similar to the "cre-ative appropriations" of Leo Strauss, Hans-Georg Gadamer, and Her-bert Marcuse?

Schematically, Heidegger's thought aids Arendt's project of reexam-ining "the whole realm of politics in light of the elementary experiences within this realm itself" in the following ways. First, the "existential an-alytic" of *Being and Time,* with its rebellion against the subject / object problematic of Descartes and Kant, suggested not only a revised con-ception of our fundamental relation to the world, but also a reformula-tion of the question of human freedom. Heidegger's conception of hu-man being as being-in-the-world displaced both the cognitive subject and the practical subject as abstract entities standing over against the world. In their place, Heidegger stressed the essentially *involved* charac-ter of *Dasein* as both understanding and acting being. This revolution-ary turn was clearly of great importance to Arendt in that it helped her to surmount the monistic, subject-centered conception of freedom as freedom of the will (or "practical reason") that dominated the Western tradition of philosophical and political thought.[6] Heidegger's concep-tion of *Dasein* as primordially both a being-in-the-world and a being-with-others aided her in placing worldliness and human plurality at the heart of human freedom, rather than at the extreme margins.

Second, Heidegger's work after *Being and Time* exposed the will to power or mastery underlying the traditional view of freedom as a form of sovereignty and action as an essentially goal-directed activity. For Arendt, Heidegger's insight into the tradition's rebellion against the finitude and frailty of the human condition provided a departure point for a critical rereading of the Western tradition from Plato to Marx. This tradition, with its persistent misinterpretation of political action as a kind of making or fabrication, repeatedly tried to overcome the "frailty, haphazardness, and contingency" of action in the public realm, with disastrous moral and political results. Heidegger's critique of the tradition's will to dominate Being thus sets the pattern for Arendt's critique of Western political philosophy's will to efface human plurality and spontaneity, which are typically seen as obstacles to the realization of the just society. (Think, in this regard, of the radical devaluation of moral disagreement we find in Plato, Aristotle, Augustine, Hobbes, Rousseau, Hegel, and, of course, Karl Marx.)

Third, Heidegger's diagnosis of the pathologies of the modern age, however mired in cultural conservatism and images of pastoral wholeness, provided Arendt with the frame for her own critique of modernity in *The Human Condition*. Heidegger's account of how the modern age places the knowing and willing subject in the structural place of God (reducing the dimensions of reality to what can be known and represented by such a subject) enabled Arendt to question the Promethean tendency of modern science and technology, along with the idea that a completely "humanized" reality will be one in which alienation is overcome.[7] "Resentment of the human condition" is seen to drive both modern science and technology, two forces that contribute mightily to our increasing "alienation from the world" and from political action, for Arendt, the most worldly of human activities.

These three themes constitute what *The Human Condition* owes positively to Heidegger. But what has made the book a classic is hardly its reformulation of abstruse Heideggerian notions into more accessible language. Its startling originality is evident in the way Arendt uses Heidegger against Heidegger, in the service of ideas he would have condemned. Arendt's subversion of Heidegger's thought is every bit as profound as her philosophical debt.

Thus, while Heidegger opened the way to a more worldly conception of freedom, he severely limited the political relevance of his conception of human being by framing it in terms of a broad distinction between authentic (*eigentlich*) and inauthentic (*uneigentlich*) existence. One can

live one's life by adhering to the given and the everyday, or one can resolutely eschew the false comfort of everything public and established and
confront the groundlessness of one's own existence. While authentic existence can never fully wrench itself free of "fallenness" and is, in fact,
dependent upon it, Heidegger leaves little doubt that the public world is
the privileged locus of inauthenticity. The "light of the public obscures
everything" because it covers over the fundamental character of human
existence as groundless, finite, and radically open or atelic.

In *The Human Condition,* Arendt appropriated Heidegger's conception of human existence as disclosedness, as open possibility divorced
from any hierarchy of ends, and turned it inside out. The *public* realm,
which for Heidegger had signified the everydayness of *Dasein,* became,
in Arendt's phenomenology, the arena of human transcendence and freedom, of *authentic* existence. According to Arendt, it is through political
action and speech on a public stage that human beings achieve a unique
identity and endow the "human artifice" with meaning. The realm of
opinion and public talk—what for Heidegger had been the arena of
"idle chatter" (*Gerede*)—is recast by Arendt as the space of disclosure
par excellence: the space where human beings are engaged in a form of
initiatory, intersubjective activity, the space that reveals both a public,
unique self and a meaningful "human artifice" or world.

Arendt's appropriation of Heidegger's deconstruction of the tradition
is every bit as critical and transformative as her appropriation of his conception of existence as disclosedness. While Heidegger's account of the
tradition was built on quasi-idealist presuppositions (these are manifest
in his 1938 declaration in the essay "The Age of the World Picture" that
"metaphysics grounds an age") and asserted a dubious linearity (an "inner logic") from Plato to Nietzsche, Arendt's radical revision was far
more limited in its claims. She hardly thought that the "destiny of Being" (*Seinsgeschick*) comes to language in the words of the great thinkers, who in Heidegger's metahistory of philosophy provide a kind of
X-ray vision into the "essential," yet hidden, history of the West.[8] She
retained the phenomenologist's focus on concrete experiences and
events. Thus, her concern with the language of theory focused, instead,
on how it imposes an alien metaphorics upon the "realm of human affairs," a set of structuring metaphors taken from fields of human activity in which human plurality plays little or no role.

For Arendt, the fact that the public / political world has been concep-
tualized by a tradition originally fixated on the experiences of contemplation and fabrication means that essential phenomena of this realm

such as human plurality have never received their theoretical due. Moreover, it means that political thinkers and actors had repeatedly construed
action as a form of making, casting human beings as the "material
cause" of the just state. The result is the baneful identification of action
with violence ("You can't make an omelet without breaking eggs") and
an enormous increase in the temptation for the best to do the worst as
they attempt to "sculpt" human material into something ordered, beautiful, whole. From Plato to Marx, the tradition gives ample evidence of
this tendency, the tendency of theorists to transpose political experience
and judgments into aesthetic or productivist terms. The result has been,
and continues to be, moral horror.

While Arendt shared Heidegger's trepidation about the way modern science and technology act in nature, setting in motion processes
that undermine the integrity of the "human artifice," she hardly subscribed to his solution. For Heidegger, the escape from the "power trip"
of Western metaphysics, science, and technology is to be found in an
attitude of releasement (*Gelassenheit*): We must abdicate the "will to
will," the will to human self-assertion and the domination of nature. For
Arendt, on the contrary, the danger posed by the existential resentment
driving modern science is not (simply) that it objectifies nature, or even
human nature. Rather, by increasing our alienation from the world, it
leads us to substitute the will to increased power for a politically engaged and morally concerned "care for the world."[9] Thus, while the
later Heidegger's diagnosis of the pathologies of modernity led him to a
"will not to will" and an intensified "thinking withdrawal," Arendt's
critical appropriation of his diagnosis led to a renewed emphasis upon
the importance of political action, moral judgment, human freedom,
and worldliness. It led her to reiterate the importance of constitutional
or republican government as a frame for sane political action and to emphasize precisely the human capacities that Heidegger rejected in the
mistaken belief that the only true form of action is thinking.[10]

But what about the charges of elitism and "political existentialism"
that have hounded Arendt, and that Wolin repeats in his review of Ettinger's book? After all, doesn't *The Human Condition* celebrate heroic,
agonal action over more associational forms of political engagement?
And doesn't Arendt's Heidegger-inspired focus on the disclosive or revelatory quality of "great" deeds come at the expense of justice, rights,
and more democratic forms of solidarity? Finally, doesn't Arendt's insistence on the relative autonomy of the public realm and political action

lead her to espouse an existentialist call to action for the sake of action, *politique pour la politique?*

There's no denying that *The Human Condition* is Grecophilic, or that her strenuous effort to distinguish political spaces and modes of action from social, economic, and other forms of activity broadly parallels efforts like that of Carl Schmitt in *The Concept of the Political*. Nor can it be denied that Arendt "aestheticizes" politics, describing action with the help of metaphors taken from the performing arts, theater in particular.

But before we charge her with being an elitist or worse in democrat's clothes, we need to be clear about her theoretical motivations. Arendt turned to the Greeks not out of a Germanic longing for an idealized past, but because she sought an understanding of political action prior to the Greek philosophical or Christian view of politics as a means to a predetermined, naturally or divinely ordained end. It was the experience of free action in a realm of civic equality, a realm marked out and guaranteed by law, that Arendt wanted to preserve in her political theory. Wherever politics is understood primarily as a means, even to an ostensibly moral end, there the experience of a plurality of equals is bound to be devalued, if not altogether effaced. Political action conceived as the vehicle to preestablished ends tempts good people to treat their fellows not as peers, but as means to the ultimate end of an eschatological form of justice. Thus, Arendt rejects the "moralizing" interpretation of action laid down by Plato and Christianity for *moral reasons*. The parallel to Kant, and to liberalism generally, should be clear.

It is for this same reason—the moral desire to respect and preserve human plurality—that Arendt "aestheticizes" action and rejects various forms of rationalism. Her "existentialism" consists in the rejection of the deeply ingrained Western assumption that there is or can be one correct or true answer to the question of how one should live, and that reason is the faculty that will deliver this answer. She shares with liberals like Isaiah Berlin and conservatives like Michael Oakeshott a deep suspicion of rationalism in politics and the pretenses of theory to guide a transformative practice. From Plato's "tyranny of reason," to the French revolutionary terror, to Marxism's catastrophic fulfillment in Stalinist totalitarianism, political rationalism has shown itself every bit as capable of generating moral horror as either religion or Romantic nationalism. Arendt is certainly not "against" reason as such in politics. Rather, she demands that we view opinion as one of our primary ratio-

nal faculties, thereby facilitating a deliberative politics from which the
tyrannizing claim to a singular moral or political truth has been eliminated.[11] Again, the preservation of civic equality and human plurality—
of human dignity—is at stake. Hence her view of the public realm in
The Human Condition as a kind of stage on which plural actors appear,
engaging in strenuous debate as well as concerted action.

Finally, Arendt's desire to view the political realm as relatively autonomous has nothing to do with establishing its hegemony as the field in
which the life-and-death struggle between friends and enemies is played
out, as in Schmitt's Hobbesian existentialism. If politics and political
action are, for her, "existentially supreme," it is because they provide
the most adequate vehicles for the human capacity to begin, to initiate.
Viewed as relatively autonomous—as not subject to the dictates of economic, biological, or historical necessity—the political realm stands
forth as the realm of human freedom. *The Human Condition* and
Arendt's other major theoretical statements are devoted to reminding
us of *this* fact, a fact obscured by rationalist philosophies of history,
schools of economic determinism, and liberal celebrations of "negative
liberty," a liberty confined to the private sphere.[12] When, in her essay
"What is Freedom?" Arendt writes that "freedom is the *raison d'être* of
politics," she succinctly sums up her hopes for the political sphere, a potential space of "tangible freedom." The distance between these hopes
(and the constitutional faith on which they rest) and Heidegger's philosophy and politics is, obviously, vast.

"MARTIN HEIDEGGER AT EIGHTY": A "WHITEWASH"?

As the Arendt-Jaspers correspondence indicates, Heidegger did not take
kindly to the violent appropriation and implicit critique of his thought
that *The Human Condition* represented. His response to receipt of a
copy of the German translation was frosty silence, and Arendt was subject to a "burst of hostility" from Heidegger and his circle, including a
pointed snub by Eugen Fink during a 1961 visit to Freiburg.[13] For all intents and purposes, contact between Arendt and Heidegger broke off
until 1967, when, with the mediation of Arendt's friend J. Glenn Gray,
she gave a lecture in Freiburg and struck "a new accord" with Heidegger.[14] This was followed, a year later, by her agreement to contribute to
Heidegger's eightieth birthday *Festschrift* an essay that was subsequently
published by the *New York Review of Books* in 1971 under the title
"Martin Heidegger at Eighty."

Both Ettinger and Wolin view "Martin Heidegger at Eighty" as a scandalous whitewash, typical of what they see as Arendt's desire to exonerate "the master" of his political past. Ettinger writes: "Arendt went to extraordinary pains to minimize and justify [sic] Heidegger's contribution to and support of the Third Reich. . . . In her tribute to Heidegger, the last act in a drama started almost half a century ago, Arendt displayed the same unquestioning generosity, loyalty, and love she had shown since the beginning."[15] Wolin attacks as "blind devotion" what he reads as a defense of her "embattled mentor," a defense that hinged upon disputing "any essential relation between Heidegger's thought and his support of Hitler" and upon denying that the "gutter born" ideology of Nazism owed anything to representatives of *Kultur* such as Heidegger.[16]

Arendt certainly did not agree with Theodor Adorno's judgment that Heidegger's philosophy was "fascist down to its most intimate components." Indeed, any objective reader of a goodly portion of Heidegger's sixty-nine-volume *Gesamtausgabe* will be impressed by just how resolutely apolitical his philosophy generally is. (I am deliberately excluding the nonphilosophical public speeches he made in his capacity as rector of Freiburg during 1933. These are, of course, craven harangues, blatant attempts to coddle the new regime. Even here, however, there is no trace of the biological racism that was the sine qua non of Nazi ideology.) But if the question of an "essential relation" between Heidegger's thought and politics is a highly contentious and by no means obvious one, what about the charge of "whitewash," of minimization and justification of Heidegger's engagement with National Socialism? What does Arendt actually *do* in her tribute essay?

The reader seeking a nest of "exculpatory" statements by Arendt will be disappointed. It is only in a long note that Arendt makes the following statement, in parentheses: "Heidegger himself corrected his own 'error' more quickly and more radically than many of those who later sat in judgment over him—he took considerably greater risks than were usual in German literary and university life during the period."[17] This statement accepts Heidegger's own account of his reasons for resigning the rectorship and the nature of his subsequent philosophical activity under the Third Reich.[18] The biographical works of Hugo Ott and Rudiger Safranski enable us, in hindsight, to charge Arendt with excessive credulity on this score.[19]

The bulk of Arendt's essay is given over not to apologetics, but to an account of Heidegger's early fame as a teacher and to an extended description of the nature of his "passionate thinking." With regard to the latter, Arendt emphasized the noninstrumental, noncognitive nature of thinking as practiced by Heidegger; a thinking that has "a digging quality peculiar to itself," an active, as opposed to contemplative, thinking that yields no results and is constantly beginning again.[20]

Such passionate thinking, so different from scholarship *about* philosophical doctrines or philosophical "problem solving," begins in wonder at what is and demands an abode in which such wonder can be experienced and extended. As Arendt put it, the "abode of thought" is one of essential seclusion from the world, while thinking itself "has only to do with things absent."[21] The famous Heideggerian thesis about the "withdrawal of Being" was, according to Arendt, a function of thinking's need to create a "place of stillness" withdrawn from the world, where the distractions of everydayness prevent both thoughtful solitude and the experience of wonder. In Arendt's words:

> Seen from the perspective of thinking's abode, "withdrawal of Being" or "oblivion of Being" reigns in the ordinary world which surrounds the thinker's residence, the "familiar realms . . . of everyday life," i.e., the loss of that which thinking—which by nature clings to the absent—is concerned. Annulment of this "withdrawal," on the other side, is always paid for by a withdrawal from the world of human affairs, and this remoteness is never more manifest than when thinking ponders exactly those affairs, training them into its own sequestered stillness.[22]

One can see where Arendt is going with this passage and how it might provide grist for those who charge her with being an apologist for Heidegger. In her view, the greatness of Heidegger's thinking was manifest in its purity, in the thoroughness of his withdrawal to thinking's "sequestered abode." When worldly events draw the thinker out from his abode, back into the realm of human affairs, he experiences a disorientation similar to that described by Plato in the *Republic*'s famous allegory of the cave. Egregious "errors" of political judgment may result. Thus, Arendt concluded her tribute by retelling the story from Plato's *Theaetetus* about Thales, whose upward glance to contemplate "higher things" leads him to stumble into a well, to the amusement of a Thracian girl who witnesses the thinker's fall. Heidegger, Arendt seems to be saying, also "stumbled" when he gave into the temptation to "change his residence and get involved in the world of human affairs." Yet, according to Arendt, "he was still young enough to learn from the shock of the collision, which, after ten short hectic months thirty-seven years ago drove him back to his residence, to settle in his thinking what he had experienced."[23]

Thanks to Hugo Ott, we know that the "collision" lasted more than ten months: twelve years is more like it. In accepting Heidegger's account of the span of his engagement with National Socialism as coterminous with his rectorship, Arendt can again be charged with excessive charity and credulity. But more troubling is the description of Heidegger's engagement as an "error." This, more than the mistaken statements about the length of his support of the Nazis, appears to support Ettinger's and Wolin's charges of "whitewash."

Yet the surface is deceptive. If we put Arendt's tribute essay together with the lengthy Heidegger critique found in the penultimate chapter of *The Life of the Mind,* we see that what at first glance appears to be an apology is, in fact, an indictment. For what Arendt draws our attention to in both places is the way Heidegger's thought focuses on the absent: Being in its withdrawal, obscured by everyday ("fallen") reality. As a "pure activity" that issues in no concrete, useful result, Heidegger's passionate thinking resembles Socrates', but with one crucial difference. Socrates performed his thinking in the agora. The aporetic arguments of the dialogues are deployed by "a citizen amongst citizens." Socratic thinking points to a kind of *ordinary* thinking we should be able to demand of everyone: a capacity to dissolve conventional moral pieties and socially given rules by reflection, the better to activate the voice of conscience. In opposition to such ordinary or Socratic thinking, Arendt posed the example of Heidegger's *extraordinary* thinking, a thinking utterly divorced from the world of appearances, which is, for Arendt, the world of politics.

What is the force of this distinction between ordinary Socratic thinking and extraordinary Heideggerian thinking? The answer emerges when we consider the relation of thinking to judgment. For Arendt, as for Kant, judging and thinking are two different faculties. The former, in its reflexive mode, ascends from particulars to universal concepts. The latter is neither a form of judgment nor a mode of cognition, but a quest for meaning beyond appearances. In the case of Socrates, the activity of thinking dissolves all ready-to-hand standards and rules for conduct. Yet Socratic thinking, because it is performed in the agora, retains its link to the world of appearances, the public world of plural human beings. Thus, Arendt can claim that Socratic thinking, which refuses to tell us how to judge or provide us with shortcuts that might avoid the labor of judgment, stimulates the capacity for judgment precisely because it throws our everyday derivation of conduct from preestablished rules out of gear. The perplexity induced by Socrates' "dissolvent" thinking is the prelude to a genuinely reflective, that is, *moral,* exercise of judgment. In "emergency situations," where most are carried away by their enthusiasm for a popular political regime, it is this capacity to think for oneself—for judging "without banisters"—that can provide salvation.[24]

Arendt's point in "Martin Heidegger at Eighty" and the Heidegger critique given in *The Life of the Mind* is that the activity of thinking, when purified of the "taint" of the world of appearances, loses its link to the activity of judging. Her surprising thesis is that pure thought is the death of judgment. This thesis, the result of her consideration of Heidegger's political idiocy, resonates with her suspicion of philosophy's traditional attitude toward the realm of human affairs. Moreover, it resonates with her portrait of the "thoughtless" Adolf Eichmann in *Eichmann in Jerusalem,* whose conduct she saw as a function of the unthinking application of clichés and "language rules" to every new situation. Heidegger and Eichmann, it turns out, are linked: Pure thought and thoughtlessness are two sides of the same phenomenon, the incapacity for judgment. Heidegger's "error" (Arendt puts the word in quotes) was no error in judgment, his engagement with National Socialism no "mistake." Rather, what it testifies to, in Arendt's view, is the *absence* of judgment.

This is a shocking and far-reaching claim. It constitutes a more profound and objective indictment of Heidegger than Ettinger's narrative of a nasty and manipulative male or Wolin's reiteration of Adorno's charge. Of course, Heidegger was no Eichmann. He was not part of the killing apparatus. Nor was he, as Ettinger and Wolin both claim, an ideologue of the party, his naive and silly idea that the National Socialist revolution could, in 1933, be given spiritual direction by a return to the thought of the pre-Socratics notwithstanding. He was a *genuine* philosopher—in Arendt's view, a great one—whose life is an object lesson in how pure thought can be, from a political point of view, indistinguishable from the greatest thoughtlessness.

The thematic of thought, thoughtlessness, and the absence of judgment I have just outlined does not lessen either Heidegger's responsibility for his support of the Nazi regime or Eichmann's responsibility for the role he played in the genocide. In typically original fashion, Arendt focuses our gaze on two representative Germans under National Socialism. Her unsettling lesson is that moral and political judgment can be extinguished by extraordinary thinking, as well as by no thinking at all. We see how far she is from any attempt to exempt genius from the responsibility inherent in citizenship, as Wolin charges, or from "justifying" Heidegger's involvement, as Ettinger wrongly asserts. If Arendt is guilty of anything, it is failing to draw more explicitly the connections between her reflections on Heidegger, the nature of thinking, and the capacity for moral and political judgment. Her failure to do so enabled critics to take phrases out of context and construct an apologia where, in fact, one finds a worldly and wise moral judgment about the "philosopher's philosopher," Heidegger.

The story of Hannah Arendt's relationship to Heidegger cannot be reduced to the stuff of soap opera or mere discipleship. From 1946 on, her public and private reflections on Heidegger, as well as her theoretical work, show an uncanny ability to arrive at an impartial judgment of a thinker to whom she had once been intimately attached. For Arendt, as for Kant, distance and impartiality were the hallmarks of judgment. Arendt's ability to appreciate Heidegger's philosophical achievement while remaining critical of its content, her intense awareness of his failings as a human being and his idiocy as a political actor, her respect for his passionate thinking and her fear of its unworldliness—all these things testify to a faculty of judgment that remained surprisingly unclouded, even when confronted by the "magician from Messkirch."

Hannah Arendt and Martin Heidegger

History and Metahistory

Annette Vowinckel

It is a striking fact that while the idea of history is a central element in the thinking of both Heidegger and Arendt, this element is to a large extent present as the object of remarkable antagonism between them.[1] It is an equally striking fact that despite this antagonism, it is precisely the raw contingencies of history that have given the relationship between these two figures—intellectual and emotional—its particular urgency and poignancy.

Let us begin with a brief review of the notion of history that Heidegger develops in *Being and Time*. A basic, often commented-upon aspect of that work is Heidegger's distinction between an "ordinary," or vulgar, understanding of history, in the sense of the real past of human lives, and a particular conception of temporality that forms the central focus of Heidegger's magnum opus. This conception, in fact, stands in opposition to both "real" history and the philosophy of history. Within it, the past is no more important than the present or the future but is simply one part of the temporal determination of life. Historicity, then, is merely one mode of temporality, and certainly not the most important one.[2] For Heidegger, it is the future that constitutes what he terms "the primary phenomenon of original and authentic temporality" insofar as *Dasein*, "being-there," can never be anything else but being-unto-death.[3] Hence, what constitutes a philosophy of historicity for Heidegger is not the search for historical terms or historical insights, but rather the analysis of temporality itself, of *Dasein*. The task of the philosopher, as he states it, is "the interpretation of the authentically historical existent on the basis of its historicity." [4] While "real" human history, as indicated, becomes so to speak a side effect of temporality here, Heidegger goes further in his criticism of historiography as a *Wissenschaft,* as scholarship.

He talks of the "essence of scholarship as a making"—the untranslatable German is "*das machenschaftliche Wesen der Wissenschaft*"—a goal-oriented or function-oriented enterprise capable of grasping the essential life of neither nature nor history. In light of such an incapacity, Heidegger views as imperative a reconsideration of the terms "chance" and "fate," developing the term *Geschick*—an old German word for fate with religious overtones, but for Heidegger involving a fusion of fate with history (*Schicksal* with *Geschichte*): in other words, *historical fate.* If, as Heidegger explains it, "fateful [*schicksalhaftes*] *Dasein* as being-in-the-world essentially exists in a being-with [*Mitsein*] with others, then its occurrence [*Geschehen*] is an occurrence-with [*Mitgeschehen*], determined by *Geschick*. With this, we signify the occurrence [*Geschehen*] of the community [*Gemeinschaft*]—of the Volk." [5]

Later, as rector of the university of Freiburg, Heidegger would define his role in terms of executing the fate of being. [6] It is worth here recalling Karl Löwith's argument that Heidegger's conception of *Seinsgeschick* was closely connected with his definition of truth as "unconcealment," *Unverborgenheit*. According to Löwith, in claiming that the identification of truth with correctness was a fundamental error, Heidegger opened the way for both arbitrary interpretations and distortions of history: "History"—so goes Löwith's summary of Heidegger—"first and finally is the emergence of the hidden into the truth as unconcealment. As an absolute prehistory of being, history is not only undatable but also unexplorable and unrecognizable." [7]

Although Arendt once directly termed Heidegger's conception of history "lamentable," [8] she never explicitly spelled out her criticism, either in public or in private. Indeed, although at first glance Arendt's own historical writings would seem to already stand in direct conflict with Heideggerian notions and Heidegger's approach, her conception of history nevertheless contains elements taken straight from Heidegger's philosophy. Arendt herself acknowledged this indirectly when, more than forty years after reading the manuscript of *Being and Time,* she described Heidegger as a philosopher who "precisely because he knew that the thread of tradition was broken, was discovering the past anew. The rumor about Heidegger put it quite simply: Thinking has come to life again; the cultural treasures of the past, believed to be dead, are being made to speak, in the course of which it turns out that they propose things altogether different from the familiar, worn-out trivialities they had been presumed to say." [9] But despite her reference to "discovering the past anew," Arendt in fact appropriated a way of thinking from her teacher that can aptly be termed unhistorical—at least to the extent that it abjured the methods of traditional academic historiography.

To define this way of thinking concretely: just as we do with Heidegger's, we find running through Arendt's work a distinction between "real," "actual" being and "unreal," "vulgar" being that forms the basis for her own version of distinction between "real" and "vulgar" history. But within the framework of such a conceptual affinity, there are significant differences. To understand their nature, it is again useful to recall one of Löwith's insights regarding Heidegger—here regarding Heidegger's argument that "real" historicity needs to be defended against the vulgar interpretations of history.[10] As a result of such a stance, Löwith correctly suggests, the reality of the social world remained "as far removed from Heidegger's 'essential' thinking as from the private existentialism of Jaspers and Sartre." [11] But where Jaspers, in defining "greatness" as the very opposite of the "vulgar," had in mind the Greek notion of great deeds and thoughts, Heidegger was referring to what he described as the "'greatness' of fate," as the "moments of the highest peaks of Being"—and in the historical moment of 1933, as we are aware, to the "magnificence" and "greatness of this [German] eruption"—or *Aufbruch*.[12]

In Arendt's writing, the distinction between real and vulgar history takes a markedly different form. It is expressed as a distinction between the social and the political—and it is such a distinction that frames Arendt's understanding of what constitutes history. While the masses—what the German renders as *man*—are the subject of social life, the individual is the subject of a political action that alone allows for "greatness." As is the case for Jaspers, for Arendt, "greatness" does not mean the greatness of any historical fate or destiny—hence any teleological political movement—but, exclusively, the greatness of a single person or deed. And in a strikingly inverse process, while Heidegger's writing is permeated by a fear of *Selbstentfremdung*—the alienation of the individual subject from himself or herself[13]—Arendt repeatedly warns us of the individual's alienation from the commonly shared world—the process of *Weltentfremdung*.[14] This said, we are in a position to formulate a guarded criticism. The problem with Arendt is not that she makes a fetish of the "real," in the sense of a reality beyond political life, but that she makes a fetish of the political itself, thereby running the risk of obscured vision in the face of crucial social and historical questions.

In any event, the element of Arendt's historical thinking most directly shaped by her early confrontation with Heidegger's philosophy is her intuitive approach to the past. Heidegger had announced that truth is to be found through a phenomenology of "unconcealment"—*Entbergung* —not by a system. This principle had already been formulated by Husserl in the following, eloquent terms: "Everything that presents itself . . . in 'intuition' originally . . . [is] simply to be taken the way it appears." [15] Such an approach is clearly manifest in the first part of *The Origins of Totalitarianism* in Arendt's use of Proust as a main historical source for her description of nineteenth-century France.

In this section of her important study, Arendt draws a picture of nineteenth-century French anti-Semitism. To do so, she justly relies on Proust as an acute observer of the integration of the Jews into French bourgeois society. It is, of course, important to keep in mind that Proust's masterpiece was not intended as a contribution to historical research— not even in the sense of a historical narrative—but was ultimately an analytic processing of personal memories and observations. In this respect, it is useful to note the sensitive description of Proust's manner of memorializing the past offered by Samuel Beckett in his early essay on Proust. Evoking the general Bergsonian framework of Proustian epistemology, Beckett distinguishes between a "willful" and an "unwillful" way of remembering. What he calls "voluntary" memory is, in actuality, not a form of memory, but "the application of a concordance to the Old Testament." [16] "Involuntary" memory generates "what has been registered by our extreme inattention and stored in that ultimate and inaccessible dungeon of our being to which Habit does not possess the key. . . . From this deep source Proust hoisted his world. His work is not an accident but its salvage is an accident." [17]

As Arendt sees it, Proust's "genius" was based on the fact that he was both part of French society and an outsider. Consequently, "all events appeared to him as they are reflected in society and reconsidered by the individual, so that reflections and reconsiderations constitute the specific reality and texture of Proust's world." [18] In the "mute and uncommunicative solitude" into which he withdrew in order to write his work, "his inner life, which insisted on transforming all worldly happening into inner experience, became like a mirror in whose reflection truth might appear." [19] This, for Arendt, is what gives Proust's cycle of novels the kind of philosophical depth that according to Heidegger facilitates the revelation of truth. In his essay, Beckett describes the Proustian transformation of "worldly happenings" into "inner experience" thus: in the depth of memory's dungeon "is stored the essence of ourselves, the best of our many selves and their concretions that simplists call the world," and—now let us take note—a "pearl that may give the lie to our carapace of paste and pewter." [20]

Strikingly, Beckett is here making use of the same pearl image from Shakespeare's "Tempest" (act 1, scene 2) that Arendt takes up in her 1968 introduction to the collection of Benjamin's essays titled *Illumina-tions*.[21] For Benjamin, this "pearl diving," as Arendt calls it, is in fact a deliberate process, not a form of involuntary memory. But this deliberate act is nonetheless guided by intuition—a notion surely owing a considerable debt to Proust's theory of remembering. In his essay "The Image of Proust" in *Illuminations,* Benjamin describes Proust as following his sense of smell, rather than his vision, when recording his memories. In order to understand Proust, we read, one has to

> place himself in a special stratum—the bottommost—of this involuntary memory, one in which the materials of memory no longer appear singly, as images, but tell us about a whole, amorphously and formlessly, indefinitely and weightily, in the same way as the weight of his net tells a fisherman about his catch. Smell—that is the sense of weight of someone who casts his nets into the sea of *temps perdu*.[22]

Instead of systematically investigating the past, Benjamin practiced the art of "collecting," and he collected mainly books and quotations. His project was, as he put it, "to spring a specific epoch out of the homogenous course of history . . . a specific life out of the epoch . . . a specific work out of the life's work. The gain consists in the preserving and transcending [or, more tellingly, annulling: Benjamin's term is *aufheben*] of the life's work *within* the work; the epoch *within* the life's work; and the entirety of history's course *within* the epoch." [23] According to Arendt, Benjamin's pearl diving and the new approach to history it implied were required by the fact that the continuous thread of tradition and authority had been broken: no guidelines were any longer available connecting the present with the past. The new approach offered an answer to the question of how to both destroy and conserve history. And what matters most in our context is that, according to Arendt, this method had more in common with "Heidegger's great sense for what has become pearls and corals that started as living bone" than with "the dialectic subtleties of his Marxist friends." [24] In turn, we can observe that as mediated by figures such as Proust and Benjamin, Arendt's own approach to the idea of history has much in common with the Heideggerian conception of truth—*aletheia*[25]—and its momentary revelation, as well as with the general Heideggerian phenomenology of intuition.

It is thus not so surprising that Arendt's appraisal of Heidegger's philosophical method is the key to her defense of her former teacher on the occasion of his eightieth birthday. While in her 1946 *Partisan Review* essay titled "What is Existenz-Philosophy?" Arendt had ventured to pose the question of whether "Heidegger's philosophy has not generally been taken too seriously," [26] she now stressed that the "pathways" of his thinking "may safely be called *Holzwege,* wood-paths"—a citation, of course, of Heidegger's collection of essays covering the years from 1935 to 1946—"which, just because they lead nowhere outside the wood and 'abruptly leave off in the untrodden,' are incomparably more agreeable to him who loves the wood and feels at home in it than the carefully laid out problem-streets on which scurry the investigations of philosophical specialists and historians of ideas." [27]

Once Arendt's own assessment is thus acknowledged—an assessment unmistakably pointing to a perceived philosophical affinity—we can move toward a deeper understanding of an important, basic difference between Heidegger's and Arendt's conceptions of history. Let us begin by noting Arendt's insistence (in any event well grounded), emerging after the war in her American academic context, that historiography, in contrast with the "real" sciences, never deals with universally valid laws, but rather with particular events that need to be understood in their particularity. As she bluntly explains it: "Whoever in the historical sciences honestly believes in causality actually denies the subject of his own science." [28] For historical methodology, this means, again in Arendt's words, "forget causality. Instead: analysis of the elements of the event. In the center is the event into which the elements have abruptly crystallized." [29] These sentences, arguing for a historical discipline liberated from linear, cause-and-effect thinking, stand in interesting relation to Heidegger's observation, most likely proffered sometime in the late 1930s: "the fact that in history, one [i.e., *man,* with its intimation of the vulgar sense of *man*—"self"] confirms 'chance' and 'fate' as codeterminate, simply proves the monopoly on rule enjoyed by causal thinking, in as far as 'chance' and 'fate' only represent the inexact and unclear connection of cause and effect." [30]

To summarize briefly: Heidegger chose to break what he perceived as causal thinking's *universal* "monopoly on rule" by proposing a quasi-teleological *Seinsgeschick*—a "fate of being"—that happened to serve as his justification of an embrace of Nazi politics. In contrast, Arendt made her skepticism toward the *specific* causal thinking at work in one kind of history and her belief that a new beginning is possible even under the grimmest circumstances the basis for a specific theory of action in the here and now. In doing so, she explicitly opposed Heidegger's *general* disinterest in particular events, as well as his contention that the past is only one aspect of temporality, hence of secondary importance. She likewise refused to share his universal criticism of scientific research, his contempt for all the empirical sciences as "machinations."

Where Heidegger is always very much concerned with death and mortality, Arendt is increasingly concerned with birth and natality. In her later writing, these concepts are applied not only to the political realm, in which every action is perceived as a new beginning with incalculable effects, but also to the general capacity for thinking, marked by the ever-present possibility of breaking away from a mere reckoning with consequences: the possibility for an onset of a new way of thinking. Likewise, where Heidegger is always concerned with temporality as the defining aspect of being-there, Arendt increasingly focuses on escaping from such temporality, centering her thought, for instance, on spatial concepts, speaking of the polis as the space for the great deeds that grant great men their immortality.[31]

Although Arendt, despite her implicit distinction in the above-cited *Partisan Review* article between weaker and stronger historiographical modes, never really warmed up to history as an academic discipline, she was always enthusiastic about the art of narrative, or, in her own words, "telling stories," which, she explained, "contains the sense of things without committing the mistake of naming it." Such storytelling, she continues, "leads to a harmony and reconciliation with things as they really are, and perhaps we can allow it implicit possession of that final word we expect on the day of judgment."[32] This idea of storytelling was clearly influenced not only by Kant,[33] but by a theological-teleological way of thinking to which Arendt stood in methodological opposition. It represented Arendt's personal approach to coming to terms with her past, and she occasionally applied it herself, not only in some of her scholarly works, but also, at one point, in her writing about Heidegger. In her 1953 notebook, we find a sketch titled "Heidegger the Fox":

> Heidegger proudly says: "People say Heidegger's a fox." Now this is the true story of Heidegger the fox: Once upon a time there was a fox who so badly lacked slyness that he not only stepped into traps time and again but could not tell a trap from a nontrap. This fox suffered from still another affliction:

Something was wrong with his fur so that he had absolutely no natural protection against the rigors of a fox life. After having spent his entire youth falling into the traps of others so that . . . not a single piece of his own fur was
left, he decided to completely withdraw from the fox world and started digging a fox den. In his hair-raising ignorance of traps as well as nontraps . . .
he came up with an idea radically new and unheard of among foxes: He
constructed a trap in the form of a fox den, placed himself inside it, and pretended it was an ordinary den (not out of slyness but because he had always
confused the traps set for other foxes with dens). But then he decided, in his
own way, to become sly, to turn the trap he's made himself, that fitted only
him, into a trap for others. This move again revealed his great ignorance of
trapping: Nobody could fall into his trap because he himself was in it. This
bothered him—after all, everybody knows that sometimes foxes fall into
traps, despite all their wit. Why should a fox trap constructed not by any fox,
but by the fox most experienced in trapping, not be the equal of traps set by
human beings and hunters? Apparently, because the trap was not recognizable as such clearly enough. So it occurred to our fox to decorate his trap
most beautifully and put up signs announcing very clearly: Come everyone,
here is a trap, the most beautiful trap in the world. Henceforth it was clear
that no fox could ever fall into this trap unintentionally. Still, many foxes
came by. For this trap served as our fox's den. Whoever wanted to visit him
where he was at home had to get into his trap. To be sure, everyone could
come and go except for him. It was literally tailor-made for him. But the fox
living in the trap proudly said: So many fall into my trap, I've become the best
of all foxes. And there was even a grain of truth in it: Nobody knows traps
and trapping better than who's been sitting in one all life long." [34]

The reward for telling a story, as Arendt indicated, was "to be at
peace with the world." [35] At the same time, she made clear that one
could tell a story only after it had come to an end—that only then could
the message be grasped, hence that "we are . . . entangled in a life-long
story whose end we do not know." [36] In this respect, the fable about Heidegger the fox is only an interim report. Heidegger survived Arendt by
three months, thereby denying her a chance ever to tell her own tale.
Thus it remains to the historian to make sense of this story, which lasted
almost exactly half a century.

It is always difficult to pin down fine differences between inspiration,
influence, and intellectual dependence, especially when dealing with figures as complex as Heidegger and Arendt. It is apparent that Arendt
could never shrug off a figure she assumed—along with many other
thinkers of her time and ours—to be one of the greatest of modern philosophers. This does not, however, mean, as Elzbieta Ettinger suggests,
that the relationship amounted to an intellectual dependence. It may,
however, mean that for Arendt, who was only eighteen years old when

she and Heidegger began their long affair, it was rather more difficult to resist Heidegger's charismatic mix of personality and philosophy. From a historical vantage, it is an extraordinarily naive assumption that because Arendt was Jewish, she ought to have had a second sense of the path Heidegger's life would take a few years later—her failure to do so rendering her a "self-hating" Jew, a priori.[37] In fact, many Jewish intellectuals and artists who themselves grew up in a general context of German-Jewish *Bildung* (figures as varied as Karl Löwith, Leo Strauss, and Walter Benjamin—as well as, some time later, the poet Paul Celan) were just as fascinated by his personality and his philosophy as their non-Jewish contemporaries. And we can note in conclusion that this fascination has permeated, quite problematically, the postwar literary-cultural scene up to the present day.

Notes

PREFACE

1. Certain additions and omissions should, however, be noted. The talks presented at the conference by Shlomo Avineri, Antonia Gruenenberg, and Robert Wistrich could not be included here. The papers by Walter Laqueur and Susan Neiman and the contribution by Dana Villa on "Totalitarianism, Modernity and the Tradition" were not presented at the conference but form part of the present volume.

2. The *Chronicle of Higher Education,* January 16, 1998, pp. A17–A18, featured a lengthy article by Haim Watzman, "Conference Showcases Hannah Arendt's Strengths—and Weaknesses," as did the Italian newspaper *Le Repubblica* in a piece by Susanna Nirenstein entitled "Hannah Arendt Gerusalemme toglie l'embargo." A detailed report of the conference by Mae Cohen, "Hannah Arendt in Jerusalem," appeared in the *Congress Monthly* 65, no. 2 (March–April 1998), pp. 9–11. Various German newspapers carried accounts of the conference. Israeli radio and television interviewed various participants and the Canadian Broadcasting Company devoted an entire program to its problematics (December 28, 1997).

3. This description was suggested to me by Michael Marrus as, rather bemused, we observed the dynamics of this session unfold. Clearly, these are merely impressions. It should also be noted that there were many who, even on that occasion, did not go along with these reverential sentiments.

STEVEN ASCHHEIM, "INTRODUCTION"

1. The nature of and reasons behind this reception are well analyzed in Seyla Benhabib, "Introduction: Why Hannah Arendt?" in *The Reluctant Modernism*

of Hannah Arendt, Modernity and Political Thought 10 (Thousand Oaks, Calif.: Sage, 1996). See also the introduction to Richard J. Bernstein, *Hannah Arendt and the Jewish Question* (Cambridge, Mass.: MIT Press, 1996). The most powerful postmodern reading to date can be found in Dana R. Villa, *Arendt and Heidegger: The Fate of the Political* (Princeton: Princeton University Press, 1996). For the relation to identity politics and feminism, see Bonnie Honig, ed., *Feminist Interpretations of Hannah Arendt* (University Park: The Pennsylvania State University Press, 1995). For a post-Marxist reading, see Phillip Hansen, *Hannah Arendt: Politics, History, and Citizenship* (Stanford, Calif.: Stanford University Press, 1993).

2. See the revised and enlarged edition, *Eichmann in Jerusalem: A Report on the Banality of Evil* (New York: Viking, 1964). An older view, that Arendt's portrait in *The Origins of Totalitarianism* of the powerful centrality of the Jew in the economy and polity of the absolutist state replicates the Nazi version, is held by some leading Israeli historians and political scientists to this day. See Tom Segev, *The Seventh Million: The Israelis and the Holocaust,* translated by Haim Watzman (New York: Hill and Wang, 1993), p. 360.

3. Indeed, I recognize that the very title "Hannah Arendt in Jerusalem" has a rather provocative ring, conjuring up, as it intentionally does, Arendt's extremely contentious *Eichmann in Jerusalem.* The title was suggested by Prof. Wolfgang Schieder when the idea of this conference was broached. It appears, however, that this theme confirms the existence of a Zeitgeist. In the recent special issue devoted to Hannah Arendt, *History and Memory* 8, no. 2 (fall–winter 1996), both Richard Wolin and Jose Brenner have similar titles. See "The Ambivalences of German-Jewish Identity: Hannah Arendt in Jerusalem" and "Eichmann, Arendt, and Freud in Jerusalem," respectively. Moreover, Idith Zertal presented a paper (which I have not yet seen) entitled "Arendt in Zion" at a 1997 international colloquium on Arendt in Potsdam. See also Amos Elon's insightful "The Case of Hannah Arendt," in the *New York Review of Books* (November 6, 1997), pp. 25–29. I came upon this piece only after writing my own article, but many of its conclusions are very similar to my own.

4. That *Eichmann in Jerusalem* finally appeared in Hebrew only in 2000 is made all the more scandalous by Arendt's comment to Karl Jaspers in 1966: "the Hebrew edition of *Eichmann* is finally coming out in Israel. I think the war between me and the Jews is over." See Letter 394, March 26, 1966, in Hannah Arendt and Karl Jaspers, *Correspondence, 1926–1969,* edited by Lotte Köhler and Hans Saner, translated by Robert Kimber and Rita Kimber (New York: Harcourt Brace Jovanovich, 1992), p. 632. See also Tom Segev, *The Seventh Million,* p. 465.

5. For some of the relevant writings, see her *Rahel Varnhagen: The Life of a Jewish Woman,* translated by Richard and Clara Winston, revised edition (New York: Harcourt Brace Jovanovich, 1974), a collection of her Jewish essays edited by Ron H. Feldman, *The Jew as Pariah: Jewish Identity and Politics in the Modern Age* (New York: Grove Press, 1978), and her *Essays in Understanding, 1930–1954,* edited by Jerome Kohn (New York: Harcourt and Brace, 1994).

6. This is, to be sure, still a rather fringe, avant-garde affair. But it is signifi-

cant that the Tel Aviv journal *History and Memory* recently devoted a special issue to Arendt. See "Hannah Arendt and *Eichmann in Jerusalem,*" *History and
Memory* 8, no. 2 (fall–winter 1996). The hall in which Richard Bernstein gave
his 1997 lecture in Jerusalem on "Arendt and the Banality of Evil" was packed
beyond capacity. To be sure, these were all English-language events. Nevertheless, a Hebrew panel on Arendt held in Jerusalem in March 1997 under the auspices of the Leo Baeck Institute publication met with similar interest.

7. One concrete example of the ambivalence and complexity, indeed perhaps
also the cynicism and confusion, that Arendt felt with regard to the earthly Jerusalem may be found in a letter to Mary McCarthy: "Jerusalem will be an altogether different proposition, and probably much less rewarding for you than
Florence or Venice. On the other hand there is no book on Jerusalem and the
market possibilities are certainly very high. Also, and more important, Jerusalem is the only city I know that gives you an idea what a city in antiquity was
like. It has been frozen through religion, and though I would not know what
exactly to *do* with this, I have always been impressed by the enormous quiet
significance that is present in every stone." See her letter of August 28, 1959,
in *Between Friends: The Correspondence of Hannah Arendt and Mary Mc-
Carthy, 1949–1975,* edited by Carol Brightman (New York: Harcourt Brace,
1995), p. 62.

8. For her appreciation of the extraordinary nature of that experience
("nothing comparable to it is to be found even in the other areas of Jewish assimilation") and the challenge of historically understanding it, see her preface to
Rahel Varnhagen, p. xvii.

9. See Dan Diner, "Hannah Arendt Reconsidered: On the Banal and the Evil
in Her Holocaust Narrative," *New German Critique* no. 71 (spring–
summer 1997).

10. For a superb portrait of this tradition, see George L. Mosse, *German
Jews beyond Judaism* (Bloomington: Indiana University Press, 1983). "The
trouble with the educated philistine was not that he read the classics but that he
did so prompted by the ulterior motive of self-perfection, remaining quite unaware . . . that Shakespeare or Plato might have to tell him more important
things than how to educate himself . . . he fled into a region of 'pure poetry' in
order to keep reality out of his life . . . or to look at it through a veil of 'sweet-
ness and light.'" "The Crisis in Culture," in Arendt's *Between Past and Future:
Six Exercises in Political Thought* (Cleveland, Ohio: Meridian Books, 1961). See
also *Rahel Varnhagen,* especially pp. 9–10.

11. See "Die jüdische Armee—der Beginn einer jüdischen Politik?" *Aufbau*
7, no. 46 (November 14, 1941). Robert Meyerson's 1972 doctoral dissertation
at the University of Minnesota, "Hannah Arendt: Romantic in a Totalitarian
Age, 1928–1963," contains useful information about these earlier years.

12. The relevant biographical information is to be found in the still-
definitive biography by Elisabeth Young-Bruehl, *Hannah Arendt: For Love of
the World* (New Haven: Yale University Press, 1982). See Scholem's letter (119)
to Shalom Spiegel of July 17, 1941, in Gershom Scholem, *Briefe: Band I, 1914–
1947,* edited by Itta Shedletzky (Munich: C. H. Beck, 1994), p. 285.

13. Letter 394 of March 26, 1966, to Jaspers in *Correspondence,* p. 632. See her letter of October 17, 1969, in *Between Friends: The Correspondence of Hannah Arendt and Mary McCarthy, 1949–1975,* edited with an introduction by Carol Brightman (New York: Harcourt Brace & Company, 1995), p. 249. On Arendt's response to the Yom Kippur War, see her letter of October 16, 1973 (pp. 349–50), and especially note 5, where Brightman describes her reaction as one of "panic."

14. Letter 421 of October 1, 1967, in *Correspondence,* pp. 674–75.

15. This may be the very reason why Arendt was so compelling during the 1950s and early 1960s to previously unengaged nonestablishment American Jewish intellectuals. Her capacity to integrate Jewish matters into the eye of the storm of world history, to make them explanatory factors in the great catastrophes of twentieth-century history, provided a kind of dignity and importance to a previously marginalized, even derided, existence. See, for instance, Irving Howe, *The Decline of the New* (New York: Harcourt Brace, 1970), pp. 244–45, and Alfred Kazin, *New York Jew* (New York: Knopf, 1978), especially p. 299.

16. She wrote Jaspers that "many Jews such as myself are religiously completely independent of Juda*ism* yet are still Jews themselves." Letter 61, September 4, 1947, in *Correspondence,* p. 98. See, especially, chapter 2 of Michael Walzer's *Interpretation and Social Criticism* (Cambridge, Mass.: Harvard University Press, 1987).

17. For letters documenting all these qualities, see Gershom Scholem to Theodor W. Adorno, Letter 131 of February 29, 1968, and Letter 133 to Hans Paeschke of March 24, 1968, in Gershom Scholem, *Briefe: Band II, 1948–1970,* edited by Thomas Sparr (Munich: C. H. Beck, 1995), pp. 206–7, 209–10, respectively. See also the interesting comments by Raymond Aron, "The Essence of Totalitarianism according to Hannah Arendt," *Partisan Review* 60 (1993). This appeared originally in the French journal *Critique* in 1954.

18. Letter 53 of July 26, 1950, in Hannah Arendt and Hermann Broch, *Briefwechsel, 1946 bis 1951,* edited by Paul Michael Lützeler (Frankfurt am Main: Jüdischer, 1996), p. 145.

19. Letter to Gershom Scholem, July 24, 1963, reprinted in *The Jew as Pariah,* p. 247. Letter 135 to Jaspers, of September 7, 1952, in *Correspondence,* pp. 196–201. The quote appears on p. 197. Scholem recommended *Rahel Varnhagen* to Benjamin. See his *Walter Benjamin, The Story of a Friendship,* translated by Harry Zohn (Philadelphia: JPS, 1981), pp. 213–14.

20. Jaspers added that more justice would have been done to "see her not just in the context of the Jewish question but, rather, in keeping with Rahel's own intentions and reality as a human being in whose life the Jewish problem played a very large role but by no means the only one . . . everything you cite from 'enlightened' thinking is illustrated with negative examples. . . . But it was the greatness of the Enlightenment . . . that carried Rahel. . . . What starts to take shape in your work but is then lost in sociological and psychological considerations (which should not in any way be omitted but should be incorporated into a higher level) is the unconditional aspect of Rahel . . . the quality of her personal influence, the totality of her insight . . . all the things for which being a Jew

is only the outward guise and only the point of departure." See Jaspers's brilliant Letter 134, August 23, 1952, in ibid., pp. 192–96.

21. See her 1959 Lessing Prize address, "On Humanity in Dark Times: Thoughts about Lessing," in *Men in Dark Times* (New York: Harcourt Brace Jovanovich, 1968), especially p. 18, and her Letter 50 to Jaspers, December 17, 1946, in *Correspondence,* p. 70.

22. Letter of July 24, 1963, reprinted in *The Jew as Pariah,* pp. 246–47.

23. See Arendt's 1944 "Zionism Reconsidered," in *The Jew as Pariah,* especially pp. 136–38.

24. Postmodernist feminist critics, while admiring of Arendt's resistance to Scholem's definitions—seeing in his "identity politics insidious resources for the homogenizing control of behavior and the silencing of independent criticism"— take her to task for insisting on the private nature of Jewish identity: "Arendt would have done better to contest the terms of Scholem's construal of Jewishness as identity. . . . Both she and Scholem treat Jewish identity as a univocal, constative fact. . . . They disagree on whether it is a public or private fact. . . . In treating Jewish identity as constative, Arendt relinquishes the opportunity to engage or even subvert Jewish identity performatively, to explore its historicity and heterogeneity, to dislodge and disappoint its aspirations to univocity, to proliferate its differentiated possibilities." See Honig, "Toward an Agonistic Feminism: Hannah Arendt and the Politics of Identity," in Honig, ed., *Feminist Interpretations.*

25. Young-Bruehl, *Hannah Arendt,* p. 127. Unfortunately Young-Bruehl provides no explanation for this extraordinary step.

26. Arendt to Jaspers, Letter 34, January 29, 1946, in *Correspondence,* p. 29.

27. See the letter of August 8, 1936, in Hannah Arendt and Heinrich Blücher, *Briefe, 1936–1968* (Munich: Piper, 1996), pp. 38–40. The quote appears on p. 39. See also Hannah Arendt and Hermann Broch, *Briefwechsel, 1946 bis 1951,* and the remarkable letter to Blücher of August 24, 1936, in *Briefe 1936– 1968,* pp. 57–60.

28. See letter 49, November 28, 1955, in Hannah Arendt and Kurt Blumenfeld, *". . . In keinem Besitz verwurzelt": Die Korrespondenz,* edited by Ingeborg Nordmann and Iris Pilling (Hamburg: Rotbuch, 1995), pp. 135–36.

29. Hannah Arendt, *The Origins of Totalitarianism* (Cleveland: Meridian Books, 1958), p. 66. The work appeared first in 1951.

30. On the atmosphere of the Weimar Republic, see "German Jews beyond Liberalism: The Radical Jewish Revival in the Weimar Republic," in my *Culture and Catastrophe: German and Jewish Confrontations with National Socialism and Other Crises* (New York: NYU Press, 1996). On Kafka, see especially her "Franz Kafka: A Revaluation" in *Essays in Understanding,* pp. 69–80, written originally in 1944. In her famous essay "The Jew as Pariah: A Hidden Tradition," Kafka is, of course, one of her main examples. See *The Jew as Pariah,* especially pp. 81–89.

31. See her essay "Walter Benjamin: 1892–1940," in *Men in Dark Times,* p. 195.

32. Ibid., p. 190.

33. Letter 285 of April 13, 1961, written to Jaspers from the Pension Reich,

Beth Hakerem, in *Correspondence,* pp. 434–36. The quote appears on p. 435. The last sentence of this paragraph softens things a little: "The major impression, though, is of very great poverty."

34. The debate is by now exceedingly well known. Less familiar is Scholem's reply to Arendt, in a letter only recently published, regarding her belief that if the Jews had "been unorganized and leaderless," the number of victims would have been considerably less. Had the Jews done that, Scholem argues, "we would have reproached them now." More organization, we would claim, would have helped to save lives. See Letter 66 to Hannah Arendt, August 12, 1963, in *Briefe, Band II,* 107–8. The most comprehensive review of responses can be found in Richard I. Cohen, "Breaking the Code: Hannah Arendt's *Eichmann in Jerusalem* and the Public Polemic—Myth, Memory, and Historical Imagination," *Michael* 13 (1993): 29–85. The quote appears on p. 84. See also his contribution to the present volume.

35. McCarthy's review "The Hue and Cry." See footnote 6 of *Between Friends,* p. 167. Ibid., Arendt to McCarthy, June 23, 1964, p. 168.

36. See Scholem's published letter of June 23, 1963, to Arendt in their exchange over the Eichmann book, reprinted in *The Jew as Pariah,* pp. 240–45. We have already examined Arendt's response to Scholem's accusation of lacking *ahavat Israel.* It is only fair to point out, however, that as Scholem emphasizes in his later reply, he described her as belonging to the Jewish people in order to distance himself from those who regarded her as no longer part of it. See his Letter 66 to Arendt of August 12, 1963, in Gershom Scholem, *Briefe, Band II, 1948–1970,* edited by Thomas Sparr (Munich: C. H. Beck, 1995), pp. 105–8. The quote appears on p. 106.

37. Letter 331 to Jaspers, July 20, 1963, in *Correspondence,* especially pp. 510–11; Letter 336, October 20, 1963, pp. 521–25. Letter 338, October 25, 1963, p. 527.

38. This is reprinted in *The Jew as Pariah,* pp. 131–63.

39. See Scholem's Letter 131 to Arendt of January 28, 1946, in *Briefe, Band I,* pp. 309–14.

40. See her reply to Scholem, July 24, 1963, reprinted in *The Jew as Pariah,* p. 246, and Scholem's Letter 133 to Hans Paeschke, March 24, 1968, in *Briefe, Band II,* p. 210.

41. Scholem's Letter 131 to Hannah Arendt, in *Briefe, Band I,* p. 310.

42. As it does for the person they both deeply admired, Walter Benjamin.

43. David Suchoff, "Gershom Scholem, Hannah Arendt, and the Scandal of Jewish Particularity," *The Germanic Review* 72, no. 1 (winter 1997): 57–76. The quotes appear on pp. 57–58. I thank Paul Mendes-Flohr for drawing my attention to this piece.

44. For Scholem's attitude, see Letter 133 in *Briefe, Band II,* pp. 209–10. Arendt's Letter 65 to Kurt Blumenfeld, January 9, 1957, in *". . . In keinem Besitz verwurzelt,"* pp. 174–77. The quote appears on p. 176.

45. Dana Villa has most recently and radically underlined these aspects of Arendt's thought in his *Arendt and Heidegger.*

46. Elzbieta Ettinger, *Hannah Arendt / Martin Heidegger* (New Haven: Yale

University Press, 1995), never goes beyond the merely gossipy. The links and differences are best analyzed in Villa, *Arendt and Heidegger*. See also Bernstein, *Hannah Arendt and the Jewish Question*, pp. 191–92, n. 6.

47. See the suggestive piece by Bonnie Honig, "Toward an Agonistic Feminism," in Honig, ed., *Feminist Interpretations*, pp. 135–66. The quote appears on p. 149.

48. "Arendt's warnings," writes Amos Elon, "displayed considerable foresight. Today's readers may be more willing to accept both her essays and her book [*Eichmann*] on their merits." See his "The Case of Hannah Arendt," p. 25. See, for instance, her letter to Blücher of October 18, 1955, in *Briefe*, p. 413, where she writes of "this little land, where one always sees the borders. It is sadder and less embittered than I thought. Perhaps because my environment has remained relatively reasonable, above all, the very charming children. . . . The anxiety is very great and overshadows everything, and expresses itself in that one wants to see and hear nothing. Ultimately, the 'activist elements' will naturally gain the upper hand. . . . Everyone, whoever opens their mouth, is vehemently nationalist: One should have expelled (*rausjagen*) Arabs who stayed in the country, and so on." Ibid., Letter of October 22, 1955, pp. 414–16. See also the remarkable Letter 61 of September 4, 1947, to Jaspers defining her attitude toward Judaism and its future, Zionism, and the "extraordinary" achievements in Palestine in *Correspondence*, pp. 96–99, especially p. 96. For a balanced treatment of this whole question see chapter 5, "Zionism: Jewish Homeland or Jewish State?" in Bernstein, *Hannah Arendt*. Letter to Blücher of April 20, 1961, in *Briefe*, p. 522. See her "To Save the Jewish Homeland: There Is Still Time" in *The Jew as Pariah*, p. 191.

49. Many of the essays from this period have been republished in *Essays in Understanding*. See especially "Approaches to the 'German Problem,'" "Organized Guilt and Universal Responsibility," "The Image of Hell," "Social Science Techniques and the Study of Concentration Camps," and others. Arendt, "What Remains? The Language Remains: A Conversation with Günter Gaus," in ibid., p. 14. See her letter of July 19, 1947, in "*. . . In keinen Besitz,*" p. 43.

50. Much history writing is a matter of tone, context, and underlying motivation. In the *Historikerstreit* of the 1980s, Ernst Nolte was widely perceived as employing the thesis of Nazi-Soviet equivalence as a way of softening or relativizing the indictment against National Socialist atrocities. No one would have dreamed of accusing Arendt of this.

Saul Friedlander has incisively analyzed the differences between the original "totalitarian" school and the *Historikerstreit* approach. Both employed the comparative method, but the former never sought to relativize, but "ultimately maintained the Nazi case as the ne plus ultra, in relation to which the other crimes were measured." See his "A Conflict of Memories? The New German Debates about the 'Final Solution,'" *The Leo Baeck Memorial Lecture* 31 (New York: Leo Baeck Institute, 1987), especially pp. 7–10.

51. Raul Hilberg's pathbreaking *The Destruction of the European Jews* (Chicago: Quadrangle Books) did not appear until 1961. For the rather absurd, yet symptomatic, tensions between Hilberg and Arendt, see Hilberg's *The Poli-*

tics of Memory: The Journey of a Holocaust Historian (Chicago: Ivan R. Dee, 1996), especially pp. 147–57. See also Arendt's Letter 351 to Jaspers, April 20, 1964, in *Correspondence,* pp. 549–51.

52. See Friedlander's "From Anti-Semitism to Extermination: A Historiographical Study of Nazi Policies toward the Jews and an Essay in Interpretation," *Yad Vashem Studies* 16 (1984), p. 16. Kazin, *New York Jew,* p. 298.

53. I have dealt with all this at length in "Nazism, Culture, and *The Origins of Totalitarianism:* Hannah Arendt and the Discourse of Evil," *New German Critique* 70 (winter 1997): 117–39.

54. Arendt, "Nightmare and Flight," in *Essays in Understanding,* p. 134. She contrasted this with "death," which "became the fundamental problem after the last war." See *Origins,* 459, and her Letter 109 to Jaspers of March 4, 1951, in *Correspondence,* p. 166.

55. For an interesting review of the background and genesis of these theories, see Leon Bramson, *The Political Context of Sociology* (Princeton: Princeton University Press, 1961).

56. She wrote this in 1945. See her "Approaches to the German Problem," in *Essays in Understanding,* p. 108. See also Ernst Gellner, "From Koenigsberg to Manhattan (Or Hannah, Rahel, Martin, and Elfriede; or Thy Neighbour's *Gemeinschaft*)" in *Culture, Identity, and Politics,* edited by Ernst Gellner (Cambridge: Cambridge University Press, 1987), and Richard Wolin, "Hannah and the Magician: An Affair to Remember," *The New Republic,* October 9, 1995, 27–37.

57. While this is so, Arendt also consistently criticized Zionism for its desire to believe in the eternality of anti-Semitism and its political instrumentalization of this condition. This prompted Scholem, in his critique of "Zionism Reconsidered," to comment that he did indeed believe in its "eternality" as witnessed by the fact that, despite all rational analyses, it seemed to renew itself in ever-new constellations. Letter 131 to Arendt, January 28, 1946, in *Briefe, Band I,* p. 310.

58. For a sustained comparative analysis, see my "Post-Holocaust Mirrorings of Germany: Hannah Arendt and Daniel Goldhagen," *Tel Aviver Jahrbuch für Deutsche Geschichte* 26 (1997). See also my "Archetypes and the German-Jewish Dialogue: Reflections Occasioned by the Goldhagen Affair," *German History* 15, no. 2 (1997). See Arendt's letter to Blumenfeld, July 19, 1947, in "*. . . In keinem Besitz,*" p. 43.

59. Arendt, "Social Science Techniques and the Study of Concentration Camps," in *Essays in Understanding,* p. 235.

60. See Moshe Zimmermann, "Chameleon and Phoenix: Israel's German Image," *Tel Aviver Jahrbuch für deutsche Geschichte* 26 (1997).

61. Arendt, "Nightmare and Flight," in *Essays in Understanding,* p. 134.

62. For one perspective on this see chapter 7, "From Radical Evil to the Banality of Evil: From Superfluousness to Thoughtlessness," in Bernstein, *Hannah Arendt.* On her earlier struggles with a kind of "demonizing" tendency see chapter 6, "Hannah Arendt and Karl Jaspers: Friendship, Catastrophe, and the Possibilities of German-Jewish Dialogue," in my *Culture and Catastrophe.* For the

various critics who took Arendt to task for such "demonizing," see my "Nazism, Culture, and *The Origins of Totalitarianism.*"

63. Letter 43 to Jaspers, August 17, 1946, in *Correspondence,* pp. 51–56. The quote appears on p. 54.

64. Ibid. Letter 277 to Jaspers, February 5, 1961, p. 423.

65. Arendt, *Origins,* p. 290.

66. This has already begun. Thus, Adi Ophir, quoting Arendt to the effect that "totalitarian solutions may well survive the fall of totalitarian regimes," adds: "Indeed, they have survived, even in the State of the survivors." See his piece "Between Eichmann and Kant: Thinking on Evil and Arendt" in *History and Memory*'s special volume "Hannah Arendt and *Eichmann in Jerusalem.*" The brilliant article by Leora Y. Bilsky, "When Actor and Spectator Meet in the Courtroom: Reflections on Hannah Arendt's Concept of Judgment," demonstrates a sophisticated and critical knowledge of Arendt and a willingness and ability to employ her categories in ways that were not available ten years ago.

67. See Hilberg, *The Politics of Memory,* p. 147. In a communication on November 4, 1997, Antonia Gruenenberg informed me that the Hannah Arendt is an intercity express that goes from Stuttgart to Hamburg-Altona and (on the way back) from Kiel to Stuttgart. The postage stamp, she reports, has been sold out.

68. Letter 338, October 25, 1963, in *Correspondence,* p. 527.

AGNES HELLER, "HANNAH ARENDT ON TRADITION AND NEW BEGINNINGS"

1. Hannah Arendt, *Between Past and Future: Eight Exercises in Political Thought* (Harmondsworth: Penguin Books, 1977).

2. Arendt here makes obvious reference to Apostle Paul's discussion of the treasure that one must preserve. Paul's words had been frequently used against the Stoics, the Gnostics, and the Manicheans, among others, and also by Augustine, to whom Arendt frequently refers, particularly in presenting her concept of natality.

3. In the preface of part 1 of *The Origins of Totalitarianism* (New York: Harcourt Brace, 1951.) Arendt tells the reader what she means by "comprehension": "Comprehension, in short, means the unpremeditated, attentive facing up to, and resisting of, reality—whatever it may be or might have been" (p. xiv).

4. *The Origins of Totalitarianism,* p. 267.

5. François Furet: *The Passing of an Illusion: The Ideal of Communism in the Twentieth Century,* translated by Deborah Furet (Chicago: University of Chicago Press, 1999).

6. Arendt, *The Origins of Totalitarianism,* pp. 478–79.

7. Hannah Arendt, *The Human Condition* (New York: Doubleday, 1959), pp. 222, 296.

8. Hannah Arendt, *On Revolution* (New York: Viking, 1965), pp. 29–30.

9. Ibid., p. 123.

10. Ibid., p. 235.

ALBRECHT WELLMER, "HANNAH ARENDT ON REVOLUTION"

1. Hannah Arendt, *On Revolution* (London: Faber and Faber, 1963).
2. These oppositions had been worked out in Arendt's *The Human Condition* (Chicago: University of Chicago Press, 1958).
3. Arendt, *On Revolution,* p. 285.
4. "If we equate these spaces of freedom . . . with the political realm itself, we shall be inclined to think of them as islands in a sea or as oases in a desert." Ibid., p. 279.
5. See Hannah Arendt, "The Rights of Man: What Are They?" in *Modern Review* 3, no. 1 (1949): 30, 34 ff.
6. See *On Revolution,* p. 271.
7. This is not the original English text, but a retranslation from Hannah Arendt's German version of *On Revolution,* in which she has added the phrase "perhaps of all peoples of the earth." See Hannah Arendt, *Über die Revolution* (Munich: Piper, 1963), p. 341. The original English sentence is: "It was nothing more or less than this hope for a transformation of the state, for a new form of government that would permit every member of the modern egalitarian society to become a 'participator' in public affairs, that was buried in the disasters of twentieth-century revolutions." *On Revolution,* p. 268.
8. See Hannah Arendt, "What Is Authority?" in *Between Past and Future* (New York: Penguin Books, 1977), pp. 125 ff.
9. Dana R. Villa, *Arendt and Heidegger: The Fate of the Political* (Princeton: Princeton University Press, 1996).
10. Jürgen Habermas, "Reconciliation through the Public Use of Reason: Remarks on John Rawls's Political Liberalism," and John Rawls, "Reply to Habermas," *The Journal of Philosophy* 92, no. 3 (1995).
11. See my "Conditions of a Democratic Culture," in Albrecht Wellmer, *Endgames: The Irreconcilable Modernity* (Boston: MIT Press, 1998).
12. Quoted in Arendt, *On Revolution,* p. 239.

WALTER LAQUEUR, "THE ARENDT CULT"

1. The increasing interest in the life and work of Hannah Arendt is in stark contrast to the decline of interest in a figure such as Herbert Marcuse. While Marcuse was a towering figure in the 1960s and 1970s as far as publicity was concerned, he was half-forgotten by the 1990s. During the past ten years, only a very few books about Marcuse have been published, including admittedly one in Greek and another in Bulgarian. The publication of Marcuse's *Collected Works* has not continued. *Sic transit. . . .*
   A Marcuse admirer notes this fact with regret: "Since his death in 1979, Herbert Marcuse's star has been steadily waning. The extent to which his work is ignored in progressive circles is curious." Douglas Kellner, "A Marcuse Renaissance?" in *From the New Left to the Next Left,* edited by John Bokina and Timothy Lukes (Lawrence, Kans., 1994). Kellner rightly notes that Marcuse did not anticipate the postmodern attacks on reason. But Hannah Arendt did not antici-

pate these attacks, either, and the fact that Marcuse has fallen into oblivion has mainly to do with the general decline of interest in Marxism in its various forms (including anti-Marxism). But the Benjamin cult is based not on his politics (to the extent that there was such a thing), but on his influence on those engaged in literary and cultural studies.

2. One example for this trend should suffice: "Because the Eichmann study drew upon the analysis in *The Origins of Totalitarianism* in important ways still not recognized, and this lack of recognition mars the work of contemporary theorists of totalitarianism such as Claude Lefort, Cornelius Castoriadis, and Agnes Heller, who consciously follow in Arendt's footsteps, the controversy surrounding it brought to the fore more than the question of Arendt's accuracy in dealing with the Holocaust, the primary target of the critical attack on Arendt's position. It also raised the issue of the experimental context and content of totalitarian rule, and thus the possibility of forms of total control to be found in all states, including democratic ones. In short, *Eichmann in Jerusalem* is a powerful contribution to political theory, a contribution not yet sufficiently recognized." Philip Hansen, *Hannah Arendt: Politics, History, and Citizenship* (Stanford, Ca., 1993), p. 11.

3. This refers, for instance, to the writings of Adrienne Rich, Mary O'Brien, Hannah Pitkin, and Wendy Brown. For a discussion of these and other writings, see Mary Hawkes, "Arendtian Politics: Feminism as a Test Case," *Journal of Women's History* (spring 1996). Also Bonnie Honig, *Feminist Interpretations of Hannah Arendt* (University Park, Pa., 1995) and various articles in *Hypatia* throughout 1996.

4. For an analysis of the Sartre cult, see A. Boschetti, *Sartre et les "Temps Modernes"* (Paris, 1985).

5. For Marcuse's political predictions, some only recently uncovered, see Herbert Marcuse, *Feindanalysen* (Lüneburg, 1998).

6. In a long television interview, which was not to be shown in his lifetime, I asked Ben-Gurion of what American Zionist leader he thought most highly. Without hesitation, Ben-Gurion replied: "Magnes." When I argued that this was an unlikely choice, because they had been political adversaries for so long, the former prime minister waved this argument aside: "But he came to Palestine, the others did not" (Brandeis University archives).

7. According to several writers, this article was first submitted to *Commentary*, but rejected. However, when Arendt submitted her article, *Commentary* did not even exist. It was not to be a Zionist organ, and Eliot Cohen, its first editor, was much in sympathy with Hannah Arendt's views. But Arendt submitted an article that was about three times as long as any published by *Commentary*. That it was controversial goes without saying. Thus wrote Kurt Blumenfeld, one of her closest friends, in a letter to Martin Rosenblueth: "a hotchpotch (*Mischmasch*) of someone half educated in these things" expressing "extreme resentment, spite, and nastiness" (*bis zum Aberwitz übersteigerten Resentiment, voller Gehässigkeit und Gemeinheit*, January 17, 1946). Blumenfeld wrote on the same occasion that these feats of character had induced him once before to break off relations with Hannah Arendt. *Commentary* did publish in later years articles by Hannah Arendt critical of official Zionist policy.

8. Various collections of Arendt's correspondence have been published—with Karl Jaspers, Martin Heidegger, Kurt Blumenfeld, Mary McCarthy, and Hermann Broch. The most revealing are, not surprisingly, the letters exchanged with her husband, Heinrich Blücher, even though only about three hundred out of four handred letters have been published. Derogatory passages referring to third persons have been deleted, according to the editors, because of considerations of defamation. Few authors have so far made use of these letters, even though they have been accessible for a number of years. The editors ought to be congratulated for providing detailed and helpful introductions. However, the explanations provided are far from being perfect. Thus, Leo Löwenthal is mixed up with Richard Löwenthal, Ludwig Marcuse with Herbert Marcuse; and a few minutes' research would have shown that Otto Heller was the author of the then famous book *Der Untergang des Judentums*.

9. I am thinking in this context of the Marxism of *Neu Beginnen* rather than the Frankfurt School, with its apodictic statements equating fascism and capitalism, with fascism a perverted truth of liberalism, proclaiming, on one hand, that "there are no more anti-Semites" and on the other imputing to the United States the intention to exterminate the Jews. The Frankfurt School never succeeded in coming to terms with totalitarianism, fascism, and anti-Semitism. It interpreted anti-Semitism psychologically as paranoia (of the German middle class) and Horkheimer toward the end of his life conceded that Herzl's warnings of 1900 were more to the point than the essays of the Frankfurt School forty years later. Such arguments were unlikely to appeal to Hannah Arendt. Her mistakes were on a higher level of sophistication. See Ehrhard Bahr, "The Anti-Semitism Studies of the Frankfurt School: The Failure of Critical Theory," in *Foundations of the Frankfurt School of Social Research,* edited by Judith Marcus and Zoltan Tar (New Brunswick, N.J., 1984), and Erich Cramer, *Hitler's Antisemitismus und die Frankfurter Schule: Kritische Faschismustheorie und geschichtliche Realität* (Düsseldorf, 1979).

10. In a small way, I also became a victim of Hannah Arendt's paranoia. I had reviewed Jakob Robinson's *And the Crooked Shall Be Made Straight,* which took Arendt to task for many errors of fact, mostly minor, in her book on the Eichmann trial. I was not impressed by Robinson's scholarship. The title of the review, "Footnotes to the Holocaust," reflected fairly accurately the tenor. But I also noted that Miss Arendt's book was deficient in both factual knowledge and scholarship. Hannah Arendt did not like this, and in an answer more than twice as long as my original review (the *New York Review of Books,* November 11, 1965, and January 20, 1966), she suggested that I was not only an admirer of Dr. Robinson, but in some mysterious way also his employee. I was at the time director of the Wiener Library in London, Robinson a leading figure in the Claims Conference. The assignment of this organization was, *inter alia,* to support institutions such as the Wiener Library. However, for reasons that one can only surmise, Robinson and his colleagues did not make any significant contribution to the Wiener Library. In other words, I had no reason whatsoever to feel, to put it cautiously, an obligation, let alone a debt of gratitude toward Dr. Robinson. Hannah Arendt might not have known this, but, in any case, it would have hardly prevented her from scenting a conspiracy.

11. The Eichmann book was reissued in Germany in 1986, twenty years after it had first appeared, with a longish preface by Hans Mommsen, one of the leading functionalists. Again, ten years later, in the midst of the Goldhagen controversy, a German author wrote: "In 1964 Hannah Arendt supplied the required explanation [in the form] of her theory of the 'banality of evil.' . . . The responsibility for Nazi terror did not lie with the abject character and morals of the Germans, but with their having been enlisted in the totalitarian bureaucratic apparatus. Stereotypes of the desk criminal who signs with equanimity orders of murder and deportation, and of a 'book keeper mentality' of underlings ensconced in their routines—these stereotypes make a career as explanatory models and in this fashion the evil-doers and ugly German disappeared. . . . This explains the lasting success of Arendt's thesis in Germany; elsewhere hardly anyone took this banality nonsense seriously because evil is never banal." Mathias Broeckers, "Das Böse ist niemals banal." *Tageszeitung, TAZ*, Berlin, September 10, 1996, quoted in Avraham Barkai, "German Historians Face Goldhagen," in *Yad Vashem Studies* 24 (Jerusalem, 1998): 310–11.

Whether Hannah Arendt, as moral philosopher, would have fully subscribed to the functionalist conception as it later emerged is not certain. These debates took place only in later years. But it can hardly be disputed that, in certain crucial ways, her Eichmann book paved the way for this conception. It ought to be added that the "banality of evil" found literary expression first, in only slightly different formulation, in the introduction to Joseph Conrad's *Under Western Eyes*. Bröcker's assertion that this idea was taken seriously nowhere but in Germany is not correct. It also had a certain following in the United States, but in a different context—the moral relativism of the postmodern movement.

SUSAN NEIMAN, "THEODICY IN JERUSALEM"

The following abbreviations are used for citing Arendt's work: *EiJ, Eichmann in Jerusalem: A Report on the Banality of Evil* (Viking, 1963); *EU, Essays in Understanding 1930–1954*, edited by Jerome Kohn (Harcourt Brace, 1994); *BPF, Between Past and Future* (Viking, 1961); *MDT, Men in Dark Times* (Harcourt Brace Jovanovich, 1968); *T, Thinking* (Harcourt Brace Jovanovich, 1971); *W, Willing* (Harcourt Brace Jovanovich, 1978); *Lectures, Lectures on Kant's Political Philosophy* (University of Chicago Press, 1982); *BF, Between Friends: The Correspondence of Hannah Arendt and Mary McCarthy* (Harcourt Brace, 1995); *V, Ich will verstehen, Selbstauskünfte zu Leben u. Werk* (Piper, 1996). Translations of texts not available in English are my own. This essay was written while I was a fellow at the Institute of Advanced Studies of the Shalom Hartman Institute, whose generous support has enabled me to write. I am grateful to the number of people who took time to offer comments on the first version of this text and am particularly indebted to conversations with Richard Bernstein, Dan Diner, Burton Dreben, Ruth Gavison, Eva Illouz, Irad Kimhi, Claudio Lange, Menachem Lorberbaum, James Ponet, Shira Wollosky, and Shoshana and Yirmayahu Yovel.

1. Noting this phenomenon in his "Hannah Arendt Reconsidered," Dan Diner suggests that the depth of the controversy can be understood by reference

to fundamental questions of Jewish self-definition raised by the book. *Babylon,* nos. 16–17 (1996). My emphasis on metaphysical issues is compatible with the political interpretation Diner offers. Passion is usually overdetermined.

2. It is possible that Arendt would have found the project of defining evil a suspicious one from the outset, as is suggested by the following passage from her essay on Isak Dinesen: "It is true that storytelling reveals meaning without committing the error of defining it, that it brings about consent and reconciliation with things as they really are, and that we may even trust it to contain by implication that last word which we expect from the 'day of judgment.'" *Men in Dark Times,* 105. The implication that a definition of something like evil would be in error leaves us all the more in need of understanding the point of Arendt's claim of the banality of evil.

3. For thoughtful criticism on this score, see especially Richard Bernstein, *Hannah Arendt and the Jewish Question,* chapter 8 (MIT Press, 1996), and Seyla Benhabib, *The Reluctant Modernism of Hannah Arendt,* chapter 6 (Sage, 1996).

4. These general questions can only be sketched in the present essay, which is part of a longer study tracing the modern problem of evil. See Susan Neiman, "Metaphysics, Philosophy: Rousseau and the Problem of Evil," in *Reclaiming the History of Ethics: Essays for John Rawls,* edited by Andrews Reath, Christine Korsgaard, and Barbara Hermann (Cambridge University Press, 1997), and *Evil in Modern Thought: An Alternative History of Philosophy* (Harvard University Press, forthcoming).

5. On Arendt's use of the image of hell and comparisons with Celan's, see Shira Wollosky, *Language Mysticism* (Stanford University Press, 1995), p. 164.

6. See Susan Neiman, *The Unity of Reason: Rereading Kant* (Oxford University Press, 1994).

7. Arendt herself repeats this in recalling that not Nietzsche but Hegel is the source of the claim that God is dead. See *Willing.*

8. Though two months earlier she wrote to a certain Herr Meier-Cronemeyer: "That what I'm really concerned with is 'to create the foundations of a new political morality' is of course true, though I never formulated it like that out of modesty." Elisabeth Young-Bruehl, *Hannah Arendt: For Love of the World* (Yale University Press, 1982), 526.

9. A similar suggestion is made by Albrecht Wellmer in his incisive "Hannah Arendt on Judgment: The Unwritten Doctrine of Reason," in *Hannah Arendt: Twenty Years Later,* edited by Larry May and Jerome Kohn (MIT Press, 1996).

10. Immanuel Kant, *Critique of Pure Reason, B,* 172–73.

11. The maxims are to think for oneself, to think oneself in the place of others, and to think consistently. Arendt comments: "These are not matters of cognition; truth compels, one doesn't need any maxims. Maxims apply and are needed only for matters of opinion and in judgments" *Lectures on Kant's Political Philosophy,* 71.

12. See, expanding on her remarks in the Gaus interview, the April 13, 1965, letter to Jaspers: "What troubles me so much about all this is the alienation from reality, that people ignore reality in favor of their bright ideas" (footnote 13, p. 15).

13. These are the interesting reasons for her protest at being called a philosopher, which ignore the less interesting professional matters from which even the most self-confident are never entirely free. As she acknowledges in the Gaus interview, Arendt was never really recognized by the philosopher's guild of the country in which she made her home. How much this has to do with Arendt and how much this has to do with the state of professional philosophy in America are questions that remain open. The use of scare quotes in her disclaimer in the opening paragraph of *Thinking* ("I have neither claim nor ambition to be a 'philosopher'") suggests an uncharacteristic coyness on the subject.

14. Whether Arendt was right to read him this way depends on one's understanding of the equation of the real and the rational and of a host of other points of Hegel interpretation that I cannot adjudicate. *That* this was her reading seems clear.

15. Young-Bruehl, *Hannah Arendt,* 177.

16. Arendt summarizes: "The Hegelian escape from concern with politics into an interpretation of history is no longer open. Its tacit assumption was that historical events and the entire stream of past happenings could make sense and, despite all evil and negative aspects, disclose positive meaning to the backward-directed glance of the philosopher. . . . Hegel's grandiose effort to reconcile spirit with reality depended entirely on the ability to harmonize and see something good in every evil. It remained valid only as long as 'radical evil' (of which, among philosophers, only Kant had the conception, if hardly the concrete experience) had not happened. Who would dare to reconcile himself with the reality of extermination camps, or play the game of thesis-antithesis-synthesis until his dialectics have discovered 'meaning' in slave labor?" "Concern with Politics in Recent European Philosophical Thought," *Essays in Understanding,* 444.

17. Quoted in Jerome Kohn, "Evil and Plurality," in *Hannah Arendt: Twenty Years Later,* 155.

18. Whether this is a correct interpretation of the Book of Job itself is questionable, but Kant held the appeal to God's inscrutability to imply the "abhorrent" implication that there is meaningful order and purpose in the world, even if we will never grasp it, and this is to mock reality.

19. On Arendt's interest in Kant's discussion of beauty as evidence that we do, see *Between Friends,* 268, and *Lectures on Kant's Political Philosophy.*

20. See Benhabib, *The Reluctant Modernism of Hannah Arendt,* Bernstein, *Hannah Arendt and the Jewish Question,* and Wellmer, "Hannah Arendt on Judgment." Jerome Kohn, "Evil and Plurality," in *Hannah Arendt: Twenty Years Later,* is a careful attempt to show that *The Life of the Mind* satisfies more objections than most critics have charged. Henry Allison's "Reflections on the Banality of (Radical) Evil: A Kantian Analysis" suggests that the lack of depth of Arendt's notion of evil makes it unavailable for theoretical analysis. Allison's interesting suggestion is too brief to explain the ways in which evil should be less analyzable than other surface phenomena. Benhabib's emphasis on the role of narrative and the nonfoundationalist character of Arendt's thought is more successful.

21. In this, as in other aspects, Arendt's discussion is very close to Rousseau's.

22. As Bernstein (148) points out, the comparison of evil to a fungus may well stem from Jaspers's metaphor of evil as bacteria. Jaspers's letter also refers to the Nazis as banal.

23. See her discussion in "The Eggs Speak Up," in *Essays in Understanding*, 272.

24. Bernstein writes that Arendt introduced the discussion of the *Judenräte* to show the "total moral collapse of European society" (*Hannah Arendt and the Jewish Question*, 163). I would add: to show that this collapse was not a function of wrong intentions.

25. See, in particular, Wellmer, "Hannah Arendt on Judgment."

26. I am especially indebted to Burton Dreben and Irad Kimhi for thinking about these questions.

27. Arendt's discussion here is clearly prompted by her study of totalitarianism, and it is precisely her disinterest in intention that allows her to discuss Stalinism and Nazism together. The leftist reluctance to do so stems from understandable repugnance at comparing two movements whose intentions were so opposed to each other. As Arendt was well aware, the one was directed toward realizing the very concept of humanity born in the French Revolution that the other is dedicated to destroying. Arendt seeks a moral view that acknowledges both this fact and the fact that it is less significant than the way in which both movements created hell on earth—in what she insists is a literal sense.

28. *Lectures on Kant's Political Philosophy*, 68, tell us that judgment is fundamentally other-directed.

29. This is, of course, a Kantian critique, which may lead us to question the consistency of Kant's own formulation of the relationship between good will and morality, particularly in light of his views about punishment. But these questions must be the subject of another investigation.

30. This astuteness was not confined to Arendt, but shared by many intelligent writers who took the trouble to open their eyes to all that made postwar Germany a veritable classroom for the study and practice of moral judgment. Postwar German literature offers abundant testimony.

31. "Totalitarian terror achieved its most terrible triumph when it succeeded in cutting the moral person off from the individualist escape and in making the decisions of conscience absolutely questionable and equivocal. When a man is faced with the alternative of betraying and thus murdering his friends or of sending his wife and children, for whom he is in every sense responsible, to their death; when even suicide would mean the immediate murder of his own family—how is he to decide? The alternative is no longer between good and evil, but between murder and murder." *The Origins of Totalitarianism*, 452.

32. "And if you go through such times as those of totalitarianism, the first thing you know is this: you never know how someone will act. You are always experiencing the surprise of your life! This applies to all levels of society and to the most various distinctions among people." "On Hannah Arendt," in *Ich will verstehen*, 85. See also her remark: "In such things there are nothing but *Einzelfälle* [individual cases]." Young-Bruehl, *Hannah Arendt*, 350.

33. Again, Eichmann's capacity to give a reasonable interpretation of the Categorical Imperative must function as a warning against viewing morality as a matter of general law—which is not, of course, how Kant himself viewed it.

34. In "Understanding and Politics," Arendt undertakes to deny the statement: *tout comprendre c'est tout pardonner.* Her discussion is suggestive, but far too brief for a point of such magnitude for her account.

35. At one point, she states the relation to be even stronger: "to think and to be fully alive are the same." *Thinking,* 178.

36. See Jean Améry's brilliant and devastating *Jenseits von Schuld und Sühne* (Szczesny, 1966). I discuss Améry's position as well as his own attack on it in "Jean Améry," in *The Yale Companion to Jewish Writing and Thought in Germany,* edited by Sander Gilman and Jack Zipes (Yale University Press, 1997).

37. For discussion of Nazi success in negating the bases of instrumental reasoning, see Dan Diner, "Historical Understanding and Counterrationality: The *Judenrat* as Epistemological Vantage," in *Probing the Limits of Representation: Nazism and the "Final Solution,"* edited by Saul Friedlander (Harvard University Press, 1992).

38. Though she devoted some attention to the former question. See especially her "Social Science Techniques and the Study of Concentration Camps," in *Essays in Understanding,* 232–48. For Rawls's discussion of the reasonable and the rational, see his *Political Liberalism,* chapter 1 (Columbia University Press, 1993).

39. Hannah Arendt and Karl Jaspers, Letter 50, December 17, 1946, in *Correspondence, 1926–1969,* edited by Lotte Köhler and Hans Saner, translated by Robert Kimber and Rita Kimber (New York: Harcourt Brace Jovanovich, 1992), p. 69.

40. In a late letter, Arendt recalled a central feature of the legend: not even the thirty-six know they are the righteous ones for whose sake the world is saved. Young-Bruehl, *Hannah Arendt,* 377. She might have added that this impossibility of knowledge leaves something both free and precarious in the fact of righteousness itself.

41. Had the trial taken place, *per impossible,* in Bonn, Arendt would have written a very different book. As the title suggests, the centrality of place is conscious, and a number of remarks that offended Israeli audiences were clearly not the result of oversight but deliberate critique. Nevertheless, I am indebted to two conversations for convincing me that Arendt simply misjudged some features of the trial. Shlomo Avineri reminded me that the state of Israel has been plagued by the advice of Diaspora Jews from its inception, which, however intelligent, is bound to have an oracular quality removed from just that daily commitment to political reality of which Arendt was aware. Shoshana Yovel pointed out that what was needed in 1961 in Israel was closer to catharsis than theodicy. In the climate of silence that had accompanied the experience of the Shoah, the victims' need to speak was experienced as collectively liberating. As Arendt herself would tell us, "All sorrows can be borne if you put them into a story." *Men in Dark Times,* 104. One can learn about judgment in more ways than one.

BERNARD CRICK, "ARENDT AND *THE ORIGINS OF TOTALITARIANISM*"

1. See my "On Rereading *The Origins of Totalitarianism*," in *Hannah Arendt: The Recovery of the Public World*, edited by M. A. Hill (New York: St. Martin's Press, 1979), pp. 27–47.

2. Hannah Arendt, *The Origins of Totalitarianism*, 1st edition (New York: Harcourt Brace, 1951), pp. 431–32.

3. Margaret Canovan, *Hannah Arendt: A Reinterpretation of Her Political Thought* (Cambridge, Cambridge University Press, 1992), pp. 6–7 and 17–23.

4. As notably Ronald Beiner has pointed out, she sees political judgment, even action, as much closer to Kant's aesthetics than to his concept of practical reason. See his *Political Judgement* (London: Methuen, 1983), which arose out of his Oxford D.Phil. dissertation, "Hannah Arendt and Political Judgement."

MICHAEL HALBERSTAM, "HANNAH ARENDT ON THE TOTALITARIAN SUBLIME"

Portions of this essay are adapted from chapter 9 of my *Totalitarianism and the Modern Conception of Politics* (New Haven: Yale University Press, 1999), reprinted by permission of Yale University Press. I am grateful to Meili Steele for his careful reading of an earlier draft of this paper and to members of the University of South Carolina Political Theory Workshop for their comments. I wish to thank Kate Brown, Tom Huhn, Maureen Mahon, Sean McCann, Joe Rouse, and Betsy Traube for their valuable comments. Work on this paper was also supported by a Mellon Fellowship at Wesleyan University's Center for the Humanities.

1. See Ramin Jahanbegloo, *Conversations with Isaiah Berlin* (London: P. Halban, 1992), pp. 82–83: "she produces no arguments, no evidence of serious philosophical or historical thought. It is all a stream of metaphysical associations." Quoted by Seyla Benhabib in *The Reluctant Modernism of Hannah Arendt* (Thousand Oaks, Calif.: Sage, 1996).

2. Hannah Arendt, *The Origins of Totalitarianism* (New York: Harcourt Brace Jovanovich, 1979), p. 466. Also, p. 465: "Terror is the realization of the law of movement; its chief aim is to make it possible for the force of nature or of history to race freely through mankind, unhindered by any spontaneous human action."

3. Ibid., pp. 478, 459, 470, 303, 474, 476, 466.

4. The first edition of *The Origins of Totalitarianism* appeared in 1948. Arendt added the essay "Ideology and Terror" to the 1958 revised edition.

5. "Whereas in Germany itself—though it was very different in the occupied territories—there was a certain horrific predictability to the terror, so that non-targeted groups were relatively safe as long as they kept out of trouble and retained a low profile, the very unpredictability of Stalinist terror meant that no one could feel safe. By the later 1930's Stalin had turned the terror against the party, the army high command, economic managers, the members of his own Politburo, and even the secret police itself." Ian Kershaw and Moshe Lewin,

"Afterthoughts," in *Stalinism and Nazism: Dictatorships in Comparison,* edited by Ian Kershaw and Moshe Lewin (Cambridge: Cambridge University Press, 1997), p. 355. See also Dan Diner, "Nationalsozialismus und Stalinismus," in *Kreisläufe* (Berlin: Berlin Verlag, 1995), p. 67: "Under Stalinism fear was pervasive—a genuine regime of terror . . . Stalin's rule was totalitarian in the highest degree—a characterization that cannot validly be applied to National Socialism in the same way."

6. George L. Mosse, *The Nationalization of the Masses* (Ithaca: Cornell University Press, 1975), p. 4.

7. For a comparative analysis, see *Stalinism and Nazism,* edited by Kershaw and Lewin. For a reassessment of the totalitarian paradigm, see *The Totalitarian Paradigm after the End of Communism,* edited by Achim Siegel (Amsterdam: Rodophi, 1998).

8. To mention just one, anti-Semitism and racism, which she makes one of the elements of totalitarianism's genesis, though they did drive National Socialism, weren't essential parts of Bolshevik ideology. For a reconsideration of Arendt's theory of totalitarianism, see Friedrich Pohlmann, "The 'Seeds of Destruction' in Totalitarian Systems: An Interpretation of the Unity of Hannah Arendt's Political Philosophy," in Siegel, *The Totalitarian Paradigm.*

9. Clearly the periodization of Soviet and Nazi rule is important to Arendt's totalitarianism thesis. Arendt's model applies best to Nazi rule between 1939 and 1945 in Germany and to Stalin's rule in the Soviet Union between 1929 and his death in 1953. Both regimes brought periods of relative civil peace after their accession to power. The National Socialists did make war on their population, on the "enemy within" (as did Stalin against the peasants and many others). The distinction between "ethnic Germans" and non-ethnic Germans is somewhat artificial. To a certain degree, it relies on Nazi racial distinctions. Jews and Communists were Germans (and, often enough, nationalists!) too. They were part of the mainstream of German society. "Germans," like "Frenchmen," identified themselves regionally and locally before nationalism. See Mosse, *The Nationalization of the Masses,* for the nationalization of Germany, and Eugene Weber, *Peasants into Frenchmen* (Stanford, Calif.: Stanford University Press, 1976), for the case of France. In mid-1933, 11 percent of all practicing German physicians were Jews. Jews still made up more than 16 percent of all practicing lawyers. They were citizens, culture bearers, employers, employees, fiduciaries, and neighbors. Saul Friedlander's *Nazi Germany and the Jews* (New York: Harper Collins, 1998) quickly communicates the sense of utter bewilderment that must strike any observer of the "system of terror" put into action during the accession to power in 1933 (p. 17). Accordingly, while Kershaw and Lewin insist that Hitler did not rule by terror, they do not, of course, deny that terror pervaded the system or that its comparative analysis is no longer of interest to historians (*Stalinism and Nazism,* pp. 8–9).

10. Friedrich Pohlmann, "The 'Seeds of Destruction,' " p. 227.

11. Ibid., p. 229.

12. "For a month he was absorbed in the histories of ancient and modern art in order to gather evidence to demonstrate the basically revolutionary and disruptive character of Hegel's fundamental categories; like the young Russian rad-

icals of this period he looked upon them as being, in Herzen's phrase, 'The algebra of revolution.' 'Too frightened to apply them openly,' wrote Herzen, 'in the storm-tossed ocean of politics, the old philosopher set them afloat in the tranquil inland lake of aesthetic theory.'" Isaiah Berlin, *Karl Marx* (New York: Oxford University Press, 1963), p. 76. See also Louis Dupré, *Marx's Social Critique of Culture* (New Haven: Yale University Press, 1984), p. 262: "Marx's early aesthetic reflections set up an ideal of cultural integration that gradually came to dominate his entire work." On the relevance of the aesthetic for the conservative revolutionaries in Germany see, for example, Fritz Stern, *The Politics of Cultural Despair* (1961; Berkeley: University of California Press, 1974). See also Joseph Chytry, *The Aesthetic State: A Quest in Modern German Thought* (Berkeley: University of California Press, 1989).

13. Margaret Canovan, *Hannah Arendt: A Reinterpretation of Her Political Thought* (Cambridge: Cambridge University Press, 1992), p. 5.

14. See, for example, Dana Villa, *Arendt and Heidegger: The Fate of the Political* (Princeton: Princeton University Press, 1996). See also my *Totalitarianism and the Modern Conception of Politics,* chapter 7.

15. Canovan, *Hannah Arendt,* p. 3.

16. Villa, *Arendt and Heidegger.*

17. Charles Taylor, *Hegel* (Cambridge: Cambridge University Press, 1975), p. 187.

18. Ibid., p. 403.

19. Jean Hyppolite, *The Genesis and Structure of Hegel's Phenomenology of Spirit,* translated by Samuel Cherniak and John Heckman (Evanston, Ill.: Northwestern University Press, 1974), p. 454.

20. I am indebted to Joe Rouse for this way of putting things.

21. "What emerges . . . is of course the demand for 'absolute freedom' from all previous restrictions and cultural restraints. What Hegel describes here is a kind of contextless freedom, a nihilistic yearning for oblivion or a 'freedom of the void' which is often associated with the modern desire for revolution and total emancipation." Steven Smith, *Hegel's Critique of Liberalism* (Chicago: University of Chicago Press, 1989), p. 87.

22. Jean-Jacques Rousseau, *On the Social Contract,* in *Social Contract,* introduced by Ernest Barker (London: Oxford University Press, 1960), p. 181. For a feminist critique of the social contract, see Carol Pateman, "The Fraternal Social Contract," in *Contemporary Political Philosophy,* edited by Robert E. Goodin and Philip Pettit (London: Blackwell, 1996). Feminist critiques of the social contract generally begin with Hegel's critical insight into the formalism and abstraction of the idea of the social contract.

23. Immanuel Kant, *Political Writings,* edited by Hans Reiss (Cambridge: Cambridge University Press, 1991), pp. 41–54.

24. Hegel would stress the retreat from politics and into the self that characterizes Kant's moral philosophy. Taylor, *Hegel,* pp. 187–88.

25. "Sein Zweck ist der allgemeine Zweck, seine Sprache das allgemeine Gesetz, sein Werk das allgemeine Werk." G. W. F. Hegel, *Die Phänomenologie des Geistes* (Hamburg: Meiner, 1952), p. 416, *The Phenomenology of Spirit,* p. 357.

26. Ibid., p. 359. Fichte was regarded as a supporter of the Jacobin policies of Robespierre. On this see Smith, *Hegel's Critique of Liberalism*, p. 85. And Hegel has Fichte's version of idealism in mind when he addresses the Jacobin reign of terror. Fichte advocated a "police state" and was explicit about carrying the perspective of the theoretical subject into the realm of practical affairs: "To subject all irrational nature to himself, to rule over it without restraint and according to his own laws is the ultimate end of man; which *ultimate end* is perfectly unattainable. . . . But he may and should constantly approach nearer to it—and thus the *unceasing approximation* to this end is his true *vocation* as man." Johann Gottlieb Fichte, *The Vocation of the Scholar,* in *The Popular Works,* translated by William Smith (London: John Chapman, 1848) 1:183, cited by Smith, *Hegel's Critique of Liberalism,* p. 83.

27. Arendt, *The Origins of Totalitarianism,* p. 341: "Totalitarianism uses violence not so much to frighten people . . . as to realize constantly its ideological doctrines and its practical lies. Totalitarianism will not be satisfied to assert, in the face of contrary facts, that unemployment does not exist; it will abolish unemployment as part of its propaganda, and in the end eliminate the unemployed."

28. Pohlmann, "The 'Seeds of Destruction,'" pp. 234–35.

29. Arendt, "What Is Freedom?" in *Between Past and Future* (New York: Viking, 1968), p. 164.

30. Arendt, "Mankind and Terror," in *Essays in Understanding,* edited by Jerome Kohn (New York: Harcourt Brace, 1994), p. 300.

31. Arendt does, however, want to distinguish sharply between revolutionary politics and totalitarian politics. She argues that revolutionary politics culminates in a new constitution of liberty, that is, in a new legal code, whereas totalitarianism engages in "permanent revolution." But this is not how Hegel reads the French Revolution.

32. Arendt to Jaspers, March 4, 1951, in *Correspondence 1926–1969,* edited by Lotte Köhler and Hans Saner, translated by Robert Kimber and Rita Kimber (New York: Harcourt Brace Jovanovich, 1992), p. 166, cited by Steven Aschheim, *Culture and Catastrophe* (New York: NYU Press, 1996), p. 110.

33. Eric Voegelin, "A Review of *The Origins of Totalitarianism,*" *Review of Politics* (January 1953): 63–98.

34. Ibid., p. 74.

35. See especially her essay "Religion and Politics" in *Essays in Understanding* for her rejection of a secularization thesis.

36. "A correct estimation of the role of the 'Analytic of the Sublime' in the *Third Critique* must find its function not simply in completing the architectonic articulation of aesthetic judgments but much more in demonstrating a connection between aesthetic experience in general and the ultimate nature of the self. Kant confirmed this point by terming his consideration of the sublime a *Kritik des Geistesgefühls,* a critique of spiritual feeling [Kant, *First Introduction to the Third Critique* §12:54 (A.A. 20:250)] . . . the sublime was the aesthetic experience which par excellence symbolized the moral dimension of human existence." John H. Zammito, *The Genesis of Kant's Critique of Judgment* (Chicago: The University of Chicago Press, 1992), pp. 278–79.

37. Arendt, *The Origins of Totalitarianism,* p. 461.

38. Ibid., p. 474.

39. Edmund Burke, *A Philosophical Enquiry into the Origin of Our Ideas of the Sublime and Beautiful,* edited by James T. Boulton (Notre Dame: University of Notre Dame Press, 1986), p. 58.

40. Ibid., pp. 39–43, 64, and part 2, section 3.

41. Cited by Ernest Tuveson, *The Imagination as a Source of Grace* (Berkeley: University of California Press, 1960), p. 59.

42. Ibid., pp. 61, 58.

43. Kant, *Critique of Judgment,* trans. J. H. Bernard (New York: Hafner, 1951), §28, 100–101.

44. "Bold overhanging, and as it were threatening rocks; clouds piled up in the sky, moving with lightning flashes and thunder peals; volcanoes in all their violence of destruction; hurricanes with their track of devastation; the boundless ocean in a state of tumult; the lofty waterfall of a mighty river, and such like— these exhibit our faculty of resistance as insignificantly small in comparison with their might. But the sight of them is the more attractive, the more fearful it is, provided only that we are in security; and we willingly call these objects sublime, because they raise the energies of the soul above their accustomed height and discover in us a faculty of resistance of a quite different kind, which gives us courage to measure ourselves against the apparent almightiness of nature. Now, in the immensity of nature and in the insufficiency of our faculties to take in a standard proportionate to the aesthetical estimation of the magnitude of its *realm,* we find our own limitation, although at the same time in our rational faculty we find a different, nonsensuous standard, which has that infinity itself under it as a unity, in comparison with which everything in nature is small, and thus in our mind we find a superiority to nature even in its immensity. And so also the irresistibility of its might, while making us recognize our own [physical] impotence, considered as beings of nature, discloses to us a faculty of judging independently of and a superiority over nature, on which is based a kind of self-preservation entirely different from that which can be attacked and brought into danger by external nature. Thus humanity in our person remains unhumiliated, though the individual might have to submit to this dominion. In this way nature is not judged to be sublime in our aesthetical judgments in so far as it excites fear, but because it calls up that power in us (which is not nature) of regarding as small the things we *care about* (goods, health, and life), and of regarding its might (to which we are no doubt subjected in respect of these things) as nevertheless without any dominion over us and our personality to which we must bow where our highest fundamental propositions, and their assertion or abandonment, are concerned. Therefore nature is here called sublime merely because it elevates the imagination to a presentation of those cases in which the mind can make felt the proper sublimity of its destination, in comparison with nature itself." Kant, *Critique of Judgment,* §28, A 104–5. Italics indicate my changes in the translation. Kant uses the same word, *Sorge, besorgt sein,* that Heidegger uses in *Being and Time.* This is not coincidental. Heidegger's leave taking from care in the "resolute anticipation of death" (*Entschlossenheit*) of the second half

of *Being and Time* is explicitly making use of the experience of the sublime and its history in the German tradition.

45. Burke, *Enquiry*, p. 57: "In this case the mind is so entirely filled with its object, that it cannot entertain any other."

46. Kant, *Critique of Judgment*, §29, 116.

47. Zammito, *The Genesis of Kant's Critique of Judgment*, p. 277.

48. Arendt, "What Is Freedom?" in *Between Past and Future*, p. 147.

49. In *The Birth of Tragedy*, Nietzsche uses the experience of sublime terror precisely in this manner to level all distinctions between reality and appearances in the "Apollinian" world, that is, in our everyday social and perceptual experience. He later repudiated the work as the product of, among other things, "an illness contracted at the front."

50. Nietzsche, *Birth of Tragedy*; Kierkegaard, *Fear and Trembling*; Kant, *Critique of Judgment*; Dostoyevsky, *Crime and Punishment*; Heidegger, *Being and Time*; Sartre, *Being and Nothingness*.

51. The original title of Arendt's *The Origins of Totalitarianism* was *The Burden of Our Time* (London: Secker and Warburg, 1951).

52. See, e.g., Nietzsche's attempt at a self-criticism in the preface to later editions of *The Birth of Tragedy*, in *The Case of Wagner*, in his chapter "On Those Who Are Sublime" in *Zarathustra*, and in many other writings.

53. Arendt, "What Is Existentialism?" in *Essays in Understanding*, pp. 176–77: "The fascination that the idea of nothingness has held for modern philosophy does not necessarily suggest a nihilistic bias in that philosophy. If we consider the problem of nothingness in our context of a philosophy in revolt against philosophy as pure contemplation and if we see it as an attempt to make us the master of Being and thus enable us to pose the philosophical questions that will enable us to progress immediately to action, the idea that Being is really nothingness is of inestimable value. Proceeding from this idea, man can imagine that he stands in the same relationship to Being as the Creator stood before creating the world, which, as we know, was created *ex nihilo*. Then too, designating Being as nothingness brings with it the attempt to put behind us the definition of Being as what is given and to regard human actions not just as god-like but as divine. This is the reason—though it is not one Heidegger admits to—why in his philosophy nothingness suddenly becomes active and begins to nihilate [*nichten*]. Nothing tries, as it were, to destroy the givenness of Being and nihilatingly [*nichtend*] to usurp Being's place. If Being, which I have not created, is the business of a being that I am not and do not know, then nothingness is perhaps the truly free domain of man. Since I cannot be a world-creating being it could perhaps be my role to be a world-destroying being."

54. Ibid., p. 187.

55. Adam Müller, "Von der Idee des Staates" (1809), in *Deutsche Vergangenheit und deutscher Staat*, edited by Paul Kluckhohn (Leipzig: Philip Reclam, 1935), pp. 200–226.

56. "Adam Müller Rennaissance" in *Kölnische Zeitung*, nos. 502 and 510 (September 9 and September 17, 1932).

57. "Den Staat als ein durchaus lebendiges Ganzes und in der Bewegung [als

Idee] gefasst." Kluckhohn, "Einleitung," in *Deutsche Vergangenheit und deutscher Staat,* pp. 20, 212–13. See Müller, "Von der Idee des Staates," pp. 212 ff.

58. Adam Müller, "Vorlesungen über die deutsche Wissenschaft und Literatur," cited by Kluckhohn, "Einführung," *Deutsche Vergangenheit und deutscher Staat,* p. 20.

59. Müller, "Von der Idee des Staates," p. 212: "Der Staat ruht ganz in sich; unabhängig von menschlicher Willkür und Erfindung, kommt er unmittelbar und zugleich mit dem Menschen daher, wo der Mensch kommt, aus der Natur: aus Gott, sagten die Alten."

60. Similar arguments were made by antiliberals during the 1920s such as Carl Schmitt. See Stephen Holmes, *The Anatomy of Antiliberalism* (Cambridge, Mass.: Harvard, 1993), especially chapter 1. In spite of this, or perhaps because of it, Schmitt launched a vociferous critique of Adam Müller and other Romantics in *Political Romanticism* (1925), translated by Guy Oakes (Cambridge, Mass.: MIT Press, 1986). Schmitt especially seizes on Müller's opportunism and hypocrisy. Müller changed his theoretical allegiances according to his political fortunes. He also offered the Prussian minister Hardenberg his services as a secret journalistic provocateur for the Prussian state. Hardenberg turned him down. Schmitt's own political opportunism matches Müller's in every respect, except that Schmitt was more successful. Still condemning the Nazi Party in a book published in 1932, he quickly acceded to Hitler's request in 1933 to establish the constitutional legitimacy of the National Socialist state retroactively. Arendt is likely to have read Schmitt's book on Romanticism. Her essay appears to draw on it.

61. Müller, "Von der Idee des Staates," p. 214: "*Der Staat ist die Totalität der menschlichen Angelegenheiten, ihre Verbindung zu einem lebendigen Ganzen. Schneiden wir auch nur das unbedeutendste Teil des menschlichen Wesens aus diesem Zusammenhange für immer heraus, trennen wir den menschlichen Charakter auch nur an irgendeiner Stelle vom bürgerlichen, so können wir den Staat als Lebenserscheinung oder als Idee worauf es hier ankommt, nicht mehr empfinden.*"

62. Arendt, *The Origins of Totalitarianism,* p. 469.

63. Ibid., p. 469.

64. Arendt's turn to Montesquieu as a resource for political thinking also is in direct opposition to Müller's rejection of Montesquieu as the representative of the mistaken bourgeois differentiation of the state into different spheres. See Müller, "Von der Idee des Staates," pp. 220–21.

65. A similar defense of Hegel's quasi-messianism is provided by Shlomo Avineri: while "Hegel's vision of the state [as the sublime march of the spirit of world history on earth] invests it with the positive role of being itself the embodiment of man's self-consciousness . . . this, however, also reflects the potentially critical attitude Hegel develops against the state. The state embodies man's highest relationship to other human beings yet this function of the state is conditional, not absolute. In order to qualify for such a role, the state has to reflect the individual's self-consciousness." *Hegel's Theory of the Modern State* (New York: Cambridge University Press, 1989), p. 181.

66. Commentators take issue with precisely this conflation of the experience

of victims on the one hand and perpetrators and bystanders on the other. In *Hitler's Willing Executioners* (New York: Vintage, 1997), Daniel Goldhagen, for example, argues that "contrary to Arendt's assertions, the perpetrators were not such atomized, lonely beings [as Arendt claims]. They decidedly belonged to their world and had plenty of opportunities, which they obviously used, to discuss and reflect upon their exploits" (p. 581, n. 23). Kant and those who follow his analysis of the sublime regard an aesthetic distance to the threat, that is, a removal from immediate threat, as a condition of its functioning as an aesthetic experience. It is such aesthetic distance that makes possible the experience of a threat to one's existence as a source of delight. On this reading, the bystanders would be the ones to experience the "loss of world" as sublime.

67. Arendt, "On the Nature of Totalitarianism," in *Essays in Understanding,* p. 357.

68. George Mosse describes the significance of the sublime for nationalism and for an emerging tradition of political religion in Europe from an objectivating point of view: "Ernst Moritz Arndt, the poet of German unity, said in 1814 that Christian prayer should accompany national festivals, but even when such obvious linkage vanished the national cult retained not only the forms of Christian liturgy intact, but also the ideal of beauty: the 'beauty of holiness' which was exemplified by Christian churches. This tradition, fused with classicism, led to such artistic forms as could inspire political action. Both in the French Revolution and in Pietism, the ideal of inner-directed creative activity had already pushed outward into the political realm. The artistic and the political had fused." *Nationalization of the Masses,* p. 15. See Isaiah Berlin, "A Remarkable Decade," in *Russian Thinkers* (New York: Viking Press, 1978), p. 119, for some of the factors that contributed to the tremendous influence of German Romanticism on the birth of the Russian intelligentsia. Admittedly, this essay leaves unexplored the connections that would need to be made in order to show that aesthetic categories are relevant in the Russian case.

69. It is well known that Thomas Mann based the figure of the Romantic, revolutionary Marxist Naphta on Georg Lukács, whom Mann met in 1922. Lukács, who was later to become a Stalinist, was then in exile for his participation in the 1919 revolution in Hungary. Mann was one of the first to anticipate the totalitarian paradigm in his fusion of reactionary and communist sensibilities in the figure of Naphta. See István Hermann's "Introduction" to Judith-Marcus Tar, *Thomas Mann und Grygory Lucács* (Cologne: Böhlau, 1982).

DANA R. VILLA, "TOTALITARIANISM, MODERNITY, AND THE TRADITION"

1. See, for example, Stuart Hampshire's characterization of the Nazi regime in his *Innocence and Experience* (Cambridge, Mass.: Harvard University Press, 1989), pp. 66–72.

2. This is precisely what John Gunnell has done in his stimulating study *Political Theory: Tradition and Interpretation* (Cambridge, Mass.: Winthrop Publishers, 1979).

3. See Elisabeth Young-Bruehl, *Hannah Arendt: For Love of the World*

(New Haven: Yale University Press, 1983), pp. 200–203 for a good discussion of Arendt's general approach to totalitarianism as a phenomenon, one that emphasizes understanding, rather than causal explanation.

4. In a note to her essay "Martin Heidegger at Eighty" in *Heidegger and Modern Philosophy*, edited by Michael Murray (New Haven: Yale University Press, 1978), Arendt writes: "We are still surrounded by intellectuals and so-called scholars, not only in Germany, who, instead of speaking of Hitler, Auschwitz, genocide, and 'extermination' as a policy of permanent depopulation, prefer, according to their inspiration and taste, to refer to Plato, Luther, Hegel, Nietzsche, or to Heidegger, Jünger, or Stefan George, in order to dress up the horrible gutter-born phenomenon with the language of the humanities and the history of ideas" (p. 302).

5. See, for example, Arendt's remarks in the lecture "Concern with Politics in Recent European Thought" in *Essays in Understanding, 1930–1954*, edited by Jerome Kohn (New York: Harcourt Brace, 1994), p. 431, or those in her tribute to Heidegger in "Martin Heidegger at Eighty" in *Heidegger and Modern Philosophy*, p. 302.

6. Hannah Arendt, "A Reply to Eric Voegelin," in *Essays in Understanding*, p. 405.

7. Hannah Arendt, "Understanding and Politics," in *Essays in Understanding*, p. 309.

8. See the second sentence of Arendt's "On the Nature of Totalitarianism: An Essay in Understanding," in *Essays in Understanding*: "Totalitarianism is the most radical denial of human freedom" (p. 328).

9. Hannah Arendt, "What Is Authority?" in *Between Past and Future* (New York: Penguin Books, 1968), pp. 95–97. See also Arendt, "Ideology and Terror: A Form of Government," in *Totalitarianism: Part Three of the Origins of Totalitarianism* (New York: Harcourt Brace Jovanovich, 1968), p. 159, and Arendt, "On the Nature of Totalitarianism," p. 331.

10. Arendt, "On the Nature of Totalitarianism," pp. 339, 353. Cf. "Ideology and Terror," p. 172.

11. Arendt, "On the Nature of Totalitarianism," pp. 336–37.

12. Ibid., p. 330.

13. Arendt, *The Origins of Totalitarianism*, p. 456; Arendt, "Mankind and Terror," in *Essays in Understanding*, p. 304; "On the Nature of Totalitarianism," pp. 328, 342.

14. Arendt, *The Origins of Totalitarianism*, p. 457.

15. Arendt, Arendt, "Mankind and Terror," pp. 297–98; also "On the Nature of Totalitarianism," p. 345.

16. Arendt, "Mankind and Terror," p. 305.

17. Arendt, "Ideology and Terror," p. 163. Cf. Arendt, "On the Nature of Totalitarianism," p. 341.

18. See Arendt, *Eichmann in Jerusalem*.

19. Arendt, "Mankind and Terror," p. 302.

20. Arendt, *The Origins of Totalitarianism*, pp. 439–41.

21. Ibid., p. 471.

22. Arendt, "Ideology and Terror," p. 159.

23. Ibid., p. 162. Needless to say, the very notion of lawfulness is altered when totalitarianism shifts the focus away from positive law (understood as the relatively permanent yet mutable framework that "translates" universal principles for particular men in particular societies) to the "laws of motion" of Nature or History. As Arendt puts it in "On the Nature of Totalitarianism," "The very term 'law' has changed its meaning; from denoting the framework of stability within which human actions were supposed to, and were permitted to, take place, it has become the very expression of these motions themselves" (p. 341).

24. Arendt, "On the Nature of Totalitarianism," p. 353.

25. Arendt, "Ideology and Terror," p. 159.

26. Arendt, "On the Nature of Totalitarianism," pp. 341–43. See also Arendt, "Mankind and Terror," p. 306. I should note that Arendt's emphasis tends to shift depending on context: When assessing totalitarianism's relation to structures of positive law, she stresses its lawlessness (see, for example, "Mankind and Terror," p. 300), but when analyzing the source of its restless activism, she emphasizes its adherence to natural or historical "laws of movement" (see, for example, "On the Nature of Totalitarianism," p. 340).

27. Arendt, "Ideology and Terror," p. 160.

28. Ibid., p. 163.

29. Margaret Canovan, *Hannah Arendt: A Reinterpretation of Her Political Thought* (New York: Cambridge University Press, 1992), p. 13.

30. Arendt, "On the Nature of Totalitarianism," p. 357: "If it were true that there are eternal laws ruling supreme over all things human and demanding of each human being only total conformity, then freedom would be only a mockery, some snare luring one away from the right path; then homelessness would be only a fantasy, an imagined thing, which could be cured by the decision to conform to some recognizable universal law."

31. Arendt, "Ideology and Terror," p. 163. Cf. "On the Nature of Totalitarianism," pp. 342–44. For terror as the essence of totalitarianism, see also "Mankind and Terror," pp. 302–5.

32. "Ideology and Terror," p. 164.

33. Arendt, *The Origins of Totalitarianism*, p. 469.

34. Ibid., p. 438.

35. Ibid.

36. Arendt, "Mankind and Terror," p. 304.

37. Arendt, *The Origins of Totalitarianism*, p. 455.

38. Ibid., pp. 438, 437.

39. Ibid., pp. 447–57.

40. Ibid., p. 457.

41. Arendt, "Mankind and Terror," pp. 305–6.

42. See, for example, Arendt's essay "What Is Freedom?" in *Between Past and Future*, p. 168.

43. See Hannah Arendt, *The Human Condition* (Chicago: University of Chicago Press, 1958), p. 176.

44. Ibid., pp. 38–46.

45. Ibid., p. 322.

46. See Friedrich Nietzsche, *On the Genealogy of Morals,* translated by Walter Kaufmann (New York: Vintage Books, 1989), essay 3, section 9.

47. In "Understanding and Politics," Arendt writes of the totalitarian attempt "to rob man of his nature under the pretext of changing it" (p. 316).

48. See, in this regard, Arendt's invocation of the choral ode from Sophocles' *Oedipus at Colonus* at the end of *On Revolution.* In her translation: "Not to be born prevails over all meaning uttered in words; by far the best in life, once it has appeared, is to go as swiftly as possible whence it came." As George Kateb points out in his *Hannah Arendt: Politics, Conscience, Evil* (Totowa, N.J.: Rowman and Allanheld, 1984), the only thing that redeems life from this tragic wisdom is, in her view, the possibility of political action and freedom (p. 1).

49. Arendt, "Mankind and Terror," pp. 229, 306.

50. Kateb, *Hannah Arendt,* p. 66.

51. Arendt, "Ideology and Terror," pp. 173–75.

52. Ibid., pp. 172, 173.

53. See especially Arendt, *The Human Condition,* pp. 175–99, and my discussion in *Arendt and Heidegger* (Princeton: Princeton University Press, 1996), pp. 90–99.

54. See Seyla Benhabib, *The Reluctant Modernism of Hannah Arendt* (Thousand Oaks, Calif.: Sage, 1996), for a good discussion of what she calls "the narrative structuration of action" in Arendt's work.

55. See, in this regard, Arendt's contention in the essay "Understanding and Politics" that stupidity (understood as the inability to think and to judge) has, with the death of common sense (the *sensus communis,* our "feeling for the world"), become our shared destiny (p. 314).

56. Arendt, *The Origins of Totalitarianism,* p. ix. Cf. the preface to part 1, p. xv.

57. Arendt, "The Image of Hell," in *Essays in Understanding,* pp. 201–2. As Arendt says in her interview with Günter Gaus: "No one ever blamed someone if he 'coordinated' [with the regime] because he had to take care of his wife or child. The worst thing was that some people really believed in Nazism: For a short time, many for a very short time. But that means that they made up ideas about Hitler, in part terrifically interesting things! Completely fantastic and interesting and complicated things! Things far above the ordinary level! I found that grotesque. Today I would say that they were trapped by their own ideas. That is what happened." "What Remains? The Language Remains," in *Essays in Understanding,* p. 11. It seems clear that Heidegger was one of the people Arendt was thinking of when she made this statement.

58. Canovan, *Hannah Arendt,* p. 64.

59. Arendt, draft of "Karl Marx and the Tradition of Western Political Thought," quoted in Canovan, p. 64. This was a lecture Arendt delivered at Princeton in 1953.

60. Arendt, "Project: Totalitarian Elements in Marxism" (Guggenheim book proposal), quoted in Canovan, p. 64.

61. Arendt, *The Human Condition,* pp. 94–101.

62. Arendt, "The Ex-Communists," in *Essays in Understanding,* p. 396.

63. See, for example, Arendt, "What Is Authority?" in *Between Past and Future*, p. 111.

64. Arendt, *The Human Condition*, pp. 50–53.

65. Canovan, *Hannah Arendt*, p. 73.

66. Arendt, "On the Nature of Totalitarianism," p. 355.

67. See, for example, the treatments given it by Jürgen Habermas in *Theory and Practice* (Boston: Beacon Press, 1973) and Seyla Benhabib in *Critique, Norm, and Utopia* (New York: Columbia University Press, 1987).

68. Arendt, *The Human Condition*, pp. 220–30.

69. As Arendt puts it: "Action, as distinguished from fabrication, is near possible in isolation; to be isolated is to be deprived of the capacity to act. Action and speech need the surrounding presence of others no less than fabrication needs the surrounding presence of nature for material, and of a world in which to place the finished product. Fabrication is surrounded by and in constant contact with the world: action and speech are surrounded by and in contact with the web of the acts and words of other men." *The Human Condition*, p. 188.

70. Ibid., p. 190.

71. Arendt, "Ideology and Terror," p. 163; "On the Nature of Totalitarianism," p. 343.

72. Arendt, *The Human Condition*, p. 185. Cf. Arendt's citation of Pascal's famous description of Plato and Aristotle as "amusing themselves" when they turned to consider the "madhouse" of human affairs in Arendt, *Lectures on Kant's Political Philosophy,* edited by Ronald Beiner (Chicago: University of Chicago Press, 1982), p. 22.

73. Arendt, *The Human Condition*, pp. 185, 195.

74. Ibid., p. 195.

75. Ibid., pp. 225–30. Cf. Arendt, "What Is Authority?" in *Between Past and Future*, pp. 104–15. While Aristotle hardly relies on the craftsmanship analogy to anything like the degree that Plato does, and while he emphatically distinguishes between *praxis* and *poiesis, phronesis* and *techne* in the *Nicomachean Ethics,* Arendt still regards him as succumbing to desire to interpret action as a kind of making. I have tried to reconstruct Arendt's argument against Aristotle in chapter 2 of *Arendt and Heidegger.*

76. This is made clear by the alternatives posed in the dialogue *Protagoras* between Socrates' "art of measurement" and Protagoras's allegory of democratic education and judgment.

77. See the famous allegory of the cave in Plato, *Republic,* book 7.

78. The leitmotif of unity runs throughout the *Republic* and takes a variety of forms, from the communism of the Guardians to what Eric Voegelin has called "the somatic unity of the polis." See especially Plato, *Republic,* 423–24, 432a.

79. See ibid., 472c, 484dl, and (especially) 500d.

80. Arendt, "What Is Authority?" p. 110. Cf. Arendt, *The Human Condition,* pp. 225–26.

81. Arendt, "What Is Authority?" p. 97. This reading of the tradition—and of Plato's role in it—obviously has the closest affinities with Heidegger's metahistory of philosophy. It is interesting to note, in this regard, that Arendt specifically cites Heidegger's great essay "Platon's Lehre von der Wahrheit," with its

contrast between correctness (*orthotes*) and discovery or unconcealedness (*Unverborgenheit*). See Arendt, "What Is Authority?" p. 291, n. 16.

82. Arendt, *The Human Condition*, p. 229.

83. Ibid., p. 143.

84. See Martin Heidegger, "Letter on Humanism," in Heidegger, *Basic Writings*, edited by David Farrell Krell (New York: Harper and Row, 1977), pp. 193–94, for a discussion of the "technical relation" set up between thinking and acting by Plato and Aristotle. See also my discussion in *Arendt and Heidegger*, pp. 227–28.

85. Arendt, *The Human Condition*, p. 229.

86. See volume 1 of Karl Popper's *The Open Society and Its Enemies* (Princeton University Press, 1960) and Andre Glucksmann, *The Master Thinkers* (Harper and Row, 1980).

87. Arendt, "What Is Authority?" pp. 95–100.

88. See Arendt's comments on the supposedly "scientific" character of totalitarian ideology in "Ideology and Terror," pp. 166–72. For similar conclusions reached from a perspective not very friendly to Arendt, see Isaiah Berlin, "The Pursuit of an Ideal," in *The Crooked Timber of Humanity* (New York: Vintage Books, 1992).

89. One of the primary differences between the totalitarian project of fabricating mankind and more traditional teleologies is precisely the ongoing, literally endless quality of the former. As long as it exists, totalitarianism must manifest the law of motion of Nature or History, that is, it must keep itself in motion and find ever new groups to eliminate. Otherwise, the motion of Nature or History (the locus of the totalitarian sense of reality as the hidden movement behind appearances) comes to an end, which would be an insupportable contradiction for the totalitarian mind. See Arendt, "Ideology and Terror," p. 162, and "On the Nature of Totalitarianism," p. 341.

90. Arendt, "On the Nature of Totalitarianism," p. 354.

91. See Leo Strauss, *The City and Man* (Chicago: University of Chicago Press, 1963), p. 127.

92. See Philippe Lacoue-Labarthe, *Heidegger, Art, and Politics*, translated by Chris Turner (Oxford: Blackwell, 1990), p. 77.

93. Arendt, "Mankind and Terror," p. 306.

94. Arendt, "Ideology and Terror," p. 158.

95. See Arendt's discussion of the meaning of creative capacity of political action in *The Human Condition*, pp. 175–88. It is precisely this capacity that separates action, in Arendt's mind, from both work and labor.

96. See Hannah Arendt, *On Revolution*.

97. See Judith Shklar, "The Liberalism of Fear," in *Liberalism and the Moral Life*, edited by Nancy Rosenblum, editor (Cambridge, Mass.: Harvard University Press, 1989).

98. Arendt, *The Origins of Totalitarianism*, p. vii.

99. Arendt, "On the Nature of Totalitarianism," p. 344.

100. Judith Shklar, *Ordinary Vices* (Cambridge, Mass.: Harvard University Press, 1984), pp. 5–9.

101. Arendt, "Mankind and Terror," p. 302.

102. Of course, Arendt discusses both constitutionalism and civil rights at some length in *On Revolution,* but she is remarkably dismissive of both. It is interesting to note Arendt's own shift in her discussion of the nature of totalitarian evil, namely, from the Kantian idea of radical evil to her celebrated and widely misunderstood notion of the "banality of evil" in *Eichmann in Jerusalem.* For a good analysis of the issues involved in this shift, see Richard Bernstein's essay "Did Hannah Arendt Change Her Mind?" in *Hannah Arendt: Twenty Years Later,* edited by Jerome Kohn and Larry May (Cambridge, Mass.: MIT Press, 1996).

103. This is clear from her analysis of the "right to have rights," to membership in a political community, as more fundamental than the "rights of man" and as the precondition for the effectiveness of the latter. See Arendt, *The Origins of Totalitarianism,* pp. 290–302.

LILIANE WEISSBERG, "IN SEARCH OF THE MOTHER TONGUE"

1. In regard to recent feminist readings of Hannah Arendt's work, see Bonnie Honig, ed., *Feminist Interpretations of Hannah Arendt* (University Park: Pennsylvania State University Press, 1995); see also the recent anthologies edited by Larry May and Jerome Kohn, *Hannah Arendt: Twenty Years Later* (Cambridge, Mass.: MIT Press, 1996), and by Craig Calhoun and John McGowan, *Hannah Arendt and the Meaning of Politics* (Minneapolis: University of Minnesota Press, 1997).

2. For example, Peter Fuss, "Hannah Arendt's Concept of Political Community," in *Hannah Arendt: The Recovery of the Public World,* edited by Melvyn A. Hill (New York: St. Martin's Press, 1979), 157–76; Lisa Jane Disch, *Hannah Arendt and the Limits of Philosophy* (Ithaca, N.Y.: Cornell University Press, 1994), and Seyla Benhabib, *The Reluctant Modernism of Hannah Arendt,* Modernity and Political Thought 10 (Thousand Oaks, Calif.: Sage, 1996).

3. See Hannah Arendt, *The Origins of Totalitarianism* (New York: Harcourt Brace, 1951), as well as her later work. In regard to the notion of the "example," see Hannah Arendt, *Lectures on Kant's Political Philosophy,* edited by Ronald Beiner (Chicago: University of Chicago Press), 84.

4. Arendt's "Eichmann in Jerusalem" was published in five consecutive issues in the *New Yorker* between February 16 and March 16, *1963. Eichmann in Jerusalem: A Report on the Banality of Evil* appeared in *1963,* as well. A revised version of the book was issued two years later by Viking Press in New York. The German edition of *Eichmann in Jerusalem* was issued in 1964 by Piper Verlag, Munich.

5. Arendt, "Was bleibt? Es bleibt die Muttersprache (1964): Ein Gespräch mit Günter Gaus," in Arendt, *Gespräche mit Hannah Arendt,* edited by Adelbert Reif (Munich: Piper, 1976), 9–34. The interview was originally aired by the Zweites Deutsches Fernsehen, a public television station. It is translated as "What Remains? The Language Remains" in *Essays in Understanding, 1930–1954,* edited by Jerome Kohn (New York: Harcourt Brace, 1994).

6. See, for example, Sander Gilman, *Jewish Self-Hatred: Anti-Semitism and*

the Hidden Language of the Jews (Baltimore: Johns Hopkins University Press, 1986), 74–76.

7. Arendt, quoted in "Was bleibt? Es bleibt die Muttersprache," 15.

8. Arendt, letter to Heinrich Blücher, February 14, 1950, in Hannah Arendt and Heinrich Blücher, Briefe, 1936–1968, edited by Lotte Köhler (Munich: R. Piper, 1996), 214.

9. Theodor W. Adorno, "Engagement," Noten zur Literatur, Gesammelte Schriften 11 (Frankfurt am Main: Suhrkamp, 1974), 422.

10. Arendt, "Was bleibt? Es bleibt die Muttersprache," 24.

11. Karl Kraus, Die dritte Walpurgisnacht (1933); first sentence of part 1: "As to Hitler, nothing comes to my mind." The book appeared posthumously (Munich: Kösel, 1952).

12. See, for example, the last section of collected writings relating to the Eichmann book in Hannah Arendt, The Jew as Pariah: Jewish Identity and Politics in the Modern Age, edited by Ron H. Feldman (New York: Grove Press, 1978), 225–79.

13. Arendt herself uses the word "banal" only once, toward the end of her study on Eichmann, but this book bears, of course, the subtitle A Report on the Banality of Evil.

14. Arendt, letter to Karl Jaspers, December 17, 1946; Hannah Arendt and Karl Jaspers, Correspondence, 1926–1969, edited by Lotte Köhler and Hans Saner, translated by Robert Kimber and Rita Kimber (New York: Harcourt Brace Jovanovich, 1992), 70.

15. See Elisabeth Young-Bruehl, Hannah Arendt: For the Love of the World, (New Haven: Yale University Press, 1982), 56. For a more extended treatment of Hannah Arendt's work on Rahel Varnhagen, see my introduction to Arendt's Rahel Varnhagen: The Life of a Jewess, edited by Liliane Weissberg, translated by Richard Winston and Clara Winston (Baltimore: Johns Hopkins University Press, 1997), 3–65. This introduction offers an earlier version of my discussion of Günter Gaus's interview with Arendt following the publication of her Eichmann in Jerusalem.

16. The first edition, edited by Karl August Varnhagen von Ense, was published in three volumes in 1834 (Berlin: Duncker und Humblot). Arendt's personal, annotated copy is deposited in the Leo Baeck Institute's archive in New York. Hannah Arendt, Rahel Varnhagen: The Life of a Jewess, translated by Richard Winston and Clara Winston (London: East and West Library, 1957). For a critical edition of this translation, see Rahel Varnhagen: The Life of a Jewess (Baltimore: Johns Hopkins University Press, 1997), which is the edition I have cited throughout this essay, and Rahel Varnhagen: Lebensgeschichte einer deutschen Jüdin aus der Romantik (Munich: R. Piper, 1959).

17. Compare Arendt's preface to Rahel Varnhagen, which elaborates on her approach.

18. Bernard Lazare, L'Antisémitisme, son histoire et ses causes (Paris: L. Chailley, 1894). Arendt encountered Lazare's work through her association with Kurt Blumenfeld, a leader of the German Zionist organization. In 1948, she edited a selection of Lazare's writings entitled Job's Dungheap: Essays on Jewish Nationalism and Social Revolution (New York: Schocken Books, 1948).

19. Arendt, *Rahel Varnhagen,* 255.

20. Ibid., 258–59.

21. Arendt, "The Jew as Pariah: The Hidden Tradition" is included in *The Jew as Pariah,* 67–95. See the German version, Arendt, "Die verborgene Tradition," 63, in *Die verborgene Tradition: Acht Essays* (Frankfurt am Main: Suhrkamp, 1976), 63.

22. Arendt, "Die verborgene Tradition," 63.

23. Arendt, "The Jew as Pariah," 83. The German version states it more strongly: "The new, aggressive way of thought . . . is a goal-oriented aggression." See "Die verborgene Tradition," 65.

24. Arendt, "The Jew as Pariah," 84.

25. See Arendt, "Franz Kafka," *Die verborgene Tradition,* 88–89. Compare, for example, Arendt's essay on Lessing and his notion of "Humanity," "On Humanity in Dark Times: Thoughts about Lessing," translated by Clara Winston and Richard Winston, in *Men in Dark Times* (New York: Harcourt Brace & World, 1968), 3–31.

26. Arendt, "Franz Kafka," 96.

27. The essay "Walter Benjamin: 1892–1940," translated by Harry Zohn, serves in a revised version as an introduction to Walter Benjamin, *Illuminations* (New York: Harcourt Brace & World, 1968), 1–55, and was also included in *Men in Dark Times,* 153–206.

28. See Arendt, letter to Karl Jaspers, September 7, 1952, in *Correspondence,* 197.

29. See the extended discussion of Benjamin's notion in Michael Jennings, *Dialectical Images: Walter Benjamin's Theory of Literary Criticism* (Ithaca, N.Y.: Cornell University Press, 1987).

30. Case 67, Arendt Papers, Library of Congress, Washington, D.C.

31. Walter Benjamin, *Berliner Kindheit um Neunzehnhundert,* was first published posthumously and, edited by Theodor W. Adorno in 1950, is reprinted in *Gesammelte Schriften* 4, 1, edited by Tillman Rexroth (Frankfurt am Main: Suhrkamp, 1972), 235–304. Benjamin, "Franz Kafka: On the Tenth Anniversary of His Death," translated by Harry Zohn, in *Illuminations,* 111–40. The essay appeared first in the *Jüdische Rundschau* in 1934.

32. Walter Benjamin, *Berliner Kindheit um Neunzehnhundert,* 302–4. Benjamin, "Franz Kafka," 134.

33. See Arendt, letter to Heinrich Blücher, August 2, 1941; *Briefe, 1936–1968,* 127 and 127 n.

34. Arendt sent Mary McCarthy her essay on Benjamin before it was published in the *New Yorker.* See McCarthy's letter to Arendt, September 19, 1967, in Hannah Arendt and Mary McCarthy, *Between Friends: The Correspondence between Hannah Arendt and Mary McCarthy, 1949–1975,* edited by Carol Brightman (New York: Harcourt, Brace, 1995), 204–5. McCarthy later received the full manuscript of *Men in Dark Times.* See her letter to Arendt, December 16, 1968, in *Between Friends,* 224. For the figure of the little hunchback, see the Brothers' Grimm fairy tale "Das Lumpengesindel."

35. McCarthy, letter to Arendt, December 16, 1968, in *Between Friends,* 225.

AMNON RAZ-KRAKOTZKIN,
"BINATIONALISM AND JEWISH IDENTITY"

1. Most of these essays were republished by Ron Feldman in Hannah Arendt, *The Jew as Pariah: Jewish Identity and Politics in the Modern Age* (New York: Grove Press, 1978).

2. See the descriptions and analysis of Richard J. Bernstein, *Hannah Arendt and the Jewish Question* (Cambridge, Mass.: MIT press, 1996), pp. 101–22, and Martine Leibovici, *Hanna Arendt, une Juive* (Paris: Desclée de Brouwer, 1998), pp. 365–422. Both provide illuminating discussions on the role of the binational attitude in her entire political thinking. For a description of her Zionist involvement, see also Elisabeth Young-Bruehl, *Hannah Arendt: For Love of the World* (New Haven: Yale University Press, 1982), pp. 173–81, 223–31.

3. See Susan Lee Hattis, *The Bi-National Idea in Palestine during Mandatory Times* (Tel Aviv: Shikmona, 1970); Shalom Ratzabi, "The Personalities of Central Europe in 'Brit Shalom' Society," (Ph.D. dissertation, Tel Aviv University, 1995; in Hebrew); Ahron Kedar, "The Ideas of 'Brit Shalom,'" in *Zionist Ideology and Policy* (Jerusalem, 1978; in Hebrew). Elkana Margalit, "Binationalism: An Interpretation of Zionism, 1941–1947," *Studies in Zionism* 4 (1981): 275–312; Hagit Lavski, "German Zionists and the Emergence of Brit Shalom," *Essential Papers on Zionism*, edited by Y. Reinharz and A. Shapira (New York: New York University Press, 1996), 648–70; Meir Margalit, "The Establishment of the 'Ichud' and the Response of the Yishuv to the Reorganization of 'Brit-Shalom,'" *Zionism* 20 (1996): 151–73; in Hebrew).

4. Hannah Arendt, "Zionism Reconsidered," in *The Jew as Pariah*, p. 131.

5. "To Save the Jewish Homeland—There Is Still Time" (May 1948), republished in *The Jew as Pariah*, 178–92.

6. On Magnes's activity, see Arthur Goren, ed., *Dissenter in Zion: From the Writings of Judah L. Magnes* (Cambridge, Mass.: Harvard University Press, 1982).

7. Martin Buber, *A Land of Two Peoples,* edited with commentary by Paul Mendes-Flohr (New York: Oxford University Press, 1983). Gershom Shalom, *Od Davar (Explications and Implications of Jewish Heritage and Renaissance),* vol. 2, edited by Avraham Shapira (Tel Aviv: Am Oved, 1989; in Hebrew).

8. As Edward Said notes, what is not less surprising is that her biographer, Young-Bruehl, mentioned this (p. 456), without any awareness of the contradictions. Edward Said, *The Politics of Dispossession: The Struggle for Palestinian Self-Determination, 1969–1994* (London: Chatto and Windus, 1994), p. 89. Young-Bruehl represents the way Arendt's political texts are often read—as apolitical or "moral." Reading her critically, however, is the only way to follow her own attitude and her self-definition as a political thinker.

9. This was already challenged by many Palestinian observers. See Edward Said, *The Question of Palestine,* revised edition (New York: Vintage, 1992). Said's reading of Zionism "from the standpoint of its victims" provides Arendt's observations their relevant meaning and can direct us to read her into the present political situation in Palestine. See also Edward Said and Christopher Hitch-

ens, eds., *Blaming the Victims: Spurious Scholarship and the Palestinian Question* (London: Verso, 1988).

10. Among them: Benny Morris, Simcha Flapen, Avi Shlaim, Ilan Pappe, Tom Segev, and others.

11. See Bernstein, *Hannah Arendt and the Jewish Question,* pp. 38 ff. Interestingly, later left-wing critics, including those known as "post-Zionists," showed hardly any interest in the writings and observations of Arendt and her contemporaries. One of the reasons for this is their studies on the version of events advanced by the Communist Party, which supported the partition plan and regarded its failure only as the result of a conspiracy of the colonial powers and Arab reactionary leaders. This perception prevented discussion of the plan itself and enabled the acceptance of the Zionist version. Arendt's critical attitude toward Soviet policy led to her exclusion, even by critical writers of the Left. In that context, the role of the Soviet Union in support of partition, and especially in the establishment of Jewish state, was suppressed.

12. Arendt, "Zionism Reconsidered," in *The Jew as Pariah,* 136 ff. These aspects were later elaborated by historians and sociologists such as Gershon Shafir, Baruch Kimmerling, Lev Greenberg, Yoav Peled, Oren Yiftachel, and others.

13. Hannah Arendt, "Peace or Armistice in the Near East?" (1950), in *The Jew as Pariah,* pp. 203, 202.

14. See my "Peace without Arabs: The Discourse of Peace and the Limits of Consciousness," in *After Oslo,* edited by George Giacaman and Dag Jörund Lönning (London: Pluto Press, 1998), pp. 59–76.

15. On Scholem's activity, see David Biale, *Gershom Scholem—Kabbalah and Counter-History,* second edition (Cambridge, Mass.: Harvard University Press, 1982). On the role of "Brit Shalom" in relation to the German background, see the discussions of Ratzabi and Lavski above, note 3. Gershom Scholem, "Bernai Ka Mipalgey?" 2, 1931. Republished in *Od Davar,* p. 75 (in Hebrew).

16. Ibid.

17. This perception has lately been challenged by scholars like Moshe Idel, Yehudah Liebes, and others. See especially Idel's *Messianic Mystique* (New Haven: Yale University Press, 1999).

18. I have discussed this elsewhere. See my "The Golem of Scholem: Messianism and Zionism in the Writings of Rabbi Avraham Isaac HaKohen Kook and Gershom Scholem," in *Politik und Religion in Judentum,* edited by Christoph Miething (Tübingen: Max Niemeyer, 1999).

19. In several letters, Scholem sharply opposed Arendt's reconsideration of Zionism. See Gershom Scholem, *Briefe,* edited by Itta Shedletzki, the Leo Baeck Institute nos. 129–131 (Munich: Beck, 1994), pp. 302–14. See also Shedletzki's comments, pp. 447–54.

20. Bernstein, *Hannah Arendt and the Jewish Question,* 156.

21. Leibovici, *Hannah Arendt,* 376–81.

22. Like Benjamin, they both related and responded in different ways to Carl Schmitt's political theology. See Christoph Schmidt's observations in his "Der heretische Imperativ: Gershom Scholems Kabbalah als politische Theologie?" *Sonderdruck: Zeitschrift für Religions—und Geistesgeschichte* 50, no. 1 (1998): 61–83.

23. Gershom Scholem, "Redemption through Sin," in Scholem, *The Messianic Idea in Judaism* (1938; New York: Schocken, 1971), 78–141. Scholem also developed this perspective in later writings on messianism.

24. Arendt, "Jewish History—Revised," in *The Jew as Pariah*, 96–105. First published in *Jewish Frontier*, March 1948, pp. 34–38.

25. Arendt, *The Jew as Pariah*, pp. 55–121; *The Origins of Totalitarianism*, enlarged edition (New York: Meridian Books, 1958), 54–88.

26. Arendt, "Zionism Reconsidered," 165–68.

27. In this, Arendt adopted the common perception of Jewish history. As was correctly noted by Robert Liberles, here she ignored her close friend Salo W. Baron, who already in 1928 criticized the "lachrymose approach to Jewish History." Robert Liberles, *Salo W. Baron—Architect of Jewish History* (New York: New York University Press, 1995), pp. 10–12.

28. Gershom Scholem, *Walter Benjamin: The Story of a Friendship*, translated by Harry Zohn (New York: Schocken, 1988).

29. Gershom Scholem, *Shabbetai Zvi: The Mystic Messaiah* (Princeton: Princeton University Press, 1973), p. 286. This description refers to his own image as a historian.

30. Hannah Arendt, "Introduction," in Walter Benjamin, *Illuminations*, edited with an introduction by Hannah Arendt, translated by Harry Zohn (New York: Schocken, 1969), p. 34.

31. I have tried to develop this line elsewhere. See my "Exile within Sovereignty," *Theory and Criticism* 4 (1993): 23–46, and *Theory and Criticism* 5 (1994): 114–32 (in Hebrew).

32. This attitude was recently developed by Azmi Bishara. On these grounds, he also emphasized the demand for cultural autonomy for the Arab citizens of Israel. See his "The Arab Minority in Israel, *Theory and Criticism* 3 (1992): 7–20. At the same time, Bishara clarifies that the main issue in Israel is not only the separation of religion from the state, but also the separation of national identity and the state. Bishara developed a binational perspective on many occasions, in both his writings and his political activity as member of the Knesset.

MOSHE ZIMMERMANN, "HANNAH ARENDT, THE EARLY 'POST-ZIONIST'"

1. David Watson, *Arendt* (London, 1992), p. 73; Elisabeth Young-Bruehl, *Hannah Arendt: For Love of the World* (New Haven, 1982), pp. 109, 99.

2. Young-Bruehl, *Hannah Arendt*, chapters 3 and 6; Watson, *Arendt*, chapter 4; Seyla Benhabib, *The Reluctant Modernism of Hannah Arendt* (Thousand Oaks, Calif., 1996), chapter 2. Even Richard J. Bernstein, in *Hannah Arendt and the Jewish Question* (Cambridge, Mass., 1996), does not allocate more than 10 percent of his book to this chapter of her life (pp. 101–22). Benhabib, *The Reluctant Modernism of Hannah Arendt*, p. 36. As Benhabib says, perhaps "the earliest articulation in her thought of local council democracy emerges in the context of her reflections on Jewish-Arab politics in Palestine" (p. 42).

3. Quoted in Young-Bruehl, pp. 361, 139.

4. Hannah Arendt and Kurt Blumenfeld. ". . . *In keinem Besitz verwurzelt*":

Die Korrespondenz, edited by Ingeborg Nordmann and Iris Pilling (Hamburg, 1995), pp. 174–75.

5. Hannah Arendt, "Die 'sogenannte Jüdische Armee,'" May 22, 1942, in *Hannah Arendt: Die Krise des Zionismus,* edited by Eike Geisel & Klaus Bittermann (Berlin, 1989), pp. 182–83, 190.

6. Hannah Arendt, "The Jewish State: Fifty Years After" (May 1946), in *The Jew as Pariah: Jewish Identity and Politics in the Modern Age,* edited by Ron H. Feldman (New York, 1978), p. 172.

7. Hannah Arendt, "Die Krise des Zionismus" (October–November 1942), in *Die Krise des Zionismus,* p. 188.

8. Hannah Arendt, *Eichmann in Jerusalem: A Report on the Banality of Evil* (New York, 1963), p. 8.

9. Hannah Arendt, "Ceterum Censeo" (December 26, 1941), in *Die Krise des Zionismus,* p. 171.

10. Arendt, "Die Krise des Zionismus," p. 193.

11. Arendt, "Ceterum Censeo," pp. 172–73.

12. Hannah Arendt and Karl Jaspers, *Correspondence, 1926–1969,* edited by Lotte Köhler and Hans Saner, translated by Robert Kimber and Rita Kimber (New York, 1992), letter of September 4, 1947, p. 99. Hannah Arendt, "The Jewish State: Fifty Years After," p. 175.

13. Hannah Arendt and Heinrich Blücher, *Briefe, 1936–1968,* edited by Lotte Köhler (Munich, 1996), letter of October 22, 1955, p. 415.

14. Arendt to Jaspers, letter of December 23, 1960, *Correspondence,* p. 416.

15. Arendt to Blücher, letter of April 20, 1961, *Briefe,* p. 522.

16. Arendt, *Eichmann in Jerusalem,* p. 6.

17. Arendt, "Zionism Reconsidered," pp. 141, 147. Hannah Arendt, "To Save the Jewish Homeland," in *The Jew as Pariah,* p. 183.

18. Arendt, "To Save the Jewish Homeland," p. 183.

19. Hannah Arendt, "Balfour-Deklaration und Palästina-Mandat" (May 19, 1944), in *Die Krise des Zionismus,* pp. 207–10.

20. Young-Bruehl, *Hannah Arendt,* p. 223. Arendt, "Zionism Reconsidered," p. 132.

21. Hannah Arendt, "Neue Vorschläge zur jüdisch-arabischen Verständigung" (August 25, 1944), in *Die Krise des Zionismus,* pp. 215–16.

22. Arendt, "Zionism Reconsidered," p. 138.

23. Arendt, "To Save the Jewish Homeland," p. 189.

24. Arendt to Blücher, letter of October 22, 1955, *Briefe,* p. 415.

25. Arendt to Jaspers, letter of December 23, 1960, *Correspondence,* p. 416.

26. Hannah Arendt, "Peace or Armistice in the Mid-East" (1950), in *The Jew as Pariah,* p. 208.

27. Arendt to Jaspers, letter of September 4, 1947, p. 98. Arendt, "Zionism Reconsidered," p. 140.

28. Benhabib, *The Reluctant Modernism of Hannah Arendt,* p. 46.

29. Arendt, "To Save the Jewish Homeland," p. 187.

30. Arendt to Blücher, letter of October 22, 1955, *Briefe,* p. 415.

31. Hannah Arendt, "Can the Jewish-Arab Question Be Solved?" in *Die Krise des Zionismus,* p. 189.

32. Arendt, "To Save the Jewish Homeland" (May 1948), in *The Jew as Pariah,* p. 191.

33. Ibid., p. 192.

34. Arendt, "Peace or Armistice in the Mid-East," pp. 217 ff.

35. Hannah Arendt, "This Means You," "Ceterum Censeo," "Papier und Wirklichkeit," "Die 'sogenannte Jüdische Armee'" (1941–42) in *Die Krise des Zionismus,* pp. 167–83.

36. "Die 'sogenannte Jüdische Armee,'" pp. 182–83. This shows that at least Hannah Arendt did not have to wait another three years in order to discover the enormity of the catastrophe.

37. Hannah Arendt, "Sprengstoff-Spiesser" (June 16, 1944), in *Die Krise des Zionismus,* p. 213.

38. Arendt, "To Save the Jewish Homeland," p. 181.

39. *New York Times,* December 4, 1948.

40. Arendt, *Eichmann in Jerusalem,* p. 5.

41. Ibid., p. 191.

42. Arendt, "Zionism Reconsidered," p. 134.

43. Ibid., p. 160.

44. Arendt to Blücher, letter of April 4, 1961, *Briefe,* p. 518.

45. Arendt, *Eichmann in Jerusalem,* p. 108.

46. Ibid., p. 245.

47. Arendt, "Ceterum Censeo," p. 173.

48. Yet, true to her general vision of a transnational future, she still hoped for a federal Europe that would "render the Jewish problem solvable and may guarantee Jewish settlement in Palestine." Arendt, "Krise des Zionismus."

49. Arendt, "Zionism Reconsidered," pp. 150, 156.

50. Cf. Bernstein, *Hannah Arendt and the Jewish Question,* p. 103.

51. Arendt, "Zionism Reconsidered," p. 146.

52. Arendt to Jaspers, letter of September 7, 1952, *Correspondence,* p. 197.

53. Arendt to Jaspers, letter of September 4, 1947, ibid., p. 98.

54. Arendt, "The Jewish State: Fifty Years After," p. 170.

55. *New York Times,* December 4, 1948.

56. Arendt to Blücher, letter of October 22, 1955, *Briefe,* p. 415.

57. Arendt to Blücher, letter of May 6, 1961, p. 531.

58. Blumenfeld to Arendt, letter of October 1952, ". . . *In keinem Besitz verwurzelt,"* p. 73.

59. Arendt to Blücher, letter of October 22, 1955, *Briefe,* p. 415.

60. Arendt to Blücher, letter of April 20, 1961, *Briefe,* p. 522.

61. Blumenfeld to Arendt, letter of November 5, 1954, ". . . *In keinem Besitz verwurzelt,"* p. 113.

62. Arendt to Blumenfeld, letter of January 14, 1946, ". . . *In keinem Besitz verwurzelt,"* p. 39.

63. Arendt, "The Jewish State: Fifty Years After," p. 177.

64. See, for example, "Peace or Armistice in the Mid-East," pp. 208–9. Arendt to Jaspers, letter of September 4, 1947, *Correspondence,* p. 98.

65. Arendt, "Peace or Armistice in the Mid-East," pp. 212–14.

66. Arendt to Blücher, letter of October 22, 1955, *Briefe,* p. 415.

67. Arendt, "To Save the Jewish Homeland," p. 186.

RICHARD J. BERNSTEIN, "HANNAH ARENDT'S ZIONISM?"

The following abbreviations are used for citing Arendt's work. *EU:* Hannah Arendt, *Essays in Understanding: 1930–1954,* edited by Jerome Kohn (New York: Harcourt Brace, 1994). *JP: The Jew as Pariah: Jewish Identity and Politics in the Modern Age,* edited by Ron H. Feldman (New York: Grove Press, 1978). *OT: The Origins of Totalitarianism* (New York: Harcourt Brace Jovanovich, 1973). *HAKJ:* Hannah Arendt and Karl Jaspers, *Correspondence 1926–1969,* edited by Lotte Köhler and Hans Saner (New York: Harcourt Brace Jovanovich, 1992).

1. In *Hannah Arendt and the Jewish Question* (Cambridge, Mass.: MIT Press, 1996). I have closely followed the development of Arendt's growing interest in and ambivalence toward Zionism. See especially chapter 4, "Zionism: Jewish Homeland or Jewish State?"

MICHAEL R. MARRUS, "*EICHMANN IN JERUSALEM*"

1. Hannah Arendt, *The Jew as Pariah: Jewish Identity and Politics in the Modern Age,* edited by Ron H. Feldman (New York: Grove Press, 1978), 241; Richard I. Cohen, "Breaking the Code: Hannah Arendt's *Eichmann in Jerusalem* and the Public Polemic. Myth, Memory, and Historical Imagination," *Michael* 13 (1993): 57; Richard Wolin, "The Ambivalences of German Jewish Identity," *History and Memory* 8 (fall–winter 1996): 29.

2. Alfred Kazin, *New York Jew* (New York: Knopf, 1978), 218. See Cohen, "Breaking the Code," 29–85.

3. Kazin, *New York Jew,* 91; Dagmar Barnow, *Visible Spaces: Hannah Arendt and the German-Jewish Experience* (Baltimore: Johns Hopkins University Press, 1990), chapter 2.

4. Hannah Arendt, *Eichmann in Jerusalem: A Report on the Banality of Evil* (New York: Viking, 1965), 294.

5. Arendt to Jaspers, in Hannah Arendt and Karl Jaspers, *Correspondence 1926–1969,* edited by Lotte Köhler and Hans Saner, translated by Robert Kimber and Rita Kimber (New York: Harcourt Brace Jovanovich, 1992), 414–15.

6. Ibid., 415.

7. David Ben-Gurion, "The Eichmann Case as Seen by Ben-Gurion," *New York Times Magazine,* December 18, 1960, 7.

8. Arendt, *Eichmann in Jerusalem,* 3, 18.

9. Arendt to Jaspers, *Correspondence,* 423.

10. Ibid., 417.

11. Arendt, *Eichmann in Jerusalem,* 3, 18.

12. Arendt to Jaspers, *Correspondence,* 434–35, 437. Arendt continued: "My first impression: On top, the judges. . . . Below them, the prosecuting at-

torneys, Galicians, but still Europeans. Everything is organized by a police force that gives me the creeps, speaks only Hebrew, and looks Arabic. Some downright brutal types among them. They would obey any order. And outside the door, the oriental mob, as if one were in Istanbul or some other half-Asiatic country. In addition, and very visible in Jerusalem, the peies and caftan Jews, who make life impossible for all the reasonable people here." Ibid., 435.

13. Arendt, *Eichmann in Jerusalem*, 3–4.

14. Arendt to Jaspers, *Correspondence*, 434.

15. Arendt, *Eichmann in Jerusalem*, 7.

16. Ibid., 19.

17. Ibid., 229.

18. Ibid., 54.

19. Ibid., 257.

20. Ibid., 268–69.

21. Ibid., 253.

22. Arendt, *The Jew as Pariah*, 228.

23. Ibid., 295.

24. Arendt, *Eichmann in Jerusalem*, 159, emphasis mine.

25. Ibid., 268.

26. International Military Tribunal, *Trial of the Major War Criminals before the International Military Tribunal, Nuremberg, 14 November 1945–1 October 1946*, 42 vols. (Nuremberg: International Military Tribunal, 1947), 1:179–81. On the place of the Jews in the proceedings, I have written "The Holocaust at Nuremberg," *Yad Vashem Studies* 26 (1998): 4–45.

27. Arendt, *Eichmann in Jerusalem*, 279, 18.

28. Ibid., 272.

29. Ibid., 273.

30. Arendt, *The Jew as Pariah*, 275.

31. Ibid., 253.

32. Elisabeth Young-Bruehl, *Hannah Arendt: For Love of the World* (New Haven: Yale University Press, 1982), 373.

33. Arendt, *The Jew as Pariah*, 235.

YAACOV LOZOWICK, "MALICIOUS CLERKS"

1. Gideon Hausner, *Justice in Jerusalem* (New York: Schocken, 1968), pp. 298 ff.

2. Raul Hilberg's *The Destruction of the European Jews* (Chicago: Quadrangle, 1961), was published concurrently with the trial, and there is no indication that the prosecution was even aware of it.

3. Hannah Arendt, *The Origins of Totalitarianism* (New York: Meridian Books, 1958).

4. Hannah Arendt, *Eichmann in Jerusalem: A Report on the Banality of Evil* (1963; New York: Penguin, 1992).

5. Arendt, *Eichmann in Jerusalem*, pp. 287–88. Italics in the original.

6. For example: "Our investigation of the desk killer has led to the conclusion that he is no aberration, but the product of the developmental logic of

modernity itself; a human type already present *in nuce* in the modern bureaucrat. Marcuse's one dimensional man, Adorno's subjectless subject. Heidegger's they-man and Weber's specialist and man of order, all possess the characteristics out of which the desk murderer, so clearly delineated by Hannah Arendt, can be molded. All that is needed for this transformation to occur is a situation in which a policy of genocide again becomes a necessity of state and an ideology with which to 'justify' such a policy to the population at large. Arendt's philosophical anthropology constitutes a warning of the menacing potential which lies hidden within the very interstices of modernity." Alan Milchman and Alan Rosenberg, "The Holocaust as Portent: Hannah Arendt and the Etiology of the Desk Killer," in G. Jan Colijn and Marcia S. Littell, *The Netherlands and Nazi Genocide.* Papers of the Twenty-First Annual Scholars Conference (Lewiston / Queenston / Lampeter, N.Y.: Edwin Mellon Press, 1992), pp. 300–301.

7. The best description of this is to be found in part 2, chapter 3, "Von der 'Abwehr' zur Prävention," in Ulrich Herbert, *Best: Biographische Studien über Radikalismus, Weltanschauung und Vernunft, 1903–1989* (Bonn: Dietz, 1996).

8. Shlomo Aronson, *Heydrich und die Anfänge des SD und der Gestapo* (Stuttgart: Freie Universität, 1971); George C. Browder, *Foundations of the Nazi Police State: The Formation of Sipo and SD* (Lexington: University of Kentucky Press, 1989).

9. Arendt, *Eichmann in Jerusalem,* p. 32; Adolf Eichmann, *Ich, Adolf Eichmann: Ein historischer Zeugenbericht,* edited by Rudolf Aschenauer (Leoni: Druffel, 1980), p. 65.

10. National Archives microfilm reel T-175 r.411 fr. 2935416–451. A copy can be found at Yad Vashem Archives JM.4712.

11. Hans Safrian, *Die Eichmann Männer* (Vienna: Europaverlag, 1993).

12. National Archives T-175 r.410 fr.2934993–5003, copy at Yad Vashem Archives JM.4711.

13. Yad Vashem Archives, Eichmann trial documents (TR.3) 1278, 1663, TR.3–1265, TR.3–321, 930, 1086.

14. Yad Vashem Archives TR.3–535, 537, 1280, TR.3–1278.

15. Yad Vashem Archives TR.3–306, 744, 746, 1048.

16. Shmuel Spector, "Aktion 1005—Effacing the Murder of Millions," *Holocaust and Genocide Studies* 5, no. 2 (1990); TR.10–767b, pp. 575–77; Eichmann, *Interrogation,* 1:264–65.

17. Christopher Browning, *The Final Solution and the German Foreign Office* (New York: Holmes and Meier, 1978).

18. 1 Js 1/65 (RSHA), Vermerk in the case of Bosshammer, Hartmann, Hunsche, Woehm, 30.4.1969 (Yad Vashem Archives TR.-10.767); 1 Js 1/65 (RSHA), indictment of Bosshammer, 23.4.1971 (Yad Vashem Archives TR.10–754). There are large quantities of additional materials generated in these proceedings, most of them in the office of the prosecutor in Berlin.

19. For example, see the testimony of Elisabeth Marks, who was eighteen years old when she began to work in the department, at the height of its activity. TR.10–754, pp. 485–86, TR.10–767c, pp. 946–48.

20. The single most important documentary source about the SS in the Netherlands is the summary of the evidence prepared for the trial of Harster,

Zoepf, and Slottke by the prosecution in Munich, 14Js 48/59. Yad Vashem Archives TR.10–1243. And see also Zentrale Stelle der Landesjustizverwaltungen, Ludwigsburg (ZSL), 107 AR 689/66 (Yad Vashem Archives TR.10–1284).

21. Jacob Presser, *The Destruction of the Dutch Jews* (New York: E. P. Dutton, 1969), p. 144. He brings eyewitness testimony to the fact that the SS found much to laugh about when arrested Jews were detained in the courtyard of their headquarters.

22. For example, see the protocol of a meeting of the SS officers in France who dealt with Jewish matters, 30.6.1942: Yad Vashem Archives TR.3–59.

23. Perhaps the single most important research project to demonstrate this was Michael Marrus and Robert O. Paxton, *Vichy France and the Jews* (New York: Basic Books, 1981). Their central thesis, now accepted by all mainstream historians, is that the Vichy government acted against its Jews of its own volition.

24. The most accessible collection of the relevant documentation is to be found in Serge Klarsfeld, *Vichy-Auschwitz: Die Zusammenarbeit der deutschen und französischen Behörden bei der "Endlösung der Judenfrage" in Frankreich* (Nördlingen: Delphi Politik, 1989).

25. Ibid., pp. 132, 403; TR.3–698, 8.7.42.

26. The clash of wills between the Italian and the German authorities over the fate of the Jews in the Italian zone can be found in Daniel Carpi, *Between Mussolini and Hitler: The Jews and the Italian Authorities in France and Tunisia* (Hanover, N.H.: Brandeis University Press, 1994), pp. 163 ff. (for the Italian side) and in Klarsfeld, *Vichy-Auschwitz,* pp. 520 ff. (for the German side), as well as in the documentation from the Eichmann trial (Yad Vashem Archives TR.3)

27. The best description of these actions is in Safrian, *Die Eichmann Männer,* chapters 8, 9, and 10.

HANS MOMMSEN, "HANNAH ARENDT'S INTERPRETATION OF THE HOLOCAUST"

1. See F. A. Krummacher, ed., *Die Kontroverse: Hannah Arendt, Eichmann und die Juden* (Munich, 1964).

2. The correspondence has been published in Hannah Arendt, *The Jew as Pariah: Jewish Identity and Politics in the Modern Age,* edited by Ron H. Feldman (New York, 1978), pp. 240 ff.

3. See the German edition, Hannah Arendt, *Eichmann in Jerusalem: Ein Bericht von der Banalität des Bösen,* 5th edition (Munich, 1987), pp. 175 ff. In the English edition, pp. 121–22, 133–34.

4. Letter from Jaspers to Arendt, December 13, 1963, Hannah Arendt and Karl Jaspers, *Briefwechsel 1926–1969,* edited by Lotte Köhler and Hans Saner (Munich, 1985), p. 578. This edition is available in English: *Correspondence, 1926–1969,* edited by Lotte Köhler and Hans Saner, translated by Robert Kimber and Rita Kimber (New York: Harcourt Brace Jovanovich, 1992).

5. Cf. Hans Mommsen, "The Realization of the Unthinkable: The 'Final Solution of the Jewish Question' in the Third Reich," in *The Policies of Genocide. Jews and Soviet Prisoners of War in Nazi Germany,* edited by Gerhard Hirsch-

feld (London, 1986), pp. 126–27; cf. Christopher Browning: "Beyond 'Intentionalism' and 'Functionalism': The Decision for the Final Solution Reconsidered," in Browning, *The Path to Genocide: Essays on Launching the Final Solution* (Cambridge, 1992), pp. 111 ff.

6. Hannah Arendt, *The Origins of Totalitarianism* (New York, 1951).

7. See Raul Hilberg, *The Destruction of the European Jews,* 1st edition (Chicago, 1961); cf. Hilberg's complaint in *Unerbetene Erinnerung: Der Weg eines Holocaust-Forschers* (Frankfurt, 1994); cf. letter from Arendt to Jaspers, April 20, 1964, in *Briefwechsel,* p. 586.

8. Cf. letter from Jaspers to Arendt, December 14, 1960, *Briefwechsel,* 447–48. Eichmann's report was published by *Life* under the title *Eichmann Tells His Own Damning Story,* editions of November 28 and December 5, 1960.

9. Arendt to Jaspers, letter of December 23, 1960, in *Briefwechsel,* p. 453.

10. Arendt, *Origins of Totalitarianism,* p. 433. The German edition used instead the term *"das radikale Böse,"* p. 701; cf. Elisabeth Young-Bruehl, *Hannah Arendt: Leben und Werk* (Frankfurt, 1986), p. 446, and Seyla Benhabib, "Identity, Perspective, and Narrative—Hannah Arendt's 'Eichmann in Jerusalem,'" in *History and Memory* 8, no. 2 (1996): 44.

11. Cf. Young-Bruehl, *Hannah Arendt,* pp. 474–75.

12. Cf. *Eichmann in Jerusalem,* p. 111, where Arendt draws the conclusion that the totality of moral destruction produced by Nazi rule with respect to the upper classes in almost all European societies included the Jewish notables, too.

13. Arendt to Jaspers, letter of December 2, 1960, in *Briefwechsel,* p. 446. The quote is from the English translation, pp. 409–10.

14. See her criticism of the Nuremberg trial and the Jerusalem court for having overlooked the "unprecedentedness" of the crimes against humanity and for referring to historical analogies. *Eichmann in Jerusalem,* pp. 250 ff.

15. Arendt, *The Origins of Totalitarianism,* pp. 648 and 681.

16. Letter from Jaspers to Arendt, December 13, 1963, in *Briefwechsel,* p. 578.

17. See Benhabib, "Identity, Perspective, and Narrative," who concludes that Arendt's general position consisted in an *"anthropological universalism"* (p. 53).

18. George Iggers, *Deutsche Geschichtswissenschaft,* 2d edition (Munich, 1971), pp. 310 ff.

19. Letter from Helmuth James von Moltke to Lionel Curtis, April 18, 1942, in Michael Balfour and Julian Frisby, *Helmuth von Moltke: Leader against Hitler* (London, 1971), p. 185.

20. See Hans Mommsen, "The German Resistance against Hitler and the Restoration of Politics," in *Resistance against the Third Reich, 1933–1945,* edited by Michael Geyer and John Boyer (Chicago, 1994), pp. 151–66.

21. Arendt, *The Origins of Totalitarianism,* pp. 293, 298.

22. Arendt, *Eichmann in Jerusalem,* pp. 253–54. Letter from Arendt to Jaspers, December 23, 1960, in *Briefwechsel,* p. 454.

23. Arendt, *Eichmann in Jerusalem,* pp. 255–56.

24. Letter from Arendt to Jaspers, February 5, 1961, in *Briefwechsel,* p. 459.

25. Arendt, *The Origins of Totalitarianism,* pp. 377–78.

26. Ibid., p. 397.

27. Letter from Arendt to Mary McCarthy, September 10, 1963, in Hannah Arendt and Mary McCarthy, *Im Vertrauen: Briefwechsel 1949–1975*, edited by Carol Brightman (Munich, 1995), p. 234.

28. Mommsen, *Eichmann*, pp. xvi–xvii.

29. Ernst Klee, *"Euthanasie" im NS-Staat: Die Vernichtung "lebensunwerten Lebens,"* 2d edition (Frankfurt, 1985); Hans-Waler Schmuhl, *Rassnhygiene, National-Sozialismus, Euthanasie: Von der Verhütung zur Vernichtung "lebensunwerten Lebens," 1890 bis 1945* (Göttingen, 1987).

30. Letter from Arendt to Jaspers, April 13, 1961, in *Briefwechsel*, p. 471.

31. Arendt, *The Origins of Totalitarianism*, pp. 336, 343–44.

32. Hannah Arendt, "Ideology and Terror," *Review of Politics* 15 (1953): 323–24; Ingeborg Nordensen, *Hannah Arendt* (Frankfurt, 1994), pp. 95–96.

33. See Fritz Stern, *The Politics of Cultural Despair* (New York, 1963). Cf. Hans Mommsen, *The Rise and Fall of Weimar Democracy* (Chapel Hill, 1996), pp. 311 ff.

34. Cf. her letter to Jaspers on April 13, 1961, in *Briefwechsel*, p. 471.

35. See Christopher Browning, *Ordinary Men: Reserve Police Battalion 101 and the Final Solution in Poland* (New York, 1992), pp. 184 ff.; see also Browning, "Ordinary Men or Ordinary Germans," in *Unwilling Germans: The Goldhagen Debate,* edited by Robert R. Shandley (Minneapolis, 1998), pp. 55–74.

36. Hannah Arendt, *Elemente und Ursprünge totaler Herrschaft* (Berlin, 1968), 256; cf. my introduction to *Eichmann in Jerusalem,* new edition (Munich, 1986), p. xxv.

LEORA BILSKY, "BETWEEN JUSTICE AND POLITICS"

I would like to thank the participants in the faculty seminar in the Tel Aviv Law School and participants in the seminar of the American Bar Foundation for their comments on drafts of this paper. The paper is part of a book tentatively titled *Israeli Political Trials: The Struggle over Israeli Collective Identity* (University of Michigan Press, forthcoming).

1. Cr. C. (Jm.) 40/61 *Attorney General v. Adolf Eichmann,* P.M. 45 (1965), 3.

2. Lawyers also provide contrasting (uninterrupted) narratives in their opening and closing statements.

3. Gideon Hausner, *Justice in Jerusalem* (New York, 1966), pp. 322–24; *The Eichmann Trial: Prosecution's Opening Statement* (Jerusalem, 1974; in Hebrew), p. 7.

4. Hannah Arendt, *Eichmann in Jerusalem: A Report on the Banality of Evil,* revised edition (New York, 1994), pp. 223–25, 19–20, 268–70, 277–79.

5. Hausner, *Justice in Jerusalem*, p. 465.

6. By "correct," I refer to their wish to provide the master story that will determine the temporal and spatial framework of the trial, the choice of protagonists, the question of voice, and so on. Both Arendt and Hausner understood the centrality of the trial's narrative for all subsequent stories, hence the fierce contest between them.

7. The distinction between "author" and "storyteller" according to Arendt has to do with her understanding of the nature of our agency as human beings and our recognition of our interdependence, our reliance on others' points of view and stories. "Nobody is the author or the producer of his own life story. In other words, the stories, the result of action and speech, reveal an agent, but this agent is not an author. . . . Somebody began it and is its subject in the twofold sense of the word, namely, its actor and sufferer, but nobody is its author." Hannah Arendt, *The Human Condition* (Chicago, 1958), p. 184.

8. Another spatial division is geographical. Hausner wanted to include in his trial's narrative the fate of all the Jewish centers in Europe, Western, Central, and Eastern. Arendt, on the other hand, argued that the trial's narrative should be limited to Western and Central Europe, where Eichmann's actions took place.

9. Hausner, *Justice in Jerusalem*, p. 340. Cr. C. 124/53 *Attorney General* v. *Gruenwald*, 44 P.M. 3 (1965).

10. Cr. C. 124/53 *Gruenwald*, p. 51; Cr. A. 232/55 *Attorney General* v. *Gruenwald* P.D. 12(3) (1958), 2017. For further elaboration on this topic, see Leora Bilsky, "Justice or Reconciliation: The Politicization of the Holocaust in the Kastner Trial," in *Lethe's Law: Justice, Law, and Ethics in Reconciliation,* edited by Emilios Christodoulidis and Scott Veitch (forthcoming).

11. The Kastner trial was not the first time the victims were put on trial. In the 1950s, several criminal trials were conducted against Jewish policemen and *Kapos*. Nevertheless, the Kastner trial was the first one against a Jewish leader who cooperated with the Nazis. Hannah Yablonka, "The Law of Punishment for Nazis and Their Collaborators," *Kathedra* 82 (1996): 135–52 (in Hebrew).

12. These "repeat players" included Gabriel Bach, who was the assistant to the attorney general, Judge Benjamin Halevi, Justice Simon Agranat, and a long line of witnesses including Joel Brand, Hansi Brand, Pinchas Freudiger, and others.

13. Hausner, *Justice in Jerusalem*, p. 341.

14. Hansi Brand's testimony in *The Eichmann Trial: Testimonies* (Jerusalem, 1974; in Hebrew), 7:933.

15. Hausner, *Justice in Jerusalem*, p. 341. Pinchas Freudiger's testimony in *The Eichmann Trial: Testimonies* 7:734–74 (in Hebrew). The official transcript is not supposed to include remarks from the audience, but in Freudiger's case, as Arendt reported (*Eichmann in Jerusalem*, p. 124), the witness replied, "What could we have done? What could we have done?" and the presiding judge responded, "I do not think this is an answer to the question," a question that was raised by the audience, not the court. The judge's and the witness's words are, no doubt, relevant to the official transcript, but they do not appear there. Compare to the transcript of Yehiel Dinur's testimony, where traces of his confusion and collapse on the witness stand are evident.

16. "That the prosecution in Jerusalem, so careful not to embarrass the Adenauer administration, should have avoided, with even greater and more obvious justification, bringing this chapter of the story into the open was almost a matter of course" (*Eichmann in Jerusalem*, p. 119). "The testimony of Mrs. Charlotte Salzberger on Theresienstadt . . . permitted us to cast at least a glance into this neglected corner of what the prosecution kept calling the 'general picture'"

(Ibid., p. 120); "they were only too glad not to 'elaborate' on this side of their story" (Ibid., p. 121); "the gravest omission from the 'general picture' was that of a witness to testify to the cooperation between the Nazi rulers and the Jewish authorities" (Ibid., p. 124).

17. Arendt, *Eichmann in Jerusalem*, pp. 112–34. Hausner, *Justice in Jerusalem*, pp. 294–95.

18. Pnina Lahav, *Judgment in Jerusalem: Chief Justice Simon Agranat and the Zionist Century* (Berkeley, 1997), pp. 121–65; Hannah Yablonka, "The Law for Punishment of the Nazis and Their Collaborators," 135–52 (in Hebrew). The only "legitimate" voices at the time were those of survivors who belonged to the Jewish resistance and underground.

19. Michael Keren, "Ben Gurion's Theory of Sovereignty: The Trial of Adolf Eichmann," in *Politics and Leadership in Israel,* edited by Ronald W. Zweig (London, 1991), p. 46. Hausner, who tried to facilitate the move from accusing the victims to accusing the victimizers and who therefore attempted to create a wall between the trials, had to walk a fine line because the Jewish leaders who negotiated with Eichmann, such as Hansi Brand and Pinchas Freudiger, were among the most relevant witnesses for proving Eichmann's guilt, since they met him face to face. For elaboration on this point, see Leora Bilsky, "Breaking the Acoustic Wall between Kastner's Trial and Eichmann's Trial," in *Forum for Israeli Legal History,* edited by Ron Harris and Sandy Kedar (forthcoming).

20. Letter from Arendt to Karl Jaspers, December 23, 1960, in *Correspondence, 1926–1969,* edited by Lotte Köhler and Hans Saner, translated by Robert Kimber and Rita Kimber (New York, 1992), pp. 414, 417.

21. The criticism of Arendt's book concentrated on two issues: the inclusion of the chapter on the *Judenräte* and her thesis about the banality of evil. Both these issues, the critics argued, obscured the distinction between victims and perpetrators. Lionel Abel, "The Aesthetics of Evil: Hannah Arendt on Eichmann and the Jews," *Partisan Review* (summer 1963): 211; Marie Syrkin, "Hannah Arendt: The Clothes of the Empress," *Dissent* (autumn 1963): 341; Marie Syrkin, "Miss Arendt Surveys the Holocaust," *Jewish Frontier* (May 1963): 7. In some reviews, Arendt was even accused of taking it upon herself to provide the legal defense for Eichmann. See, for example, Norman Podhoretz, "Hannah Arendt on Eichmann—A Study in the Perversity of Brilliance," *Commentary* (September 1963): 201.

22. Arendt to McCarthy, October 3, 1963, in *Between Friends: The Correspondence of Hannah Arendt and Mary McCarthy 1949–1975,* edited by Carol Brightman (New York, 1995), p. 151.

23. Arendt, *Eichmann in Jerusalem*, p. 5: "And Ben-Gurion, rightly called the 'architect of the state,' remains that invisible stage manager of the proceedings . . . in the courtroom he speaks with the voice of Gideon Hausner, the Attorney General, who, representing the government, does his best, his very best, to obey his master. And if, fortunately, his best often turns out not to be good enough, the reason is that the trial is presided over by someone who serves Justice as faithfully as Mr. Hausner serves the State of Israel." Ibid., pp. 253. 119–21, 124, 225.

24. Ibid., pp. 125–26.

25. Arendt might have thought that understanding the background of the total moral collapse could better serve the dictates of justice because it would have served to question traditional legal doctrines about criminal responsibility within a criminal state. See my article "When Actor and Spectator Meet in the Courtroom: Reflections on Hannah Arendt's Concept of Judgment," *History and Memory* 8, no. 2 (1996): 137–73. However, as I argue below, Arendt's interest in the moral collapse under Nazi totalitarian regime went beyond the issue of assigning legal responsibility. She worried about the possible repetition of this phenomenon in the future and therefore sought to comprehend its historical origins.

26. Hannah Arendt, "Truth and Politics," in *Between Past and Future: Eight Exercises in Political Thought* (New York, 1968), p. 227: "[The controversy] may also serve as an example of what happens to a highly topical subject when it is drawn into that gap between past and future which is perhaps the proper habitat of all reflections."

27. Peter Brooks and Paul Gewirtz, eds., *Law's Stories, Narrative and Rhetoric in the Law* (New Haven, 1996), pp. 2–13.

28. Elazar Weinrib, "The Fall and Rise of the Historical Narrative," *Zmanim* 52 (1995): 20–29 (in Hebrew); Hans Kellner, "Narrativity in History: Post-Structuralism and Since," *History and Theory* 26 (1987): 1–29.

29. As Ben-Gurion, Israel's prime minister, declared: "We want to establish before the nations of the world how millions of people, because they happened to be Jews, and one million babies, because they happened to be Jewish babies, were murdered by the Nazis." Quoted in Arendt, *Eichmann in Jerusalem*, p. 9. See also Tom Segev, *The Seventh Million: The Israelis,* translated by Haim Watzman (New York, 1993), p. 333.

30. "The judicial process has ways of its own, laid down by law, and these do not change, whatever the subject of the trial may be. . . . The court does not have at its disposal the tools required for the investigation of general questions. Accordingly, its ability to describe general events is inevitably limited." Cr. C. (Jm.) 40/61 *Attorney General* v. *Adolf Eichmann*, p. 16.

31. Walter Benjamin, "The Storyteller," in *Illuminations,* translated by Harry Zohn (New York, 1968), p. 86.

32. Moreover, for Benjamin, the unique quality of judgment through storytelling comes from the fact that it always springs from a human experience and remains close to it.

33. Hayden White, "The Value of Narrativity in the Representation of Reality," in *On Narrative,* edited by W. J. T. Mitchell (Chicago, 1981), p. 20. See also pp. 14, 22. White cites Croce: "where there is no narrative there is no history," and Peter Gay: "Historical narration without analysis is trivial, historical analysis without narration is incomplete" (p. 6).

34. Robert Cover, "Nomos and Narrative," in *Narrative, Violence, and the Law,* edited by Martha Minow, Michael Ryan, and Austin Sarat (Ann Arbor, 1992), p. 96.

35. The question of audience is treated by Arendt in the first pages of her book (9–12). Arendt criticizes the supposed "lessons" directed to the different audiences (the world, world Jewry, Israelis, Arabs) advocated by Ben-Gurion

and carried forward by Hausner. She does not discuss the audience of her report (readers of the *New Yorker*) and how imagining this audience has shaped her narrative. Jennifer Ring discusses this issue in *The Political Consequences of Thinking: Gender and Judaism in the Work of Hannah Arendt* (Albany, 1997) pp. 91–108.

36. White, "The Value of Narrativity," p. 13.

37. See Saul Friedlander, ed., *Probing the Limits of Representation: Nazism and the "Final Solution"* (Cambridge, Mass., 1996).

38. Arendt to Jaspers, December 23, 1960, in *Correspondence*, p. 417.

39. For discussions of the cyclical structure of Jewish historiography, see Yosef Hayim Yerushalmi, *Zakhor: Jewish History and Jewish Memory* (Seattle, 1982), and Amos Funkenstein, *Perceptions of Jewish History* (Berkeley, 1993), 54–55.

40. Arendt, *Eichmann in Jerusalem*, p. 13. Arendt notes that the trial revealed that all rumors about Eichmann's connection with Haj Amin el Husseini, the former Mufti of Jerusalem, were unfounded.

41. For a discussion of the reasons for this omission in the Nuremberg trials see Lawrence Douglas, "Film as Witness: Screening *Nazi Concentration Camps* before the Nuremberg Tribunal," *Yale Law Journal* 105 (1995): 449, 459–63, and Michael R. Marrus, "The Holocaust at Nuremberg," *Yad Vashem Studies* 26 (1998): 5.

42. Enacted by the Law for Punishment of the Nazis and Their Collaborators (1950).

43. Arendt, *Eichmann in Jerusalem*, p. 19.

44. White, "The Value of Narrativity," p. 18.

45. A narrative account is authorized by the court by reproducing it as eyewitness testimony, going through cross-examination, and receiving the stamp of approval from the judgment of the court.

46. Arendt to Mary McCarthy, September 20, 1963, in *Between Friends*, p. 148. Arendt insists on the nature of her book as a "report" on several occasions in her correspondence with McCarthy. Ibid., pp. 146, 147, 148, 152.

47. Arendt, "Truth and Politics," pp. 264, 238–39.

48. Hausner, *Justice in Jerusalem*, p. 291.

49. Arendt, "Truth and Politics," p. 262.

50. Arendt explained that recounting the facts is not enough for history telling because "reality is different from, and more than, the totality of facts and events. . . . Who says what is—always tells a story, and in this story the particular facts lose their contingency and acquire some humanly comprehensible meaning." "Truth and Politics," pp. 261–62.

51. "The political function of the storyteller—historian or novelist—is to teach acceptance of things as they are. Out of this acceptance, which can also be called truthfulness, arises the faculty of judgment." Arendt, "Truth and Politics," p. 262.

52. In fact, Hausner's frame for his story can be explained in light of the two preceding Holocaust trials, Kastner's and the Nuremberg Tribunal's. Kastner's trial, which took place in Israel during the 1950s, produced a public narrative divided by political affiliations and did not produce catharsis or closure. For this

reason, Hausner decided to split the story in two and not to discuss the *Judenräte* behavior in the trial of Eichmann. The Nuremberg trials obliterated the Jewish story because they adopted a limited interpretation of crimes against humanity within the framework of waging an aggressive war. As a reaction to this, Ben-Gurion decided to conduct a trial in Israel that would tell the story of the Jewish victims under the Nazi regime. To facilitate this story, Hausner had to emphasize the framework of "crimes against the Jewish people." Together, the two previous trials can explain the prosecutorial decisions of Hausner in the Eichmann trial.

53. Even though the Supreme Court inverted the verdict of the trial court, its judgment did not provide the needed closure to the affair. This might stem from the fact that the judgment was rendered after the assassination of Kastner and hence could be understood as a gesture of clearing his name. Another reason might stem from the structural difference between a trial court and an appellate court. In the first, the dramaturgical elements are strong, and therefore the trial tends to capture the imagination of the public. The appellate court is generally concerned with questions of law, and not of fact. It does not admit witnesses and reaches its decisions on the basis of documents.

54. The survivors experienced feelings of shame and self-blame for their actions under Nazi rule. Their survival was interpreted by a large part of the Israeli public as a sign of their culpability. The trials of the 1950s against *Kapos* (Jewish functionaries), culminating in the Kastner trial, only enhanced these feelings because the survivors saw themselves standing in the defense box together with the accused. Only with the Eichmann trial, which put Eichmann in the defense box and assigned the role of witnesses for the prosecution to the survivors, could they begin to overcome these feelings.

55. Hausner's framework was also compatible with the Zionist narrative of the negation of the Diaspora, which depicts the life of Jews in the Diaspora as a monolithic story of persecutions and assigns to the Jew the role of the eternal, passive victim.

56. Arendt, *Eichmann in Jerusalem*, p. 119.

57. Arendt, "Truth and Politics," p. 236.

58. For Arendt, collective self-deception is more dangerous than simple lying because it is accompanied with violence toward individuals within the group who try to resist this mechanism and because it is more likely to succeed on a larger scale. Ibid., p. 253. The connections between speech, community, and reality are captured in Arendt's interpretation of the notion of "common sense," *sensus communis*. See *The Human Condition*, p. 208.

59. Ibid., p. 258.

60. Ibid.

61. Arendt first dealt with the connection between self-deception and reiterations in her biography of Rahel Varnhagen. Hannah Arendt, *Rahel Varnhagen: The Life of a Jewess,* edited by Liliane Weissberg, translated by Richard Winston and Clara Winston (Baltimore, 1997). Arendt writes about the "lessons" that Rahel learned from her experience of self-deception (pp. 163–64): "For to the world and in the world the only things of permanence were those that could be communicated. Uncommunicated and incommunicable things which had

been told to no one and had made no impression upon anyone, which had never entered the consciousness of the ages and had sunk without importance into the chaos of oblivion—such things were condemned to reiteration; they had to be reiterated because although they had really happened, they had found no permanent resting-place in reality. . . . It took reiteration to make Rahel learn to dread forgetting. Pure continuance of life, with accompanying loss of her own history, could only mean 'leaping from hell to hell forever.'" Arendt connects the need to tell one's story with the fear of reiteration. Not telling her story condemns Rahel to repeat the same experience with no gain in knowledge. Forgetting cannot erase the experience—it just leaves it with no "resting-place," thus condemning her to repeat it. Translating these insights to the collective level, it seems that the importance of telling the story of the Jewish *Judenräte* in the court of law had a therapeutic purpose, in Arendt's view. It enabled a community to relate a story out of the past experiences of its people and thus to find a place for these experiences in a history. This gives the past a "permanent place" and hence allows the community to break away from the cycle of repetitions.

62. Arendt, *Eichmann in Jerusalem*, p. 269.

63. Ibid, p. 273: "It is in the very nature of things human that every act that has once made its appearance and has been recorded in the history of mankind stays with mankind as a potentiality long after its actuality has become a thing of the past" (p. 273).

64. This can also be seen in the choice of beginning—Hausner's opening statement begins with the Holocaust of the Jews, while Arendt's report begins with a chapter on Eichmann's biography.

65. Arendt, *Eichmann in Jerusalem*, p. 12.

66. Arendt to Jaspers, December 23, 1960, *Correspondence*, p. 417. Arendt's exclusion of the testimonies of victims about their suffering can be explained by her understanding of the private / public division. A trial falls under the public realm, from which she excludes the body and the emotions embodied in the victims' testimonies. See Arendt, *The Human Condition*, pp. 22–78.

67. Arendt, *Eichmann in Jerusalem*, p. 211. This either / or choice (survivor's testimonies versus documents) also points to the existence of two separate worlds created by the totalitarian regime, worlds that are difficult to bridge: the world of the victim (testimonies) and the world of the perpetrators (documents).

68. Hausner, *Justice in Jerusalem* p. 291. The dilemma was even more complicated because the survivors who actually knew Eichmann were often Jewish functionaries. Moreover, many of the survivors (hence the potential witnesses) were from Hungary, and in their testimonies they were likely to bring forward the Kastner affair. Thus, the procedural decision to rely on oral testimonies had the potential to undermine the narrative framework that excluded the chapter on the *Judenräte*.

69. Lawrence L. Langer, *Holocaust Testimonies: The Ruins of Memory* (New Haven, 1991).

70. Hausner, *Justice in Jerusalem*, p. 294.

71. Arendt, *Eichmann in Jerusalem*, pp. 223–24. Hausner also describes the effects of "deep memory" on the testimony of Kastner's partner, Joel Brand, who was sent from Hungary to promote the plan of "trucks for blood." Hausner

writes: "I realized that the man was no more than a receptacle for memories. He had no present; his life had stopped long ago . . . for every day ten thousand Hungarian Jews were being sent to their deaths." Ibid., p. 344.

72. To enable their testimonies, Hausner relaxed the ordinary framework of questions and answers of a courtroom investigation. Arendt harshly criticized this divergence from the trial's procedure: "[The prosecution] simply refused to guide its witnesses. The witnesses behaved like speakers at a meeting chaired by the Attorney General, who introduced them to the audience before they took the floor." Arendt, *Eichmann in Jerusalem*, p. 121. Arendt was unaware of the possible effect of the Kastner trial, where the survivors' voices were erased under the framework of the lawyer's questions on this procedural decision. See, for example, the testimony of Danzig (Cr. C. 123/53 *Gruenvald*, pp. 85–88; Cr. A. 232/55 *Gruenvald*, p. 2117).

73. For an elaboration of the internal conflict in Arendt between the two traditions, see Ring, *Political Consequences*, pp. 231–41.

74. Hannah Arendt, *Thinking* (New York, 1971), p. 112. Arendt is probably thinking about the hierarchy embedded in the relations between the one who speaks (God) and the one who obeys (the Jewish subject). This hierarchy is due less to the difference between sight and hearing, however, than to the fact that God is *both* the one who sees everything and the one who speaks, while the Jewish subject can only hear the voice of God, without seeing its face.

75. In *Lectures on Kant's Political Philosophy*, Arendt suggests that the faculty of judgment springs from our sense of taste, which is more subjective than the sense of sight. Hannah Arendt, *Lectures on Kant's Political Philosophy*, edited by Ronald Beiner (Chicago, 1982), p. 64.

76. For example, the defense attorney in Kastner's trial used the adversarial structure of the testimonies to reenact in the courtroom the tragic choice between prominent Jews (the witnesses for the prosecution) and the masses who were sent to extermination (the witnesses for the defense). See Bilsky, *Reconciliation or Justice*. For a general discussion of the dramaturgical qualities of courtroom representation of the past, see Mark Osiel, *Mass Atrocity, Collective Memory, and the Law* (New Brunswick, N.J., 1997).

77. Milner Ball, "The Play's the Thing: An Unscientific Reflection on Courts under the Rubric of Theater," *Stanford Law Review* 28 (1975): 81. For example, many rape victims complain of a second symbolic rape that they experience in their cross-examination in the courtroom. The difference between a "healthy" and a "pathological" reenactment seems to lie in the different settings for representing a traumatic past experience. When the courtroom provides a forum for a controlled repetition of a painful past, it can empower the victim who relates the experience. When the speech situation in the courtroom repeats the same structures of the powerlessness of the victim outside the courtroom, it can be harmful for her. For an elaboration of the importance of the speech setting for the telling of a traumatic past experience, see Susan J. Brison, "Outliving Oneself: Trauma, Memory, and Personal Identity," in *Feminists Rethink the Self*, edited by Diana Tietjens Meyers (Boulder, Colo., 1997), pp. 12–39.

78. Dori Laub, "An Event without a Witness: Truth, Testimony, and Survival, in *Testimony—Crises of Witnesses in Literature, Psychoanalysis, and His-*

tory, edited by Shoshana Felman and Dori Laub (New York, 1992), pp. 80–82. Shoshana Felman, "The Return of the Voice: Claude Lanzmann's *Shoah*," in *Testimony*, p. 208: "The Nazis see to it that both the Jews and the extermination will remain unseen, invisible: the death camps are surrounded, for that purpose, with a screen of trees." Arendt discusses this point in her article on concentration camps: Hannah Arendt, "Social Science Techniques and the Study of Concentration Camps," *Jewish Social Studies* 12 (1950): 49, 59–60: "Most difficult to imagine and most gruesome to realize is perhaps the complete isolation which separated the camps from the surrounding world as if they and their inmates were no longer part of the world of the living. . . . From the moment of his arrest, nobody in the outside world was supposed to hear of the prisoner again; it is as if he had disappeared from the surface of the earth."

79. Arendt explains how a totalitarian system works to produce "holes of oblivion" into which all deeds, good and evil, disappear. Arendt, *Eichmann in Jerusalem*, p. 232.

80. In the Eichmann trial, the willingness to give voice to the suffering of the victims was intended to make them *visible*, to give them a public stage.

81. Douglas, "Film as Witness."

82. Cited in Felman and Laub, *Testimony*, p. 210, quoting from the film *Shoah* by Claude Lanzmann: "The Germans even forbade us to use the words 'corpse' or 'victim.' The dead were blocks of wood, shit. The Germans made us refer to the bodies as *Figuren*, that is, as puppets, as dolls, or as *Schmattes*, which means 'rags.'"

83. Arendt, "Concentration Camps," p. 60: "Total domination is achieved when the human person, who somehow is always a specific mixture of spontaneity and being conditioned, has been transformed into a completely conditioned being whose reactions can be calculated even when he is led to certain death." Indeed, one of the strongest motivations of victims to survive was to tell the story. Hausner cites the words of one survivor: "When I was hiding out in Warsaw after the ghetto revolt, I thought I was the only Jew who had remained alive out of the millions of Jews in Poland. I knew I had to live to tell the world what had happened, after Hitler's defeat." Hausner, *Justice in Jerusalem*, 293. See also Primo Levi, *The Drowned and the Saved*, translated by Raymond Rosenthal (New York, 1988).

84. This could explain some of the differences between the Eichmann trial and the trial of the prison camp guard John (Ivan) Demanjuk that took place in Israel in 1986 because the testimonies of survivors had to be heard against a very different historical and social background.

85. Isaiah Trunk, *Judenrat: The Jewish Councils in Eastern Europe under Nazi Occupation* (New York, 1972), pp. 561–69.

86. If we take into account this silence of the survivors during the 1950s, we see that the omission of the chapter on Kastner from Eichmann's trial was intended by Hausner to enable the testimonies of survivors. Arendt was wrong to think that the silencing was only on Hausner's side. If she had had her way and the Kastner affair had become a central chapter in the Eichmann trial, it might be that the result would have been the continued silencing of Holocaust survivors. As an outsider to Israeli society, Arendt enjoyed a perspective that al-

lowed her to develop a counterstory, but she also suffered from a lack of understanding of internal processes within Israeli society in relation to the Holocaust.

87. This is especially important in light of survivors' testimonies about Nazis' remarks that no one would believe their story if they survived.

88. See Leora Bilsky, "Giving Voice to Women: An Israeli Case Study," *Israel Studies* 3 (1998).

89. One man will always be left alive to tell the story." In a letter to McCarthy, Arendt explains how she came to change her mind about the existence of "holes of oblivion" after the Eichmann trial. Arendt to McCarthy, September 20, 1963, in *Between Friends*, p. 147.

90. Arendt, *Eichmann in Jerusalem*, p. 229.

RICHARD I. COHEN, "A GENERATION'S RESPONSE
TO *EICHMANN IN JERUSALEM*"

1. For a more extensive study of the controversy, see my "Breaking the Code: Hannah Arendt's *Eichmann in Jerusalem* and the Public Polemic—Myth, Memory, and Historical Imagination," *Michael* 8, edited by Dina Porat and Shlomo Simonsohn (Tel Aviv, 1993): 29–85, and references there to older literature. My thanks to the director of The Diaspora Research Institute of Tel Aviv University for permission to reproduce portions of that essay in this article. My thanks to Yael Richler of the Hebrew University for her assistance with this paper.

2. Raul Hilberg, *The Politics of Memory: The Journey of a Holocaust Historian* (Chicago, 1996), pp. 147–57.

3. See Steven E. Aschheim, "Archetypes and the German-Jewish Dialogue: Reflections Occasioned by the Goldhagen Affair," *German History* 15 (1997): 240–50. *Eichmann in Jerusalem* also has been translated into Spanish, Portuguese, and Swedish.

4. See the enlightening discussion by Richard J. Bernstein on this issue in *Hannah Arendt and the Jewish Question* (Cambridge, Mass., 1996), pp. 147–53; also, idem, "Did Hannah Arendt Change Her Mind? From Radical Evil to the Banality of Evil," *Hannah Arendt: Twenty Years Later,* edited by Larry May and Jerome Kohn (Cambridge, Mass., 1996), pp. 136–44.

5. Cf. Seyla Benhabib, "Identity, Perspective, and Narrative in Hannah Arendt's *Eichmann in Jerusalem,*" *History and Memory* 8 (1996): 37. Benhabib claims that the issue of the detention of Eichmann and the Israeli trial was also a major source of conflict over the book. To my mind, it did not figure prominently in the controversy in the 1960s.

6. See, for example, Shmuel Ettinger, "Jew-Hatred in Its Historical Context," *Antisemitism through the Ages,* edited by Shmuel Almog (Oxford, 1988), pp. 2–3; cf. Arthur Hertzberg, *The French Enlightenment and the Jews* (New York, 1968), pp. 6–7. It would be interesting to pursue this issue further, because no attempt has been made to document the extent to which Arendt's thesis of anti-Semitism has been integrated into the study of the phenomenon. See Steven E. Aschheim, "Nazism, Culture and *The Origins of Totalitarianism:* Hannah Arendt and the Discourse of Evil," *New German Critique* 70 (1997): 117–39, esp. 117–21.

7. This argument and its ensuing polemic were published in the Hebrew journal *Zion,* 1992–1993; however, the discussion resonated in various academic circles. Yuval's arguments will appear in English in *Two Nations in Your Womb: Perceptions of Jews and Christians,* to be published by the University of California Press.

8. Cf. the argument made by Amos Funkenstein, "Jewish History among Thorns," *Zion* 40 (1995): 335–47 (in Hebrew), p. xxii (English abstract).

9. Christopher R. Browning, *Ordinary Men: Reserve Police Battalion 101 and the Final Solution in Poland* (New York, 1992), p. 216.

10. Hannah Arendt, *Rahel Varnhagen: The Life of a Jewess,* first complete edition, edited by Liliane Weissberg, translated by Richard Winston and Clara Winston (Baltimore, 1997), pp. 148–49.

11. Browning, *Ordinary Men,* p. 216. Gertrude Himmelfarb, *On Looking into the Abyss: Untimely Thoughts on Culture and Society* (New York, 1995), p. 44.

12. Daniel J. Goldhagen, *Hitler's Willing Executioners: Ordinary Germans and the Holocaust* (New York, 1996), p. 406.

13. Aschheim, "Archetypes and the German-Jewish Dialogue."

14. Aron Zeitlin, "A Book on the Eichmann Trial," *Der Tog-Morgen Zhurnal* (New York), November 12, 1965, p. 6; similarly Dagmar Barnouw, in *Visible Spaces: Hannah Arendt and the German-Jewish Experience* (Baltimore, 1990), has pointed to Lionel Abel's need to continue to believe in the "dimensions of the monstrous, the ineffable."

15. Frederick Brodnitz, "Hannah Arendt und das deutsche Judentum," in *Die Kontroverse Hannah Arendt: Eichmann und die Juden,* edited by F. A. Krummacher (Munich, 1964), p. 148.

16. Leo Mindlin, "during the week . . . as I see it," *The Jewish Floridian,* March 15, 1963. This article appeared in a brochure distributed by the Anti-Defamation League of the B'nai B'rith in March 1963 to combat the negative effect of Arendt's book.

17. Hannah Arendt, *Eichmann in Jerusalem: A Report on the Banality of Evil,* revised and enlarged edition (New York, 1965), pp. 282–83; idem, "The Formidable Dr. Robinson: A Reply to the Jewish Establishment," *New York Review of Books* 5, no. 12 (January 20, 1966): 26–30; Arendt to this author, November 9, 1971. See also Elisabeth Young-Bruehl, *Hannah Arendt: For Love of the World* (New Haven, 1982), pp. 348–49. Mary McCarthy also spoke of a conspiracy atmosphere. *Times Literary Supplement,* June 25, 1964. See also *Between Friends: The Correspondence of Hannah Arendt and Mary McCarthy, 1949–1975,* edited by Carol Brightman (New York, 1995), p. 166.

18. In her letter to me of November 11, 1971, Arendt returned to her previous claim (see Arendt, "The Formidable Robinson," p. 29) that Ben-Gurion intervened to prevent the publication by Schocken Press. Gershom Schocken, the editor of *Ha'aretz,* adamantly rejected this presumption in an interview with me on November 22, 1971, maintaining inter alia that this was completely contrary to Ben-Gurion's attitude toward freedom of speech. Moreover, there seems to be no evidence of a positive attitude toward her book in Israel during the 1960s

or 1970s. Other than the translation of several long passages of her book in *Ha'aretz,* no other evidence confirms this contention. Interestingly, Young-Bruehl, in *Hannah Arendt,* p. 398, quotes a letter from Arendt to Jaspers from March 26, 1966, in which the former writes: "Also, the Hebrew edition of *Eichmann* is finally out in Israel. I think that the war between me and the Jews is over." A Hebrew edition of the book was published in 2000 and is arousing a certain amount of interest. See also Tom Segev, *The Seventh Million: The Israelis and the Holocaust* (New York, 1993).

19. Young-Bruehl, *Hannah Arendt,* p. 348.

20. Walter Laqueur, "Hannah Arendt in Jerusalem: The Controversy Revisited," in *Western Society after the Holocaust,* edited by Lyman H. Legters (Boulder, Colo., 1987), p. 116.

21. Robert Weltsch, "Could German Jews Have Helped Themselves?" *The Jewish Chronicle,* October 18, 1963, p. 7. Weltsch emphasized the inability of imagination and rational powers to understand what he considered "irrational days." He even found wanting the book by Jacob Robinson, *The Crooked Shall Be Made Straight,* because it failed to convey the total bankruptcy of human society that the period symbolized. Though he never wrote a specific response to Arendt, Weltsch countered her arguments on certain occasions but was distressed that too much had been made of her book while the essential issues were still overlooked. He thus called for a cessation of the discussion. See Robert Weltsch, "The Attitude to Jews as a Standard of Man," *Ha'aretz,* February 11, 1966, p. 3; idem, "Wenn Granen zur Statistik wird . . . ," *Aufbau,* February 7, 1964. See also Young-Bruehl, *Hannah Arendt,* pp. 351–52.

22. B. Z. Goldberg, "A Book by a Jewish Woman: Why A. Eichmann Is Cleared and the Jews Are to Blame," *Der Tog-Morgen Zhurnal* (New York), May 26, 1963, p. 5.

23. Irving Howe, *A Margin of Hope: An Intellectual Autobiography* (New York, 1982), p. 270.

24. Alfred Kazin, *New York Jew* (London, 1978), p. 200. See also Robert B. Westbrook, "The Responsibility of Peoples: Dwight Macdonald and the Holocaust," *Holocaust Studies Annual* 1 (1983): 43. Westbrook's discussion of the New York intellectuals and the Holocaust is particularly relevant here.

25. Howe, *A Margin of Hope,* p. 253.

26. Lionel Abel, "The Aesthetics of Evil: Hannah Arendt on Eichmann and the Jews," *Partisan Review* 30 (1963): 210–30. Abel's position was also forcefully presented at a special public meeting held by the editors of *Dissent* in New York in 1963. See two descriptions of the meeting: Young-Bruehl, *Hannah Arendt,* p. 360, and Howe, *A Margin of Hope,* p. 274.

27. On Abel's attitude toward Arendt's thesis, see the remarks by Arendt and Mary McCarthy in *Between Friends,* pp. xxxi, 147–49, 152.

28. Marie Syrkin, "Hannah Arendt: Clothes of the Empress," *Dissent* 10 (1963): 344–52. See also idem, "Miss Arendt Surveys the Holocaust," *Jewish Frontier* (May 1963): 7–14, where Syrkin wrote much less vitriolically. For Arendt's response to this piece, see Young-Bruehl, *Hannah Arendt* pp. 360–61. Syrkin later upped her opposition to the book in two other articles: "Arguments:

More on Eichmann," *Partisan Review* 31 (1964): 253–55, and "Setting the Record Straight," *Midstream* 12 (1966): 66–70.

29. Norman Podhoretz, "Hannah Arendt on Eichmann—A Study in the Perversity of Brilliance," *Commentary* 34 (1963): 205.

30. M. Geltman, "Hannah Arendt and Her Critics," *National Review* 16 (November 17, 1963): 1007. In a similar spirit, see J. I. Fishbein, "Was There an Alternative?" *The Sentinel,* May 23, 1963, p. 7; H. Golden, "Hannah Arendt and the Eichmann Trial," *The Carolina Israelite* 21 (1963): 11–12.

31. Norman Fruchter, "Arendt's Eichmann and Jewish Identity," *Studies on the Left* 5 (1965): 22–42; idem, "Reply," *Studies on the Left* 5 (1965): 74–79. This was a reply to an essay by two Jews of leftist leanings who took issue with the premise of Fruchter's argument. See Louis Harap and Morris Schappes, "On Arendt's Eichmann and Jewish Identity," *Studies on the Left* 5 (1965): 54–73. See Young-Bruehl, *Hannah Arendt,* pp. 360–61.

32. [Jacob Robinson], "A Report on the Evil of Banality: The Arendt Book," *Facts* 15 (1963): 263. Jacob Robinson, *And the Crooked Shall Be Made Straight: A New Look at the Eichmann Trial* (New York, 1965). The book was translated into Hebrew in 1966 and French in 1968. For a discussion of the background to his book see Young-Bruehl, *Hannah Arendt,* pp. 355–57.

33. Ibid., pp. 24, 225. Podhoretz, "Hannah Arendt," 205.

34. Midge Decter, Review of *And the Crooked Shall Be Made Straight, New Politics* 4 (1966): 80–81.

35. H. M. Sachar, "Objectivity and Jewish Social Science," *American Jewish Historical Quarterly* 55 (1965–66): 439. See also essays by E. Bortniker, *The Jewish News* (Newark), July 21, 1963, p. 13; R. Meister, "Missed Opportunity," *New Leader* 49 (1966): 24–25; Léon Poliakov, "L'histoire ne s'écrit pas avec des si . . . ," *Les Nouveaux Cahiers* 2 (1966): 7–9; idem., "The Eichmann Trial," *Commentary* 43 (1967): 86–90.

36. Walter Laqueur, "Footnotes to the Holocaust," *New York Review of Books* 5 (November 11, 1965): 20–22.

37. Robert Lowell, "Letter to the Editor," *New York Times Book Review,* June 23, 1963, p. 4. See also R. Paret, "Qui n'est pas Adolf Eichmann?" *Preuves* 17 (1967): 8–17.

38. Dwight Macdonald, "Argument: More on Eichmann," *Partisan Review* 31 (1964): 265. On this letter, Arendt wrote to McCarthy, "Dwight wrote them an excellent and very furious letter on the subject." *Between Friends,* p. 147.

39. Mary McCarthy, "The Hue and the Cry," *Partisan Review* 31 (1964): 82–94; idem, "Arguments: More on Eichmann," *Partisan Review* 31 (1964): 275–78; Paret, "Qui n'est pas," 10–11. See McCarthy's letter to Arendt of September 24, 1963, and Arendt's to McCarthy of February 2, 1964, *Between Friends,* pp. 149, 160.

40. A. E. Mayhew, "The Lessons of the 'Normal Man' who Helped Kill Millions," *Commonweal* 78 (July 12, 1963): 429.

41. Dwight Macdonald, "Argument," 124. On Macdonald's intercession on behalf of Arendt, see Young-Bruehl, *Hannah Arendt,* p. 359.

42. R. H. Glauber, "The Eichmann Case," *The Christian Century* 80 (May 22, 1963): 682.

43. According to the *New York Times,* over a hundred letters were received in reply to the article, and Arendt was asked, in an unprecedented gesture, to respond. She declined, as she did on many similar occasions during the polemic. Michael A. Musmanno, "A Man with an Unspotted Conscience," *New York Times Book Review,* May 19, 1963, pp. 1, 40–41. Arendt referred to this review as another one of the political attempts to falsify the content of the book and added: "I cannot do anything against it . . . because an individual is powerless by definition and the power of the image-makers is considerable—money, personnel, time, connections etc." Letter of September 21, 1963, to McCarthy, *Between Friends,* p. 147.

44. Michael A. Musmanno, "Eichmann in Jerusalem: A Critique," *Chicago Jewish Forum* 21 (summer 1963): 285; idem, "Did the 6,000,000 Kill Themselves?" *The National Jewish Monthly* 78 (1963): 11, 54. It is interesting to note how the response to Arendt colored for many their view of Hilberg's book, even for those like Musmanno, who previously held it in high regard. Idem, "The Perishable Record of an Infamy," *Chicago Jewish Forum* 20 (1961–62): 110–12.

45. See also Konrad Kellen, "Reflections on *"Eichmann in Jerusalem,"* *Midstream* 9 (1963): 25–35.

46. Hugh Trevor-Roper, "How Innocent was Eichmann?" *The Sunday Times,* October 13, 1963; also in *Jewish Affairs* 19 (1964): 4–10, later in Krummacher, *Die Kontroverse.*

47. R. H. S. Crossman, "The Case against Arendt," *The Observer,* October 13, 1963, p. 25.

48. See Krummacher, *Die Kontroverse.*

49. Rolf Schroers, "Der banale Eichmann und seine Opfer," *Merkur* 18 (1964): 578–83; also in Krummacher, *Die Kontroverse.* See also F. K. Fromme, "Die Banalität des Bösen," *Frankfurter Allgemeine Zeitung,* September 29, 1964.

50. Golo Mann, "Le procès Eichmann vu par Hannah Arendt," *Cahiers Pologne-Allemagne: Faits et Documents* 20 (1964): 34–41. Also in Krummacher, *Die Kontroverse.*

51. W. Scheffler, "Hannah Arendt und der Mensch im totälitaren Staat," *Aus Politik und Zeitgeschichte: Beilage zur Wochenzeitung, "Das Parlament,"* no. 45/64 (November 4, 1964): 19–38.

52. H. Köpke, "Die Nazi-Verbrechen sind wiederholbar: Adolf Eichmann war kein Dämon. Zu Hannah Arendts heftig umstrittenen Buch," *Frankfurter Rundschau,* September 19, 1964.

53. H. E. Holthusen, "Hannah Arendt, Eichmann, und die Kritiker," *Vierteljahrshefte zur Zeitgeschichte* 13 (1965): 178–90.

54. Mann, "Le Procès," 40.

55. Hannah Arendt, *Eichmann in Jerusalem: Ein Bericht von der Banalität des Bösen* (Munich, 1996). An English translation of Mommsen's introduction was published in his collection of essays *From Weimar to Auschwitz: Essays in German History,* translated by Phillip O'Connor (Cambridge, 1991).

56. Hannah Arendt, *The Jew as Pariah: Jewish Identity and Politics in the Modern Age,* edited by Ron H. Feldman (New York, 1978), pp. 47–48.

57. Bernstein, *Hannah Arendt and the Jewish Question,* introduction.

58. To mention but a few utilized for this paper, see Bernstein, *Hannah*

Arendt and the Jewish Question; Benhabib, "Identity, Perspective and Narrative"; Margaret Canovan, *Hannah Arendt: A Reinterpretation of Her Political Thought* (Cambridge, 1992); Shiraz Dossa, "Hannah Arendt on Eichmann: The Public, the Private and the Evil," *The Review of Politics* 46 (1984): 163–82. See also Dana R. Villa, "The Banality of Philosophy: Arendt on Heidegger and Eichmann," *Hannah Arendt: Twenty Years Later,* edited by Larry May and Jerome Kohn (Cambridge, Mass., 1996).

59. Villa, "The Banality of Philosophy," p. 184.

60. Alan Milchman and Alan Rosenberg, "Hannah Arendt and the Etiology of the Desk Killer: The Holocaust as Portent," *History of European Ideas* 14 (1992): 219, 223–25. A recent work treating aspects of Arendt's attitude toward the legal and moral issues of the trial reached me as this article was in press. See Barry Sharpe, *Modesty and Arrogance in Judgment: Hannah Arendt's "Eichmann in Jerusalem"* (Westport, 1999).

GABRIEL MOTZKIN, "LOVE AND *BILDUNG* FOR HANNAH ARENDT"

1. George L. Mosse, *German Jews beyond Judaism* (Cincinnati: Hebrew Union College Press, 1985); David Sorkin, *The Transformation of German Jewry, 1780–1840* (Oxford: Oxford University Press, 1987).

2. Hannah Arendt, "We Refugees," in *The Jew as Pariah: Jewish Identity and Politics in the Modern Age,* edited by Ron H. Feldman (New York: Grove, 1978), pp. 55–66; originally published in *Menorah Journal* 31 (January 1943): 69–77. See also Hannah Arendt, "The Jew as Pariah: A Hidden Tradition," *Jewish Social Studies* 6, no. 2 (April 1944): 99–122; reprinted in *The Jew as Pariah,* pp. 67–90. For a discussion of the categories of pariah and parvenu in *Rahel Varnhagen,* see Seyla Benhabib, *The Reluctant Modernism of Hannah Arendt* (Thousand Oaks, Calif.: Sage, 1996), pp. 8, 36. For a discussion of these categories in Arendt's early thought, see Richard J. Bernstein, *Hannah Arendt and the Jewish Question* (Cambridge: Polity Press, 1996).

3. Denis de Rougemont, *L'amour et l'occident* (1938, 1956; Paris: Plon, 1972).

4. Ibid., pp. 78–86, 426.

5. Hannah Arendt, *Der Liebesbegriff bei St. Augustin: Versuch einer philosophischen Interpretation* (Berlin: Julius Springer, 1929); English translation: *Love and Saint Augustine,* with an interpretive essay by Joanna V. Scott and Judith C. Stark (Chicago: University of Chicago Press, 1996). Hannah Arendt, *Rahel Varnhagen: The Life of a Jewish Woman,* revised edition (New York: Harcourt Brace Jovanovich, 1974).

6. Arendt, *Der Liebesbegriff bei St. Augustin,* p. 18.

7. Ibid., pp. 18 ff.

8. Ibid., pp. 19, 20.

9. Ibid., p. 32.

10. Ibid., p. 70

11. Ibid., pp. 70–71.
12. Ibid., p. 84.
13. Ibid., p. 86.
14. Ibid., p. 90.
15. Arendt, *Rahel Varnhagen,* pp. 3, 4.
16. Ibid., p. 9.
17. Ibid., p. 11.
18. Ibid.
19. Ibid. Hannah Arendt, *Eichmann in Jerusalem. A Report on the Banality of Evil,* revised edition (New York: Penguin Books, 1977), p. 52.
20. Arendt, *Rahel Varnhagen,* p. 11.
21. Ibid., p. 13.
22. Ibid., pp. 15–17.
23. Ibid., p. 20.
24. Ibid., pp. 20, 21, 22, 49.

ANSON RABINBACH, "GERMAN AS PARIAH, JEW AS PARIAH"

1. Hannah Arendt, "Karl Jaspers: A Laudatio," in *Men in Dark Times* (New York: Harcourt, Brace & World, 1968), 71–80.
2. Ibid., 74.
3. Ibid., 75.
4. Margaret Canovan, "Socrates or Heidegger? Hannah Arendt's Reflections on Philosophy and Politics," *Social Research* 57, no. 1 (spring 1990): 150.
5. For an elaboration of this theme, see Anson Rabinbach, *In the Shadow of Catastrophe: German Intellectuals between Apocalypse and Enlightenment* (Berkeley: University of California Press, 1997), 129–65.
6. Karl Jaspers to Hannah Arendt, March 30, 1930. *Correspondence, 1926–1969,* edited by Lotte Köhler and Hans Saner, translated by Robert Kimber and Rita Kimber (New York: Harcourt Brace Jovanovich, 1992), 10. All subsequent references to the English-language edition are noted as *Correspondence.*
7. Jaspers to Arendt, March 30, 1930, *Correspondence,* 10.
8. Arendt to Jaspers, March 24, 1930, *Correspondence,* 11.
9. Seyla Benhabib, "The Pariah and Her Shadow," *Political Theory* 23 (February 1995): 5–24. Also see Seyla Benhabib, *The Reluctant Modernism of Hannah Arendt* (Newbury Park, Calif.: Sage Publications, 1996).
10. Hannah Arendt, "The Jew as Pariah: A Hidden Tradition," *Jewish Social Studies* 6, no. 2 (April 1944): 99–122. Reprinted in *The Jew as Pariah: Jewish Identity and Politics in the Modern Age,* edited by Ron H. Feldman (New York: Grove Press, 1978), 67–91.
11. Karl Jaspers, *Max Weber* (Munich: E. Piper, 1988), 78.
12. Arendt to Jaspers, January 1, 1933, *Correspondence,* 16.
13. Jaspers to Arendt, January 3, 1933, *Correspondence,* 17.
14. Hannah Arendt, "Zionism Reconsidered," in *The Jew as Pariah,* 131–

64, and in Hannah Arendt, *Die Krise des Zionismus: Essays und Kommentare* 2, edited by Eike Geisel and Klaus Bittermann, translated by Eike Geisel (Berlin: Edition Tiamant, 1989).

15. Karl Jaspers, "Bemerkungen zu Max Weber's politischem Denken," in *Max Weber,* 126.

16. Dolf Sternberger, "Jaspers und der Staat," *Karl Jaspers Werk und Wirkung: Zum 80 Geburtstag Karl Jaspers* (R. Piper: Munich, 1963), 133, 134.

17. Ralf Dahrendorf, "Kulturpessimismus vs. Fortschrittshoffnung: Eine Notwendige Abgrenzung," *Stichworte zur "Geistigen Situation der Zeit,"* vol. 1, *Nation und Republik,* edited by Jürgen Habermas (Frankfurt am Main: Suhrkamp, 1979), 223.

18. Karl Jaspers, *Die Schuldfrage* (Heidelberg: Lambert Schneider, 1946), 26.

19. Jaspers frequently stated that he expected that it would take at least twenty years for there to be free elections in Germany. See Rabinbach, *In the Shadow of Catastrophe,* 141.

20. Hannah Arendt, "Karl Jaspers as Citizen of the World," *The Philosophy of Karl Jaspers,* edited by Paul Arthur Schilpp (La Salle, Ill.: Open Court, 1981), 541, 543.

21. Carl Schmitt, *Ex Captivitate Salus: Erfahrungen der Zeit 1945/47* (Cologne, 1950), 70. Cited in Helmut Lethen, *Verhaltenslehren der Kälte; Lebensversuche zwischen den Kriegen* (Frankfurt am Main: Suhrkamp, 1994), 219.

22. Karl Jaspers, "Philosophical Autobiography," in *The Philosophy of Karl Jaspers,* 64.

23. Ibid.

24. Karl Jaspers, "Geleitwort für die Zeitschrift 'Die Wandlung' 1945," in Karl Jaspers, *Hoffnung und Sorge: Schriften zum deutschen Politik, 1945–1965* (Munich: Piper, 1965), 27.

25. See Klaus von Beyme, "Karl Jaspers—Vom philosophischen Aussenseiter zum Preceptor Germaniae," in *Heidelberg 1945,* edited by Jürgen C. He, Hartmut Lehmann, and Volker Sollin (Stuttgart: Franz Steiner, 1996), 120–48.

26. On Jaspers's admiration for Rector Bauer, see Eike Wolgast, "Karl Heinrich Bauer—Der erste Heidelberger Nachkriegsrektor: Weltbild und Handeln, 1945–1946," in *Heidelberg 1945,* 107–29.

27. Letter from Karl Jaspers to Fritz Ernst, cited in *Karl Jaspers: Erneuerung der Universität. Rede und Schriften, 1945/6,* edited by Renato de Rosa (Heidelberg: Lambert Schneider, 1986), 412. According to Jaspers, when Penham confronted him, demanding to know who had drafted the senate document, Jaspers assumed responsibility, though it was apparently Ernst who had drafted it.

28. Page references in parentheses refer to Karl Jaspers, *Die Schuldfrage* (Piper: Munich, 1965), my translation.

29. Jaspers to Arendt, September 18, 1946, *Correspondence,* 58.

30. Memorandum for the officer in charge. 307th Counter Intelligence Corps Detachment Headquarters, Seventh United States Army, February 23, 1946. I am indebted to Professor Daniel Penham for providing me with the original text of this document.

31. Hannah Arendt to Kurt Blumenfeld, October 14, 1952, in Hannah Arendt and Kurt Blumenfeld *". . . In keinem Besitz verwurzelt": Die Korre-*

spondenz, edited by Ingeborg Nordmann and Iris Pilling (Hamburg: Rotbuch, 1995), 68.

32. Elisabeth Young-Bruehl, *Hannah Arendt: For Love of the World* (New Haven, 1982), 216.

33. Arendt was successful in securing a translation published by the Dial Press as *The Question of German Guilt,* translated by E. B. Ashton (New York, 1947).

34. Jaspers to Arendt, October 16, 1946, *Correspondence,* 62, 63. Also see the discussion of this theme in Agnes Heller and Ferenc Féher, *The Postmodern Political Condition* (New York: Columbia University Press, 1989), 85.

35. Heinrich Blücher to Hannah Arendt, July 15, 1946, in Hannah Arendt and Heinrich Blücher, *Briefe, 1936–1968,* edited by Lotte Köhler (Munich: Piper, 1996), 146.

36. Young-Bruehl, *Hannah Arendt,* 216.

37. Arendt to Jaspers, August 17, 1946, *Correspondence,* 53.

38. Ibid., 54.

39. Jaspers to Arendt, October 19, 1946, *Correspondence,* 62, 63.

40. Jaspers to Arendt, May 16, 1947, *Correspondence,* 87.

41. Ibid.

42. Arendt to Jaspers, August 17, 1946, *Correspondence,* 56.

43. Arendt to Jaspers, June 30, 1947, *Correspondence,* 90.

44. Hannah Arendt, "The Moral of History," in *The Jew as Pariah,* 107.

45. Arendt to Jaspers, June 30, 1947, *Correspondence,* 91.

46. Arendt to Jaspers, September 7, *Correspondence,* 1952, 197.

47. Ibid.

48. Richard J. Bernstein, *Hannah Arendt and the Jewish Question* (Cambridge, Mass.: MIT Press, 1996).

49. Martin Heidegger to Karl Jaspers, March 25, 1950, in Martin Heidegger and Karl Jaspers, *Briefwechsel, 1920–1963,* edited by Walter Biemel and Hans Saner (Frankfurt am Main: Vittorio Klostermann; Munich: R. Piper, 1990), 199.

50. Karl Jaspers, *Notizen zu Martin Heidegger,* edited by Hans Saner (Munich: R. Piper, 1989), 130.

51. See Willy Brandt, foreword to Karl Jaspers, *Freiheit und Wiedervereinigung* (Munich: R. Piper, 1990), iii.

52. Dan Diner, "Negative Symbiose: Deutsche und Juden nach Auschwitz," *Babylon: Beiträge zur jüdischen Gegenwart* 1 (1986): 9–21.

PETER BAEHR, "THE GRAMMAR OF PRUDENCE"

I am grateful to Volker Meja, Stuart Pierson, Stephen Riggins, Hedda Schuurman, and especially Judith Adler for their helpful comments on this article.

1. Unless other stated, all references to the Arendt-Jaspers correspondence are to Hannah Arendt and Karl Jaspers, *Correspondence, 1926–1969,* edited by Lotte Köhler and Hans Saner, translated by Robert Kimber and Rita Kimber (New York: Harcourt Brace, 1992). The first number refers to the letter number, the second number refers to the relevant page of the English translation.

2. Writing of the conversations that took place between Arendt and Jaspers after 1949, Lotte Köhler and Hans Saner contend that "they were able to say anything and everything to each other without screening their thoughts or filing the rough edges and that they always felt an affinity in their mode of thought, despite their disagreement about details," a quality that "formed the basis of their trust" (*Correspondence*, p. viii).

3. Hannah Arendt, "Hannah Arendt on Hannah Arendt," in *Hannah Arendt: The Recovery of the Public World*, edited by Melvyn A. Hill (New York: St. Martin's Press, 1979), p. 339.

4. Karl Jaspers, "Philosophical Autobiography," in *The Philosophy of Karl Jaspers*, augmented edition, with a new section on Martin Heidegger, edited by Paul Arthur Schilpp (1957; La Salle, Ill.: Open Court, 1981), p. 67.

5. On matters held back from Jaspers, see Elzbieta Ettinger, *Hannah Arendt / Martin Heidegger* (New Haven: Yale University Press), pp. 112–17.

6. Karl Jaspers, *Max Weber: Deutsches Wesen im politischen Denken, im Forschen, und Philosophieren* (Oldenburg: Gerhard Stalling, 1932), p. 7. The phrase comes from a passage in which Jaspers is reminding his contemporaries of the "greatness" Weber had embodied before and during the First World War. The series in which this book appeared ("Schriften an die Nation") and its publisher, Stalling, were closely associated with the National Socialist movement.

7. Jaspers, "Philosophical Autobiography," p. 57. "Max Weber was the last genuine national German; genuine because he represented the spirit of Baron von Stein, of Gneisenau, of Mommsen, not the will to power for one's own empire—at any price and above all others."

8. Jaspers claimed that the subtitle of the book was a suggestion of the publisher (*Correspondence*, no. 23, 17). The offending expression "*deutsches Wesen*" was dropped in subsequent editions of the book's subtitle (though not, incidentally, from the introductory remarks themselves), no doubt partly in response to Arendt's objections and partly because Jaspers was addressing a different audience from the young nationalist opponents of the Weimar Republic he had originally sought to influence. Henceforth, the book appeared as *Max Weber, Politiker-Forscher-Philosoph* (Bremen: Johannes Storm, 1946). All of Jaspers's major statements on Weber have been translated into English. They are conveniently located in *Karl Jaspers on Max Weber*, edited by John Dreijmanis, translated by Robert J. Whelan (New York: Paragon House, 1989).

The history of Jaspers's *Max Weber* book warrants a short essay in its own right. Suffice it to note here that the first English translation by "Ralph Manheim," a pseudonym, in *Leonardo, Descartes, Max Weber: Three Essays* (London: Routledge and Kegan Paul, 1965), pp. 189–274, expunges the paragraph to which Arendt had objected in 1933. (It is restored in the Whelan translation.) Other deletions include the section entitled "The German Mission in World History." Interestingly, though Arendt's letters to Jaspers (*Correspondence*, no. 348, 546, February 19, 1964; no. 351, 550–51, April 20, 1964) offer a number of suggestions designed to tone down the essay's nationalistic cadence, or at least place it in historical context, the omission of the "*deutsches Wesen*" paragraph is *not* among them. Even so, it has vanished from the Manheim translation.

9. See the subtle discussion in Dagmar Barnouw's *Visible Spaces: Hannah*

Arendt and the German-Jewish Experience (Baltimore: Johns Hopkins University Press, 1990), pp. 36–37.

10. "Karl Jaspers: A Laudatio," in *Men in Dark Times* (New York: Harcourt Brace, 1968), pp. 76–77.

11. I have amended slightly the translation. See Hannah Arendt and Karl Jaspers, *Briefwechsel, 1926–1969,* edited by Lotte Köhler and Hans Saner (Munich: Piper, 1985), p. 82.

12. But see *Correspondence,* no. 46, 63, October 19, 1946 (and Arendt's reply, no. 50, 70, December 17, 1946), and no. 52, 71–72, January 1, 1947. A more rounded discussion than I provide here can be found in Steven E. Aschheim, *Culture and Catastrophe: German and Jewish Confrontations with National Socialism and Other Crises* (London: Macmillan, 1996), pp. 97–114.

13. This is translated by Robert and Rita Kimber as "Dedication to Karl Jaspers," in *Hannah Arendt: Essays in Understanding 1930–1954,* edited by Jerome Kohn (New York: Harcourt Brace, 1994), pp. 212–16.

14. Cf. Jaspers's "Philosophical Autobiography" on "the two meanings" of Germany, pp. 64–65.

15. The perplexities that surrounded Jaspers's move to "European Basel" are well documented in the correspondence. See especially *Correspondence,* no. 63, 101–3, January 30, 1948.

16. Moved in part by some of his wife's earlier promptings, Blücher had communicated with Jaspers indirectly by sending a letter to Arendt in Basel (January 29, 1950) and then asking *her* (in a letter of February 4) to convey to the great man a passage the first letter contained, provided she found it appropriate. In this "sketch," Blücher sings Jaspers's praises, signaling a change of heart from his previous angry criticisms of, among other things, Jaspers's cerebral, insufficiently visceral analysis of "German guilt" (July 15, 1946). See, respectively, Hannah Arendt and Heinrich Blücher, *Briefe, 1936–1968,* edited with an introductory essay by Lotte Köhler (Munich: Piper, 1996), pp. 197–200, 201–4, 146–49. Hereafter cited as *Briefe.*

17. *Correspondence,* no. 217, 335, November 23, 1957.

18. The two men continued to rehearse their views on Germany, nationalism, and freedom in *Correspondence,* no. 264, 399–402; no. 266, 403; no. 291, 442–45; no. 295, 450–52; no. 300, 463–66.

19. For the books, see *Sechs Essays* (Heidelberg: L. Schneider, 1948) and *On Revolution* (New York: Viking Press, 1963), which is dedicated to "Gertrud and Karl Jaspers, In reverence—in friendship—in love."

20. "Karl Jaspers: A Laudatio," pp. 76–77 and 74, respectively.

21. Hannah Arendt, "Karl Jaspers zum fünfundachtzigsten Gerburtstag," in *Erinnerungen an Karl Jaspers,* edited by Klaus Piper and Hans Saner (Munich: Piper, 1974), p. 314. See also *Correspondence,* no. 423, 677, February 20, 1968. The sentence "Loyalty is the sign of truth" [*Treue ist das Zeichen der Wahrheit*] is from Heinrich = *Briefwechsel,* p. 712. Also, see Elisabeth Young-Bruehl, *Hannah Arendt: For Love of the World* (New Haven: Yale University Press, 1892), pp. 200, 510–11, n. 49. That people today often view loyalty as a weakness, or as a poor reason for devotion, shows clearly its erosion as a virtue. This is no ground to conclude, however, that Hannah Arendt—who also had a

penchant for invoking the language of sin, evil, honor, blasphemy, and heroism—concurred with this modern disparagement. For an illuminating discussion, see Henry Louis Gates, Jr., "The End of Loyalty," *New Yorker,* March 9,
1998, pp. 34–44.

22. The context is an exchange between them on the Rahel Varnhagen book
and Jaspers's wish "to defend against you and Blumenfeld the many remarkable
people who have lived as German Jews." He continues: "What it comes to in the
end is that I will never cease claiming you as a 'German' (you know that, of
course), although, as Monsieur [Heinrich Blücher] would say, I am, along with
you and many other Germans, 'not a German,' namely, not in the political sense
(even though I am a German according to my passport, but that gives me no
pleasure)." *Correspondence,* no. 138, 204, December 29, 1952.

23. Quoted by Martin Green, in *The von Richthofen Sisters: The Triumphant
and the Tragic Modes of Love* (New York: Basic Books, 1974), pp. 172–73.

24. Weber's death in 1920 made it seem "as though the world had changed.
The great man, who had justified its existence to my consciousness and had
given it a soul (and meaning) was no longer with us." Weber was "the last genuine national German," whose "political thought coined my own." Jaspers,
"Philosophical Autobiography," pp. 32, 57. Weber was "the greatest German of
our era," a conviction Jaspers says he has lived with for "half a century" (1958
preface to "Max Weber: Politician, Scientist, Philosopher," in *Karl Jaspers on
Max Weber,* p. 31). And in lecture notes penned in 1960–61, Jaspers remarks
that for the past fifty years "I never philosophized without thinking of Max Weber. I asked, What would he say? . . . I have been under his influence since 1909.
When he died in 1920, I felt as if the German world had lost its heart." "Max
Weber: Concluding Characterization," in *Karl Jaspers on Max Weber,* pp. 140–
41; cf. p. 157.

When, in May 1967, Jaspers learned of Weber's love affair with Else Jaffe (née
Else von Richthofen), he was deeply shocked. The man who—as he put it to
Marianne Weber—"war die Wahrheit selber," was truth itself, had turned out
to have had a clandestine, adulterous relationship. Before his death in 1969,
Jaspers was considering a reevaluation of his previous estimate of Weber. On this,
see John Dreijmanis's introduction to *Karl Jaspers on Max Weber,* pp. xix–xx.

25. "One more 'case': Max Weber's sister—Lily Schaefer, a wonderful, sovereign personality, a friend of Gertrud's—committed suicide because of a complicated situation that would be too involved to recount here. . . . Max Weber
spoke at the graveside. I don't think I ever saw him as shaken as on that occasion. He had loved his sister very much. He celebrated the freedom of man, who
is able to take his own life. 'It gave me what I could; now it's enough.' The minister was relegated to just standing there." *Correspondence,* no. 402, 653, August 17, 1966.

26. See also the reproduction of Jaspers's handwritten note recalling this last
visit on p. 792 of the *Correspondence,* no. 396, n. 3.

27. On the relationship between friendship and truth, see Hannah Arendt,
"On Humanity in Dark Times: Thoughts about Lessing," in *Men in Dark Times,*
pp. 3–31, esp. 28.

28. Jaspers's never-completed project on representative types of independent thinking was prompted by Arendt's *Eichmann in Jerusalem* and the ferocious response it received from its critics. When Jaspers's failing health made him unequal to pursuing the enterprise, Arendt successfully persuaded him to abandon it. See *Correspondence*, no. 347, 543, January 29, 1964; no. 355, 560, July 27, 1964; no. 393, 631–32, March 9, 1966.

29. On a previous occasion, following a visit in which Arendt's book on Rahel Varnhagen was discussed, Jaspers sensed that "a conflict has emerged" but one that nonetheless had taken place on "the basis of reliable solidarity we share." *Correspondence*, no. 168, 262, July 15, 1955. For Arendt's reply, see no. 169, 263, August 6, 1955.

30. *Correspondence*, no. 107, 163, January 7, 1951; no. 129 (Jaspers to Blücher), 186–87, July 21, 1952.

31. *Correspondence*, no. 91, 139, August 4, 1949. The tribute reminds one of Jaspers's feelings for Weber. See also no. 92, 140, September 1, 1949.

32. For instance, Hannah Arendt, *The Human Condition* (Chicago: University of Chicago Press, 1958), p. 79, and "Hannah Arendt on Hannah Arendt," p. 327 ("I have a great respect for Marx").

33. *The Human Condition*, pp. 277–78 n. 34.

34. Particularly in light of the praise that Arendt showers on Weber in *The Human Condition*. See footnotes 44 and 45 below.

35. The reference to the Weberian notion of "ideal type" is lost in the English translation of Robert and Rita Kimber, which renders *idealtypisch* as "archetypically." See *Briefwechsel*, p. 245.

36. *Correspondence*, no. 147, 225–26, September 15, 1953.

37. Jaspers, "Philosophical Autobiography," p. 67.

38. The bulk of Weber's "methodological" reflections are to be found in a series of essays that were published posthumously as *Gesammelte Aufsätze zur Wissenschaftslehre* (Tübingen: J. C. B. Mohr [Paul Siebeck], 1922). See also part 1 of *Economy and Society*, edited by Guenther Roth and Claus Wittich, translated by various translators (1922, 1968; Berkeley: University of California Press, 1978). To the best of my knowledge, Arendt does not discuss the material contained in either work.

39. Blücher was in complete agreement with his wife. For Blücher, Weber's construction of "*Idealtypenschemata*" was far less interesting than, and was in some ways a diversion from, his passionate interest in politics and the "grief" he felt for his country, a sorrow so deep that it "had eaten away his heart." See Arendt to Blücher, August 1, 1941, in *Briefe*, p. 123, and Blücher to Arendt, August 2, 1941, pp. 125–26.

40. Hannah Arendt, "Religion and Politics," in *Essays in Understanding*, pp. 378, 388 n. 24. Arendt had previously criticized Gerth's use of "Max Weber's category of 'charismatic leadership'" in *The Origins of Totalitarianism* (1951; New York: Harcourt Brace, 1966), pp. 361–62 n. 57, though in this case, it is not entirely clear from the context whether it is Gerth or the category itself that is fundamentally at fault. Cf. *The Origins of Totalitarianism*, p. 305 n. 1.

41. Max Weber, *Economy and Society*, p. 1112. Arendt might have said with more plausibility that the objective of ideal-type construction, on Weber's account, was not to draw parallels, but to discern unique personalities and conjunctures.

Arendt's view of the ideal type itself is actually more complex than at first it seems. Her early remarks seem to damn it. Hence, to the examples I have already cited one might add her reply to Ben Halpern, whose use of "Max Weber's method of constructing *Idealtypen* . . . proves how difficult it seems to be to avoid 'a type of reasoning which [is] . . . in essence metaphysical.'" Hannah Arendt, "About Collaboration," [1948], in *The Jew as Pariah,* edited by Ron H. Feldman (New York: Grove Press, 1978), p. 238. In her later comments and writings, however, she appears to endorse the ideal type, albeit without any sustained attempt at definition or analysis. "Hannah Arendt on Hannah Arendt," p. 329; *The Life of the Mind,* volume 1, *Thinking* (New York: Harcourt Brace, 1978), p. 169.

42. Hannah Arendt, "A Reply to Eric Voegelin," in *Essays in Understanding,* p. 404. That the "most evaluative" statement can also be the best, that is, the "most precise and accurate description of what actually happened," is also argued by Roy Bhaskar (drawing on Isaiah Berlin) in *The Possibility of Naturalism: A Philosophical Critique of the Contemporary Human Sciences* (Brighton: Harvester, 1979), pp. 75–76.

Arendt would also have been perfectly aware that the phrase *sine ira et studio* was coined by Tacitus in his very partisan attack on the Augustan Principate. See *Annals,* 1:1 in Tacitus, *The Annals of Imperial Rome,* translated with an introduction by Michael Grant (Harmondsworth: Penguin, 1977), p. 32.

43. Where Arendt appears to commend Weber's *personal* qualities (e.g. "imposing patriotism" and "intellectual sobriety"), as distinct from the formal attributes of his historical writings, her remarks are loaded with double entendres in which appreciation is not clearly demarcated from implied criticism.

44. Weber's historical study *Agraverhältnisse im Altertum* was published in two versions, the first in 1898 and the second, duly expanded, in 1909. Arendt is referring to the 1909 version, republished in *Gesammelte Aufsätze zur Sozial- und Wirtschaftsgeschichte,* edited by Marianne Weber (Tübingen: J. C. B. Mohr [Paul Siebeck], 1924), pp. 1–288. It has been translated by R. I. Frank with the misleading title *The Agrarian Sociology of Ancient Civilizations* (London: New Left Books, 1976). Arendt described Weber's essay as "remarkable" (*The Human Condition,* p. 66; cf. p. 119 n. 70).

45. See *The Human Condition* on the "greatness of Max Weber's discovery of the economic power that comes from an otherworldliness directed toward the world" and the "greatness of Max Weber's discovery about the origins of capitalism," pp. 252 n. 2 and 254, respectively.

46. "In his methodological essays between 1903 and 1906 Weber has in mind economics whenever he writes of 'our science.'" Guenther Roth, "'Value-Neutrality' in Germany and the United States," in *Scholarship and Partisanship: Essays on Max Weber,* edited by Reinhard Bendix and Guenther Roth (Berkeley: University of California Press, 1971), p. 37 n. 6.

47. In her discussion of the Protestant ethic thesis in *The Human Condition* (p. 277), Arendt refers to Weber as a "historian." She did so for good reason. Sociology is not mentioned in *The Protestant Ethic and the Spirit of Capitalism,* nor is the ideal-type method described there as a sociological method. On the contrary, it is presented as an element of "historical concept" formation. *The Protestant Ethic and the Spirit of Capitalism,* translated by Talcott Parsons (1904–1905; London: George Allen and Unwin, 1930), p. 48.

Elisabeth Young-Bruehl suggests that Arendt's critique of Karl Mannheim adduced "The Protestant Ethic" as a sociological work (*Hannah Arendt,* p. 84). This may have been implied—Arendt quotes from the version of the essay in *Religionssoziologie*—but is nowhere specifically stated. Indeed, it is just as possible that Arendt was citing this essay as an *alternative* to sociology, a usage consistent with her later description of it as a "historical" study. See "Philosophy and Sociology" (1930), in *Essays in Understanding,* p. 40.

48. Max Weber, "Politics as a Vocation," in *From Max Weber: Essays in Sociology,* edited by H. H. Gerth and C. Wright Mills (London: Routledge and Kegan Paul, 1948), pp. 77–128, esp. 77 and 121.

49. For a systematic analysis of Weber's Caesarist view of politics, see Peter Baehr, *Caesar and the Fading of the Roman World: A Study in Republicanism and Caesarism* (New Brunswick, N.J.: Transaction Books, 1998), pp. 165–254.

50. "Power is the probability that one actor within a social relationship will be in a position to carry out his own will despite resistance, regardless of the basis on which this probability rests." Weber, *Economy and Society,* p. 53. "Power is never the property of an individual"; it "corresponds to the human ability not just to act but to act in concert." Hannah Arendt, "On Violence," in *Crises of the Republic* (Harmondsworth: Penguin, 1973), p. 113. In Arendt's lexicon, Weber is describing a mixture of "strength" and "violence." Note, too, pp. 119–20, where Arendt distinguishes "legitimacy" from "justification." For Arendt's earlier analysis on power, see *The Human Condition,* pp. 200–201.

51. Hannah Arendt, *On Revolution* (Harmondsworth: Penguin, 1965), p. 270. Arendt was particularly interested in the way modern societies *transform* people into "masses" or (a different phenomenon) "mobs." See also *Origins of Totalitarianism,* pp. 106–7, "on the fundamental error of regarding the mob as identical with rather than as a caricature of the people" and on the connection of the mob ("the residue of all classes") to plebiscitary rule, and p. 308, distinguishing "masses" from "classes" and "citizens." In Weber's political sociology and political journalism, by contrast, there is no clear analytical distinction between "people" and "masses," or even between "masses" and "mobs." Documentation in Baehr, *Caesar and the Fading of the Roman World,* pp. 236–42.

52. Its Platonic root is examined in *The Human Condition,* pp. 220–30. Also, *On Revolution,* p. 276 (that "the essence of politics is rulership" is a contention that Arendt believes to be "profoundly untrue"). Moreover, while Weber adapts the concept of *Herrschaft* to embrace voluntary obedience, whatever the ground of its justification, Arendt formulates it in its darkest colors to denote "illegality." Hence the German translation she gave to *The Origins of Totalitarianism, Elemente und Ursprünge totaler Herrschaft.* See also "On the

Nature of Totalitarianism: An Essay in Understanding," in *Essays in Under-standing*, p. 330, though the expression Arendt uses there, following Kant, is *Formen der Beherrschung*.

For an important discussion of the complexity surrounding the term *Herr-schaft*, see Melvin Richter, *The History of Political and Social Concepts: A Criti-cal Introduction* (New York: Oxford University Press, 1995), pp. 58–78.

53. Weber, "Politics as a Vocation," p. 121. Arendt, on the other hand, dis-tinguished between those who seek to make the world "good" (a highly danger-ous enterprise), that is, to make the world consistent with some religious norm of goodness, and those concerned to act scrupulously and with moral concern in each of their actions. In the first case, a person is trying to bend the world to make it conform to an interior ethical standard (*The Human Condition*, pp. 73–78); in the second, a person avoids treating others as means (even as means to the "good") and attempts to secure not his or her own soul, but a world stable and free enough to allow human plurality and freedom. Also, contrast Weber's commendation of *Sachlichkeit* ("objectivity," "matter-of-factness") in "Politics as a Vocation," p. 115, with Arendt's warning of the distortions to which it is subject in *Eichmann in Jerusalem* (1963; New York: Viking, 1965), p. 69. Cf. "Peace or Armistice in the Near East?" (1950), "In a world like ours . . . in which politics in some countries has long since outgrown sporadic sinfulness and entered a new stage of criminality, uncompromising morality has suddenly changed its old function of merely keeping the world together and has become the only medium through which true reality, as opposed to the distorted and es-sentially ephemeral factual situations created by crimes, can be perceived and planned." *The Jew as Pariah*, p. 217.

54. See Hannah Arendt, "Hermann Broch" (1955), in *Men in Dark Times*, p. 148. And for a similar formulation, "The Eggs Speak Up" (c. 1950), in *Es-says in Understanding*, p. 281.

55. Max Weber, *Economy and Society*, pp. 4, 22–26. Contrast also Weber's discussion of "freedom" in *Roscher and Knies: The Logical Problems of His-torical Economics*, translated by Guy Oakes (1903, 1905–1906; New York: Free Press, 1975), pp. 191–98, with Hannah Arendt, "What Is Freedom?" in *Between Past and Future: Eight Exercises in Political Thought* (New York: Vi-king, 1961), pp. 143–71. Like Arendt, Weber refused to equate "freedom" with "freedom of will." But his alternative formulation is, in other respects, the an-tithesis of hers. For Weber, the historical investigation of an actor's freedom is tantamount to a specification of the "rational analysis of . . . motivation." An action—for instance, a decision—is free to the degree that it is not externally coerced or emotionally directed but rather unfolds through a process of delib-eration in which "ends" are matched by the appropriate "means." For Arendt, freedom is the capacity for making beginnings, and hence for *interrupting* the flow of events and means-ends chains.

Weber's attempt to develop a model of "causality" appropriate to the study of social relations was another area with which Arendt had little sympathy: We-ber, *Roscher and Knies*, pp. 144–45, 195–98; Max Weber, "Critical Studies in the Logic of the Cultural Sciences" (1906; New York: Free Press, 1949), pp. 164–

88; Arendt, "Understanding and Politics: (The Difficulties of Understanding)" (1954), in *Essays in Understanding,* p. 319: ("Causality . . . is an altogether alien and falsifying category in the historical sciences"), and p. 325 n. 13.

56. I am greatly simplifying and telescoping Arendt's account. For a sophisticated treatment of it, see Ronald Beiner, "Hannah Arendt on Judging," in Hannah Arendt, *Lectures on Kant's Political Philosophy,* edited with an interpretive essay by Ronald Beiner (Chicago: University of Chicago Press, 1982), pp. 89–157.

57. *The Human Condition,* pp. 189, 195; see also "Hermann Broch: 1886–1951" in *Men in Dark Times,* pp. 147–48, and *The Life of the Mind,* volume 2, *Willing* (New York: Harcourt Brace Jovanovich, 1978), pp. 123–24. A helpful clarification of this point is offered by Elisabeth Young-Bruehl when she says that planning and policy making are not, appearances to the contrary, ruled out by Arendt's concept of action. "Planning is not precluded, but action that fails to achieve its end may nevertheless be meaningful or great. . . . Action engaged in only for the sake of an end may, on the other hand, adopt any means or pervert human relations by making them into a means." *Hannah Arendt,* p. 494.

58. "The only aspect of politics where Arendt did think that craftsmanship was called for was in setting up the framework for political action: drawing up a constitution to set the stage or construct the areas for free politics." Margaret Canovan, "Politics and Culture: Hannah Arendt and the Public Realm" (1985), in *Hannah Arendt: Critical Essays,* edited by Lewis P. Hinchman and Sandra K. Hinchman (Albany, N.Y.: State University of New York Press, 1994), p. 184.

59. Jaspers himself was more dubious: *Correspondence,* no. 234, 359–60, December 31, 1958.

60. Hannah Arendt, "Rosa Luxemburg," in *Men in Dark Times,* p. 43.

61. Max Weber, "The National State and Economic Policy" (1895), in *Reading Weber,* edited by Keith Tribe, translated by Ben Fowkes (London: Routledge, 1989), p. 198. On Weber's imperialism and "liberal nationalism," see Wolfgang J. Mommsen, *Max Weber and German Politics, 1890–1920,* translated by M. S. Steinberg (1959; Chicago: University of Chicago Press, 1984), pp. 137, 205–7, 210–11.

62. Quoted in Marianne Weber, *Max Weber: A Biography,* translated by Harry Zohn, with an introduction by Guenther Roth (1926; New Brunswick, N.J.: Transaction Books, 1988), pp. 521–22, emphasis in the original. Cf. Arendt, *The Origins of Totalitarianism,* pp. 327–28.

63. As part of *Leonardo, Descartes, Max Weber: Three Essays.* See note 8 above.

64. Arendt, "On Violence," p. 106.

65. Many previous commentators have drawn attention to this fact. Among them, see especially Margaret Canovan, *Hannah Arendt: A Reinterpretation of Her Political Thought* (Cambridge: Cambridge University Press, 1992), p. 185; Seyla Benhabib, *The Reluctant Modernism of Hannah Arendt* (London: Sage, 1996), p. 49; Jürgen Habermas, "Hannah Arendt's Communications Concept of Power" (1977), in *Hannah Arendt: Critical Essays,* pp. 211–29; Lewis P. Hinchman and Sandra K. Hinchman, "Existentialism Politicized:

Arendt's Debt to Jaspers" (1991), in *Hannah Arendt: Critical Essays,* pp. 143–78, at p. 155.

66. See Hannah Arendt, "Karl Jaspers: Citizen of the World?" in *Men in Dark Times,* p. 85; Hinchman and Hinchman, "Existentialism Politicized," p. 151.

DANA R. VILLA "APOLOGIST OR CRITIC?"

1. Elisabeth Young-Bruehl, *Hannah Arendt: For Love of the World* (New Haven: Yale University Press, 1982).

2. Elzbieta Ettinger, *Hannah Arendt / Martin Heidegger* (New Haven: Yale University Press, 1995).

3. Hannah Arendt and Martin Heidegger, *Briefe 1925 bis 1975,* edited by Ursula Ludz (Frankfurt: Vittorio Klostermann, 1998).

4. I provide an overview in a longer version of this essay in Dana Villa, *Politics, Philosophy, Terror: Essays on the Thought of Hannah Arendt* (Princeton: Princeton University Press, 1999), chapter 3.

5. Quoted in Ettinger, *Hannah Arendt / Martin Heidegger,* p. 114.

6. See Arendt's essay "What Is Freedom?" in Hannah Arendt, *Between Past and Future* (New York: Penguin Books, 1968).

7. See especially Heidegger's essays "The Age of the World-Picture" and "The Question Concerning Technology," both in Heidegger, *The Question Concerning Technology and Other Essays* (New York: Harper and Row, 1977).

8. See Arendt's Heidegger critique in Arendt, *The Life of the Mind,* volume 2, *Willing* (New York: Harcourt Brace Jovanovich, 1978), chapter 15.

9. Hannah Arendt, *The Human Condition* (Chicago: University of Chicago Press, 1958), chapter 6.

10. See Martin Heidegger, "Letter on Humanism," in *Basic Writings* (New York: Harper & Row, 1977).

11. See Arendt, *On Revolution* (New York: Penguin Books, 1963), p. 229: "opinion and judgment obviously belong among the faculties of reason, but the point of the matter is that these two, politically most important, rational faculties have been almost entirely neglected by the tradition of political as well as philosophical thought."

12. It is hardly the case that Arendt denigrates the latter, as her analyses of totalitarianism make clear. See Hannah Arendt, "Ideology and Terror," in *The Origins of Totalitarianism* (New York: Harcourt Brace Jovanovich, 1973), especially pp. 462–64. Her critical point, best developed in *On Revolution,* is that being a "participant in government" and "public happiness" are dimensions of freedom most cherished by those who have experienced them but all too often are seen as a needless burden by those who have not.

13. Hannah Arendt and Karl Jaspers, *Correspondence: 1926–1969,* edited by Lotte Köhler and Hans Saner (New York: Harcourt Brace Jovanovich, 1992), pp. 447, 453, and 457. Arendt recounts being snubbed by Fink during a visit to Freiburg in a letter dated August 6, 1961, in which she also tells of Heidegger's failure to get in touch with her. In a subsequent letter, responding to Jaspers's

astonishment at Heidegger's hostile behavior, she writes: "it is intolerable to him that my name appears in public, that I write books, etc. I have really fibbed to him about myself all the while, behaving as though none of this existed. . . . But suddenly this fib became quite boring to me and I have paid for my change of mind with a knock on the nose."

14. See Young-Bruehl, *Hannah Arendt*, p. 442.

15. Ettinger, *Hannah Arendt / Martin Heidegger*, p. 10.

16. Richard Wolin, "Hannah and the Magician," *The New Republic*, October 15, 1995, pp. 34–35.

17. Hannah Arendt, "Martin Heidegger at Eighty," in *Heidegger and Modern Philosophy*, edited by Michael Murray (New Haven: Yale University Press, 1978), p. 302.

18. See the text of Heidegger's posthumously published interview with *Der Spiegel*, reprinted in *Martin Heidegger and National Socialism*, edited by Gunther Nesler and Emil Kettering (New York: Paragon House, 1990).

19. See Hugo Ott, *Martin Heidegger: A Political Life*, translated by Allan Blunden (New York: Basic Books, 1993), and Rudiger Safranski, *Ein Meister aus Deutschland: Heidegger und seine Zeit* (Munich: Carl Hanser, 1994).

20. Arendt, "Martin Heidegger at Eighty," pp. 296–97.

21. Ibid., p. 299.

22. Ibid., p. 300.

23. Ibid., pp. 300–301.

24. The preceding paragraph outlines the argument Arendt makes in her 1971 essay "Thinking and Moral Considerations," *Social Research* 38, no. 3 (fall 1971): 417–46.

ANNETTE VOWINCKEL, "HANNAH ARENDT AND MARTIN HEIDEGGER"

1. I would like to thank Joel Golb for his comments and suggestions on a draft of this essay.

2. See Heidegger's famous discussion of "being unto death" in *Being and Time*, especially the following passage: "As a way of being, of *Dasein*, history [*Geschichte*] has its roots so essentially in the future that death, as the characterized possibility of being-there, throws back anticipatory existence onto its factual thrownness, only so endowing having-been-ness [*Gewesenheit*] with its own particular priority within the historical. Authentic being-unto-death, that is, the finitude of temporality, is the hidden ground of the historicity of *Dasein*." *Sein und Zeit* (Tübingen, 1963, p. 386.)

3. Ibid., p. 329.

4. Ibid., p. 10.

5. Ibid., p. 384.

6. In Karl Löwith's succinct words: "His 'leadership' ['*Führung*'] of Freiburg implied claim of being 'led,' himself, by the 'inexorability' of a historical 'mandate'—one casting the German *Volk* into the stamp of its *Geschichte*." Heidegger, *Denker in dürftiger Zeit* (Göttingen, 1960), p. 51; cf. Martin Heidegger, *Die Selbstbehauptung der deutschen Universität* (Breslau, 1933), p. 5.

7. Heidegger, *Denker in dürftiger Zeit,* p. 53.

8. Letter from Arendt to Heinrich Blücher, June 13, 1952, in Hannah Arendt and Heinrich Blücher, *Briefe, 1938–1968,* edited by Lotte Köhler (Munich, 1996), p. 288.

9. Hannah Arendt, "Martin Heidegger at Eighty," *New York Review of Books* 17, no. 6 (October 21, 1971), p. 51.

10. Heidegger, *Sein und Zeit,* pp. 375–76.

11. Heidegger, *Denker in dürftiger Zeit,* pp. 54–55.

12. Heidegger, *Grundfragen der Philosophie* (Frankfurt am Main, 1984), p. 55, and *Die Selbstbehauptung der deutschen Universität* (Breslau, 1933), p. 22. See also the notorious passage in *Einführung in die Metaphysik* (Frankfurt am Main, 1983), p. 207f.: "That which presently is passed about as the philosophy of National Socialism, but which has absolutely nothing to do with this movement's inner truth and greatness (namely, with the encounter between planetarily determined technology and modern humanity)—that is fishing around in the murky water of 'value' and 'totality.'"

13. Cf. *Sein und Zeit,* p. 322: "The *Man*-self most loudly and frequently says 'me-me' [*Ich-Ich*] because that self *is* basically *not authentically* itself and evades the authentic possibility of being."

14. Hannah Arendt, *Vita activa, oder Vom tätigen Leben* (Munich, 1989), p. 249.

15. Martin Heidegger, *Zur Bestimmung der Philosophie* (1919; Frankfurt am Main, 1987), p. 109; cf. Edmund Husserl, *Ideen zu einer reinen Phänomenologie und phänomenologischen Philosophie I* (Halle am der Saale, 1913), p. 43. See also Heidegger, *Zur Bestimmung der Philosophie,* pp. 116–17. In a letter to Elisabeth Blochmann, Heidegger phrased the same idea this way: "The new life we desire, or that desires within us, has renounced being universal, that is, ungenuine and shallow [*flächig*] (super-ficial [*ober-flächig*])—its property is originality—not the artificially constructed, but the evidence of total intuition." Martin Heidegger to Elisabeth Blochmann, May 1, 1919, in Martin Heidegger and Elisabeth Blochmann, *Briefwechsel, 1918–1969,* edited by Joachim W. Storck (Marbach am Neckar, 1989), p. 15.

16. Samuel Beckett, *Marcel Proust* (London, 1931), p. 19.

17. Ibid., pp. 18–19.

18. Hannah Arendt, *The Origins of Totalitarianism* (New York, 1951), p. 80. In a footnote, Arendt mentions Emanuel Levinas's essay "L'autre dans Proust" (1947) as a source of inspiration.

19. Hannah Arendt, *The Origins of Totalitarianism,* p. 80. Beckett describes Proust's technique as follows: "From this Janal, trinal, agile monster or Divinity: Time—a condition of resurrection because an instrument of death; Habit—an infliction in so far as it opposes the dangerous exaltation of the one and a blessing in so far as it palliates the cruelty of the other; Memory—a clinical laboratory stocked with poison and remedy, stimulant and sedative: from Him the mind turns to the one compensation and miracle of evasion tolerated by His tyranny and vigilance. This accidental and fugitive salvation in the midst of life may supervene when the action of involuntary memory is stimulated by the negligence or agony of Habit, under no other circumstances, nor necessarily then.

Proust has adopted this mystic experience as the Leitmotiv of his composition."
Marcel Proust, p. 22.

20. Ibid., pp. 18–19. The similarity of the pictures used by Proust and Benjamin is evident: While Proust's main character, Swann, evokes his memories through the "long-forgotten taste of a madeleine steeped in an infusion of tea" that "conjures in all the relief and color of its essential significance from the shallow well of a cup's inscrutable banality" (21), Benjamin dives into the past as if into an ocean.

21. Arendt knew Benjamin's *Geschichtsphilosophische Thesen* long before they were published, since Benjamin had given her the manuscript in 1940 in southern France before he committed suicide. Today this manuscript is in the Arendt papers in the Library of Congress (Cont. 7, Doc. No. 020950–58).

22. Walter Benjamin, "The Image of Proust," in *Illuminations,* edited with an introduction by Hannah Arendt, translated by Harry Zohn (New York, 1969), p. 214.

23. Walter Benjamin, "Über den Begriff der Geschichte," in *Gesammelte Werke,* vol. 1, part 2 (Frankfurt am Main, 1980), p. 703. Compare Heidegger's well-known definition: "The artwork opens, in its own way, the being of what is [*das Sein des Seienden*]. This opening, i.e., unconcealing, i.e., the truth of what is, takes place in the work. In the artwork, the truth of what is has settled into the work." "Vom Ursprung des Kunstwerks," in *Holzwege* (Frankfurt am Main, 1963), p. 28.

24. Hannah Arendt, "Walter Benjamin," in *Menschen in finsteren Zeiten* (Munich, 1989), p. 238.

25. See Ernst Vollrath, "Hannah Arendt und Martin Heidegger," in *Heidegger und die praktische Philosophie,* edited by Annemarie Gethmann-Siefert and Otto Pöggeler (Frankfurt am Main, 1989), p. 358.

26. Hannah Arendt, "What Is Existenz Philosophy?" in *Partisan Review* 13 (1946): 46 n.

27. Arendt, "Martin Heidegger at Eighty," p. 51.

28. Arendt, "Understanding and Politics," in *Partisan Review* 20 (1953): 388. This sentence and the following one—"Within the framework of causality, events in the sense of something irrevocably new can never happen; history without events would be the dead monotony of sameness, unfolded in time."—are crossed out in the manuscript but included in the published version. See Library of Congress, Cont. 63, File "The Difficulties of Understanding," published 1953, p. 14. We also find this passage in an unpublished paper titled "On the Nature of Totalitarianism" (Library of Congress, Cont. 76, p. 7).

29. Hannah Arendt, "Denktagebuch," 4 (May–June 1951), German Literary Archives, Marbach am Neckar, pp. 37–38. Along with evoking, perhaps, the key Heideggerian notion crystallized in his term *Ereignis* ("event"), this passage may remind us of a passage in a postwar letter from Heidegger to Arendt: "that a half moment *of suddenness* can be 'more full of being' [*seiender*]; that human beings must prepare themselves for this *Seyn* and learn another sort of memory; that with all this something most high very much awaits them." Martin Heidegger to Hannah Arendt, April 12, 1950, German Literary Archives, Marbach am Neckar.

30. Martin Heidegger, *Beiträge zur Philosophie* (Frankfurt am Main, 1989), p. 147. This was written in the late 1930s.

31. See Gary Raymond Olsen, "The Effort to Escape from Temporal Consciousness as Expressed in the Thought and Work of Hermann Hesse, Hannah Arendt, and Karl Löwith" (Ph.D. diss., University of Arizona, 1973). See also Dana R. Villa, "Beyond Good and Evil: Arendt, Nietzsche, and the Aestheticization of Political Action," *Political Theory* 20 (1992): 298.

32. Hannah Arendt, "Isak Dinesen," in *Menschen in finsteren Zeiten*, p. 125.

33. Hannah Arendt, "A Reply [to Eric Voegelin's review of *Origins of Totalitarianism*]," *Review of Politics* 15 (1953), p. 79.

34. Hannah Arendt, "Denktagebuch," 17 (July 1953), pp. 15–18.

35. Hannah Arendt, *Between Past and Future* (New York, 1969), p. 8.

36. Arendt, *Vita activa*, p. 184.

37. Richard Wolin, in his review of Ettinger's book, takes such a stance (at least implicitly) in speaking of Arendt's Jewish problem. Wolin's piece apparently suffers from a crude identification of Arendt's admiration for the philosopher of *Being and Time*, on the one hand, with, on the other hand, an alleged absorption of Nazi and anti-Jewish prejudices. See Wolin, "Hannah and the Magician," *The New Republic*, October 9, 1995, pp. 27–37.

Contributors

STEVEN E. ASCHHEIM holds the Vigevani Chair of European Studies at the Hebrew University, Jerusalem, where he teaches cultural and intellectual history. He is the author of *Brothers and Strangers: The East European Jew in German and German-Jewish Consciousness, 1800–1923* (1982); *The Nietzsche Legacy in Germany, 1890–1990* (1992); *Culture and Catastrophe: German and Jewish Confrontations with National Socialism and Other Crises* (1996); *In Times of Crisis: Essays on European Culture, Germans, and Jews* (2001); and *Scholem, Arendt, and Klemperer: Intimate Chronicles in Turbulent Times* (2001).

PETER BAEHR teaches in the Department of Politics and Sociology, Lingnan University, Hong Kong. His publications include *Caesar and the Fading of the Roman World* (1998) and *Founders, Classics, and Canons* (2001). He is also the editor of *The Portable Hannah Arendt* (2000).

RICHARD J. BERNSTEIN is the Vera List Professor of Philosophy and chair of the Department of Philosophy of the New School for Social Research. His recent books include *Freud and the Legacy of Moses* (1998); *Hannah Arendt and the Jewish Question* (1996); and *The New Constellation: The Ethical-Political Horizons of Modernity/Postmodernity*. He is currently a fellow of the Wissenschaftskolleg zu Berlin, where he is working on a book dealing with the problem of evil.

LEORA BILSKY is a senior lecturer on the Faculty of Law at Tel Aviv University and has recently been a fellow at the program in Ethics and the Professions at Harvard University. Her main areas of interest are feminism, law and philosophy, political trials, and the Holocaust. In her work on political trials she has looked at the history of Israeli law and the legacy of the Holocaust and the work of Hannah Arendt. She is the editor of a special issue of *Theoretical Inquiries in Law* on "Judging and Judgment in the Shadow of the Holocaust" (2000). She is currently writing a book tentatively titled *Political Trials: The Struggle over Israel's Collective Identity,* forthcoming from the University of Michigan Press.

RICHARD I. COHEN holds the Paulette and Claude Kelman Chair in French Jewry Studies at the Hebrew University of Jerusalem. He is the author of *The Burden of Conscience: French-Jewish Leadership during the Holocaust* (1987) and *Jewish Icons: Art and Society in Modern Europe* (1998). In addition, he is the editor of the diary of Raymond-Raoul Lambert, *Carnet d'un témoin, 1940–1943* (1985) and *The French Revolution and Its Historical Impact* (1991, Hebrew) and coeditor of *Art and Its Uses: The Visual Image and Modern Jewish Society* (1991); *From Court Jews to the Rothschilds: Art, Patronage, and Power, 1600–1800* (1996); and the Historical Society of Israel's quarterly journal *Zion* (Hebrew).

BERNARD CRICK is emeritus professor of politics and honorary fellow of Birkbeck College, University of London, and of University College London. Among his books are *In Defence of Politics* (5th ed., 2000); *Political Theory and Practice* (1973); *George Orwell: A Life* (1980); *Essays on Politics and Literature* (1988); *Political Thoughts and Polemics* (1989); *Essays on Citizenship* (2000); and *Crossing Borders* (2001).

MICHAEL HALBERSTAM is author of *Totalitarianism and the Modern Conception of Politics* (1999). He taught philosophy at the University of South Carolina for four years. During his final year in the philosophy department he was a Mellon Fellow at Wesleyan University's Center for the Humanities. He is currently completing a law degree at Stanford University.

AGNES HELLER teaches philosophy at the New School for Social Research in New York. A student of Georg Lukács and a Hungarian dissident, she is the recipient of the Hungarian Szechenyi National Prize and the Hannah Arendt Prize. She has received several honorary degrees and is the author of several dozen books. Among these are *A Philosophy of History* (1993); *An Ethics of Personality* (1996); *A Theory of Modernity* (1999); and *The Time is Out of Joint: Shakespeare as Philosopher of History* (2000).

WALTER LAQUEUR is university professor emeritus at Georgetown University. He was director of the Institute of Contemporary History and Wiener Library in London from 1965 to 1991 and the founder and editor of the *Journal of Contemporary History*. He has been serving as chair of the International Research Council at CSIS Washington. Among his books on German, Russian, and Middle Eastern history in the nineteenth and twentieth centuries, the most recent is *Generation Exodus* (2001).

YAACOV LOZOWICK is the director of the Yad Vashem Archives in Jerusalem. He is the author of *Hitler's Bureaucrats: The Nazi Security Police and the Banality of Evil* (German, 2000, and Hebrew, 2001).

MICHAEL R. MARRUS is the Chancellor Rose and Ray Wolfe Professor of Holocaust Studies and dean of the School of Graduate Studies at the University of Toronto. He is the author of *The Politics of Assimilation: French Jews at the Time of the Dreyfus Affair* (1971); *Samuel the Unwanted: European Refugees in the Twentieth Century* (1985); *The Holocaust in History* (1987); and; *Bronfman: The Life and Times of Seagram's Mr. Sam* (1991). He is coauthor, with Robert O. Paxton, of *Vichy France and the Jews* (1981) and editor of *The Nuremberg War Crimes Trial, 1945–46: A Documentary History* (1997).

HANS MOMMSEN studied history and German literature at the universities of Marburg and Tübingen and has taught at Harvard, Berkeley, the Hebrew University of Jerusalem, and Georgetown University. He has published widely on the legacy of National Socialism and the Holocaust. In 1999–2000 he was the Senior Shapiro Scholar in Residence at the U.S. Holocaust Memorial Museum in Washington, D.C.. He is the author of *The Rise and Fall of Weimar Democracy, Die Geschichte des Volkswagenwerks und seiner Arbeiter im Dritten Reich* (with Manfred Grieger), and two collections of articles, *Von Weimar nach Auschwitz: Zur Geschichte Deutschlands in der Weltkriegsepoche* (1999) and *Alternative zu Hitler: Studien zur Geschichte des deutschen Widerstandes.*

GABRIEL MOTZKIN is director of the Institute of Arts and Letters and associate professor of history, philosophy, and German literature at the Hebrew University of Jerusalem. He is the author of *Time and Transcendence: Secular History, the Catholic Reaction, and the Rediscovery of the Future* (1992) and numerous articles on the philosophy of history.

SUSAN NEIMAN was professor of philosophy at Yale University and Tel Aviv University and is currently director of the Einstein Forum, Potsdam. She is the author of *Slow Fire: Jewish Notes from Berlin; The Unity of Reason: Rereading Kant;* and *Evil in Modern Thought* (forthcoming), as well as a number of essays.

ANSON RABINBACH is professor of history and director of the Program in European Cultural Studies at Princeton University. He is also coeditor of *New German Critique: An Interdisciplinary Journal of German Studies*. His recent publications include *In the Shadow of Catastrophe: German Intellectuals between Apocalypse and Enlightenment* (1997).

AMNON RAZ-KRAKOTZKIN is a lecturer in the department of history at Ben-Gurion University. He studies both early-modern Christian-Jewish discourse and Zionist historical consciousness. Among his publications are *Censorship, Hebraism and Modern Jewish Discourse: The Catholic Church and Hebrew Literature in the Sixteenth Century; Exile within Sovereignty* (Hebrew); *Orientalism, Jewish Studies, and Israeli Society* (Hebrew); and *Redemption, Colonialism, and the Nationalization of Jewish History*. His book *Binationalism and the Critique of Zionism* is forthcoming in Hebrew and French.

DANA R. VILLA teaches political theory at the University of California, Santa Barbara. He is the author of *Socratic Citizenship* (2001); *Politics, Philosophy, Terror: Essays on the Thought of Hannah Arendt* (1999); and *Arendt and Heidegger: the Fate of the Political* (1996). He is also the editor of *The Cambridge Companion to Hannah Arendt* (2000).

ANNETTE VOWINCKEL holds a postdoctoral fellowship at the Institute for Cultural Studies at Humboldt University, Berlin, where she is working on a book about Renaissance conceptions of man. She is the author of *Hannah Arendt: Geschichte und Geschichtsbegriff* (2001).

LILIANE WEISSBERG is Joseph B. Glossberg Term Professor in the Humanities, professor of German and comparative literature, and chair of the Program in Comparative Literature and Literary Theory at the University of Pennsylvania. Her publications on German and American literature, literary theory, and German-Jewish cultural studies include *Cultural Memory and the Construction of Identity* (with Dan Ben-Amos, 1999) and *Romancing the Shadow: Poe and Race* (with J. Gerald Kennedy, 2001). Her critical edition of Hannah Arendt's *Rahel Varnhagen: The Life of a Jewess* appeared in 1997.

ALBRECHT WELLMER has taught philosophy in Frankfurt am Main, Toronto, New York, and Constance. Currently he holds the Chair of Aesthetics, Hermeneutics, and Sciences Humaines at the Free University of Berlin. His English publications include *Critical Theory of Society* (1971); *The Persistence of Modernity: Essays on Aesthetics, Ethics, and Postmodernism* (1991); *Cultural-Political Interventions in the Unfinished Project of Enlightenment* (coeditor, 1992); and *Endgames: The Irreconcilable Nature of Modernity* (1998).

MOSHE ZIMMERMANN is professor of German history and director of the Richard Koebner Center for German History at the Hebrew University, Jerusalem. He is the author of *Wilhelm Marr: The Patriarch of Antisemitism* (1986); *Wende in Israel: Zwischen Nation and Religion* (1996); *Die deutschen Juden, 1914–1945* (Munich, 1997); and *Deutsch Juedisch* (2000). He is also the editor of the Hebrew volume *The Third Reich: A Historical Evaluation* (2000).

Index

Text: 10/13 Sabon
Display: Sabon
Composition: G&S Typesetters, Inc.
Printing and binding: Haddon Craftsmen, Inc.